Just like Mom made

1,000 Family Favorites

by Janet Briggs and Jennifer Olski

Reiman Media Group, Inc.

Greendale, Wisconsin • Pleasantville, New York

©2007 Reiman Media Group, Inc.
5400 S. 60th St., Greendale WI 53129
All rights reserved.

Editors: Janet Briggs and Jennifer Olski

Art Directors: Lori Arndt, Edwin Robles, Jr.
Layout Designers: Kathy Crawford, Catherine Fletcher
Proofreaders: Linne Bruskewitz, Victoria Soukup Jensen
Cover Photographer: Jim Wieland
Cover Food Stylist: Sarah Thompson
Cover Set Stylist: Delores Schaefer

Vice President and Executive Editor, Books: Heidi Reuter Lloyd
Vice President and Publisher, Adult Trade Books: Harold Clarke
President, Food & Entertaining: Suzanne M. Grimes
President and Chief Executive Officer: Mary G. Berner

Pictured on front cover: Bumbleberry Pie, page 421

International Standard Book Number (10): 0-89821-597-8
International Standard Book Number (13): 978-0-89821-597-7
Library of Congress Control Number: 2007928163

For more Reader's Digest products and information, visit
www.rd.com (in the United States), www.rd.ca (in Canada).

Printed in China
1 3 5 7 9 10 8 6 4 2

Table of Contents

Introduction   4

Breakfast, Lunch & Starters

    Appetizers & Beverages   5

    Breakfast & Brunch   39

    Soups & Sandwiches   63

Perfect Partners

    Salads & Sides   107

    Dressings, Sauces & Condiments   171

    Breads, Muffins, Biscuits & Rolls   183

Main Attractions

    Beef   213

    Pork   263

    Poultry   311

    Fish & Seafood   357

Sweet Sensations

    Candy   373

    Cookies, Bars & Brownies   387

    Pies & Tarts   411

    Cakes   431

    Desserts   453

Index   477

About this cookbook...

Imagine sitting down to a meal of all the delicious dishes you remember from your childhood. Platters of tender roasts, comforting potatoes and seasoned vegetables at dinnertime. Stacks of fluffy pancakes and waffles, sweet pastries and moist muffins for breakfast or brunch. Bowls of steaming, chunky soup and mile-high sandwiches on crusty, homemade bread at lunchtime. Desserts so rich and creamy, you can hardly pass up a second serving!

You likely have a few of these special recipes tucked away in your own collection. But if you're the kind of cook who's always on the lookout for classic, home-style recipes or you're curious about what cooking gems you might be missing, then *1,000 Family Favorites* is your dream come true!

We sifted through piles of recipes from thousands of great family cooks just like you and whittled down the bunch to our very favorites. These recipe sensations include classic dishes and their tasty variations, regional favorites, celebrated prize winners and a few quirky recipes too good to pass up! Plus, every recipe in this cookbook had to be good enough to make you say, "It's just like Mom made!"

That's why we chose each recipe based on taste, appeal and originality. When appropriate, we also updated them for current food safety and preparation standards, revised ingredient lists and added a few of our own notes to help guarantee cooking success.

So grab your shopping list and get ready to pore through this tempting treasury of old-fashioned recipes. You're certain to come across a recipe that will become one of your own family favorites. Enjoy!

—*Janet Briggs and Jennifer Olski*

Breakfast ∽ Lunch ∽ & Starters

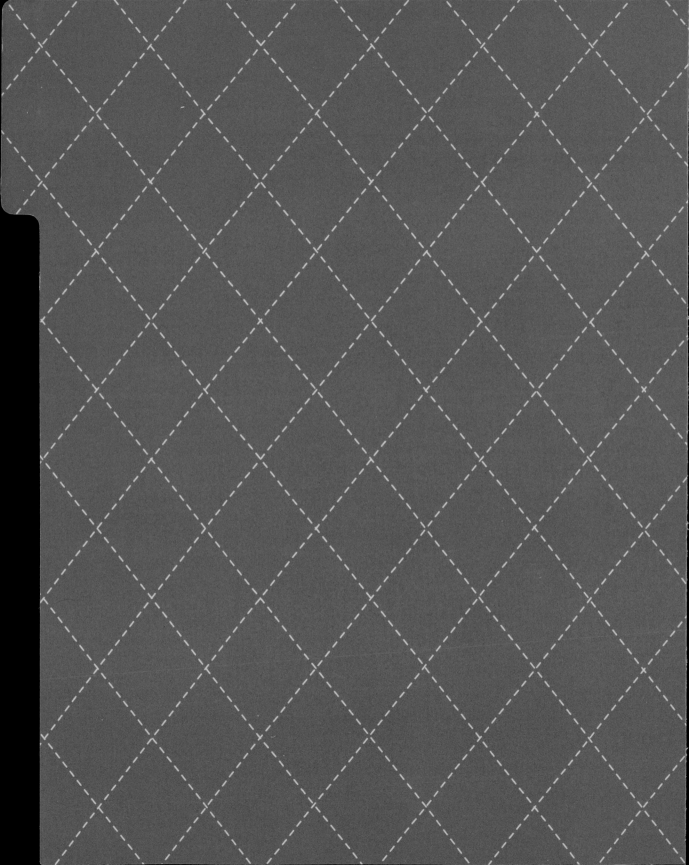

Appetizers & Beverages

Cheesy Artichoke Garlic Loaf

1 loaf (20 inches) French bread, halved lengthwise

1/2 cup butter

6 garlic cloves, minced

2 tablespoons sesame seeds

1-1/2 cups (12 ounces) sour cream

1/4 cup grated Parmesan cheese

2 tablespoons minced fresh parsley

2 teaspoons lemon-pepper seasoning

2 cups (8 ounces) cubed Monterey Jack cheese

1 can (14 ounces) water-packed artichoke hearts, rinsed, drained and chopped

1 can (2-1/4 ounces) sliced ripe olives, drained

1 cup (4 ounces) shredded cheddar cheese

1 medium tomato, chopped

Additional parsley

Carefully hollow out top and bottom of bread, leaving 1/4-in. shells; set aside. Cut removed bread into small cubes.

In a skillet, melt butter. Add the bread cubes, garlic and sesame seeds; cook and stir until butter is absorbed. Remove from the heat.

In a bowl, combine sour cream, Parmesan, parsley, lemon-pepper, Monterey Jack cheese, artichokes, olives and bread mixture. Spoon into bread shells; sprinkle with cheddar cheese. Place on ungreased baking sheets.

Bake at 350° for 30 minutes or until heated through. Sprinkle with tomato and additional parsley. Refrigerate any leftovers. **Yield:** 10-12 servings.

Deviled Ham and Egg Appetizer

6 hard-cooked eggs
3/4 cup finely chopped fully
   cooked ham
1/4 cup mayonnaise

1 tablespoon sweet pickle relish
2 teaspoons prepared mustard
1/8 teaspoon salt
Dash pepper

Slice eggs in half lengthwise. Remove yolks to a small bowl; set whites aside. Mash yolks; stir in ham, mayonnaise, relish, mustard, salt and pepper. Spoon into the egg whites. Cover and chill until ready to serve. **Yield:** 1 dozen.

Mandarin Chicken Bites

1 cup all-purpose flour
1/2 teaspoon salt
1/4 teaspoon pepper
1 pound boneless skinless
   chicken breasts, cut into 2-inch
   cubes

2 tablespoons butter
1 can (11 ounces) mandarin
   oranges, drained
2/3 cup orange marmalade
1/2 teaspoon dried tarragon

In a large resealable plastic bag, combine the flour, salt and pepper. Add chicken, a few pieces at a time, and shake to coat.

   In a skillet, brown chicken in butter until juices run clear. In a saucepan, combine the oranges, marmalade and tarragon; bring to a boil. Pour over chicken; stir gently to coat. Serve warm with toothpicks. **Yield:** 12-15 servings.

Frappe Mocha

1 teaspoon instant coffee
   granules
1/4 cup boiling water

1 cup milk
4-1/2 teaspoons chocolate syrup
1/2 cup crushed ice

In a small bowl, dissolve coffee granules in water. Pour into ice cube tray; freeze. In a blender, combine the milk, chocolate syrup and ice cubes; cover and process until smooth. Add crushed ice; blend. Serve immediately. **Yield:** 2 servings.

Party Barbecued Franks

2 teaspoons cornstarch
2 tablespoons cold water
1 jar (18 ounces) peach preserves

1 cup barbecue sauce
2 packages (1 pound *each*)
  miniature hot dogs *or*
  smoked sausages

In a large saucepan, combine the cornstarch and water until smooth. Stir in the preserves and barbecue sauce. Bring to a boil; cook and stir for 2 minutes or until thickened. Stir in hot dogs until coated. Cover and cook for 5 minutes or until heated through. **Yield:** 20 servings.

Chili Cheese Dip

1/4 to 1/2 pound ground beef
1 can (15 ounces) chili con carne
  without beans
1 pound process American
  cheese, cubed

1 can (4 ounces) chopped green
  chilies
Tortilla chips

In a saucepan, cook beef over medium heat until no longer pink; drain. Add chili, cheese and green chilies. Heat over medium-low, stirring frequently, until cheese melts. Serve warm with chips. **Yield:** 12 servings.

Tangy Turkey Meatballs

2 cups soft bread crumbs
1/2 cup finely chopped onion
2 pounds ground turkey

1 jar (12 ounces) currant jelly
1 bottle (12 ounces) chili sauce

In a bowl, combine the bread crumbs, onion and turkey. Shape into 1-in. balls. Place in a lightly greased 13-in. x 9-in. x 2-in. baking dish. Combine jelly and chili sauce; pour over meatballs.

Cover and bake at 350° for 40 minutes. Uncover; bake 10 minutes longer or until meat is no longer pink. **Yield:** about 5 dozen.

Super Nachos

1/4 pound lean ground beef
1 tablespoon chopped onion
1/8 teaspoon salt
Dash pepper
3/4 cup refried beans
2 tablespoons chopped green chilies

1/4 cup taco sauce
1 cup (4 ounces) shredded cheddar cheese
2 tablespoons sour cream
Tortilla chips, optional

In a small nonstick skillet, cook beef and onion over medium heat until meat is no longer pink; drain. Sprinkle with salt and pepper; set aside.

Spread refried beans on bottom of 9-in. pie plate coated with nonstick cooking spray. Top with meat mixture and chilies. Drizzle with taco sauce. Sprinkle with cheese.

Bake, uncovered, at 400° for 10-15 minutes or until heated through and cheese is melted. Garnish with sour cream. Serve with tortilla chips if desired. **Yield:** 2-3 servings.

Perfect Scalloped Oysters

2 cups crushed butter-flavored crackers (about 50)
1/2 cup butter, melted
1/2 teaspoon salt
Dash pepper

1 pint shucked oysters *or* 2 cans (8 ounces *each*) whole oysters, drained
1 cup heavy whipping cream
1/4 teaspoon Worcestershire sauce

In a bowl, combine the cracker crumbs, butter, salt and pepper; sprinkle a third into a greased 1-1/2-qt. baking dish. Arrange half of the oysters over crumbs. Top with another third of the crumb mixture and the remaining oysters.

Combine cream and Worcestershire sauce; pour over oysters. Top with remaining crumb mixture. Bake, uncovered, at 350° for 30-40 minutes or until top is golden brown. **Yield:** 8 servings.

Strawberry Punch

1 can (46 ounces) pineapple
   juice, chilled
2-1/4 cups water
1 can (6 ounces) frozen pink
   lemonade concentrate, thawed

3/4 cup sugar
1 quart strawberry ice cream
2-1/2 quarts ginger ale, chilled

In a punch bowl, combine the first four ingredients. Add ice cream; stir gently. Add ginger ale; stir gently. Serve immediately. **Yield:** 6 quarts.

Honey Cereal Bites

6 cups puffed wheat cereal
2 cups salted peanuts
1/4 cup sesame seeds, toasted

1/2 cup packed brown sugar
1/4 cup honey
1/4 cup butter

In a large bowl, combine the cereal, peanuts and sesame seeds. In a small saucepan, cook brown sugar, honey and butter over low heat, stirring frequently until smooth. Pour over cereal mixture and toss to coat.

Spread in two ungreased 13-in. x 9-in. x 2-in. baking pans. Bake at 275° for 45 minutes, stirring every 15 minutes. Cool. Store in an airtight container. **Yield:** 9-10 cups.

Fruity Popcorn Balls

6 quarts plain popped popcorn
3 cups (about 36) large
   marshmallows

3 tablespoons butter
3 tablespoons fruit-flavored
   gelatin (any flavor)

Place popcorn in a large bowl. In a medium saucepan, cook and stir the marshmallows, butter and gelatin over low heat until smooth. Pour over popcorn; mix well. Butter hands and form popcorn mixture into 3-in. balls. **Yield:** about 2 dozen.

Zucchini Spread

1 cup finely shredded zucchini
1 cup (4 ounces) shredded sharp
  cheddar cheese
1/2 cup chopped walnuts

1 teaspoon lemon juice
3/4 cup mayonnaise
1/2 teaspoon salt
1/4 teaspoon pepper

Place zucchini in cheesecloth or a strainer; squeeze out excess moisture. In a bowl, combine zucchini with remaining ingredients. Cover and refrigerate for at least 1 hour or overnight. Serve with crackers or raw vegetables. **Yield:** about 2 cups.

Grape Juice Crush

3/4 cup grape juice concentrate
3/4 cup lemonade concentrate
1 can (6 ounces) frozen orange
  juice concentrate, thawed

6 cups water
4 cups cold ginger ale
Crushed ice

In a 1-gallon container, combine the concentrates and water. Refrigerate until well chilled. Just before serving, slowly add the ginger ale. Serve over ice. **Yield:** about 3 quarts.

Stuffed Mushrooms

16 to 18 large fresh whole
  mushrooms
1 small onion, chopped
1 garlic clove, minced
2 tablespoons butter
8 butter-flavored crackers,
  crushed

3 ounces pepperoni *or* summer
  sausage, finely chopped
1/4 cup grated Parmesan cheese
1 tablespoon minced fresh
  parsley
1/8 teaspoon pepper

Remove stems from mushrooms; set caps aside. Mince the stems. In a skillet, saute the stems, onion and garlic in butter until soft. Remove from the heat and stir in remaining ingredients. Firmly stuff into mushroom caps; place on a greased baking sheet. Bake at 375° for 15-20 minutes or until tender. **Yield:** about 1-1/2 dozen.

Peachy Yogurt Shake

3/4 cup milk
2 cups sliced peaches
1 cup peach-flavored yogurt

1 cup crushed ice
2 tablespoons sugar
2 drops almond extract

In a blender container, place all ingredients in the order indicated; cover and process until smooth. **Yield:** 3-4 servings.

Ham and Cheese Spread

1 package (8 ounces) cream cheese
1/4 cup mayonnaise
1/2 pound boiled *or* leftover baked ham, cut in small pieces

4 tablespoons fresh parsley, *divided*
1/4 teaspoon ground mustard
1/4 teaspoon Tabasco sauce
1 tablespoon chopped green onion

Combine all ingredients except 2 tablespoons of parsley in food processor or blender; cover and pulse until ham is minced. Do not over process. Roll into a ball; chill until firm.

Coat outside of ball with reserved chopped parsley. Serve with a variety of crackers. **Yield:** 24 appetizer servings.

Mexican Pizza

1 tube (8 ounces) refrigerated crescent rolls
2 cups prepared thick chili
1/2 cup sliced ripe olives
1/4 cup chopped onion

3/4 cup shredded cheddar cheese
1/2 cup crushed corn chips
Avocado slices, shredded lettuce, chopped tomatoes *and/or* sour cream, optional

Unroll the crescent roll dough; pat into the bottom and up the sides of an ungreased 13-in. x 9-in. x 2-in. baking pan. Pinch edges together to seal. Bake at 400° for 10 minutes.

In a bowl, combine the chili, olives and onion. Spread evenly over baked crust. Sprinkle with cheese and corn chips. Bake for 8-10 minutes or until bubbly. Top with avocado, lettuce, tomatoes and/or sour cream if desired. **Yield:** 6-8 servings.

Fruit Slush

2 cups sugar
3 cups boiling water
1 can (12 ounces) frozen orange
   juice concentrate, undiluted

6 to 8 bananas, sliced
1 can (20 ounces) crushed
   pineapple
1 bottle (20 ounces) lemon-lime
   soda

Dissolve sugar in boiling water. Add the orange juice concentrate, bananas and pineapple, stirring until orange juice is dissolved. Stir in soda; pour into a large container or several small containers and freeze. Thaw for about 1 hour or until slushy before serving. **Yield:** 8-10 servings.
   Variation: Add fresh sliced peaches or seedless grapes.

Beef 'n' Cheddar Biscuits

1 pound ground beef, browned
   and drained
4 tablespoons bottled barbecue
   sauce

2 tubes (4-1/2 ounces *each*)
   refrigerated biscuits
1 cup (4 ounces) shredded
   cheddar cheese

Combine ground beef and barbecue sauce in a small bowl; set aside. Place one biscuit in each of 12 greased muffin cups; press firmly into the bottom and up the sides. Spoon 1 to 2 tablespoons of beef mixture into each cup; sprinkle with cheese.
   Bake at 350° for 15-18 minutes or until biscuits are golden and cheese is melted. Serve immediately. **Yield:** 1 dozen.

Easy Peanut Butter Pretzels

1/2 cup peanut butter chips
3/4 to 1 teaspoon shortening

8 pretzel rods
Assorted sprinkles, optional

In a 1-cup microwave-safe bowl, combine peanut butter chips and shortening. Microwave, uncovered, at 50% power until melted, stirring every 30 seconds. Dip pretzels in peanut butter mixture. Place on waxed paper and dust with sprinkles if desired. Cool completely. **Yield:** 8 servings.
   Editor's Note: This recipe was tested with an 850-watt microwave.

Tomato-Cheese Snack Bread

2 cups biscuit/baking mix
2/3 cup milk
3 medium tomatoes, peeled and cut into 1/4-inch slices
1 medium onion, finely chopped
2 tablespoons butter
1 cup (4 ounces) shredded cheddar cheese
3/4 cup sour cream
1/3 cup mayonnaise
3/4 teaspoon salt
1/4 teaspoon pepper
1/4 teaspoon dried oregano
Paprika

In a bowl, combine biscuit mix and milk just until moistened. Turn onto a floured surface; knead 10-12 times. Press onto the bottom and 1 in. up the sides of a greased 13-in. x 9-in. x 2-in. baking dish. Arrange tomato slices over top.

In a skillet, saute onion in butter until tender; remove from the heat. Stir in the cheese, sour cream, mayonnaise, salt, pepper and oregano. Spoon over tomatoes. Sprinkle with paprika.

Bake at 400° for 20-25 minutes or until browned. Let stand for 10 minutes before cutting. Serve warm. Refrigerate leftovers. **Yield:** 12-15 servings.

Barbecued Meatballs

1 pound lean ground beef
1/2 cup dry bread crumbs
1/3 cup minced onion
1/4 cup milk
1 egg, beaten
1 tablespoon snipped fresh parsley
1 teaspoon salt
1/2 teaspoon pepper
1 teaspoon Worcestershire sauce
1/4 cup vegetable oil
1 bottle (12 ounces) chili sauce
1 jar (10 ounces) grape jelly

In a mixing bowl, combine the first nine ingredients. Shape into 1-inch balls. Heat oil in a large skillet; brown meatballs on all sides. Remove meatballs and drain fat. In same skillet, combine chili sauce and jelly. Heat over medium, stirring constantly, until jelly has melted. Return meatballs to skillet; heat through. Serve warm in a chafing dish. **Yield:** about 5 dozen.

Tomato Fondue

1 garlic clove, halved
1/2 cup condensed tomato soup, undiluted
1-1/2 teaspoons ground mustard
1-1/2 teaspoons Worcestershire sauce
10 slices process American cheese, cubed
1/4 to 1/3 cup milk
1 package (16 ounces) miniature hot dogs *or* smoked sausages, warmed
Cubed French bread

Rub garlic clove over the bottom and sides of a small fondue pot or slow cooker; discard garlic and set fondue pot aside.

In a small saucepan, combine the tomato soup, mustard and Worcestershire sauce; heat through. Add cheese; stir until melted. Stir in milk; heat through.

Transfer to prepared fondue pot and keep warm. Serve with hot dogs and bread cubes. **Yield:** About 1 cup.

Nutty Caramel Popcorn

4 quarts popped popcorn
1-1/3 cups pecan halves, toasted
2/3 cup whole unblanched almonds, toasted
1-1/3 cups sugar
1 cup butter
1/2 cup light corn syrup
2 teaspoons vanilla extract

Place popcorn in a large greased bowl. Sprinkle pecans and almonds over top; set aside. In a heavy saucepan, combine the sugar, butter and corn syrup; cook and stir over medium heat until a candy thermometer reads 300°-310° (hard-crack stage). Remove from the heat; stir in vanilla. Immediately pour over popcorn mixture; toss gently. Spread on greased baking sheets. When cool, break into small pieces. Store in airtight containers. **Yield:** about 20 cups.

Editor's Note: We recommend that you test your candy thermometer before each use by bringing water to a boil; the thermometer should read 212°. Adjust your recipe temperature up or down based on your test.

Salmon Pate

1 can (14-3/4 ounces) salmon, drained, bones and skin removed
1 package (3 ounces) cream cheese, softened
1 tablespoon lemon juice
1 teaspoon prepared horseradish

1 teaspoon grated onion
1/4 teaspoon salt
1/8 teaspoon pepper
1/8 teaspoon Liquid Smoke, optional
Garnishes (sliced almonds, stuffed green olive, celery stalk, parsley)

In a bowl, flake the salmon. Add the cream cheese, lemon juice, horseradish, onion, salt, pepper and Liquid Smoke if desired; mix well.

On a platter, mold mixture into a fish shape. Arrange almonds to resemble scales. Use slice of olive for eye, thin strips of celery for the tail. Garnish with parsley. Cover and chill until serving time. Serve with buttery crackers. Refrigerate leftovers. **Yield:** 16 servings.

Bacon-Wrapped Water Chestnuts

1 pound sliced bacon
2 cans (8 ounces *each*) whole water chestnuts, rinsed and drained

1 cup ketchup
3/4 cup packed brown sugar

Cut bacon strips into thirds; wrap a strip around each water chestnut and secure with toothpicks. Place in an ungreased 15-in. x 10-in. x 2-in. baking pan. Bake at 375° for 25 minutes or until bacon is crisp.

Meanwhile, in a small saucepan, combine ketchup and brown sugar; cook and stir over medium heat until sugar is dissolved. Remove chestnuts to paper towels; drain. Dip in ketchup mixture; place in a lightly greased 13-in. x 9-in. x 2-in. baking pan. Spoon remaining sauce over chestnuts. Bake 10 minutes longer. **Yield:** about 5 dozen.

Peanut Butter 'n' Jelly Shake

2 cups cold milk
1 ripe banana, sliced
2 tablespoons peanut butter
2 tablespoons jam, jelly *or* preserves (any flavor)
1/2 teaspoon vanilla extract

Place all of the ingredients in a blender; cover and process for 3 minutes or until smooth. Serve in chilled glasses. **Yield:** 1-2 servings (2-1/2 cups).

Fruity Thirst Quencher

4 cups water
3/4 cup sugar
1 envelope (.15 ounce) unsweetened strawberry starfruit soft drink mix *or* unsweetened soft drink mix of your choice
1/2 cup orange juice
1/4 cup lemon juice
1/2 cup crushed pineapple

In a 3-qt. pitcher, combine the water, sugar and soft drink mix. Stir until sugar and mix are dissolved. Add the orange juice, lemon juice and pineapple; mix well. Refrigerate until serving. **Yield:** about 5 cups.

Sweet and Sour Chicken Nuggets

1/2 cup fine dry bread crumbs
2 teaspoons lemon-pepper seasoning
4 boneless skinless chicken breast halves, cubed
3 tablespoons vegetable oil

SAUCE:
2 tablespoons sugar
2 tablespoons ketchup
2 tablespoons soy sauce
2 tablespoons white vinegar

In a bowl or plastic bag, combine bread crumbs and lemon-pepper seasoning. Add chicken pieces, a few at a time, and shake to coat.

Heat oil in a skillet over medium heat. Cook and stir chicken in oil for about 5 minutes or until juices run clear. In a small saucepan, combine sauce ingredients; cook and stir until heated through. Serve with chicken. **Yield:** 6-8 servings.

Ham Pickle Pinwheels

- 1 package (8 ounces) cream cheese, cubed
- 1/4 pound sliced Genoa salami
- 1 tablespoon prepared horseradish
- 7 slices deli ham
- 14 to 21 okra pickles *or* dill pickle spears

In a food processor, add the cream cheese, salami and horseradish; cover and process until blended. Spread over ham slices.

Remove stems and ends of okra pickles. Place two or three okra pickles or one dill pickle down the center of each ham slice. Roll up tightly and wrap in plastic wrap. Refrigerate for at least 2 hours. Cut into 1-in. slices. **Yield:** about 3-1/2 dozen.

Frosted Hazelnuts

- 2 egg whites
- 1 cup sugar
- 2 tablespoons water
- 1 teaspoon salt
- 1/2 teaspoon *each* ground cloves, cinnamon and allspice
- 4 cups hazelnuts *or* filberts

In a medium bowl, lightly beat egg whites. Add the sugar, water, salt and spices; mix well. Let stand for 5 minutes or until sugar is dissolved. Add hazelnuts; stir gently to coat.

Spread into two greased 15-in. x 10-in. x 1-in. baking pans. Bake at 275° for 50-60 minutes or until crisp. Remove to waxed paper to cool. Store in airtight containers. **Yield:** 6 cups.

Easy Mint Hot Chocolate

- 6 Andes chocolate mints
- 16 ounces chocolate milk
- Mini marshmallows, optional

In a small saucepan, melt the mints over low heat. Slowly whisk in chocolate milk until well blended; heat but do not boil. Pour into mugs; top with mini marshmallows if desired. **Yield:** 2 servings.

Cheese Straws

4 cups (1 pound) shredded cheddar cheese
1/2 cup butter

2 cups all-purpose flour
1 teaspoon cayenne pepper

Bring cheese and butter to room temperature; mix them together by hand. Add flour and cayenne; mix well. Use a cookie press with a star or zigzag end to make strips on ungreased baking sheets.

Bake at 350° for 12-14 minutes or until golden brown and as crisp as desired. **Yield:** 10 dozen.

Creamy Red Pepper Dip

1 garlic clove, peeled
1 package (8 ounces) cream cheese, cubed
1/2 cup roasted sweet red peppers, drained
2 green onions, cut into 2-inch pieces

2 tablespoons lemon juice
1/2 teaspoon ground cumin
1 medium sweet yellow pepper, halved
Assorted fresh vegetables

In a food processor, process garlic until minced. Add the cream cheese, red peppers, onions, lemon juice and cumin; cover and process until smooth. Spoon into pepper halves. Serve with vegetables. **Yield:** about 1-1/2 cups.

Pickled Eggs

2 cups white vinegar
1 medium onion, thinly sliced
2 tablespoons sugar
2 teaspoons mixed pickling spices

2 teaspoons curry powder
1 teaspoon salt
12 hard-cooked eggs, peeled

In a medium saucepan, combine the first six ingredients; bring to a boil. Reduce heat; simmer, uncovered, until onion is tender, about 5 minutes.

Place six eggs each in two 1-qt. jars with tight-fitting lids. Pour half of the hot vinegar mixture into each jar; cover with lids. Refrigerate several hours or overnight. **Yield:** 1 dozen.

Dried Beef Spread

1 package (2-1/2 ounces) sliced dried beef

2 packages (8 ounce *each*) cream cheese, cubed

2 tablespoons milk

1 tablespoon chopped green onion

1/2 teaspoon dill weed

1/4 teaspoon hot pepper sauce

Crackers *or* party rye bread

Place beef in a food processor or blender; cover and process until chopped. Add the cream cheese, milk, onion, dill and hot pepper sauce; cover and process until well blended. Serve with crackers or bread. **Yield:** 2 cups.

Hamburger-Broccoli Dip

1 package (10 ounces) frozen chopped broccoli

1/2 pound ground beef

1/2 teaspoon salt

1 pound process cheese (Velveeta), cubed

1 can (10 ounces) diced tomatoes with mild green chilies

Corn chips

Cook broccoli according to package directions; drain and set aside. In a skillet, cook beef and salt over medium heat until meat is no longer pink; drain. Reduce heat. Add cheese; cook and stir until cheese is melted. Add tomatoes and broccoli; mix well. Serve with chips. **Yield:** 8-10 servings.

Crab-Stuffed Celery

1 carton (8 ounces) whipped chive cream cheese

1/2 cup crabmeat, drained, flaked and cartilage removed *or* imitation crabmeat

1 tablespoon mayonnaise

1/2 teaspoon lemon juice

1/8 teaspoon onion salt

1/8 teaspoon garlic salt

6 celery ribs, cut into serving-size pieces

In a bowl, combine the first six ingredients; mix well. Transfer to a small resealable plastic bag. Cut a small hole in the corner of the bag; pipe mixture into celery sticks. Store in the refrigerator. **Yield:** 2 dozen.

Tiny Taco Meatballs

2 eggs
1 medium onion, finely chopped
1 envelope taco seasoning
1/2 teaspoon salt

1/4 teaspoon pepper
2 pounds ground beef
Taco sauce, optional

In a bowl, combine the first five ingredients. Crumble beef over mixture and mix well. Shape into 1-in. balls. Place meatballs on a greased rack in a shallow baking pan. Bake at 400° for 14-18 minutes or until meat is no longer pink. Serve with taco sauce if desired. **Yield:** 14-16 servings.

Westerfield Wassail

32 ounces cranberry juice cocktail
2 cups apple juice
1 cup sugar
1 lemon, sliced

2 cinnamon sticks
3/4 teaspoon whole cloves
12 to 24 whole allspice
2 cups red wine, optional

In large saucepan, combine the cranberry juice, apple juice and sugar. Place the lemon slices, cinnamon sticks, cloves and allspice on a double thickness of cheesecloth; bring up corners of cloth and tie with kitchen string to form a bag. Place in the saucepan. Bring to a boil. Reduce heat; cover and simmer for 30 minutes. Discard spice bag. Stir in wine if desired and heat through (do not boil). Serve warm. **Yield:** 12-1/2 cups.

Orange Colada

1 can (6 ounces) frozen orange
    juice concentrate, thawed
6 ounces frozen nonalcoholic
    pina colada mix

1 cup milk
2 tablespoons lemon juice
1-1/2 cups crushed ice
Orange slices

In a blender container, combine first four ingredients; cover and process until smooth. Add ice and process until blended. Serve in a chilled glass. Garnish with an orange slice. Serve immediately. **Yield:** 6 servings.

Black Bean Salsa

1 can (15 ounces) black beans, *divided*

2 tablespoons lime juice

2 to 4 tablespoons chopped fresh cilantro

1 medium onion, chopped

1 garlic clove, minced

3 plum tomatoes, seeded and chopped

Salt to taste

Tortilla chips

Drain beans, reserving 1 tablespoon liquid. In a mixing bowl, combine lime juice, half the beans and the reserved bean liquid. Mash until smooth. Stir in remaining beans, cilantro, onion, garlic, tomatoes and salt. Serve with tortilla chips. **Yield:** 4-6 servings.

Blueberry Milk Shake

1 cup milk

2 tablespoons lemon juice

1 pint vanilla ice cream

1 cup fresh *or* frozen blueberries

1 tablespoon sugar

1 tablespoon grated lemon peel

Place all ingredients in a blender container; cover and process on high until smooth. Pour into glasses. Refrigerate any leftovers. **Yield:** 3-4 servings.

Crab-Stuffed Deviled Eggs

12 hard-cooked eggs

1 can (6 ounces) crabmeat, drained, flaked and cartilage removed *or* 1 cup finely chopped imitation crabmeat

2/3 cup mayonnaise

1/2 cup finely chopped celery

1/2 cup chopped slivered almonds

2 tablespoons finely chopped green pepper

1/2 teaspoon salt

Slice eggs in half lengthwise. Remove yolks and set whites aside. In a bowl, mash yolks. Stir in the crab, mayonnaise, celery, almonds, green pepper and salt. Stuff or pipe into egg whites. Refrigerate until ready to serve. **Yield:** 2 dozen.

Creamy Shrimp Dip

1 package (8 ounces) cream cheese, softened
1/2 cup mayonnaise
4 green onions, chopped
1/2 teaspoon celery seed
1/2 teaspoon garlic powder
2 cans (6 ounces *each*) tiny shrimp, rinsed and drained
Potato chips *or* crackers

In a bowl, combine the first five ingredients; mix well. Stir in shrimp. Refrigerate until serving. Serve with chips or crackers. **Yield:** 2 cups.

Dairy Hollow House Herbal Cooler

8 bags Red Zinger tea
1 quart (4 cups) boiling water
1 can (12 ounces) frozen apple juice concentrate
4-1/2 cups cold water
1 orange, sliced
1/2 lemon, sliced
Mint sprig to garnish

Steep tea in boiling water in glass container; cool until lukewarm. Remove tea bags. Add apple juice concentrate, cold water, orange and lemon slices. Chill thoroughly. Serve coolers over ice with a sprig of mint. **Yield:** 8 servings.

Curried Chicken Balls

2 packages (3 ounces *each*) cream cheese, softened
2 tablespoons orange marmalade
2 teaspoons curry powder
3/4 teaspoon salt
1/4 teaspoon pepper
3 cups finely minced cooked chicken
3 tablespoons minced green onion
3 tablespoons minced celery
1 cup finely chopped almonds, toasted

In a mixing bowl, combine first five ingredients. Beat until smooth. Stir in chicken, onion and celery. Shape into 1-in. balls; roll in almonds. Cover and chill until firm (can refrigerate up to 2 days). **Yield:** about 5 dozen appetizers.

Buttery Chicken Spread

1 package (8 ounces) cream
   cheese, softened
3 cups shredded cooked chicken
1 cup butter, softened
1/4 cup minced fresh parsley
2 tablespoons minced onion

1 teaspoon lemon juice
1/2 to 1 teaspoon dill weed
1/8 teaspoon salt
Dash ground cinnamon
Party bread, toast *or* crackers

In a bowl, combine the first nine ingredients. Transfer to a small crock or serving dish. Cover and chill at least 1 hour. Let stand at room temperature for 20 minutes before serving. Serve with bread, toast or crackers. **Yield:** 20-25 servings (3-1/2 cups).

Crunchy Swiss-n-Ham Snacks

2 cups ground fully cooked ham
2 cups stiff mashed potatoes
1 cup (4 ounces) shredded Swiss
   cheese
1/3 cup mayonnaise

1/4 cup finely chopped onion
1 egg, beaten
1 teaspoon prepared mustard
1/4 teaspoon pepper
1-1/4 cups crushed cornflakes

In a bowl, combine the first eight ingredients. Cover and refrigerate for 1 hour or until easy to handle. Shape into 1-in. ball; roll in cornflakes until coated. Place in a lightly greased 15-in. x 10-in. x 1-in. baking pan.

Bake at 350° for 25-30 minutes or until golden brown. Serve warm. Refrigerate any leftovers. **Yield:** about 5 dozen.

Mini Garlic Bread

4 to 5 tablespoons butter
1/2 teaspoon dill weed
1/2 teaspoon garlic powder

1/2 teaspoon Italian seasoning
4 hot dog rolls, sliced

In a mixing bowl, combine the butter, dill weed, garlic powder and Italian seasoning. Spread on cut sides of each roll. Place on baking sheet; broil until golden brown. **Yield:** 4 servings.

Crab Roll-Ups

1 package (10 ounces) frozen chopped spinach, thawed and squeezed dry
1 envelope vegetable soup mix
1/2 cup mayonnaise
1/2 cup sour cream
1 package (8 ounces) imitation crabmeat, chopped
1 package (8 ounces) cream cheese, softened
1/4 cup mango chutney *or* chutney of your choice
1/8 teaspoon garlic powder
1/8 teaspoon onion powder
12 flour tortillas (8 inches), room temperature

In a large bowl, combine the spinach, soup mix, mayonnaise and sour cream; cover and refrigerate for 1 hour.

In another large bowl, combine the crab, cream cheese, chutney, garlic powder and onion powder; cover and refrigerate for 1 hour.

Spread the spinach mixture on six tortillas. Spread the crab mixture on remaining tortillas. Place one crab tortilla over each spinach tortilla. Roll up tightly, jelly-roll style, and wrap in plastic wrap. Refrigerate for at least 30 minutes.

Cut each roll into seven slices. Refrigerate any leftovers. **Yield:** about 7 dozen.

Eggnog Dip

1-1/2 cups eggnog
2 tablespoons cornstarch
1/2 cup sour cream
1/2 cup heavy whipping cream
1 tablespoon sugar
1/2 teaspoon rum extract, optional
Assorted fruit and pound cake cubes

In a saucepan, combine the eggnog and cornstarch until smooth. Bring to a boil; cook and stir for 2 minutes. Remove from the heat; stir in sour cream. Cool completely.

In a large mixing bowl, beat whipping cream and sugar until stiff peaks form. Fold into eggnog mixture with extract if desired. Cover and refrigerate overnight. Serve with fruit and cake cubes. **Yield:** about 2-1/2 cups.

Editor's Note: This recipe works best with commercially prepared eggnog.

Chutney Stuffed Eggs

12 hard-cooked eggs
6 bacon strips, cooked and finely crumbled

1/4 cup chutney, chopped
3 tablespoons mayonnaise

Cut eggs in half lengthwise; remove yolks and set whites aside. In a bowl, mash the yolks. Add the bacon, chutney and mayonnaise; mix well. Pipe or spoon into egg whites. Refrigerate until serving. **Yield:** 12 servings.

Ham 'n' Cheese Puffs

1 cup water
1/2 cup butter
1 cup all-purpose flour
1/2 teaspoon ground mustard
4 eggs

1 cup finely chopped fully cooked ham
1/2 cup shredded sharp cheddar cheese
Warm prepared cheese sauce, optional

In a heavy saucepan over medium heat, bring water and butter to a boil. Add flour and mustard all at once; stir until a smooth ball forms. Remove from the heat; let stand for 5 minutes. Add eggs, one at a time, beating well after each addition. Beat until smooth. Stir in the ham and cheese (cheese does not have to melt).

Drop batter by tablespoonfuls 2 in. apart onto greased baking sheets. Bake at 400° for 30-35 minutes or until golden. Serve warm or cold with cheese sauce for dipping if desired. **Yield:** about 4-1/2 dozen.

Apple Pie a la Mode Shake

1 cup plain nonfat yogurt
1/2 cup applesauce, frozen
2 tablespoons brown sugar

1/2 teaspoon ground cinnamon
1/2 teaspoon vanilla extract

Combine all ingredients in a blender until smooth. **Yield:** 1-2 servings (1-1/2 cups).

Banana Smoothie

2 cups milk
2 medium ripe bananas

1/4 cup honey
1/2 teaspoon vanilla extract

Combine all ingredients in a blender until smooth. **Yield:** 3-4 servings (3-1/2 cups).

Cheese Olive Appetizers

1 package (16 ounces) hot roll mix
3/4 cup warm water (110° to 115°)
1 egg
1/4 cup butter, melted
1 cup (4 ounces) shredded cheddar cheese
1 tablespoon poppy seeds

TOPPING:
2 cups (8 ounces) shredded cheddar cheese
1 cup sliced stuffed olives
1/3 cup butter, melted
1 egg, beaten
1 tablespoon dried minced onion
1 teaspoon Worcestershire sauce

In a large bowl, dissolve yeast from hot roll mix in warm water. Add egg, butter, cheese and poppy seeds. Add flour from mix; blend well. Press into a greased 15-in. x 10-in. x 1-in. baking pan. Cover and let rise in a warm place until doubled, about 45 minutes. Combine topping ingredients; spread over dough. Bake at 400° for 20-25 minutes or until golden brown. Cut into squares; serve warm. **Yield:** About 4 dozen.

Mustard Dip

1 can (14 ounces) sweetened condensed milk
1/4 cup ground *or* prepared mustard

3 tablespoons prepared horseradish
1 tablespoon Worcestershire sauce

In a bowl, combine all the ingredients until smooth (mustard will thicken as it stands). Store in the refrigerator. **Yield:** 1-1/2 cups.

Editor's Note: To make hot and sippy dip for pretzels and egg rolls, use ground mustard. To make a milder, sweeter sauce that's very good with ham and turkey, use prepared mustard.

Onions and Cream Appetizer

2 cups water
1 cup sugar
1/4 cup white vinegar
1 teaspoon celery seed

6 cups sliced sweet onions,
  separated into rings
1 cup mayonnaise
Assorted crackers

In a large saucepan, combine the first four ingredients; bring to a boil. Drop onion rings into boiling mixture; cook for 5 minutes. Cover and remove from the heat. Let stand for 20-30 minutes or until onions are transparent; drain. Cool.

In a bowl, whisk the mayonnaise until smooth; stir in onions. Cover and refrigerate overnight. Serve with crackers. **Yield:** 3 cups.

Pepperoni Bread

1 French *or* Italian sandwich roll
  (about 4 to 5 inches long)
2 to 3 tablespoons pizza sauce

8 slices pepperoni
1/4 cup shredded part-skim
  mozzarella cheese

Slice roll in half lengthwise. Place on baking sheet. Spread pizza sauce over each half. Top with pepperoni. Sprinkle with mozzarella cheese.

Bake at 350° for 10 minutes or until heated through. Broil 4 in. from the heat for 2 minutes or until cheese is bubbly and golden brown. **Yield:** 2 servings.

Cranberry Apple Punch

2 quarts water
2 cups sugar
1 can (16 ounces) frozen orange
  juice concentrate, thawed
1 can (12 ounces) frozen
  lemonade concentrate, thawed

2 quarts cranberry juice
1 quart apple juice
2 cups prepared tea, cooled
Orange, lemon and lime slices

In a large saucepan, heat water and sugar until dissolved. Cool; pour into a large punch bowl. Add the next five ingredients. Garnish with orange, lemon and lime slices. Chill with an ice ring. **Yield:** 6-1/2 quarts.

Chocolate Banana Smoothie

3 cups whole milk, *divided*
2 large bananas, cut into pieces

1/2 teaspoon vanilla extract
1/2 cup chocolate syrup

In a blender container, combine 1-1/2 cups milk, bananas, vanilla and chocolate syrup. Blend until smooth. Add remaining milk and blend again. Serve immediately. **Yield:** 4-6 servings (4 cups).

Tex-Mex Bean Dip

6 green onions, chopped, *divided*
1 can (16 ounces) refried beans
1 cup (8 ounces) sour cream
1 package (8 ounces) cream cheese, softened
1 cup (4 ounces) shredded cheddar cheese

1 cup (4 ounces) shredded Monterey Jack cheese
1 can (4 ounces) green chilies, chopped
1 package taco seasoning
Tortilla chips

Set aside 1 tablespoon green onion. Place the remaining green onions in a fondue pot or chaffing dish. Add the beans, sour cream, cream cheese, cheeses, green chilies and taco seasoning; mix well. Heat and stir until cheese is melted. Top with reserved onions. Serve warm with tortilla chips. **Yield:** 40 appetizer servings.

Cottage-Cauliflower Spread

1 cup (8 ounces) cream-style cottage cheese
2 cups cooked cauliflowerets
1 cup grated Parmesan cheese
2 garlic cloves, minced

2 tablespoons grated onion
4-1/2 teaspoons chopped fresh oregano
Freshly ground black pepper
Whole wheat crackers

In a mixing bowl, combine cottage cheese and cauliflower. Mix until almost smooth. Stir in Parmesan cheese, garlic, onion, oregano and pepper. Spoon into a greased 1-qt. baking dish. Bake at 400° for 20 minutes. Serve with crackers. **Yield:** about 3-1/2 cups.

Aunt Shirley's Liver Pate

3/4 cup butter, *divided*
1-1/4 pounds chicken livers, halved
1/4 cup chopped onion
2 teaspoons Worcestershire sauce

1 tablespoon minced fresh parsley
1/4 cup sliced stuffed olives
Additional parsley, optional
Crackers

In a large skillet, melt 1/2 cup butter. Add chicken livers, onion, Worcestershire sauce and parsley. Saute over medium heat for 6-8 minutes or until chicken is no longer pink. Remove from the heat; cool for 10 minutes.

Transfer to a blender; cover and process until smooth. Melt the remaining butter; cool to lukewarm. Add to blender and process until blended.

Pour into a 2-1/2-cup mold that has been lined with plastic wrap. Cover and chill for 8 hours or overnight. Before serving, unmold pate onto a chilled plate. Press olives on top of pate; garnish with parsley if desired. Serve with crackers. **Yield:** 8-10 servings (2-1/4 cups).

Hawaiian Roll-Ups

1/2 cup milk
1 teaspoon prepared mustard
3 drops Worcestershire sauce
1 cup soft bread crumbs
2/3 cup packed brown sugar
1 teaspoon dried minced onion
1 teaspoon salt

1/4 teaspoon pepper
1-1/2 pounds lean ground beef
14 thin slices deli ham
14 bacon strips, halved widthwise
1 can (8 ounces) pineapple tidbits, undrained

In a large bowl, combine the first eight ingredients. Crumble beef over the mixture and mix well. Spread beef mixture over ham slice. Roll up, starting with a short side. Cut in half widthwise; wrap a bacon slice around each. Secure with toothpicks.

Place in an ungreased 13-in. x 9-in. x 2-in. baking dish. Pour pineapple over roll-ups. Cover and bake at 375° for 30 minutes. Uncover; bake 30 minutes longer or until heated through. **Yield:** 28 roll-ups.

Breaded Asparagus Sticks

2 pounds asparagus spears
1-1/2 cups grated Parmesan cheese
1-1/2 cups fresh bread crumbs
2 eggs, beaten
1/2 teaspoon salt
Dash hot pepper sauce
2 tablespoons butter
2 tablespoons olive oil
Grated Parmesan cheese, optional

Cook the asparagus in a small amount of water until crisp-tender. Drain well. Combine 1-1/2 cups cheese and the bread crumbs on a plate.

In a shallow bowl, stir together eggs, salt and pepper sauce. Dip each asparagus spear in egg mixture and roll in crumbs to coat well. Chill for 20 minutes.

In a skillet, heat butter and oil on medium-high. Brown the spears in a single layer, turning carefully. Remove and keep warm while browning remaining spears. Serve with additional Parmesan cheese, if desired. **Yield:** 6 servings.

Cheesy Mushroom Appetizers

2 tubes (8 ounces *each*) refrigerated crescent rolls
2 packages (8 ounces *each*) cream cheese, softened
3 cans (4 ounces *each*) mushroom stems and pieces, drained and chopped
1-1/4 teaspoons garlic powder
1/2 teaspoon Cajun seasoning
1 egg
1 tablespoon water
2 tablespoons grated Parmesan cheese

Unroll crescent dough into two long rectangles; seal the seams and perforations. In a mixing bowl, combine the cream cheese, mushrooms, garlic powder and Cajun seasoning. Spread over dough to within 1 in. of edges. Roll up each rectangle, jelly-roll style, starting with a long side; seal edges. Place seam side down on a greased baking sheet.

Beat egg and water; brush over dough. Sprinkle with cheese. Bake at 375° for 20-25 minutes or until golden brown. Cut into slices. **Yield:** 16 appetizers.

Hot Chocolate Mix

1 package (8 quarts) nonfat dry milk

1 jar (6 ounces) nondairy coffee creamer

1 container (16 ounces) dry chocolate milk mix

1/2 cup confectioners' sugar

Place ingredients in a very large bowl. Stir until well blended. Store in airtight container. For each serving, add 1/4 cup chocolate mix to 2/3 cup hot water. **Yield:** 3-qts. dry mix.

Almond Tea

1 can (12 ounces) frozen lemonade concentrate, thawed

1 cup sugar

3 to 4 tablespoons unsweetened instant tea

1 tablespoon almond extract

1 tablespoon vanilla extract

14 cups water

In a 1-gallon container, combine the first five ingredients. Add 8 cups water; stir to blend. Add the remaining water. Serve over ice. **Yield:** 16 servings (4 quarts).

Rhubarb Punch

3 quarts diced fresh *or* frozen rhubarb

4-1/2 cups sugar

3 quarts water

1 can (6 ounces) frozen orange juice concentrate, thawed

3 tablespoons lemon juice

Lemon-lime soda

In a heavy saucepan, bring rhubarb, sugar and water to a boil. Boil for 15 minutes; cool and strain. Stir in orange and lemon juices. Chill.

For each serving, combine 1/2 cup rhubarb syrup and 12 ounces soda. Serve in chilled glass. **Yield:** 24 servings (12 ounces each).

Editor's Note: If using frozen rhubarb, measure rhubarb while still frozen, then thaw completely. Drain in a colander, but do not press liquid out.

Hot Wings

4 pounds whole chicken wings
Oil for deep-fat frying
1/4 cup butter
1/4 cup honey
1/4 cup barbecue sauce
4 to 6 tablespoons hot pepper sauce

3 tablespoons cider vinegar
3 tablespoons prepared mustard
1/4 teaspoon garlic salt
Celery and carrot sticks
Blue cheese *or* ranch salad dressing

Cut wings into three sections; discard wing tip section. In an electric skillet or deep-fat fryer, heat oil to 350°. Fry chicken wings, a few at a time, about 9 minutes or until golden. Drain on paper towels; place in a large bowl.

In a saucepan, combine the next seven ingredients; cook and stir 5-10 minutes. Pour over cooked wings; let stand for 10 minutes.

With a slotted spoon, remove wings from sauce and place in a single layer on greased baking sheets. Bake at 350° for 15 minutes. Serve hot with vegetable sticks and dressing for dipping. **Yield:** 12-16 servings.

Old-Fashioned Popcorn Balls

2 quarts popped popcorn
1 cup sugar
1/3 cup corn syrup
1/3 cup water

1/4 cup butter
1/2 teaspoon salt
1 teaspoon vanilla extract

Place popcorn in a baking pan and keep warm in a 200° oven while preparing syrup. In a large saucepan, combine the sugar, corn syrup, water, butter and salt. Cook over medium heat until mixture comes to a boil, stirring constantly. Continue cooking without stirring until the temperature reaches 270° on a candy thermometer. Remove from the heat. Add vanilla; stir just enough to mix. Slowly pour over the popcorn. Cool just enough to handle. Shape into balls with buttered hands. **Yield:** 1 dozen.

Editor's Note: We recommend that you test your candy thermometer before each use by bringing water to a boil; the thermometer should read 212°. Adjust your recipe temperature up or down based on your test.

Hot Bacon Cheese Spread

1 unsliced round loaf (1 pound)
   Italian bread
2 cups (8 ounces) shredded
   Monterey Jack cheese
1 cup (4 ounces) shredded
   Parmesan cheese

1 cup mayonnaise
1/4 cup chopped onion
5 bacon strips, cooked and
   crumbled
1 garlic clove, minced

Cut top fourth off loaf of bread; carefully hollow out bottom, leaving a 1-in. shell. Cube removed bread and set aside. Combine the remaining ingredients; spoon into bread bowl. Replace top. Place on an ungreased baking sheet.

    Bake at 350° for 1 hour or until heated through. Serve with reserved bread cubes. **Yield:** 2 cups.

    Editor's Note: Reduced-fat or fat-free mayonnaise may not be substituted for regular mayonnaise in this recipe.

Sweet-And-Sour Meatballs Appetizer

2 cups soft bread crumbs
1/2 cup milk
1/2 cup lean ground beef
1/2 pound bulk pork sausage
1 can (8 ounces) whole water
   chestnuts, finely chopped and
   drained

1 tablespoon soy sauce
1/2 teaspoon garlic powder
1/4 teaspoon onion salt
Prepared sweet-and-sour sauce,
   optional

In a bowl, combine bread crumbs and milk; set aside. Meanwhile, combine ground beef, sausage, water chestnuts, soy sauce, garlic powder and onion salt. Add to bread crumb mixture; mix well. Form into 1-1/2-in. meatballs. Place meatballs on a greased rack in a shallow baking pan.

    Bake at 350° for about 20 minutes or until a meat thermometer reads 160°; drain. Serve with sweet-and-sour sauce if desired. **Yield:** 3-4 dozen.

Nutty Beef Turnovers

1 pound ground beef	2 teaspoons sugar
1-1/2 cups chopped nuts	1/4 teaspoon ground cinnamon
1 medium onion, chopped	2 loaves (1 pound *each*) frozen
2 garlic cloves, minced	bread dough, thawed
1 tablespoon Worcestershire sauce	

In a skillet, cook the beef, nuts, onion and garlic over medium heat until meat is no longer pink; drain. Remove from the heat. Stir in the Worcestershire sauce, sugar and cinnamon.

On a floured surface, roll each portion of dough into a 12-in. square. Cut each into four squares. Place about 1/4 cup meat mixture in center of each square. Moisten edges of pastry with water; fold over filling, forming a triangle. Press edges with a fork to seal. Place on ungreased baking sheets. Bake at 350° for 20 minutes or until golden brown. **Yield:** 8 servings.

Roasted Corn and Avocado Dip

1 cup fresh corn	1 can (3-1/2 ounces) jalapeno peppers, drained and chopped
2 tablespoons vegetable oil	
2 large avocados, peeled	1/2 teaspoon salt
3 tablespoons lime juice	1/4 teaspoon ground cumin
2 garlic cloves, minced	Tortilla chips
2 tablespoons minced onion	

In a shallow baking dish, combine corn and oil. Bake, uncovered, at 400° for 12-15 minutes or until lightly browned, stirring several times. Cool.

Meanwhile, chop 1 avocado and set aside. Mash the other avocado in a bowl; add the lime juice, garlic, onion, jalapenos, salt and cumin. Fold in chopped avocado and the corn. Cover and chill. Serve with tortilla chips. **Yield:** 2-1/2 cups.

Editor's Note: When cutting or seeding hot peppers, use rubber or plastic gloves to protect your hands. Avoid touching your face.

Tasty Tortilla Roll-Ups

2 packages (one 8 ounces, one
    3 ounces) cream cheese,
    softened
1/4 cup minced green onions
3 tablespoons chopped green
    chilies and jalapeno peppers
3 tablespoons chopped ripe
    olives

3 tablespoons diced pimientos,
    drained
3 tablespoons finely chopped
    pecans *or* walnuts
1/8 teaspoon garlic powder
5 flour tortillas (8 inches)

In a small mixing bowl, beat cream cheese. Stir in green onions, green chilies, olives pimientos, pecans and garlic powder. Spread over tortillas. Roll up tightly. Wrap in plastic wrap. Refrigerate for at least 2 hours. Cut into 1/2-in. pieces. **Yield:** 2-1/2 dozen.

Editor's Note: When cutting or seeding hot peppers, use rubber or plastic gloves to protect your hands. Avoid touching your face.

Swiss 'n' Bacon Pizza

2 tubes (12 ounces *each*)
    refrigerated buttermilk biscuits
1 pound sliced bacon, cooked
    and crumbled
1 medium tomato, chopped

1 medium onion, chopped
1 cup (4 ounces) shredded Swiss
    cheese
1/2 cup mayonnaise
1 teaspoon dried basil

Split each biscuit into two halves. Press onto a greased 14-in. pizza pan, sealing seams. In a bowl, combine the remaining ingredients; spread over crust.

Bake at 350° for 20-23 minutes or until golden brown. Cut into thin wedges. **Yield:** 8-12 servings.

Editor's Note: Reduced-fat or fat-free mayonnaise may not be substituted for regular mayonnaise in this recipe.

Sausage Bacon Tidbits

1-1/2 cups herb-seasoned stuffing
    mix
1/4 cup butter
1/4 cup water

1/4 pound bulk pork sausage
1 egg, beaten
1 pound sliced bacon

Place stuffing mix in a bowl. In a saucepan, heat butter and water until butter is melted. Pour over stuffing. Add sausage and egg; mix well. Refrigerate for at least 1 hour.

Shape into 1-in. balls. Cut bacon strips in half; wrap a strip around each stuffing ball and secure with a toothpick. Place in a ungreased 15-in. x 10-in. x 1-in. baking pan.

Bake, uncovered, at 375° for 20 minutes. Turn; bake 15 minutes longer or until bacon is crisp. Drain on paper towels; serve warm. **Yield:** about 2-1/2 dozen.

Hot Crab Dip

1 package (8 ounces) cream
    cheese, softened
1/4 cup shredded Monterey Jack
    cheese
2 tablespoons milk
1/2 teaspoon prepared horseradish
1/4 teaspoon salt
1/4 teaspoon dill weed

Dash pepper
1 can (6 ounces) crabmeat,
    drained, flaked and cartilage
    removed
1/4 cup sliced green onions
Additional dill weed, optional
Sliced French bread

In a mixing bowl, combine the cream cheese, Monterey Jack cheese, milk, horseradish, salt, dill and pepper. Stir in crab and onions. Spread evenly into an ungreased 9-in. pie plate. If desired, sprinkle with additional dill. Bake, uncovered, at 375° for 15 minutes. Serve with bread. **Yield:** 12 servings.

Tasty Pork Nuggets

1 cup cornflake crumbs
1/3 cup toasted wheat germ
3 tablespoons sesame seeds
1-1/2 teaspoons dried parsley flakes
1/2 teaspoon paprika
1/2 teaspoon ground mustard
1/2 teaspoon celery salt

1/2 teaspoon onion powder
1/4 teaspoon lemon-pepper
    seasoning
1/4 teaspoon salt, optional
1 pound lean boneless pork, cut
    into 1-inch x 1-1/2-inch cubes
1 cup plain nonfat yogurt

Combine the cornflake crumbs, wheat germ, sesame seeds, parsley, paprika, mustard, celery salt, onion powder, lemon-pepper and salt if desired; set aside.

Dip pork cubes in yogurt, then roll in crumb mixture. Arrange pork in a single layer on a 13-in. x 9-in. x 2-in. baking pan coated with nonstick cooking spray.

Bake at 400° for 15-18 minutes or until juices run clear. For a crispier coating, broil for 2-3 minutes after baking. **Yield:** 2-1/2 dozen.

Speedy Pizza Rings

2 medium zucchini (about 2-inch
    diameter), cut into 1/4-inch
    slices
1 can (8 ounces) pizza sauce
1 package (3 ounces) sliced
    pepperoni

1 cup (4 ounces) shredded
    part-skim mozzarella cheese
Sliced jalapeno peppers and ripe
    olives, optional

Arrange zucchini in a single layer on a large microwave-safe plate coated with nonstick cooking spray. Microwave, uncovered, on high for 2-1/4 minutes. Spread 1 teaspoon pizza sauce on each zucchini round; top each with a slice of pepperoni. Heat, uncovered, for 1-1/2 minutes. Sprinkle each with cheese, jalapenos and olives if desired. Microwave 30-50 seconds longer or until cheese is melted. **Yield:** 10-12 servings.

Editor's Note: When cutting or seeding hot peppers, use rubber or plastic gloves to protect your hands. Avoid touching your face. This recipe was tested in a 1,100-watt microwave.

Easy Egg Rolls

1 pound ground beef, cooked
and drained
1 package (16 ounces) coleslaw
mix
2 tablespoons soy sauce
1/2 teaspoon garlic powder
1/4 teaspoon ground ginger
Onion powder to taste
2 packages (16 ounces *each*) egg
roll wrappers
1 tablespoon all-purpose flour
Vegetable oil for frying

In a bowl, combine the first six ingredients. Place a heaping table-
spoonful of beef mixture in the center of one egg roll wrapper. Fold
bottom corner over filling. Fold sides toward center over filling.

In a small bowl, combine flour and enough water to make a paste.
Moisten top corner of egg roll wrapper with paste; roll up tightly to seal.
Repeat. In an electric skillet, heat 1 in. of oil to 375°. Fry egg rolls for
3-5 minutes or until golden brown. **Yield:** 40 egg rolls.

Editor's Note: Fill egg roll wrappers one at a time, keeping the others
covered until ready to use.

Curry Carrot Dip

1 small onion, chopped
2 teaspoons canola oil
4 medium carrots, sliced
1/3 cup water
1/4 teaspoon salt
1/4 teaspoon pepper
1/4 teaspoon curry powder
2 tablespoons mayonnaise
2 teaspoons prepared mustard
Assorted raw vegetables

In a nonstick skillet, saute onion in oil. Add the carrots, water, salt,
pepper and curry. Bring to a boil. Reduce heat; cover and simmer for 6
minutes or until vegetables are tender. Uncover; cook for 8 minutes or
until liquid has evaporated. Cool.

Transfer to a food processor or blender; cover and process until
smooth. Add mayonnaise and mustard; mix well. Serve with vegetables.
Yield: 1 cup.

Breakfast & Brunch

Viennese Pancakes

2/3 cup all-purpose flour
1/2 cup milk
1/3 cup water
1 egg
1/8 teaspoon salt

FILLING:
1 package (8 ounces) cream
cheese, softened

6 tablespoons sugar
2 eggs, *separated*
1/4 cup raisins, chopped
1/4 cup sliced almonds
1 teaspoon grated lemon peel
1/8 teaspoon salt
2 teaspoons brown sugar
Additional sliced almonds, optional

In a mixing bowl, combine flour, milk, water, egg and salt; beat until smooth. Cover and let stand for 1 hour.

In a lightly greased 8-in. skillet over medium-high heat, add 2-3 tablespoons batter; lift and tilt skillet to cover bottom. Cook until lightly browned; turn and brown the other side. Repeat with remaining batter, greasing skillet as needed. Stack pancakes with waxed paper between layers.

For filling, beat cream cheese and sugar in a mixing bowl until light and fluffy. Beat in egg yolks. Stir in raisins, almonds, lemon peel and salt. Place 1 tablespoon filling down the center of each pancake; set remaining filling aside. Roll up pancakes and place seam side down in a greased 12-in. x 8-in. x 2-in. baking dish.

In a small bowl, beat egg whites until stiff; fold in reserved filling. Spoon over pancakes; sprinkle with brown sugar and almonds if desired.

Bake, uncovered, at 350° for 20-25 minutes or until edges are lightly browned. **Yield:** 13 pancakes.

Breakfast Pizza

1 tube (8 ounces) refrigerated
  crescent rolls
1 pound bulk pork sausage
1 can (4 ounces) sliced
  mushrooms, drained

1 cup (4 ounces) shredded
  part-skim mozzarella cheese
1 cup (4 ounces) shredded
  cheddar cheese

Separate crescent roll dough into eight triangles and place on an ungreased 12-in. round pizza pan with points toward the center. Press over bottom and up sides to form a crust; seal perforations. Bake at 350° for 10 minutes.

Meanwhile, crumble sausage into a skillet. Cook over medium heat until no longer pink. Drain; place over crust. Sprinkle with mushrooms and cheeses.

Bake at 350° for 15 minutes or until cheese is melted. **Yield:** 8-10 servings.

Pull-Apart Morning Rolls

1 cup chopped walnuts
1 package (3.4 ounces) instant
  butterscotch pudding mix
1/2 cup packed brown sugar
1/2 teaspoon ground cinnamon

2 packages (13-1/2 to 15 ounces
  each) frozen dinner roll dough,
  thawed
1/2 cup butter, melted

Sprinkle walnuts in the bottom of a well-greased 10-in. fluted tube pan. Combine pudding mix, brown sugar and cinnamon. Roll each dinner roll in butter and then in brown sugar mixture; coat well. Place each roll in pan. Cover and refrigerate overnight. Remove from refrigerator 30 minutes before baking.

Bake at 350° for 30-35 minutes or until golden brown. Cool for 10 minutes in pan before removing to a serving platter. **Yield:** 16-20 servings.

Corned Beef Hash and Eggs

1 package (32 ounces) frozen cubed hash browns

1-1/2 cups chopped onion

1/2 cup vegetable oil

4 to 5 cups chopped cooked corned beef

1/2 teaspoon salt

8 eggs

Salt and pepper to taste

2 tablespoons minced fresh parsley

In a large ovenproof skillet, cook hash browns and onion in oil until potatoes are browned and onion is tender. Remove from the heat; stir in corned beef and salt. Make eight wells in the hash browns. Break one egg into each well. Sprinkle with salt and pepper. Cover and bake at 325° for 20-25 minutes or until eggs reach desired doneness. Garnish with parsley. **Yield:** 4 servings.

Zucchini Oven Omelet

2 cups chopped zucchini

1/4 cups chopped green pepper

1/4 cup vegetable oil

6 eggs, lightly beaten

2 tablespoons grated Parmesan cheese

1 tablespoon half-and-half cream

1 tablespoon butter, melted

1/2 teaspoon salt

1/8 teaspoon pepper

1/2 cup shredded cheddar cheese

In a 10-in. ovenproof skillet, saute zucchini and green pepper in oil until tender, about 3 minutes. Combine eggs, Parmesan cheese, cream, butter, salt and pepper; pour over the vegetable mixture. Cook and stir gently for 3 minutes or until eggs are set on bottom. Top with cheese.

Bake at 350° for 5-7 minutes or until eggs are set and cheese is melted. **Yield:** 4-6 servings.

Brunch Tidbits Bread

1-1/2 cups (6 ounces) shredded cheddar cheese
3/4 cup chopped green olives
3/4 cup chopped ripe olives
1/2 cup mayonnaise
1/4 cup sliced green onions
1/4 teaspoon pepper
4 English muffins, split

In a bowl, combine cheese, olives, mayonnaise, onions and pepper. Spread on English muffins; cut into fourths. Place on an ungreased baking sheet and bake at 350° for 8-10 minutes or until bubbly. Or freeze and bake frozen at 350° for 18-20 minutes. **Yield:** 8 servings.

Curried Scrambled Egg

1 egg
1 teaspoon water
1 teaspoon finely chopped chives
1/8 to 1/4 teaspoon curry powder
1 teaspoon olive oil

In a small bowl, beat the egg, water, chives and curry powder. Pour oil into a small skillet: add egg mixture. Cook and stir gently over medium heat until egg is set. **Yield:** 1 serving.

Creamed Ham and Eggs

3 tablespoons butter
1/4 cup all-purpose flour
1/2 teaspoon ground mustard
1/8 teaspoon pepper
2 cups milk
1/2 teaspoon Worcestershire sauce
3 hard-cooked eggs, diced
2 cups cubed fully cooked ham
3 slices toast, cut into triangles

In a saucepan, melt butter. Add flour, mustard and pepper; cook until bubbly. Gradually add milk and Worcestershire sauce. Bring to a boil; cook and stir for 2 minutes or until thickened. Stir in eggs and ham; heat through. Serve hot over toast. **Yield:** 2-3 servings.

Spanish-Style Breakfast Bake

4 cups cooked long grain rice
2 cups (8 ounces) shredded cheddar cheese, *divided*
12 bacon strips, cooked and crumbled, *divided*
1 can (15 ounces) tomato sauce
1/2 cup bottled chili sauce
12 eggs
12 thinly sliced green pepper rings

In a bowl, combine rice, 1-1/2 cups cheese, 1/2 cup crumbled bacon, tomato sauce and chili sauce. Pat firmly into a greased 13-in. x 9-in. x 2-in. baking dish. Using the back of a spoon, make twelve 2-in. wells in the rice mixture. Cover and bake at 350° for 25 minutes.

Remove from the oven; break an egg into each well. Press a green pepper ring around each egg. Cover and bake for another 30-35 minutes or until eggs reach desired doneness. Sprinkle with remaining cheese and bacon; cover and let stand for 5-10 minutes or until cheese is melted. **Yield:** 12 servings.

Overnight Caramel French Toast

1 cup packed brown sugar
1/2 cup butter
2 tablespoons light corn syrup
12 slices bread
1/4 cup sugar
1 teaspoon ground cinnamon, *divided*
6 eggs
1-1/2 cups milk
1 teaspoon vanilla extract

In a small saucepan, bring the brown sugar, butter and corn syrup to a boil over medium heat, stirring constantly. Remove from the heat. Pour into a greased 13-in. x 9-in. x 2-in. baking dish. Top with six slices of bread. Combine sugar and 1/2 teaspoon cinnamon; sprinkle half over the bread. Place remaining bread on top. Sprinkle with remaining cinnamon-sugar; set aside.

In a large bowl, beat the eggs, milk, vanilla and remaining cinnamon. Pour over bread. Cover and refrigerate for 8 hours or overnight.

Remove from the refrigerator 30 minutes before baking. Bake, uncovered, at 350° for 30-35 minutes. **Yield:** 6 servings.

Pennsylvania Dutch Potato Doughnuts

2-1/2 cups mashed potatoes *or* riced potatoes (no milk, butter *or* seasoning added)

1 cup milk

3 eggs, lightly beaten

2 tablespoons butter, melted

2 cups sugar

2 tablespoons baking powder

5 cups all-purpose flour

Oil for deep-fat frying

GLAZE:

2 cups confectioners' sugar

5 tablespoons half-and-half cream

1/2 teaspoon vanilla extract

In a large bowl, combine potatoes, milk, eggs and butter. Combine sugar, baking powder and 2 cups flour; stir into potato mixture. Add enough remaining flour to form a soft dough. Divide dough in half. Turn onto a lightly floured surface; roll each half to 1/2-in. thickness. Cut with a 2-3/4-in. doughnut cutter.

In a electric skillet or deep-fat fryer, heat oil to 375°. Fry doughnuts, a few at a time, until golden, about 2 minutes. Turn with a slotted spoon and fry 2 minutes more or until golden brown. Drain on paper towels. Repeat until all doughnuts are fried.

Combine glaze ingredients and drizzle over warm doughnuts. Serve immediately. **Yield:** about 4 dozen.

Spiced Date Oatmeal

2 cups apple juice

1 cup quick-cooking oats

1/2 cups chopped dates

1/4 teaspoon ground cinnamon

Dash ground nutmeg

Milk

Coconut, optional

In a saucepan, bring apple juice to a boil. Stir in oats; cook 1 minute. Remove from the heat; stir in dates, cinnamon and nutmeg. Cover and let stand for 5 minutes. Serve with milk and sprinkle with coconut if desired. **Yield:** 2 servings.

Down-on-the-Farm Breakfast

8 bacon strips, cut into 1/4-inch
  pieces
1 package (5-1/4 ounces)
  au gratin potatoes mix
2-1/4 cups boiling water
2/3 cup milk
1/4 cup chopped green pepper
2 tablespoons chopped onion
1/4 teaspoon dried thyme
6 eggs
Dash pepper
1/2 cup shredded cheddar cheese

In a large skillet, cook bacon over medium heat until crisp. Drain, reserving 2 tablespoons drippings in the skillet with the bacon. Stir in contents of au gratin potato mix, water, milk green pepper, onion and thyme. Bring to a boil, stirring frequently. Reduce heat; cover and simmer, stirring occasionally, for 20 minutes.

Transfer to an ungreased 2-qt. baking dish. Make six indentations in potato mixture with a spoon. Break eggs into indentations. Sprinkle with pepper. Cover and bake at 350° for 20 minutes or until eggs reach desired doneness. Sprinkle with cheese. **Yield:** 6 servings.

Hearty Sausage Loaf

2 loaves (1 pound *each*) frozen
  bread dough, thawed
1 pound bulk pork sausage
1 garlic clove, minced
1/8 teaspoon fennel seed
3 eggs, lightly beaten
2 cups (8 ounces) shredded
  part-skim mozzarella cheese
1/4 cup grated Romano *or*
  Parmesan cheese
1 tablespoon butter, melted

Allow dough to rise until nearly doubled. Meanwhile, in a skillet, cook sausage with garlic and fennel seed over medium heat until no longer pink. Drain and cool. Add eggs and cheeses; mix well.

Punch dough down and roll each loaf into a 16-in. x 12-in. rectangle. Place half of the sausage mixture on each rectangle, spreading to within 1 in. of edges. Roll jelly-roll style, starting at the narrow end. Place on a greased baking sheet.

Bake at 375° for 30-35 minutes. Brush with melted butter while warm. **Yield:** 16-20 servings.

Pigs in a Blanket

2 cups all-purpose flour
1 teaspoon baking soda
1 teaspoon baking powder
1 teaspoon salt
2 eggs, lightly beaten
2-1/4 cups buttermilk
1/4 cup vegetable oil

16 to 18 pork sausage links, cooked

SYRUP:
1 cup sugar
1 cup packed brown sugar
1/2 cup water
1/2 teaspoon vanilla extract
1/2 teaspoon maple flavoring

In a large mixing bowl, combine the flour, baking soda, baking powder and salt. Combine eggs, buttermilk and oil; blend into dry ingredients.

Pour batter by 1/4 cupfuls onto a lightly greased hot griddle; turn when bubbles form on top of pancakes. Cook until the second side is golden brown. Roll each pancake around a sausage link.

For syrup, in a small saucepan, combine sugars and water; bring to a boil. Stir in flavorings. Serve warm with pancakes. **Yield:** 16-18 pancakes (1-1/2 cups syrup).

Banana Fritters

2 eggs
1/2 cup milk
1 teaspoon vegetable oil
1 cup all-purpose flour
1 teaspoon baking powder

1 teaspoon salt
4 large firm bananas
Oil for deep-fat frying
Confectioners' sugar, optional

In a bowl, beat eggs, milk and oil. Combine flour, baking powder and salt; stir into egg mixture until smooth. Cut bananas into quarters (about 2 in. long). Dip each banana piece into batter to coat.

In an electric skillet or deep-fat fryer, heat oil to 375°. Fry banana pieces, two to three at a time, until golden brown.

Drain on paper towels. Dust with confectioners' sugar if desired. **Yield:** 6-8 servings.

Scrumptious Breakfast Fruit Soup

6 cups water

4 tablespoons quick-cooking tapioca

1 cinnamon stick (2 inches)

1 can (29 ounces) sliced peaches with syrup

2-1/2 cups assorted dried fruits, chopped

1 cup pitted prunes

1 cup raisins

Juice of 1 lemon

In a large heavy saucepan, combine water, tapioca and cinnamon stick; let stand for 5 minutes. Bring to a boil; reduce heat and simmer, stirring frequently, for 15 minutes or until tapioca begins to thicken. Add remaining ingredients and cook over medium heat for 25 minutes, stirring frequently. Remove from the heat; cover and let stand for 30 minutes. Remove cinnamon stick. Fruit will continue to plump. Serve warm or cold. **Yield:** 8-10 servings.

Yogurt Honey Fruit Bowl

1/4 teaspoon cornstarch

1/8 teaspoon salt

1/4 cup honey

4 teaspoons lemon juice

1 egg yolk, lightly beaten

1 carton (8 ounces) plain yogurt

1 carton (8 ounces) frozen whipped topping, thawed

4 cups chopped mixed fruit

1/2 cup chopped nuts

1/2 cup granola without raisins

In a small saucepan, combine cornstarch and salt. Blend in honey and lemon juice; cook over medium-low heat until thickened and bubbly, stirring constantly. Cook and stir 2 minutes longer. Gradually stir half of the hot mixture into the egg yolk; return all to the saucepan and cook for 2 minutes. Remove from the heat; blend in yogurt. Cool completely.

Fold in whipped topping. Layer a fourth of the fruit, yogurt mixture, nuts and granola in a serving bowl. Repeat layers, ending with granola. Refrigerate. **Yield:** 6-8 servings.

Blueberry Brunch Loaf

1/4 cup butter, softened
3/4 cup packed brown sugar
1 egg
1 tablespoon grated orange peel
2-1/4 cups all-purpose flour
1 tablespoon baking powder
1/2 teaspoon salt
1/2 cup milk

1/4 cup orange juice
1 cup fresh *or* frozen blueberries

GLAZE:
1/2 cup confectioners' sugar
2 teaspoons butter, softened
1/2 teaspoon grated orange peel
1 to 1-1/2 tablespoons milk

In a mixing bowl, cream butter and brown sugar. Stir in egg and orange peel. Combine flour, baking powder and salt; add to creamed mixture alternately with milk and juice, mixing thoroughly after each addition. Fold in blueberries. Pour into a greased 9-in. x 5-in. x 3-in. loaf pan.

Bake at 350° for 50-55 minutes or until a toothpick comes out clean. Cool in pan 10 minutes before removing to a wire rack.

For glaze, combine sugar, butter and orange peel. Gradually add milk until glaze is spreadable; drizzle over warm bread. **Yield:** 1 loaf.

Early-Riser Muffins

2 cups all-purpose flour
2 tablespoons sugar
1 teaspoon baking powder
1/2 teaspoon salt
1/4 teaspoon ground mustard

1 egg, lightly beaten
1 cup milk
1/3 cup butter, melted
3/4 cup finely chopped ham
3/4 cup shredded cheddar cheese

In a bowl, combine flour, sugar, baking powder, salt and mustard. Combine egg, milk and butter; stir into dry ingredients just until moistened. Fold in ham and cheese. Fill greased or paper-lined muffins cups about two-thirds full.

Bake at 400° for 20-25 minutes or until a toothpick comes out clean. Cool in pan for 10 minutes before removing to a wire rack. **Yield:** about 1 dozen.

Individual Egg Bakes

8 bacon strips
1 cup ketchup, chili-pepper
    ketchup *or* salsa

8 eggs
Salt and pepper to taste
Chopped fresh parsley, optional

Partially cook bacon in microwave or oven until about halfway done (do not overcook); drain. Spray eight 10-oz. custard cups with nonstick cooking spray. Line each cup with one bacon strip. Spoon 2 tablespoons ketchup or salsa on top of bacon. Break one egg into each cup; season with salt and pepper. Place cups on a baking sheet.

Bake, uncovered, at 375° for 18-20 minutes or until eggs reach desired doneness. Let stand for 2 minutes. Run a knife around edge of cups; slip eggs out of cups onto a serving platter.

Spoon sauce from the custard cups over eggs. Garnish with parsley if desired. **Yield:** 8 servings.

Ham and Cheese Waffles

3 eggs
2 cups milk
1/3 cup vegetable oil
2 1/2 cups all-purpose flour
2 teaspoons baking powder
1/2 teaspoon salt

1-1/2 cups (6 ounces) shredded
    part-skim mozzarella cheese
1/2 to 3/4 cup cubed fully cooked
    ham *or* Canadian bacon
Fried eggs, optional

In a bowl, beat eggs, milk and oil. Combine flour, baking powder and salt; add to egg mixture and beat until smooth. Fold in cheese and ham or bacon.

Bake in a waffle iron according to manufacturer's directions until golden brown. Top each waffle with a fried egg if desired. **Yield:** 8-10 waffles (6-1/2 inches).

Feather-Light Breakfast Puffs

1/3 cup shortening
1 egg
1-1/2 cups all-purpose flour
1/2 cup sugar
1-1/2 teaspoons baking powder
1/2 teaspoon salt

1/4 teaspoon ground nutmeg
1/2 cup milk

TOPPING:
1/2 cup sugar
1 teaspoon ground cinnamon
6 tablespoons butter, melted

In a mixing bowl, beat shortening and egg. Combine the flour, sugar, baking powder, salt and nutmeg. Stir into egg mixture alternately with milk (batter will be stiff). Fill greased or paper-lined muffin cups about two-thirds full.

Bake at 350° for 15-20 minutes or until toothpick comes out clean. For topping combine sugar and cinnamon. When puffs are removed from the oven, immediately roll each in butter and then into cinnamon-sugar. Serve hot. **Yield:** about 1 dozen.

Wake-Up Bacon Omelet

2 to 4 bacon strips, diced
2 eggs
2 tablespoons water

2 teaspoons minced chives
3 to 5 drops hot pepper sauce
Salt and pepper to taste

In an 8-in. nonstick skillet, cook bacon over medium heat until crisp. Using a slotted spoon, remove bacon to paper towel to drain; discard drippings.

In a small bowl, beat eggs; add water, chives, hot pepper sauce, salt pepper and bacon. Pour into the same skillet; cook over medium heat. As eggs set, lift edges, letting uncooked portion flow underneath. When eggs are set, fold omelet in thirds. **Yield:** 1 serving.

Canadian Bacon Breakfast

6 tablespoons Dijon mustard

6 tablespoons honey

6 English muffins, split and toasted

2 tablespoons butter

12 slices Canadian bacon *or* thinly sliced ham

1 thinly sliced peeled tart apple

5 egg whites

1 cup (4 ounces) shredded cheddar cheese

1/2 teaspoon paprika

Combine mustard and honey; spread 1 tablespoon on each toasted muffin half. In a large skillet, melt butter. Add Canadian bacon and heat through; remove to paper towels to drain. Cook apple slices in the drippings until tender. Arrange bacon on muffins; top with apple slices. Place on a baking sheet.

In a mixing bowl, beat egg whites until stiff peaks form. Fold in cheese and paprika; spread over apples. Broil muffins until tops are puffed and golden brown. **Yield:** 6 servings.

Freezer French Toast

4 eggs

1 cup milk

2 tablespoons sugar

1 teaspoon vanilla extract

1/4 teaspoon ground nutmeg

10 slices day-old French bread (3/4 inch thick)

1 to 2 tablespoons butter, melted

In a large bowl, beat eggs, milk, sugar, vanilla and nutmeg. Place bread in a well-greased 13-in. x 9-in. x 2-in. baking dish. Pour egg mixture over bread. Let soak for several minutes, turning once to coat. Freeze until firm. Package in airtight containers.

To bake, place bread on a well-greased baking sheet. Dot with butter. Bake at 450° for 7 minutes; turn and bake 10-12 minutes longer or until golden brown. **Yield:** 4-5 servings.

Fried Shredded Wheat

4 large shredded wheat biscuits
3/4 cup milk

Oil for frying
Maple syrup

Soak cereal in milk for 5 minutes on each side. Remove with a slotted spoon; drain slightly. Fry in a large skillet until brown on both sides, pressing down while frying. Serve with syrup. **Yield:** 4 servings.

Pork Sausage Ring

2 eggs
1/2 cup milk
1-1/2 cups finely crushed saltines

1 cup finely chopped apple
2 pounds bulk pork sausage
Scrambled eggs

In a large bowl, beat eggs and milk. Add cracker crumbs, apple and sausage; mix well. Pat into a greased 6-cup ring mold.

Bake at 350° for 1-1/4 hours. Drain; unmold onto serving platter. Fill center with scrambled eggs. **Yield:** 10-12 servings.

Orange-Pecan Baked Apples

6 medium baking apples cored
1/4 cup orange marmalade
2 tablespoons finely chopped pecans

Ground cinnamon
Ground nutmeg

Place apples in a shallow ungreased baking pan; add a small amount of water to pan.

In a small bowl, combine marmalade and pecans. Fill center of apples with marmalade mixture; sprinkle with cinnamon and nutmeg.

Bake, uncovered, at 350° for 60-70 minutes or until apples are tender. **Yield:** 6 servings.

Vanilla Granola

6 cups quick-cooking oats
1 cup chopped walnuts
1/2 cup flaked coconut
1/2 cup sesame seeds
2/3 cup vegetable oil

1/2 cup honey
1/2 cup packed brown sugar
2 tablespoons water
1-1/2 teaspoons vanilla extract

In a large bowl, toss oats, walnuts, coconut and sesame seeds. In a saucepan over medium heat, cook oil, honey, brown sugar, water and vanilla, stirring until sugar is dissolved (do not boil). Pour over oat mixture and stir to coat evenly. Pour into two greased 13-in. x 9-in. x 2-in. baking pans.

Bake at 275° for 50-60 minutes or until golden brown, stirring every 15 minutes. Cool, stirring occasionally. Store in an airtight container. **Yield:** 8 cups.

Graham-Streusel Coffee Cake

STREUSEL:
1-1/2 cups graham cracker crumbs
1 cup packed brown sugar
3/4 cup chopped pecans
2/3 cup butter, melted
2 teaspoons ground cinnamon

CAKE:
1 package (18-1/4 ounces) white cake mix with pudding
3 eggs, lightly beaten
1 cup water
1/4 cup vegetable oil

In a bowl, combine streusel ingredients; set aside. In a mixing bowl, combine cake mix, eggs, water and oil. Beat on low speed until mixed; beat on medium speed for 2 minutes. Pour half into a greased 13-in. x 9-in. x 2-in. baking pan. Sprinkle with half of the streusel. Carefully spread remaining batter over streusel. Top with remaining streusel.

Bake at 350° for 35-40 minutes or until toothpick comes out clean. **Yield:** 12-16 servings.

Honey-Baked French Toast

3 eggs
4 tablespoons honey, *divided*
1-1/2 teaspoons ground cinnamon
1 cup milk

15 slices day-old French bread (cut diagonally 3/4 inch thick)
3 tablespoons brown sugar
2 tablespoons butter, melted
Maple syrup

In a bowl, beat eggs with 2 tablespoons honey and cinnamon; stir in milk. Dip bread into egg mixture.

In a greased 13-in. x 9-in. x 2-in. baking pan, arrange three rows of five slices of bread, overlapping slices slightly. Cover and chill 8 hours or overnight. Remove from refrigerator 30 minutes before baking. Sprinkle brown sugar over bread; drizzle with butter and remaining honey.

Bake at 350° for 30 minutes. Serve with syrup. **Yield:** 6-8 servings.

Buttermilk Coffee Cake

2-1/2 cups all-purpose flour
1 cup packed brown sugar
3/4 cup sugar
3/4 cup vegetable oil
1 teaspoon salt
1 egg, lightly beaten
1 cup buttermilk
1 teaspoon baking soda

TOPPING:
1 cup chopped pecans
1/4 cup packed brown sugar
1/4 cup sugar
1 tablespoon all-purpose flour
3/4 teaspoon ground cinnamon
1/2 teaspoon ground nutmeg

In a mixing bowl, combine flour, sugars, oil and salt. Remove 1/2 cup and set aside. To remaining flour mixture, add egg, buttermilk and baking soda; mix well. Pour into a greased 15-in. x 10-in. x 1-in. baking pan.

To reserved flour mixture add all topping ingredients; mix well. Sprinkle over batter. Bake at 350° for 25-30 minutes or until toothpick comes out clean. **Yield:** 20-24 servings.

Country Sausage Gravy

1 pound bulk pork sausage
1 can (10-3/4 ounces) condensed
  cream of chicken soup,
  undiluted
1-1/4 cups milk
1/2 teaspoon ground mustard
1/4 teaspoon seasoned salt
1/4 teaspoon pepper
1 cup (8 ounces) sour cream
Warm biscuits

Crumble sausage into a heavy skillet. Cook over medium heat until no longer pink. Drain and set aside. In the same skillet, combine soup and milk; add mustard, seasoned salt and pepper. Bring to a boil. Reduce heat; add sausage and sour cream. Simmer until heated through (do not boil). Serve over warm biscuits. **Yield:** 4-6 servings (3-1/2 cups gravy).

Garden Fresh Breakfast

8 ounces fresh mushrooms,
  sliced
1 cup chopped zucchini
1/2 cup chopped green pepper
1/4 cup sliced green onions
2 tablespoons butter
1 medium tomato, diced and
  seeded
4 eggs
2 tablespoons water
2 tablespoons Dijon mustard
1/2 teaspoon salt
1/4 teaspoon pepper
1 cup (4 ounces) shredded
  Monterey Jack cheese
Paprika

In a large skillet, saute mushrooms, zucchini, green pepper and onions in butter for 5 minutes or until tender. Drain off juices. Stir in tomato.

In a bowl, beat the eggs, water, mustard, salt and pepper. Pour over vegetables. Cover and cook over medium heat for 5-10 minutes or until eggs are set. Sprinkle with cheese and paprika. Cut into wedges to serve. **Yield:** 4-6 servings.

Pear-Oatmeal Breakfast Pudding

1 can (29 ounces) pear halves

2 cups milk

2 tablespoons brown sugar, *divided*

1 tablespoon butter

1/4 teaspoon salt

1/4 teaspoon ground cinnamon

1-1/2 cups old-fashioned oats

1/4 cup raisins

Half-and-half cream *or* additional milk

Drain pears, reserving 1 cup syrup in a saucepan. Set pears aside. To the syrup, add milk, 1 tablespoon brown sugar, butter, salt and cinnamon; heat until simmering. Dice all but two pear halves; stir into syrup mixture. Add oats and raisins. Heat until bubbly. Pour into a greased 1-1/2-qt. baking dish.

Bake at 350° for 20 minutes; stir. Slice remaining pear halves; arrange over top. Sprinkle with remaining brown sugar. Bake 10-15 minutes longer. Serve hot with cream or milk. **Yield:** 6 servings.

Bacon-Potato Burritos

8 bacon strips

1-1/2 cups frozen Southern-style hash brown potatoes

2 teaspoons minced dried onion

4 eggs

1/4 cup milk

1 teaspoon Worcestershire sauce

1/4 teaspoon salt

1/4 teaspoon pepper

1 cup (4 ounces) shredded cheddar cheese

6 flour tortillas (8 inches)

Salsa

In a large skillet, cook bacon over medium heat until crisp; drain on paper towels. Brown potatoes and onion in drippings. In a bowl, beat eggs; add milk, Worcestershire sauce, salt and pepper. Pour over potatoes; cook and stir until eggs are set. Crumble bacon and stir into eggs. Sprinkle with cheese. Meanwhile, warm tortillas according to package directions. Spoon egg mixture down center of tortillas; fold in sides of tortilla. Serve with salsa. **Yield:** 4-6 servings.

Mixed Grain and Wild Rice Cereal

8 cups water, *divided*	1/2 cup chopped dates
1/2 cup uncooked wild rice, rinsed	1/3 cup packed brown sugar
1/2 cup medium pearl barley	3 tablespoons butter
1/2 cup old-fashioned oats	1/2 teaspoon ground cinnamon
1/2 cup raisins	Honey, optional

In a saucepan, combine 2 cups water and wild rice; bring to a boil. Cover and simmer for 20 minutes; drain. Place in a greased 2-1/2-qt. baking dish; add the barley, oats, raisins, dates, brown sugar, butter, cinnamon and remaining water.

Cover and bake at 375° for 1 hour and 40 minutes or until grains are tender, stirring occasionally. **Yield:** 8-10 servings.

Ethan's Apple-Nut Pancakes

2 cups all-purpose flour	2 cups buttermilk
1/2 cup toasted wheat germ	2 eggs, lightly beaten
2 teaspoons baking powder	1/2 cup applesauce
1 teaspoon baking soda	1 tablespoon molasses
1 teaspoon salt	1/2 cup chopped walnuts
1 teaspoon ground cinnamon	1 apple, peeled and grated

In a large mixing bowl, combine flour, wheat germ, baking powder, baking soda, salt and cinnamon. Combine buttermilk, eggs, applesauce and molasses; add to dry ingredients and mix well. Fold in walnuts and apple.

Pour batter by 1/4 cupfuls onto a lightly greased hot griddle; turn when bubbles form on top of pancakes. Cook until second side is golden brown. **Yield:** 20-22 pancakes.

Hot Jam Breakfast Sandwiches

1/4 cup butter
1/4 cup flaked coconut
1/2 cup apricot jam

1/2 teaspoon ground cinnamon
12 slices raisin bread

In a bowl, mix butter and coconut; stir in jam and cinnamon. Spread between slices of bread. Grill on a greased skillet until golden brown on both sides. **Yield:** 6 servings.

Wake-Up Sandwiches

4 ounces cream cheese, softened
2 tablespoons milk
1 package (2-1/2 ounces) sliced corned beef, chopped
1/2 cup shredded Swiss cheese

2 hard-cooked eggs, chopped
3 English muffins, split and toasted
Sliced hard-cooked egg, optional
Minced fresh parsley, optional

In a bowl, combine cream cheese and milk until smooth. Fold in corned beef, cheese and chopped eggs. Spread 1/3 cup mixture on each toasted muffin half.

Bake at 450° for 10-12 minutes or until heated through. If desired, garnish each half with an egg slice and parsley. **Yield:** 2-3 servings.

Puffed Eggnog Pancake

2 tablespoons butter
3 eggs
2/3 cup eggnog

1/2 cup all-purpose flour
1/4 cup sliced almonds
2 teaspoons sugar

Place butter in a 10-in. cast iron skillet; place in a 425° oven for 2-3 minutes or until melted.

In a mixing bowl, beat eggs until fluffy. Add eggnog and flour; beat until smooth. Pour into hot skillet. Sprinkle with almonds and sugar.

Bake for 16-18 minutes or until puffed and browned. Serve pancake immediately. **Yield:** 4-6 servings.

Crispy Breakfast Slices

3 cups water	1/2 teaspoon ground nutmeg
1/4 cup sugar	2 cups quick-cooking oats
1 teaspoon salt	Butter
1/2 teaspoon ground cinnamon	Maple syrup, optional

In a saucepan, bring water, sugar, salt, cinnamon and nutmeg to a boil. Stir in oats. Return to a boil; cook 1 minute. Remove from the heat; cover and let stand for 5 minutes. Pour into a greased 9-in. x 5-in. x 3-in. loaf pan. Cover and refrigerate overnight.

Unmold and cut into 1/2-in. slices. Fry in butter in a skillet over medium heat until browned, about 6-8 minutes. Serve with syrup if desired. **Yield:** 8 servings.

Asparagus-Chicken Pie

1 cup cooked fresh asparagus	3 eggs
1 unbaked pastry shell (9 inch)	1-1/3 cups half-and-half cream
1 cup cooked chicken, chopped	2 teaspoons all-purpose flour
3 bacon strips, cooked and crumbled	1/2 teaspoon salt
1/3 cup shredded process cheese, (Velveeta)	Paprika

Arrange asparagus in bottom of pie shell. Top with chicken, bacon and cheese. In a small bowl, beat eggs; stir in cream, flour and salt. Pour into shell. Sprinkle with paprika.

Bake at 375° for 45-50 minutes or until a knife inserted near the center comes out clean. Let stand for 5 minutes before cutting. **Yield:** 6 servings.

Quick and Easy Waffles

2 cups biscuit/baking mix
2 eggs, lightly beaten

1/2 cup vegetable oil
7 ounces lemon-lime soda

In a mixing bowl, combine biscuit mix, eggs and oil. Add soda and mix well. Bake in a preheated waffle iron according to the manufacturer's directions until golden brown. **Yield:** 4-5 waffles.

Salmon Scramble

8 eggs
3/4 cup milk
1/2 teaspoon salt
1/8 teaspoon pepper

1 can (7-1/2 ounces) pink salmon, drained *or* 1 cup smoked salmon, flaked and cartilage removed
1/2 cup shredded Monterey Jack cheese
1/4 cup minced fresh parsley

In a bowl, beat eggs, milk, salt and pepper. Stir in salmon, cheese and parsley. In a greased skillet, cook and stir gently over medium heat until eggs are set, about 3-5 minutes. **Yield:** 4-6 servings.

Fried Cornmeal Mush

4 cups water, *divided*
1 cup cornmeal
1 teaspoon salt

Oil for frying
Maple syrup

Bring 3 cups water to a boil. Combine remaining water with cornmeal and salt; stir into boiling water. Stir until mixture returns to a boil. Reduce heat; cover and simmer for 1 hour, stirring occasionally.

Pour into a greased 9-in. x 5-in. x 3-in. loaf pan. Chill for 8 hours or overnight. Slice 1/2 in. thick.

Fry in a large skillet in oil until browned on each side. Serve with syrup. **Yield:** 14-16 servings.

Home-Style Hominy Casserole

1 pound bulk pork sausage
1 can (15-1/2 ounces) white hominy, drained
12 eggs
1/4 cup milk
1/4 teaspoon pepper
8 ounces process cheese (Velveeta), sliced

Crumble sausage into a large skillet. Cook over medium heat until no longer pink; drain. Add hominy; stir until heated through, about 5 minutes.

In a large bowl, beat eggs, milk and pepper. Add to hominy mixture; cook and stir gently until eggs are set. Pour into a greased 2-qt. baking dish. Cover with cheese slices.

Place under broiler until cheese is melted. **Yield:** 8-10 servings.

Southwest Skillet Dish

4 tablespoons butter
5 to 6 cups thinly sliced peeled uncooked potatoes
6 slices fully cooked ham, cubed
Salsa
1 can (4 ounces) chopped green chilies
1 cup (4 ounces) shredded Colby cheese

In a 10-in. cast-iron skillet, melt butter over medium heat. Fry potatoes until lightly browned and tender. Add ham and cook until heated through. Sprinkle with chilies and cheese. Remove from the heat and cover until the cheese is melted. Serve in the skillet. Top with salsa. **Yield:** 4-6 servings.

Rice-Crust Quiche

2-1/2 cups warm cooked rice
1/4 cup butter
1-1/2 cups finely chopped fully cooked ham
1 cup (4 ounces) shredded cheddar cheese
1 cup (4 ounces) shredded Swiss cheese

Several drops of hot pepper sauce
3 eggs
1/2 cup milk
1/8 teaspoon paprika
1/8 teaspoon garlic powder
1/8 teaspoon onion powder
Chopped fresh parsley

With the back of a spoon, press the rice into a greased 9-in. pie plate to form a crust. Drizzle with butter. Bake at 350° for 3 minutes; remove from the oven. Combine ham, cheeses and hot pepper sauce; sprinkle over rice. Beat eggs, milk, paprika, garlic powder and onion powder; pour over ham over mixture. Sprinkle with parsley. Bake at 350° for 30 minutes or until a knife inserted near the center comes out clean. Let stand for 5-10 minutes before cutting. **Yield:** 6 servings.

Cheesy Egg Casserole

4 cups (16 ounces) shredded Monterey Jack cheese
1 tablespoon all-purpose flour
2 cups (8 ounces) shredded sharp cheddar cheese

1 pound sliced bacon, cooked and crumbled
12 eggs
1 cup milk

Toss Monterey Jack cheese with flour; place in the bottom of a greased 13-in. x 9-in. x 2-in. baking dish. Top with cheddar cheese; sprinkle with bacon. Beat eggs and milk; pour over all. Cover and chill 8 hours or overnight. Remove from refrigerator 30 minutes before baking.

Bake, uncovered, at 325° for 40-45 minutes or until a knife inserted near the center comes out clean. Let stand for 5 minutes before cutting. **Yield:** 12-16 servings.

Soups & Sandwiches

Farmhouse Chicken Soup

1 broiler/fryer chicken (3 to 3-1/2 pounds)
2 quarts water
1 large onion, chopped
1/2 cup chopped celery
1 cup diced carrots
2 garlic cloves, minced
2 teaspoons salt
1/2 teaspoon pepper
1/2 teaspoon poultry seasoning
1/4 teaspoon crushed red pepper flakes

SPAETZLE:
1-1/2 cups all-purpose flour
1/2 teaspoon salt
1/8 teaspoon baking powder
1/8 teaspoon ground nutmeg
2 eggs, well beaten
1/2 cup milk
1 tablespoon minced fresh parsley

Place the chicken and water in a Dutch oven or soup kettle. Slowly bring to a boil; reduce heat. Add the onion, celery, carrots, garlic, salt, pepper, poultry seasoning and red pepper flakes. Cover and simmer for 1 hour or until chicken is tender.

Remove chicken from broth; cool. Skim fat from broth. Remove meat from bones; discard bones and skin. Cut meat into bite-size pieces; return to broth. Cover and simmer.

For spaetzle, combine the flour, salt, baking powder and nutmeg in a small bowl. Stir in the eggs, milk and parsley; blend well. With a rubber spatula, push batter through a large-hole grater or colander into simmering soup. Simmer, uncovered, for 10 minutes or until spaetzle float to the top. **Yield:** 10-12 servings (about 3 quarts).

Cajun Corn Soup with Shrimp

1/2 cup vegetable oil
1/2 cup all-purpose flour
1 small onion, chopped
1/3 cup green onions, chopped
2 quarts hot water *or* heated chicken broth
2 cans (14-1/2 ounces) stewed tomatoes, cut up

8 cups cut corn *or* 4 cans (16 ounces *each*) whole-kernel corn, drained
2 pounds peeled, deveined shrimp
Salt to taste
Pepper to taste

In a heavy 8-qt. Dutch oven, combine oil and flour until smooth. Cook over medium-high heat for 5 minutes, stirring constantly. Reduce heat to medium. Cook and stir about 5 minutes more or until mixture is reddish-brown (the color of a penny). Add onion and green onions. Cook for 5 minutes, stirring often. Turn heat to high. Add hot water or broth, tomatoes and corn. Bring to boil; reduce heat. Cover and simmer for 15 minutes. Add shrimp; simmer about 5 minutes more, until shrimp turn pink. Season to taste with salt and pepper. **Yield:** 12 servings.

Turkey Tomato Club

1/2 cup mayonnaise
1 tablespoon cider vinegar
2 teaspoons sugar
1/4 teaspoon salt
1/8 teaspoon pepper
4 cups thinly sliced cabbage
1 round loaf (1 pound) sourdough bread

10 bacon strips, cooked and drained
6 tomato slices
1 cup thinly sliced cucumber
1/2 pound thinly sliced smoked turkey

Combine the first five ingredients in a bowl. Add cabbage; toss. Set aside for 30 minutes. Cut a thin slice off the top of the bread; hollow out bottom half, leaving a 1-in. shell. (Discard removed bread or save for another use.) Place half of the cabbage mixture in bottom of loaf. Layer with bacon, tomato, cucumber and turkey; top with remaining cabbage mixture. Replace bread top. Cut into wedges. **Yield:** 6-8 servings.

Favorite Chili

3-1/2 pounds beef chuck roast, cut into 1/2-inch cubes
1/4 cup vegetable oil
2 cups chopped onion
3 medium green peppers, chopped
5 garlic cloves, minced
2 cans (28 ounces *each*) diced tomatoes, undrained
2 cups water
1 can (12 ounces) tomato paste
1/3 cup chili powder
1/4 cup sugar
1 tablespoon salt
2 teaspoons dried oregano
3/4 teaspoon pepper
1 can (16 ounces) pinto beans, rinsed and drained
1/4 cup cornmeal
Shredded cheddar cheese and additional chopped onion, optional

In a Dutch oven or soup kettle, brown beef in oil; drain. Add the onion, green peppers and garlic; cook until tender. Add next eight ingredients; bring to a boil. Reduce heat; cover and simmer for 2 hours, stirring occasionally. Add beans and cornmeal; simmer for 15 minutes, stirring frequently. Garnish with cheese and onion if desired. **Yield:** 14-16 servings (4 quarts).

Hearty Krautwiches

4 hard-cooked eggs, *divided*
1 can (14 ounces) sauerkraut, well drained
1/3 cup Russian salad dressing
1 medium red onion
6 onion buns, split
8 ounces thinly sliced salami
6 slices Muenster cheese
6 ounces sliced liverwurst
6 lettuce leaves
Additional Russian salad dressing, optional

In a small bowl, chop one egg; stir in sauerkraut and salad dressing. Chop half of the onion; add to sauerkraut mixture. Slice remaining eggs and onion; set aside. On bun bottoms, layer salami, cheese, liverwurst, lettuce, onion and about 1/3 cup of sauerkraut mixture. Top each with sliced eggs and additional salad dressing if desired. Replace bun tops. **Yield:** 6 servings.

Hearty Steak Soup

1/2 cup butter

1 cup all-purpose flour

6 cups water

2 pounds ground round steak *or* ground beef, browned and drained

1 cup chopped onion

1 cup chopped celery

1 package (20 ounces) frozen mixed vegetables, thawed

1 can (28 ounces) diced tomatoes, undrained

1 tablespoon seasoned salt

1 teaspoon salt

1 teaspoon pepper

2 tablespoons browning sauce

In a large saucepan, melt butter. Stir in flour until smooth paste. Add water. Bring to a boil; cook and stir for 2 minutes or until thickened. Add beef, onion, celery, mixed vegetables, tomatoes, seasonings and browning sauce. Bring to a boil; reduce heat and simmer 20-30 minutes or until the vegetables are tender. **Yield:** 8-10 servings (4 quarts).

Hot Turkey Salad Pitas

1 medium navel orange, peeled and quartered

1 cup fresh *or* frozen cranberries

1/2 cup green grapes

1/2 cup sugar

1/8 teaspoon ground ginger *or* 3/4 teaspoon minced fresh gingerroot

2 cups cubed cooked turkey

1 celery rib, chopped

1/2 cup mayonnaise

1/2 teaspoon salt

1/8 teaspoon pepper

2 pita breads (6 inches), halved

For relish, place the orange, cranberries, grapes, sugar and ginger in a blender or food processor. Cover and process until finely chopped. Set aside 1/2 cup. Cover and refrigerate remaining relish.

In a bowl, combine the turkey, celery, mayonnaise, salt, pepper and reserved relish. Spoon into pita halves. Place on an ungreased baking sheet.

Bake, uncovered, at 375° for 8-10 minutes or until heated through. Serve with the chilled relish. **Yield:** 2-4 servings.

Toasted Apple-Cheese Sandwiches

6 slices white *or* French bread
2 tablespoons mayonnaise
6 slices cheddar cheese
1 medium tart apple, peeled, cored and cut crosswise into six rings

1 tablespoon brown sugar
12 bacon strips, cooked and drained

In a broiler, toast one side of each slice of bread. Spread untoasted side with mayonnaise. Top with cheese and apple; sprinkle with brown sugar. Cross two strips of bacon over each. Broil 6 in. from the heat for 2-3 minutes or until cheese melts. **Yield:** 6 servings.

Lasagna in a Bun

1/2 pound ground beef
1 medium onion, diced
1 can (8 ounces) tomato sauce
1 teaspoon Italian seasoning, *divided*
1/2 teaspoon salt
1 cup (4 ounces) shredded part-skim mozzarella cheese, *divided*

1/2 cup ricotta cheese
1 egg white
3 tablespoons grated Parmesan cheese
6 small submarine *or* hoagie buns (8 inches)

In a skillet, cook beef and onion over medium heat until meat is no longer pink; drain. Add tomato sauce, 1/2 teaspoon Italian seasoning and salt. Cook for 5 minutes or until heated through. Meanwhile, combine 1/2 cup mozzarella, ricotta, egg white, Parmesan and remaining Italian seasoning; mix well.

Cut a thin slice off the top of each bun. Carefully hollow out bun bottoms, leaving a 1/4-in. shell. (Discard removed bread or save for another use). Spoon meat mixture into buns; top with the cheese mixture. Sprinkle with remaining mozzarella. Replace bun tops. Wrap each in heavy-duty foil. Place on a baking sheet.

Bake at 400° for 25 minutes or until heated through. **Yield:** 6 servings.

Black Bean Potato Chili

1 pound dried black beans
6 cups water
1 can (28 ounces) diced tomatoes, undrained
1 pound ground beef, cooked and drained
4 medium potatoes, peeled and cubed
2 medium onions, chopped
1 can (16 ounces) enchilada sauce
1 envelope chili seasoning
1 tablespoon sugar
2 teaspoons salt
1 teaspoon garlic powder

Place the beans in a soup kettle or Dutch oven; add water to cover by 2-in. Bring to a boil; boil for 2 minutes. Remove from the heat; cover and let stand for 1-4 hours or until beans are softened. Drain and discard liquid. Add 6 cups water to the beans; bring to a boil. Reduce heat; cover and simmer for 2 hours or until beans are almost tender. Add remaining ingredients. Cover and simmer for 1 hour or until soup reaches desired consistency. **Yield:** 12 servings (3 quarts).

Ham and Spinach Loaf

1 pound fully cooked ham
1/3 cup mayonnaise
1 tablespoon Dijon mustard
1/4 cup chopped pistachios, toasted
2 cups packed fresh spinach
1 package (3 ounces) cream cheese, softened
1 tablespoon milk
2 teaspoons dill weed
1 loaf (1 pound) French bread

In a food processor, process ham until minced or ground. Transfer to a medium bowl; add mayonnaise, mustard and pistachios. Mix well; set aside. Rinse spinach in cold water. Cook in a large skillet with only water clinging to the leaves until limp; drain.

In a food processor, process spinach, cream cheese, milk and dill until smooth; set aside. Cut bread in half lengthwise; hollow out top and bottom, leaving a 1/2-in. shell. (Discard removed bread or save for another use.) Spread spinach mixture inside top and bottom halves of bread. Pack ham mixture into bottom half, mounding slightly. Replace bread top and wrap tightly with foil. Chill for at least 2 hours. **Yield:** 6 servings.

Rosemary's Ham Reubens

8 ounces fully cooked ham, julienned

8 ounces Swiss cheese, julienned

3/4 cup mayonnaise

1 can (8 ounces) sauerkraut, drained

1 teaspoon caraway seed

8 slices rye bread

Dijon mustard, optional

Combine ham, cheese, mayonnaise, sauerkraut and caraway. Lightly toast the bread. Spread mustard on toast if desired; top with filling. Place on a baking sheet; broil 6 in. from the heat for 2-3 minutes or until cheese melts. **Yield:** 4-8 servings.

ABC Soup

1 pound ground beef

1 medium onion, chopped

2 quarts tomato juice

1 can (15 ounces) mixed vegetables, undrained

1 cup water

2 beef bouillon cubes

1 cup alphabet pasta *or* small pasta

Salt and pepper to taste

In a large saucepan, cook beef and onion over medium heat until the meat is no longer pink; drain. Add tomato juice, vegetables, water and bouillon; bring to a boil. Add pasta. Cook, uncovered, for 6-8 minutes or until pasta is tender, stirring frequently. Add salt and pepper. **Yield:** 10-12 servings (2-3/4 quarts).

Chicken-Apple Croissants

2 cups diced cooked chicken

1 cup diced peeled apple

3/4 cup mayonnaise

1/2 cup halved green grapes

1/4 cup sliced almonds, toasted

1/2 teaspoon seasoned salt

1/4 teaspoon pepper

6 croissants *or* hard rolls, split

6 lettuce leaves

In a bowl, combine the first seven ingredients. Spoon about 1/2 cup onto each croissant; top with lettuce. **Yield:** 6 servings.

Spinach Bisque

1/2 cup chopped onion
2 tablespoons butter
1/3 cup all-purpose flour
1/2 to 1 teaspoon salt
1/8 teaspoon ground nutmeg
2-1/2 cups milk

1 cup water
3/4 cup cubed process American cheese
1 package (10 ounces) frozen chopped spinach, thawed and drained
Oyster crackers, optional

In a 3-qt. saucepan, saute onion in butter until tender. Stir in the flour, salt and nutmeg until smooth. Gradually whisk in milk and water. Bring to a boil; cook and stir for 2 minutes or until thickened. Reduce heat. Add cheese; cook and stir until melted. Add spinach; cover and simmer for 4-5 minutes or until heated through. Serve with oyster crackers if desired. **Yield:** 5-6 servings.

Easy Stromboli

1 tablespoon active dry yeast
1 cup warm water (110° to 115°)
3 tablespoons vegetable oil
1/2 teaspoon salt
2-3/4 to 3-1/4 cups all-purpose flour
1 cup pizza sauce
1 pound bulk pork sausage, cooked and drained

1 can (4 ounces) mushroom stems and pieces, drained
1 package (3-1/2 ounces) sliced pepperoni
1 cup (4 ounces) shredded part-skim mozzarella cheese

In a mixing bowl, dissolve yeast in warm water. Add oil, salt and 2 cups flour. Beat until smooth. Stir in enough remaining flour to form a soft dough. Turn onto a floured surface; knead until smooth and elastic, about 6-8 minutes. Cover and let rest for 10 minutes.

Roll dough into a 14-in. x 12-in. rectangle. Transfer to a greased 15-in. x 10-in. x 1-in. baking pan. Spoon pizza sauce to within 1/2 in. of edges. Top with sausage, mushrooms, pepperoni and cheese. Roll up jelly-roll style, starting with a long side; pinch seam to seal and tuck ends under.

Bake at 400° for 30-35 minutes or until golden brown. Serve warm. Refrigerate leftovers. **Yield:** 1 loaf.

Veggie Delights

1/2 cup thinly sliced onion rings
2 cups sliced fresh mushrooms
3 tablespoons butter, *divided*
1/4 teaspoon salt
1/4 teaspoon pepper
1/4 teaspoon garlic powder
1/8 teaspoon onion powder
1/8 teaspoon celery seed

4 French rolls, split
8 thin green pepper rings
8 slices Colby-Monterey Jack cheese *or* cheddar cheese, halved
8 thin slices tomato
20 thin slices zucchini
8 thin sweet red pepper rings
1/4 cup sliced stuffed olives

In a skillet, saute onion rings and mushrooms in 1 tablespoon butter until tender. Sprinkle with salt and pepper; set aside. Combine remaining butter with garlic powder, onion powder and celery seed; spread over cut sides of rolls. Broil 4-5 in. from the heat for 1-2 minutes or until lightly browned.

Place about 1/4 cup mushrooms mixture on the bottom of each roll. Layer with green pepper rings and two cheese slices. On top halves, layer tomato and zucchini slices, red pepper rings, olives and remaining cheese. Broil 4 in. from the heat for 3-4 minutes or until cheese is bubbly. Put tops and bottoms of sandwiches together. **Yield:** 4 servings.

Sweet 'n' Sour Pockets

1/3 cup mayonnaise
1/3 cup sour cream
1/2 teaspoon Dijon mustard
1 can (8 ounces) pineapple tidbits, drained
5 pita pocket breads (6 inches), halved

10 lettuce leaves
10 slices (1 ounce *each*) fully cooked ham
1/2 cup chopped green pepper
1/2 cup chopped red onion

In a small bowl, combine mayonnaise, sour cream and mustard. Cover and chill for 1 hour. Just before serving, stir pineapple into mayonnaise mixture. Fill each pita half with lettuce, ham, 2 tablespoons pineapple mixture, green pepper and onion. **Yield:** 5 servings.

Humpty-Dumpty Sandwich Loaf

1 unsliced loaf (1 pound) Italian bread
1/3 cup mayonnaise
1/3 cup sweet pickle relish
4 teaspoons prepared mustard
1 garlic clove, minced
Pinch pepper

4 hard-cooked eggs, chopped
1 cup diced celery
1 cup diced fully cooked ham
3 tablespoons chopped onion
2 tablespoons butter, melted, optional

Slice off the top third of the loaf; set top aside. Hollow out the bottom of the loaf, leaving a 1-in. shell. Crumble part of the removed bread to measure 3/4 cup; set aside. (Discard remaining bread or save for another use.)

In a bowl, combine mayonnaise, relish, mustard, garlic and pepper. Stir in eggs, celery, ham, onion and reserved bread. Stuff loaf; replace top.

To serve immediately, cut into 4-in. pieces. To serve hot, brush with butter; wrap in foil. Place on a baking sheet. Bake at 400° for 25 minutes. **Yield:** 4 servings.

Garlic Oatmeal Soup

1 quart water, *divided*
1/2 cup quick-cooking oats
3 chicken bouillon cubes
2 garlic cloves, minced

1 cup (4 ounces) shredded cheddar cheese
1/4 teaspoon dried basil
1/4 teaspoon salt
Dash pepper

In a small saucepan over medium heat, bring 1 cup water to a boil. Add oats and cook for 1 minute, stirring occasionally. Cover and set aside for 5 minutes. Add bouillon, garlic and remaining water; bring to a boil. Reduce heat and simmer for 10 minutes, stirring occasionally. Add cheese, basil, salt and pepper; cook and stir until cheese is melted. **Yield:** 4 servings.

Mock Monte Cristos

3 tablespoons mayonnaise

12 slices white bread

6 ounces fully cooked ham, thinly sliced

6 slices process Swiss cheese

6 ounces cooked turkey, thinly sliced

2 tablespoons Dijon mustard

3 eggs, beaten

3/4 cup milk

2 tablespoons confectioners' sugar, optional

1/4 teaspoon salt, optional

2 cups crushed crisp rice cereal

1/2 cup sour cream

1/4 cup strawberry jam

Spread mayonnaise on six slices of bread; top each with ham, cheese and turkey. Spread mustard on remaining bread; place over turkey. In a shallow dish, combine eggs, milk, and confectioners' sugar and salt if desired. Dip each sandwich into egg mixture, then into crushed cereal.

Place on a greased 15-in. x 10-in. x 1-in. baking pan. Bake at 425° for 7 minutes. Turn and bake 5-7 minutes more or until golden brown. Combine sour cream and jam; serve as a dip with hot sandwiches. **Yield:** 6 servings.

Summer Garden Soup

1 cup chopped onion

4 to 6 garlic cloves, minced

2 tablespoons olive oil

3 cups chopped fresh tomatoes

1 cup fresh or frozen cut green beans

1 tablespoon minced fresh basil or 1 teaspoon dried basil

1 teaspoon minced fresh tarragon or 1/4 teaspoon dried tarragon

1/2 teaspoon minced fresh dill or pinch dill weed

1/4 teaspoon salt, optional

1/4 teaspoon pepper

3-1/2 cups chicken broth

1 cup fresh or frozen peas

1 cup sliced zucchini or yellow summer squash

In saucepan, saute onion and garlic in oil until onion is tender. Add tomatoes, beans, basil, tarragon, dill, salt if desired and pepper; simmer for 10 minutes. Add broth, peas and zucchini; simmer for 5-10 minutes or until vegetables are crisp-tender. **Yield:** 8 servings (2 quarts).

Nutty Shrimp Salad Sandwiches

2 cups cooked salad shrimp

3 kiwifruit, peeled, sliced and quartered

3/4 cup shredded carrots

1/2 cup mayonnaise

1/2 cup chopped pecans

1/8 teaspoon ground nutmeg

Lettuce leaves

3 pita breads (6 inches), halved

In a medium bowl, combine the first six ingredients. Line pita halves with lettuce; spoon about 1/2 cup shrimp mixture into each. **Yield:** 6 servings.

Fried Chicken Pitas

3 cups thinly sliced fried chicken (including crispy skin)

1 cup bottled coleslaw dressing

1/3 cup crumbled cooked bacon

2 tablespoons chopped green onions with tops

1/4 teaspoon ground mustard

1/8 teaspoon pepper

6 pita bread halves

In a medium bowl, combine chicken, dressing, bacon, onions, mustard and pepper. Spoon into pita bread. **Yield:** 6 servings.

Pepper Soup

1 pound ground beef

1 *each* large green, sweet red and yellow pepper, chopped

1 large onion, chopped

1 can (46 ounces) V8 juice

1/2 to 1 teaspoon cayenne pepper

Salt and pepper to taste

In a saucepan, cook beef, peppers and onion over medium heat until meat is no longer pink; drain. Add the remaining ingredients; bring to a boil. Reduce heat; simmer, uncovered, for 15 minutes or until vegetables are tender. **Yield:** 8 servings (2 quarts).

Baked Chili

6 bacon strips, diced

1-1/2 pounds ground beef

1 large onion, thinly sliced

1/2 cup chopped green pepper

2 cans (16 ounces *each*) kidney beans, rinsed and drained

1 can (14-1/2 ounces) diced tomatoes, undrained

1 can (6 ounces) tomato paste

4-1/2 teaspoons chili powder

1-1/2 teaspoons salt

1/4 teaspoon dried oregano

1/4 teaspoon ground cumin

1/8 teaspoon rubbed sage

In a large saucepan, cook bacon over medium heat until crisp; remove with a slotted spoon and drain on paper towels. Cook beef, onion and green pepper in drippings over medium heat until meat is no longer pink; drain. Remove from the heat; add the remaining ingredients. Stir in bacon; mix well.

Transfer to an ovenproof Dutch oven or greased 13-in. x 9-in. x 2-in. baking dish. Cover and bake at 350° for 45 minutes. Uncover and bake 15 minutes longer or until thick and bubbly. **Yield:** 6-8 servings (about 2 quarts).

Beef Ravioli Soup

1 cup sliced celery

1/2 cup chopped onion

1 cup sliced carrots

2 tablespoons vegetable oil

4 cups beef broth

1/8 teaspoon pepper

1/4 teaspoon crushed red pepper flakes

1 can (15 ounces) beef ravioli

1/4 cup chopped fresh parsley

Grated Parmesan cheese

In a large kettle, saute celery, onion and carrots in oil for 3 minutes; add broth and seasonings. Bring to a boil. Reduce heat; simmer, covered, about 15 minutes or until the vegetables are tender. Stir in the ravioli and heat through. Garnish with parsley and Parmesan cheese. **Yield:** 4-6 servings (1-1/2 qts.).

Pizza Buns

2 pounds ground beef
1 cup chopped onion
1 garlic clove, minced
1 cup ketchup
1/4 teaspoon ground mustard
1/2 teaspoon dried oregano

1 tablespoon Worcestershire sauce
2 cans (4 ounces *each*) mushrooms, drained
Shredded part-skim mozzarella cheese
Buttered hamburger buns

In a skillet, cook ground beef with onion and garlic over medium heat until meat is no longer pink; drain. Combine the ketchup, mustard, oregano and Worcestershire sauce; stir into beef mixture. Add mushrooms and mix well. Simmer 15 minutes or until heated through. Spoon onto buttered hamburger buns; sprinkle with mozzarella cheese. Place on baking sheets; heat under broiler until cheese melts. **Yield:** 10-12 servings.

Vegetarian Chili

1 medium green pepper, chopped
1 medium onion, chopped
3 garlic cloves, minced
1 tablespoon vegetable oil
2 cans (14-1/2 ounces *each*) Mexican-style stewed tomatoes
1 can (16 ounces) kidney beans, rinsed and drained

1 can (15 ounces) pinto beans, rinsed and drained
1 can (11 ounces) whole kernel corn, drained
2-1/2 cups water
1 cup uncooked long grain rice
1 to 2 tablespoons chili powder
1-1/2 teaspoons ground cumin

In a Dutch oven, saute green pepper, onion and garlic in oil until tender. Stir in all remaining ingredients; bring to a boil. Reduce heat; cover and simmer for 25-30 minutes or until rice is cooked, stirring occasionally. If thinner chili is desired, add additional water. **Yield:** 11 servings.

Mom's Chicken Soup

1 chicken (about 2-1/2 to 3 pounds) with giblets, quartered

2-1/2 quarts water

1 tablespoon salt

1 medium onion

6 whole peppercorns

6 celery stalks (leaves reserved), *divided*

6 whole carrots, *divided*

2 cups cooked rice *or* cooked fine egg noodles

1/4 cup chopped fresh parsley

3 to 4 drops yellow food coloring

Put chicken, giblets, water, salt, onion, peppercorns, 3 stalks celery, all the celery leaves and 3 carrots in a soup kettle. Cover and slowly bring to a boil. Skim off the foam. Reduce heat to simmer and cook for 2 hours or until meat is tender. Remove meat, vegetables and peppercorns. Discard cooked vegetables and peppercorns. Strain stock, if desired.

Chill stock, then skim fat layer. Dice remaining celery and carrots; add to the stock. Cook until the vegetables are tender.

Meanwhile, remove chicken from the bones and dice. Add chicken, cooked rice or noodles and parsley. Heat through. Stir in food coloring. **Yield:** 10-12 servings.

Quick Calzones

2 cups (8 ounces) shredded part-skim mozzarella cheese

1 carton (15 ounces) ricotta cheese

6 ounces diced fully cooked ham *or* sliced pepperoni

1 teaspoon garlic powder

2 loaves (1 pound *each*) frozen bread dough, thawed

Warmed spaghetti *or* pizza sauce, optional

In a large bowl, combine the cheeses, ham and garlic powder. Divide each loaf into eight pieces.

On a floured surface, roll each portion into a 5-in. circle. Place filling in the center of each circle. Bring dough over filling; pinch seams to seal.

Place seam side down on greased baking sheets. Bake at 375° for 30-35 minutes or until golden brown. Serve warm with sauce if desired. Refrigerate leftovers. **Yield:** 16 servings.

Make-Ahead Saucy Sandwiches

24 slices white sandwich bread
1-1/2 cups diced cooked chicken
1 can (10-3/4 ounces) condensed cream of mushroom soup, undiluted
1/2 cup prepared chicken gravy
1 can (8 ounces) water chestnuts, drained and chopped
1 jar (2 ounces) chopped pimientos, drained
2 tablespoons chopped green onions
Salt and pepper to taste
5 eggs
1/3 cup milk
2 bags (6 ounces *each*) ridged potato chips, crushed

Trim crusts from bread. (Discard or save for another use.) In a medium bowl, combine chicken, soup, gravy, water chestnuts, pimientos, onions, salt and pepper. Spread on 12 slices of bread; top with remaining bread. Wrap each in foil and freeze.

In a bowl, beat eggs and milk. Unwrap sandwiches; dip frozen sandwiches in egg mixture and then in potato chips.

Place on greased baking sheets. Bake at 325° for 50-60 minutes or until golden brown. **Yield:** 12 servings.

Cheesy Chicken Corn Soup

2 cans (14-1/2 ounces *each*) chicken broth
1 can (10 ounces) diced tomatoes and green chilies, undrained
2 cup shredded cooked chicken
2 cups frozen corn
1-1/2 cups water, *divided*
1/4 cup finely chopped onion
Dash pepper
1/2 cup all-purpose flour
1 pound process American cheese, cubed

In a large saucepan, combine the broth, tomatoes, chicken, corn, 1 cup water, onion and pepper. Bring to a boil. Reduce heat; simmer, uncovered, for 5 minutes or until the corn is tender.

Combine the flour and remaining water until smooth; stir into the soup. Bring to a boil; cook and stir for 2 minutes or until thickened. Reduce heat to low; stir in the cheese until melted. **Yield:** 9 servings (about 2 quarts).

Creamy Turkey Melt

1/2 cup chopped red onion	1/3 cup sour cream
5 tablespoons butter, softened, *divided*	2 cups cubed cooked turkey
1 package (3 ounces) cream cheese, cubed	8 slices dark rye *or* pumpernickel bread
	4 slices Swiss cheese

In a saucepan, saute onion in 1 tablespoon butter until tender. Reduce heat to low. Add cream cheese and sour cream; cook and stir until smooth. Add turkey; cook until heated through (do not boil). Spoon 1/2 cup filling onto four slices of bread; top with a slice of cheese. Spread outside of bread with remaining butter. In a skillet over medium heat, cook sandwiches until lightly browned on both sides. **Yield:** 4 servings.

Broccoli, Hamburger And Cheese Soup

1-1/2 cups water	1/4 teaspoon salt
2 chicken bouillon cubes	1/8 teaspoon pepper
3 cups frozen broccoli	2 cups milk
1/4 cup finely chopped onion	1 cup cubed process cheese (Velveeta)
2 tablespoons butter	1 pound ground beef, browned and drained
3 tablespoons all-purpose flour	

In a saucepan, bring water to a boil; add bouillon and stir until dissolved. Add broccoli; cook according to package directions. Do not drain. Remove from the heat; set aside.

In a large saucepan, cook onion in butter until tender. Add flour, salt and pepper; stir until well blended. Remove from the heat and stir in enough milk to make a smooth paste; stir in remaining milk. Return to heat. Bring to a boil; cook and stir for 1 minute or until thickened. Add cheese, ground beef, broccoli and cooking liquid. Cook until heated through and the cheese is melted, stirring occasionally. Serve hot. **Yield:** 6 servings, (6-1/2 cups).

Hearty Muffuletta Loaf

1 unsliced loaf (1 pound) French bread
1/2 cup olive oil
1/3 cup red wine vinegar
1 teaspoon dried oregano
2 garlic cloves, minced
1 cup (4 ounces) shredded part-skim mozzarella cheese
1 jar (6-1/2 ounces) marinated artichoke hearts, drained and chopped
1/2 cup sliced stuffed olives
1 can (2-1/4 ounces) sliced ripe olives, drained
1/2 cup sliced fresh banana peppers
1/4 cup chopped red onion
1/4 pound sliced Genoa salami
1/4 pound sliced Cotto salami
1/4 pound sliced pepperoni
1/4 pound sliced provolone cheese

Cut bread in half lengthwise; hollow out top and bottom, leaving a 1-in. shell. (Discard removed bread or save for another use.) Combine the oil, vinegar, oregano and garlic; brush half on the inside of shell. Add the mozzarella cheese, artichoke hearts, olives, peppers and onion to the remaining oil mixture. Spoon into bottom of bread shell; layer with meats and cheese. Replace bread top. Wrap tightly in plastic wrap; refrigerate until ready to serve. **Yield:** 8 servings.

Lamb and Potato Stew

2 pounds lean lamb stew meat, cut into 1-inch pieces
1/2 cup chopped onion
4 to 6 medium potatoes, peeled and diced
4 carrots, diced
1-1/4 cups water
1 can (14-1/2 ounces) diced tomatoes, undrained
1/2 cup diced celery
1-1/2 teaspoons salt
1/2 teaspoon pepper
1/2 teaspoon garlic powder
1/2 teaspoon dried thyme
1/2 teaspoon dried basil
1 to 2 bay leaves

In a large kettle or Dutch oven, combine all ingredients. Cover and bake at 325° for 1-1/2 to 2-1/2 hours or until tender. Discard bay leaves before serving. **Yield:** 8 servings (2 quarts).

Turkey BLT

2 tablespoons mayonnaise
1 tablespoon spicy brown
  mustard
1 tablespoon honey
2 large pumpernickel rolls, split
4 slices cooked turkey

4 bacon strips, cooked and
  drained
2 slices Swiss cheese
4 slices tomato
Lettuce leaves

In a small bowl, combine mayonnaise, mustard and honey; spread on cut sides of rolls. On bottom halves of rolls, layer turkey, bacon and cheese. Broil 4 in. from the heat for 2-3 minutes or until cheese begins to melt. Top with tomato and lettuce; replace roll tops. **Yield:** 2 servings.

Chicken Salad on Buns

2 cups diced leftover cooked
  chicken
1/4 pound process American
  cheese, diced
1 to 2 tablespoons pickle relish

1/4 cup mayonnaise
2 tablespoons chopped onion
2 tablespoons chopped green
  pepper
Kaiser rolls

In a bowl, combine first six ingredients. Spoon about 1/3 cup onto each roll. Wrap each tightly in foil. Bake at 300° for 20-30 minutes or until heated through. **Yield:** 6-8 servings.

Gazpacho

1 can (46 ounces) vegetable juice
1 can (10-1/2 ounces) condensed
  beef consomme, undiluted
2 cups chopped cucumber
2 cups chopped tomatoes
1 cup chopped green pepper

1/2 cup chopped onion
1/2 cup chopped celery
1/3 cup red wine vinegar
2 tablespoons fresh lemon juice
2 garlic cloves, minced
3 to 4 drops hot pepper sauce

In a large bowl, combine all ingredients. Cover and chill for 2-3 hours before serving. Serve cold. **Yield:** 12 servings (3 quarts).

Liverwurst Deluxe

4 onion rolls, split
4 teaspoons prepared mustard
1/3 to 1/2 pound liverwurst, sliced 1/4 inch thick
1/2 pound cooked turkey breast, sliced

8 bacon strips, cooked and drained
2 slices onion, separated into rings
Dill pickle slices
4 slices cheddar cheese

Spread rolls with mustard. On bottoms of rolls, layer liverwurst, turkey, bacon, onion, pickles and cheese; replace tops. **Yield:** 4 servings.

California Clubs

1/2 cup ranch salad dressing
1/4 cup Dijon mustard
8 slices sourdough bread, toasted
4 boneless skinless chicken breast halves, cooked and sliced

1 large tomato, sliced
1 medium ripe avocado, peeled and sliced
12 bacon strips, cooked and drained

In a small bowl, combine salad dressing and mustard; spread on each slice of bread. On four slices of bread, layer the chicken, tomato, avocado and bacon. Top with remaining bread. **Yield:** 4 servings.

Tomato Soup with a Twist

1 can (10-3/4 ounces) condensed tomato soup, undiluted
1 tablespoon creamy peanut butter

1-1/3 cups milk
2 tablespoons shredded cheddar cheese
Additional cheddar cheese

In a saucepan, combine the soup and peanut butter. Gradually stir in milk. Add cheese; cook and stir until peanut butter and cheese is melted and soup is heated through. Garnish with additional cheese. **Yield:** 2 servings.

Tomato-Bacon Rarebit

1 tablespoon butter
1 tablespoon all-purpose flour
2/3 cup milk
1 teaspoon Worcestershire sauce
1/4 teaspoon ground mustard
1/4 teaspoon salt
1/8 teaspoon pepper

1/8 teaspoon paprika
2 cups (8 ounces) shredded sharp cheddar cheese
4 slices white bread, toasted
12 bacon strips, cooked and drained
2 medium tomatoes, sliced

In a saucepan, melt butter over medium heat. Stir in the flour until smooth. Gradually stir in milk. Bring to a boil; cook and stir for 2 minutes or until thickened. Reduce heat to low; add Worcestershire sauce, mustard, salt, pepper, paprika and cheese. Cook and stir until cheese is melted.

Place toast on plates; top each piece with three bacon strips, two slices of tomato and cheese sauce. **Yield:** 4 servings.

Turkey Cabbage Soup

1 pound lean ground turkey
2 medium onions, chopped
1 tablespoon vegetable oil
3 pounds potatoes, peeled and cut into 1-inch pieces
3 medium carrots, sliced
1 small head cabbage, chopped
1 can (49-1/2 ounces) reduced-sodium chicken broth

1 tablespoon prepared Dijon mustard
1-1/2 teaspoons prepared horseradish
3/4 teaspoon salt
1/2 teaspoon pepper
2 teaspoons cornstarch
1 tablespoon cold water

In a Dutch oven or large soup kettle, cook turkey and onions in oil over medium heat until turkey is no longer pink; drain. Add the potatoes, carrots, cabbage, broth, mustard, horseradish, salt and pepper; bring to a boil. Reduce heat; cover and simmer for 15-20 minutes or until potatoes are tender, stirring occasionally.

Combine cornstarch and cold water until smooth; gradually stir into soup. Bring to a boil; cook and stir for 2 minutes or until slightly thickened. **Yield:** 10 servings (about 3-1/2 quarts).

Chickenwiches

1 cup finely chopped cooked
  chicken
1/2 cup chopped celery
1/4 cup mayonnaise
2 tablespoons sliced stuffed
  green olives
2 tablespoons minced fresh
  parsley

2 teaspoons lemon juice
1/4 teaspoon salt
Dash pepper
6 slices sandwich bread
6 bacon strips, cooked and
  crumbled

In a medium bowl, combine the first eight ingredients. Spread on three slices of bread; sprinkle with bacon. Top with remaining bread. **Yield:** 3 servings.

Sweet Succotash Chili

1 pound dry lima beans
2 pounds ground beef
4 medium onions, chopped
3 tablespoons olive oil
1/4 cup paprika
3 tablespoons ground cumin
3 garlic cloves, minced

1 teaspoon salt
1 can (49-1/2 ounces) chicken
  broth
1 can (28 ounces) crushed
  tomatoes
4 cups frozen corn

Place beans in a Dutch oven or soup kettle; cover with water. Bring to a boil; boil for 2 minutes. Remove from the heat; let stand for 1-4 hours or until beans are softened. Drain beans and discard liquid.

In a 6-qt. Dutch oven or soup kettle, cook beef and onions over medium heat until meat is no longer pink and onions are tender; drain. Add beans, paprika, cumin, garlic and salt. Stir in chicken broth and tomatoes; bring to a boil. Reduce heat; cover and simmer for 1 hour. Add corn; cover and simmer for 1 hour or until beans are tender. **Yield:** 12-16 servings (4 quarts).

Meat Loaf Sandwiches

1/2 cup salsa
1 tablespoon Worcestershire sauce
1/8 teaspoon salt
1/8 teaspoon cayenne pepper
1/8 teaspoon pepper
1/2 cup diced sharp cheddar cheese
1/2 cup diced Swiss cheese
1/2 cup chopped dill pickle
1 can (2-1/4 ounces) sliced ripe olives, drained
1/3 cup chopped red onion
1/3 cup dry bread crumbs
1 egg
3 tablespoons crumbled blue cheese
2 pounds bulk pork sausage
14 to 16 hard rolls, split
Dijon mustard

In a large bowl, combine the first five ingredients. Add the next eight ingredients; mix well. Add the sausage; mix well. Press into an ungreased 9-in. x 5-in. x 3-in. loaf pan.

Bake at 350° for 1 hour; drain often. Increase temperature to 375° and bake 30 minutes longer or until a meat thermometer reads 160°; drain. Cool in pan for 30 minutes. Remove from pan; cover and chill overnight. Cut into 1/2-in.-thick slices. Spread rolls with mustard and top with meat loaf slices. **Yield:** 14-16 servings.

Autumn Soup

1 can (28 ounces) stewed tomatoes
1 pound ground beef
1 cup chopped onion
1 cup diced carrot
1 cup diced celery
1 cup diced peeled potato
1 cup diced peeled rutabaga
1 bay leaf
1/8 teaspoon dried basil
4 cups water

Puree tomatoes in a blender or food processor; set aside. In a skillet, cook ground beef over medium heat until no longer pink; drain. Stir in tomatoes and remaining ingredients. Bring to a boil; reduce heat and simmer 25-30 minutes or until the vegetables are tender. Discard bay leaf before serving. **Yield:** 8-10 servings (10 cups).

Pepper Lover's BLT

1/4 cup mayonnaise
1 tablespoon diced pimientos
1/8 teaspoon coarsely ground pepper
1/4 teaspoon hot pepper sauce
8 slices sourdough bread, toasted
4 teaspoons Dijon-mayonnaise blend

6 tablespoons shredded sharp cheddar cheese
4 pickled jalapeno peppers *or* green chilies, thinly sliced
12 bacon strips, cooked and drained
8 tomato slices
4 lettuce leaves
8 thin slices cooked turkey

In a small bowl, combine mayonnaise, pimientos, pepper and hot pepper sauce. Chill for at least 1 hour.

Spread four slices of toast with Dijon-mayonnaise blend. Sprinkle with cheese; top with jalapenos, bacon, tomato, lettuce, turkey. Spread mayonnaise mixture on remaining slices of toast; place over turkey. **Yield:** 4 servings.

Editor's Note: When cutting or seeding hot peppers, use rubber or plastic gloves to protect your hands. Avoid touching your face.

Quick Bean Soup

1 medium onion, chopped
2 medium carrots, chopped
2 celery ribs, chopped
2 cups water
2 cans (15 ounces *each*) navy *or* great northern beans
1 can (28 ounces) diced tomatoes, undrained

1 pound smoked sausage, cut into 1/2-inch slices and halved
1 teaspoon salt
1/2 teaspoon garlic salt
1/2 teaspoon paprika
1/2 teaspoon dried marjoram
1/2 teaspoon dried thyme
1/2 teaspoon pepper

In a 3-qt. saucepan, combine onion, carrots, celery and water. Bring to a boil; boil for 5 minutes. Add the remaining ingredients; mix well. Heat through. **Yield:** 6-8 servings (about 2-1/4 quarts).

Cream of Asparagus Soup

4 cups fresh asparagus, washed, trimmed and cut in 1/2-inch pieces

2 cups water, *divided*

1/4 cup very finely diced green onions

5 tablespoons butter

5 tablespoons flour

1/2 to 1 teaspoon salt

1/4 teaspoon white pepper

4 cups milk

1 tablespoon chicken bouillon granules

In a large saucepan, bring asparagus and 1 cup water to a boil. Cook, uncovered, for 3-5 minutes or until tender-crisp. Drain, reserving liquid. Set asparagus aside.

In a saucepan, saute onions in butter. Stir in the flour, salt and pepper until blended; gradually stir in the milk, bouillon, remaining water and reserved cooking liquid. Bring to a boil; cook and stir for 2 minutes or until thickened. Stir in reserved asparagus. Heat through and serve. **Yield:** 6 servings.

Carrot Soup

1 medium onion, chopped

2 tablespoons butter

2-1/2 cups chicken broth

1 pound carrots, sliced

2 large potatoes, peeled and cubed

1-1/2 cups milk

1/4 teaspoon salt

1/4 teaspoon pepper

Shredded Swiss cheese and minced fresh parsley, optional

In a 3-qt. saucepan, saute onion in butter until tender. Add broth, carrots and potatoes; bring to a boil. Reduce heat and simmer for 15-20 minutes or until vegetables are tender. Remove from the heat; cool slightly.

Transfer to a blender; cover and process until blended. Return to pan. Stir in milk, salt and pepper; heat through (do not boil). Garnish with cheese and parsley if desired. **Yield:** 6 servings.

Southwestern Chicken Soup

1 can (10-1/2 ounces) condensed beef broth

1 can (12 ounces) tomato paste

1 can (15-1/2 ounces) kidney beans, rinsed and drained

1 can (11 ounces) Mexicorn, drained

1-1/2 cups diced cooked chicken

3 green onions, sliced

2 to 3 tablespoons chili powder

1 can (4 ounces) chopped green chilies

1-2/3 cups water

In a large saucepan, combine beef broth and tomato paste. Add remaining ingredients. Cover and simmer for 10 minutes. **Yield:** 6 servings.

Deviled English Muffins

1/3 cup chili sauce

1-1/2 teaspoons ground mustard

1-1/2 teaspoons Worcestershire sauce

1 teaspoon dried minced onion

1 teaspoon salt

Pepper to taste

1 pound ground beef

6 English muffins, split

In a bowl, combine the first six ingredients. Crumble beef over mixture and mix well. Spread meat mixture over muffin halves. Place on an ungreased baking sheet. Broil 4 in. from the heat for 10 minutes or until no longer pink. **Yield:** 6 servings.

Hot Chicken Heroes

2 cups cubed cooked chicken

1/2 cup cubed process American cheese

1/2 cup chopped onion

1/2 cup mayonnaise

1/4 cup chopped green pepper

1/4 teaspoon salt

1/4 teaspoon pepper

4 submarine rolls (6 inches)

In a medium bowl, combine the first seven ingredients. Spread on rolls; wrap each in heavy-duty foil and bake at 325° for 20 minutes. **Yield:** 4 servings.

Crab Bisque

1/2 cup chopped celery
2 tablespoons chopped onion
1/4 cup butter
1/4 cup all-purpose flour
2-1/2 cups milk
2 beef bouillon cubes
1 cup half-and-half cream

1 can (6 ounces) crabmeat,
drained
1/2 cup sliced fresh mushrooms
1/2 teaspoon dried basil
1/4 teaspoon garlic powder
1/4 to 1/2 teaspoon Creole
seasoning
1/8 to 1/4 teaspoon pepper

In a 3-qt. saucepan over medium heat, saute celery and onion in butter until tender. Stir in flour; gradually add milk. Bring to a boil; cook and stir for 2 minutes or until thickened. Add the bouillon, cream, crab, mushrooms, basil, garlic powder, 1/4 teaspoon Creole seasoning and 1/8 teaspoon pepper. Reduce heat; cover and simmer for 45 minutes, stirring frequently. Season to taste with remaining Creole seasoning and pepper if desired. **Yield:** 4 servings.

Editor's Note: The following spices may be substituted for the Creole seasoning: 1/2 teaspoon *each* paprika and garlic powder, and a pinch *each* cayenne pepper, dried thyme and ground cumin.

Triple Tasty Sandwich Spread

1/2 to 2/3 cup mayonnaise
1 tablespoon Dijon mustard
1 tablespoon finely chopped
onion
1 tablespoon minced jalapeno
pepper
1 teaspoon Worcestershire sauce

1/2 pound fully cooked ham,
ground
1/2 pound Genoa salami, ground
1/4 cup finely chopped sweet
pickle
3 hard-cooked eggs, chopped
12 slices whole wheat bread,
toasted

Combine the first five ingredients in a medium bowl. Stir in ham, salami, pickle and eggs. Spoon about 1/2 cup between slices of whole wheat toast. **Yield:** 6 servings.

Editor's Note: When cutting or seeding hot peppers, use rubber or plastic gloves to protect your hands. Avoid touching your face.

Kielbasa Cabbage Soup

1 small head cabbage, coarsely chopped

1 medium onion, chopped

4 to 6 garlic cloves, minced

2 tablespoons olive oil

4 cups water

3 tablespoons cider vinegar

1 to 2 tablespoons brown sugar

1 pound smoked kielbasa *or* Polish sausage, halved, cut into 1/2-inch pieces

4 medium potatoes, peeled and cubed

3 large carrots, chopped

1 teaspoon caraway seeds

1/2 teaspoon pepper

In a Dutch oven or soup kettle, saute the cabbage, onion and garlic in oil for 5 minutes or until tender. Combine water, vinegar and brown sugar; add to cabbage mixture. Stir in remaining ingredients. Bring to a boil. Reduce heat; cover and simmer for 60-70 minutes or until vegetables are tender. **Yield:** 8-10 servings.

Italian-Sausage Pepper Sandwiches

2 uncooked Italian sausage links

1 small red onion, thinly sliced

1/2 medium green pepper, julienned

1/2 medium sweet red pepper, julienned

1 garlic clove, chopped

1 tablespoon canola oil

1 large tomato, seeded and chopped

1/2 teaspoon dried oregano

Salt and pepper to taste, optional

2 French *or* submarine rolls, split and toasted

In a skillet, cook sausage over medium heat until browned. Let stand until cool enough to handle. Cut into 1/2-in. slices. Return to pan and cook until no longer pink; drain and set aside.

In same skillet, saute the onion, green pepper, red pepper and garlic in oil until crisp-tender. Add the sausage, tomato, oregano and salt and pepper if desired. Cook until tomatoes are heated through. Spoon sausage mixture into rolls. **Yield:** 2 servings.

Church Supper Chili

2-1/2 pounds ground beef
1/2 cup chopped green pepper
1 cup chopped celery
2 cups chopped onion
1 garlic clove, minced
3 tablespoons chili powder
2 teaspoons salt
1/2 teaspoon pepper

1 can (14-1/2 ounces) diced
  tomatoes, undrained
1 can (46 ounces) tomato juice
1 bottle (32 ounces) V8 juice
2 cans (16 ounces *each*) kidney
  beans, rinsed and drained
2 cans (16 ounces *each*) hot
  chili beans

In a large Dutch oven or soup kettle, cook beef over medium heat until no longer pink; drain. Add green pepper, celery, onion and garlic; cook until tender. Add spices, tomatoes and juices. Bring to a boil. Reduce heat; simmer, uncovered for 20 minutes. Add beans and simmer 20 minutes longer. **Yield:** 20-24 servings.

Grilled Blue Cheese Sandwiches

1-1/2 cups sliced fresh mushrooms
2 tablespoons chopped onion
1/2 cup mayonnaise, *divided*
2 cups (8 ounces) shredded
  cheddar cheese
1/4 cup crumbled blue cheese
1 teaspoon yellow *or* Dijon
  mustard

1 teaspoon Worcestershire sauce
1/4 teaspoon salt
1/8 teaspoon cayenne pepper
12 slices white *or* wheat bread
2 to 4 tablespoons butter

In a skillet, saute mushrooms and onion in 3 tablespoons mayonnaise for 5 minutes or until mushrooms are tender; cool. In a bowl, combine cheeses, mustard, Worcestershire sauce, salt, cayenne, mushroom mixture and remaining mayonnaise. Spread 1/3 cup on six slices of bread; top with remaining bread. Melt 2 tablespoons butter in a large skillet. Add sandwiches and cook until each side is golden brown and cheese is melted, adding additional butter if necessary. **Yield:** 6 servings.

Special Ham 'n' Cheese Sandwiches

1 package (3 ounces) cream
  cheese, softened
2 tablespoons sweet pickle relish
1 tablespoon Dijon mustard

1/2 cup shredded cheddar cheese
2 ounces fully cooked ham,
  finely chopped
4 slices of bread *or* 2 buns

In a small bowl, combine cream cheese, pickle relish and mustard. Stir
in cheese and ham. Spread 1/2 cup between slices of bread or in buns.
Yield: 2 servings.

Curried Chicken Pita Pockets

3/4 cup mayonnaise
1 teaspoon soy sauce
1 teaspoon lemon juice
1/2 teaspoon curry powder
1 small onion, finely chopped
2-1/2 cups cubed cooked chicken

1-1/2 cups halved seedless green
  grapes
3/4 cup chopped celery
1/2 cup sliced almonds
10 pita breads, halved

In a large bowl, combine the first five ingredients. Stir in chicken, grapes
and celery; refrigerate. Just before serving, add almonds. Stuff about 1/4
cup into each pita half. **Yield:** 10 servings.

Sweet Potato Stew

1 can (14-1/2 ounces) beef broth
3/4 pound lean ground beef
2 medium sweet potatoes,
  peeled and cut into 1/2-inch
  cubes
1 small onion, finely chopped

1/2 cup V8 juice
2 teaspoons golden raisins
1 garlic clove, minced
1/2 teaspoon dried thyme
Pinch cayenne pepper

In a large saucepan, bring broth to a boil. Crumble beef into broth. Cover
and cook for 3 minutes, stirring occasionally. Add remaining ingredients;
return to a boil. Reduce heat; simmer, uncovered, for 15 minutes or until
meat is no longer pink and potatoes are tender. **Yield:** 4 servings.

Egg Salad Tuna Wraps

12 hard-cooked eggs, chopped
2 cans (6 ounces *each*) tuna,
   drained and flaked
2 celery ribs, chopped
1/2 cup sweet pickle relish
1/2 cup mayonnaise

3 tablespoons dry onion
   soup mix
1 tablespoon minced fresh
   parsley
1/2 teaspoon pepper
Lettuce leaves, optional
6 flour tortillas (10 inches)

In a bowl, combine the first eight ingredients. Place lettuce leaves on tortillas if desired. Top each with about 3/4 cup egg mixture; roll up tightly. Serve immediately or wrap in plastic wrap and refrigerate. **Yield:** 6 servings.

Herbed Pasties

1-1/2 pounds ground beef
1 medium onion, chopped
2 beef bouillon cubes
1/4 cup boiling water
1-1/2 cups (6 ounces) shredded
   cheddar cheese
1 cup sliced fresh mushrooms
1 celery rib, diced
1/4 cup grated Parmesan cheese

3/4 teaspoon dill weed
3/4 teaspoon dried thyme
1/2 teaspoon dried rosemary,
   crushed
Salt and pepper to taste
2 packages (11 ounces *each*) pie
   crust mix
1 egg
1 tablespoon water

In a skillet, cook beef and onion over medium heat until meat is no longer pink; drain well. Dissolve bouillon in water; stir into meat mixture. Add the cheddar cheese, mushrooms, celery, Parmesan cheese and seasonings; mix well.

Prepare pie crusts according to package directions. Divide dough into four portions. On a floured surface, roll each into a 14-in. square. Cut each into four 7-in. squares. Place a scant 1/2 cup meat mixture in the center of each square. Moisten edges of pastry with water and fold over filling, forming a triangle. Press edges with a fork to seal. Make a 1-in. slit in the top of each triangle.

Place on two ungreased baking sheets. Beat egg and water; brush over pastry. Bake at 375° for 30-35 minutes or until golden brown. **Yield:** 16 servings.

Chili Rellenos Sandwiches

1 can (4 ounces) chopped green
   chilies, drained
6 slices bread
3 slices Monterey Jack cheese

2 eggs
1 cup milk
2 to 4 tablespoons butter
Salsa, optional

Mash chilies with a fork; spread on three slices of bread. Top with cheese and remaining bread. In a shallow bowl, beat eggs and milk; dip the sandwiches.

   Melt 2 tablespoons of butter in a large skillet. Cook sandwiches until golden brown on both sides and cheese is melted, adding additional butter if necessary. Serve with salsa if desired. **Yield:** 3 servings.

Vegetable Bean Soup

1-1/2 cups chopped onion
1 cup sliced celery
3 medium carrots, sliced
2 to 3 garlic cloves, minced
1 tablespoon vegetable oil
2 cans (14-1/2 ounces *each*)
   chicken broth
2 cans (15 ounces *each*) navy *or*
   great northern beans, rinsed
   and drained, *divided*

2 cups broccoli florets
1/2 teaspoon dried rosemary,
   crushed
1/4 teaspoon dried thyme
1/2 teaspoon salt
1/4 teaspoon pepper
1 cup fresh spinach

In a Dutch oven or soup kettle, saute onion, celery, carrots and garlic in oil until tender. Add broth, one can of beans, broccoli and seasonings; bring to a boil. Reduce heat; simmer, uncovered, for 5-7 minutes.

   Place remaining beans in a blender or food processor; cover and process until smooth. Add to the soup along with the spinach; simmer for 2 minutes or until heated through. **Yield:** 8 servings (2 quarts).

Stuffed Ham Slices

1 package (8 ounces) cream
cheese, softened
3/4 cup minced celery
1/2 cup shredded cheddar cheese
1/3 cup minced fresh parsley
1/4 cup mayonnaise

2 tablespoons minced onion
1 unsliced loaf (1 pound) Italian
bread
8 slices (1 ounce *each*) fully
cooked ham
3 to 4 whole dill pickles, sliced
lengthwise

In a bowl, combine the first six ingredients. Cut bread in half lengthwise; spread each half with the cheese mixture. On the bottom half, layer half the ham, pickle slices and remaining ham. Replace top of loaf. Wrap tightly in plastic wrap; chill for at least 2 hours before serving. **Yield:** 8 servings.

French Onion Soup

1/4 cup butter
2 pounds onions, thinly sliced
1 tablespoon sugar
4 tablespoons all-purpose flour
3 cans (14-1/2 ounces *each*) beef
broth
2 cups water
1 teaspoon salt

1 teaspoon dried minced onion
1 teaspoon beef bouillon
granules
1/4 teaspoon garlic salt
1/4 teaspoon pepper
8 slices French bread, toasted
1 cup (4 ounces) shredded Swiss
cheese

In a Dutch oven or soup kettle, melt butter. Add onions and sugar; cook over low heat until lightly browned, about 1 hour.

Sprinkle flour over onions and stir until blended. Gradually stir in broth. Add the water, salt, dried onion, bouillon, garlic salt and pepper.

Bring to a boil; cook and stir for 2 minutes. Reduce heat; cover and simmer for 45 minutes.

Ladle soup into ovenproof bowls. Top with a slice of toasted bread; sprinkle with cheese. Place on a baking sheet. Bake at 400° for 5 minutes. **Yield:** 8 servings.

Grandmother's Chicken 'n' Dumplings

1 large chicken (6 pounds)
2 teaspoons salt
4 quarts water
2 tablespoons white vinegar
1 large onion, sliced
2 carrots, washed and chopped
2 stalks celery, washed and sliced

DUMPLINGS:
2 cups all-purpose flour
1-1/2 teaspoons salt
1 egg
1/2 cup reserved chicken broth

Place chicken, salt, water, vinegar, onion, carrots and celery in large soup kettle, adding more water, if necessary, to cover chicken. Slowly bring to a boil. Cover; reduce heat to simmer. Cook until meat nearly falls from the bone. Strain off broth, reserving chicken meat. Remove and discard skin, bones and vegetables. Cut or tear meat into bite-size pieces. Reserve 1 cup broth; cool to lukewarm.

To make dumplings, combine flour and salt. Make a "well" in flour; add egg. Gradually stir 1/4 cup broth into egg, picking up flour as you go. Continue until flour is used up, adding additional broth as needed, and dough is consistency of pie dough. Pour any remaining reserved broth back into soup kettle.

Turn dough onto floured surface; knead in additional flour to make stiff dough. Allow dough to rest 15 minutes. Roll out dough on floured surface as if for pie crust (circle about 17 in. round). Cut into pieces 1 in. square. Dust with additional flour; let dry for 30 to 60 minutes.

Bring chicken broth to boil (you should have about 4 qts.). Drop squares into boiling broth; reduce heat to a slow simmer. Cover; simmer for 10 minutes. Uncover; cook until a dough dumpling tests done, about 30 minutes. Dust with pepper and add reserved chicken meat. **Yield:** 8-10 servings.

Creamy Egg Salad Sandwiches

1 package (3 ounces) cream cheese, softened
2 tablespoons butter, softened
1 tablespoon mayonnaise
1 teaspoon finely chopped onion
1 teaspoon sugar
1/2 teaspoon prepared horseradish

1/2 teaspoon lemon juice
1/4 teaspoon salt
1/8 teaspoon pepper
Dash garlic powder
6 hard-cooked eggs, chopped
8 slices rye bread

In a medium bowl, combine the first 10 ingredients until smooth. Stir in eggs. Chill for 1 hour. Spread 1/2 cup onto four slices of bread. Cover with remaining bread. **Yield:** 4 servings.

White Christmas Chili

1 pound dried navy beans
6 cups turkey *or* chicken broth
1 cup chopped onion
4 garlic cloves, minced
1 teaspoon white pepper
1/2 teaspoon crushed red pepper flakes
1/4 to 1/2 teaspoon curry powder

1/4 teaspoon ground cumin
2 pounds turkey *or* chicken breast, cooked and cubed
1 can (15-1/4 ounces) white sweet corn
1 cup heavy whipping cream
Chopped green and sweet red peppers, optional

Place beans in a large saucepan or Dutch oven; cover with water. Bring to a boil and boil for 2 minutes. Remove from the heat and soak for 1-4 hours or until beans are softened. Drain and rinse beans; return to the pan. Add broth, onion, garlic and seasonings.

Cover and simmer for 1-1/2 hours or until beans are tender. Add turkey and corn; simmer for 15 minutes. Add cream just before serving; heat through. If desired, garnish individual servings with peppers. **Yield:** 12-14 servings (3 quarts).

Curried Acorn Squash Soup

3 medium acorn squash, halved
and seeded
1/2 cup chopped onion
3 to 4 teaspoons curry powder
2 tablespoons butter

3 cups chicken broth
1 cup half-and-half cream
1/2 teaspoon ground nutmeg
Salt and pepper to taste
Crumbled cooked bacon, optional

Place the squash cut side down in a greased shallow baking pan. Bake at 350° for 35-40 minutes or until the squash is almost tender.

In a saucepan, saute onion and curry powder in butter until onion is tender. Remove from the heat; set aside. Carefully scoop out squash; add pulp to saucepan. Gradually add broth. Cook over medium heat for 15-20 minutes or until squash is very tender. Cool slightly.

In a food processor or blender, process the squash mixture until smooth; return to saucepan. Stir in cream, nutmeg, salt and pepper. Cook over low heat until heated through (do not boil). Garnish with bacon if desired. **Yield:** 4-6 servings.

Cream of Zucchini Soup

2 cups sliced zucchini
1/2 cup chopped onion
1/2 cup chopped carrot
1 tablespoon butter
2 cups chicken broth
3/4 teaspoon dried tarragon

1/2 teaspoon salt
1/4 teaspoon pepper
1/4 to 1/2 teaspoon garlic powder
2 cups milk
Paprika and additional zucchini,
optional

In a large saucepan over medium heat, saute zucchini, onion and carrot in butter for 5 minutes. Add broth, tarragon, salt, pepper and garlic powder; bring to a boil. Reduce heat; cover and simmer for 15-20 minutes or until vegetables are tender. Cool slightly.

Puree in a blender or food processor; return to pan. Add milk; heat through. Garnish with paprika and zucchini if desired. **Yield:** 4 servings.

Three-Cheese Tomato Melt

1/4 cup shredded cheddar cheese

2 tablespoons shredded
part-skim mozzarella cheese

1 tablespoon grated Parmesan
cheese

2 tablespoons mayonnaise

1/8 teaspoon garlic powder

4 slices tomato

2 bagels *or* English muffins, split
and toasted

Combine the cheeses, mayonnaise and garlic powder; set aside. Place a tomato slice on each bagel half; broil 5 in. from the heat for 1-2 minutes or until tomato is warm. Spread about 1 tablespoon cheese mixture over each tomato; broil 2-3 minutes longer or until cheese is melted. **Yield:** 2 servings.

Tarragon Chicken Salad

3/4 cup sour cream

3/4 cup mayonnaise

1 cup finely chopped celery

1/4 cup minced fresh tarragon *or* 1
tablespoon dried tarragon

5 cups cubed cooked chicken

In a medium bowl, combine sour cream, mayonnaise, celery and tarragon; stir in chicken. Refrigerate for 2-3 hours. **Yield:** 4-6 servings.

Mom's Monday Lunch Potato Soup

8 bacon strips, diced

1 small onion, chopped

1-1/2 cups leftover mashed potatoes

1 can (10-3/4 ounces) condensed
cream of chicken soup,
undiluted

2 cups milk

1/2 teaspoon salt, optional

1/8 teaspoon pepper

2 tablespoons chopped fresh
parsley

In a 3-qt. saucepan, cook bacon until crisp; remove to paper towels to drain. Saute onion in the drippings until tender. Add the potatoes and soup and stir until smooth. Gradually stir in milk. Cook over medium heat, stirring constantly. Stir in bacon, salt if desired and pepper. Cook until heated through. Garnish with parsley. **Yield:** 3-4 servings.

Vegetable Tuna Sandwiches

2 packages (3 ounces *each*) cream cheese, softened, *divided*

6 tablespoons mayonnaise, *divided*

1/4 teaspoon salt

1/8 teaspoon pepper

1 can (6 ounces) tuna, drained and flaked

3 tablespoons finely chopped celery

3 tablespoons finely chopped green pepper

1 cup shredded carrots

2 tablespoons finely chopped onion

8 slices white bread

4 slices whole wheat bread

In a large bowl, combine one package of cream cheese, 3 tablespoons mayonnaise, salt and pepper until smooth. Add tuna, celery and green pepper; mix well. In another bowl, combine carrots, onion and remaining cream cheese and mayonnaise. Spread 1/3 cup tuna mixture on four slices of white bread; top with a slice of whole wheat bread. Spread 1/4 cup carrot mixture on the whole wheat bread; top with a slice of white bread. **Yield:** 4 servings.

Pea Soup for a Crowd

1 pound dry navy beans *or* whole yellow peas

3 cups (1-1/2 pounds) dry yellow split peas

2 pounds smoked pork shoulder *or* picnic ham

3-1/2 quarts water

4 celery ribs, chopped

3 large carrots, shredded

2 cups chopped onion

1-1/4 teaspoons salt

1 teaspoon pepper

Rinse and sort beans. Place in a Dutch oven or soup kettle; cover with water. Bring to a boil; boil for 2 minutes. Remove from the heat; let stand 1-4 hours or until beans are softened. Drain beans and discard liquid. Rinse and sort split peas. Place beans in an 8-qt. roaster. Add remaining ingredients.

Cover and bake at 350° for 5-7 hours or until peas are tender and soup is thick, stirring occasionally. Remove pork; allow to cool. Cut into chunks, discarding bone and fat. Return meat to pan; heat through. **Yield:** 20-26 servings (6-1/2 quarts).

Meatball Noodle Soup

1 egg
1 tablespoon dry bread crumbs
1 teaspoon dried parsley flakes
1/2 teaspoon salt
1/8 teaspoon pepper

Pinch dried oregano
1 pound lean ground beef
2 cans (14-1/2 ounces *each*) chicken broth
1 cup uncooked fine egg noodles

In a bowl, combine the first six ingredients. Crumble beef over mixture and mix well. Shape into 1/2-in. balls; set aside.

In a large saucepan, bring broth to a boil; add meatballs. Reduce heat; simmer, uncovered, for 20 minutes. Add noodles; cook 15 minutes longer or until the meat is no longer pink and the noodles are tender. **Yield:** 4 servings.

Mexican Pork Stew

2-1/2 pounds lean boneless pork, cut into 1-inch cubes
1 garlic clove, minced
1 cup chopped onion
1 can (14-1/2 ounces) no-salt-added whole tomatoes, undrained and diced
1 to 2 cans (4 ounces *each*) chopped green chilies

1 tablespoon minced fresh cilantro *or* parsley
2 teaspoons dried oregano
2 bay leaves
1 tablespoon cornstarch
1 tablespoon water

In a large skillet coated with nonstick cooking spray, brown pork and garlic. Add onion, saute until tender. Stir in tomatoes, chilies, cilantro, oregano and bay leaves; cover and simmer for 40 minutes or until pork is tender and no longer pink.

Combine cornstarch and water until smooth; stir into skillet. Bring to a boil; cook and stir for 2 minutes or until thickened. Discard bay leaves. **Yield:** 10 servings.

Bacon Veggie Roll-Ups

1/2 pound sliced bacon, diced
3 medium zucchini, diced
1 small onion, chopped
1 jalapeno pepper, seeded and chopped

1 small tomato, chopped
1 teaspoon chicken bouillon granules
1-1/2 cups (6 ounces) shredded cheddar cheese
8 flour tortillas (10 inches)

In a skillet, cook bacon over medium heat until crisp. Remove to paper towels. Drain, reserving 1 teaspoon drippings. In the drippings, cook zucchini, onion, jalapeno, tomato and bouillon for 5-10 minutes or until zucchini is almost tender, stirring occasionally. Sprinkle with cheese and bacon. Spoon down the center of tortillas and roll up. **Yield:** 8 servings.

Editor's Note: When cutting or seeding hot peppers, use rubber or plastic gloves to protect your hands. Avoid touching your face.

Dilled Chicken Soup

1 chicken (4 to 5 pounds), quartered
3 carrots, peeled
1 small sweet potato, peeled
4 celery stalks with leaves, cut up
1 small parsnip, peeled and sliced

1 large onion, peeled and quartered
Few sprigs fresh dill
Water
Salt and pepper to taste
8 ounces thin egg noodles, cooked and drained

Place chicken, vegetables and dill in a large kettle. Add water to cover, about 2-1/2 qts. Cover and slowly bring to a boil over high heat. Skim foam. Add salt and pepper; simmer, covered, for 2 hours.

Remove chicken and vegetables; set aside to cool. Pour the broth through a strainer. Slice carrots and dice chicken; return to broth. Discard all other vegetables and bones. Add noodles to soup and heat through. **Yield:** 10 servings.

Ham-Stuffed Bread

1 tablespoon active dry yeast
1 cup warm milk (110° to 115°)
1 egg
1/2 cup vegetable oil
1/2 teaspoon salt
2-3/4 to 3-1/4 cups all-purpose flour

FILLING:
1 small onion, chopped
1/3 cup vegetable oil
2 medium tomatoes, chopped
1 garlic clove, minced
Salt and pepper to taste
1/2 pound fully cooked ham, chopped
1 teaspoon cider vinegar
1/2 teaspoon dried oregano

In a mixing bowl, dissolve yeast in warm milk. Add the egg, oil and salt; beat until smooth. Stir in enough flour to form a stiff dough. Place in a greased bowl, turning once to grease top. Cover and let rise in a warm place until doubled, about 1 hour.

Meanwhile, in a skillet, saute onion in oil until tender. Add tomatoes, garlic, salt and pepper. Cook over medium heat until liquid is absorbed, about 30 minutes. Remove from the heat. Add ham, vinegar and oregano; mix well. Cool.

Punch dough down. Turn onto a lightly floured surface; roll into a 14-in. x 12-in. rectangle. Spread filling over dough to within 1/2 in. of edges. Roll up jelly-roll style, starting with a long side; pinch seam to seal and tuck ends under. Place seam side down on a greased baking sheet. Do not let rise.

Bake at 375° for 18-22 minutes or until golden brown. Remove from pan to a wire rack. Serve warm. Refrigerate leftovers. **Yield:** 1 loaf.

Turkey Barley Soup

1-1/2 cups sliced carrots
1-1/2 cups sliced fresh mushrooms
1 cup thinly sliced celery
1 cup chopped onion
2 tablespoons vegetable oil

9 cups turkey broth
2 cups cubed cooked turkey
1/2 cup medium pearl barley
2 bay leaves
1/4 teaspoon pepper

In a 3-qt. saucepan, saute carrots, mushrooms, celery and onion in oil for 20 minutes or until tender. Add remaining ingredients; bring to a boil. Reduce heat; cover and simmer for 50-60 minutes or until barley is tender. Discard bay leaves before serving. **Yield:** 6-8 servings (2 quarts).

Arkansas Travelers

1 pound turkey breast
1 block (5 ounces) Swiss cheese
1 avocado, peeled and pitted
1 large tomato

10 bacon strips, cooked and crumbled
1/3 to 1/2 cup ranch salad dressing
10 slices whole wheat bread, toasted

Chop turkey, cheese, avocado and tomato into 1/4-in. cubes; place in a large bowl. Add bacon and dressing. Spoon 1/2 cup between two slices of toast. **Yield:** 6 servings.

Thanksgiving Sandwiches

2 cups cubed cooked turkey
3/4 cup dried cranberries
1 celery rib, chopped
1/2 cup chopped pecans, toasted

3/4 cup honey-mustard salad dressing
4 whole wheat pita breads (6 inches), halved
Lettuce leaves, optional

In a bowl, combine the turkey, cranberries, celery and pecans. Add dressing and toss to coat. If desired, line pita halves with lettuce; fill with turkey mixture. **Yield:** 4-8 servings.

Sausage 'n' Spinach Pockets

1/2 pound bulk pork sausage
1/3 cup chopped onion
1 garlic clove, minced
1 cup chopped fresh spinach
1/4 cup chopped fresh mushrooms
3/4 cup shredded part-skim
  mozzarella cheese
1/2 teaspoon salt

1/4 teaspoon pepper
2 tablespoons grated Parmesan
  cheese, optional
2 tubes (8 ounces *each*)
  refrigerated crescent rolls
1 egg
1 tablespoon water
1 tablespoon cornmeal

In a large skillet, cook sausage, onion and garlic over medium heat until meat is no longer pink; drain. Remove from the heat; stir in spinach and mushrooms. Add mozzarella cheese, salt, pepper and Parmesan cheese if desired; mix well and set aside.

Separate crescent dough into eight rectangles; seal perforations and flatten slightly to 5-in. x 4-1/2-in. rectangles. Place about 1/3 cup sausage mixture on half of each rectangle to within 1/2 in. of edges. Beat egg and water; brush on edges of dough. Bring unfilled half of dough over filling; press edges with a fork to seal. Brush tops with egg mixture. Sprinkle the cornmeal on a greased baking sheet; place pockets on baking sheet.

Bake at 350° for 15-20 minutes or until golden brown. **Yield:** 8 servings.

Chicken Tortellini Soup

2 cans (14-1/2 ounces *each*)
  chicken broth
2 cups water
1-1/2 cups frozen mixed vegetables
3 boneless skinless chicken
  breast halves, cut into 1-inch
  cubes

1 package (9 ounces) refrigerated
  cheese tortellini
2 celery ribs, thinly sliced
1 teaspoon dried basil
1/2 teaspoon dried oregano
1/2 teaspoon garlic salt
1/4 teaspoon pepper
Breadsticks, optional

In a 3-qt. saucepan, combine the first 10 ingredients; bring to a boil. Reduce heat; cover and simmer for 20 minutes. Serve with breadsticks if desired. **Yield:** 8 servings (about 2 quarts).

Chicken Stew

2 pounds boneless skinless
  chicken breasts, cut into 1-inch
  cubes
2 cans (14-1/2 ounces *each*)
  fat-free chicken broth
3 cups cubed peeled potatoes
1 cup chopped onion
1 cup sliced celery
1 cup thinly sliced carrots

1 teaspoon paprika
1/2 teaspoon pepper
1/2 teaspoon rubbed sage
1/2 teaspoon dried thyme
1 can (6 ounces) no-salt-added
  tomato paste
1/4 cup cold water
3 tablespoons cornstarch

In a 5-qt. slow cooker, combine the first 11 ingredients; cover and cook
on high for 4 hours.

Mix water and cornstarch until smooth; stir into stew. Cook, covered,
30 minutes more or until the vegetables are tender. **Yield:** 10 servings.

Dilly Cheese Soup

4-1/2 cups water
4 medium potatoes, peeled and
  cubed
1/2 cup uncooked long grain rice
3 to 4 tablespoons minced fresh
  dill
2 tablespoons chopped onion

1 to 2 chicken bouillon cubes
1/4 teaspoon salt
1/4 teaspoon pepper
8 ounces process American
  cheese, cubed
1/2 cup sour cream

In a soup kettle or Dutch oven, combine the first eight ingredients; bring
to a boil. Reduce heat; cover and simmer for 15 minutes or until
potatoes are tender. Add the cheese and sour cream; heat and stir just
until cheese is melted (do not boil). **Yield:** 6-8 servings (2 quarts).

Spiced Rhubarb Soup

8 cups diced fresh *or* frozen rhubarb, thawed

3-1/2 cups water, *divided*

1 cup sugar

4 cinnamon sticks (3 inches)

1/4 teaspoon salt

3 tablespoons plus 1-1/2 teaspoons cornstarch

1 lemon slice

4 tablespoons reduced-fat sour cream

In a large saucepan, bring rhubarb, 3-1/4 cups water, sugar, cinnamon sticks and salt to a boil. Reduce heat; simmer, uncovered, for 20 minutes or until rhubarb is tender. Discard cinnamon sticks. Strain rhubarb mixture; discard pulp. Return liquid to the pan; bring to a boil.

Combine cornstarch and remaining water until smooth; stir into saucepan. Cook and stir for 2 minutes or until thickened. Remove from the heat; add lemon slice. Cover and refrigerate until chilled. Discard lemon slice. Ladle soup into bowls. Garnish each serving with 1 table-spoon sour cream. **Yield:** 4 servings.

Pumpkin Chili

3 pounds ground beef

1 medium onion, chopped

2 cans (16 ounces *each*) hot chili beans

2 bottles (12 ounces *each*) chili sauce

2 cans (10-3/4 ounces *each*) condensed tomato soup, undiluted

1 cup canned pumpkin

2 teaspoons pumpkin pie spice

1 teaspoon sugar

1 teaspoon salt

1 teaspoon pepper

1 teaspoon chili powder

In a large Dutch oven, cook beef and onion over medium heat until meat is no longer pink; drain. Stir in the remaining ingredients. Add water if desired to reduce thickness. Bring to a boil. Reduce heat; cover and simmer for 1 hour. **Yield:** 11 servings.

Wild Rice Soup

1 large meaty ham bone
1 large onion, chopped
Water
1-1/2 cups uncooked wild rice,
    rinsed and drained
6 tablespoons butter
6 tablespoons all-purpose flour
2 cups heavy whipping cream
3 egg yolks

3 jars (4-1/2 ounces *each*) sliced
    mushrooms
1 can (14-1/2 ounces) chicken
    broth
1/2 teaspoon white pepper
1 teaspoon dried thyme
1 tablespoon chopped parsley
Milk

Place ham bone, onion and 3 qts. water in an 8-qt. soup kettle or Dutch oven; slowly bring to a boil. Reduce heat; simmer for 2-1/2 hours. Remove ham bone. When cool enough to handle, remove meat from the bone; set aside. Discard bone. Add wild rice to stock. Simmer for 1 hour more or until tender. Remove from the heat; drain and reserve stock. Set rice and onion aside. Add enough water to stock to make 2 qts.; set aside.

In the same kettle, melt butter. Stir in flour until smooth. Gradually stir in reserved stock. Bring to a rapid boil over high heat; cook and stir for 3 minutes or until slightly thickened. Remove from the heat.

In a mixing bowl, combine cream and yolks. Add 1 cup stock to egg mixture, then stir into kettle. Return soup to heat; heat gently over medium-low (do not boil). Add reserved rice, onion and ham along with mushrooms, chicken broth, pepper, thyme and parsley. Thin with milk if necessary. **Yield:** 12-16 servings (4 quarts).

Cool Cucumber Sandwich

1 tablespoon prepared ranch
    salad dressing
2 slices bread, toasted

12 to 15 thin cucumber slices
2 bacon strips, cooked
1 slice tomato

Spread salad dressing on one side of each slice of toast. Layer cucumber, bacon and tomato on one slice of bread; top with second slice of bread. **Yield:** 1 serving.

Perfect Partners

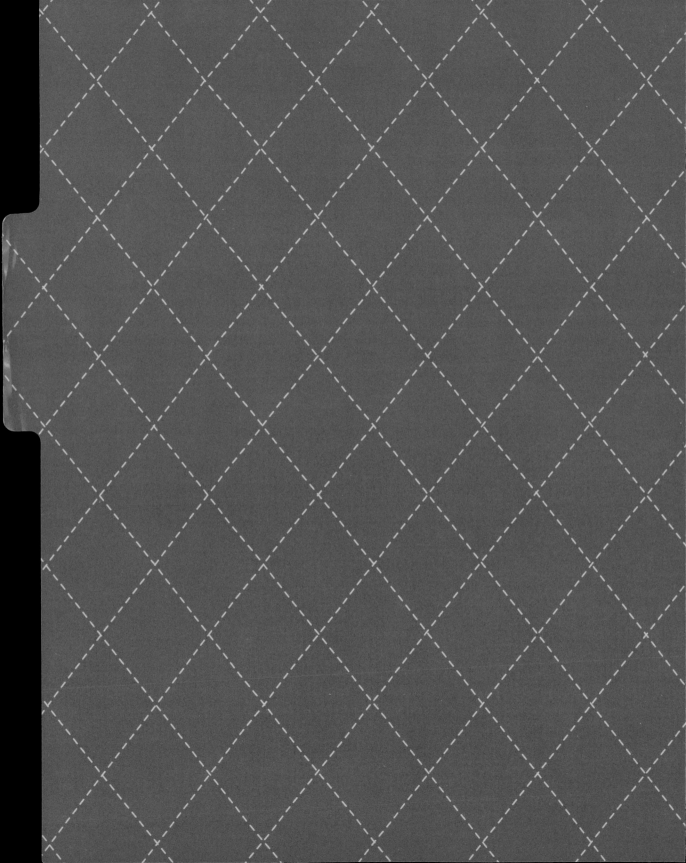

Sides & Salads

Layered Vegetable Loaf

FIRST LAYER:
- 2 eggs, beaten
- 1 cup chopped cooked broccoli
- 1/2 cup shredded cheddar cheese
- 1 tablespoon butter, melted
- 1/4 teaspoon onion salt

SECOND LAYER:
- 2 eggs, beaten
- 1 cup cooked rice
- 1/2 cup shredded part-skim mozzarella cheese
- 1/2 cup chopped sweet red pepper
- 1 tablespoon butter, melted
- 1/4 teaspoon onion salt

THIRD LAYER:
- 2 eggs, beaten
- 1 cup mashed cooked carrots
- 1/2 cup shredded cheddar cheese
- 1 tablespoon butter, melted
- 1/4 teaspoon onion salt

SAUCE:
- 2 tablespoons butter
- 2 tablespoons all-purpose flour
- 1 cup milk
- 1/4 teaspoon onion salt
- 1/8 teaspoon pepper

Combine first layer ingredients; pour into a greased 8-in. x 4-in. x 2-in. loaf pan. Combine second layer ingredients and spread over first layer. Combine third layer ingredients and spread over second layer.

Bake at 325° for 60-70 minutes or until a knife inserted near the center comes out clean. Run a knife around edges to loosen; cool in pan to room temperature.

For sauce, melt butter in a small saucepan; stir in flour until smooth. Gradually add the milk, onion salt and pepper. Bring to a boil over medium heat; cook and stir for 2 minutes or until thickened.

Unmold loaf onto a serving platter; serve with sauce. **Yield:** 8-10 servings.

Instant Party Potatoes

3 cups water
4 tablespoons butter
1 teaspoon salt
3/4 cup milk
1 package (8 ounces) cream
   cheese, softened

1 cup (8 ounces) sour cream
1 teaspoon garlic powder
1 teaspoon dried minced onion
2-2/3 cups instant potato flakes
Paprika, optional

In a saucepan, bring the water, butter and salt to a boil. Add the milk, cream cheese, sour cream, garlic powder and minced onion; stir in potato flakes.

Spoon into a greased 2-qt. baking dish. Sprinkle with paprika if desired. Bake, uncovered, at 350° for 30 minutes. **Yield:** 8-10 servings.

Cabbage-Potato Saute

4 cups shredded cabbage
1/2 cup water
1/4 cup grated raw potato

1 tablespoon butter
Pinch salt and pepper
1 tablespoon white vinegar

In a saucepan, cook cabbage in water until tender, stirring occasionally; drain. Add the potato, butter, salt and pepper. Stir in vinegar. Cook and stir over low heat for 5 minutes. **Yield:** 4 servings.

Dad's Onion Rings

4 medium onions, sliced 1/4 inch
   thick
Cold water
3/4 cup all-purpose flour
1 egg, beaten

2/3 cup milk
1 teaspoon sugar
1/2 teaspoon salt
1 tablespoon vegetable oil
Oil for deep-fat frying

Separate onion slices into rings; soak in water 30 minutes. Meanwhile, in a small bowl, beat the flour, egg, milk, sugar, salt and oil together. Drain onions and pat dry. With a fork, dip rings into batter.

In an electric skillet, heat 1 in. oil to 375°. Fry, a few rings at a time, for 2-3 minutes or until golden brown. Drain on paper towels. Keep warm in a 300° oven while frying remaining rings. **Yield:** 4-6 servings.

Herbed Egg Noodles

8 ounces uncooked wide egg
noodles
3 tablespoons butter
1 garlic cloves, minced
1/4 teaspoon salt
1/4 teaspoon dill weed
1/4 teaspoon dried thyme

Cook noodles according to package directions. Meanwhile, in a skillet, melt butter. Stir in the garlic, salt, dill and thyme. Drain noodles and add to butter mixture; toss to coat. Serve warm. **Yield:** 4 servings.

Basil Beans

1 pound fresh green beans,
trimmed
1 tablespoon minced fresh basil
or 1 teaspoon dried basil
1 tablespoon butter
1/2 teaspoon salt
1/8 teaspoon pepper

Place beans in a saucepan and cover with water; bring to a boil. Cook, uncovered, for 8-10 minutes or until crisp-tender; drain.

Place beans in a serving dish. Add the basil, butter, salt and pepper. Toss until butter is melted and beans are evenly coated. Serve immediately. **Yield:** 4 servings.

Crown Jewel Patties

1 egg
1-1/2 cups mashed cooked carrots
1/2 cup finely chopped onion
1/4 cup mayonnaise
2 tablespoons vegetable oil
1/4 teaspoon salt
1/8 teaspoon pepper
3 cups soft bread crumbs
2 cups crushed cornflakes

In a mixing bowl, beat egg. Add the carrots, onion, mayonnaise, oil, salt and pepper; mix well. Add the bread crumbs and mix thoroughly. (If mixture is to wet to handle, add more crumbs.) Shape into 10 to 12 patties; coat with cornflakes.

Place on a greased baking sheet. Bake at 375° for 25 minutes or until heated through. **Yield:** 5-6 servings.

Blue Cheese Green Beans

4 teaspoons half-and-half cream

1 tablespoon white wine vinegar

1 tablespoon crumbled blue cheese

1-1/2 teaspoons grated Parmesan cheese

1/4 teaspoon dried oregano

1/8 teaspoon salt

1/8 teaspoon pepper

Pinch sugar

2 tablespoons olive oil

1 pound fresh green beans, trimmed

4 bacon strips, cooked and crumbled

Place the first eight ingredients in a blender; cover and process until combined. While processing, gradually add oil in a steady stream; process until smooth. Set aside.

Place the beans in a large saucepan and cover with water; bring to a boil. Cook, uncovered, for 8-10 minutes or until crisp-tender. Drain and place in a serving bowl. Drizzle with the blue cheese mixture and sprinkle with bacon. **Yield:** 4 servings.

Curried Turkey and Rice Salad

4-1/2 cups chicken broth

2 cups uncooked long grain rice

1 to 2 teaspoons curry powder

1/2 teaspoon ground ginger

1/2 teaspoon ground turmeric

1/4 cup olive oil

1/4 cup lemon juice

2 cups cubed cooked turkey

1 cup golden raisins

1 can (8 ounces) water chestnuts, drained and chopped

1/2 cup chopped green pepper

1/2 cup chopped sweet red pepper

1/2 cup mayonnaise

1/2 cup sour cream

1/2 cup slivered almonds, toasted

Salt and pepper to taste

In a saucepan, bring broth to a boil; add rice, curry, ginger and turmeric. Reduce heat; cover and simmer for 25 minutes or until all of the broth is absorbed. Remove from the heat. Add oil and lemon juice; mix well.

Transfer to a large bowl; cover and chill. Just before serving, add the remaining ingredients and mix well. **Yield:** 8-10 servings.

Fluffy Fruit Salad

1 can (20 ounces) pineapple chunks, drained
1 can (17 ounces) fruit cocktail, drained
1 can (16 ounces) sliced pears, drained and cut into chunks
1 can (15 ounces) mandarin oranges, drained
1 jar (10 ounces) maraschino cherries, drained
1 carton (12 ounces) frozen whipped topping, thawed
2 cups (16 ounces) sour cream
1/2 cup sugar
1 tablespoon fresh lemon juice
Dash salt
1/2 cup chopped walnuts

In a large bowl, combine all the fruit. In another bowl, combine the whipped topping, sour cream, sugar, lemon juice and salt; fold into fruit mixture. Cover and chill. Just before serving, stir in nuts. **Yield:** 12-16 servings.

Apple Cider Salad

1-3/4 cups apple cider *or* juice, *divided*
1 package (3 ounces) cherry gelatin
1 cup chopped peeled apple
1 envelope unflavored gelatin
1/4 cup cold water
1 cup applesauce
1 package (3 ounces) cream cheese, softened
1 can (5 ounces) evaporated milk
Red *or* green food coloring, optional

In a small saucepan, bring 1 cup apple cider to a boil. Remove from the heat; stir in cherry gelatin until dissolved. Stir in remaining cider. Chill until mixture begins to thicken. Stir in apples. Pour into a 6-cup mold coated with nonstick cooking spray; chill until set.

Meanwhile, sprinkle unflavored gelatin over cold water; let stand for 1 minute. In a saucepan, whisk applesauce and cream cheese until smooth. Add milk and unflavored gelatin; cook and stir over low heat for 4 minutes or until gelatin is completely dissolved. Add food coloring if desired.

Chill until mixture begins to thicken. Pour over first layer. Chill until set. Unmold onto a serving platter. **Yield:** 6-8 servings.

Potatas Forradas

3 tablespoons butter, melted
Garlic salt to taste
4 medium potatoes, cooked and
  peeled

1/2 teaspoon dried cilantro
Salt to taste
4 bacon strips
1 green onion, thinly sliced

In a small bowl, combine butter and garlic salt. Brush over potatoes. Sprinkle with cilantro and salt. Wrap a bacon slice around each potato; secure with a toothpick.

Place in an ungreased baking dish; bake at 375° for 25-30 minutes or until bacon is crisp. Sprinkle with green onion before serving. **Yield:** 4 servings.

Tangy Cabbage Salad

1 can (8 ounces) pineapple
  chunks
2/3 cup mayonnaise
1/2 cup sugar

4 cups chopped cabbage
2 large tart apples, chopped
2/3 cup miniature marshmallows
1/2 cup chopped walnuts

Drain pineapple, reserving 2 tablespoons juice in a small bowl. Set pineapple aside. Stir mayonnaise and sugar into juice.

In a large bowl, combine the cabbage, apples, marshmallows, walnuts and pineapple. Just before serving, add dressing and toss to coat. **Yield:** 8-10 servings.

New Potatoes with Dill

1 pound unpeeled new potatoes,
  julienned
2 tablespoons butter

1 teaspoon snipped fresh dill *or*
  1/2 teaspoon dill weed
1/2 teaspoon seasoned salt

In a greased 11-in. x 7-in. x 2-in. baking dish, arrange potatoes in a single layer. Dot with butter; sprinkle with dill and salt. Cover and bake at 425° for 20-25 minutes or until tender, stirring once. **Yield:** 4 servings.

Skillet Seasoned Rice

1/4 cup uncooked long grain rice
1 green onion with top, cut into 1-inch pieces
1 tablespoon butter

1/8 teaspoon *each* dried tarragon, thyme, basil, parsley flakes and pepper
1/2 cup reduced-sodium chicken broth

In a small saucepan, cook rice and onion in butter until onion is tender. Add the seasonings; cook for 1 minute. Add broth; bring to a boil. Reduce heat; cover and simmer for 15 minutes or until liquid is absorbed and rice is tender. **Yield:** 1 serving.

Creamy Cauliflower Salad

1 cup (8 ounces) sour cream
1/2 cup French salad dressing
2 teaspoons caraway seeds
1/2 teaspoon salt

1 large head cauliflower, broken into florets and thinly sliced
1/2 cup minced celery leaves
1/4 cup thinly sliced green onions

In a large bowl, combine the sour cream, salad dressing, caraway seeds and salt. Add the cauliflower, celery leaves and onions; toss. Refrigerate for 2-3 hours before serving. **Yield:** 10-12 servings.

Parmesan Potato Sticks

2 pounds Russet potatoes
1/2 cup butter, melted
1/2 cup fine dry bread crumbs
1/2 cup grated Parmesan cheese

1/2 teaspoon salt
1/8 teaspoon garlic powder
1/8 teaspoon black pepper

Scrub and peel potatoes; cut lengthwise into quarters. Cut each quarter into 3 strips. Place the butter in a shallow dish. Combine the remaining ingredients in another shallow dish. Roll potato strips in melted butter, then coat with bread crumb mixture.

Place potato sticks in a single layer on a baking sheet. Drizzle remaining melted butter over potatoes. Bake at 400° for 30-35 minutes or until potatoes are tender. **Yield:** 6 servings.

Hungarian Cabbage with Noodles

5 slices bacon, diced

2 teaspoons sugar

1 teaspoon salt

6 cups chopped cabbage (1-inch squares)

3 cups cooked noodles (4 ounces uncooked)

1 cup (8 ounces) sour cream

Paprika

In a skillet, cook bacon over medium heat until crisp. Using a slotted spoon, remove to paper towels. Stir sugar and salt into bacon drippings. Add cabbage, stirring until cabbage is coated with bacon drippings. Cover and cook 7 to 10 minutes. Add cooked noodles and bacon, stirring to blend. Adjust seasoning to taste.

Spoon into 2-qt. baking dish; cover tightly. Bake at 325° for 45 minutes. Uncover; spread sour cream over top and sprinkle with paprika. Bake 5 minutes longer. **Yield:** 10 servings.

Mini Molded Salads

1 package (6 ounces) lemon gelatin

2 cups boiling water

1 package (3 ounces) cream cheese, softened

1 cup heavy whipping cream, *divided*

1 cup thinly sliced celery

1 cup sliced stuffed olives

SHRIMP SAUCE:

2 hard-cooked eggs, chopped

1 cup mayonnaise

1 can (4-1/4 ounces) tiny shrimp, rinsed and drained

1 jar (2 ounces) chopped pimientos, drained

1/4 cup minced fresh parsley

2 tablespoons minced onion

1 tablespoon lemon juice

1/2 teaspoon salt

1/4 teaspoon pepper

In a bowl, dissolve gelatin in boiling water. Chill until syrupy, about 30-45 minutes. Meanwhile, beat cream cheese and 1 tablespoon cream in a mixing bowl until smooth.

In another bowl, beat remaining cream until soft peaks form; fold into cream cheese mixture. Fold in the celery, olives and gelatin. Pour into seven 6-oz. custard cups or molds coated with nonstick cooking spray; cover and chill until firm.

In a bowl, combine the sauce ingredients. Cover and chill. Unmold salads onto individual plates. Serve with sauce. **Yield:** 7 servings.

Hopping John

1/2 pound sliced bacon, cut into 1-inch pieces

1/2 cup chopped green *or* sweet red pepper

2 celery ribs, chopped

6 green onions, sliced

1 cup uncooked long-grain rice

2 cups water

Salt and pepper to taste

1 teaspoon ground red pepper

1/2 teaspoon dried basil

1/4 teaspoon dried thyme

1/4 teaspoon dried oregano

1 bay leaf

1 can (15 ounces) black-eyed peas, drained

In a skillet, cook bacon over medium heat until crisp. Using a slotted spoon, remove to paper towels; drain, reserving 2 tablespoons drippings. Saute the pepper, celery and onions in drippings until almost tender. Add the rice, water and seasonings. Cover and simmer for 10 minutes. Add peas and bacon; cook for 10 minutes. Discard bay leaf. **Yield:** 4-6 servings.

Chinese Noodle Slaw

1 medium head cabbage, chopped (about 10 cups)

5 green onions with tops, chopped

2 packages (3 ounces *each*) Ramen noodles

1/2 cup butter

1 tablespoon sesame seeds

1/2 cup slivered almonds

DRESSING:

1/2 cup vegetable oil

1 tablespoon soy sauce

1/3 cup sugar

1/4 cup white vinegar

In a large bowl, combine cabbage and onions; chill. Meanwhile, break noodles into small pieces. (Save the seasoning packets for another use.)

In a saucepan, melt butter over medium-low heat; brown noodles, sesame seeds and almonds in butter, stirring frequently. Drain on paper towels; keep at room temperature.

In a mixing bowl, whisk together all the dressing ingredients. Twenty minutes before serving, toss noodle mixture with cabbage and onions. Pour dressing over and toss well. **Yield:** 10 servings.

Artichoke 'n' Olive Salad

2 jars (6 ounces *each*) marinated
artichokes, undrained

1 can (6 ounces) pitted ripe
olives, drained

1 jar (5 ounces) stuffed olives,
drained

1 jar (3-1/4 ounces) cocktail
onions, drained

1 cup banana pepper rings,
drained

1 can (8 ounces) tomato sauce

In a large bowl, combine the artichokes, olives, onions and pepper rings.
Add tomato sauce; mix well. Let stand at room temperature for 15
minutes. Serve with a slotted spoon. **Yield:** 8-10 servings.

Cranberry Gelatin Salad

2 packages (3 ounces *each*)
cherry *or* cranberry gelatin

2 cups boiling water

1 package (12 ounces) fresh *or*
frozen cranberries

1-1/2 medium seedless oranges,
quartered

1-3/4 cups sugar

2 cans (8 ounces *each*) crushed
pineapple, undrained

1 cup chopped celery

1/2 cup chopped walnuts

In a large bowl, dissolve gelatin in boiling water. In a food processor,
finely chop cranberries and oranges. Transfer to a bowl; stir in sugar
until dissolved. Add the pineapple, celery and nuts. Stir in gelatin. Chill
for at least 6 hours. **Yield:** 16-20 servings.

Apple Cottage Cheese Salad

3 cups cottage cheese

2 small apples, chopped

1/4 cup raisins

2 teaspoons poppy seeds

2 tablespoons lemon juice

2 tablespoons honey

1/2 cup salted sunflower kernels,
optional

In a bowl, combine the cottage cheese, apples, raisins and poppy seeds.
Combine the lemon juice and honey; add to apple mixture. Chill. Just
before serving, stir in sunflower kernels if desired. **Yield:** 10 servings.

Warm Asparagus Salad

2 cups asparagus pieces
4 bacon strips
1 small red onion, thinly sliced
  and separated into rings
2 tablespoons white vinegar

1 tablespoon sugar
1/2 teaspoon minced fresh parsley
Salt to taste
1 medium tomato, chopped
4 cups torn mixed greens

Cook the asparagus until crisp-tender. Drain. In a skillet, cook bacon over medium heat until crisp. Remove to paper towels.

In same skillet, sauté onion in drippings until soft; stir in the vinegar, sugar, parsley and salt. Crumble bacon. Stir in the asparagus, bacon and tomato into skillet. Pour mixture over mixed greens and toss. Serve immediately. **Yield:** 4 servings.

Mushroom 'n' Tomato Salad

6 tablespoons olive oil
2 tablespoons lemon juice
1/2 teaspoon salt
1/4 teaspoon pepper
1 pound fresh mushrooms,
  quartered

16 cherry tomatoes, halved
3 tablespoons minced chives
2 tablespoons sesame seeds,
  toasted

In a large bowl, whisk together the oil, lemon juice, salt and pepper. Add mushrooms; toss to coat. Chill for at least 1 hour. Just before serving, stir in tomatoes and chives; sprinkle with sesame seeds. **Yield:** 6-8 servings.

Creamed Spinach

2 packages (10 ounces *each*)
  frozen chopped spinach,
  thawed and well drained

2 cups (16 ounces) sour cream
1 envelope onion soup mix

In a large bowl, combine all the ingredients. Spoon into a greased 1-qt. baking dish. Cover and bake at 350° for 25-30 minutes or until heated through. **Yield:** 4 servings.

Two-Bean Tuna Salad

1 can (16 ounces) kidney beans, rinsed and drained

1 can (15 ounces) garbanzo beans *or* chickpeas, rinsed and drained

1 can (6 ounces) tuna in water, drained and flaked

2/3 cup chopped celery

1/2 cup sliced pimiento-stuffed olives

1/3 cup sliced green onions

1/4 cup chopped green pepper

1/4 cup minced fresh parsley

DRESSING:

1/3 cup olive oil

2 tablespoons lemon juice

2 tablespoons white wine vinegar

1 teaspoon paprika

1/2 teaspoon ground mustard

1/2 teaspoon salt

1/4 teaspoon sugar

1/4 teaspoon pepper

In a large bowl, combine the first eight ingredients. In a jar with tight-fitting lid, combine dressing ingredients. Pour over salad; toss to coat. Cover and chill for at least 2 hours. **Yield:** 6-8 servings.

Tortellini Bake

1 package (10 ounces) refrigerated cheese tortellini

1 tablespoon olive oil

1 small zucchini, diced

1 yellow squash, diced

1 onion, diced

1 sweet red pepper, diced

1 teaspoon dried basil

1/2 teaspoon pepper

1/2 teaspoon salt

1 cup (4 ounces) shredded part-skim mozzarella cheese

1 cup half-and-half cream

Cook tortellini according to package directions. Meanwhile, heat oil in a skillet; cook the zucchini, squash, onion, red pepper and seasonings until vegetables are crisp-tender.

Drain tortellini and rinse in hot water. Combine tortellini, mozzarella and cream with vegetable mixture. Transfer to a 1-1/2-qt. baking dish.

Bake, uncovered, at 375° for 20 minutes or until heated through. **Yield:** 6-8 servings.

Sour Cream Potato Salad

6 cups diced cooked potatoes
1 cup chopped celery
1/2 cup chopped seeded peeled
   cucumber
1/2 cup chopped green pepper
1/4 cup sliced green onions
6 hard-cooked eggs

1 cup (8 ounces) sour cream
1/2 cup mayonnaise
1 tablespoon prepared mustard
4 teaspoons white vinegar
1-1/2 teaspoons salt
1/2 teaspoon pepper
1 teaspoon celery seed, optional

In a large bowl, combine the first five ingredients. Remove egg yolks
from whites. Chop whites and add to potato mixture; toss lightly.

In a bowl, mash yolks with the sour cream, mayonnaise, mustard,
vinegar, salt, pepper and celery seed if desired. Fold in potato mixture.
Refrigerate for at least 6 hours. **Yield:** 8-10 servings.

Acorn Squash with Spinach Stuffing

3 small acorn squash
1 cup chopped celery
3 green onions, chopped
1 tablespoon vegetable oil
1 package (10 ounces) fresh
   spinach, chopped

1/2 teaspoon salt, divided
6 tablespoons dry bread crumbs
2 tablespoons chopped pecans
1 tablespoon butter

Cut squash in half; discard seeds. Place squash cut side down in an
ungreased 15-in. x 10-in. x 1-in. baking pan. Fill pan with hot water to
a depth of 1/2 in. Bake, uncovered, at 350° for 40 minutes.

Meanwhile, in a skillet, saute celery and onions in oil until tender.
Add the spinach and 1/4 teaspoon salt; cook and stir until spinach is
wilted.

In a bowl, combine the bread crumbs, pecans and remaining salt.
Drain water from baking pan. Turn squash cut side up. Stuff with
spinach mixture; sprinkle crumb mixture over top. Dot with butter. Bake
15 minutes longer or until the squash is tender. **Yield:** 6 servings.

Cheesy Broccoli Rice

1 pound ground beef
1 medium onion, diced
1 garlic clove, minced
3 cups cooked long grain rice
2 cups fresh *or* frozen chopped
   broccoli, thawed

2 cups (8 ounces) shredded
   cheddar cheese
2 tablespoon grated Parmesan
   cheese

In a skillet, cook beef, onion and garlic over medium heat until the meat is no longer pink; drain. Stir in the rice, broccoli and cheddar cheese.

Transfer to a greased 13-in. x 9-in. x 2-in. baking dish. Sprinkle with Parmesan cheese. Bake, uncovered, at 350° for 30-40 minutes or until heated through. **Yield:** 8 side-dish servings or 4 main-dish servings.

Nutty Carrot Salad

1/3 cup mayonnaise
2 tablespoons peanut butter

2 cups shredded carrots
1/3 cup raisins

In a bowl, combine the mayonnaise and peanut butter. Stir in carrots and raisins. Cover and refrigerate until serving. **Yield:** 3-4 servings.

Roasted Root Veggies

3 large red potatoes, cut into
   1-inch cubes
1 large red onion, cut into
   wedges
2 medium turnips, peeled and
   quartered
5 medium carrots, halved and
   quartered

2 medium parsnips, peeled and
   cut into 1/4-inch strips
1 small rutabaga, peeled and cut
   into 3/4-inch cubes
2 tablespoons vegetable oil
1 teaspoon dried thyme
1/8 teaspoon pepper

Toss all of the ingredients in a large bowl; transfer to a 15-in. x 10-in. x 1-in. baking pan coated with nonstick cooking spray. Bake, uncovered, at 375° for 1 to 1-1/2 hours or until vegetables are tender, stirring frequently. **Yield:** 15 servings.

Picnic Peas

1 cup chopped green pepper
1 cup chopped onion
1 cup minced celery
1 tablespoon vegetable oil
1 tablespoon sugar
1 bay leaf

1 can (15 ounces) black-eyed peas, rinsed and drained
1 can (14-1/2 ounces) diced tomatoes, liquid reserved
1/2 teaspoon salt
1/4 teaspoon pepper
4 bacon strips, cooked and crumbled

In a skillet, saute the green pepper, onion and celery in oil. Add the sugar, bay leaf, peas, tomatoes, half the tomato liquid, salt and pepper. Reduce heat and simmer 15 minutes. Discard bay leaf. Transfer to a bowl; sprinkle with bacon. Serve hot or at room temperature. **Yield:** 6 servings.

Sesame Zucchini

4 cups thinly sliced zucchini
2 tablespoons sesame seeds

Salt and garlic powder to taste
2 tablespoons vegetable oil

In a skillet, sauté the zucchini, sesame seeds, salt and garlic powder in oil for 2-3 minutes or until zucchini is crisp-tender. **Yield:** 6 servings.

Italian Broccoli Salad

2-1/2 pounds fresh broccoli
1 pound sliced bacon, cooked and crumbled
1 jar (5-1/4 ounces) pimiento-stuffed olives, drained and sliced

1 cup sliced green onions
1 bottle (16 ounces) Italian salad dressing
1 cup mayonnaise
3/4 cup shredded Parmesan cheese

Parboil broccoli; cool and cut into bite-size pieces. Place in a large bowl; add the bacon, olives and onions.

In a small bowl, combine salad dressing, mayonnaise and Parmesan cheese. Pour over vegetables and toss. Serve immediately. **Yield:** 10-12 servings.

Pocket Veggies

1 *each* medium green, sweet red
and yellow pepper, julienned
1 cup fresh baby carrots
1 cup fresh whole green beans
4 medium plum tomatoes,
quartered

3 tablespoons olive oil
3 tablespoons white vinegar
2 teaspoons dried oregano
1/2 teaspoon pepper

Combine the peppers, carrots and beans; divide between four pieces of
heavy-duty foil (about 12 in. x 12 in.). Top with the tomatoes.

In a jar with tight-fitting lid, combine the oil, vinegar, oregano and
pepper; shake well. Drizzle over vegetables. Fold foil around vegetables
and seal the edges tightly.

Grill, covered, over indirect heat for 15-20 minutes or until tender.
Yield: 12 servings.

Broiled Zucchini with Rosemary Butter

3 tablespoons butter, softened
1/4 cup finely chopped green
onions
1 to 2 tablespoons minced fresh
rosemary *or* 1 to 2 teaspoons
dried rosemary, crushed

1 teaspoon lemon juice
1/2 teaspoon grated lemon peel
1/4 teaspoon pepper
1/8 teaspoon cayenne pepper
4 medium zucchini

In a bowl, combine the first seven ingredients; set aside. Cut zucchini
lengthwise into 1/2-in. slices. Place on a broiler pan coated with
nonstick cooking spray. Broil 4 in. from the heat for 10-12 minutes or
until crisp-tender, turning occasionally. Spread with rosemary butter;
serve immediately. **Yield:** 4 servings.

Colorful Cauliflower Salad

1 large head cauliflower, broken into florets and thinly sliced

1 can (2-1/4 ounces) sliced ripe olives, drained

1 medium green pepper, chopped

1/2 cup chopped onion

1/4 cup chopped pimientos

DRESSING:

1/2 cup vegetable oil

3 tablespoons lemon juice

3 tablespoons white wine vinegar

1 teaspoon salt

1/2 teaspoon sugar

1/4 teaspoon pepper

In a large bowl, combine the cauliflower, olives, green pepper, onion and pimientos. In a jar with a tight-fitting lid, combine all the dressing ingredients; shake well. Pour over vegetables; toss to coat. Refrigerate overnight. **Yield:** 8-10 servings.

Elbow Macaroni Salad

1 package (7 ounces) elbow macaroni

3 hard-cooked eggs, chopped

1-1/2 cups cubed cheddar cheese

1-1/2 cups chopped celery

1 medium green pepper, chopped

1 jar (2 ounces) sliced pimientos, drained

3/4 cup mayonnaise

4 teaspoons lemon juice

3/4 teaspoon salt

1/4 teaspoon pepper

8 bacon strips, cooked and crumbled

Cook macaroni according to package directions; drain and rinse in cold water. Place in a large bowl; add the next five ingredients. In a small bowl, combine the mayonnaise, lemon juice, salt and pepper. Pour over salad and toss. Cover and chill for at least 1 hour. Just before serving, add bacon and toss. **Yield:** 6-8 servings.

Zucchini-Garlic Pasta

1 package (16 ounces) wagon wheel pasta *or* other specialty shape pasta

1/2 pound sliced bacon, diced

1 medium onion, chopped

4 to 6 garlic cloves, minced

2 to 3 medium zucchini (about 1-1/2 pounds), halved and sliced

1/2 teaspoon salt

3 tablespoons lemon juice

1/4 cup grated Romano *or* Parmesan cheese

Cook pasta according to package directions. Meanwhile, in a large skillet, cook bacon over medium heat until crisp. Using a slotted spoon, remove to paper towels; drain, reserving 2 tablespoons of drippings. In same skillet, saute onion and garlic in reserved drippings for 3 minutes or until tender. Add the zucchini and salt; cook 6 minutes longer or until tender.

Drain pasta and add to the zucchini mixture. Add lemon juice and bacon; toss. Transfer to a serving bowl or platter; sprinkle with cheese. **Yield:** 6-8 servings.

Baked Stuffed Tomatoes

6 medium tomatoes

STUFFING:

1 cup garlic/cheese croutons, crushed

2 tablespoons grated Parmesan cheese

2 tablespoons grated process cheese (Velveeta) *or* cheddar cheese

4 tablespoons melted butter

1/2 teaspoon salt

1/4 teaspoon freshly ground pepper

Chopped fresh parsley for garnish

Hollow out a funnel-shaped hole in each tomato to make room for stuffing. In a bowl, combine all the stuffing ingredients. Spoon into tomatoes; sprinkle with parsley.

Place tomatoes in baking dish; cover tomatoes with aluminum foil to prevent over-browning of stuffing. Bake at 350° for 30 minutes or cook on grill until done. **Yield:** 6 servings.

Tomato Mozzarella Bake

3 tablespoons butter, softened, *divided*

8 slices French bread (1 inch thick)

2/3 cup chopped green pepper

1/3 cup chopped onion

2 garlic cloves, minced

4 eggs

4 bacon strips, cooked and crumbled

2 teaspoons sugar

1 teaspoon salt

1 teaspoon dried oregano

1/2 teaspoon pepper

2 medium tomatoes

1 cup (4 ounces) shredded part-skim mozzarella cheese

Spread 2 tablespoons butter over both sides of bread slices. Place on a baking sheet; bake at 400° until lightly toasted, about 3 minutes on each side. Cut into 1-in. cubes. Reduce heat to 350°.

In a large skillet, saute the green pepper, onion and garlic in remaining butter until tender. In a large bowl, lightly beat the eggs. Stir in bread cubes, vegetable mixture, bacon, sugar, salt, oregano and pepper.

Transfer to a greased 11-in. x 7-in. x 2-in. baking dish. Cut each tomato into four thick slices; arrange over the top. Sprinkle with cheese. Bake, uncovered, at 350° for 30-35 minutes or until a knife inserted near the center comes out clean. **Yield:** 6-8 servings.

Fiesta Black Bean Salad

2 cans (15 ounces *each*) black beans, rinsed and drained

1 can (11 ounces) whole kernel corn, drained

1 medium tomato, seeded and diced

1/4 cup thinly sliced green onions

DRESSING:
1/4 cup vegetable oil

2 tablespoons cider vinegar

1 tablespoon fresh lime juice

2 tablespoons minced fresh cilantro

1/2 teaspoon garlic powder

1/4 to 1/2 teaspoon ground turmeric

1/4 teaspoon cayenne pepper

Dash pepper

In a large bowl, combine the first four ingredients. In a small bowl, whisk together the dressing ingredients. Pour over black bean mixture; gently stir to coat. Cover and chill for at least 2 hours. **Yield:** 12 servings.

Skillet Vegetables

3 carrots, thinly sliced
1 large onion, chopped
1/2 medium head cabbage, chopped
1/2 medium green pepper, chopped
2 tablespoons olive oil
2 garlic cloves, minced

2 tablespoons Worcestershire sauce
1 tablespoon minced fresh parsley
1 teaspoon caraway seeds
1 teaspoon dried Italian seasoning
1/2 teaspoon celery salt

In a large skillet, sauté the carrots, onion, cabbage and green pepper in oil for 5 minutes. Add the remaining ingredients; cook and stir about 5 minutes longer or until the vegetables are cooked to desired doneness. **Yield:** 8 servings.

Candied Acorn Squash Rings

2 acorn squash, cut into 1-inch rings and seeded

2/3 cup packed brown sugar
1/2 cup butter, softened

Arrange squash in a shallow baking pan; cover with foil. Bake at 350° for 35-40 minutes or until tender. Combine sugar and butter; spread over squash. Bake uncovered, for 15-20 minutes, basting occasionally. **Yield:** 6 servings.

Fried Green Tomatoes

1/2 cup all-purpose flour
1/4 cup cornmeal
1/4 cup grated Parmesan cheese
1/2 teaspoon dried oregano

1/2 teaspoon salt
1/8 teaspoon pepper
3 to 4 green tomatoes, cut into 1/2-inch slices
Oil for deep-fat frying

Combine the flour, cornmeal, Parmesan cheese, oregano, salt and pepper. Coat tomato slices with flour mixture.

In a skillet, heat 1 in. oil over medium. Fry tomatoes for 2-3 minutes per side until tender and lightly browned. Drain on paper towels. Serve immediately. **Yield:** 4-6 servings.

Scalloped Corn

1 can (14-3/4 ounces) cream-style corn
2 eggs, beaten
1/2 cup crushed saltines (about 14 crackers)
1/4 cup grated carrot
1/4 cup chopped sweet red pepper
1/4 cup butter, melted
1/4 cup evaporated milk
1 tablespoon chopped celery
1 tablespoon chopped onion
1/2 teaspoon salt
1/2 teaspoon pepper
1/2 cup shredded cheddar cheese
Paprika

In a large bowl, combine the first 11 ingredients. Spoon into four greased 8-oz. baking dishes. Sprinkle with cheese and paprika. Bake, uncovered, at 350° for 25-30 minutes or until set. **Yield:** 4 servings.

Editor's Note: A 1-qt. baking dish may be used in place of the individual baking dishes.

Sweet Potato Balls

2 cups mashed sweet potatoes
12 large marshmallows
3/4 cup finely crushed cornflakes
1/2 cup packed brown sugar
1/4 cup butter
2 tablespoons milk

Mold a spoonful of the sweet potatoes around each marshmallow; roll in cornflake crumbs. Place in a greased shallow 1-1/2-qt. baking dish.

In a saucepan, bring the brown sugar, butter and milk to a boil; pour over the balls. Bake, uncovered, at 350° for 15 minutes. **Yield:** 1 dozen.

Zesty Buttered Peas

2 tablespoons butter
1 package (10 ounces) frozen peas, thawed
1 cup sliced celery
1/2 cup chopped onion
1 tablespoon minced fresh savory *or* 1-1/2 teaspoons dried savory
1/2 teaspoon salt, optional
2 tablespoons diced pimientos

Melt butter in a heavy saucepan; add the peas, celery, onion, savory and salt if desired. Cover and cook over medium heat for 6-8 minutes or until vegetables are tender. Stir in pimientos. **Yield:** 6 servings.

Cranberry Nut Stuffing

2 medium onions, chopped
2 celery ribs, chopped
1/2 cup butter
6 cups cubed crustless day-old bread
1/2 cup chopped walnuts *or* hazelnuts

1-1/2 teaspoons poultry seasoning
1/2 teaspoon salt
1/2 teaspoon pepper
1 cup chopped fresh cranberries
3 eggs, beaten
1-1/2 cups chicken broth
2 tablespoons brown sugar

In a skillet, saute onions and celery in butter until tender; transfer to a large bowl. Stir in the bread cubes, nuts, poultry seasoning, salt and pepper. Add cranberries; toss lightly to mix.

In a small bowl, combine the eggs, broth and brown sugar; pour over bread mixture. Mix lightly until bread is moistened. Place in a greased 2-qt. baking dish.

Cover and bake at 325° for 45 minutes. Uncover; bake 15 minutes longer or until heated through. **Yield:** 6-8 servings.

Mixed Greens with Mushrooms

6 cups mixed salad greens
1 cup halved cherry tomatoes
1/2 pound fresh mushrooms, sliced

DRESSING:
1 tablespoon red wine vinegar
1 tablespoon lemon juice
1 tablespoon thinly sliced green onion

1 tablespoon Dijon mustard
1 tablespoon minced fresh parsley
1/4 teaspoon salt, optional
1/8 teaspoon sugar
1/8 teaspoon dried tarragon
Dash pepper

In a large bowl, toss greens, tomatoes and mushrooms. In a small bowl, whisk together the dressing ingredients; pour over salad and toss to coat. Serve immediately. **Yield:** 8 servings.

Zesty Carrots

1-1/2 pounds carrots, peeled
  2 tablespoons grated onion and juice
  1 tablespoon prepared horseradish
1/2 cup mayonnaise
1/4 cup shredded cheddar cheese

1/2 teaspoon salt
1/4 teaspoon pepper

TOPPING:
  1 cup soft bread crumbs
1/4 cup butter, melted
  1 teaspoon paprika

Slice carrots 1/4 in. thick; cook in small amount of water for 5 minutes. Drain; reserve 1/4 cup cooking water for sauce.

In a bowl, combine the onion and juice, horseradish, mayonnaise, cheese, salt, pepper and reserved cooking water. Add carrots. Transfer to a greased 2-qt. baking dish.

Combine topping ingredients; sprinkle over carrot mixture. Bake, uncovered, at 350° for 20 minutes. **Yield:** 8 servings.

Spinach Salad Ring

  2 envelopes unflavored gelatin
  1 can (10-1/2 ounces) condensed beef broth
1/4 cup water
  2 tablespoons lemon juice
1/2 teaspoon salt
  1 cup mayonnaise

1 package (10 ounces) frozen chopped spinach, thawed and squeezed dry
4 hard-cooked eggs, chopped
1/4 pound sliced bacon, cooked and crumbled
1/4 cup thinly sliced green onions
Cherry tomatoes, optional

In a saucepan, sprinkle gelatin over broth; let stand for 5 minutes. Cook over low heat until gelatin is dissolved. Add the water, lemon juice and salt; mix well.

Place mayonnaise in a bowl. Gradually add broth mixture, stirring constantly until smooth. Chill until slightly thickened, about 40 minutes. Fold in the spinach, eggs, bacon and onions. Pour into a 6-cup mold coated with nonstick cooking spray. Cover and chill until firm.

When ready to serve, unmold onto a platter; garnish with tomatoes if desired. **Yield:** 10-12 servings.

Cheddar Cauliflower

1 medium head cauliflower,
  broken into florets
1/4 cup water
1 cup (8 ounces) sour cream
2 teaspoons minced chives

1/4 teaspoon salt
1/8 teaspoon pepper
1-1/2 cups (6 ounces) shredded
  cheddar cheese

Place the cauliflower and water in a 2-qt. microwave-safe dish. Cover and microwave on high for 4-1/2 minutes; stir. Cook 4-6 minutes longer or until tender. Drain.

Combine the sour cream, chives, salt and pepper; spoon over the cauliflower. Sprinkle with cheese. Microwave, uncovered, on high for 1-1/2 minutes or until cheese is melted. **Yield:** 6 servings.

Editor's Note: This recipe was tested in a 1,100-watt microwave.

Grandma's Apple Salad

1 cup mayonnaise
1/2 cup milk
2 tablespoons sugar
5 tart apples, diced

1-1/2 cups sliced celery
1-1/2 cups miniature marshmallows
1 cup salted peanuts

In a bowl, combine the mayonnaise, milk and sugar until smooth. Add the apples, celery and marshmallows. Just before serving, stir in peanuts. **Yield:** 10-12 servings.

Italian-Style Peas

1 small onion, diced
4 ounces diced fully cooked lean
  ham
4 teaspoons olive oil

1 package (16 ounces) frozen
  peas
1/2 teaspoon salt
1/4 teaspoon dried oregano
1/4 teaspoon pepper

In a nonstick skillet, saute onion and ham in oil until onion is tender. Add the remaining ingredients. Reduce heat; cover and cook until peas are tender. **Yield:** 4 servings.

Stove-Top Macaroni and Cheese

1 package (7 ounces) elbow
macaroni
1/4 cup butter
1/4 cup all-purpose flour
1/2 teaspoon salt

Pinch pepper
2 cups milk
2 cups (8 ounces) shredded
cheddar cheese
Paprika, optional

Cook macaroni according to package directions. Meanwhile, in a medium saucepan, melt butter over medium heat. Stir in flour, salt and pepper until smooth; gradually add milk. Bring to a boil; cook and stir for 2 minutes or until thickened. Reduce heat; add cheese, stirring until melted. Drain macaroni; add to cheese sauce and stir to coat. Sprinkle with paprika if desired. **Yield:** 4-6 servings.

Rosy Raspberry Salad

3 packages (3 ounces *each*)
raspberry gelatin
3 cups boiling water

3 cups raspberry sherbet
1 package (12 ounces)
unsweetened frozen
raspberries

In a large bowl, dissolve gelatin in boiling water. Add sherbet and stir until melted. Chill until syrupy. Add raspberries. Pour into an 8-cup mold coated with nonstick cooking spray. Cover and chill until firm. **Yield:** 12-14 servings.

Ratatouille

3 tablespoons olive oil
3 medium zucchini, cut into
1/2-inch slices
2 large tomatoes, peeled and
chopped
1 large onion, chopped

1 green pepper, cut into strips
1/4 cup minced fresh parsley
1 tablespoon minced fresh basil
or 1 teaspoon dried basil
1/2 teaspoon salt
1/4 teaspoon pepper

In a large Dutch oven, heat oil over medium-high. Add all the remaining ingredients; cook and stir for 5 minutes. Reduce heat; cover and simmer for 15 minutes or until vegetables are tender, stirring occasionally. **Yield:** 6-8 servings.

Almond Asparagus

3 tablespoons butter, *divided*
3 tablespoons bread crumbs
1 garlic clove, minced
1/2 teaspoon dill weed
1/2 cup sliced almonds
1/4 cup grated Parmesan cheese
1 pound fresh asparagus, trimmed and cut into 1-inch pieces
1 tablespoon lemon juice

In a skillet, melt 2 tablespoons butter over medium heat. Stir in the bread crumbs, garlic and dill; saute until crumbs are golden brown. Remove from the heat; stir in the almonds and cheese. Set aside.

Cook asparagus in a small amount of water until crisp-tender. Drain; heat with remaining butter. Sprinkle with lemon juice. Spoon asparagus into a serving dish and top with the reserved crumb mixture. **Yield:** 4-6 servings.

Spinach Cheese Bake

3 tablespoons butter
3 tablespoons all-purpose flour
1-1/2 cups milk
8 ounces process cheese (Velveeta), shredded
1 package (10 ounces) frozen chopped spinach, thawed and drained
1-1/2 cups soft bread crumbs
3 eggs, lightly beaten
1/2 teaspoon garlic salt
1/4 teaspoon dried oregano
1/4 teaspoon pepper

In a saucepan, melt butter. Stir in flour until smooth; gradually add milk. Bring to a boil; cook and stir for 2 minutes or until thickened. Remove from the heat; add cheese, stirring until melted. Add the spinach, bread crumbs, eggs and seasonings; mix well.

Spoon into an ungreased 1-1/2-qt. baking dish. Bake, uncovered, at 350° for 45-50 minutes or until lightly browned. **Yield:** 6-8 servings.

Nutty Mandarin Salad

TOASTED ALMONDS:
  2 tablespoons sugar
  1 tablespoon butter
  1 tablespoon water
  1/2 cup sliced almonds

DRESSING:
  1/2 cup vegetable oil
  1/2 cup tarragon *or* white wine vinegar
  2-1/2 teaspoons sugar
  2 teaspoons minced fresh parsley
  1/2 teaspoon salt
  1/2 teaspoon dried tarragon
  1/2 teaspoon Dijon mustard
  1/4 teaspoon pepper

SALAD:
  8 cups torn romaine
  6 cups torn Bibb lettuce
  1 can (15 ounces) mandarin oranges, drained
  1 cup thinly sliced green onions

In a skillet, cook the sugar, butter and water over medium heat until a syrup is formed, stirring constantly. Add almonds; cook and stir for 4-6 minutes or until almonds are coated and browned. Set aside.

In a jar with tight-fitting lid, combine the dressing ingredients; shake well. In a large bowl, combine the greens, oranges and onions. Break almonds apart and add to salad. Add dressing and toss. Serve immediately. **Yield:** 12-14 servings.

Green Beans with Mushrooms

  2 cloves garlic, minced
  1/4 pound small, fresh mushrooms, trimmed and sliced
  1 tablespoon butter
  1 medium red onion, cut in thin strips
  1 pound fresh green beans, trimmed
Fresh ground pepper
  1 teaspoon dill weed
  2 tablespoons toasted almonds *or* pine nuts

In a skillet, saute garlic and mushrooms in butter until tender. Stir in onion; set aside.

Steam or cook beans in small amount of water until tender-crisp; drain. Combine beans and mushroom mixture; add pepper and dill. Garnish with nuts. Serve immediately. **Yield:** 6 servings.

Vegetable Pancakes

1/2 medium onion, finely chopped
2 medium potatoes, peeled and shredded
3 carrots, shredded
2 cups packed fresh spinach, sliced

1/4 head lettuce, finely sliced
2 eggs, lightly beaten
1 cup all-purpose flour
1 teaspoon baking powder
1 teaspoon salt
1/8 teaspoon pepper

In a bowl, combine all of the vegetables. Stir in eggs; mix well. Combine dry ingredients; add to vegetables.

Drop batter by 1/4 cupfuls onto a hot well-greased skillet. Spread into 4-in. circles. Cook until brown on each side. **Yield:** 4-6 servings.

Baked Hominy and Cheese

1 egg
2 cans (15-1/2 ounces *each*) white *or* yellow hominy, rinsed and drained
12 ounces process cheese (Velveeta), cubed
3/4 cup milk

1/2 small onion, finely chopped
3 bacon strips, cooked and crumbled
1 tablespoon butter, melted
1/4 teaspoon pepper
Chopped fresh parsley, optional

In a large bowl, beat egg. Add the hominy, cheese, milk, onion, bacon, butter and pepper; mix well. Spoon into a greased 11-in. x 7-in. x 2-in. baking dish.

Bake, uncovered, at 350° for 45 minutes or until bubbly and top begins to brown. Let stand a few minutes before serving. Garnish with parsley if desired. **Yield:** 8 servings.

Tangy Cauliflower

1 medium head cauliflower
1 tablespoon water
1/2 cup mayonnaise

1-1/2 teaspoons prepared mustard
1/2 teaspoon ground mustard
1/2 cup shredded sharp cheddar cheese

Place cauliflower in a microwave-safe dish. Add water. Cover and microwave on high for 9-11 minutes or until tender. Combine the mayonnaise, prepared mustard and ground mustard; spread over the cauliflower. Sprinkle with cheese.

Microwave, uncovered, on high for 30 seconds or until the cheese is melted. **Yield:** 6-8 servings.

Editor's Note: This recipe was tested in a 1,100-watt microwave.

Swiss Bake

1 package (26 ounces) frozen shredded hash browns, thawed
2 cups (8 ounces) shredded Swiss cheese
3 cups frozen chopped broccoli, thawed and well drained

2 cups heavy whipping cream
1/2 cup chopped onion
1/2 cup butter, melted
1 teaspoon salt
1/4 teaspoon pepper

Combine all the ingredients; pour into a greased 13-in. x 9-in. x 2-in. baking dish. Bake, uncovered, at 350° for 1 hour or until golden brown. **Yield:** 10-12 servings.

Autumn Squash Bake

9 cups diced peeled Hubbard squash
2 medium pears, cut into 1-inch pieces

1 cup fresh *or* frozen cranberries
1 tablespoon butter
2 tablespoons water

Combine all ingredients in a 3-qt. baking dish coated with nonstick cooking spray. Cover and bake at 350° for 50-55 minutes or until squash is tender. **Yield:** 14 servings.

Patio Salad

1/2 cup sour cream
1/3 cup mayonnaise
2 tablespoons white vinegar
1 tablespoon sugar
1/2 teaspoon ground mustard
1/4 teaspoon salt

4 cups fresh corn, cooked
1 cup diced celery
1 cup diced unpeeled cucumber
2 tomatoes, seeded and diced
1/2 cup chopped onion

In a small bowl, combine the sour cream, mayonnaise, vinegar, sugar, mustard and salt; set aside.

In a large bowl, combine the corn, celery, cucumber, tomatoes and onion. Add dressing and toss lightly. Cover and chill until ready to serve. **Yield:** 8-10 servings.

Molded Cherry-Pineapple Salad

2 envelopes unflavored gelatin
1/4 cup cold water
1 can (20 ounces) crushed pineapple, undrained
1 package (8 ounces) cream cheese
1/2 cup sugar

2 tablespoons lemon juice
2 tablespoons maraschino cherry juice
1 cup heavy whipping cream, whipped
12 maraschino cherries, halved

In a medium saucepan, sprinkle gelatin over cold water; let stand for 1 minute. Add the pineapple, cream cheese, sugar and juices; cook over medium heat until cream cheese is melted and gelatin is dissolved, stirring often.

Chill until syrupy. Fold in cream and cherries. Pour into a 6-cup mold coated with nonstick cooking spray. Cover and chill until firm. **Yield:** 8-10 servings.

Spectacular Spaghetti Squash

1 medium spaghetti squash
(about 3 pounds)

8 ounces fresh mushrooms,
sliced

1 medium zucchini, sliced

1 medium sweet red pepper,
julienned

3 cups sugar snap peas

6 green onions, chopped

2 garlic cloves, minced

2 tablespoons olive oil

1 tablespoon butter

2 medium tomatoes, chopped

1 tablespoon minced fresh basil
  or 1 teaspoon dried basil

1/2 teaspoon garlic salt

1/8 teaspoon pepper

3/4 cup shredded Parmesan cheese

Cut squash in half lengthwise; scoop out seeds. Place squash cut side down in a baking dish. Fill pan with hot water to a depth of 1/2 in. Cover and bake at 375° for 50-60 minutes or until tender.

When cool enough to handle, scoop out the squash and separate strands with a fork. Place squash in a large serving bowl and keep warm. Discard shells.

Meanwhile, in a skillet, sauté the mushrooms, zucchini, red pepper, peas, onions and garlic in oil and butter for 15 minutes or until tender. Add the tomatoes, basil, garlic salt and pepper; heat through. Pour over squash. Sprinkle with Parmesan cheese. **Yield:** 10-12 servings.

Sauerkraut Side Dish

1 medium onion, thinly sliced

2 tablespoons butter

1 can (27 ounces) sauerkraut,
rinsed and drained

3 medium tart apples, peeled
and sliced

1 large potato, peeled and
shredded

1 cup chicken broth

2 tablespoons brown sugar

1 teaspoon caraway seeds

1/2 teaspoon salt

Additional brown sugar, optional

In a large saucepan, saute onion in butter until tender. Add sauerkraut, apples, potato, broth, sugar, caraway and salt; mix well. Cover and simmer for 20 minutes or until the apples are tender. Sprinkle with additional brown sugar if desired. **Yield:** 8 servings.

Authentic Spanish Rice

1 tablespoon bacon drippings *or* vegetable oil
3/4 cup long-grain white rice
1/2 cup chopped onion
1 garlic clove, minced
3 small canned tomatoes, diced
2 tablespoons tomato juice
2 cups hot water
1/2 teaspoon salt

In a skillet, heat bacon drippings over medium-high heat. Add rice; cook and stir until rice is golden brown. Add onion and garlic; stir and cook for 3 minutes.

Add the remaining ingredients. Cook, uncovered, on medium heat for 20 minutes, stirring only once after 10 minutes. Check rice for doneness by tasting a few top grains. If rice is firm, add a little water; cover and cook 5 minutes longer. **Yield:** 6 servings.

Cauliflower Lettuce Salad

1 head iceberg lettuce, torn
1 small head cauliflower, broken into florets
3/4 pound sliced bacon, cooked and crumbled
1/4 cup finely chopped red onion
1/4 cup sugar
1/4 cup grated Parmesan cheese
1 cup mayonnaise

In a large bowl, layer the lettuce, cauliflower, bacon, onion, sugar and cheese. Spread mayonnaise over the top; do not toss. Cover and chill for 2 hours or overnight. Toss just before serving. **Yield:** 8 servings.

Fruity-Toot-Toot

1 carton (8 ounces) frozen whipped topping, thawed
1/2 of a 3-ounce package of raspberry gelatin
1 can (20 ounces) pineapple tidbits, drained
1 can (16 ounces) fruit cocktail, drained
2 large apples, diced
2 large firm bananas, sliced

In a large bowl, combine whipped topping and gelatin. Stir in fruit. Cover and chill until ready to serve. **Yield:** 12-16 servings.

Carrot Casserole

1 pound carrots, sliced
2 eggs
1 cup chopped celery
1/2 cup chopped onion

1 tablespoon minced fresh
  parsley
3/4 cup butter, melted
1 teaspoon salt
8 cups cubed day-old bread

In a saucepan, cover carrots with water and cook until very tender. Drain and mash. In a large bowl, beat eggs; add the celery, onion, parsley, butter and salt. Stir in carrots. Add bread cubes and mix well.

Pour into greased 2-qt. baking dish. Bake, uncovered, at 350° for 30-40 minutes or until set. **Yield:** 8-10 servings.

Lemon Rice Pilaf

1 cup uncooked jasmine *or* long
  grain white rice
1 cup sliced celery
1 cup thinly sliced green onions

2 tablespoons butter
1 tablespoon grated lemon peel
1 teaspoon salt
1/4 teaspoon pepper

Cook rice according to package directions. Meanwhile, in a skillet, saute celery and onions in butter until tender. Add the rice, lemon peel, salt and pepper; toss lightly. Cook and stir until heated through. **Yield:** 4-6 servings.

Harvard Beets

3 cups sliced raw beets *or* 2 cans
  (16 ounces *each*) sliced beets
1/2 cup sugar
1 tablespoon all-purpose flour

1/2 cup white vinegar
1/2 teaspoon salt
2 tablespoons butter

In a saucepan, place raw beets and enough water to cover. Cook until tender, about 15-20 minutes. Drain, reserving 1/4 cup liquid. (If using canned beets, drain and reserve 1/4 cup juice.)

In another saucepan, combine the sugar, flour, vinegar and reserved beet juice. Cook over low heat until thickened. Stir in beets, salt and butter. Simmer for 10 minutes. **Yield:** 6-8 servings.

Four-Bean Salad

1/2 cup vegetable oil
1/2 cup honey
1/2 cup white vinegar
1 tablespoon water
1/8 teaspoon salt
1/8 teaspoon pepper
1 can (16 ounces) kidney beans, rinsed and drained

1 can (15 ounces) garbanzo beans *or* chickpeas, rinsed and drained
1 can (14-1/2 ounces) wax beans, drained
1 can (14-1/2 ounces) green beans, drained
1/4 cup chopped onion
1 jar (2 ounces) chopped pimientos, drained

In a bowl, whisk together the first six ingredients. Add the remaining ingredients; toss to coat. Cover and chill for at least 6 hours. **Yield:** 8-10 servings.

Sheepherder's Potatoes

5 to 6 medium potatoes (about 2 pounds), cooked, peeled and sliced
12 bacon strips, cooked and crumbled
1 large onion, chopped
6 eggs

1/4 cup milk
1 teaspoon salt
1/2 teaspoon pepper
2 tablespoons dried parsley flakes
1/2 teaspoon dried thyme
1/2 cup shredded cheddar cheese

In a greased 13-in. x 9-in. x 2-in. baking dish, layer the potatoes, bacon and onion. In a bowl, beat the eggs, milk, salt, pepper, parsley and thyme. Pour over potato mixture.

Bake, uncovered, at 350° for 15 minutes or until eggs are almost set. Sprinkle with cheese; bake 5 minutes longer or until cheese is melted and eggs are set. **Yield:** 6-8 servings.

Ham, Turkey and Wild Rice Salad

5 cups cooked wild rice
1/2 cup Western salad dressing
1 cup cubed fully cooked ham
1 cup cubed cooked turkey
1 cup thinly sliced celery
1 cup frozen peas, thawed
2/3 cup thinly sliced radishes

1/2 cup finely chopped onion
1 cup mayonnaise
2 teaspoons prepared mustard
1/4 to 1/2 teaspoon curry powder
1/2 teaspoon salt
1/4 teaspoon pepper

In a large bowl, combine rice and salad dressing; cover and chill overnight. Add the ham, turkey, celery, peas, radishes and onion. In a small bowl, combine the mayonnaise, mustard, curry, salt and pepper. Stir into salad. Cover and refrigerate for at least 2 hours. **Yield:** 8-10 servings.

Marinated Onion Salad

3 medium sweet onions, thinly sliced
4 cups boiling water
4 medium cucumbers, thinly sliced
1 cup (8 ounces) plain yogurt
1 teaspoon lemon juice

1-1/2 teaspoons salt
1/8 teaspoon pepper
Dash Worcestershire sauce
Dash white vinegar
1 teaspoon dill weed, optional
2 tablespoons minced fresh parsley

Separate onions into rings and place in a large bowl; pour water over onions. Let stand 1 minute; drain. Add cucumbers.

In a small bowl, combine the yogurt, lemon juice, salt, pepper, Worcestershire sauce, vinegar and dill if desired. Pour over onion mixture; toss to coat. Cover and chill until ready to serve. Sprinkle with parsley. Serve with a slotted spoon. **Yield:** 16-20 servings.

Fresh Vegetable Kabobs

2 medium ears fresh corn, cut into 2-inch pieces

2 medium zucchini, cut into 1-inch pieces

8 boiling *or* pearl onions *or* 1 package (8 ounces) boiling onions, cooked

1/2 cup butter, melted

2 tablespoons minced fresh chives

2 tablespoons minced fresh parsley

1/2 teaspoon garlic salt

Thread the corn, zucchini and onions alternately on four large metal or soaked wooden skewers. Combine butter, chives, parsley and garlic salt. Place skewers on a broiler pan; broil for about 8-10 minutes, turning and brushing with butter mixture every 2 minutes. **Yield:** 4 servings.

Baked Corn Casserole

1/4 cup butter

2 packages (3 ounces *each*) cream cheese, softened

1 can (15-1/4 ounces) whole kernel corn, drained

1 can (14-3/4 ounces) cream-style corn

1 can (4 ounces) chopped green chilies

1/2 cup chopped onion

1 can (2.8 ounces) french-fried onions, *divided*

In a large bowl, beat together butter and cream cheese. Stir in the kernel corn, cream-style corn, chilies and chopped onion; mix well. Pour into a greased 8-in. square baking dish.

Bake, uncovered, at 350° for 15 minutes. Remove from the oven; stir in half of the fried onions. Sprinkle remaining fried onions on top. Bake 15 minutes longer. **Yield:** 8-10 servings.

Southern Potato Salad

5 medium potatoes, peeled and cubed
Water
6 hard-cooked eggs, chopped
1/2 cup thinly sliced green onions
1/4 cup chopped sweet pickles
1 teaspoon prepared mustard
1 teaspoon celery seed
1 cup mayonnaise
Salt and pepper to taste

Cook potatoes in boiling water until tender. Drain and chill. Add eggs, onions and pickles; toss well. Stir in the mustard, celery seed and mayonnaise. Season with salt and pepper and mix well. Cover and chill until ready to serve. **Yield:** 6-8 servings.

Skinny Fries

2 medium baking potatoes, peeled and cut into 1/4-inch julienned slices
1 tablespoon butter, melted
1/4 teaspoon salt
1/8 teaspoon pepper

Place potatoes in a bowl; drizzle with butter and toss to coat. Transfer to a lightly greased 15-in. x 10-in. x 1-in. baking pan.

Bake, uncovered, at 400° for 45 minutes until golden brown, turning once. Sprinkle with salt and pepper. **Yield:** 2 servings.

Noodle Nibblers

2 cups uncooked bow tie pasta
Oil for deep-fat frying
1/2 cup grated Parmesan cheese
1 teaspoon dried oregano
1 teaspoon dried parsley flakes
1/2 teaspoon garlic salt
1/4 teaspoon onion powder

Cook pasta according to package directions; drain. Pat dry with paper towels. In an electric skillet or deep-fat fryer, heat oil to 375°. Fry bow ties, a few at a time, for 1-1/2 minutes or until golden brown. Drain on paper towels.

Combine remaining ingredients in a resealable plastic bag; add warm bow ties and shake to coat. Serve warm or cold. **Yield:** 3 cups.

Twice-Baked Sweet Potatoes

4 medium sweet potatoes
2 tablespoons butter
1/2 teaspoon salt
1/3 cup orange juice

1 small ripe banana, mashed
1/4 cup chopped pecans
Flaked coconut (optional)

Scrub and pierce the potatoes; bake at 375° for 45-60 minutes or until tender. Cut a slice off top of each potato and scoop out the pulp, leaving skins intact.

Mash potatoes with butter, salt, orange juice and banana. Spoon mixture into shells and top with the chopped pecans. Sprinkle lightly with coconut, if desired. Bake 12 to 15 minutes longer or until heated through. **Yield:** 4 servings.

Potato Volcano

8 to 10 medium russet potatoes, peeled and cubed
1/4 to 1/2 cup milk
3 tablespoons butter
1/2 teaspoon salt

CHEESE SAUCE:
1 tablespoon butter
1 tablespoon all-purpose flour
3/4 cup milk
1-1/2 cups cubed process cheese (Velveeta)
Salt and pepper to taste

Place potatoes in a large saucepan and cover with water. Cover and bring to a boil; cook for 20-25 minutes or until very tender. Drain well; mash with milk. Add butter and salt; beat until fluffy. Mound potato mixture about 4 in. high on a 9-in. broiler-proof pan; set aside.

In a saucepan, melt butter; stir in flour until smooth. Gradually add milk. Bring to a boil; cook and stir for 2 minutes or until thickened. Reduce heat. Add cheese, salt and pepper; stir until the cheese is melted.

With a large spoon, form a well 3 to 3-1/2 in. deep and 2-in. wide in the potato mixture. Pour cheese sauce into the well and drizzle down the sides. Broil 4 to 6 in. from the heat for 10 minutes or until the cheese sauce is browned and bubbling. **Yield:** 6 servings.

Cranberry Cabbage Salad

3/4 cup fresh *or* frozen cranberries, halved
1/4 cup sugar
6 cups shredded cabbage
1 cup seedless green grapes, halved
1/2 cup thinly sliced celery
1/4 cup orange juice
3 tablespoons mayonnaise
1/2 teaspoon salt

Toss cranberries with sugar and set aside. In a large bowl, combine the cabbage, grapes and celery. Add cranberries and toss.

Combine the orange juice, mayonnaise and salt; pour over salad and toss to coat. Serve immediately. **Yield:** 6-8 servings.

Nutty Coleslaw

6 cups shredded cabbage
1 cup dry roasted salted peanuts

DRESSING:
2 eggs
1/2 cup half-and-half cream
2 tablespoons all-purpose flour
2 tablespoons sugar
1/2 teaspoon ground mustard
1/2 teaspoon paprika
1/2 teaspoon salt
1/3 cup cider vinegar
2 tablespoons vegetable oil
2 tablespoons water

Place cabbage and peanuts in a large salad bowl; set aside. In a mixing bowl, beat eggs and cream until frothy; set aside.

In a small saucepan, combine remaining dressing ingredients. Cook and stir over medium-high heat until thickened and bubbly. Reduce heat; cook and stir 2 minutes longer. Remove from the heat. Stir a small amount of hot filling into egg yolks; return all to pan, stirring constantly. Return to heat; cook and stir over low heat until mixture thickens and coats a spoon. Set aside to cool. Pour over cabbage; toss to coat. Cover and refrigerate. **Yield:** 8-10 servings.

Turkey-Blue Cheese Pasta Salad

1 package (16 ounces) small
  pasta shells, cooked, drained
  and cooled
3 cups cubed cooked turkey *or*
  chicken
1 cup diced green pepper

1/4 cup chopped onion
1 cup blue cheese salad dressing
1/4 cup sour cream
2 teaspoons celery seed
1/4 teaspoon pepper
1/2 teaspoon salt, optional

In a large bowl, combine the pasta, turkey, green pepper and onion. In a small bowl, combine the dressing, sour cream, celery seed, pepper and salt if desired; pour over salad and toss. Serve immediately. **Yield:** 12 servings.

Onion Pie

6 to 8 medium onions, thinly
  sliced
2 tablespoons vegetable oil
6 eggs

1 cup soft bread crumbs
1/2 cup grated Parmesan cheese
1/2 cup minced fresh parsley

In a large skillet, saute onions in oil until soft but not browned; drain well. In a mixing bowl, beat eggs. Add the bread crumbs, Parmesan cheese, parsley and onions; mix well.

Place in a greased 10-in. pie pan. Bake at 350° for 35-40 minutes or until a knife inserted near the center comes out clean. **Yield:** 6-8 servings.

Tomato Barley Salad

4 cups cold cooked medium
  pearl barley
1/3 cup grated Parmesan cheese
1/4 cup vegetable oil
1-1/2 teaspoons minced fresh basil
  or 1/2 teaspoon dried basil

1 garlic clove, minced
1/2 teaspoon salt
1/4 to 1/2 teaspoon pepper
4 cups halved cherry tomatoes
2 cups frozen corn, thawed

Place barley in a large bowl. In a small bowl, combine the cheese, oil, basil, garlic, salt and pepper. Pour over barley and toss to coat. Add tomatoes and corn; toss to combine. Cover and refrigerate for 2 hours. **Yield:** 12 servings.

Zucchini Patties

2 cups shredded zucchini
1/2 cup shredded cheddar cheese
1/3 cup biscuit/baking mix
3 tablespoons grated onion
1/2 teaspoon salt

1/2 teaspoon dried basil
1/4 teaspoon pepper
2 eggs, lightly beaten
2 tablespoons butter

In a bowl, combine first seven ingredients. Stir in eggs; mix well. Shape into six patties, using about 1/4 cup of zucchini mixture for each patty.

In a skillet, melt butter; cook patties for 4-5 minutes on each side or until lightly browned. **Yield:** 4-6 servings.

Glazed Beets

1 can (16 ounces) sliced or diced beets
2 tablespoons sugar
1 tablespoon cornstarch

1/4 teaspoon salt
3 to 4 tablespoons white vinegar
2 tablespoons butter

Drain beets, reserving 1/3 cup juice. In a saucepan, combine the sugar, cornstarch and salt. Stir in beet juice and vinegar until smooth. Bring to a boil over medium-high heat; cook and stir for 2 minutes or until thickened. Add beets and butter; heat through. **Yield:** 4 servings.

Greek Rice Salad

4 cups cooked brown rice
2 cups julienned cooked turkey breast
2 cups halved cherry tomatoes
1 cup halved ripe olives
3/4 cup plain yogurt

3 to 4 tablespoons minced fresh mint
2 tablespoons red wine vinegar
1/2 teaspoon lemon-pepper seasoning
1/2 cup crumbled feta cheese, optional

In a large bowl, combine the rice, turkey, tomatoes and olives. In a small bowl, combine the yogurt, mint, vinegar and lemon-pepper. Pour over rice mixture; toss to coat. Sprinkle with cheese if desired. **Yield:** 8 servings.

Broccoli Tomato Cups

1-1/2 cups soft bread crumbs,
  divided
1 cup grated Parmesan cheese,
  divided
6 to 8 medium tomatoes

2 cups chopped broccoli
1 cup (4 ounces) shredded
  cheddar cheese
3/4 cup mayonnaise
Salt and pepper to taste

Combine 1/2 cup of bread crumbs and 1/4 cup Parmesan cheese; set aside. Cut a thin slice off the top of each tomato; scoop out pulp and place in a strainer to drain. Place tomatoes upside down on paper towels.

Cook the broccoli until crisp-tender; drain. Chop tomato pulp and place in a large bowl. Add the broccoli, cheddar cheese, mayonnaise, salt, pepper and remaining crumbs and Parmesan; mix gently.

Stuff tomatoes; place in a greased 11-in. x 7-in. x 2-in. baking dish. Sprinkle with reserved crumb mixture. Bake, uncovered, at 375° for 30-40 minutes. **Yield:** 6-8 servings.

Garbanzo Avocado Salad

3 medium tomatoes, diced
2 medium avocados, diced
1 can (15 ounces) garbanzo
  beans *or* chickpeas, rinsed and
  drained
1 cup cubed Monterey Jack
  cheese
1/4 cup chopped onion
6 tablespoons olive oil

1/4 cup lemon juice
1 garlic clove, minced
2 teaspoons Worcestershire
  sauce
3/4 teaspoon salt
1/2 teaspoon hot pepper sauce
1/4 teaspoon pepper
5 bacon strips, cooked and
  crumbled

In a large bowl, combine the first five ingredients. In a small bowl, whisk together the oil, lemon juice, garlic, Worcestershire sauce, salt, hot pepper sauce and pepper; pour over vegetables and toss. Cover and refrigerate for at least 1 hour. Just before serving, add bacon and toss. **Yield:** 8-10 servings.

Golden Corn Puff

1 package (16 ounces) frozen corn, thawed
1 large tomato, seeded and chopped
4 tablespoons butter, *divided*
3 tablespoons all-purpose flour
1/2 teaspoon salt

1/8 teaspoon pepper
Dash cayenne pepper
1 cup milk
1 cup (4 ounces) shredded sharp cheddar cheese
4 eggs, *separated*
1/4 teaspoon cream of tartar

In a skillet, saute corn and tomato in 1 tablespoon butter until tomato is heated through; set aside. In a large saucepan, melt the remaining butter; stir in flour, salt, pepper and cayenne until smooth. Gradually add milk. Bring to a boil; cook and stir for 2 minutes or until thickened. Remove from the heat. Add cheese and the reserved corn mixture.

In a small mixing bowl, beat egg yolks until thick and lemon-colored, about 3 minutes. Stir in 1/3 cup hot corn mixture; return all to the pan, stirring constantly. Cool to room temperature.

In another mixing bowl, beat egg whites until soft peaks form. Add cream of tartar; beat until stiff peaks form. Gently fold into corn mixture.

Transfer to a greased 2-1/2-qt. baking dish. Bake, uncovered, at 350° for 40-45 minutes or until thermometer reads 160° and top is golden brown. Let stand for 5 minutes before serving. **Yield:** 4-6 servings.

Skillet Stuffing

1/2 cup crushed corn bread stuffing *or* crumbled day-old corn bread
1/2 cup cooked rice
2 hard-cooked eggs, chopped
1/2 cup chicken broth
1/4 cup chopped celery

2 tablespoons chopped onion
2 tablespoons butter
1 teaspoon minced fresh parsley
1/4 teaspoon poultry seasoning, optional
Salt and pepper to taste

In a bowl, combine the first four ingredients; set aside. In a skillet, saute celery and onion in butter until vegetables are tender. Add the corn bread mixture and seasonings; mix well. Cook over medium heat until lightly browned. **Yield:** 2 servings.

Mary's Caesar Salad

1 hard-cooked egg
2 to 4 tablespoons mayonnaise
2 tablespoons lemon juice
1 garlic clove, minced
3 tablespoons red wine vinegar
1 to 3 teaspoons sugar
1 teaspoon Worcestershire sauce
1/2 teaspoon salt
1/4 teaspoon ground mustard
1/4 teaspoon pepper
1/2 cup olive oil
1 large bunch romaine, torn
3/4 cup Caesar-flavored salad croutons
1/4 cup grated Parmesan cheese
1 can (2 ounces) anchovy fillets, optional

Place the first 10 ingredients in a blender or food processor; cover and process until egg is chopped. While processing, add oil and blend until smooth.

In a large bowl, toss romaine, croutons and Parmesan cheese. Add dressing; toss to coat. Top with anchovies if desired. **Yield:** 10 servings.

Chopped Salad

1 can (6 ounces) pitted ripe olives, drained and chopped
1 jar (5 ounces) stuffed olives, drained and chopped
1 large cucumber, seeded and chopped
1 large green pepper, chopped
1 large tomato, chopped
1 small onion, chopped
1 bottle (8 ounces) Catalina salad dressing

In a large bowl, combine all the ingredients. Serve immediately or cover and refrigerate. **Yield:** 8-10 servings.

Sour Cream Cucumber Salad

1/2 cup sour cream
2 teaspoons sugar
1 teaspoon white vinegar
1 teaspoon salt
1/2 teaspoon dill weed
4 medium cucumbers, sliced

In a large bowl, combine the sour cream, sugar, vinegar, salt and dill. Add cucumbers; toss to coat. Cover and chill for at least 30 minutes. **Yield:** 8-10 servings.

Potato Casserole

5 to 6 medium potatoes, cooked, peeled and diced
3/4 cup butter, melted, *divided*
1 jar (2 ounces) chopped pimientos, drained
1/2 cup chopped green pepper
1 cup evaporated milk
1-1/2 teaspoons salt
1/4 teaspoon pepper
3/4 cup shredded cheddar cheese
24 saltine crackers, crushed (about 1 cup)

In a large bowl, combine the potatoes, 1/2 cup butter, pimientos, green pepper, milk, salt, pepper and cheese. Mix thoroughly; transfer to a greased 13-in. x 9-in. x 2-in. baking dish. Sprinkle with crackers. Drizzle with remaining butter. Bake, uncovered, at 350° for 45 minutes. **Yield:** 10-12 servings.

Corn Wheels with Lime Butter

4 medium ears of corn
2 tablespoons butter
2 tablespoons fresh lime juice
1/2 teaspoon pepper, optional

Using cleaver or large knife, cut corn into 1-in. lengths. In a large pot, bring water to boil over high heat. Add corn wheels; cover and boil 2 minutes. Melt butter; mix with the lime juice.

Transfer corn to serving platter and drizzle with lime-butter. Sprinkle with pepper, if desired. **Yield:** 4 servings.

Salmon Salad

2 cans (14-3/4 ounces *each*) salmon, drained, bones and skin removed
2 celery ribs, sliced
1 large apple, peeled and chopped
5 green onions, sliced
1/2 cup mayonnaise
2 teaspoons minced fresh dill *or* 3/4 teaspoon dill weed
3/4 teaspoon minced fresh basil *or* pinch dried basil
1/4 teaspoon garlic salt
1/4 teaspoon minced fresh tarragon *or* pinch dried tarragon

Flake salmon into a bowl. Add all the remaining ingredients; stir gently. Cover and chill until ready to serve. **Yield:** 8 servings.

Colorful Antipasto

3 ounces cheddar cheese, cut into 1/4-inch cubes

3 ounces Monterey Jack cheese, cut into 1/4-inch cubes

2-1/2 ounces sliced pepperoni

1/2 cup pitted ripe olives

1/2 cup broccoli florets

1/2 cup cauliflowerets

1/2 cup diced green pepper

1/4 cup *each* diced sweet red pepper, yellow pepper, onion and celery

DRESSING:

1/3 cup white wine vinegar

1/4 cup olive oil

1 tablespoon chopped fresh parsley

1 tablespoon sugar

1 teaspoon dried oregano

1/4 to 1/2 teaspoon crushed red pepper flakes

1/4 teaspoon minced garlic

1/4 teaspoon salt

In a large bowl, combine the cheeses, pepperoni, olives and vegetables. In a small bowl, combine dressing ingredients. Stir into the vegetable mixture. Cover and refrigerate for at least 4 hours. Store in the refrigerator for up to 5 days. **Yield:** 10 servings (5 cups).

Quick Pantry Salad

4-1/2 cups cooked elbow macaroni

1 can (16 ounces) kidney beans, rinsed and drained

1 can (15-1/4 ounces) whole kernel corn, drained

2 cups cubed cooked turkey *or* chicken

1 small cucumber, seeded and chopped

2 celery ribs, thinly sliced

1 cup shredded carrots

1/2 cup chopped green pepper

1/2 cup chopped onion

1/2 cup frozen peas, thawed

6 hard-cooked eggs, chopped

1 cup mayonnaise

1/4 cup milk

1/2 teaspoon salt

1/4 to 1/2 teaspoon poultry seasoning

1/4 to 1/2 teaspoon ground cumin

1/4 teaspoon pepper

In a large bowl, combine the first 11 ingredients. Combine the mayonnaise, milk and seasonings in a small bowl. Pour over salad and toss to coat. Serve immediately or refrigerate until ready to serve. **Yield:** 16-18 servings.

Creamy Veggie Vermicelli

2 cups fresh broccoli florets
2 cups cut fresh asparagus
   (1-inch pieces)
1/4 cup butter, cubed
8 ounces uncooked vermicelli
2 packages (3 ounces *each*)
   cream cheese, cubed

1 cup milk
3/4 cup grated Parmesan cheese
1/4 teaspoon salt
1/4 teaspoon pepper
1 tablespoon grated lemon peel

In a large skillet, saute the broccoli and asparagus in butter for 8-10 minutes or until crisp-tender. Meanwhile, cook vermicelli according to package directions.

In a large saucepan, cook and stir the cream cheese and milk over medium heat until smooth. Add Parmesan cheese, salt and pepper; cook 2 minutes longer or until blended. Remove from the heat.

Stir lemon peel into the vegetables. Drain vermicelli; place in a large serving bowl. Add vegetables and cheese sauce; toss to coat. Serve immediately. **Yield:** 4-6 servings.

Three Bean Casserole

1 can (16 ounces) red kidney
   beans, rinsed and drained
1 can (15 ounces) garbanzo
   beans *or* chickpeas, rinsed and
   drained
1 can (15-1/4 ounces) lima beans,
   rinsed and drained
1 pound lean ground beef
1 large onion, chopped

1 garlic clove, minced
1/4 cup packed brown sugar
1/2 teaspoon salt
Dash pepper
2 tablespoons prepared mustard
1/2 cup ketchup
1 teaspoon ground cumin
1/4 cup water
1 tablespoon white vinegar

In a 2-1/2-qt. baking dish, combine beans; set aside. In a skillet, cook the beef, onion and garlic over medium heat until beef is no longer pink. Remove from the heat; drain. Add all the remaining ingredients to skillet; mix well. Stir beef mixture into beans.

Bake at 350° for about 45 minutes or until heated through.
Yield: 6-8 servings.

Broccoli Supreme

1 pound fresh broccoli spears
1/2 tablespoon butter
1/4 cup seasoned bread crumbs

1 hard-cooked egg, chopped
Salt and pepper to taste

Place broccoli and a small amount of water in a saucepan; cover and cook for 8-10 minutes or until crisp-tender.

In a small skillet, melt butter. Add bread crumbs and toss to coat. Cook and stir over medium heat until warmed, about 1 minute. Remove from the heat and stir in egg.

Drain broccoli; season with salt and pepper. Sprinkle with crumb topping. **Yield:** 4 servings.

Surprise Potatoes

6 medium white potatoes, peeled

1 cup heavy whipping cream
Salt and pepper to taste

Shred the potatoes and rinse in cold water. Drain thoroughly. Place in a greased 9-in. square baking pan; pour cream over all and sprinkle with salt and pepper.

Cover with foil and bake at 325° for 1-1/2 hours. Uncover; bake 30 minutes longer or until lightly browned on top. **Yield:** 6 servings.

Baked Rhubarb

4 cups fresh *or* frozen diced rhubarb
4 cups cubed bread

1-1/2 cups sugar
1/2 cup butter, melted

In a bowl, combine rhubarb, bread cubes and sugar; toss to coat. Add butter; mix well. Turn into an 11-in. x 7-in. x 2-in. baking pan. Bake at 350° for 40-45 minutes or until golden. Serve warm. **Yield:** 6 servings.

Editor's Note: If using frozen rhubarb, measure rhubarb while still frozen, then thaw completely. Drain in a colander, but do not press liquid out.

Creamed Asparagus and Tomato

2 pounds fresh asparagus
   spears, trimmed
1/3 cup mayonnaise
1-1/4 teaspoons lemon juice

1/4 teaspoon salt
Pinch pepper
1 medium tomato, peeled, diced
   and drained

Cook the asparagus in boiling salted water until tender, about 10 minutes. Meanwhile, in a small saucepan, heat the mayonnaise, lemon juice, salt and pepper over low heat until heated through. Stir in tomato and remove from the heat. Drain the asparagus and place in a serving dish; top with tomato mixture. **Yield:** 6-8 servings.

Peppery Corn Salad

2 cans (15-1/4 ounces *each*)
   whole kernel corn, drained
1 medium green pepper,
   chopped
1 medium sweet red pepper,
   chopped

1 medium onion, chopped
1/4 cup mayonnaise
1/4 teaspoon cayenne pepper
Dash garlic salt

In a bowl, combine all the ingredients. Cover and refrigerate for at least 2 hours. Store in the refrigerator. **Yield:** 6-8 servings.

Spicy Spaghetti Salad

1 package (7 ounces) spaghetti
1 can (10 ounces) diced tomatoes
   with green chilies, undrained
1/2 cup mayonnaise
1/2 cup chopped pimiento-stuffed
   olives

1/4 cup chopped celery
1/4 cup chopped onion
2 garlic cloves, minced
1/4 teaspoon salt
1/4 teaspoon ground cumin

Break spaghetti in half and cook according to package directions. Meanwhile, combine remaining ingredients in a large bowl. Drain spaghetti; rinse in cold water. Add to tomato mixture and toss. Cover and refrigerate for at least 2 hours. **Yield:** 4 servings.

Fruity Pasta Salad

1 can (20 ounces) pineapple
  chunks
2 eggs, lightly beaten
3 tablespoons lemon juice
2 tablespoons sugar
1 tablespoon butter
1/4 teaspoon salt
1-1/4 cups heavy whipping cream,
  whipped

6 to 7 cups cooked cooled spiral
  pasta
1 can (11 ounces) mandarin
  oranges, drained
2 medium apples, diced
2 cups miniature marshmallows
1 cup halved seedless green
  grapes
1/4 cup maraschino cherries

Drain pineapple, reserving 3 tablespoons juice in a saucepan. Set
pineapple aside. To juice, add eggs, lemon juice, sugar, butter and salt;
cook and stir over medium heat for 3-4 minutes or until thickened and a
thermometer reads 160°. Cool to room temperature. Fold in whipped
cream.

In a large bowl, combine the pasta, oranges, apples, marshmallows,
grapes and pineapple. Fold in dressing. Cover and chill. Garnish with
cherries. **Yield:** 12-14 servings.

Hot Curried Fruit

2 cans (8 ounces *each*) pineapple
  chunks
1 can (15-1/4 ounces) peach
  halves
1 can (15 ounces) pear halves
2 tablespoons cornstarch
2 tablespoons brown sugar

1 tablespoon sugar
1 teaspoon curry powder
1 jar (14 ounces) spiced apple
  rings, drained
1 jar (6 ounces) maraschino
  cherries, drained

Drain the pineapple, peaches and pears, reserving juices; set the fruit
aside. In a saucepan, combine the cornstarch, sugars and curry powder.
Gradually stir in reserved juices until smooth. Bring to a boil; cook and stir
for 2 minutes or until thickened.

Stir in apple rings and reserved fruit; heat through. Remove from the
heat; stir in cherries. **Yield:** 8-10 servings.

Classic Red Beans 'n' Rice

1 pound dried kidney beans
2 quarts water
1 ham hock
2 bay leaves
1 teaspoon onion powder
1 pound ground beef
1 large onion, chopped
1 garlic clove, minced
1 teaspoon salt
1/2 teaspoon pepper
Hot cooked rice

Sort beans and rinse with cold water. Place beans in a Dutch oven; add water to cover by 2 in. Bring to a boil; boil for 2 minutes. Remove from the heat; cover and let stand for 1 to 4 hours or until beans are softened.

Drain and rinse beans, discarding liquid. Return to Dutch oven. Add 2 qts. water, ham hock, bay leaves and onion powder. Bring to a boil. Reduce heat; cover and simmer for 1 hour.

In a skillet, cook the beef, onion, garlic, salt and pepper over medium heat until meat is no longer pink; drain. Add to bean mixture. Simmer, uncovered, for 1 hour. Discard bay leaves.

Remove ham hock; allow to cool. Remove meat from bones; discard bone. Cut meat into bite-size pieces and return to broth. Heat through. Serve over rice. **Yield:** 8 servings.

Creamy Citrus Salad

1 package (6 ounces) orange gelatin
2 cups boiling water
1 can (6 ounces) frozen orange juice concentrate, thawed
2 cans (11 ounces *each*) mandarin oranges, drained
1 can (20 ounces) crushed pineapple, undrained
1 cup cold milk
1 package (3.4 ounces) instant lemon pudding mix
1 cup heavy whipping cream, whipped

In a large bowl, dissolve gelatin in boiling water; stir in orange juice concentrate. Cool until partially set. Fold in oranges and pineapple. Pour into a greased 13-in. x 9-in. x 2-in. dish. Chill until firm.

In a small bowl, whisk milk and pudding mix for 2 minutes; let stand for 2 minutes or until soft-set. Fold in cream. Spread over gelatin. Chill for 30 minutes. **Yield:** 12-14 servings.

Green Chili 'n' Rice Casserole

3 cups cooked long grain rice
1-1/2 cups (6 ounces) shredded
  cheddar cheese
1-1/2 cups (12 ounces) small-curd
  cottage cheese
1 can (4 ounces) chopped green
  chilies, drained

1/3 cup milk
1/3 cup chopped roasted red
  peppers
1 can (8-3/4 ounces) whole
  kernel corn, drained
1/4 cup grated Parmesan cheese

In a greased 2-qt. baking dish, combine the first seven ingredients. Sprinkle with Parmesan cheese. Cover and bake at 350° for 30-35 minutes or until heated through. **Yield:** 6-8 servings.

Mini Green Bean Casserole

2 cups frozen cut green beans
1 can (4 ounces) mushroom
  stems and pieces, drained
1 tablespoon cornstarch

1/2 teaspoon ground mustard
3/4 cup chicken broth
1 tablespoon butter
3/4 cup french-fried onions

In a greased 1-qt. baking dish, combine the beans and mushrooms. In a small bowl, combine cornstarch and mustard; gradually stir in broth until smooth. Pour over the vegetables. Dot with butter.

Bake, uncovered, at 375° for 25-30 minutes. Sprinkle with onions. Bake 5 minutes longer. **Yield:** 2 servings.

Herbed Broccoli Spears

1 pound fresh broccoli, cut into
  spears
1 medium tomato, chopped
1 garlic clove, minced

1/2 teaspoon onion salt
1/4 teaspoon dried basil
1/4 teaspoon dried oregano
1 tablespoon olive oil

Place 1 in. of water and broccoli in a saucepan. Bring to a boil. Reduce heat; cover and simmer for 5-8 minutes or until crisp-tender.

In a skillet, saute the tomato, garlic, onion salt, basil and oregano in oil for 1 minute or until heated through. Drain broccoli; top with tomato mixture and stir gently. **Yield:** 6 servings.

Apple-Strawberry Peanut Salad

3 medium apples, cubed
1 to 2 cups sliced strawberries
1 cup thinly sliced celery
1/2 cup mayonnaise

3 tablespoons honey
3/4 teaspoon celery seed
3/4 cup salted peanuts

In a large bowl, combine the apples, strawberries and celery. In a small bowl, combine the mayonnaise, honey and celery seed. Just before serving, add peanuts to fruit mixture and drizzle with dressing. **Yield:** 6-8 servings.

Tangerine Carrots

1 pound carrots, thinly sliced
4 teaspoons sugar
2 teaspoons cornstarch

1/8 teaspoon salt
1 cup tangerine *or* orange juice
1-1/2 teaspoons grated tangerine
   or grated orange peel

Place 1 in. of water and carrots in a saucepan; bring to a boil. Reduce heat; cover and simmer for 8-10 minutes or until tender. Drain and set aside.

In the same pan, combine the sugar, cornstarch and salt. Gradually stir in juice and peel. Bring to a boil; cook and stir for 2 minutes or until thickened. Return carrots to pan; heat through. **Yield:** 4 servings.

Corn Medley

1/4 cup butter
1/4 cup chopped onion
4-1/2 cups diced peeled yellow
   summer squash (about 4
   squash)

3 cups fresh corn
3 large tomatoes, peeled and
   diced
1-1/4 teaspoons salt
1/4 teaspoon pepper

Melt butter in a large saucepan over medium heat. Saute onion in butter until soft, about 3-5 minutes. Add the remaining ingredients; bring to a boil. Reduce heat; cover and simmer for 10-15 minutes or until the vegetables are tender. **Yield:** 10 servings.

Mother's Manicotti

CREPES:
1 cup all-purpose flour
1 cup water
2 eggs
1 tablespoon vegetable oil
Dash salt

FILLING:
1 carton (15 ounces) ricotta
cheese
3/4 cup shredded part-skim
mozzarella cheese
3 tablespoons grated Parmesan
or Romano cheese
1 tablespoon chopped fresh
parsley
1 egg, beaten
1 jar (28 ounces) spaghetti sauce
Additional shredded Parmesan *or*
Romano cheese

Place flour in a bowl; whisk in water, eggs, oil and salt until smooth. Pour a generous 1/8 cup into a greased hot 8-in. skillet; turn to coat. Cook over medium heat until set; do not brown. Repeat with remaining batter (makes 10-12 crepes). Stack crepes between waxed paper; set aside.

For filling, in a bowl, combine the cheeses, parsley and egg. Spread half the spaghetti sauce in the bottom of an 11-in. x 7-in. x 2-in. baking dish. Spoon 3 tablespoons of the cheese mixture down the center of each crepe; roll up. Place seam side down over spaghetti sauce; pour remaining sauce over crepes. Sprinkle with Parmesan or Romano cheese.

Bake, uncovered, at 350° for 30 minutes or until bubbly. **Yield:** 6-8 servings.

Stuffed Cucumbers

1 medium cucumber
1/2 teaspoon salt
1 package (3 ounces) cream
cheese, softened
1/4 cup chopped green pepper
2 tablespoons chopped onion
1/2 teaspoon Worcestershire sauce
1/8 teaspoon pepper
Dash paprika
French salad dressing, optional

Cut cucumber in half lengthwise. Scoop out seeds and pulp, leaving a 1/4-in. shell. Place seeds and pulp in a colander. Sprinkle with salt; drain for 30 minutes.

Meanwhile, combine the cream cheese, green pepper, onion, Worcestershire sauce and pepper. Stir in 2-3 tablespoons of the drained pulp. Spoon into cucumber shells; sprinkle with paprika. Refrigerate until serving. Serve with French dressing if desired. **Yield:** 2 servings.

Mixed Vegetable Side Dish

1 cup sliced celery
1/2 cup chopped onion
2 garlic cloves, minced
3 tablespoons butter
1-1/3 cups reduced-sodium chicken broth

1/4 cup water
4 cups cubed peeled potatoes
1 cup julienned carrots
1/4 teaspoon pepper
1 tablespoon chopped fresh parsley

In a skillet, saute the celery, onion and garlic in butter until tender. Add the broth, water, potatoes, carrots and pepper. Bring to a boil; reduce heat. Cover and simmer 15-20 minutes or until potatoes are tender. Uncover; simmer for 5 minutes or until broth has slightly thickened, stirring occasionally. Sprinkle with parsley; serve immediately. **Yield:** 10 servings.

Old-Fashioned Baked Beans

2 pounds dried navy beans
4 quarts water
2 large onions, chopped
1/2 pound bacon *or* salt pork, cut into 1/2-inch pieces

1-1/2 cups ketchup
1/2 cup molasses
1/2 cup packed brown sugar
2 tablespoons prepared mustard
1 tablespoon salt

Sort beans and rinse with cold water. Place beans in a Dutch oven or soup kettle; add water to cover by 2 in. Bring to a boil; boil for 2 minutes. Remove from the heat; cover and let stand for 1 to 4 hours or until beans are softened.

Drain and rinse beans, discarding liquid. Return to Dutch oven; add 4 qts. water. Bring to a boil. Reduce heat; cover and simmer for 1 hour or until the beans are almost tender. Drain and reserve liquid. Combine beans with the remaining ingredients.

Transfer to two ungreased 2-1/2-qt. baking dishes or bean pots. Add 1-1/2 cups reserved cooking liquid to each dish; stir to combine.

Cover and bake at 300° for 3 hours or until beans are tender and reach desired consistency, stirring every 30 minutes. Add reserved cooking liquid during baking as needed. **Yield:** 16-18 servings.

Asparagus with Blue Cheese Sauce

1/2 pound fresh asparagus spears

2 ounces cream cheese, softened

3 tablespoons evaporated milk
or half-and-half cream

1/8 teaspoon salt

1 to 2 tablespoons crumbled
blue cheese

In a small saucepan, cook asparagus in a small amount of water until crisp-tender. Meanwhile, in another saucepan, whisk cream cheese, milk and salt over low heat until smooth. Stir in blue cheese and heat through. Drain asparagus and top with sauce. **Yield:** 2 servings.

Lime Pear Salad

1 package (3 ounces) cream
cheese, softened

1 package (3 ounces) lime
gelatin

1 can (16 ounces) pear halves

2 cups vanilla ice cream,
softened

In a mixing bowl, beat cream cheese and gelatin until smooth. Drain pears, reserving syrup; set pears aside. If necessary, add enough water to syrup to measure 1 cup.

In a small saucepan, bring syrup to a boil; remove from the heat. Gradually add to gelatin mixture, beating until smooth. Stir in ice cream until dissolved. Mash pears and fold into gelatin mixture. Pour into a 6-cup mold coated with nonstick cooking spray. Cover and chill until firm. **Yield:** 6-8 servings.

Garlic-Buttered Pasta

2 cups uncooked small pasta
shells, alphabet pasta *or* ring
macaroni

3 to 4 garlic cloves, minced

1/2 cup butter

1/4 cup grated Parmesan cheese

2 tablespoons minced fresh
parsley

1/4 teaspoon salt

1/8 teaspoon pepper

Cook pasta according to package directions. Meanwhile, in a large saucepan, saute garlic in butter. Remove from the heat. Drain pasta; add to garlic butter. Stir in the Parmesan cheese, parsley, salt and pepper; toss to coat. **Yield:** 4 servings.

Apples, Berries and Yams

2 tablespoons butter
3 apples, peeled and cut into chunks
1 can (23 ounces) yams, drained

1/2 teaspoon ground nutmeg
1 can (16 ounces) whole-berry cranberry sauce
1/2 cup orange marmalade

In a skillet, melt butter over medium heat. Saute apples in butter until crisp-tender. Place apples and yams in a greased 3-qt. baking dish. Sprinkle with the nutmeg. Combine cranberry sauce and marmalade. Spoon over yams. Bake, uncovered, at 350° for 30 minutes or until heated through. **Yield:** 8-10 servings.

Cranberry Baked Beans

1 can (16 ounces) jellied cranberry sauce
1 can (8 ounces) tomato sauce
2 cans (31 ounces *each*) pork and beans, undrained

1 tablespoon prepared mustard
1/2 cup chopped onion
6 bacon strips, halved
3 tablespoons brown sugar

In a large bowl, combine the cranberry sauce, tomato sauce, beans, mustard and onion. Place in a greased 13-in. x 9-in. x 2-in. baking dish. Lay bacon on top. Sprinkle with brown sugar. Bake, uncovered, at 350° for 1 hour or until heated through. **Yield:** 12-16 servings.

My Mother's Mac and Cheese

2 cups elbow macaroni, cooked and drained
1 can (28 ounces) tomatoes with liquid, cut up
1/2 teaspoon onion salt, optional

1/4 teaspoon pepper
2 cups (8 ounces) shredded cheddar cheese, *divided*
2 tablespoons butter

In a bowl, combine the macaroni, tomatoes, onion salt if desired, pepper and 1-1/2 cups cheddar cheese. Pour into a greased 2-qt. baking dish. Dot with butter. Bake, uncovered, at 350° for 45 minutes. Sprinkle with remaining cheese; bake 15 minutes longer or until cheese is melted. **Yield:** 4 servings.

Acorn Cabbage Bake

2 large acorn squash
1 tablespoon butter
2 cups shredded cabbage
1 medium onion, chopped
1 medium apple, chopped
1/2 pound pork sausage, cooked and drained

2 tablespoons slivered almonds
3/4 teaspoon salt
1/2 teaspoon ground sage
1/4 teaspoon ground thyme
1/4 teaspoon pepper

Cut squash in half; remove seeds. Place cut side down in a 13-in. x 9-in. x 2-in. baking dish. Add 1/2 in. of water to pan. Cover and bake at 400° for 20 minutes or until tender. Cool; scoop out pulp (should have about 4 cups).

In a large skillet over medium heat, melt butter. Saute the cabbage, onion and apple until tender, about 5 minutes. Add the sausage, almonds, salt, sage, thyme and pepper; mix well. Remove from the heat and add squash. Place in a greased 2-qt. baking dish.

Bake, uncovered, at 350° for 30 minutes or until heated through. **Yield:** 8 servings.

Turkey Shrimp Salad

12 cups cooked elbow macaroni
6 cups cubed cooked turkey
2 cups cooked deveined salad shrimp
1 cup thinly sliced celery
1/2 cup thinly sliced green onions
1 can (20 ounces) pineapple chunks, drained
1 can (16 ounces) sliced peaches, drained and diced

1 can (14 ounces) sweetened condensed milk
1/2 cup lemon juice
1/2 cup vegetable oil
1/4 cup Dijon mustard
1/2 teaspoon salt
1/8 teaspoon lemon-pepper seasoning
Hard-cooked eggs, sliced, optional
Orange slices, optional

In a large bowl, combine the first seven ingredients. In a small bowl, combine the milk, lemon juice, oil, mustard, salt and lemon-pepper. Pour over salad; toss to coat. Cover and chill for at least 2 hours. Garnish with eggs and oranges if desired. **Yield:** 20-22 servings.

Homemade Noodles

6 to 7 cups all-purpose flour
1-1/2 teaspoons salt
6 eggs, beaten

1 cup water
1 tablespoon vegetable oil
Melted butter and minced fresh
  parsley, optional

In a large bowl, combine 6 cups flour and salt. Make a well in the center; add eggs and water. Mix with a wooden spoon until well combined. Gather into a ball; knead on a well-floured surface until smooth, about 10 minutes. If necessary, add remaining flour to keep dough from sticking to work surface and hands. Cover with a towel; let stand for 10 minutes.

Divide dough into eight portions. On a lightly floured surface, roll each portion into a 1/16-in.-thick square. Let stand, uncovered, for 10 minutes.

Roll up jelly-roll style. Using a sharp knife, cut into 1/4-in. slices. Unroll noodles and dry in a single layer on paper towels for 1 hour before cooking.

To cook, bring salted water to a rapid boil. Add noodles and oil to boiling water; cook for 2 minutes or until tender but not soft. Drain; toss with butter and parsley if desired. **Yield:** 24 servings.

Lima Bean Casserole

8 bacon strips, diced
1 medium onion, chopped
1 can (10-3/4 ounces) condensed
  tomato soup, undiluted
5 slices process American
  cheese, cut into 1/2-inch pieces

1 package (16 ounces) frozen
  baby lima beans, cooked and
  drained
Additional cheese slices, optional

In a large skillet, cook bacon over medium heat until crisp. Using a slotted spoon, remove to paper towel; drain, reserving 1 tablespoon of the drippings. Saute onion in drippings until tender. Stir in the soup, cheese, beans and bacon. Cover and simmer over low heat for 5 minutes or until the cheese is melted. Spoon into an ungreased 1-1/2-qt. baking dish.

Cover and bake at 350° for 20-30 minutes or until bubbly and beans are tender. Garnish with additional cheese if desired. **Yield:** 8-10 servings.

Old-Fashioned Potatoes Anna

3 eggs, *separated*
2 cups mashed potatoes
(without added milk and
butter)
3/4 cup shredded cheddar cheese

2 teaspoons finely chopped
green onion
2 teaspoons finely chopped
sweet red pepper
Salt and pepper to taste

In a bowl, beat egg yolks. Add the potatoes, cheese, onion, red pepper, salt and pepper. In a mixing bowl, beat egg whites until stiff peaks form; fold into potato mixture.

Place in a greased 1-1/2-qt. baking dish. Cover and bake at 400° for 20 minutes. **Yield:** 4-6 servings.

Chicken Tortellini Salad

8 ounces tortellini, cooked,
drained and cooled
1 cup cubed cooked chicken
3/4 cup frozen peas, thawed
1/2 cup mayonnaise
1/2 cup diced part-skim mozzarella
cheese

1/2 cup Parmesan ranch salad
dressing
2 tablespoons minced green
onions
2 tablespoons finely chopped
sweet red pepper
1 tablespoon minced fresh
parsley

In a large bowl, combine all the ingredients. Cover and refrigerate until ready to serve. **Yield:** 6 servings.

Apple-Cinnamon Coleslaw

2 cups shredded cabbage
1-1/2 cups chopped apples
1/2 cup raisins
1/2 cup chopped walnuts, optional

1 cup (8 ounces) vanilla yogurt
2 tablespoons apple juice
1/4 teaspoon ground cinnamon

In a medium bowl, toss the cabbage, apple, raisins and walnuts if desired. Combine the yogurt, apple juice and cinnamon. Pour over cabbage mixture and toss to coat. Chill until ready to serve. **Yield:** 4-6 servings.

Stuffing Balls

1/3 cup butter
1/2 cup chopped celery
1/4 cup chopped onion
5 cups soft bread cubes
1 cup chopped walnuts
1 teaspoon salt

1/2 teaspoon poultry seasoning
1/4 teaspoon pepper
1/2 cup chopped parsley
1/4 cup chicken broth
1 egg, well beaten

In a skillet, melt butter. Saute celery and onion until tender. Transfer to a large bowl. Add all the remaining ingredients and blend well. Shape mixture into eight balls. Place on a greased baking sheet. Bake at 375° for about 20 minutes or until a thermometer reads 160°. **Yield:** 8 servings.

Creamed Sweet Peas

1 tablespoon all-purpose flour
1/4 cup sugar
2/3 cup milk

2 cups fresh sweet peas *or* frozen peas, thawed
1/4 teaspoon pepper

In a medium saucepan, combine the flour, sugar and milk. Stir in peas and pepper; bring to a boil. Reduce heat; simmer for 10-12 minutes or until peas are heated through and sauce has thickened. **Yield:** 4 servings.

Green Bean Bundles

1 pound fresh green beans, trimmed
8 bacon strips, partially cooked
1 tablespoon finely chopped onion

3 tablespoons butter
1 tablespoon white wine vinegar
1 tablespoon sugar
1/4 teaspoon salt

Cook the beans until crisp-tender. Wrap about 15 beans in each bacon strip; secure with a toothpick. Place on a foil-covered baking sheet. Bake at 400° for 10-15 minutes or until bacon is done.

In a skillet, saute onion in butter until tender. Add the vinegar, sugar and salt; heat through. Remove bundles to a serving bowl or platter; pour sauce over and serve immediately. **Yield:** 8 servings.

Pesto Pasta Salad

1 package (16 ounces) spiral pasta, cooked, drained and cooled

1 cup julienned fully cooked ham

1 cup julienned carrots

1 cup thinly sliced celery

1 cup frozen peas, thawed

1 cup sliced fresh mushrooms

1 cup julienned zucchini

1 cup cubed Monterey Jack cheese

1/2 cup grated Parmesan cheese

1/2 cup thinly sliced green onions

1/3 cup chopped radishes

1 can (6 ounces) medium pitted ripe olives, drained and halved

1 jar (2 ounces) chopped pimientos, drained

PESTO DRESSING:

3 to 5 garlic cloves

2 cups loosely packed fresh basil leaves

3/4 cup grated Parmesan *or* Romano cheese

1/4 cup slivered almonds

3/4 teaspoon salt

1/2 teaspoon dried tarragon

1/4 teaspoon pepper

1/8 teaspoon sugar

1 cup olive oil

1/2 cup white wine vinegar

1 cup whole almonds, toasted

In a large bowl, combine the first 13 ingredients; set aside. For dressing, process garlic in a blender or food processor until finely chopped. Add the basil, cheese, slivered almonds, salt, tarragon, pepper and sugar. Process 15-30 seconds or until coarsely chopped. While processing, gradually add oil until mixture is smooth. Add the vinegar and process until blended. Pour over salad; toss to coat. Just before serving, add whole almonds. **Yield:** 18-20 servings.

Tomato Crouton Casserole

1 can (28 ounces) diced tomatoes, undrained

2 cups seasoned stuffing croutons, *divided*

1 small onion, chopped

1 tablespoon sugar

1/4 teaspoon dried oregano

1/4 teaspoon salt

1/8 teaspoon pepper

3 tablespoons butter

In a greased 2-qt. baking dish, combine tomatoes and 1 cup croutons. Stir in the onion, sugar, oregano, salt and pepper. Dot with butter; sprinkle with remaining croutons. Bake, uncovered, at 375° for 30-35 minutes. **Yield:** 6 servings.

Dressings, Sauces & Condiments

Hot Bacon Dressing

3/4 pound sliced bacon, diced

1/2 cup chopped onion

2 cups water

1 cup cider vinegar

1-1/2 cups sugar

1 jar (2 ounces) diced pimientos, drained

2 tablespoons Dijon mustard

1 teaspoon salt

1/4 teaspoon pepper

3 tablespoons cornstarch

2 tablespoons cold water

In a large skillet, cook bacon over medium heat until crisp. Using a slotted spoon, remove bacon to paper towels; set aside. Drain, reserving 2 tablespoons drippings in the skillet. Add onion and saute until tender; remove from the heat. Add the water, vinegar, sugar, pimientos, mustard, salt, pepper and bacon; mix well.

Combine cornstarch and cold water until smooth; stir into skillet. Bring to a boil; cook and stir for 2 minutes or until thickened.

Serve warm over fresh spinach or mixed greens. Refrigerate leftovers and reheat before serving. **Yield:** about 4 cups.

Milly's Salad Dressing

1 bottle (8 ounces) sweet-sour celery seed salad dressing

1 cup mayonnaise

2 tablespoons sweet pickle relish

2 tablespoons water

4 teaspoons Dijon-mayonnaise blend

3/4 teaspoon prepared horseradish

In a small bowl, combine all the ingredients; stir until well blended. Store in the refrigerator. **Yield:** 2 cups.

Chocolate Peanut Butter

1/2 cup butter, cubed

1/2 cup honey

1/4 cup baking cocoa

1-1/3 cups creamy peanut butter

1/4 teaspoon vanilla extract

Melt butter in a small saucepan. Stir in honey and cocoa until smooth. Remove from the heat; stir in peanut butter and vanilla. Refrigerate. **Yield:** 2-1/4 cups.

Elegant Holiday Ham Glaze

Juice and grated peel of 1 orange

Juice and grated peel of 1 lemon

1 cup sweet red wine *or* cranberry juice

1/2 cup light corn syrup

1/2 teaspoon ground mustard

1 can (16 ounces) whole-berry cranberry sauce

Drippings from a baked ham, optional

2 tablespoons cornstarch, optional

2 tablespoons cold water, optional

In a saucepan, combine orange and lemon juices and peel, wine or cranberry juice, corn syrup and mustard. Bring to a boil. Reduce heat; simmer, uncovered, for 30 minutes. Add the cranberry sauce and ham drippings if desired; heat through.

If a thicker glaze is desired, bring just to a boil. Combine cornstarch and water until smooth; stir into glaze. Cook and stir until slightly thickened. Serve warm over sliced ham. **Yield:** 3-1/2 cups.

Roasted Garlic Spread

2 large garlic heads
1 teaspoon olive oil
1 to 2 tablespoons butter
1 to 2 tablespoons all-purpose
flour

1 teaspoon chicken bouillon
granules
2/3 cup boiling water
Italian *or* French bread, sliced

Remove papery outer skin from garlic (do not peel or separate cloves). Brush with oil. Wrap each head in heavy-duty aluminum foil.

Bake at 425° for 30-35 minutes or until softened. Cool for 10-15 minutes. Cut top off garlic heads, leaving root end intact.

In a small saucepan, melt butter. Squeeze softened garlic into pan. Stir in flour until blended. Dissolve bouillon in water; gradually add to garlic mixture. Bring to a boil; cook and stir for 2 minutes or until thickened. Serve with bread. **Yield:** about 1/2 cup.

Maple-Dijon Salad Dressing

3/4 cup olive oil
1/4 cup balsamic vinegar
1/4 cup maple syrup

1/4 cup Dijon mustard
2 garlic cloves, minced
1/4 teaspoon pepper

In a jar with a tight-fitting lid, combine all the ingredients; shake well. Store in the refrigerator. Shake before serving. **Yield:** 1-2/3 cups.

White Sauce for Pasta

2 tablespoons butter
3 tablespoons all-purpose flour
2 tablespoons butter-flavored
granules

1 tablespoon reduced-sodium
chicken bouillon granules
1-1/2 cups boiling water
1 cup fat-free milk
Pepper to taste

In a saucepan, melt butter. Stir in the flour, butter-flavored granules and bouillon until blended; gradually add water and milk. Bring to a boil; cook and stir for 2 minutes or until thickened. Season with pepper. **Yield:** 2 cups.

Microwave Hollandaise Sauce

4 tablespoons butter, *divided*
3 tablespoons all-purpose flour
1 cup milk

2 egg yolks
2 tablespoons lemon juice
1/2 teaspoon salt

In a 1-qt. microwave-safe dish, heat 2 tablespoons butter, uncovered, on high for 20 seconds or until melted. Whisk in flour until smooth. Gradually add the milk. Microwave, uncovered, on high for 45 seconds; whisk lightly. Heat 45 seconds longer or until thickened. Whisk in the remaining butter until melted.

In a small bowl, beat egg yolks; add a small amount of hot milk mixture. Return all to the 1-qt. dish, stirring constantly. Whisk in the lemon juice and salt until combined. Microwave, uncovered, on high for 30-60 seconds or until thermometer reads 160°. Refrigerate leftovers. **Yield:** 1-1/4 cups.

Editor's Note: This recipe was tested in a 1,100-watt microwave.

Honey Mustard Dressing

2 quarts mayonnaise
4 cups (32 ounces) sour cream
12 ounces honey

12 ounces Dijon mustard
6 tablespoons mustard seed
Salad greens

Combine the mayonnaise, sour cream, honey, mustard and mustard seed until smooth. Serve over salad greens. **Yield:** about 4 quarts.

Salt Substitute

1 tablespoon garlic powder
1 teaspoon *each* dried parsley
    flakes, basil, marjoram and
    thyme
1 teaspoon rubbed sage

1 teaspoon pepper
1 teaspoon onion powder
1/2 teaspoon ground mace
1/2 teaspoon cayenne pepper

In a small bowl, combine all ingredients. Store in an airtight container. Use to season pork, chicken or fish. **Yield:** 1/4 cup.

Tangy Poppy Seed Dressing

1/2 cup vegetable oil
1/4 cup white wine vinegar
1 tablespoon honey
1 teaspoon poppy seeds

1 teaspoon Dijon mustard
1/8 teaspoon garlic powder
1/8 teaspoon salt

In a jar with a tight-fitting lid, combine the first seven ingredients; shake well. Store in the refrigerator. Shake before serving. **Yield:** 3/4 cup.

Mushroom Pasta Sauce

2 cans (14-1/2 ounces *each*) diced tomatoes, undrained
2 cans (10-3/4 ounces *each*) condensed tomato soup, undiluted
2 cans (7 ounces *each*) pizza sauce

1 can (8 ounces) mushroom stems and pieces, drained
1 teaspoon dried oregano
1 teaspoon dried basil
1 garlic clove, minced

In a large saucepan, combine all the ingredients. Bring to a boil, stirring frequently. Reduce heat; simmer, uncovered, for 15 minutes. Remove from the heat; cool. Transfer to freezer bags or containers. Freeze for up to 3 months. **Yield:** about 7 cups.

Light Pesto

4 ounces Romano cheese, cut into 1-inch pieces
6 garlic cloves
2-2/3 cups loosely packed fresh basil
1/3 cup chopped walnuts

3/4 teaspoon salt
1/8 teaspoon pepper
1/4 cup lemon juice
Hot cooked spaghetti

In a food processor, combine Romano cheese and garlic; cover and process for 30 seconds. Add the basil, nuts, salt and pepper; cover and process until combined, about 15 seconds. While processing, add the lemon juice; process about 15 seconds longer or until combined. Toss with spaghetti. **Yield:** 5 servings.

Cheddar Cheese Sauce

1/2 cup butter
1/2 cup all-purpose flour
1 teaspoon salt
1/2 teaspoon pepper

4 cups milk
2 cups (8 ounces) shredded cheddar cheese
6 hot baked potatoes

In a saucepan, melt butter over medium heat. Stir in the flour, salt and pepper until smooth. Gradually add milk. Bring to a boil; cook and stir for 2 minutes or until thickened. Reduce heat; add the cheese. Cook and stir until cheese is melted.

Serve 1-1/2 cups of cheese sauce with the baked potatoes. Refrigerate remaining sauce. **Yield:** 5-1/2 cups.

Sweet Dill Refrigerator Pickles

2 cups sugar
2 cups white vinegar
2 cups water
1/4 cup salt

3 quarts sliced unpeeled cucumbers
1 large onion, sliced
3/4 to 1 cup minced fresh dill

In a saucepan, combine the sugar, vinegar, water and salt. Bring to a boil and boil 1 minute. In a large nonmetallic container, combine cucumbers, onion and dill. Pour dressing over; cool. Cover and refrigerate at least 3 days before serving. Stir occasionally. **Yield:** 3-1/2 quarts.

Lemon Curd

1 cup butter
2 cups sugar
3 eggs, lightly beaten

1/2 cup lemon juice
1 tablespoon grated lemon peel

In the top of a double boiler over boiling water, melt butter. Stir in the sugar, eggs, lemon juice and peel. Cook over simmering water for 1 hour or until thickened, stirring occasionally. Pour into containers. Store in the refrigerator. Spread over scones, biscuits or toast. **Yield:** 3 cups.

Raspberry Vinegar

3 cups fresh raspberries
4 cups white wine vinegar

1/2 cup sugar

Rinse the berries and air-dry on paper towels. Place berries in a 6-cup sterilized jar; set aside. In large saucepan, combine vinegar and sugar; bring almost to a boil over low heat, stirring constantly, until sugar is dissolved (do not boil).

Pour hot vinegar mixture over berries; cover jar tightly and let stand at room temperature 48 hours. Strain through several layers of cheesecloth into a clean, sterilized bottle or jar. Seal tightly with a cork or lid. Store in cool dark place. **Yield:** 4 cups.

Lemon Butter Topping

1/2 cup butter, softened
2-1/2 tablespoons lemon juice

2 teaspoons grated lemon peel

In a small mixing bowl, cream butter until softened. Add juice and peel. Blend until well mixed. Drop by tablespoonfuls onto waxed paper. Freeze until firm.

Remove to a resealable plastic bag. Top piping hot vegetables or fish with 1-2 lemon balls just before serving. **Yield:** 8 tablespoon-size balls.

Evelyn's Original Roquefort Dressing

1 carton (8 ounces) sour cream
1/2 cup mayonnaise
1 teaspoon tarragon vinegar
1 teaspoon Worcestershire sacue
1 teaspoon lemon juice

1/2 teaspoon garlic salt
1/2 teaspoon garlic powder
1/2 teaspoon onion salt
Few drops hot pepper sauce
1 package (4 ounces) crumbled blue cheese

In a bowl, combine the ingredients in the order given. Store, covered, in the refrigerator. **Yield:** About 1 pint.

Blue Cheese Dressing

6 ounces blue cheese, crumbled
2 cups mayonnaise
1 cup (8 ounces) sour cream
2 tablespoons vegetable oil
2 tablespoons white vinegar
1 teaspoon garlic salt
1 teaspoon onion salt
1 teaspoon salt
1/2 teaspoon pepper

Place all the ingredients in a blender; cover and process on medium speed until smooth, about 1 minute. Cover and refrigerate. **Yield:** 3 cups.

Tarragon Butter

1 cup butter, softened
2 tablespoons minced fresh tarragon *or* 2 teaspoons dried tarragon
2 tablespoons minced fresh parsley
1 teaspoon fresh *or* dried chives
1 garlic clove, minced
Dash pepper

In a bowl, combine all the ingredients. Store in the refrigerator. Spread butter on French bread before toasting in oven, season cooked vegetables with it or use when cooking fish. **Yield:** 1 cup.

All Seasons Marinade

3/4 cup soy sauce
1/2 cup vegetable oil
1/2 cup red wine vinegar
1/3 cup lemon juice
1/4 cup Worcestershire sauce
2 tablespoons ground mustard
2 tablespoons minced fresh parsley
1-1/2 teaspoons pepper
1 teaspoon salt
2 garlic cloves, minced

In a jar with a tight-fitting lid, combine all the ingredients; shake well. Cover and refrigerate up to 2 weeks. Use as a marinade of beef, pork, chicken or shrimp. **Yield:** 2 cups.

French Salad Dressing

1-1/2 cups vegetable oil
1 cup ketchup
3/4 cup sugar
1/2 cup white vinegar

1 small onion, chopped
1 teaspoon lemon juice
1 teaspoon paprika
1/2 teaspoon salt

In a blender or food processor, combine all the ingredients; cover and process until smooth. Store in the refrigerator. **Yield:** about 3-1/3 cups.

Zesty Buttermilk Salad Dressing

2/3 cup fat-free plain yogurt
1/2 cup buttermilk
1/4 cup reduced-fat mayonnaise
1 tablespoon minced fresh parsley
1-1/2 teaspoons minced fresh basil *or* 1/2 teaspoon dried basil

1 teaspoon sugar
1 teaspoon minced fresh oregano *or* 1/4 teaspoon dried oregano
1/2 teaspoon minced fresh garlic
1/8 teaspoon salt

In a food processor or blender, combine the yogurt, buttermilk and mayonnaise; cover and process until smooth. Add the remaining ingredients; cover and process until blended. Cover and refrigerate for at least 1 hour before serving. **Yield:** 1-1/3 cups.

Salad Croutons

1 tablespoon olive oil
1 garlic clove, minced

1 cup cubed day-old bread
Pinch onion salt

Pour the oil into an 8-in. square baking dish; add garlic. Bake at 325° until garlic is golden, about 3-4 minutes. Add bread and onion salt; stir to coat. Bake 10-12 minutes longer or until the bread is lightly browned, stirring frequently. Store in an airtight container. **Yield:** 3/4 cup.

Chivey Potato Topper

1 package (8 ounces) cream cheese, softened
1/3 cup half-and-half cream
1 to 3 tablespoons snipped fresh chives

1-1/2 teaspoons lemon juice
1/2 teaspoon garlic salt
Baked potatoes

In a small bowl, beat cream cheese and cream. Stir in the chives, lemon juice and garlic salt; mix well. Serve on baked potatoes. **Yield:** 8 servings.

Fresh Salsa

8 medium tomatoes, chopped
3/4 cup sliced green onions
1/3 cup finely chopped fresh cilantro
1/3 cup chopped onion
2 small jalapeno peppers, finely chopped (seeded if desired)
1 can (2-1/4 ounces) sliced ripe olives, drained

3-1/2 teaspoons fresh lime juice
1 tablespoon cider vinegar
1 tablespoon vegetable oil
1 to 2 teaspoons chili powder
1 to 2 teaspoons ground cumin
1 teaspoon garlic powder
1 teaspoon dried oregano
1/4 teaspoon salt

Combine all ingredients in a large bowl. Cover and refrigerate overnight. Keeps up to 1 week. **Yield:** 8 cups.

Editor's Note: When cutting or seeding hot peppers, use rubber or plastic gloves to protect your hands. Avoid touching your face.

Paprika Salad Dressing

1/2 cup sour cream
1/4 cup mayonnaise
2 tablespoons steak sauce
1/4 teaspoon salt

1/2 teaspoon paprika
1/4 teaspoon celery seed
1/8 teaspoon hot pepper sauce
Torn salad greens

In a small bowl, combine the first seven ingredients with a wire whisk. Serve over salad greens. Refrigerate leftovers. **Yield:** 1 cup.

Sweet-and-Sour Dressing

1-1/2 cups sugar
2 teaspoons dried minced onion
1/2 teaspoon salt
1/2 teaspoon chili powder
1/2 teaspoon ground mustard

1/4 teaspoon crushed red pepper flakes
1 cup white vinegar
1 cup vegetable oil
1/4 to 1/2 cup light corn syrup

In a bowl, combine sugar and seasonings. Add vinegar; stir until sugar is dissolved. Whisk in oil and corn syrup until well blended. Store in the refrigerator. **Yield:** 3 cups.

Horseradish Sauce

2 tablespoons butter
2 tablespoons all-purpose flour
1 cup milk
1/4 cup half-and-half cream
1/2 teaspoon salt
1/2 teaspoon sugar

1/4 teaspoon pepper
1/4 teaspoon ground mustard
Pinch ground nutmeg
2 to 3 tablespoons prepared horseradish
1 tablespoon lemon juice

In a saucepan, melt butter. Stir in flour until smooth; gradually add milk and cream. Bring to a boil; cook and stir for 2 minutes. Remove from the heat; add the seasonings, horseradish and lemon juice. Serve over roast beef or spread on beef sandwiches. **Yield:** 1-1/4 cups.

Orange Barbecue Sauce

4 cups ketchup
1 cup prepared mustard
1 cup orange juice
1 large onion, finely chopped

1/2 cup packed brown sugar
4 teaspoons Liquid Smoke, optional
4 garlic cloves, minced
2 teaspoons pepper

In a large saucepan, combine all the ingredients; bring to a boil. Reduce heat; simmer, uncovered, for 30 minutes. Refrigerate for up to 1 week. Use as a basting or dipping sauce for pork, poultry or beef. **Yield:** 4 cups.

Cherry Honey Relish

1 can (16 ounces) tart cherries
  with liquid
1/2 cup raisins
1/2 cup honey
1/4 cup packed brown sugar
1 tablespoon cider vinegar

1/2 teaspoon ground cinnamon
1/8 teaspoon ground cloves
1/2 cup coarsely chopped pecans
1 tablespoon cornstarch
1 tablespoon water

In a saucepan, combine cherries with liquid, raisins, honey, brown sugar, vinegar, cinnamon and cloves. Cook, uncovered, over medium heat for 10-15 minutes or until sugar is dissolved and mixture is hot. Remove from heat; stir in pecans.

Combine cornstarch and water until smooth. Gradually stir into cherry mixture. Bring to a boil; cook and stir for 2 minutes or until thickened. Serve over slices of hot cooked chicken or turkey. **Yield:** 2-1/2 cups.

Chunky Applesauce

30 medium tart apples, peeled
  and quartered (about 11
  pounds)
4 cups water

2 tablespoons ground cinnamon
Sugar substitute equivalent to 8
  teaspoons sugar

Place apples and water in a large kettle. Cover and cook over medium-low heat for 30-40 minutes or until apples are tender; remove from the heat. Using a potato masher, mash apples to desired consistency. Stir in cinnamon and sweetener. Serve warm or cold. **Yield:** 14 cups.

Breads, Muffins, Biscuits & Rolls

Hot Cross Buns

2 packages (1/4 ounce *each*)
  active dry yeast
1/2 cup warm water (110° to 115°)
3/4 cup warm milk (110° to 115°)
1/2 cup sugar
1/3 cup butter, melted
1 teaspoon salt
1 teaspoon ground cinnamon
1/2 teaspoon ground allspice
3 eggs

3/4 cup raisins
1 tablespoon grated lemon peel
1 tablespoon grated orange peel
4-1/2 cups all-purpose flour
1 tablespoon cold water

ICING:
1 cup confectioners' sugar
1-1/2 teaspoons butter, softened
1/4 teaspoon vanilla extract
3 to 4 teaspoons milk

In a large mixing bowl, dissolve yeast in warm water. Add milk, sugar, butter, salt, cinnamon and allspice; mix well. Beat in 2 eggs. Stir in the raisins, lemon and orange peel and enough flour to form a soft dough.

Turn onto a floured surface; knead until smooth and elastic, about 10 minutes. Place in a greased bowl, turning once to grease top. Cover and let rise in a warm place until doubled, about 1 hour.

Punch dough down. Turn onto a lightly floured surface; divide into 24 pieces. Shape each into a ball. Place 2 in. apart on greased baking sheets. Cover and let rise until doubled, about 30 minutes.

Beat remaining egg with water; brush over rolls. Bake at 375° for 20-25 minutes or until browned. Remove from pans to wire racks to cool.

For icing, in a small bowl, combine sugar, butter, vanilla and enough milk to achieve a piping consistency. Pipe an "X" on top of each bun.
Yield: 2 dozen.

Sticky Apple Biscuits

1/4 cup honey
1/4 cup packed brown sugar
2 tablespoons butter, melted
2 tablespoons water
1/3 cup pecan halves

BISCUITS:
2 cups all-purpose flour
2 teaspoons baking powder
1/2 teaspoon salt
1/2 teaspoon ground cinnamon

3 tablespoons shortening
3 tablespoons cold butter
2/3 cup milk
1/2 cup diced peeled tart apple

FILLING:
3 tablespoons butter, softened
2 tablespoons applesauce
1 tablespoon honey
1/4 cup packed brown sugar
3 tablespoons raisins

In a small bowl, combine the honey, brown sugar, butter and water. Divide between 12 greased muffin cups. Sprinkle with pecans; set aside.

In a large bowl, combine the flour, baking powder, salt and cinnamon. Cut in shortening and butter until mixture resembles coarse crumbs. Stir in milk and apple just until moistened.

Turn onto a floured surface. Pat into a 10-in. x 8-in. rectangle, about 12 in. thick. Spread with butter, then applesauce; drizzle with honey. Sprinkle with brown sugar and raisins. Roll up jelly-roll style, starting with a long side. Cut into 12 biscuits. Place cut side down over pecan mixture in muffin cups.

Bake at 425° for 20-25 minutes or until golden brown. Cool for 1 minute before inverting onto a serving platter. Serve warm. **Yield:** 1 dozen.

Monkey Bread

2 tubes (7-1/2 ounces *each*)
  refrigerated buttermilk biscuits
1 cup packed brown sugar
1 teaspoon ground cinnamon

1 teaspoon ground nutmeg
1/2 cup butter, melted
1/2 cup chopped nuts
1/2 cup maple syrup

Cut each biscuit into quarters. In a small bowl, combine the brown sugar, cinnamon and nutmeg. Dip biscuits in butter, then roll in sugar mixture. Layer half the biscuits in a 10-in. fluted pan; sprinkle with half the nuts. Repeat layers. Pour syrup over top.

Bake at 350° for 25-30 minutes or until golden brown. Immediately invert onto a serving platter. Serve warm. Refrigerate leftovers. **Yield:** 1 loaf.

Banana Nut Bread

1/2 cup butter, softened
1-1/2 cups sugar
2 eggs
3 medium ripe bananas, mashed
1/3 cup buttermilk
4 cups all-purpose flour
1 teaspoon baking powder
1 teaspoon baking soda
1 teaspoon salt
1-1/2 cups grated peeled uncooked potatoes
1 cup chopped walnuts

In a mixing bowl, cream butter and sugar. Add eggs; mix well. Combine bananas and buttermilk. Combine the flour, baking powder, baking soda and salt; add to creamed mixture alternately with banana mixture. Stir in potatoes and walnuts.

Transfer to two greased 9-in. x 5-in. x 3-in. loaf pans. Bake at 350° for 40-45 minutes or until a toothpick inserted near the center comes out clean. Cool for 10 minutes before removing from pans to wire racks. **Yield:** 2 loaves.

Veggie Loaves

2 tablespoons active dry yeast
1/2 cup warm water (110° to 115°)
2 cups milk
1/3 cup vegetable oil
2 egg whites
3 tablespoons honey
2 cups chopped cabbage
2 large carrots, sliced
1 large celery rib, cut into chunks
1/2 cup cornmeal
1 tablespoon salt
5 to 6 cups whole wheat flour

In a large mixing bowl, dissolve yeast in warm water. In a blender or food processor, combine the milk, oil, egg whites, honey and vegetables. Cover and process until smooth. Add cornmeal, salt and vegetable mixture to yeast mixture; mix well. Stir in enough flour to form a stiff dough.

Turn onto a floured surface; knead until smooth and elastic, about 8-10 minutes. Do not let rise. Divide in half. Shape into two loaves. Place in two greased 9-in. x 5-in. x 3-in. loaf pans. Cover and let rise in a warm place until doubled, about 1 hour.

Bake at 350° for 35-40 minute or until browned. Remove from pans to wire racks to cool. Store in the refrigerator. **Yield:** 2 loaves.

Sugar-Topped Applesauce Muffins

2 cups biscuit/baking mix
1/4 cup sugar
1 teaspoon ground cinnamon
1 egg
1/2 cup applesauce

1/4 cup milk
2 tablespoons vegetable oil

TOPPING:
1/4 cup sugar
1/4 teaspoon ground cinnamon
2 tablespoons butter, melted

In a bowl, combine the biscuit mix, sugar and cinnamon. In another bowl, beat the egg, applesauce, milk and oil. Stir into dry ingredients just until moistened.

Fill greased or paper-lined muffin cups two-thirds full. Bake at 400° for 10-12 minutes or until a toothpick inserted near the center comes out clean. Cool for 5 minutes before removing from pan to a wire rack.

In a small bowl, combine sugar and cinnamon. Dip muffin tops in melted butter, then in cinnamon-sugar. **Yield:** 1 dozen.

Quick Homemade Bread

2-1/2 cups water
1/2 cup butter
1/3 cup sugar
3 tablespoons instant
   potato flakes

2 packages (1/4 ounce *each*)
   quick-rise yeast
1 teaspoon salt
6 cups all-purpose flour *or*
   bread flour
Vegetable oil

Heat water and butter to 125°-130°. In a large mixing bowl, combine with remaining ingredients except oil to form a stiff batter. Place in a greased bowl; oil top of dough. Cover and let rise in a warm place until doubled, about 30-45 minutes. Punch dough down.

On a lightly floured surface, knead dough until smooth and elastic, about 4-6 minutes. Divide dough into three portions. Shape into loaves and place in greased 9-in. x 5-in. x 3-in. loaf pans; oil tops of loaves. Cover and let rise until doubled, about 30 minutes.

Bake at 350° until bread sounds hollow when tapped, about 30-35 minutes. Remove from pans and cool on wire racks. **Yield:** 3 loaves.

Mom's Buttermilk Biscuits

2 cups all-purpose flour
2-1/4 teaspoons baking powder
3/4 teaspoon salt
1/4 teaspoon baking soda
1/3 cup shortening
3/4 cup buttermilk

In a large bowl, combine the dry ingredients. Cut in shortening until mixture resembles coarse crumbs. Stir in buttermilk just until moistened.

Turn onto a lightly floured surface. Roll to 1/2-in. thickness; cut with a floured 2-1/2-in. biscuit cutter. Place 1 in. apart on an ungreased baking sheet. Bake at 450° for 8-10 minutes or until golden brown. Serve warm. **Yield:** 1 dozen.

Cheery Cherry Bread

3 eggs, lightly beaten
2-1/2 cups all-purpose flour
2 cups grated carrots
1-1/2 cups flaked coconut
1 cup sugar
1/2 cup milk
1/2 cup vegetable oil
1 teaspoon baking powder
1 teaspoon baking soda
1/2 cup maraschino cherries

In a mixing bowl, combine the first nine ingredients. Fold in cherries. Spoon into three greased 8-in. x 4-in. x 2-in. loaf pans. Bake at 350° for 40-45 minutes or until a toothpick inserted near the center comes out clean. Cool for 10 minutes before removing from pans to wire racks to cool. **Yield:** 3 loaves.

Savory Biscuits

2 tubes (12 ounces *each*) refrigerated buttermilk biscuits
1/2 cup shredded Monterey Jack cheese
1/2 cup shredded cheddar cheese
3 tablespoons butter, melted
3/4 teaspoon dried basil
1/4 teaspoon dried oregano
1/8 teaspoon dill weed
1/8 teaspoon garlic powder

Separate each tube of biscuits into 10 biscuits; place in a single layer in a greased 11-in. x 7-in. x 2-in. baking pan. Sprinkle with cheeses. Drizzle with butter; sprinkle with seasonings. Bake at 350° for 25-30 minutes or until golden brown. Serve warm. **Yield:** 20 biscuits.

Sour Cream Herb Bread

3 to 3-1/4 cups all-purpose flour
1/4 cup sugar
1 package (1/4 ounce) active dry yeast
1 teaspoon salt
1/2 teaspoon celery seed
1/2 teaspoon dill seed

1/2 teaspoon dried minced onion
1 cup (8 ounces) sour cream
1/2 cup water
3 tablespoons plus 2 teaspoons butter, *divided*
1 egg
1 teaspoon sesame seeds

In a large mixing bowl, combine 2 cups flour, sugar, yeast, salt, celery seed, dill seed and onion. In a small saucepan, heat the sour cream, water and 3 tablespoons butter to 120°-130°. Add to dry ingredients; beat just until moistened. Add egg; beat until smooth. Stir in enough remaining flour to form a firm dough.

Turn onto a floured surface; knead until smooth and elastic, about 6-8 minutes. Place in a greased bowl, turning once to grease top. Cover and let rise in a warm place until doubled, about 70 minutes.

Punch dough down. Turn onto a lightly floured surface; shape into a round loaf. Place in a greased 2-qt. round baking dish. Cover and let rise until doubled, about 40 minutes.

Bake at 350° for 35-40 minutes or until golden brown. Melt remaining butter; brush over bread. Sprinkle with sesame seeds. Remove from pan to a wire rack to cool. **Yield:** 1 loaf.

Baking Powder Drop Biscuits

2 cups all-purpose flour
2 tablespoons sugar
4 teaspoons baking powder
1/2 teaspoon cream of tartar

1/2 teaspoon salt
1/2 cup shortening
2/3 cup milk
1 egg

In a bowl, combine the first five ingredients. Cut in shortening until the mixture resembles coarse crumbs. In a bowl, whisk milk and egg. Stir into crumb mixture just until moistened.

Drop by heaping spoonfuls 2 in. apart onto an ungreased baking sheet. Bake at 450° for 10-12 minutes or until golden brown. Serve warm. **Yield:** 1 dozen.

Easy Oat Bran Muffins

2 cups oat bran cereal
1/4 cup packed brown sugar
2 teaspoons baking powder
1 egg *or* 2 egg whites, lightly beaten

1 cup milk
1/4 cup dark molasses
2 tablespoons vegetable oil

In a large bowl, combine the cereal, brown sugar and baking powder. Combine the egg, milk, molasses and oil. Add to dry ingredients and stir just until moistened.

Fill greased or paper-lined muffin cups three-fourths full. Bake at 425° for 15-17 minutes or until toothpick inserted near the center comes out clean. Cool for 5 minutes before removing from pan to a wire rack. **Yield:** 8-10 muffins.

Cinnamon Walnut Crescents

3 egg yolks
1 cup (8 ounces) sour cream
1 package (1/4 ounce) active dry yeast
3 cups all-purpose flour
1/2 teaspoon salt

1 cup cold butter
1 cup finely chopped walnuts
1 cup sugar
2 teaspoons ground cinnamon
Confectioners' sugar icing, optional

In a small bowl, beat yolks; stir in sour cream and yeast. Let stand for 10 minutes. In a large bowl, combine flour and salt; cut in butter until mixture resembles coarse crumbs. Add sour cream mixture and stir well. Shape into a ball; cover with plastic wrap and refrigerate 8 hours or overnight.

Combine walnuts, sugar and cinnamon; sprinkle a fourth of the mixture on a flat surface. Divide dough into four portions; set three aside. On walnut-sprinkled surface, roll one portion into an 8-in. circle; turn dough over and press walnut mixture into both sides. Cut into 16 wedges. Roll up each wedge into a crescent shape, starting with the wide end. Place point down 1 in. apart on greased baking sheets. Repeat three more times with remaining walnut mixture and dough.

Bake at 350° for 20-25 minutes or until golden brown. Cool on wire racks. Drizzle with icing if desired. **Yield:** about 5 dozen.

English Muffin Loaf

3 cups all-purpose flour
1 package (1/4 ounce) active dry
  yeast
1-1/2 teaspoons sugar
1 teaspoon salt

1/8 teaspoon baking soda
1 cup milk
1/4 cup water
Cornmeal

In a large mixing bowl, combine 2 cups flour, yeast, sugar, salt and baking soda. In a saucepan, heat milk and water to 120°-130°. Add to dry ingredients; beat until smooth. Stir in remaining flour (batter will be stiff). Do not knead.

Grease an 8-in. x 4-in. x 2-in. loaf pan and sprinkle with cornmeal. Spoon batter into prepared pan. Cover and let rise in a warm place until doubled, about 45 minutes.

Bake at 400° for 30-35 minutes or until golden brown. Remove from pan to a wire rack to cool. **Yield:** 1 loaf.

Four-Grain Bread

1 cup quick-cooking oats
2 cups boiling water
2 tablespoons butter, softened
2 packages (1/4 ounce *each*)
  active dry yeast
1/3 cup warm water (110° to 115°)

1/2 cup cornmeal
1/2 cup whole wheat flour
1/2 cup honey
2 teaspoons salt
5 to 6 cups all-purpose flour
Additional butter, melted

In a large mixing bowl, combine the oats, boiling water and butter; cool to 110°-115°, stirring occasionally. In a small bowl, dissolve yeast in warm water. Add to oat mixture. Add the cornmeal, whole wheat flour, honey, salt and 3 cups all-purpose flour. Beat until smooth. Stir in enough remaining all-purpose flour to form a soft dough.

Turn onto a floured surface; knead until smooth and elastic, about 6-8 minutes. Place in a greased bowl, turning once to grease top. Cover and let rise in a warm place until doubled, about 1 hour.

Punch dough down. Turn onto a lightly floured surface; divide in half. Shape each portion into a loaf. Place in two greased 9-in. x 5-in. x 3-in. loaf pans. Cover and let rise until doubled, about 45 minutes.

Bake at 350° for 40-45 minutes or until golden brown. Remove from pans to wire racks. Brush with melted butter. Cool. **Yield:** 2 loaves.

Skillet Rolls

1 package (1/4 ounce) active dry yeast
1/4 cup warm water (110° to 115°)
1 cup warm buttermilk (110° to 115°)
1/4 cup butter, softened
1/4 cup sugar
1 teaspoon salt
1/4 teaspoon baking soda
1 egg
4 to 4-1/2 cups all-purpose flour
1 tablespoon cornmeal
1 tablespoon butter, melted

In a large mixing bowl, dissolve yeast in warm water. Add buttermilk, butter, sugar, salt, baking soda and egg. Beat until blended. Stir in enough flour to form a soft dough.

Turn onto a floured surface; knead until smooth and elastic, about 6-8 minutes. Place in a greased bowl, turning once to grease top. Cover and let rise in a warm place until doubled, about 1 hour.

Punch dough down. Turn onto a lightly floured surface; knead for 5 minutes. Divide into 24 pieces. Shape each into a ball.

Grease a 12-in. ovenproof skillet and sprinkle with cornmeal. Place rolls in prepared pan. Cover and let rise until doubled, about 40 minutes.

Drizzle melted butter over rolls. Bake at 375° for 18-20 minutes or until golden brown. Remove from skillet to a wire rack to cool. **Yield:** 2 dozen.

Editor's Note: Warmed buttermilk will appear curdled.

Sage Cornmeal Biscuits

1-1/2 cups all-purpose flour
1/2 cup cornmeal
3 teaspoons baking powder
1/2 to 3/4 teaspoon rubbed sage
1/2 teaspoon salt
1/3 cup shortening
3/4 cup milk

In a bowl, combine the first five ingredients. Cut in shortening until mixture resembles coarse crumbs. Stir in milk just until moistened.

Turn onto a lightly floured surface. Roll to 3/4-in. thickness; cut with a floured 2-in. biscuit cutter. Place 2 in. apart on an ungreased baking sheet. Bake at 450° for 10-12 minutes or until browned. Serve warm. **Yield:** 10 biscuits.

Pimiento-Stuffed Olive Bread

3 cups biscuit/baking mix
2 tablespoons sugar
1 egg
1-1/2 cups buttermilk
1 cup (4 ounces) shredded Swiss cheese

1 cup pimiento-stuffed olives
3/4 cup chopped walnuts
1 package (8 ounces) cream cheese, softened
1 teaspoon minced chives

In a large bowl, combine biscuit mix and sugar. In another bowl, beat egg and buttermilk. Stir into dry ingredients just until moistened. Fold in the Swiss cheese, olives and walnuts.

Transfer to a greased 9-in. x 5-in. x 3-in. loaf pan. Bake at 350° for 50-55 minutes or until a toothpick comes out clean. Cool for 10 minutes before removing from pan to a wire rack.

In a mixing bowl, combine cream cheese and chives. Serve with bread. Refrigerate leftovers. **Yield:** 1 loaf.

Roasted Red Pepper Muffins

1 teaspoon cornmeal
1-3/4 cups all-purpose flour
3 tablespoons sugar
2 teaspoons baking powder
1/2 teaspoon coarsely ground pepper, *divided*
1/4 teaspoon salt

1 egg
3/4 cup buttermilk
1/4 cup vegetable oil
2/3 cup chopped roasted sweet red pepper
1/2 cup shredded part-skim mozzarella cheese

Grease muffin cups and sprinkle with the cornmeal; set aside. In a large bowl, combine the flour, sugar, baking powder, 1/4 teaspoon pepper and salt. In another bowl, beat the egg, buttermilk and oil. Stir into dry ingredients just until moistened. Fold in red pepper and cheese.

Fill prepared muffin cups two-thirds full. Sprinkle with remaining pepper. Bake at 400° for 20-25 minutes or until a toothpick inserted near the center comes out clean. Cool for 5 minutes before removing from pan to a wire rack. Serve warm. Refrigerate leftovers. **Yield:** 1 dozen.

Cranberry Scones

1-1/2 cups butter, softened
1/2 cup fresh *or* frozen cranberries
2 tablespoons confectioners' sugar
1/2 teaspoon grated orange peel

SCONES:
2-1/2 cups all-purpose flour

2/3 cup sugar
2-1/2 teaspoons baking powder
1/2 teaspoon baking soda
3/4 cup cold butter
1 cup chopped fresh *or* frozen cranberries
3/4 cup buttermilk

In a mixing bowl, cream butter. Stir in cranberries, confectioners' sugar and orange peel; mix well. Cover and refrigerate for at least 1 hour.

Meanwhile, combine the dry ingredients in a bowl. Cut in butter until mixture resembles coarse crumbs. Add cranberries. Stir in buttermilk just until moistened.

Turn onto a lightly floured surface; gently knead 6-8 times. Divide in half. Pat each half into an 8-in. circle. Cut into eight wedges. Place 1 in. apart on ungreased baking sheets.

Bake at 400° for 15-18 minutes or until lightly browned. Remove from pans to wire racks. Serve warm with cranberry-orange butter. **Yield:** 16 scones.

Irish Soda Bread

2 cups all-purpose flour
2 tablespoons sugar
1 teaspoon baking powder
1 teaspoon baking soda
1/2 teaspoon salt

3 tablespoons cold butter
1 cup buttermilk
1/2 cup raisins
Additional butter, melted
Additional flour

In a bowl, combine the first five ingredients. Cut in butter until crumbly. Stir in buttermilk just until moistened. Fold in raisins.

Knead on a floured surface for 1 minute. Shape into a 7-in. round loaf; place on a greased baking sheet. With a sharp knife, cut a 1/4-in.-deep cross on top of the loaf.

Bake at 375° for 25-35 minutes or until golden brown. Remove from pan to a wire rack. Brush with additional butter. Cool. Dust with additional flour. **Yield:** 1 loaf.

Rye Breadsticks

1 tablespoon active dry yeast
1-1/2 cups warm water (110° to 115°), *divided*
2 tablespoons honey

2 cups whole wheat flour
1 cup rye flour
1 to 1-1/2 cups all-purpose flour

In a large mixing bowl, dissolve yeast in 1/2 cup warm water. Add honey; let stand for 5 minutes. Stir in the remaining water, whole wheat flour, rye flour and enough all-purpose flour to form a soft dough.

Turn onto a floured surface; knead until smooth and elastic, about 6-8 minutes. Do not let rise. Divide dough into 16 pieces. Roll each into a 10-in. rope. Place 2 in. apart on a greased baking sheet. Cover and let rise in a warm place until doubled, about 30 minutes.

Bake at 350° for 20-25 minutes or until golden brown. Remove to a wire rack. **Yield:** 16 breadsticks.

Cinnamon Swirl Bread

2 packages (1/4 ounce *each*) active dry yeast
1/2 cup warm water (110° to 115°)
1 cup warm milk (110° to 115°)
1/2 cup butter, softened
1 egg
1/2 cup uncooked Malt-O-Meal cereal

1/3 cup sugar
2 teaspoons salt
4 to 4-1/2 cups all-purpose flour

FILLING:
1 egg white, lightly beaten
1/2 cup sugar
1 tablespoon ground cinnamon

In a large mixing bowl, dissolve yeast in warm water. Add the milk, butter, egg, cereal, sugar, salt and 2 cups flour; mix until smooth. Stir in enough remaining flour to form a soft dough. Do not knead. Cover and let rise in a warm place until doubled, about 1-1/4 hours.

Punch dough down. Turn onto a lightly floured surface; divide dough in half. Roll each portion into a 12-in. x 7-in. rectangle. Brush with egg white. Combine sugar and cinnamon; sprinkle over rectangles. Roll up jelly-roll style, starting with a short side; pinch seams to seal and tuck ends under. Place each in a greased 8-in. x 4-in. x 2-in. loaf pan. Cover and let rise until doubled, about 30 minutes.

Bake at 375° for 40-45 minutes or until golden brown. Remove from pans to cool on wire racks. **Yield:** 2 loaves.

Iones's Parker House Rolls

1 package (1/4 ounce) active dry
   yeast
1 teaspoon sugar
1/4 cup warm water (110° to 115°)
1 cup milk

1/2 cup butter, *divided*
1/3 cup sugar
1 teaspoon salt
3-1/2 to 4 cups all-purpose
   flour, *divided*

Dissolve yeast and 1 teaspoon sugar in warm water; set aside. In a saucepan, heat milk, 1/3 cup butter, 1/3 cup sugar and salt to 110°-115°. Stir until butter melts. Pour into a large mixing bowl and add 2 cups flour and yeast mixture. Beat until smooth. Stir in enough remaining flour to form a stiff dough.

Turn out onto a floured surface and knead until smooth and elastic, about 6-8 minutes. Shape into a ball and place in a greased bowl turning once to grease top. Cover and let rise until doubled, about 1 hour.

Punch dough down. Turn onto a lightly floured surface; divide in half. Cover and let rest for 10 minutes. Form dough into desired dinner roll shapes.

Place on greased baking pans. Melt remaining butter and brush over rolls. Let rise for 30 minutes. Bake at 375° for 12-15 minutes or until golden. **Yield:** about 24 rolls.

Best-Ever Blueberry Muffins

2-1/2 cups all-purpose flour
1 cup sugar
2-1/2 teaspoons baking powder
1/4 teaspoon salt

2 eggs, lightly beaten
1 cup buttermilk
1/4 cup butter, melted
1-1/2 cups fresh blueberries

In a large bowl, combine the flour, sugar, baking powder and salt. Combine the eggs, buttermilk and butter; stir into dry ingredients just until moistened. Fold in blueberries.

Fill greased or paper-lined muffin cups three-fourths full. Bake at 400° for 20-24 minutes or until toothpick inserted near the center comes out clean. Cool for 5 minutes before removing from pan to a wire rack. **Yield:** about 1 dozen.

Cinnamon-Raisin Coffee Cake

2/3 cup sugar
1/2 cup vegetable oil
2 eggs
1 teaspoon vanilla extract
1-1/2 cups all-purpose flour
1 teaspoon baking soda
1/4 teaspoon salt

1 cup (8 ounces) plain yogurt
1/2 cup raisins

TOPPING:
1/2 cup walnuts, chopped
1/3 cup packed brown sugar
2 teaspoons ground cinnamon

In a mixing bowl, beat the sugar, oil, eggs and vanilla until smooth. Combine the flour, baking soda and salt; add to the sugar mixture alternately with yogurt. Stir in raisins. Pour half of the batter into a greased 9-in. square baking pan.

Combine topping ingredients; sprinkle half over batter. Top with remaining batter and topping. Cut through batter with a knife to swirl the topping.

Bake at 350° for 30-35 minutes or until a toothpick inserted near the center comes out clean. Cool on a wire rack. **Yield:** 9 servings.

Morning Glory Muffins

4 cups all-purpose flour
2-1/2 cups sugar
4 teaspoons baking soda
4 teaspoons ground cinnamon
1 teaspoon salt
2 cups vegetable oil
6 eggs, lightly beaten

4 teaspoons vanilla extract
4 cups grated peeled apples
1 cup raisins
1 cup flaked coconut
1 cup shredded carrots
1 cup chopped walnuts

In a large bowl, combine the flour, sugar, baking soda, cinnamon and salt. Whisk together the oil, eggs and vanilla; stir into dry ingredients just until moistened. Fold in the apples, raisins, coconut, carrots and nuts.

Fill greased or paper-lined muffin cups two-thirds full. Bake at 350° for 25-30 minutes or until a toothpick inserted near the center comes out clean. Cool for 5 minutes before removing from pans to wire racks. **Yield:** about 3 dozen.

Blueberry Streusel Coffee Cake

1/2 cup butter, softened
1-3/4 cups sugar
2 eggs
2 teaspoons vanilla extract
3-1/2 cups all-purpose flour
2 tablespoons baking powder
1 teaspoon salt

1-1/2 cups milk
3 cups fresh *or* frozen
   blueberries

STREUSEL TOPPING:
3/4 cup sugar
1/2 teaspoon ground cinnamon
1/3 cup cold butter

In a mixing bowl, cream butter and sugar. Beat in eggs and vanilla.
Combine the flour, baking powder and salt; add to creamed mixture
alternately with the milk. Fold in blueberries. Pour into a greased 13-in.
x 9-in. x 2-in. baking pan.

For topping, combine sugar and cinnamon. Cut in butter until mixture
resembles coarse crumbs. Sprinkle over batter. Bake at 375° for 35-40
minutes or until a toothpick inserted near the center comes out clean.
Cool in pan on a wire rack. **Yield:** 12-16 servings.

Editor's Note: If using frozen blueberries, do not thaw before adding
to batter.

Golden Cheese Yeast Bread

6 to 7 cups all-purpose flour
2 cups (8 ounces) shredded
   cheddar cheese
3 tablespoons sugar

2 packages (1/4 ounce *each*)
   active dry yeast
2 teaspoons salt
2 cups warm milk (120° to 130°)
1 egg

In a large mixing bowl, combine 3 cups flour, cheese, sugar, yeast and
salt. Add milk and egg; beat on low speed until smooth. Stir in enough
remaining flour to form a soft dough.

Turn onto a floured surface; knead until smooth and elastic, about
6-8 minutes. Place in a greased bowl, turning once to grease top. Cover
and let rise in a warm place until doubled, about 1 hour.

Punch dough down. Turn onto a lightly floured surface; divide in half
and shape into two loaves. Place in two greased 9-in. x 5-in. x 3-in. loaf
pans. Cover and let rise until doubled, about 45 minutes.

Bake at 375° for 25-30 minutes or until golden brown. Remove from
pans to cool on wire racks. **Yield:** 2 loaves.

Chocolate Cinnamon Rolls

1 package (1/4 ounce) active dry yeast
3/4 cup warm water (110° to 115°)
1/4 cup shortening
1 teaspoon salt
1/4 cup plus 3 tablespoons sugar, *divided*
1 egg

1/3 cup baking cocoa
2-1/4 cups all-purpose flour
1 tablespoon butter, softened
1-1/2 teaspoons ground cinnamon

QUICK WHITE ICING:
1 cup confectioners' sugar
1/2 teaspoon vanilla extract
1-1/2 tablespoons milk

In a large mixing bowl, dissolve yeast in warm water. Add shortening, salt, 1/4 cup sugar, egg, cocoa and 1 cup flour; beat for 2 minutes. Stir in remaining flour and blend with a spoon until smooth. Do not knead. Cover and let rise in a warm place until doubled, about 1 hour.

Stir dough down and turn onto a well-floured surface (dough will be soft). Roll in a 12-in. x 9-in. rectangle. Carefully spread with butter.

Combine cinnamon and remaining sugar; sprinkle over butter. Roll up jelly-roll style, starting with a long side; pinch seam to seal. Cut into 12 pieces and place in a greased 9-in. square baking pan. Cover and let rise until doubled, about 45 minutes. Bake at 375° for 25 minutes.

Meanwhile, for icing, beat all ingredients together in a small mixing bowl until mixture is desired spreading consistency. Frost rolls while still warm. **Yield:** 1 dozen.

Date Nut Bread

1-1/2 cups chopped dates
1-1/2 cups hot water
2 tablespoons butter, softened
2-1/4 cups all-purpose flour
1-1/2 cups sugar

3/4 cup coarsely chopped walnuts
1-1/2 teaspoons baking soda
1-1/2 teaspoons salt
2 eggs, beaten
1-1/2 teaspoons vanilla extract

In a bowl, combine the dates, water and butter; let stand for 5 minutes. In a large bowl, combine the flour, sugar, walnuts, baking soda and salt. Stir in the eggs, vanilla and date mixture just until moistened.

Pour into two greased 8-in. x 4-in. x 2-in. loaf pans. Bake at 375° for 45-50 minutes or until a toothpick inserted near the center comes out clean. Cover loosely with foil if top browns to quickly. Cool for 10 minutes before removing from pans to wire racks. **Yield:** 2 loaves.

Montana Mountain Muffins

4 cups all-purpose flour

4 cups whole bran cereal

1-1/2 cups sugar

1 tablespoon baking soda

4 teaspoons baking powder

2 teaspoons salt

2 cups cold coffee

2 cups milk

6 eggs, beaten

1-1/2 cups vegetable oil

2 teaspoons vanilla extract

2 cups raisins

In a large mixing bowl, stir together the first six ingredients. Combine remaining ingredients. Stir into dry ingredients just until moistened. Cover and refrigerate until ready to bake. Batter will keep for several weeks.

When ready to bake, stir batter and fill greased muffin cups 2/3 full. Bake at 350° for about 20 minutes or until a toothpick inserted near the center comes out clean. Cool for 5 minutes before removing from pans to wire racks. **Yield:** about 5 dozen.

Golden Dinner Rolls

5-1/2 to 6 cups all-purpose flour

1/2 cup sugar

2 packages (1/4 ounce *each*) active dry yeast

1-1/2 teaspoons salt

1 cup milk

2/3 cup water

1/4 cup butter, softened

2 eggs

Melted butter

In a large mixing bowl, combine 2 cups flour, sugar, yeast and salt. In a saucepan, heat the milk, water and butter to 120°-130°. Add to dry ingredients; beat on medium speed for 2 minutes. Add eggs and 3/4 cup flour. Beat on high for 2 minutes. Stir in enough remaining flour to form a stiff dough.

Turn onto a floured surface; knead until smooth and elastic, about 6-8 minutes. Place in a greased bowl, turning once to grease top. Cover and let rest for 20 minutes.

Punch dough down. Turn onto a lightly floured surface; divide into 24 pieces. Shape each into a ball. Place 3 in. apart on greased baking sheets. Brush with melted butter. Cover and refrigerate for 2 to 24 hours. Remove from the refrigerator 15 minutes before baking.

Bake at 350° for 15-20 minutes or until golden brown. Remove from pan to wire racks. **Yield:** 2 dozen.

Caraway Puffs

1 package (1/4 ounce) active dry yeast
1/4 cup warm water (110° to 115°)
1 cup warm cottage cheese (110° to 115°)
1 egg

2 tablespoons sugar
1 tablespoon butter, softened
2 teaspoons caraway seeds
1 teaspoon salt
1/4 teaspoon baking soda
2-1/3 cups all-purpose flour

In a large mixing bowl, dissolve yeast in warm water. Add the cottage cheese, egg, sugar, butter, caraway seeds, salt, baking soda and 1-1/3 cups flour; beat on low speed for 30 seconds. Beat on high for 3 minutes. Stir in the remaining flour (batter will be stiff). Do not knead. Cover and let rise in a warm place until doubled, about 45 minutes. Stir dough down.

Spoon into greased muffin cups. Cover and let rise until doubled, about 35 minutes. Bake at 400° for 12-14 minutes or until golden brown. Cool in pan for 1 minute. Serve immediately. **Yield:** 1 dozen.

Cinnamon Chip Raisin Scones

CINNAMON CHIPS:
3 tablespoons sugar
2 teaspoons shortening
2 teaspoons corn syrup
1 tablespoon ground cinnamon

SCONES:
1-2/3 cups bread or all-purpose flour

2 tablespoons sugar
2 teaspoons baking powder
1/2 teaspoon salt
1/3 cup cold butter
1/2 cup evaporated milk
1/2 cup raisins
Additional evaporated milk

In a bowl, combine the sugar, shortening, corn syrup and cinnamon with a fork until crumbly and evenly blended. Spread onto a foil-lined baking sheet. Bake at 250° for 30-40 minutes or until melted and bubbly. Cool completely; break into small pieces.

In a bowl, combine the flour, sugar, baking powder and salt. Cut in butter until the mixture resembles coarse crumbs. Stir in milk just until moistened. Gently stir in raisins and cinnamon chips.

Turn onto a lightly floured surface. Roll to 1/2-in. thickness; cut with a floured 2-in. biscuit cutter.

Line a baking sheet with foil and grease the foil. Place scones 1 in. apart on foil. Brush tops lightly with additional milk. Bake at 400° for 14-16 minutes or until golden brown. Serve warm. **Yield:** 15 scones.

Cheddar Biscuits

2 cups all-purpose flour
2 teaspoons baking powder
1 teaspoon baking soda
1/2 teaspoon salt
3/4 cup shredded cheddar cheese
1/3 cup shortening
1 cup buttermilk

In a bowl, combine the first four ingredients. Cut in cheese and shortening until crumbly. Add buttermilk; stir until just moistened.

Turn onto a lightly floured surface; knead 8-10 times. Roll out to 1/2-in. thickness; cut with a 2-1/2-in. biscuit cutter. Place on an ungreased baking sheet. Bake at 425° for 10-12 minutes or until golden brown. Serve warm. **Yield:** 16 biscuits.

Bacon Onion Breadsticks

2 tablespoons active dry yeast
2 cups warm milk (110° to 115°), *divided*
1 teaspoon sugar
1/2 cup butter, melted
1-1/4 teaspoons salt, *divided*
5-1/2 to 6 cups all-purpose flour
1 pound sliced bacon, diced
1 medium onion, chopped
1/4 teaspoon pepper
1 egg, beaten
Coarse salt

In a large mixing bowl, dissolve yeast in 1 cup warm milk. Add sugar; let stand for 5 minutes. Add the butter, 1 teaspoon salt and remaining milk; mix well. Stir in enough flour to form a soft dough.

Turn onto a floured surface; knead until smooth and elastic, about 6-8 minutes. Place in a greased bowl, turning once to grease top. Cover and let rise in a warm place until doubled, about 1-1/2 hours.

Meanwhile, in a skillet, cook bacon and onion over medium heat until bacon is crisp; drain. Add pepper and remaining salt. Cool completely. Punch dough down. Turn onto a floured surface; knead bacon mixture into dough. Roll dough into a 14-in. square. Brush with egg; sprinkle with coarse salt. Cut dough in half lengthwise and in thirds crosswise. Cut each section into six strips. Place 2 in. apart on greased baking sheets. Cover and let rise until doubled, about 30 minutes.

Bake at 375° for 15-20 minutes or until golden brown. Remove from pans to wire racks to cool. **Yield:** 3 dozen.

Lemon Blueberry Drop Scones

2 cups all-purpose flour
1/3 cup sugar
2 teaspoons baking powder
1 teaspoon grated lemon peel
1/2 teaspoon baking soda
1/4 teaspoon salt
1 cup (8 ounces) lemon yogurt

1 egg
1/4 cup butter, melted
1 cup fresh *or* frozen blueberries

GLAZE:
1/2 cup confectioners' sugar
1 tablespoon lemon juice
1/2 teaspoon grated lemon peel

In a large bowl, combine the first six ingredients. In another bowl, combine the yogurt, egg and butter. Stir into dry ingredients just until moistened. Fold in blueberries.

Drop by heaping tablespoonfuls 2 in. apart onto a greased baking sheet. Bake at 400° for 15-18 minutes or until lightly browned. Remove from pan to a wire rack. Combine glaze ingredients; drizzle over warm scones. **Yield:** 14 scones.

Editor's Note: If using frozen blueberries, do not thaw before adding to batter.

Bishop's Bread

1 cup sugar
3 eggs
1/2 teaspoon almond extract
1/2 teaspoon vanilla extract
1-1/2 cups all-purpose flour
1-1/2 teaspoons baking powder
1 teaspoon salt
1 cup whole almonds

1 cup chopped walnuts
1 cup chopped dates
1/2 cup *each* red and green maraschino cherries, drained and halved
1 milk chocolate candy bar with almonds (7 ounces), broken into bite-size pieces

In a large mixing bowl, beat the sugar, eggs and extracts. In another bowl, combine the flour, baking powder and salt; stir in the almonds, walnuts, dates, cherries and candy bar. Stir into egg mixture until blended.

Pour into a greased and floured 9-in. x 5-in. x 3-in. loaf pan. Press down firmly to eliminate air spaces. Bake at 300° for 2 hours. Cool for 10 minutes before removing from pan to a wire rack to cool. **Yield:** 1 loaf.

Tomato Bread

2 packages (1/4 ounce *each*) active dry yeast	3 tablespoons sugar
1/4 cup warm water (110° to 115°)	2 tablespoons butter, melted
2 cups warm tomato juice (110° to 115°)	1 teaspoon salt
1/4 cup ketchup	1/2 teaspoon dried basil
1/4 cup grated Parmesan cheese	1/2 teaspoon dried oregano
	6-3/4 to 7-1/4 cups all-purpose flour

In a large mixing bowl, dissolve yeast in warm water. Add the tomato juice, ketchup, Parmesan cheese, sugar, butter, salt, basil, oregano and 3 cups flour. Beat until smooth. Stir in enough remaining flour to form a soft dough.

Turn onto a floured surface; knead until smooth and elastic, about 6-8 minutes. Place in a greased bowl, turning once to grease top. Cover and let rise in a warm place until doubled, about 1 hour.
Punch dough down. Divide in half. Cover and let rest for 10 minutes. Shape into loaves. Place in two greased 9-in. x 5-in. x 3-in. loaf pans. Cover and let rise until doubled, about 45 minutes.

Bake at 375° for 25-30 minutes or until golden brown. Remove from pans to wire racks to cool. **Yield:** 2 loaves.

Sunshine Biscuits

2 cups all-purpose flour	1/2 teaspoon salt
1 cup cornmeal	3/4 cup cold butter
2 tablespoons sugar	1 egg, lightly beaten
4-1/2 teaspoons baking powder	1 cup milk
3/4 teaspoon cream of tartar	

In a bowl, combine the flour, cornmeal, sugar, baking powder, cream of tartar and salt. Cut in butter until mixture resembles coarse crumbs. Combine egg and milk; stir into flour mixture just until moistened. Let stand for 5 minutes.

Turn onto a floured surface; knead for about 1 minute. Pat or roll out to 3/4-in. thickness; cut with a 3-in. biscuit cutter. Place 2 in. apart on a greased baking sheet. Bake at 450° for 10-12 minutes. Serve warm. **Yield:** 1 dozen.

Frosted Cinnamon-Raisin Biscuits

2 cups all-purpose flour
1/4 cup sugar
2 teaspoons baking powder
1 teaspoon salt
1/4 teaspoon baking soda
1/3 cup shortening
2/3 cup buttermilk

1/3 cup raisins
1-1/2 teaspoons ground cinnamon

FROSTING:
1-1/2 cups confectioners' sugar
2 tablespoons butter, softened
1-1/2 teaspoons vanilla extract
3 to 5 teaspoons warm water

In a large bowl, combine the first five ingredients; cut in shortening until mixture resembles coarse crumbs. Stir in buttermilk just until moistened. Turn onto a floured surface; sprinkle with raisins and cinnamon. Knead 8-10 times.

Drop batter into 12 mounds 2 in. apart on a greased baking sheet. Bake at 425° for 12-16 minutes or until golden brown.

For frosting, combine the sugar, butter, vanilla and enough water to achieve desired consistency. Frost warm biscuits. Serve immediately. **Yield:** 1 dozen.

Easy Crescent Rolls

1 package (1/4 ounce) active dry yeast
1 cup warm water (110° to 115°)
3 eggs

4 to 4-1/2 cups all-purpose flour
1/2 cup sugar
1 teaspoon salt
1/2 cup shortening

In a small bowl, dissolve yeast in warm water. In a mixing bowl, beat eggs until light. Add to yeast mixture; set aside. In a large mixing bowl, combine 1 cup flour, sugar and salt. Cut in shortening until mixture resembles coarse crumbs. Stir in yeast mixture. Stir in enough remaining flour until dough leaves the side of the bowl and is soft (dough will be sticky). Do not knead. Cover and refrigerate overnight.

Punch dough down. Turn onto a well-floured surface; divide into thirds. Roll each into a 12-in. circle; cut each circle into 12 wedges. Roll up wedges from wide end and place with pointed end down 2 in. apart on greased baking sheets. Curve ends to form a crescent shape. Cover and let rise in a warm place until doubled, about 45 minutes.

Bake at 375° for 10-12 minutes or until light golden brown. Remove from pans to wire racks. **Yield:** 3 dozen.

Spinach Cheese Muffins

2 cups all-purpose flour
1/4 cup grated Parmesan cheese
2 tablespoons chopped green onions
1 tablespoon baking powder
1/4 teaspoon salt
1 egg

1-1/4 cups milk
1/3 cup butter, melted
1/2 cup chopped fresh spinach *or* 1/4 cup frozen chopped spinach, thawed and well drained
1/2 cup shredded Swiss cheese
Additional Parmesan cheese

In a large bowl, combine the flour, Parmesan cheese, onions, baking powder and salt. In another bowl, beat the egg, milk and butter. Stir into dry ingredients just until moistened. Fold in spinach and Swiss cheese.

Fill greased muffin cups three-fourths full. Sprinkle with additional Parmesan cheese. Bake at 400° for 18-20 minutes or until a toothpick inserted near the center comes out clean. Cool for 5 minutes before removing from pan to a wire rack. Serve warm. Refrigerate leftovers. **Yield:** 1 dozen.

Corn Scones

3-1/2 cups all-purpose flour
2 tablespoons baking powder
1 teaspoon ground mustard
1/2 teaspoon salt
3/4 cup cold butter

1-1/2 cups (6 ounces *each*) shredded cheddar cheese
1 can (15 ounces) cream-style corn
2 eggs, lightly beaten
2 tablespoons milk

In a medium bowl, combine the flour, baking powder, mustard and salt. Cut in butter until mixture resembles coarse crumbs. Stir in cheese, corn and eggs until a soft dough forms.

Turn onto a floured surface, gently knead 10-12 times or until dough is no longer sticky. Roll out to 1-in. thickness; cut with a 2-1/2-in. or 3-in. cutter.

Place on an ungreased baking sheet. Brush with milk. Bake at 425° for 20-25 minutes or until golden brown. Serve warm. **Yield:** 10-15 scones.

Almond Apricot Bread

2-1/2 cups all-purpose flour
1/2 cup sugar
1/2 cup packed brown sugar
3 teaspoons baking powder
1 teaspoon salt
2 jars (4 ounces *each*) apricot baby food, *divided*
1 egg
3/4 cup milk

3 tablespoons vegetable oil
1 teaspoon almond extract
2/3 cup sliced almonds, coarsely chopped
1/2 cup diced dried apricots

GLAZE:
1/2 cup confectioners' sugar
1 teaspoon milk
1/8 teaspoon almond extract

In a large bowl, combine the flour, sugars, baking powder and salt. Set aside 1 tablespoon baby food for glaze. In another bowl, beat the egg, milk, oil, extract and remaining baby food. Stir into dry ingredients just until moistened. Fold in almonds and apricots.

Pour into a greased 9-in. x 5-in. x 3-in. loaf pan. Bake at 350° for 55-65 minutes or until a toothpick inserted near the center comes out clean. Cool for 10 minutes before removing from the pan to a wire rack.

For glaze, combine the confectioners' sugar, milk, extract and reserved baby food until smooth. Drizzle over cooled bread. **Yield:** 1 loaf.

Chocolate Chip Pumpkin Bread

2/3 cup butter, softened
1 cup packed brown sugar
1 cup sugar
3 eggs
2-1/3 cups all-purpose flour
1-1/2 cups canned pumpkin

1/2 cup water
2 teaspoons baking soda
1 teaspoon ground cinnamon
1 teaspoon salt
1/2 teaspoon ground cloves
2 cups (12 ounces) semisweet chocolate chips

In a mixing bowl, cream butter, sugars and eggs. Add the flour, pumpkin, water, baking soda, cinnamon, salt and cloves. Mix thoroughly. Fold in chocolate chips.

Pour into four greased and floured 5-3/4-in. x 3-in. x 2-in. loaf pans. Bake at 350° for 45 minutes or until a toothpick inserted near the center comes out clean. Cool for 10 minutes before removing from pans to wire racks to cool. **Yield:** 4 mini loaves.

Rose's Apple Turnover Coffee Cake

FILLING:
- 1/3 cup butter
- 4 baking apples, peeled and sliced 1/2 inch thick
- 3/4 cup sugar
- 1 teaspoon grated lemon peel
- 1/2 teaspoon ground cinnamon
- 1/8 teaspoon ground mace
- 1/3 cup dried currants

DOUGH:
- 2-1/2 cups all-purpose flour, *divided*
- 3 tablespoons sugar
- 1/2 teaspoon salt
- 1 package (1/4 ounce) active dry yeast
- 3/4 cup water
- 1/3 cup butter
- 1 egg
- 1 teaspoon grated lemon peel

TOPPING:
- 3/4 cup chopped pecans
- 6 tablespoons all-purpose flour
- 1/4 cup confectioners' sugar
- 3 tablespoons butter, melted
- 1/4 teaspoon ground cinnamon

In a large saucepan, melt butter over medium heat. Add apples and cook and stir for about 8 minutes or until just tender. Stir in remaining filling ingredients. Cook 10-15 minutes, stirring until thickened. Remove from the heat; cool.

For dough, in a large mixing bowl, combine 1 cup flour, sugar, salt and yeast. In a small saucepan, combine water and butter; heat over low heat until temperature reaches 120°. Gradually add to dry ingredients; beat for 2 minutes. Beat in the egg, lemon peel and 3/4 cup flour. With mixer at high speed, beat 2 minutes. Stir in remaining flour. Cover and let stand for 20 minutes.

Meanwhile, combine topping ingredients in a small bowl; set aside. Turn dough onto a well-floured surface; divide dough in half. Using a floured rolling pin, roll each half to a 14-in. x 12-in. rectangle. Place on greased baking sheets. Spread filling down center of dough to within 1 in. of ends. On each long side, cut 1-wide strips about 3/4 in. from filling. Starting at one end, fold alternating strips at an angle across filling. Fold ends over filling. Loosely cover dough with greased waxed paper; cover paper with plastic wrap. Refrigerate at least 2 hours.

When ready to bake, uncover and let stand at room temperature for 10 minutes. Sprinkle topping over coffee cake. Bake at 375° for 30-35 minutes or until lightly browned. Remove from baking sheets to wire racks to cool. **Yield:** 2 coffee cakes (16-20 servings).

Honey White Loaves

2 packages (1/4 ounce *each*) active dry yeast
2-1/2 cups warm water (110° to 115°)
1/2 cup butter, melted

1/2 cup honey
2 eggs
1 tablespoon salt
8 to 9 cups all-purpose flour

In a large mixing bowl, dissolve yeast in warm water. Add the butter, honey, eggs, salt and 4 cups flour. Beat on low speed for 30 seconds. Beat on medium for 3 minutes. Stir in enough remaining flour to form a soft dough.

Turn onto a floured surface; knead until smooth and elastic, about 8 minutes. Place in a greased bowl, turning once to grease top. Cover and let rise in a warm place until doubled; about 1 hour.

Punch dough down. Turn onto a lightly floured surface; divide into thirds. Shape into loaves. Place in three greased 8-in. x 4-in. x 2-in. loaf pans. Cover and let rise until doubled, about 30 minutes.

Bake at 375° for 25-30 minutes or until golden brown. Remove from pans to wire racks to cool. **Yield:** 3 loaves.

Sweet Potato Biscuits

1-1/2 cups self-rising flour
2 teaspoons brown sugar
1/3 cup shortening
1 egg

1/2 cup mashed cooked sweet potatoes (without added butter *or* milk)
2 tablespoons milk

In a bowl, combine flour and brown sugar; cut in shortening until mixture resembles coarse crumbs. In another bowl, beat egg; add sweet potatoes and milk. Stir in crumb mixture just until moistened.

Turn onto a floured surface knead 10-12 times or until smooth. Roll dough to 1/2-in. thickness. Cut with a 2-1/2-in. biscuit cutter; place on an ungreased baking sheet.

Bake at 425° for 10-12 minutes or until bottoms are lightly browned. Serve warm. **Yield:** 10 biscuits.

Editor's Note: As a substitute for 1-1/2 cups self-rising flour, place 2-1/4 teaspoons baking powder and 3/4 teaspoon salt in a measuring cup. Add all-purpose flour to measure 1 cup. Combine with an additional 1/2 cup all-purpose flour.

Ginger Yeast Muffins

1 package (1/4 ounce) active dry yeast
1 cup warm water (110° to 115°)
3 cups all-purpose flour
1 cup shortening
1-1/2 cups sugar
3 eggs
1/2 cup molasses
2 teaspoons ground cinnamon
1 teaspoon salt
1/2 teaspoon baking soda
1/2 teaspoon ground ginger
1/2 cup chopped walnuts

In a small mixing bowl, dissolve yeast in warm water. Add 1-1/2 cups flour; beat until smooth. Cover and let rise in a warm place for 30 minutes.

In another mixing bowl, cream shortening and sugar. Add eggs, one at a time, beating well after each addition. Beat in molasses until smooth. Add the yeast mixture. Combine cinnamon, salt, baking soda, ginger and remaining flour; gradually add to egg mixture. Stir in nuts.

Fill greased or paper-lined muffin cups two-thirds full. Bake at 350° for 20-25 minutes or until a toothpick inserted near the center comes out clean. Cool for 5 minutes before removing from pans to wire racks. **Yield:** 2 dozen.

Zucchini Snack Bread

3 cups all-purpose flour
2-1/4 teaspoons ground cinnamon
1-1/4 teaspoons salt
1 teaspoon baking soda
1/4 teaspoon baking powder
1/4 teaspoon ground nutmeg
3 eggs
2 cups sugar
1 cup vegetable oil
1 tablespoon vanilla extract
2 cups shredded zucchini
1 cup chopped walnuts

Combine the flour, cinnamon, salt, baking soda, baking powder and nutmeg; set aside. In a mixing bowl, lightly beat eggs; stir in sugar, oil and vanilla. Add dry ingredients; stir just until moistened. Fold in zucchini and nuts; mix well (batter will be stiff).

Transfer to two greased and floured 8-in. x 4-in. x 2-in. loaf pans. Bake at 350° for 50-60 minutes or until a toothpick inserted near the center comes out clean. Cool for 10 minutes before removing from pans to wire racks. **Yield:** 2 loaves.

Cornmeal Cinnamon Rolls

2 cups milk
1/2 cup cornmeal
1/2 cup sugar
1/2 cup butter
1 tablespoon salt
2 packages (1/4 ounce *each*)
  active dry yeast
1/2 cup warm water (110° to 115°)
3 eggs, beaten
6-1/2 to 7 cups all-purpose flour

FILLING:
1-1/4 cups raisins
2 tablespoons butter, melted
3/4 cup sugar
2 teaspoons ground cinnamon
Pinch ground nutmeg, optional

FROSTING:
3-1/2 cups confectioners' sugar
2 tablespoons butter, softened
2 tablespoons cream cheese,
  softened
1/2 teaspoon almond extract
4 to 5 tablespoons milk

In a saucepan, combine milk and cornmeal. Bring to a boil over medium heat, stirring constantly. Add the sugar, butter and salt; cool to 110°-115°.

In a large mixing bowl, dissolve yeast in warm water. Add the eggs, cornmeal mixture and 2 cups flour; beat until smooth. Stir in enough remaining flour to form a soft dough.

Turn onto a floured surface; knead until smooth and elastic, about 6-8 minutes. Place in a greased bowl, turning once to grease top. Cover and let rise in a warm place until doubled, about 1 hour.

Meanwhile, place raisins in a saucepan and cover with water. Bring to a boil; remove from the heat. Cover and let stand for 15 minutes. Drain; set aside. Punch dough down. Turn onto a lightly floured surface; divide in half. Roll each into a 12-in. x 10-in. rectangle; brush with melted butter.

Combine sugar, cinnamon and nutmeg if desired; sprinkle over dough to within 1/2 in. of edges. Sprinkle with raisins. Roll up jelly-roll style, starting with a long side; pinch seam to seal. Cut each into 12 slices. Place cut side down in two greased 13-in. x 9-in. x 2-in. baking pans. Cover and let rise until doubled, about 1 hour. Bake at 375° for 20-25 minutes or until golden brown. Cool in pans on wire racks.

For frosting, combine the sugar, butter, cream cheese, extract and enough milk to achieve desired consistency. Spread or drizzle over rolls. Refrigerate leftovers. **Yield:** 2 dozen.

Wholesome Quick Bread

1 cup mashed ripe bananas
3/4 cup sugar
1/3 cup unsweetened applesauce
1/2 cup egg substitute
1 teaspoon vanilla extract
2 cups whole wheat flour
1/4 cup quick-cooking oats
1 teaspoon baking powder
1 teaspoon baking soda

1 teaspoon ground cinnamon
1/4 teaspoon ground nutmeg
3/4 cup buttermilk

TOPPING:
1/3 cup chopped pecans
2 tablespoons brown sugar
2 tablespoons quick-cooking oats
1/2 teaspoon ground cinnamon
1/4 teaspoon ground nutmeg

In a mixing bowl, combine the bananas, sugar and applesauce. Add egg substitute and vanilla; mix well. Combine the flour, oats, baking powder, baking soda, cinnamon and nutmeg; add to banana mixture alternately with buttermilk. Pour into two 8-in. x 4-in. x 2-in. loaf pans coated with nonstick cooking spray.

Combine topping ingredients; sprinkle over top. Bake at 350° for 55-60 minutes or until a toothpick inserted in the center comes out clean. Cool for 10 minutes before removing from pans to a wire rack to cool completely. **Yield:** 2 loaves (16 slices each).

Lemon-Raspberry Muffins

2 cups all-purpose flour
1 cup sugar
1 tablespoon baking powder
1/2 teaspoon salt
2 eggs, lightly beaten

1 cup buttermilk
1/2 cup vegetable oil
1 teaspoon lemon extract
1 cup fresh *or* frozen raspberries

In a large bowl, combine the flour, sugar, baking powder and salt. In a small bowl, whisk together the eggs, buttermilk, oil and lemon extract. Stir into flour mixture just until moistened. Fold in raspberries.

Fill greased or paper-lined muffin cups two-thirds full. Bake at 400° for 20-22 minutes or until center of muffin springs back when lightly touched. Cool for 5 minutes before removing from pans to wire racks. **Yield:** 15 muffins.

Editor's Note: If using frozen raspberries, do not thaw before adding to batter.

Danish Coffee Cake

1 package (1/4 ounce) active dry yeast
2 tablespoons plus 1 teaspoon sugar, *divided*
1/4 cup warm water (110° to 115°)
2-1/2 cups all-purpose flour
1/2 teaspoon salt
1/2 cup cold butter
1 egg, lightly beaten
1/2 cup heavy whipping cream

FILLING:
1 can (8 ounces) almond paste, cubed
1/4 cup packed brown sugar
1/4 cup butter, softened
1 egg
1 teaspoon water

GLAZE:
1 cup confectioners' sugar
1/4 teaspoon almond extract
2 to 3 tablespoons milk
Sliced almonds

In a small bowl, dissolve yeast and 1 teaspoon sugar in warm water; set aside. Combine the flour, salt and remaining sugar in a large bowl; cut in butter until the mixture resembles coarse crumbs. Add egg and cream to yeast mixture. Add to flour mixture; stir to form a stiff dough. Divide in half; cover and refrigerate for 3 hours.

In a mixing bowl, beat the almond paste, brown sugar and butter until smooth. On a lightly floured surface, roll each portion of dough into a 15-in. x 6-in. rectangle. Spread filling down center third of dough to within 1/2 in of edges. Beat egg and water; brush over edges of dough. Fold sides over filling; seal seam and edges. Place seam side down on greased baking sheets. Cut five to six small slits in top. Cover and let rise in a warm place for 30 minutes.

Bake at 375° for 20-25 minutes or until golden brown. Cool completely.

For glaze, combine confectioners' sugar, extract and enough milk to achieve desired consistency; drizzle over coffee cakes. Sprinkle with almonds. **Yield:** 2 coffee cakes (10-12 servings each).

Main Attractions

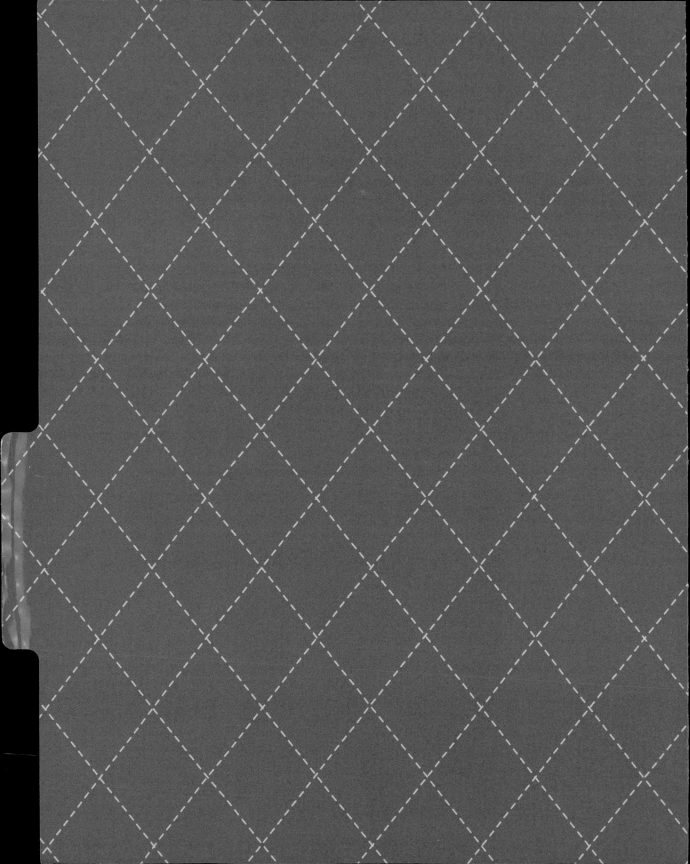

Beef

Stuffed Pizza

CRUST:
- 1 tablespoon sugar
- 2 packages (1/4 ounce *each*) active dry yeast
- 1-1/4 cups warm water (110° to 115°)
- 3-1/4 cups all-purpose flour
- 1 tablespoon salt
- 1/4 cup vegetable oil

MEAT FILLING:
- 1 pound ground beef
- 1 medium onion, chopped
- 1 can (2-1/4 ounces) sliced ripe olives, drained
- 1 can (4 ounces) sliced mushrooms, drained
- 1 package (10 ounces) frozen chopped spinach, thawed and well drained
- 2 cups (8 ounces) shredded part-skim mozzarella cheese
- 1 jar (32 ounces) spaghetti sauce

For crust, dissolve sugar and yeast in warm water; set aside. In a large mixing bowl, combine flour and salt. Stir in yeast mixture and oil; mix until dough forms a ball. Turn onto a lightly floured surface; knead for 6-8 minutes or until smooth. Place in a greased bowl, turning once to grease top. Cover and let rise in a warm place until doubled, about 1 hour.

Meanwhile, for filling, cook ground beef and onion in a skillet over medium heat until meat is no longer pink; drain and cool. Stir in the olives, mushrooms, spinach and cheese; set aside.

Punch dough down. Divide into two pieces, one slightly larger than the other. Roll out the larger piece into a 15-in. circle. Press into the bottom and up the sides of a greased 12-in. deep-dish pizza pan. Cover with meat mixture. Roll out remaining dough into a 12-in. circle; place over meat mixture. Crimp edges of crusts together to seal; gently press top crust onto meat filling. Cut a 1-in. slit in center of crust. Spread spaghetti sauce over top crust.

Bake at 475° for 35-40 minutes or until lightly browned. **Yield:** 10-12 servings.

Taco Crescents

3/4 pound ground beef
1/4 cup chopped onion
1 package (1-1/4-ounces) taco seasoning
1 can (4-1/4-ounces) chopped ripe olives, drained
2 eggs, lightly beaten
1/2 cup shredded cheddar cheese
2 tubes (8 ounces) refrigerated crescent rolls

In a skillet, cook beef and onion over medium heat until no longer pink; drain. Add taco seasoning and olives; mix well and set aside to cool. Add eggs and cheese; mix well.

On a baking sheet, separate dough. Place 2 tablespoons meat mixture on each triangle. Roll and shape into crescents. Bake at 375° for 10-15 minutes or until lightly browned. **Yield:** 8 servings.

Zucchini Lasagna

1 pound ground beef
1 medium onion, chopped
1 can (15 ounces) tomato sauce
1/2 teaspoon salt
1/2 teaspoon dried oregano
1/4 teaspoon dried basil
Dash pepper
4 medium zucchini, cut lengthwise into 1/4-inch strips
2 tablespoons all-purpose flour, *divided*
1 cup small-curd cottage cheese
1 egg
1 cup (4 ounces) shredded part-skim mozzarella cheese
1/2 cup grated Parmesan cheese

In a skillet, cook beef and onion over medium heat until meat is no longer pink; drain. Stir in the tomato sauce, salt, oregano, basil and pepper. Bring to a boil. Reduce heat; simmer, uncovered, for 10 minutes, stirring occasionally.

In a greased 11-in. x 7-in. x 2-in. baking dish, layer half of the zucchini; sprinkle with 1 tablespoon flour. In a bowl, combine the cottage cheese and egg. Spread over zucchini. Layer with half of the meat mixture, remaining zucchini and remaining flour. Top with mozzarella cheese and the remaining meat mixture. Sprinkle with Parmesan cheese.

Bake, uncovered, at 375° for 40 minutes or until heated through. Let stand for 5-10 minutes before serving. **Yield:** 4-6 servings.

Curried Meat Loaf

1 egg, beaten
1/3 cup milk
1/2 cup dry bread crumbs *or*
   old-fashioned oats
1 garlic clove, minced
1 to 2 teaspoons curry powder

1 teaspoon ground cumin
1/2 teaspoon salt
1/2 teaspoon pepper
1 cup shredded carrots
1 medium onion, chopped
1-1/2 pounds lean ground beef

In a large bowl, combine egg, milk, bread crumbs or oats, garlic, curry powder, cumin, salt, pepper, carrots and onion. Crumble beef over mixture and mix well.

Pat meat mixture into an 8-in. x 4-in. x 2-in. loaf pan. Bake at 350° for 1-1/4 hours or until a meat thermometer reads 160°. **Yield:** 6-8 servings.

Cabbage Rolls

1 medium head cabbage
1-1/2 pounds lean ground beef
1/2 cup uncooked instant rice
1/2 cup finely minced onion
1 egg, lightly beaten
1 teaspoon salt
1/2 teaspoon garlic powder
1/2 teaspoon pepper

SAUCE:
1 can (8 ounces) tomato sauce
1/3 cup ketchup
2 tablespoons brown sugar
2 tablespoons white vinegar
1/4 teaspoon salt
1/4 teaspoon pepper

Remove core from the cabbage. Place cabbage in a large saucepan and cover with water. Bring to a boil; after about 3 minutes, outer leaves should be softened enough to remove. Return to a boil; reduce heat and simmer until leaves are tender, about 10-15 minutes. Cut out the thick vein from the bottom of each leaf, making a V-shaped cut. (If leaves for rolling are too stiff, return to boiling water for 1-2 minutes.)

Combine the meat, rice, onion, egg and seasonings; mix well. Place about 2 tablespoons of meat mixture on each cabbage leaf; overlap cut ends of leaf. Fold in sides, beginning from the cut end. Roll up completely to enclose filling. Use extra leaves to line a large baking dish. Place rolls seam side down over leaves in baking dish.

Combine all sauce ingredients; pour over rolls. Cover and bake at 350° for 1-1/2 to 1-3/4 hours or until a meat thermometer reads 160° in filling. **Yield:** 6-8 servings.

Tenderloin Diane

Salt and pepper to taste
- 1 teaspoon ground mustard
- 1 pound beef tenderloin, cut into 8 slices
- 2 tablespoons butter
- 2 tablespoons sliced green onions
- 1 tablespoon lemon juice
- 2 teaspoons Worcestershire sauce

Rub salt, pepper and mustard onto both sides of the beef. In a large skillet, melt butter over medium-high heat; add beef. Cook until meat reaches desired doneness, 2 minutes on each side for medium-rare.

Remove to a serving platter; keep warm. Add the onions, lemon juice and Worcestershire sauce to the pan drippings; cook and stir for 1 minute. Spoon over meat. **Yield:** 4 servings.

Manicotti

- 1 pound ground beef
- 1/4 cup chopped onion
- 1/4 cup chopped green pepper
- 1 teaspoon salt
- 1/4 teaspoon pepper
- 1 tablespoon chopped fresh parsley
- 1 can (4 ounces) mushroom stems and pieces, drained
- 1 egg, beaten
- 1/4 cup milk
- 1/2 cup seasoned dry bread crumbs
- 8 ounces manicotti (14 tubes) manicotti, cooked and drained
- 1 jar (32 ounces) spaghetti sauce, *divided*
- 1 cup (4 ounces) shredded process cheese (Velveeta)

In a skillet, cook the beef, onion, green pepper, salt and pepper over medium heat until meat is no longer pink and vegetables are tender; drain. Stir in the parsley, mushrooms, egg, milk and bread crumbs; mix well.

Stuff filling into manicotti shells. Pour half of spaghetti sauce into a greased 13-in. x 9-in. x 2-in. baking dish. Place shells on sauce; top with remaining sauce.

Cover and bake at 350° for 25-30 minutes. Uncover; sprinkle with cheese. Bake 5 minutes longer or until cheese is melted. **Yield:** 6-8 servings.

Sausage-Stuffed French Loaf

1 loaf (1 pound) French bread
1/2 pound ground beef
1/2 pound bulk pork sausage
1 medium onion, chopped
1 cup (4 ounces) shredded
  part-skim mozzarella cheese
1 egg, beaten

1/4 cup chopped fresh parsley
1 teaspoon Dijon mustard
1/4 teaspoon pepper
1/4 teaspoon salt
1/8 teaspoon fennel seed
2 tablespoons butter
1 garlic clove, minced

Cut a thin slice off the top of the bread. Hollow out bottom half, leaving a 1/4-in. shell. In a food processor or blender, process bread crumbs until coarse; set aside 1 cup. (Discard remaining crumbs or save for another use.)

In a skillet, cook the beef, sausage and onion over medium heat until meat is no longer pink; drain. Stir in the cheese, egg, parsley, mustard, pepper, salt, fennel and reserved crumbs; mix well. Spoon into bread shell; replace bread top. Place on a large sheet of heavy-duty foil.

In a small saucepan, melt butter; add garlic and cook for 1 minute. Brush over tops and sides of loaf. Wrap foil around loaf and seal. Bake at 400° for 20 minutes or until cheese is melted. **Yield:** 6-8 servings.

Spiced Pot Roast

1/3 cup all-purpose flour
1 teaspoon salt
1/4 teaspoon pepper
1 boneless beef rump *or* chuck
  roast (3 pounds)
2 tablespoons vegetable oil
1-1/2 cups beef broth

1/2 cup chutney
1/2 cup raisins
1/2 cup chopped onion
1-1/2 teaspoons curry powder
1/2 teaspoon garlic powder
1/2 teaspoon ground ginger

Combine the flour, salt and pepper; rub over entire roast. In a Dutch oven, brown roast in oil on all sides. Combine remaining ingredients and pour over roast.

Cover and bake at 325° for 2-1/2 to 3 hours or until meat is tender. Thicken gravy if desired. **Yield:** 6-8 servings.

Baked Spaghetti

2 pounds ground beef
2 medium onions, chopped
2 cans (one 15 ounces, one 8 ounces) tomato sauce
1 can (8 ounces) sliced mushrooms, drained
1 teaspoon garlic powder
1 teaspoon dried oregano
2 packages (7 ounces *each*) uncooked spaghetti
1 package (8 ounces) cream cheese, softened
2 cups small-curd cottage cheese
1/2 cup sour cream
2 tablespoons minced chives
1/4 cup bread crumbs
1-1/2 teaspoons butter, melted

In a large skillet, cook beef and onions over medium heat until meat is no longer pink; drain. Add the tomato sauce, mushrooms, garlic powder and oregano. Bring to a boil. Reduce heat; simmer, uncovered, for 15 minutes, stirring occasionally. Meanwhile, cook the spaghetti according to package directions; drain.

In a mixing bowl, combine the cream cheese, cottage cheese, sour cream and chives; beat well. Place half of the spaghetti in a greased 4-qt. baking dish. Spoon cream cheese mixture evenly over top. Layer with remaining spaghetti and all of the beef mixture.

Toss bread crumbs and butter; sprinkle over the top. Cover and bake at 350° for 20 minutes. Uncover; bake 5-10 minutes longer until heated through. **Yield:** 12 servings.

Golden Broccoli Bake

1 pound ground beef, cooked and drained
1 can (10-3/4 ounces) condensed cream of mushroom soup, undiluted
1 package (10 ounces) frozen chopped broccoli, thawed
1 egg
2 cups (8 ounces) shredded cheddar cheese, *divided*
2 cups hot mashed potatoes (prepared with milk and butter)

In a bowl, combine the first four ingredients. Stir in 1 cup cheese. Transfer to a greased 11-in. x 7-in. x 2-in. baking dish.

In a bowl, combine potatoes with remaining cheese. Spread over the meat mixture. Bake, uncovered, at 350° for 30 minutes or until lightly browned. **Yield:** 6 servings.

Sirloin with Bernaise Sauce

1/2 teaspoon garlic salt
1/2 teaspoon pepper
1 boneless beef sirloin roast
(5 to 6 pounds)

BERNAISE SAUCE:
1/4 cup white wine vinegar
1/2 cup chopped green onions
1 tablespoon minced fresh
tarragon *or* 1 teaspoon dried
tarragon

1/4 teaspoon pepper
4 egg yolks, lightly beaten
1 tablespoon cold water
1/4 teaspoon salt
1/8 teaspoon cayenne pepper
3/4 cup cold butter
1 tablespoon minced fresh
parsley

Combine garlic salt and pepper; rub over roast. Place on a rack in a shallow roasting pan. Bake, uncovered, at 325° for 2-1/4 to 3-1/4 hours or until meat reaches desired doneness (for medium-rare, a meat thermometer should read 145°; medium, 160°; well-done, 170°). Let stand for 10-15 minutes before slicing.

Meanwhile, in a saucepan, combine the vinegar, onions, tarragon and pepper; bring to a boil. Strain, reserving liquid; discard onions and tarragon. Place egg yolks in a heavy saucepan. Gradually whisk in the water, vinegar mixture, salt and cayenne. Cook until the mixture begins to thicken, stirring constantly. Add butter, 1 tablespoon at a time, until the mixture has thickened and reaches 160°, stirring constantly. Remove from the heat; stir in parsley. Serve warm with sliced beef. **Yield:** 12 servings.

Perfect Prime Rib Roast

1/4 cup Worcestershire sauce
1-1/2 teaspoons garlic salt
1-1/2 teaspoons seasoned salt

1-1/2 teaspoons coarsely ground
pepper
1 bone-in beef rib roast (5 to 6
pounds)

In a small bowl, combine the first four ingredients; rub over the roast. Place in a large resealable plastic bag; seal and refrigerate overnight, turning often.

Place roast fat side up in a large roasting pan; pour marinade over roast. Tent with foil. Bake at 350° for 1 hour. Uncover; bake 1-1/2 hours longer or until meat reaches desired doneness (for medium-rare, a meat thermometer should read 145°; medium, 160°; well-done, 170°). Let stand for 10-15 minutes before slicing. **Yield:** 8-10 servings.

Classic Meat Loaf

1/2 cup milk
3 slices whole wheat *or* white bread, cubed
1 egg, beaten
1 medium onion, chopped
2 tablespoons chili sauce

2 teaspoons Worcestershire sauce
1 teaspoon salt
1/2 teaspoon pepper
2 to 5 drops hot pepper sauce
2 pounds lean ground beef

In a large bowl, pour milk over bread. Add the egg, onion, chili sauce, Worcestershire sauce, salt, pepper and hot pepper sauce; mix thoroughly. Crumble beef over mixture and mix well. Shape meat mixture into an 8-1/2-in. x 4-1/2-in. loaf.

Bake in a shallow pan at 350° for 1-1/4 hours or until a meat thermometer reads 160°. Drain. **Yield:** 8-10 servings.

Stuffed Sirloin Roast

9 bacon strips, *divided*
1 medium onion, chopped
3/4 cup chopped celery
1 large carrot, chopped
1/3 cup dry bread crumbs

2 teaspoons dried parsley flakes
1/4 teaspoon garlic powder
1/8 teaspoon pepper
1 boneless beef sirloin tip roast (3 to 4 pounds)

In a large skillet, cook six bacon strips over medium heat until crisp. Remove to paper towels; drain, reserving 3 tablespoons drippings. Crumble bacon and set aside. Saute the onion, celery and carrot in reserved drippings until crisp-tender. Remove from the heat; stir in the bread crumbs, parsley, garlic powder, pepper and crumbled bacon. Let stand until the liquid is absorbed.

Cut a lengthwise slit down the center of the roast to within 1/2 in. of bottom. Open roast so it lies flat; cover with plastic wrap. Flatten to 1-in. thickness. Remove plastic; spread stuffing over meat to within 1 in. of edges. Close roast and tie at 1-in. intervals with kitchen string.

Place on a rack in a shallow roasting pan. Cut remaining bacon strips in half; arrange over top of roast. Bake, uncovered, at 325° for 1-1/2 to 2 hours or until meat reached desired doneness (for medium-rare, a meat thermometer should read 145°; medium, 160°; well-done, 170°). Let stand for 10 minutes before slicing. **Yield:** 10-14 servings.

Frank's Sauerbraten

3 cups white vinegar
6 bay leaves
8 whole cloves
20 whole peppercorns
2 slices onion
2 tablespoons sugar
4 teaspoons salt
2 garlic cloves, peeled and halved
1 beef pot roast (4 to 5 pounds)
2 to 4 tablespoons vegetable oil
6 to 12 gingersnaps, crushed
Noodles *or* dumplings

In a large saucepan, combine the vinegar, bay leaves, cloves, peppercorns, onion, sugar, salt and garlic. Bring to a boil; cool to room temperature.

Place pot roast in a large glass bowl. Pour half of marinade over roast, adding enough water to cover roast. Cover and refrigerate remaining marinade. Cover and refrigerate roast for 36-48 hours, turning twice a day.

Discard marinade from roast and pat it dry. In a Dutch oven, heat the oil and brown roast on all sides. Add reserved marinade to pan; cover and simmer for 3 hours or until roast is tender.

Remove the roast; discard the bay leaves, peppercorns and cloves from pan juices. Bring juices to a boil. Add gingersnaps; cook and stir until thickened. Serve with noodles or dumplings. **Yield:** 8 servings.

Tater-Topped Casserole

1-1/2 pounds ground beef
1 package (16 ounces) frozen vegetables, thawed
1 can (2.8 ounces) french-fried onions
1/4 cup butter
1 can (10-3/4 ounces) condensed cream of celery soup, undiluted
1 can (10-3/4 ounces) condensed cream of chicken soup, undiluted
1/2 cup milk
1 package (16 ounces) frozen Tater Tots, thawed

In a large skillet, cook beef over medium heat until no longer pink; drain. In a greased 13-in. x 9-in. x 2-in. baking pan, layer the beef, vegetables and onions. Dot with butter. In a bowl, combine soups and milk; spread over vegetables. Top with Tater Tots. Bake, uncovered, at 350° for 1 hour or until golden brown. **Yield:** 6-8 servings.

Taco Rice

1 pound ground beef
1 medium onion, chopped
1 jar (16 ounces) salsa
1 can (15 ounces) tomato sauce
1 chicken bouillon cube

1-1/2 cups instant rice, cooked
Tortilla chips
Optional toppings: shredded cheddar
    cheese, kidney beans, sour cream,
    sliced ripe olives

In a skillet, cook beef and onion over medium heat until meat is no longer pink; drain. Add the salsa, tomato sauce and bouillon. Bring to a boil. Reduce heat; cover and simmer for 5 minutes. Stir in rice. Cover and simmer for 30 minutes or until rice is tender. Serve with tortilla chips and toppings of your choice. **Yield:** 4 servings.

Sweet and Spicy Steak

3 bunches green onions with
    tops
1-1/2 pounds boneless beef sirloin
    steak, cut into 1/2-inch cubes
1 tablespoon vegetable oil

1/2 cup molasses
1 teaspoon salt
1/4 teaspoon cayenne pepper
Hot cooked rice

Cut onions into 3-in. pieces; cut white portion in half lengthwise. Set aside.
    In a large skillet or wok, stir-fry beef in oil for 4-5 minutes. Add the onions, molasses, salt and cayenne. Stir-fry for 5 minutes or until heated through. Serve over rice. **Yield:** 6 servings.

Brisket with Gingersnap Gravy

1 beef brisket (about 5 pounds)
1 cup water
3/4 cup chili sauce

1 envelope onion soup mix
5 to 6 gingersnaps, crushed

Place brisket in a roasting pan. In a bowl, combine the water, chili sauce and soup mix; pour over meat. Cover and bake at 325° for 2-1/2 to 3 hours or until tender. Cool; cover and refrigerate overnight.
    Remove meat and cut into 1/4-in.-thick slices; return to the pan. Sprinkle with gingersnap crumbs. Cover and bake at 350° for 30-45 minutes or until heated through. **Yield:** 16-18 servings.
    Editor's Note: This is a fresh beef brisket, not corned beef.

Company Casserole

3 medium carrots, cut into 1-inch pieces
2 celery ribs, chopped
1 medium onion, sliced and separated into rings
1 can (14-1/2 ounces) whole tomatoes, drained
1 cup beef broth
1 can (8 ounces) sliced water chestnuts, drained
1 can (4 ounces) mushroom stems and pieces, drained
3 tablespoons quick-cooking tapioca
1 tablespoon sugar
1 teaspoon salt
2 pounds lean ground beef
Hot cooked rice *or* noodles

In a bowl, combine the first 10 ingredients. Crumble beef over mixture; toss gently. Transfer to a greased 13-in. x 9-in. x 2-in. baking dish. Cover and bake at 350° for 2 hours or until hot and bubbly. Serve over rice or noodles. **Yield:** 8 servings.

Southwestern Deep-Dish Pizza

2-1/2 cups biscuit/baking mix
1/2 cup cornmeal
3/4 cup water
1 pound ground beef
1 medium onion, diced
1 can (8 ounces) tomato sauce
2 teaspoons chili powder
1 teaspoon ground cinnamon
1 can (16 ounces) refried beans
Hot pepper sauce to taste
2 cups (8 ounces) shredded Monterey Jack *or* cheddar cheese
Salsa and sliced ripe olives, optional

In a bowl, combine biscuit mix and cornmeal. Stir in water until mixture forms a soft dough. Press onto the bottom and up the sides of a lightly greased 15-in. x 10-in. x 1-in. baking pan. Bake at 425° for 10 minutes or until lightly browned.

Meanwhile, in a skillet, cook beef and onion over medium heat until meat is no longer pink; drain. Add the tomato sauce, chili powder and cinnamon. Bring to a boil. Reduce heat; simmer, uncovered, for 5 minutes. Remove from the heat.

Combine refried beans and hot pepper sauce; spread over crust. Top with meat mixture; sprinkle with cheese. Bake at 425° for 10 minutes or until cheese is melted. Let stand for 10 minutes before cutting. Serve with salsa and olives if desired. **Yield:** 16 servings.

Stuffed Acorn Squash

2 large acorn squash, halved and seeded
1 cup water
3/4 pound ground beef
1 celery rib, chopped
1 small onion, chopped
1 medium tart apple, chopped
1 cup cooked rice
1/4 cup sunflower kernels
1 teaspoon curry powder
1 egg, beaten
5 teaspoons brown sugar, *divided*
1-1/2 teaspoons salt, *divided*
4 teaspoons butter

Invert squash in an ungreased 13-in. x 9-in. x 2-in. baking dish. Add water and cover with foil. Bake at 375° for 50-60 minutes or until tender.

Meanwhile, cook the beef, celery and onion over medium heat until meat is no longer pink and vegetables are tender; drain. Add the apple, rice, sunflower kernels and curry powder. Cook and stir for 2 minutes or until apple is tender. Remove from the heat. Stir in the egg, 1 teaspoon brown sugar and 1 teaspoon salt.

Place squash cut side up on a baking sheet. Place 1 teaspoon of the remaining brown sugar and 1 teaspoon butter in each. Sprinkle with remaining salt. Fill with meat mixture.

Bake, uncovered, at 375° for 15-20 minutes or until heated through. **Yield:** 4 servings.

Farmhouse Dinner

1 pound ground beef
2 eggs
1/4 cup milk
1 can (14-3/4 ounces) cream-style corn
1 cup soft bread crumbs
1/4 cup finely chopped onion
2 teaspoons prepared mustard
1 teaspoon salt
1/2 cup dry bread crumbs
2 tablespoons butter, melted

In a large skillet, cook beef over medium heat until no longer pink; drain and set aside.

In a large bowl, combine eggs and milk. Add the corn, soft bread crumbs, onion, mustard, salt and beef; mix well.

Transfer to a greased 9-in. square baking dish. Toss dry bread crumbs with butter; sprinkle over meat mixture. Bake, uncovered, at 350° for 30 minutes or until golden brown. **Yield:** 4-6 servings.

Beef Crescent Loaf

1-1/2 pounds ground beef
1/2 cup chopped onion
3/4 cup chopped green pepper
2 cans (11 ounces *each*) condensed cheddar cheese soup, undiluted

1 tablespoon Worcestershire sauce
1/2 teaspoon salt
1/4 teaspoon pepper
1 can (8 ounces) refrigerated crescent rolls
1/2 cup shredded cheddar cheese

In a skillet, cook beef and onion over medium heat until meat is no longer pink; drain. Stir in the green pepper, soup, Worcestershire sauce, salt and pepper; set aside.

On an ungreased baking sheet, separate crescent dough into 2 large rectangles. Join the longer sides together. Press edges and perforations together to form a 12-in. x 7-in. rectangle. Spread half of the meat mixture down the center of the rectangle to within 1 in. of edges. Set aside meat mixture. Fold longer sides of dough over meat mixture to center; seal ends.

Bake at 375° for 15 minutes. Remove from oven and spoon remaining meat mixture down center of loaf. Sprinkle with cheddar cheese; bake 10 minutes longer or until loaf is golden brown and cheese is melted. **Yield:** 10-12 servings.

Baked Nachos

2 pounds ground beef
3 cups (12 ounces) shredded Colby-Monterey Jack cheese, *divided*
3 cups salsa
1 package (10 ounces) frozen corn, thawed

1 cup (8 ounces) sour cream
1 to 2 tablespoons chili powder
1 teaspoon ground cumin
6 cups tortilla chips

In a skillet, cook beef over medium heat until no longer pink; drain. Stir in 2 cups cheese, salsa, corn, sour cream, chili powder and cumin; mix well. Pour half into a greased 13-in. x 9-in. x 2-in. baking dish. Top with half of the chips; repeat layers.

Bake, uncovered, at 350° for 25 minutes or until heated through. Sprinkle with remaining cheese. Bake 5 minutes longer or until cheese is melted. **Yield:** 8 servings.

Meaty Pita Pockets

3 medium onions, chopped
1/2 cup pine nuts
2 tablespoons vegetable oil
2 pounds ground beef
2 medium tomatoes, chopped
1/2 cup chopped green pepper
1/3 cup lemon juice
1/3 cup minced fresh parsley
3 tablespoons red wine vinegar
1-1/2 teaspoons salt
3/4 teaspoon ground allspice
1/2 teaspoon cayenne pepper
6 pita breads, halved

In a skillet, saute onions and pine nuts in oil until onions are tender and nuts are toasted. Add beef; cook over medium heat until meat is no longer pink. Drain. Stir in the tomatoes, green pepper, lemon juice, parsley, vinegar, salt, allspice and cayenne; mix well. Reduce heat; cover and simmer for 30 minutes. Spoon about 1/2 cup meat mixture into each pita half. **Yield:** 6 servings.

Beefy Enchiladas

1-1/2 pounds ground beef
1/2 cup chopped onion
1 can (16 ounces) refried beans
1/2 teaspoon salt
1/4 teaspoon pepper
2 tomatoes, chopped
10 corn tortillas (6 inches), warmed

SAUCE:
4 teaspoons butter
1/4 cup all-purpose flour
2 cups milk
1 can (10 ounces) enchilada sauce
1-1/2 cups (6 ounces) shredded cheddar cheese
3/4 cup sliced ripe olives, drained

In a skillet, cook beef and onion over medium heat until meat is no longer pink; drain. Stir in the beans, salt and pepper. Place 1/3 cup of mixture and a spoonful of tomatoes on each tortilla. Roll up and place seam side down in a 13-in. x 9-in. x 2-in. baking pan.

For sauce, melt butter in a saucepan. Stir in flour until smooth. Gradually add milk and enchilada sauce; stir until smooth. Add cheese and olives; bring to a boil over medium heat. Cook and stir for 2 minutes or until thickened. Pour over enchiladas.

Bake, uncovered, at 350° for 30 minutes or until heated through. Let stand for a few minutes before serving. **Yield:** 5-6 servings.

Cashew Noodle Casserole

2 pounds ground beef
2 large onions, chopped
1 can (4 ounces) mushroom stems and pieces, drained
1 can (10-3/4 ounces) condensed cream of chicken soup, undiluted
1-1/4 cups milk
1/4 cup soy sauce
1 teaspoon Worcestershire sauce
1/2 teaspoon pepper
8 ounces fine egg noodles, cooked and drained
2 cups (8 ounces) shredded cheddar cheese
1 package (6 ounces) chow mein noodles
1 cup whole cashews

In a skillet, cook beef and onions over medium heat until meat is no longer pink; drain. Add the mushrooms; set aside.

In a bowl, combine the soup, milk, soy sauce, Worcestershire sauce and pepper. In a greased 13-in. x 9-in. x 2-in. baking dish, layer egg noodles, beef mixture and soup mixture. Sprinkle with cheese and chow mein noodles.

Bake, uncovered, at 350° for 20 minutes or until heated through. Sprinkle with cashews. **Yield:** 8-10 servings.

Saucy Herb Hamburgers

1 egg
1/4 cup sour cream
1/4 cup dry bread crumbs
1/4 teaspoon dried parsley flakes
1/4 teaspoon dried thyme
1/4 teaspoon salt
Dash pepper
1 pound ground beef
1 cup ketchup
1/4 cup packed brown sugar
2 teaspoons prepared mustard
4 hamburger buns, split

In a bowl, combine the first seven ingredients. Crumble beef over mixture and mix well. Shape into four patties.

For the barbecue sauce, combine the ketchup, brown sugar and mustard in a small bowl.

Grill patties, uncovered, over medium-hot heat for 3 minutes on each side. Brush with barbecue sauce. Grill 4-6 minutes longer or until juices run clear, basting and turning several times. Serve on buns. **Yield:** 4 servings.

Swedish Meatballs

2 eggs, beaten
1/2 cup milk
1 cup dry bread crumbs
2 teaspoons salt
1/2 teaspoon pepper
1-1/2 teaspoons dried dill weed
1/4 teaspoon ground allspice
1/4 teaspoon ground nutmeg
1 cup chopped onion
2 tablespoons butter
2 pounds ground beef

1/2 pound ground pork

SAUCE:
1/4 cup butter
1/2 cup all-purpose flour
2 cans (14-1/2 ounces *each*) beef broth
1 pint heavy whipping cream
1/2 teaspoon dried dill weed
1/2 teaspoon salt
1/4 teaspoon pepper
Fresh dill sprigs, optional

In a large mixing bowl, combine the eggs, milk, bread crumbs and seasonings; set aside. In a skillet, saute onion in butter until soft; add egg to mixture. Crumble beef and ground pork over mixture and mix well. Cover and refrigerate for 1 hour.

Shape meat mixture into 1-1/4-in. to 1-1/2-in. balls. Place meatballs on a greased rack in a shallow baking pan. Bake, uncovered, at 350° for 20-25 minutes. Remove from the oven and place in a 3-qt. baking dish.

For sauce, melt butter in a saucepan; stir in flour until smooth. Gradually stir in broth; bring to a boil, stirring constantly. Reduce heat; stir in cream, dill, salt and pepper. Pour sauce over meatballs.

Bake, uncovered, at 350° for 40-45 minutes or until heated through and bubbly. Garnish with fresh dill if desired. **Yield:** 10-12 servings.

Pumpkin Sloppy Joes

2 pounds ground beef
1 medium onion, finely chopped
1 cup ketchup
1/2 cup tomato juice
1 teaspoon chili powder

3/4 teaspoon salt
1/4 teaspoon *each* ground cloves, nutmeg and pepper
2 cups canned pumpkin
Hamburger buns, split

In a large skillet, cook beef and onion over medium heat until meat is no longer pink; drain. Add the ketchup, tomato juice, chili powder, salt, cloves, nutmeg and pepper; mix well. Bring to a boil. Stir in pumpkin. Reduce heat; cover and simmer for 15-20 minutes. Serve on buns. **Yield:** 6-8 servings.

Roast Beef with Mushroom Sauce

2 tablespoons butter
3/4 cup thinly sliced onion
1/4 pound fresh mushrooms, sliced
2 tablespoons all-purpose flour
1/4 teaspoon ground marjoram
1/4 teaspoon garlic salt

Salt and pepper to taste
3/4 cup beef broth
1/4 cup ketchup
8 slices leftover cooked roast beef

In a skillet, melt butter over medium heat. Saute onion for 5 minutes. Add mushrooms and saute 2-3 minutes. Stir in the flour and seasonings until blended. Add broth and ketchup. Bring to a boil, stirring constantly. Reduce heat to low; simmer for 10 minutes. Add beef and heat through. **Yield:** 4 servings.

Barbecued Short Ribs

5 pounds bone-in beef short ribs, trimmed
2 medium onions, finely chopped
2 garlic cloves, minced
2 tablespoons olive oil
1 can (14-1/2 ounces) diced tomatoes, undrained
1 cup chili sauce
1/3 cup soy sauce

1/3 cup honey
1/4 cup packed brown sugar
1/4 cup ketchup
2 teaspoons chili powder
1/2 teaspoon ground ginger
1/8 teaspoon cayenne pepper
1/8 teaspoon dried oregano
1/8 teaspoon Liquid Smoke, optional

Place ribs in a Dutch oven; add water to cover by 2 in. Bring to a boil. Reduce heat; simmer, uncovered, for 1-1/2 to 2 hours or until tender.

Meanwhile, in a saucepan, saute onions and garlic in oil until tender. Add the remaining ingredients; bring to a boil. Reduce heat; simmer, uncovered, for 30 minutes, stirring occasionally.

Drain ribs. Arrange on a broiler pan and baste with barbecue sauce. Broil 4 to 5 in. from the heat for 5-10 minutes on each side or until sauce is bubbly. **Yield:** 6-8 servings.

Apple-Raisin Meat Loaf

2 eggs, beaten
1/2 cup applesauce
1 cup soft bread crumbs
1 cup crushed saltine crackers
1/2 cup chopped onion
1/2 cup chopped peeled apple

1/2 cup raisins
1-1/2 teaspoons salt
1/4 teaspoon pepper
1/4 teaspoon garlic powder
2 pounds lean ground beef

In a large bowl, combine first 10 ingredients. Crumbled ground beef over mixture and mix well. Pat into a 9-in. x 5-in. x 3-in. loaf pan.

Bake at 350° for 1-1/4 hours or until a meat thermometer reads 160°. Drain. Let stand for 5 minutes before cutting. **Yield:** 8-10 servings.

Zesty Meatball Sandwiches

SAUCE:
1-1/2 cups chopped onion
2 garlic cloves, minced
2 tablespoons olive oil
2 cans (28 ounces *each*) diced
   tomatoes, undrained
1 can (6 ounces) tomato paste
1 cup water
2 bay leaves
1 tablespoon dried oregano
2 tablespoons sugar
1 teaspoon salt
1/4 teaspoon pepper

MEATBALLS:
8 slices white bread, crusts
   removed and cubed
1/3 cup water
4 eggs, lightly beaten
1 cup grated Parmesan cheese
1/4 cup minced fresh parsley
2 garlic cloves, minced
1 teaspoon dried oregano
1 teaspoon salt
Dash pepper
2 pounds ground beef
10 to 12 Italian rolls, split

In a large saucepan or Dutch oven, saute onion and garlic in oil until tender. Add the remaining sauce ingredients; bring to a boil. Reduce heat; cover and simmer for 30 minutes. Discard bay leaves; set sauce aside.

In a large bowl, toss bread cubes with water. Add the eggs, Parmesan, parsley, garlic, oregano, salt and pepper; crumble beef over mixture and mix well. Shape into 1-1/2-in. balls. Place on an ungreased shallow baking pan.

Bake, uncovered, at 350° for 20-25 minutes; drain. Add to sauce. Simmer, uncovered, for 30 minutes. Serve on rolls. **Yield:** 10-12 servings.

Stuffed Artichokes

2 medium artichokes
Lemon juice
2 eggs
1/4 cup milk
3 tablespoons ketchup
1 cup dry bread crumbs
2 tablespoons minced fresh basil
   or 2 teaspoons dried basil
2 tablespoons minced fresh
   parsley
1 garlic clove, minced
1 pound lean ground beef
1 can (8 ounces) tomato sauce
1/4 cup water

Rinse artichokes well; trim stem. Cut 1 in. off the top. Snip the tip of each leaf with a kitchen shears. Brush cut edges with lemon juice. Spread artichoke open. Using a small knife, carefully cut around center choke. Scoop out and discard the fuzzy center.

In a saucepan, place artichokes in a steam basket over 1 in. of boiling water. Cover; steam for 20-25 minutes or until crisp-tender. Invert on a paper towel to drain.

In a bowl, combine the eggs, milk, ketchup, bread crumbs, basil, parsley and garlic. Crumble beef over mixture and mix well. Stuff meat mixture into center of artichokes and between leaves. Place in an ungreased 11-in. x 7-in. x 2-in. baking dish. Combine tomato sauce and water; pour over top.

Cover and bake at 350° for 1 to 1-1/2 hours or until meat is no longer pink. **Yield:** 4 servings.

Chop Suey

1 pound ground beef
2 beef bouillon cubes
2 cups water, *divided*
2 tablespoons cornstarch
1 can (28 ounces) chop suey
   vegetables, drained
2 tablespoons soy sauce
Cooked rice
Chow mein noodles

In a skillet, cook beef over medium heat until no longer pink; drain. Dissolve bouillon in 1-1/2 cups boiling water; add to skillet. Combine cornstarch with remaining water until smooth; stir into beef mixture. Bring to a boil; cook and stir for 2 minutes or until thickened. Add the vegetables and soy sauce; stir and cook until heated through, about 15 minutes. Serve with rice and chow mein noodles. **Yield:** 4-6 servings.

Creamy Beef Stroganoff

1 pound ground beef
1/3 cup all-purpose flour
1/2 teaspoon salt
1 can (10-3/4 ounces) condensed cream of mushroom soup, undiluted

1 can (10-1/2 ounces) beef consomme
1 tablespoon prepared mustard
8 ounces wide egg noodles, cooked and drained
1 cup (8 ounces) sour cream

In a skillet, cook beef over medium heat until no longer pink; drain. Stir in flour and salt until blended. Stir in the soup, consomme and mustard. Bring to a boil, stirring constantly. Reduce heat; simmer, uncovered, for 10 minutes. Stir in the noodles and sour cream; heat through (do not boil). **Yield:** 6-8 servings.

Mozzarella Meat Whirl

1 pound lean ground beef
1/4 pound ground pork
1/4 pound ground veal
1/2 cup dry bread crumbs
1 egg, beaten
1 tablespoon prepared mustard
1 teaspoon salt
1/8 teaspoon pepper

2 cups (8 ounces) shredded part-skim mozzarella cheese
1/4 cup chopped fresh parsley

SAUCE:
3/4 cup ketchup
1/2 cup water
1 tablespoon Worcestershire sauce

In a large mixing bowl, combine the beef, pork and veal. Add the bread crumbs, egg, mustard, salt and pepper; blend well. On waxed paper, pat meat mixture into a 14-in. x 8-in. rectangle. Cover meat with mozzarella cheese and sprinkle with parsley to within 1 in. of outer edges. Roll up jelly-roll style, starting with a short side and peeling waxed paper away while rolling. Seal seam and ends. Place seam side down in a 9-in. x 5-in. x 3-in. loaf dish.

For sauce, combine ketchup, water and Worcestershire sauce; pour over meat loaf. Bake at 350° for 1-1/4 hours or until a meat thermometer reads 160°, basting frequently. **Yield:** 6 servings.

Mexi-Corn Lasagna Dish

1 pound ground beef
2 cups fresh corn
1 can (15 ounces) tomato sauce
1 cup picante sauce
1 tablespoon chili powder
1-1/2 teaspoons ground cumin
10 flour tortillas (7 inch)

2 cups (16 ounces) 4% cottage cheese
2 eggs, lightly beaten
1/4 cup grated Parmesan cheese
1 teaspoon dried oregano
1/2 teaspoon garlic salt
1 cup (4 ounces) shredded cheddar cheese

In a skillet, cook beef over medium heat until no longer pink; drain. Add the corn, tomato sauce, picante sauce, chili powder and cumin; bring to a boil. Reduce heat; cover and simmer for 5 minutes.

Place half of the tortillas in the bottom and up the sides of a greased 13-in. x 9-in. x 2-in. baking pan. Spoon meat mixture over tortillas. Combine the cottage cheese, eggs, Parmesan, oregano and garlic salt; spread over meat mixture. Top with remaining tortillas. Cover with foil.

Bake at 375° for 30 minutes. Uncover; sprinkle with cheese. Bake 10 minutes longer or until cheese is melted. **Yield:** 12 servings.

Stuffed Green Peppers

6 medium fresh tomatoes, peeled, seeded and chopped
1 medium onion, chopped
3 celery ribs, diced
1 can (8 ounces) tomato sauce
1 cup water

2 teaspoons salt, *divided*
1/2 teaspoon pepper, *divided*
4 medium green peppers
1 pound lean ground beef
1 cup instant rice, cooked
1 teaspoon dried basil

In a large saucepan or Dutch oven, combine the tomatoes, onion, celery, tomato sauce, water, 1 teaspoon salt and 1/4 teaspoon pepper. Bring to a boil. Reduce heat; simmer, uncovered, for 10-15 minutes.

Meanwhile, cut tops off of green peppers and remove seeds; set aside. In a bowl, combine the ground beef, rice, basil and remaining salt and pepper. Fill peppers with beef mixture. Carefully place peppers in tomato sauce. Spoon some sauce over tops of peppers. Cover and simmer for 40-45 minutes or until beef is cooked and peppers are tender. **Yield:** 4 servings.

Stuffed Round Steak

2 pounds boneless beef top sirloin steaks, (about 1 pound *each*)

4 bacon strips, diced

1 medium onion, chopped

1-1/2 cups unseasoned stuffing cubes

2 tablespoons minced fresh parsley

1/2 teaspoon salt

1/2 teaspoon celery salt

1/4 teaspoon rubbed sage

1/4 teaspoon pepper

1 cup beef broth

1 can (8 ounces) tomato sauce

4-1/2 teaspoons cornstarch

2 tablespoons cold water

Flatten steaks to 1/4-in. thickness; set aside. In a large skillet, cook bacon over medium heat until crisp. Using a slotted spoon, remove to paper towels. Drain, reserving 3 tablespoons drippings.

Saute onion in reserved drippings. Add the stuffing cubes, parsley, salt, celery salt, sage, pepper and bacon. Spread over each steak to within 1 in. of edges. Roll up jelly-roll style, starting with a long side; tie with kitchen string.

Place in a greased 13-in. x 9-in. 2-in. baking dish. Pour broth over steaks. Cover and bake at 325° for 1 hour. Drizzle with tomato sauce. Bake, uncovered, for 45 minutes or until meat is tender.

Remove meat to a serving platter and keep warm. Pour drippings and loosened brown bits into a measuring cup; skim fat. In a saucepan, combine cornstarch and water until smooth; gradually stir in drippings. Bring to a boil; cook and stir for 2 minutes or until thickened. Serve with sliced steak. **Yield:** 6-8 servings.

German Skillet Meal

1 pound ground beef

1 cup chopped onion

1 cup uncooked long grain rice

2 cans (8 ounces *each*) tomato sauce

1 can (16 ounces) sauerkraut, rinsed and well drained

1/2 teaspoon caraway seed

1 cup water

1/2 teaspoon pepper

3/4 teaspoon salt, optional

In a skillet, cook ground beef and onion over medium heat until meat is no longer pink; drain. Stir in the rice, tomato sauce, sauerkraut, caraway seed, water, pepper, and salt if desired. Bring to a boil. Reduce heat; cover and simmer about 25 minutes or until the rice is tender. **Yield:** 6 servings.

Beef Pinwheels

3/4 cup vegetable oil
2/3 cup water
1/4 cup soy sauce
1 tablespoon lemon-pepper
  seasoning

2 teaspoons Worcestershire
  sauce
4 drops hot pepper sauce
1 beef flank steak (2 to 2-1/2
  pounds), trimmed

In a bowl, combine the oil, water, soy sauce, lemon-pepper, Worcestershire sauce and hot pepper sauce; set aside.

Pound steak on each side. Cut into 1/2-in. strips on the diagonal; add to marinade. Cover and refrigerate for 4 hours or overnight.

Drain marinade. Divide meat strips into eight portions. Roll and shape strips, using larger strips around edges, into pinwheels. Secure each with a skewer.

Grill over hot heat for 5-6 minutes per side or until done. **Yield:** 8 servings.

Smoky Beef Brisket

2 to 4 tablespoons Liquid Smoke
1 teaspoon pepper
1/2 teaspoon salt
1 fresh beef brisket (about 3
  pounds)
1/4 cup packed brown sugar

1 teaspoon *each* celery salt,
  garlic salt and onion salt
1 teaspoon ground nutmeg
1 teaspoon paprika
1/2 cup barbecue sauce

In a large resealable plastic bag, combine the Liquid Smoke, pepper and salt; add the brisket. Seal bag and turn to coat; refrigerate for at least 4 hours or overnight.

Drain and discard marinade. Combine the brown sugar, celery salt, garlic salt, onion salt, nutmeg and paprika; rub over meat. Wrap in a large sheet of heavy-duty foil; seal tightly. Place in an ungreased 15-in. x 10-in. x 1-in. baking pan. Bake at 325° for 4 hours or until meat is tender.

Remove brisket to a warm serving platter; skim fat from pan juices. In a saucepan over medium heat, combine 1 cup pan juices with barbecue sauce; cook and stir until thickened. Thinly slice meat across the grain; serve with sauce. **Yield:** 6-8 servings.

Editor's Note: This is a fresh beef brisket, not corned beef. The meat comes from the first cut of the brisket.

Beef Burgundy

1-1/3 cups red wine
1 small onion, sliced
2 sprigs fresh parsley, stems removed
4-1/2 teaspoons vegetable oil
1 garlic clove, crushed
1 bay leaf
1/8 teaspoon white pepper
Dash dried thyme

1 beef sirloin tip roast (about 2 pounds), cut into 1-inch cubes
2 tablespoons all-purpose flour
3 tablespoons butter, *divided*
1/2 cup beef consomme, undiluted
6 cups water
20 pearl onions
1 cup sliced fresh mushrooms
Hot cooked noodles

In a large resealable plastic bag, combine the first eight ingredients; add the beef. Seal bag and turn to coat; refrigerate for 4 hours or overnight, turning bag occasionally.

Remove meat from marinade; pat dry with paper towel. Strain marinade and set aside; discard onion, parsley and bay leaf.

Coat beef with flour. In a Dutch oven, brown meat on all sides in 2 tablespoons butter over medium-high heat. Stir in the consomme and reserved marinade. Bring to a rolling boil; boil for 1 minute. Reduce heat; cover and simmer for 1-1/2 hours or until meat is tender.

In a large saucepan, bring water to a boil. Add pearl onions; boil for 3 minutes. Drain and rinse in cold water; peel. In a skillet, saute mushrooms and onions in remaining butter until tender. Add to beef mixture. Simmer 10 minutes longer. Thicken sauce if desired. Serve over noodles. **Yield:** 6-8 servings.

Oven Porcupines

1 pound lean ground beef
1/2 cup uncooked long grain rice
1/2 cup water
1/3 cup chopped onion
1 teaspoon salt

1/4 teaspoon garlic powder
1/2 teaspoon pepper
1 can (15 ounces) tomato sauce
1 cup water
2 teaspoons Worcestershire sauce

Combine first seven ingredients; shape into 12 balls. Place meatballs in an ungreased 8-in. square baking dish. Combine remaining ingredients; pour over meatballs.

Cover with foil and bake at 350° for 1 hour. Uncover; bake 15 minutes longer or until a meat thermometer reads 160°. **Yield:** 4 servings.

Cornmeal Empanadas

FILLING:
1-1/2 pounds ground beef
1-1/2 cups thick spaghetti sauce
1/4 cup raisins
2 teaspoons chili powder
1 teaspoon brown sugar
1/2 teaspoon onion powder
1/2 teaspoon salt
1/4 teaspoon garlic powder
1/4 teaspoon ground cinnamon

CORNMEAL PASTRY:
3 cups all-purpose flour
2/3 cup cornmeal
1 teaspoon salt
1 cup shortening
1/2 cup ice water
1 egg, beaten
1 tablespoon water
Taco sauce, optional

In a large skillet, cook beef over medium heat until no longer pink;
drain. Stir in spaghetti sauce, raisins and seasonings. Bring to a boil.
Reduce heat; simmer, uncovered.

Meanwhile, for pastry, combine the flour, cornmeal and salt in a large
bowl. Cut in shortening until mixture resembles coarse crumbs.
Gradually add water, tossing with a fork until dough forms a ball. Cover
and let rest for 10 minutes.

Divide pastry into two balls; roll half out on a lightly floured surface
to a 16-in. circle. Cut into four 7-1/2-in. rounds. Place 1/2 cup filling
on each round. Combine egg and water; brush on pastry edges. Fold
dough over to form half circles; crimp edges to seal. Repeat with other
half of pastry and remaining filling.

Place on greased baking sheets; brush tops with remaining egg
mixture. Bake at 400° degrees for 25-30 minutes or until lightly
browned. Serve with taco sauce if desired. **Yield:** 8 servings.

Oriental Patties

1/4 cup soy sauce
2 to 4 tablespoons minced fresh
  cilantro
1 green onion, chopped
2 garlic cloves, minced
1 teaspoon ground ginger
7 drops hot pepper sauce
Pinch pepper
1 pound ground beef
4 hamburger buns, split

In a bowl, combine the first seven ingredients. Crumble beef over the
mixture and mix well. Shape into four patties.

Broil or grill until no longer pink. Serve on buns. **Yield:** 4 servings.

Beef Fried Rice

1-1/2 pounds ground beef
  1 cup finely chopped carrots
  1 cup finely chopped celery
1/2 cup finely chopped onion
  2 garlic cloves, minced
3/4 cup chopped fresh mushrooms
1/2 cup frozen peas, thawed
  1 tablespoon dried parsley flakes

  1 teaspoon dried basil
1/4 teaspoon ground ginger
Salt and pepper to taste
  5 cups cold cooked long grain rice
  2 eggs, scrambled
1/4 to 1/2 cup soy sauce

In a large skillet, cook beef over medium heat until no longer pink; drain, reserving 2-3 tablespoons of drippings. Stir-fry the carrots, celery, onion and garlic. Add mushrooms and peas; cook until all vegetables are tender. Add parsley, basil, ginger, salt, pepper, rice and eggs; stir until well mixed. Add soy sauce and heat through. **Yield:** 8-10 servings.

New England Boiled Dinner

  1 corned beef brisket (3 to 4 pounds)
1/2 pound sliced bacon
  6 medium carrots, halved
  1 to 2 medium turnips, quartered

  6 medium potatoes, peeled and halved
  2 medium onions, quartered
  1 small head cabbage, cored and quartered

Place brisket and enclosed seasoning packet in Dutch oven with enough water to cover. Simmer, covered, about 1 hour. Add bacon; simmer 1 to 1-1/2 hours longer or until beef is tender.

Remove brisket from Dutch oven and keep warm. Discard bacon; strain stock. Return stock to Dutch oven. Add carrots and turnips. Bring to a boil. Reduce heat; simmer, uncovered, for 10 minutes. Add potatoes and onions; simmer 15 minutes longer. Add cabbage; simmer for 10-15 minutes or until tender.

Return brisket to stock; heat through. Place meat on a large platter with vegetables around it. **Yield:** 8-10 servings.

Lemon-Herb Gyros

2 pounds ground beef
2 tablespoons minced fresh parsley
3 garlic cloves, minced
1/3 cup lemon juice
1/4 cup beef broth
2 tablespoons minced fresh oregano or 2 teaspoons dried oregano
2 beef bouillon cubes
1-1/2 teaspoons minced fresh basil or 1/2 teaspoon dried basil
1 teaspoon salt
1/4 teaspoon pepper
6 pita breads, halved
1 large onion, sliced
1 large tomato, sliced
Ranch salad dressing

In a large skillet, cook beef over medium heat until no longer pink; drain. Add the parsley and garlic; cook and stir for 2 minutes. Stir in the lemon juice, broth, oregano, bouillon, basil, salt and pepper. Bring to a boil. Reduce heat; simmer, uncovered, for 5 minutes. Spoon about 1/3 cupful into each pita half. Add onion and tomato. Drizzle with salad dressing. **Yield:** 6 servings.

Mexican Meat Loaf Roll

2 eggs, beaten
1/4 cup quick-cooking or old-fashioned oats
1 tablespoon Worcestershire sauce
1 teaspoon pepper
1-1/2 pounds lean ground beef
1 package (8 ounces) cream cheese, softened
1 can (4 ounces) chopped green chilies, drained
3/4 cup salsa

In a large bowl, combine the eggs, oats, Worcestershire sauce and pepper. Crumble ground beef over mixture and mix well. On a piece of waxed paper, pat meat mixture to an 18-in. x 9-in. rectangle. Combine cream cheese and chilies; spread over meat to within 1 in. of outer edges. Roll up jelly-roll style, starting with a short side and peeling waxed paper away while rolling. Seal seam and ends. Place seam side down in a greased 11-in. x 7-in. x 2-in. baking dish. Bake, uncovered, at 350° for 50 minutes. Drain excess fat. Top with salsa and bake 10-15 minutes longer or until a meat thermometer reads 160°. Let stand for 10 minutes before serving. **Yield:** 6-8 servings.

Short Ribs with Plums

2 to 2-1/2 pounds beef short ribs
1 tablespoon vegetable oil
1/3 cup chopped onion
1 teaspoon salt
1 teaspoon browning sauce, optional

1/4 teaspoon pepper
1 cup water, *divided*
15 pitted dried plums
1 tablespoon cornstarch
Hot cooked rice

In a large skillet, brown the meat in oil over medium heat. Remove meat; keep warm. Add onion to the drippings. Saute onion until tender, scraping the pan to loosen browned bits; drain. Add the salt, browning sauce if desired, pepper, 3/4 cup water and dried plums. Bring to a boil; return meat to the pan. Reduce heat; cover and simmer for 1 hour or until meat is tender. Remove meat; keep warm.

Skim fat from the pan. Combine the cornstarch and the remaining water until smooth. Stir into pan drippings. Bring to a boil; cook and stir for 2 minutes or until thickened. Serve with ribs and rice. **Yield:** 4 servings.

Beef-Stuffed Onions

4 large sweet onions
1/2 pound ground beef, cooked and drained
1/4 cup soft bread crumbs
1/4 cup condensed nacho cheese soup, undiluted
1/4 cup finely chopped green pepper

1/2 teaspoon dried oregano
1/2 teaspoon salt
1/2 teaspoon pepper
1/2 teaspoon beef bouillon granules
1/4 cup hot water

Cut tops off onions and peel them. Scoop out centers to within 1/4 in. of edge; set shells aside. Chop the removed onion; set aside 1/4 cup (refrigerate remaining onion for another use).

In a bowl, combine the beef, bread crumbs, soup, green pepper, oregano, salt, pepper and chopped onion. Stuff the onions. Arrange in a 9-in. microwave-safe pie plate. In a small bowl, dissolve bouillon in water. Pour over onions. Cover and microwave on high for 10-15 minutes, turning and basting after 5 minutes. **Yield:** 4 servings.

Editor's Note: This recipe was tested in a 1,100-watt microwave.

Beef Rouladen

1 pound thin cut beef round
  steak, separated into 4 pieces
Coarse-ground prepared mustard
  1/4 teaspoon dried thyme
Salt and pepper to taste
  1 medium dill pickle, quartered
    lengthwise
  3 carrots, cut into sticks, *divided*

1 small onion, cut into wedges
2 tablespoons all-purpose flour
1 tablespoon vegetable oil
2 cups water
2 beef bouillon cubes
3 tablespoons ketchup
Cooked noodles

Spread steak pieces with mustard. Sprinkle with thyme, salt and pepper. Top one edge with a piece of pickle, carrot and a wedge of onion. Roll up and secure with a toothpick. Coat each roll with flour.

In a skillet, heat oil over medium-high. Brown beef on all sides. Add the water, bouillon, ketchup and remaining carrots. Bring to a boil. Reduce heat; cover and simmer for 1 hour. Thicken gravy, if desired, and serve over noodles. **Yield:** 4 servings.

Hungarian Goulash

1 pound beef chuck *or* rump
  roast, cut into 1-inch pieces
2 tablespoons vegetable oil
1/2 cup sliced onion
1 garlic clove, minced
1/3 cup ketchup
2 to 4 tablespoons
  Worcestershire sauce
1/2 teaspoon white vinegar

1/2 teaspoon brown sugar
1-1/4 teaspoons paprika
1 teaspoon salt
1/2 teaspoon ground mustard
Dash crushed red pepper flakes
1-2/3 cups water, *divided*
1 tablespoon all-purpose flour
Hot cooked egg noodles

In a Dutch oven, brown beef in oil over medium-high heat. Add onion and garlic; cook until tender.

In a bowl, combine the ketchup, Worcestershire sauce, vinegar, brown sugar, seasonings and 1-1/2 cups water. Stir into beef. Reduce heat; cover and simmer for 2 to 2-1/2 hours or until meat is tender.

Combine flour and remaining water until smooth; stir into beef mixture. Bring to a boil; cook and stir for 2 minutes or until thickened. Serve over noodles. **Yield:** 4 servings.

Cheesy Tortilla Bake

TORTILLAS:
    1 cup all-purpose flour
    1/2 cup yellow cornmeal
    1/2 teaspoon salt
1-2/3 cups milk
    1 egg, beaten
    2 tablespoons butter, melted

FILLING:
    1 pound ground beef
1/2 cup chopped onion

1 garlic clove, minced
1 can (10-3/4 ounces) condensed tomato soup, undiluted
1/2 cup taco sauce
1 teaspoon dried oregano
1 can (2-1/4 ounces) sliced ripe olives, drained
2 cups (8 ounces) shredded cheddar cheese

In a mixing bowl, combine the flour, cornmeal and salt. Add the milk, egg and butter. Beat until smooth. Place a lightly greased small skillet over medium heat. For each tortilla, pour about 3 tablespoons batter into skillet. Lift and tilt skillet to spread batter. Return to heat. Cook until light brown; turn and brown the other side. Remove to a warm platter; repeat with remaining batter. Set aside.

For filling, cook the beef, onion and garlic over medium heat until the meat is no longer pink; drain. Stir in the soup, taco sauce, oregano and olives.

Meanwhile, cover the bottom of an 11-in. x 7-in. x 2-in. baking dish with six tortillas, overlapping as needed. Cover with half of meat mixture. Top with remaining tortillas and remaining meat mixture. Sprinkle with cheese.

Bake at 350° for 30 minutes or until heated through. Let stand for 3-5 minutes before serving. **Yield:** 8 servings.

Spaghetti-Style Rice

1 pound ground beef, cooked and drained
1 jar (15-1/2 ounces) garden-style spaghetti sauce

1-1/2 cups (6 ounces) shredded Monterey Jack cheese
1 cup uncooked instant rice
1 can (4 ounces) mushroom stems and pieces, drained

In a large bowl, combine all ingredients. Transfer to a greased 11-in. x 7-in. x 2-in. baking dish. Bake, uncovered, at 375° for 15 minutes; stir. Bake 10 minutes longer or until rice is tender. **Yield:** 4 servings.

Beef Florentine

2 pounds ground beef
1 medium onion, chopped
1 garlic clove, minced
1 package (10 ounces) frozen chopped spinach, thawed and squeezed dry
1 jar (14 ounces) spaghetti sauce
1 can (8 ounces) tomato sauce
1 can (6 ounces) tomato paste
1 teaspoon salt
1 teaspoon pepper
7 ounces elbow macaroni, cooked and drained
1 cup (4 ounces) shredded cheddar cheese
1-1/2 cups soft bread crumbs
2 eggs, lightly beaten

In a large skillet, cook beef, onion and garlic over medium heat until meat is no longer pink; drain. Cook spinach according to the package directions. Drain spinach, reserving cooking liquid; add enough water to make 1 cup. Set spinach aside.

In a small bowl, combine cooking liquid, spaghetti sauce, tomato sauce, tomato paste, salt and pepper. Stir sauce into skillet; bring to a boil. Reduce heat; simmer, uncovered, for 10 minutes.

In a large bowl, combine the macaroni, cheese, bread crumbs, eggs and cooked spinach. Spread into a greased 13-in. x 9-in. x 2-in. baking dish. Cover with meat sauce.

Bake at 350° for 30 minutes. Let stand for 5 minutes before serving.
Yield: 10-12 servings.

Corn Bread Beef Bake

1 pound ground beef
2 cans (16 ounces *each*) pork and beans
1/4 cup ketchup
2 tablespoons brown sugar
1/8 teaspoon pepper
1 package (8-1/2 ounces) corn bread/muffin mix
1/3 cup milk
1 egg

In a skillet, cook beef over medium heat until no longer pink; drain. Add the beans, ketchup, brown sugar and pepper; mix well. Transfer to a greased 11-in. x 7-in. x 2-in. baking dish.

In a bowl, mix the dry corn bread mix, milk and egg just until combined. Spoon over bean mixture. Bake, uncovered, at 350° for 35 minutes or until a toothpick inserted in the corn bread comes out clean.
Yield: 4-6 servings.

Hobo Knapsacks

2 medium potatoes, peeled and thinly sliced
2 large tomatoes, chopped
1 large onion, chopped
1 package (10 ounces) frozen mixed vegetables, thawed
1 can (4 ounces) mushroom stems and pieces, drained
1/2 cup tomato juice
1/2 cup old-fashioned oats
1 egg, beaten
1 tablespoon minced onion
1 teaspoon salt
1/4 teaspoon pepper
1 pound lean ground beef
6 (18-in. x 12 in.) sheets heavy-duty aluminum foil
Additional salt and pepper, optional

In a mixing bowl, combine potatoes, tomatoes, onion, mixed vegetables and mushrooms; set aside. In another bowl, combine the tomato juice, oats, egg, onion, salt and pepper; crumble beef over mixture and mix well.

Divide mixture into six portions; crumble each portion onto a piece of foil. Spoon the vegetable mixture over the beef mixture. Season with additional salt and pepper if desired. Tightly fold up the foil around the beef and vegetables to form a pouch. Transfer to a baking sheet.

Bake at 350° for 50-60 minutes or until the meat is cooked and the potatoes are tender. **Yield:** 6 servings.

Cheeseburger Macaroni

1 pound ground beef
1 medium onion, chopped
1 garlic clove, minced
1 can (10-3/4 ounces) condensed cheddar cheese soup, undiluted
1 can (10-3/4 ounces) condensed cream of mushroom soup, undiluted
1/2 cup milk
1/2 teaspoon dried basil
1/8 teaspoon pepper
2 cups elbow macaroni, cooked and drained
1 cup (4 ounces) shredded process cheese (Velveeta)
1/2 cup dry bread crumbs
1 tablespoon butter, melted

In a skillet, cook beef, onion and garlic over medium heat until meat is no longer pink; drain. In a bowl, combine the soups, milk, basil and pepper. Stir in beef mixture. Fold in macaroni and cheese.

Transfer to a greased 13-in. x 9-in. x 2-in. baking dish. Toss bread crumbs and butter; sprinkle over the top. Bake, uncovered, at 375° for 45 minutes or until heated through. **Yield:** 8 servings.

Baked Ziti With Fresh Tomatoes

- 1 pound ground beef
- 1 cup chopped onion
- 8 cups blanched, peeled and chopped fresh tomatoes (about 3 pounds)
- 1 teaspoon dried basil
- 1-1/2 teaspoons salt
- 1/4 teaspoon pepper
- 8 ounces ziti, cooked and drained
- 2 cups (8 ounces) shredded part-skim mozzarella cheese, *divided*
- 2 tablespoons grated Parmesan cheese

In a skillet, cook beef and onion over medium heat until beef is no longer pink; drain. Stir in the tomatoes, basil, salt and pepper. Bring to a boil. Reduce heat; simmer, uncovered, for 45 minutes, stirring occasionally. Stir in ziti and 1 cup mozzarella.

Spoon into a greased 2-1/2-qt. baking dish; sprinkle with Parmesan and remaining mozzarella. Cover and bake at 350° for 15 minutes. Uncover; bake 15 minutes longer or until heated through. **Yield:** 6 servings.

Vegetable Beef Kabobs

- 1-1/2 pounds boneless beef sirloin steak
- 2/3 cup white wine *or* beef broth
- 1/3 cup soy sauce
- 2 tablespoons vegetable oil
- 1 teaspoon minced fresh gingerroot *or* 1/4 teaspoon ground ginger
- 1 garlic clove, minced
- 1/2 teaspoon dried tarragon
- 18 small whole onions
- 3 to 4 small zucchini, cut in 1-inch slices
- 2 large sweet red peppers, cut in 1-inch pieces

Cut beef into 1-1/4-in. cubes; place in a large resealable plastic bag. In a 1-cup measuring cup, combine the wine or broth, soy sauce, oil, ginger, garlic and tarragon; pour 2/3 cup marinade over beef. Seal bag and turn to coat; let stand at room temperature for 45 minutes. Set aside remaining marinade for basting.

Drain and discard marinade from beef. Thread the meat, onions, zucchini and peppers alternately on six metal or soaked wooden skewers.

Grill over medium-hot heat for 10-12 minutes or until meat reaches desired doneness, turning and basting occasionally with reserved marinade. **Yield:** 6 servings.

Chili Rice Pie

2 cups cooked brown rice
1/4 cup shredded cheddar cheese
1 egg, beaten
1 teaspoon vegetable oil

FILLING:
1/2 pound ground beef
1/4 cup *each* finely chopped celery, onion, green pepper and sweet red pepper

1 garlic clove, minced
1 cup canned diced tomatoes, drained
1/2 cup canned kidney beans, rinsed and drained
1/4 teaspoon chili powder

In a bowl, combine the first four ingredients. Press onto the bottom and up the sides of a greased 9-in. pie plate; set aside.

For filling, cook the beef, celery, onion, peppers and garlic over medium heat until meat is no longer pink; drain. Add the tomatoes, beans and chili powder. Spoon into crust.

Bake at 325° for 40 minutes or until heated through. Let stand for 15 minutes before serving. **Yield:** 4 servings.

Cheesy Beef Stroganoff

1 pound beef sirloin tips
2 tablespoons vegetable oil
1 can (4 ounces) mushroom stems and pieces, drained
1/2 teaspoon salt
1/4 teaspoon pepper
1 can (10-3/4 ounces) condensed cream of mushroom soup, undiluted

1/2 cup milk
1 cup (8 ounces) sour cream
1/2 cup shredded part-skim mozzarella cheese
1/2 cup shredded Monterey Jack cheese
Hot cooked noodles *or* rice

In a skillet, cook beef in oil over medium-high heat until no longer pink. Add the mushrooms, salt and pepper. Combine soup and milk; add to skillet. Reduce heat; stir in sour cream. Cook 30 minutes longer (do not boil). Add cheeses; heat for 5 minutes or until melted. Serve over noodles or rice. **Yield:** 4 servings.

Mandarin Beef Skillet

1 pound ground beef
1 small onion, sliced
1 can (11 ounces) mandarin oranges
1-1/2 cups water, *divided*
1/4 cup soy sauce
3/4 teaspoon ground ginger

2 tablespoons cornstarch
3 celery ribs, sliced
1 small green pepper, chopped
1 can (8 ounces) sliced water chestnuts, drained
1 can (4 ounces) mushroom stems and pieces, drained
Hot cooked rice

In a skillet, cook beef and onion over medium heat until meat is no longer pink; drain. Drain the oranges, reserving syrup. Add syrup to the meat mixture; set oranges aside. Stir in 1 cup of water, soy sauce and ginger. Bring to a boil. Reduce heat; cover and simmer for 5 minutes.

Combine cornstarch and remaining water until smooth; stir into meat mixture. Bring to a boil; cook and stir for 2 minutes or until thickened. Add the celery, pepper, water chestnuts and mushrooms. Cover and cook over low heat for 5-7 minutes or until heated through. Serve over rice. Garnish with the oranges. **Yield:** 4-6 servings.

Corn 'n' Beef Pasta Bake

1 pound ground beef
1 medium onion, chopped
1 medium green *or* sweet red pepper, chopped
2 garlic cloves, minced
2 cups frozen corn, thawed
1 can (14-1/2 ounces) diced tomatoes, undrained

1-1/2 cups uncooked bow tie pasta
1 cup buttermilk
1 package (3 ounces) cream cheese, cubed
1 to 2 teaspoons chili powder
Salt and pepper to taste
1 cup (4 ounces) shredded Monterey Jack cheese

In a large skillet, cook the beef, onion, green pepper and garlic over medium heat until meat is no longer pink; drain. Stir in the corn, tomatoes, pasta, buttermilk, cream cheese, chili powder, salt and pepper.

Transfer to a greased 2-1/2-qt. baking dish; sprinkle with cheese. Cover and bake at 375° for 40 minutes. Uncover; bake 25-30 minutes longer or until the pasta is tender. **Yield:** 6-8 servings.

Homemade Pinwheel Noodles

2-1/4 to 2-3/4 cups all-purpose flour
4 eggs
3/4 pound ground beef
1/4 cup *each* finely chopped celery, onion and green pepper
3/4 teaspoon garlic powder

3/4 teaspoon seasoned salt
1/2 teaspoon pepper
6 cups water
1 can (10-1/2 ounces) condensed beef broth, undiluted

Place 2-1/4 cups flour in a bowl. Make a well in the center; add the eggs. Gradually mix with a wooden spoon until well blended. Knead on a floured surface until smooth, about 10 minutes. If necessary, add remaining flour to kneading surface or hands.

On a lightly floured surface, roll dough into a 16-in. x 12-in. rectangle, dusting top of dough with flour to prevent sticking. Crumble beef over dough; lightly press into dough. Sprinkle with the celery, onion, green pepper, garlic powder, seasoned salt and pepper. Roll up jelly-roll style, starting with a short side. Using a sharp knife, cut into 2-in. slices.

In a large kettle or Dutch oven, bring water and broth to a rapid boil. Drop pinwheels into the boiling liquid. Return to a gentle boil. Reduce heat; cover and simmer for 1 hour or until noodles are tender and meat is no longer pink. Serve with broth in soup bowls. **Yield:** 6 servings.

Sirloin Steak Sandwiches

1 boneless beef sirloin steak (1 pound)
4 onion rolls, split
1/4 cup mayonnaise

2 to 4 tablespoons prepared mustard
4 teaspoons prepared horseradish
4 slices Swiss cheese

Grill steak, uncovered, over medium heat for 5-8 minutes on each side or until meat reaches desired doneness (for medium-rare, a meat thermometer should read 145°; medium, 160°; well-done, 170°).

Spread cut side of roll tops with mayonnaise, mustard and horse-radish. Slice steak diagonally; place on roll bottoms. Top with cheese and roll tops. **Yield:** 4 servings.

Chicken-Fried Cube Steaks

2-1/2 cups all-purpose flour, *divided*
  2 tablespoons pepper
  1 to 2 tablespoons white pepper
  2 tablespoons garlic powder
  1 tablespoon paprika
1-1/2 teaspoons salt
  1 teaspoon ground cumin
  1/4 to 1/2 teaspoon cayenne pepper

2 cups buttermilk
2 cans (12 ounces *each*) evaporated milk
8 beef cube steaks (4 ounces *each*)
Oil for frying
  1 teaspoon Worcestershire sauce
Dash hot pepper sauce

In a shallow bowl, combine 2 cups flour and seasonings; set aside. In another bowl, combine buttermilk and evaporated milk. Remove 3-1/2 cups for gravy and set aside. Dip cube steaks into buttermilk mixture, then into flour mixture, coating well. Repeat.

In a skillet, heat 1/2 in. of oil on high. Fry steaks, a few at a time, for 5-7 minutes. Turn carefully and cook 5 minutes longer or until coating is crisp and meat is no longer pink. Remove steaks and keep warm.

Drain, reserving 1/3 cup drippings in the skillet; stir remaining flour into drippings until smooth. Cook and stir over medium heat for 5 minutes or until golden brown. Whisk in reserved buttermilk mixture; bring to a boil. Cook and stir for 2 minutes or until thickened. Add Worcestershire sauce and hot pepper sauce. Serve with steaks. **Yield:** 8 servings (4 cups gravy).

Parsley-Stuffed Flank Steak

1 beef flank steak (2 pounds)
1/2 cup minced fresh parsley

4 teaspoons chopped garlic
1/2 cup grated Romano cheese

Butterfly the flank steak, cutting horizontally from a long side to within 1/2 in. of opposite side. Open and place on a large piece of heavy-duty aluminum foil (about 18 in. square). Sprinkle the parsley, garlic and cheese over meat to within 1/2 in. of edges. Roll up tightly jell-roll style, starting with a long side. Wrap tightly in foil.

Place in a 13-in. x 9-in. x 2-in. baking dish. Bake at 325° for 1-1/2 hours or until meat reaches desired doneness (for medium-rare, a meat thermometer should read 145°; medium, 160°; well-done, 170°). Let stand for 5 minutes. Unwrap and slice steak. **Yield:** 8 servings.

Italian Beef Sandwiches

1 boneless sirloin tip roast (4 to 5 pounds)
1/2 teaspoon salt
3 medium onions, thinly sliced
3 beef bouillon cubes
7 hot banana peppers, seeded and thinly sliced

2 teaspoons Italian seasoning
1 teaspoon dried basil
1 teaspoon dried oregano
1 teaspoon garlic salt
1 teaspoon onion salt
20 to 24 hard rolls, split

Place roast on a rack in a 13-in. x 9-in. x 2-in. baking pan. Sprinkle with salt; top with onions. Add 1/2 in. of water to pan. Cover with heavy-duty foil.

Bake at 350° for 2 to 2-1/4 hours or until a meat thermometer reads 160°-170°. Remove meat; set aside until cool enough to handle. Slice thin; place in a large bowl.

Pour pan juices into a saucepan; add the bouillon, peppers and seasonings. Bring to a boil. Reduce heat; cover and simmer for 10 minutes. Pour over beef; cover and refrigerate for at least 8 hours. Reheat before serving. Serve 1/2 cup on each roll. **Yield:** 20-24 servings.

Crazy Crust Pizza

1-1/2 pounds ground beef
1 cup all-purpose flour
Dash salt and pepper
1 teaspoon Italian seasoning
2 eggs
2/3 cup milk

1/4 cup chopped onion
1 can (4 ounces) sliced mushrooms, drained
1 can (8 ounces) pizza sauce
1 cup (4 ounces) shredded part-skim mozzarella cheese

In a skillet, cook beef over medium heat until no longer pink; drain and set aside. In a small bowl, combine the flour, salt, pepper, Italian seasoning, eggs and milk; beat until smooth. Pour batter into a greased and floured 12-in. or 14-in. pizza pan. Spoon beef, onion and mushrooms over batter.

Bake at 425° for 25-30 minutes. Remove from the oven. Top with pizza sauce and top with mozzarella cheese. Bake 10-15 minutes longer or until cheese is melted. **Yield:** 4-6 servings.

Beef 'n' Pepper Stir-Fry

1-1/2 cups julienned celery
1 medium green or sweet red pepper, julienned
1 medium onion, cut into wedges
1 garlic clove, minced
3 tablespoons vegetable oil
2 tablespoons cornstarch
1-1/4 cups cold water
1 cup cubed cooked beef, pork or chicken
2 tablespoons soy sauce
1/4 teaspoon salt
Hot cooked rice

In a skillet, stir-fry the celery, green pepper, onion and garlic in oil until crisp-tender. Combine cornstarch and water until smooth; stir into vegetables. Add the beef, soy sauce and salt. Bring to a boil; cook and stir for 2 minutes or until thickened. Serve over rice. **Yield:** 4 servings.

Zesty Corn Cakes

1 pound ground beef
1 medium onion, chopped
1 small green pepper, chopped
1 celery rib, chopped
1 can (6 ounces) tomato paste
1/3 cup water
2 garlic cloves, minced
1 teaspoon chili powder
1 teaspoon salt
1/4 teaspoon pepper

CHEESE SAUCE:
8 ounces process cheese (Velveeta), cubed
2/3 cup evaporated milk
1/2 teaspoon chili powder

CORN CAKES:
1 package (8-1/2 ounces) corn bread/muffin mix
1/2 cup evaporated milk
1/4 cup water
1 egg, beaten
2 tablespoons butter, melted

In a skillet, cook beef over medium heat until no longer pink; drain. Add the next nine ingredients; mix well. Bring to a boil. Reduce heat; simmer, uncovered, for 2 minutes or until thickened.

In a saucepan, combine sauce ingredients. Cook and stir over low heat until cheese is melted.

In a bowl, combine corn cake ingredients just until moistened. Pour 1/4 cupfuls of batter onto a hot greased griddle. Turn when bubbles form on top of cake. Cook until the second side is golden brown.

Place a corn cake on four serving plates. Top each with 1/4 cup of filling. Repeat layers once. Serve with cheese sauce. **Yield:** 4 servings.

Beef 'n' Veggie Cheddar Pie

2 tablespoons all-purpose flour
1 can (10-3/4 ounces) condensed tomato soup, undiluted
1/4 cup water
1-1/2 pounds ground beef, cooked and drained
3 medium potatoes, peeled, cubed and cooked
2 cups frozen diced carrots, thawed
1 medium onion, chopped

CRUST:
1 cup all-purpose flour
1/2 teaspoon salt
1/3 cup shortening
1/2 cup shredded cheddar cheese
2 to 3 tablespoons cold water

In a bowl, combine the flour, soup and water until smooth. Stir in the beef, potatoes, carrots and onion. Spoon into an ungreased 13-in. x 9-in. x 2-in. baking dish.

For crust, combine flour and salt in a bowl. Cut in shortening until mixture resembles coarse crumbs. Add cheese and mix well. Gradually add water, tossing with a fork until a ball forms. On a lightly floured surface, roll dough to fit top of baking dish. Place over filling; trim, seal and flute edges. Cut slits in top.

Bake, at 425° for 35 minutes or until golden brown. Let stand for 10 minutes before cutting. **Yield:** 6-8 servings.

Mock Ravioli

1 pound ground beef
1 medium onion, chopped
1 garlic clove, minced
1 jar (28 ounces) spaghetti sauce
1 teaspoon salt
2 cups medium pasta shells, cooked and drained
1 package (10 ounces) frozen chopped spinach, thawed and drained
1/2 cup shredded cheddar cheese
1/2 cup grated Parmesan cheese
2 eggs, beaten
1/4 cup vegetable oil

In a skillet, cook the beef, onion and garlic over medium heat until the meat is no longer pink; drain. Stir in spaghetti sauce and salt; set aside.

In a bowl, combine the pasta, spinach, cheeses, eggs and oil. Transfer to a greased 13-in. x 9-in. x 2-in. baking dish. Top with the meat sauce.

Bake, uncovered, at 350° for 30 minutes or until heated through. **Yield:** 6-8 servings.

Lazy Lasagna

2 cups (8 ounces) shredded
   part-skim mozzarella cheese
1-1/2 cups (12 ounces) small-curd
   cottage cheese
2 eggs, beaten
1/3 cup minced fresh parsley
1 teaspoon onion powder
1/2 teaspoon dried basil
1/8 teaspoon pepper
1 jar (28 ounces) spaghetti sauce
3/4 pound ground beef, cooked
   and drained
9 uncooked lasagna noodles
1/4 cup water
Grated Parmesan cheese

In a large bowl, combine the first seven ingredients; set aside. In another bowl, combine the spaghetti sauce and beef.

Spoon a fourth of the meat sauce into a greased 13-in. x 9-in. x 2-in. baking dish. Top with three noodles and half of the cheese mixture; repeat layers once. Top with a fourth of the meat sauce, remaining noodles and remaining meat sauce. Pour water around edges. Sprinkle with Parmesan cheese.

Cover and bake at 375° for 45 minutes. Uncover; bake 15 minutes longer or until noodles are tender. Let stand for 10 minutes before cutting. **Yield:** 8-10 servings.

Willie Hoss' Meat Loaf

1 small onion, chopped
1/2 medium green pepper,
   chopped
1 can (4 ounces) mushroom
   pieces, drained
1 can (2-1/2 ounces) sliced ripe
   olives, drained
2 eggs, beaten
1 cup cracker crumbs
1 cup ketchup
1/2 to 1 teaspoon garlic powder
Salt and pepper to taste
1-1/2 pounds lean ground beef
Additional ketchup, optional

In a large bowl, combine the onion, green pepper, mushrooms, olives, eggs, cracker crumbs, ketchup, garlic powder, salt and pepper; crumble beef over mixture and mix well.

Press into a 9-in. x 5-in. x 3-in. loaf pan. Top with additional ketchup, if desired. Bake at 350° for about 1 hour or a meat thermometer reads 160°. Let stand for 15 minutes before cutting. **Yield:** 8 servings.

Pizza Casserole

1 pound ground beef	1/3 cup butter, melted
1 package (3-1/2 ounces) sliced pepperoni	1 can (15 ounces) tomato sauce
1 onion, chopped	1 cup (4 ounces) shredded Swiss cheese
1 green pepper, chopped	4 cups (16 ounces) shredded part-skim mozzarella cheese
1 can (4 ounces) sliced mushrooms	1/2 teaspoon dried oregano
7 ounces vermicelli, cooked and drained	1/2 teaspoon dried basil
	Green pepper rings, optional

In a skillet, cook the beef, pepperoni, onion and green pepper over medium heat until beef is no longer pink and vegetables are tender; drain. Stir in mushrooms; set aside.

Combine vermicelli and butter in a 13-in. x 9-in. x 2-in. baking dish; toss noodles to coat evenly. Pour 1 cup tomato sauce over noodles. Spoon half of the meat mixture over the noodles. Combine Swiss and mozzarella cheeses; sprinkle half over meat mixture. Sprinkle with oregano and basil. Repeat with remaining meat and cheese mixtures. Pour remaining tomato sauce over cheese layer.

Bake, uncovered, at 350° for 25-30 minutes or until bubbly. Garnish with green pepper rings if desired. **Yield:** 8-10 servings.

Hot Tamale Pie

1 pound ground beef	1 medium green pepper, chopped
1 medium onion, chopped	2 to 3 teaspoons taco seasoning
2 cans (14-1/2 ounces each) stewed tomatoes	Corn bread
2 cans (2-1/4 ounces each) sliced ripe olives, drained	

In a skillet, cook the beef and onion over medium heat until meat is no longer pink; drain. Add the tomatoes, olives, green pepper and taco seasoning. Cook and stir over low heat until hot and bubbly. Serve over corn bread. **Yield:** 6 servings.

Meatballs with Spaetzle

1 egg
1/4 cup milk
1/4 cup dry bread crumbs
1 tablespoon dried parsley flakes
1/2 teaspoon salt
1/4 teaspoon poultry seasoning
Dash pepper
1 pound ground beef
1 can (10-1/2 ounces) condensed beef broth, undiluted
1 can (4 ounces) mushroom stems and pieces, drained

1 medium onion, chopped
1 tablespoon all-purpose flour
1 teaspoon caraway seeds
1 cup (8 ounces) sour cream

HOMEMADE SPAETZLE:
2 cups all-purpose flour
1 teaspoon salt
2 eggs, lightly beaten
1 cup milk
2 quarts water *or* beef broth

In a bowl, combine the first seven ingredients. Crumble beef over the mixture and mix well. Shape into 1-1/2-in. balls.

In a skillet, brown meatballs; drain. Add the broth, mushrooms and onion. Bring to a boil. Reduce heat; cover and simmer for 30 minutes. Combine the flour, caraway seeds and sour cream until smooth; stir into meatball mixture. Cook over low heat until heated through and thickened, about 10 minutes.

Meanwhile, in a bowl, combine the flour, salt, eggs and milk. Let stand for 5 minutes. In a large saucepan, bring water or broth to a rapid boil. Place spaetzle batter in a colander or spaetzle press. Holding over the boiling liquid, press batter through holds of colander. Cook and stir for 5 minutes or until tender; drain. Serve meatballs and sauce over spaetzle. **Yield:** 4 servings.

Creamy Corned Beef Casserole

1 can (10 ounces) cooked corned beef *or* 1-1/2 cups cubed cooked corned beef

1 can (10-3/4 ounces) condensed cream of chicken soup, undiluted

8 ounces cheddar cheese, cubed

1 package (7 ounces) small shell pasta, cooked and drained

1 cup milk

1/2 cup chopped onion

2 bread slices, cubed

2 tablespoons butter, melted

In a bowl, combine the first six ingredients. Transfer to a greased 2-qt. baking dish. Toss bread cubes with butter; sprinkle over top.

Bake, uncovered, at 350° for 30 minutes. Cover and bake 15 minutes longer or until golden brown. Let stand for 10 minutes before serving. **Yield:** 6-8 servings.

Italian-Style Round Steak

1/4 cup all-purpose flour

1-1/2 teaspoons salt

1/4 teaspoon pepper

2 pounds boneless beef round steak, cut into serving-size pieces

2 to 3 tablespoons vegetable oil

1 cup water

1 garlic clove, minced

1 can (15 ounces) tomato sauce

1/2 pound fresh mushrooms, sliced

1 medium onion, sliced

1 small green pepper, julienned

2 teaspoons sugar

1/2 teaspoon dried oregano

1/8 teaspoon dried basil

1 package (7 ounces) spaghetti, cooked and drained

1/4 cup grated Parmesan cheese

In a large resealable plastic bag, combine the flour, salt and pepper. Add beef, a few pieces at a time, and shake to coat. In a Dutch oven, brown beef in batches in oil; drain. Add water and garlic. Bring to a boil. Reduce heat; cover and simmer for 1-1/2 hours.

Stir in the tomato sauce, mushrooms, onion, green pepper, sugar, oregano and basil. Cover and simmer 30-45 minutes longer or until the meat and vegetables are tender. Serve over spaghetti. Sprinkle with Parmesan cheese. **Yield:** 6-8 servings.

Red-Eye Beef Roast

1 boneless beef eye of round
  roast (about 3 pounds)
1 tablespoon vegetable oil
2-1/2 cups water, *divided*
1 envelope onion soup mix

3 tablespoons cider vinegar
2 tablespoons Louisiana hot
  sauce
2 tablespoons all-purpose flour

In a Dutch oven, brown roast on all sides in oil over medium-high heat; drain. Combine 3/4 cup water, soup mix, vinegar and hot sauce; pour over roast.

Cover and bake at 325° for 2-3 hours or until tender. Transfer to a serving platter and keep warm. Let stand for 10-15 minutes before slicing.

For gravy, transfer meat juices to a saucepan; skim fat. Combine flour and remaining water until smooth; stir into meat juices. Bring to a boil; cook and stir for 2 minutes or until thickened. Serve with meat. **Yield:** 10-12 servings.

Topsy-Turvy Pie

1 pound ground beef
1/2 cup chopped onion
1/4 cup chopped green pepper
1 can (8 ounces) tomato sauce
1 can (4-1/2 ounces) chopped
  ripe olives, drained

1/2 teaspoon salt
1 teaspoon chili powder

BISCUIT TOPPING:
1 cup buttermilk biscuit mix
1/4 cup milk
2 tablespoons butter, melted

In a skillet, cook the beef, onion and green pepper over medium heat until meat is no longer pink and pepper is tender; drain. Stir in the tomato sauce, olives, salt and chili powder; mix well. Pour into a 9-in. pie plate; set aside.

For topping, combine biscuit mix, milk and butter in a mixing bowl; beat 15 strokes. Turn onto a floured surface and knead 8-10 times. Roll into a 10-in. circle. Place over meat mixture; crimp edges to seal. Cut small slits in crust to vent steam.

Bake at 425° for 15-20 minutes. Let stand a few minutes before serving. **Yield:** 4-6 servings.

Sesame Flank Steak

1/4 cup sesame seeds, toasted
1/4 cup thinly sliced green onions
3 tablespoons reduced-sodium
   soy sauce
2 tablespoons vegetable oil
1 tablespoon brown sugar

1 tablespoon ground ginger
3 garlic cloves, minced
1 teaspoon ground mustard
1 teaspoon Worcestershire sauce
1-1/2 pounds beef flank steak

In a large resealable plastic bag, combine the first nine ingredients. Score steak and add to bag. Seal bag and turn to coat; refrigerate for 4 hours or overnight.

Drain and discard marinade. Grill steak, covered, over medium heat until the meat reaches desired doneness (for medium-rare, a meat thermometer should read 145°; medium, 160°; well-done, 170°). Thinly slice across the grain. **Yield:** 8 servings.

Kid-Pleasing Spaghetti

1-1/2 pounds ground beef
1 medium onion, chopped
2-1/2 cups spaghetti sauce
8 ounces spaghetti, cooked and
   drained
3 tablespoons butter

2 tablespoons all-purpose flour
1/2 teaspoon salt
1-1/2 cups milk
1-1/2 cups (6 ounces) shredded
   cheddar cheese, *divided*
1/4 cup grated Parmesan cheese

In a skillet, cook beef and onion over medium heat until meat is no longer pink; drain. Stir in spaghetti sauce. Cover and simmer for 10 minutes. Stir in spaghetti; set aside.

In a saucepan, melt butter. Stir in flour and salt until smooth. Gradually add milk. Bring to a boil; cook and stir for 2 minutes or until thickened. Remove from the heat. Add 3/4 cup cheddar cheese and Parmesan cheese, stirring until melted.

Place half of the spaghetti mixture in a greased 13-in. x 9-in. x 2-in. baking dish. Top with cheese sauce and the remaining spaghetti mixture. Sprinkle with remaining cheddar cheese.

Bake, uncovered, at 350° for 30 minutes or until heated through. **Yield:** 10 servings.

Mock Pot Roast

1/2 cup ketchup
2 eggs
1 tablespoon prepared horseradish
1/2 cup quick-cooking oats
1 teaspoon ground mustard
1 teaspoon salt
1/4 teaspoon pepper
2 pounds lean ground beef
1 teaspoon steak sauce
8 medium carrots, halved
8 small red potatoes
16 pearl onions
1 package (10 ounces) frozen peas, thawed

In a large bowl, combine the first seven ingredients. Crumble beef over mixture and mix well. Shape into a loaf in a greased 13-in. x 9-in. x 2-in. baking pan. Brush with steak sauce. Arrange the carrots, potatoes and onions around loaf.

Cover and bake at 375° for 40 minutes. Add peas. Cover and bake 30 minutes longer. Uncover; baste with pan juices. Bake 5 minutes more or until the meat is no longer pink and a meat thermometer reads 160°. **Yield:** 8 servings.

Pepper Steak

1-1/4 cups beef broth, *divided*
1/4 cup soy sauce
1-1/4 teaspoons ground ginger
1/2 teaspoon sugar
1/4 teaspoon pepper
1-1/2 pounds boneless beef round steak, cut into strips
1 garlic clove, minced
1/4 cup olive oil
4 medium green peppers, julienned
2 large tomatoes, peeled and chopped
3 tablespoons cornstarch
Hot cooked rice

In a small bowl, combine 3/4 cup broth, soy sauce, ginger, sugar and pepper; set aside.

In a skillet or wok, brown beef and garlic in oil over medium-high heat. Add peppers and tomatoes. Cook and stir until peppers are crisp-tender, about 3 minutes. Stir the soy sauce mixture and add to pan. Cover and cook until the meat is tender, about 15 minutes.

Combine cornstarch with the remaining broth until smooth; stir into pan. Bring to a boil; cook and stir for 2 minutes or until thickened. Serve over rice. **Yield:** 8 servings.

Rhubarb Beef

2 to 2-1/2 pounds beef stew
   meat, cut into 1-inch cubes
2 tablespoons butter
2 large onions, chopped
1 can (10-1/2 ounces) beef broth
1 cup water
1/4 cup lemon juice
1/4 cup chopped fresh parsley

1-1/2 teaspoons dried mint
2 teaspoons salt
1 teaspoon saffron
1/4 teaspoon pepper
2 to 3 cups sliced fresh *or* frozen
   rhubarb
Hot cooked rice

In a Dutch oven, brown beef on all sides in butter. Remove meat from pan; drain all but 2 tablespoons drippings. Saute onions in drippings until lightly browned.

Return meat to pan. Add the broth, water, lemon juice, parsley, mint, salt, saffron and pepper; cover and simmer until meat is tender, about 2 hours. Add additional water as needed. Add rhubarb during the last 15 minutes of cooking. Serve over rice. **Yield:** 6 servings.

Poached Meatballs In Lemon Sauce

1/2 cup seasoned dry bread
   crumbs
1 egg, beaten
1/2 teaspoon salt
1 teaspoon grated lemon peel
1 pound ground beef

2-1/4 cups water, *divided*
2 beef bouillon cubes
2 teaspoons cornstarch
2 tablespoons fresh lemon juice
2 egg yolks
Cooked rice

In a mixing bowl, combine the bread crumbs, egg, salt and lemon peel. Crumble ground beef over mixture and mix well. Shape into 12 meatballs, about 1-1/2 in. in diameter; set aside.

In a saucepan, bring 2 cups water to a boil; add bouillon and stir to dissolve. Gently drop meatballs into broth. Reduce heat and simmer for 10 minutes or until the meatballs are no longer pink; remove to a warm bowl.

Combine cornstarch and remaining water until smooth; stir into broth. Add lemon juice. Bring to a boil; cook and stir for 2 minutes or until thickened. Remove from the heat. Stir a small amount of broth into egg yolks; blend well. Return all to pan and bring to a gentle boil, stirring constantly. Serve sauce over meatballs. **Yield:** 4 servings.

Cheesy Casserole

1 pound ground beef
1 can (10-3/4 ounces) condensed tomato soup, undiluted
1 teaspoon salt
1/8 teaspoon pepper
1 cup (8 ounces) 4% cottage cheese

1 cup (8 ounces) sour cream
6 to 8 green onions with tops, sliced
8 ounces medium noodles, cooked and drained
1 cup (4 ounces) shredded cheddar cheese

In a skillet, cook beef over medium heat until no longer pink; drain. Add the soup, salt and pepper; cook for 5 minutes. Remove from the heat.

In a large mixing bowl, combine cottage cheese, sour cream, green onions and noodles. Layer noodle mixture alternately with meat sauce in a greased 2-qt. baking dish.

Cover and bake at 350° for 25 minutes. Uncover; sprinkle with cheese. Bake 5-10 minutes longer or until cheese is melted. **Yield:** 6-8 servings.

Open-Faced Pizza Burgers

1-1/2 pounds ground beef
1/4 cup chopped onion
1 can (15 ounces) pizza sauce
1 can (4 ounces) mushroom stems and pieces, drained

1 tablespoon sugar
1/2 teaspoon dried oregano
6 hamburger buns, split and toasted
1-1/2 cups (6 ounces) shredded part-skim mozzarella cheese

In a large skillet, cook beef and onion over medium heat until the meat is no longer pink; drain. Stir in the pizza sauce, mushrooms, sugar and oregano; heat through. Spoon onto buns; sprinkle with mozzarella cheese.

Place on ungreased baking sheets. Broil 4 in. from the heat for 2 minutes or until the cheese is melted. **Yield:** 12 servings.

Stuffed Meat Loaf

1-1/4 pounds lean ground beef
1 pound bulk hot sausage
1-1/2 cups herb-seasoned dry bread stuffing
1 egg, beaten
5 tablespoons ketchup, *divided*
3 tablespoons steak sauce, *divided*
1 cup (4 ounces) shredded cheddar cheese

1 small tomato, diced
1 small onion, diced
1/2 small green pepper, diced
8 to 10 fresh mushrooms, sliced
4 ounces thinly sliced fully cooked ham, optional
1 cup (4 ounces) shredded Swiss cheese

In a mixing bowl, combine ground beef, sausage, stuffing, egg, 3 tablespoons ketchup and 2 tablespoons steak sauce. Pat half of meat mixture into a 9-in. x 5-in. x 3-in. loaf pan. Sprinkle with cheddar cheese. Layer with the tomato, onion, green pepper, mushrooms, ham if desired and Swiss cheese. Cover with remaining meat mixture; press down firmly to seal. (Mixture may be higher than the top of the pan.)

Combine remaining ketchup and steak sauce; drizzle over top of meat loaf. Bake at 350° for 1 hour or until a meat thermometer reads 160°, draining off fat when necessary. **Yield:** 6-8 servings.

Lemon Rib Eyes

1-1/2 teaspoons dried basil
1-1/2 teaspoons dried oregano
1 teaspoon garlic powder
1/2 teaspoon salt
1/8 teaspoon pepper
2 beef rib eye steaks (8 ounces *each*)

1 tablespoon olive oil
1 tablespoon lemon juice
2 tablespoons crumbled feta, optional
1 tablespoon sliced ripe olives, optional
Lemon slices, optional

Combine the basil, oregano, garlic powder, salt and pepper; rub over steaks. In a skillet, cook steaks in oil for 11-15 minutes or until meat reaches desired doneness (for medium-rare, a meat thermometer should read 145°; medium, 160°; well done, 170°).

Transfer to a serving platter. Drizzle with lemon juice. If desired, top with cheese and olives and garnish with lemon. **Yield:** 2 servings.

Pork

Pork Tenderloin Florentine

1 pork tenderloin (1 pound)
1/8 teaspoon garlic powder
6 to 7 medium whole fresh
   mushrooms
1 package (10 ounces) frozen
   chopped spinach, thawed and
   well drained, *divided*

1/2 cup corn bread stuffing mix
3 tablespoons grated Parmesan
   cheese, *divided*
3 tablespoons butter, melted
1 tablespoon sliced green onion
Browning sauce, optional
Dash ground nutmeg

Cut a lengthwise slit down the center of the tenderloin to within 1/2 in.
of bottom. Open tenderloin so it lies flat; cover with plastic wrap.
Flatten with the flat side of a meat mallet to 1/4-in. thickness. Remove
plastic and sprinkle meat with garlic powder; set aside.

Separate caps from stems of four mushrooms; set caps aside. Chop
stems and remaining mushrooms to measure 1/2 cup. In a bowl,
combine the chopped mushrooms, half the spinach, stuffing mix,
2 tablespoons cheese, butter and onion. Spread over tenderloin.
Roll up, starting with a long edge. Secure with toothpicks.

Place seam side down in a greased 13-in. x 9-in. x 2-in. baking pan;
brush lightly with browning sauce if desired. Top with remaining
spinach; sprinkle with nutmeg. Arrange mushroom caps around meat;
sprinkle with remaining Parmesan.

Cover and bake at 350° for 30 minutes. Uncover; bake 10 minutes
longer or until a meat thermometer inserted into meat layer reads 160°.
Cut into 1-in. slices. **Yield:** 4 servings.

Teriyaki Tangerine Ribs

4 pounds country-style pork ribs
2/3 cup fresh tangerine *or* orange juice
1/3 cup light corn syrup
2 tablespoons soy sauce
1 teaspoon grated tangerine *or* orange peel
1/2 teaspoon ground ginger
1 garlic clove, minced

Place ribs meat side down on a rack in a foil-lined shallow roasting pan. Bake at 425° for 30 minutes. Drain; turn ribs. Reduce temperature to 350° and bake 30 minutes longer.

Meanwhile, combine remaining ingredients in a saucepan; bring to a boil. Remove from the heat and set aside. Remove ribs from rack; discard drippings and foil. Return ribs to pan; pour tangerine mixture over ribs.

Bake, uncovered, turning ribs often, for 30-40 minutes or until tender. **Yield:** 8 servings.

Stuffed Banana Peppers

6 to 8 mild banana peppers
1 pound bulk pork sausage
1/2 cup cooked rice
1/3 cup thinly sliced green onions
3 garlic cloves, minced
1 teaspoon salt
1/2 teaspoon pepper
1 can (8 ounces) tomato sauce
1 tablespoon water
1 teaspoon chili powder, optional
1/2 cup shredded part-skim mozzarella cheese, optional

Remove stems of peppers; cut peppers in half lengthwise. Carefully remove seeds and membrane; set aside. Combine the sausage, rice, onions, garlic, salt and pepper. Fill pepper halves. Place in a greased 13-in. x 9-in. x 2-in. baking dish. Combine the tomato sauce, water and chili powder if desired; pour over peppers.

Cover and bake at 350° for 30 minutes or until filling is cooked and set. Uncover; sprinkle with cheese if desired. Bake 5-10 minutes longer or until cheese is melted. **Yield:** 6-8 servings.

Sausage Sloppy Joes

1/2 pound bulk pork sausage
1/3 cup chopped onion
1/2 cup tomato sauce
1/4 cup water
2 tablespoons ketchup

1-1/2 teaspoons Worcestershire sauce
Dash to 1/8 teaspoon hot pepper sauce
2 hamburger buns, split

In a skillet, cook sausage and onion over medium heat until meat is no longer pink; drain. Stir in tomato sauce, water, ketchup, Worcestershire sauce and hot pepper sauce. Bring to a boil. Reduce heat; cover and simmer for 30 minutes. Serve on buns. **Yield:** 2 servings.

Old-Fashioned Pork Roast

1 boneless pork loin roast (2 to 3 pounds)
1 cup unsweetened applesauce

1 teaspoon salt
1 teaspoon rubbed sage

Place roast fat side up on a greased rack in a roasting pan. Combine applesauce, salt and sage; spread over roast.

Cover and bake at 350° for 1 hour. Uncover and bake 15 to 30 minutes longer or until a meat thermometer reads 160°. Let stand for 10 minutes before slicing. **Yield:** 8-10 servings.

Simple Sausage Ring

1 pound bulk pork sausage
2 tubes (12 ounces *each*) refrigerated biscuits

2 cups (8 ounces) shredded Monterey Jack cheese

In a skillet, cook sausage over medium heat until no longer pink; drain and set aside. Flatten each biscuit to a 3-in. diameter. Press half of the biscuits onto the bottom and 2 in. up the sides of a greased 10-in. fluted tube pan. Spoon sausage into pan; sprinkle with cheese. Top with remaining biscuits.

Bake at 350° for 20-25 minutes or until golden brown. Let stand for 10 minutes before inverting onto a serving plate. **Yield:** 8-10 servings.

Stuffed Crown Roast of Pork

1 pork crown rib roast (about 7 pounds)
1 cup chopped onion
1 cup chopped celery
6 tablespoons butter
1 can (6 ounces) frozen orange juice concentrate, thawed, undiluted, *divided*

4 cups soft bread cubes
1 teaspoon salt
1/4 teaspoon fennel seed, crushed
1/8 teaspoon pepper
1 cup fresh *or* frozen cranberries, thawed
1/2 cup honey

Place the roast with rib ends up in a shallow roasting pan. Bake, uncovered, at 325° for 2 to 2-1/2 hours or until meat thermometer inserted into meat between ribs reads 150°.

Meanwhile, saute onion and celery in butter in a skillet until tender. Stir in 1/4 cup orange juice concentrate; bring to a boil. Remove from the heat. Add the bread cubes, salt, fennel and pepper; toss lightly. Stir in cranberries; spoon into the center of roast. Bake 30 minutes longer.

Meanwhile, combine honey and remaining orange juice concentrate in a saucepan. Bring to a boil; reduce heat and simmer for 2 minutes. Brush over roast and dressing; bake 30 minutes longer or until meat thermometer reads 160°. Let stand for 15 minutes before slicing. **Yield:** 14 servings.

Sesame Pork Kabobs

3/4 cup finely chopped onion
1/2 cup soy sauce
1/4 cup sesame seeds, toasted
1/4 cup water
3 tablespoons sugar

4-1/2 teaspoons minced garlic
1-1/2 teaspoons ground ginger
1/8 teaspoon cayenne pepper
2 pork tenderloins (3/4 pound *each*), trimmed

In a large resealable plastic bag, combine the first eight ingredients. Cut pork across the grain into 1/4-in.-thick medallions; add to bag. Seal bag and turn to coat; refrigerate for at least 1 hour.

Drain and discard marinade. Thread medallions accordion-style onto metal or soaked wooden skewers. Use about 10 pieces on each skewer. Grill, uncovered, over medium heat for 9-12 minutes or until meat is no longer pink, turning often. **Yield:** 6 servings.

Marinated Pork Loin Roast

3/4 cup ketchup
1/4 cup packed brown sugar
1/4 cup white wine vinegar
1/4 cup seedless raspberry jam
1/4 cup maple-flavored syrup
2 tablespoons lemon juice
2 tablespoons Worcestershire sauce

1 teaspoon *each* dried thyme, oregano and marjoram
1 teaspoon salt
1 teaspoon pepper
1 teaspoon Dijon mustard
1 bay leaf
1/4 teaspoon ground ginger
1 boneless pork loin roast (3 pounds)

In a saucepan, combine all the ingredients except pork. Bring to a boil over medium heat; cool. Place roast in an 11-in. x 7-in. x 2-in. baking dish. Prick surface of roast with a fork; pour sauce over roast. Cover and refrigerate overnight, turning several times.

Bake, uncovered, at 325° for 1-1/2 to 2 hours or until a meat thermometer reads 160°. Let stand for 10 minutes before slicing. Discard bay leaf. **Yield:** 10 servings.

Shredded Pork Tacos

1 pork tenderloin (3/4 pound), cut into 1-inch pieces
1 teaspoon vegetable oil
1 small onion, chopped
2 garlic cloves, minced
1 can (8 ounces) tomato sauce
1 can (4 ounces) chopped green chilies
1 teaspoon chili powder

1/2 teaspoon salt
1/2 teaspoon dried oregano
1/2 teaspoon ground cumin
1/4 teaspoon pepper
2 to 4 flour tortillas (7 inches), warmed
Shredded lettuce and chopped tomato, optional

In a skillet, brown pork in oil. Remove from pan and keep warm. In same skillet, saute onion and garlic in drippings until tender. Stir in the tomato sauce, chilies, chili powder, salt, oregano, cumin and pepper. Add pork; bring to a boil. Reduce heat; cover and simmer for 20 minutes or until pork is tender.

Cool slightly; shred with two forks. Return to sauce; heat through. Serve in tortillas with lettuce and tomato if desired. **Yield:** 2 servings.

Saucy Ham and Rice

1-1/2 pounds fully cooked ham, julienned
1 tablespoon butter
1 cup chopped celery
1 cup julienned green pepper
1 small onion, cut into thin wedges

1 can (10-3/4 ounces) condensed cream of mushroom soup, undiluted
2 tablespoons prepared mustard
3/4 teaspoon dill weed
1/8 teaspoon celery salt
1 cup (8 ounces) sour cream
Hot cooked rice

In a skillet, saute ham in butter for 2 minutes. Add the celery, green pepper and onion; saute until tender. Add the soup, mustard, dill and celery salt; stir until smooth and heated through. Stir in sour cream; heat through but do not boil. Serve over rice. **Yield:** 4-6 servings.

Pork Wellington

1 boneless whole pork loin roast (2 to 3 pounds)
1/4 teaspoon salt
1/4 teaspoon pepper
4 garlic cloves, minced, *divided*
5 tablespoons olive oil, *divided*

2 cups torn fresh spinach
1-1/2 cups sliced fresh mushrooms
1/2 cup shredded part-skim mozzarella cheese
1 tube (11 ounces) refrigerated breadsticks

Slice roast in half horizontally; sprinkle with salt and pepper. In a skillet, cook roast and two garlic cloves in 3 tablespoons oil over low heat for 40 minutes, turning to brown all sides.

Meanwhile, in another skillet, cook the spinach, mushrooms and remaining garlic in remaining oil for 3-4 minutes or until soft; drain well. Remove from the heat; stir in cheese. Place breadsticks 1/2 in. apart in a greased 15-in. x 10-in. x 1-in. baking pan, stretching dough slightly so each breadstick is about 13 in. long. Lay one roast half in the center of the dough. Spread spinach filling evenly over roast. Top with other half of roast. Bring ends of a breadstick to the top of the roast, twisting and pinching to seal. Repeat with each breadstick.

Bake at 350° for 35-45 minutes or until meat thermometer reads 160°. Let stand for 10 minutes before slicing. **Yield:** 8-10 servings.

Hasty Heartland Dinner

1 package (5-1/2 ounces) au gratin potatoes
4 hard-cooked eggs, chopped
1 cup chopped fully cooked ham
1 cup frozen peas

In a microwave, cook potatoes according to package directions. Add sauce packet and milk as directed. Stir in the eggs, ham and peas.

Cover and cook on high until heated through, about 3-5 minutes, stirring occasionally. Let stand for 5 minutes before serving. **Yield:** 4 servings.

Editor's Note: This recipe was tested in a 1,100-watt microwave.

Mom's Chinese Dish

4 bacon strips, diced
2 pork tenderloins (3/4 pound *each*)
1 garlic clove, minced
3/4 cup water, *divided*
3 tablespoons soy sauce
1/4 teaspoon ground ginger
1/4 teaspoon pepper
1 large green *or* sweet red pepper, julienned
1 medium onion, julienned
3 celery ribs, cut into thin diagonal slices
2 tablespoons cornstarch
1 can (8 ounces) sliced water chestnuts, drained
1 can (8 ounces) sliced bamboo shoots, drained
Hot rice *or* chow mein noodles

In a large skillet, cook bacon over medium heat until crisp. Using a slotted spoon, remove to paper towel, reserving drippings. Cut pork into 3-in. x 1/2-in. strips.

In same skillet, stir-fry pork and garlic in bacon drippings over medium-high heat for 2-3 minutes. Carefully stir in 1/2 cup water, soy sauce, ginger and pepper. Reduce heat; cover and simmer for 3 minutes. Add the green pepper, onion and celery; Cook and stir over medium-high heat for 3 minutes or until vegetables are crisp-tender.

Combine cornstarch and remaining water until smooth; stir into skillet. Bring to a boil; cook and stir for 2 minutes or until thickened. Add the water chestnuts, bamboo shoots and bacon; heat through. Serve over rice or chow mein noodles. **Yield:** 6 servings.

Cajun Pork Roast

1 boneless pork shoulder roast
(3 to 3-1/2 pounds)
1/2 cup finely chopped onion
1 tablespoon hot pepper sauce
1 tablespoon Worcestershire sauce

1 tablespoon steak sauce
4 teaspoons prepared mustard
3 garlic cloves, minced
1 teaspoon seasoned salt

Place roast in a shallow baking pan; cut 8-10 small slits in roast. Combine remaining ingredients; press into slits and over top of roast.

Bake, uncovered, at 350° for 30 minutes. Cover and bake 1 to 1-1/2 hours longer or until a meat thermometer reads 160°. Let stand for 10 minutes before slicing. **Yield:** 8-10 servings.

Sausage Apple Roll

2 pounds bulk pork sausage
2 cups finely chopped tart apple
1 cup toasted wheat germ

1 cup soft bread crumbs
1/3 cup finely chopped onion

Pat sausage onto waxed paper to form a 14-in. x 9-in. rectangle. In a bowl, combine the apple, wheat germ, bread crumbs and onion. Spoon over sausage and gently press down; beginning at the narrow end and using the waxed paper as an aid, roll up jelly-roll style.

Place in an ungreased 13-in. x 9-in. x 2-in. baking pan. Bake at 350° for 1 hour or until a meat thermometer inserted into the center of the roll reads 160°. **Yield:** 8-10 servings.

Country-Style Pork Ribs

3/4 cup soy sauce
1/2 cup sugar
1/2 cup water

1 garlic clove, minced
4 pounds country-style pork ribs

Combine the first four ingredients; stir to dissolve sugar. Pour into a large resealable plastic bag; add ribs. Seal bag and turn to coat; refrigerate overnight, turning occasionally. Drain and discard marinade.

Grill, covered, over medium heat, turning occasionally, for 30-40 minutes or until juices run clear. **Yield:** 6-8 servings.

Citrus Pork Skillet

1/2 pound pork tenderloin, trimmed
1/2 to 3/4 teaspoon ground cumin
1/4 teaspoon pepper
1/4 teaspoon salt, optional
2 garlic cloves, minced
1 cup chicken broth

2/3 cup orange juice
2 tablespoons cider vinegar
1-1/2 teaspoons brown sugar
1 cup julienned carrots
2 tablespoons cornstarch
1/2 cup thinly sliced green onions
Hot cooked noodles, optional

Cut pork into 1/2-in. x 1/2-in. x 2-in. strips. In a large resealable plastic bag, combine the cumin, pepper and salt if desired. Add pork; seal bag and shake to coat.

In a large skillet coated with nonstick cooking spray, stir-fry pork and garlic over medium heat until pork is browned. In a bowl, combine the broth, orange juice, vinegar and brown sugar. Add carrots and 1-1/2 cups broth mixture to skillet; bring to a boil. Reduce heat; cover and simmer for 5 minutes or until carrots are tender.

Combine cornstarch and remaining broth mixture until smooth; add to skillet, stirring constantly. Bring to a boil; cook and stir for 2 minutes or until thickened. Add green onions; cook for 1 minute. Serve over noodles if desired. **Yield:** 4 servings.

Potato Ham au Gratin

1 package (1 pound) frozen tater tot potatoes, *divided*
1-1/4 cups frozen peas
1-1/2 cups diced fully cooked ham
1 cup (4 ounces) shredded Swiss cheese, *divided*

1/3 cup sliced green onions
1-1/4 cups milk
3 eggs
3/4 teaspoon salt
1/2 to 3/4 teaspoon dried tarragon
1/2 teaspoon pepper

Place half of the potatoes in a greased 11-in. x 7-in. x 2-in. baking dish. Layer with the peas, ham, 3/4 cup cheese, onions and remaining potatoes.

In a bowl, whisk the milk, eggs and seasonings; pour over potatoes. Sprinkle with remaining cheese. Bake, uncovered, at 350° for 1 hour. **Yield:** 6 servings.

Tropical Pork Kabobs

1-1/2 pounds boneless pork, cut into 3/4-inch cubes

1 medium sweet yellow pepper, cut into 1-inch pieces

1 medium sweet red pepper, cut into 1-inch pieces

1 medium zucchini, cut into 1-inch slices

12 large fresh mushrooms

1 can (20 ounces) pineapple chunks in juice, undrained

1 cup molasses

2/3 cup soy sauce

Place pork in a large resealable bag and place the peppers, zucchini and mushrooms in another large resealable plastic bag. Drain the pineapple, reserving 1/2 cup juice. Add pineapple chunks to the vegetable mixture.

Combine the molasses, soy sauce and pineapple juice. Reserve 1/2 cup for basting and refrigerate. Divide the remaining sauce between the meat and vegetables. Seal bags and turn to coat; refrigerate several hours.

Drain and discard marinade. On 12 metal or soaked wooden skewers, alternate pork, vegetables and pineapple. Grill, uncovered, over medium heat for 12-15 minutes or until the pork juices run clear, turning and basting with reserved marinade. **Yield:** 6 servings (12 kabobs).

One-Pan Pork a la Orange

2 cups dry instant chicken stuffing mix

1-1/2 cups orange juice, *divided*

4 pork cutlets

1/4 cup all-purpose flour

2 tablespoons vegetable oil

2 cups frozen baby carrots

2 cups frozen broccoli cuts

1/8 teaspoon salt

1/8 teaspoon pepper

Combine stuffing mix and 3/4 cup orange juice; let stand for 3-4 minutes or until liquid is absorbed, stirring occasionally. Flatten cutlets to 1/4-in. thickness; top each with about 1/3 cup stuffing. Roll up jelly-roll style and secure with toothpicks; coat with flour.

In a large skillet, brown roll-ups in oil; drain. Add remaining orange juice; bring to a boil. Reduce heat; cover and simmer for 7 minutes. Add remaining ingredients; cover and simmer 7-10 minutes longer or until vegetables are tender. Remove toothpicks before serving. **Yield:** 4 servings.

Cranberry-Glazed Spareribs

3 pounds pork spareribs
1/4 cup packed brown sugar
3 tablespoons all-purpose flour
1/2 teaspoon salt
1/4 teaspoon ground mustard

1/4 teaspoon ground cloves
1-3/4 cups cranberry juice
1 cup water
2 tablespoons white vinegar
1 tablespoon lemon juice

Place ribs on a rack in a foil-lined shallow roasting pan. Broil 6 in. from the heat for 12-20 minutes on each side or until browned. Remove ribs from rack; drain drippings. Return ribs to pan.

In a saucepan, combine the brown sugar, flour, salt, mustard and cloves; gradually add cranberry juice, stirring until smooth. Add the water, vinegar and lemon juice. Bring to a boil; cook and stir for 2 minutes or until thickened. Pour over ribs.

Cover and bake at 350° for 45 minutes. Uncover; bake 20-30 minutes longer or until ribs are tender. **Yield:** 4 servings.

Pork Chops with Pear Stuffing

8 pork chops (1/2 inch thick)
2 tablespoons vegetable oil
2 tablespoons butter
1/4 cup chopped celery
1/4 cup chopped onion
1-3/4 cups corn bread stuffing mix
1 fresh pear, diced

2 tablespoons chopped pecans
2 tablespoons chopped fresh
parsley
1/8 teaspoon dried thyme
1/8 teaspoon salt
Dash pepper
1/2 cup water

In a skillet, brown pork chops in oil over medium heat; drain and set aside. Add butter to skillet; saute celery and onion until tender. Remove from the heat Add the stuffing mix, pear, pecans, parsley, thyme, salt and pepper; mix well. Add water; toss gently to moisten.

Spoon a fourth of the stuffing on one pork chop; top with another chop and secure with kitchen string. Repeat with remaining chops and stuffing. Stand chops vertically, but not touching, in a deep roasting pan. Add water to a depth of 1/4 in.

Cover and bake at 350° for 30-35 minutes or until juices run clear and a meat thermometer reads 160°. Uncover; bake 5 minutes longer to brown. Remove string. **Yield:** 4 servings.

Braised Pork Chops

1/4 cup all-purpose flour
1/4 teaspoon salt
1/4 teaspoon pepper
4 pork chops (3/4 inch thick)
2 tablespoons vegetable oil
1 medium onion, sliced

3/4 cup sliced celery
1 garlic clove, minced
1 can (14-1/2 ounces) beef broth
1 teaspoon dried thyme
1 bay leaf

In a large resealable plastic bag, combine the flour, salt and pepper. Add chops; seal bag and shake to coat.

In a skillet, cook chops in oil over medium-high heat for 3 minutes on each side or until well browned. Remove chops and set aside. Cook the onion, celery and garlic in drippings until tender.

Return chops to the skillet; add broth, thyme and bay leaf. Bring to a boil. Reduce heat; simmer, uncovered, for 30 minutes or until pork juices run clear. Discard bay leaf.

Transfer chops to a serving plate. With a slotted spoon, remove celery and onion; spoon over chops. Thicken juices for gravy if desired. **Yield:** 4 servings.

Cheesy Zucchini Medley

1/2 cup uncooked long grain rice
1 pound bulk pork sausage
1/2 cup chopped onion
3-1/2 cups sliced zucchini
1 cup chopped fresh tomato

2 cans (4 ounces *each*) mushroom stems and pieces, drained
1/4 teaspoon salt
1/4 teaspoon pepper
8 ounces process cheese (Velveeta), cubed, *divided*

Cook rice according to package directions; set aside. In a large skillet, cook sausage and onion over medium heat until sausage is no longer pink; drain. Stir in the zucchini, tomato, mushrooms, salt, pepper, 6 ounces of the cheese and rice. Spoon into a greased 11-in. x 7-in. x 2-in. baking dish.

Bake, uncovered, at 325° for 50-60 minutes, stirring every 20 minutes, or until vegetables are tender. Top with remaining cheese. Bake 3-5 minutes longer or until cheese is melted. **Yield:** 6-8 servings.

Parmesan Ham Pasta

- 1 package (16 ounces) bow tie pasta
- 2 cups cubed fully cooked ham
- 1 can (4 ounces) mushroom stems and pieces, drained
- 1/2 cup butter
- 1/2 cup all-purpose flour
- 1/2 teaspoon salt
- 2 cups milk
- 1 package (10 ounces) frozen chopped spinach, thawed and squeezed dry
- 1 cup (4 ounces) shredded Parmesan cheese

Cook pasta according to package directions. Meanwhile, in a large skillet, saute ham and mushrooms in butter. Stir in flour and salt until blended. Gradually add milk. Bring to a boil; cook and stir for 2 minutes or until thickened.

Reduce heat. Stir in spinach and cheese. Cook and stir until cheese is melted. Drain pasta; stir into the ham mixture. **Yield:** 6 servings.

Barbecued Meatballs

- 1 cup quick-cooking oats
- 1 egg
- 1/3 cup evaporated milk
- 3/4 teaspoon chili powder
- 3/4 teaspoon salt
- 1/4 teaspoon pepper
- 1/8 teaspoon garlic powder
- 1-1/2 pounds ground pork
- 1 cup ketchup
- 3/4 cup packed brown sugar
- 2-1/2 teaspoons Liquid Smoke, optional
- 1/2 teaspoon lemon juice

Combine the first seven ingredients; crumble pork over mixture and mix well. Shape into 2-in. balls. Place meatballs on a greased rack in a shallow baking pan. Bake, uncovered, at 375° for 20-25 minutes or until a meat thermometer reads 160° and meatballs are no longer pink in center. Drain on paper towels. Transfer to an ungreased 2-qt. baking dish.

Meanwhile, in a saucepan, combine the ketchup, brown sugar, Liquid Smoke if desired and lemon juice; stir until brown sugar is dissolved. Pour over meatballs. Bake, uncovered, at 375° for 10-15 minutes or until meatballs are heated through. **Yield:** 6 servings.

Sausage Potato Wraps

1 pound bulk hot pork sausage
1 package (24 ounces) frozen
  O'Brien hash brown potatoes
4 eggs

1/2 cup milk
Salt and pepper to taste
12 flour tortillas (8 inches)
Sour cream and salsa, optional

In a skillet, cook sausage over medium heat until no longer pink; drain. Add potatoes; cook until lightly browned, about 15 minutes. Beat the eggs, milk, salt and pepper; add to the sausage mixture. Cook until eggs are completely set, stirring frequently. Divide mixture between tortillas; roll up tightly. Place in a greased 13-in. x 9-in. x 2-in. baking dish.

Microwave, uncovered, on high for 2-4 minutes or until heated through, or microwave individually for 30 seconds. Serve with sour cream and salsa if desired. **Yield:** 6-8 servings.

Editor's Note: This recipe was tested in a 1,100-watt microwave.

Pork Fajitas

1 pound boneless pork
2 tablespoons orange juice
2 tablespoons cider vinegar
2 garlic cloves, minced
1 teaspoon dried oregano
1 teaspoon ground cumin
1/2 teaspoon seasoned salt
1/2 teaspoon hot pepper sauce

1 medium onion, cut into thin
  wedges
1 medium green pepper,
  julienned
1 tablespoon vegetable oil
6 flour tortillas (6 inches)
Shredded lettuce, diced tomatoes,
  salsa *and/or* sour cream, optional

Cut pork into 4-in. x 1/2-in. x 1/4-in. strips; set aside. In a resealable plastic bag, combine the orange juice, vinegar, garlic, oregano, cumin, seasoned salt and hot pepper sauce; add pork. Seal bag and turn to coat; refrigerate for 1-2 hours.

In a skillet, cook pork with marinade, onion and green pepper in oil over medium heat until pork is no longer pink and vegetables are tender; drain.

Place about 3/4 cup filling down the center of each tortilla; top with lettuce, tomatoes, salsa and sour cream if desired. Fold in sides of tortillas and serve immediately. **Yield:** 6 servings.

Hot Dogs 'n' Rice

1/2 cup chopped onion
1/2 cup chopped green pepper
2 tablespoons vegetable oil
1 cup uncooked long grain rice
1-1/2 cups water, *divided*

5 hot dogs, halved lengthwise and cut into 1/2-inch slices
1 can (14-1/2 ounces) stewed tomatoes, undrained
3 tablespoons ketchup

In a large skillet, saute onion and green pepper in oil until tender. Add rice; cook and stir for 2-3 minutes. Add 1-1/4 cups water and hot dogs. Bring to a boil. Reduce heat; cover and simmer for 20-25 minutes. Add the tomatoes, ketchup and remaining water. Cover and cook until rice is tender. **Yield:** 5 servings.

Pork Chops Parmesan

1 cup crushed potato chips
1/4 cup grated Parmesan cheese
1/4 cup minced fresh parsley
2 tablespoons all-purpose flour

1/4 teaspoon pepper
4 pork chops (1/2 to 3/4 inch thick)
2 tablespoons butter

In a shallow bowl, combine the potato chips, cheese, parsley, flour and pepper. Dip pork chops into mixture, pressing firmly.

In a large skillet, cook pork chops in butter over medium-high heat for 7 minutes on each side or until juices run clear. **Yield:** 4 servings.

Depression Casserole

1 large onion, chopped
1 to 2 tablespoons vegetable oil
1/2 cup water
1/2 cup ketchup
1/4 cup cider vinegar

1 teaspoon ground mustard
1/4 teaspoon pepper
1 package (16 ounces) hot dogs, cut into 1-inch chunks
Toast points *or* cooked rice, optional

In a saucepan, saute onion in oil until tender. Stir in the water, ketchup, vinegar, mustard and pepper. Bring to a boil, stirring occasionally.

Place hot dogs in a 1-qt. baking dish; pour sauce over. Bake, uncovered, at 375° for 30 minutes or until bubbly. If desired, serve over toast points or rice. **Yield:** 5 servings.

Creole-Style Pork Roast

1 teaspoon cayenne pepper

1/2 teaspoon salt

1/4 teaspoon *each* chili powder, paprika, pepper and ground coriander

Pinch *each* ground cloves and garlic powder

1/4 cup finely chopped green pepper

1/4 cup finely chopped onion

1 tablespoon butter

1 can (4 ounces) mushroom stems and pieces, drained

1 can (6 ounces) tomato paste, *divided*

1 boneless pork shoulder roast (2 to 3 pounds)

2 tablespoons all-purpose flour

Combine all of the seasonings; set aside 1/2 teaspoon. In a saucepan over low heat, saute the green pepper, onion and remaining seasoning mixture in butter until vegetables are tender. Stir in mushrooms and half the tomato paste. Spread mixture over the roast; place in shallow baking pan.

Bake, uncovered, at 325° for 1-1/4 to 2 hours or until a meat thermometer reads 160°. Place roast on a serving platter; keep warm.

Transfer all but 2 tablespoons drippings to a measuring cup. Add enough water to measure 1-1/2 cups; set aside. Stir flour into drippings in pan. Gradually blend the 1-1/2 cups of dripping mixture into flour mixture, stirring until smooth. Add reserved seasoning mixture and remaining tomato paste. Bring to a boil over medium heat; cook and stir for 2 minutes or until thickened. Serve with roast. **Yield:** 8-10 servings.

Barbecued Ham Sandwiches

1/4 cup chopped onion

1/4 cup butter

1 cup chili sauce

3/4 cup water

2 tablespoons cider vinegar

2 tablespoons brown sugar

1 teaspoon ground mustard

1 pound shaved fully cooked ham

8 hamburger buns, split

In a saucepan or Dutch oven, saute onion in butter. Add the chili sauce, water, vinegar, brown sugar and mustard; bring to a boil. Reduce heat; cover and simmer for 20 minutes. Add ham; return to a boil. Reduce heat; cover and simmer for 10 minutes or until heated through. Spoon about 1/2 cup onto each bun. **Yield:** 8 servings.

Curried Pork and Green Tomatoes

1 large onion, minced
2 tablespoons butter
4 large fresh green tomatoes,
  cubed
1/4 cup all-purpose flour
1 to 2 teaspoons curry powder
1/2 teaspoon salt
1/4 teaspoon pepper
1/4 teaspoon sugar
Pinch ground cardamom, optional
2 cups chicken broth
2 cups cubed cooked pork
Hot cooked rice

In a medium skillet, saute onion in butter. Add tomatoes; cover and simmer for 10-12 minutes or until tender.

Combine the flour, curry, salt, pepper, sugar and cardamom if desired; slowly stir into tomatoes. Add broth and pork; simmer, uncovered, for 3-5 minutes or until sauce thickens. Serve over rice. **Yield:** 3-4 servings.

Baked Pork Chops and Apples

6 pork chops (3/4 inch thick)
1/2 teaspoon salt
1 tablespoon vegetable oil
2 medium baking apples, peeled
  and sliced
1/4 cup raisins
4 tablespoons brown sugar,
  divided
1/4 to 1/2 teaspoon ground
  cinnamon
1/8 teaspoon ground cloves
1 tablespoon lemon juice
1/4 cup apple juice
1/4 cup orange juice

Sprinkle pork chops with salt. In a skillet, brown chops in oil; set aside. Place apples and raisins in a greased 13-in. x 9-in. x 2-in. baking dish. Combine 2 tablespoons brown sugar, cinnamon and cloves; sprinkle over apples. Drizzle with lemon juice. Arrange pork chops on top. Bake, uncovered, at 325° for 40-45 minutes or until chops are tender and a meat thermometer reads 160°.

In a saucepan, combine the apple juice, orange juice and remaining brown sugar; bring to a boil. Reduce heat and simmer for 10 minutes. Pour over pork chops just before serving. **Yield:** 6 servings.

Creamy Pork Tenderloin

1/2 pound sliced bacon, cut into
   1-inch pieces
1 pork tenderloin (1 pound)
1/2 teaspoon paprika

Dash pepper
1/4 teaspoon salt, optional
1 cup heavy whipping cream

In a medium skillet, cook bacon over medium heat until it just begins to brown. Using a slotted spoon, remove to paper towels to drain; set aside. Cut pork into 1-1/2-in. slices; flatten slightly. Sprinkle with paprika, pepper and salt if desired.

Place pork in an ungreased 8-in. square baking dish. Sprinkle with bacon. Bake, uncovered, at 350° for 25-30 minutes or until pork juices run clear. Pour cream over the top. Bake 5-10 minutes longer or until the cream is slightly thickened. **Yield:** 4 servings.

Jambalaya

2 tablespoons vegetable oil
1 cup minced onion
1 cup minced green pepper
4 garlic cloves, minced
12 small pork sausage links, cut
   into 1-inch pieces
1-1/2 cups cooked cubed chicken
1-1/2 cups cooked cubed ham
1 can (28 ounces) tomatoes, cut
   up and liquid reserved

1 cup uncooked long-grain rice
1 can (14-1/2 ounces) chicken
   broth
3 tablespoons chopped parsley
1 teaspoon salt
1/2 to 1 teaspoon ground black
   pepper
1/2 to 3/4 teaspoon dried thyme

In heavy skillet, heat oil over medium. Saute the onion, green pepper, garlic and sausage until vegetables are tender. Add chicken and ham; cook for 5 minutes. Add all the remaining ingredients.

Transfer to a 2-qt. baking dish. Bake, covered, at 350° for 1 hour or until rice is tender and liquid absorbed. **Yield:** 8 servings.

Ham Balls with Mustard Dill Sauce

2 eggs, lightly beaten
1/2 cup crushed cornflakes
2-1/3 cups milk, *divided*
1/4 cup chopped onion
6 teaspoon prepared mustard,
   divided
Dash pepper
   1 pound ground fully cooked
   ham
1 pound ground pork
2 tablespoons vegetable oil
3 tablespoons butter
3 tablespoons all-purpose flour
1 cup (8 ounces) sour cream
1 teaspoon salt
1/2 teaspoon dill weed

In a bowl, combine the eggs, cornflake crumbs, 1/3 cup milk, onion, 2 teaspoons mustard and pepper; crumble ham and pork over mixture and mix well. Shape into 1-in. balls.

In a large skillet, brown ham balls in oil over medium heat. Cook for 15-20 minutes or until juices run clear.

Meanwhile, in a saucepan, melt butter; stir in flour. Gradually add remaining milk, stirring constantly. Bring to a boil; cook and stir for 2 minutes or until thickened. Reduce heat; stir in the sour cream, salt, dill and remaining mustard; heat through (do not boil).

Place ham balls on a serving platter and top with sauce. **Yield:** 8-10 servings.

Applesauce-Sauerkraut Spareribs

3 to 3-1/2 pounds country-style
   pork ribs
1 teaspoon vegetable oil
1 can (32 ounces) sauerkraut
2 cups applesauce
2 cups thinly sliced onion
3/4 cup chicken broth
3/4 cup apple juice

In a large skillet, brown ribs in oil over medium-high heat. Arrange ribs in an ungreased 13-in. x 9-in. x 2-in. baking dish. Rinse and squeeze sauerkraut; layer sauerkraut, applesauce and onion over ribs. Combine broth and apple juice; pour over all.

Cover and bake at 350° for 1-3/4 hours; uncover and bake 15 minutes longer or until onion just begins to brown. **Yield:** 6 servings.

Ham Fried Rice

2 eggs, lightly beaten
1-1/2 teaspoons canola oil
3/4 cup cold cooked rice
2/3 cup diced fully cooked ham
3/4 teaspoon garlic powder

1/4 teaspoon ground ginger
Dash pepper
Dash chili powder, optional
1-1/2 teaspoons soy sauce

In a small skillet, cook and stir eggs in oil over medium heat until eggs are completely set. Remove and set aside. In same skillet, cook the rice, ham, garlic powder, ginger, pepper and chili powder if desired until heated through. Stir in soy sauce and reserved eggs. Serve immediately. **Yield:** 2 servings.

Bratwurst Potato Skillet

3 medium red potatoes
1 pound fully cooked bratwurst *or* Polish sausage, cut into 1/2-inch slices
2 teaspoons thinly sliced green onion
1-1/2 teaspoons vegetable oil
1-1/2 cups white wine *or* chicken broth
1 teaspoon dried thyme
1 teaspoon dried marjoram

1 tablespoon sugar
1 tablespoon Dijon mustard
3 teaspoons minced fresh parsley, *divided*
3 teaspoons minced chives, *divided*
1 to 2 teaspoons cider vinegar
1/2 teaspoon salt
1/4 teaspoon pepper
2 egg yolks, lightly beaten

Place potatoes in a saucepan and cover with water; cover and bring to a boil over medium-high heat. Cook for 15-20 minutes or until tender; drain. Cool slightly; cut into cubes and keep warm.

In a large skillet, saute sausage and onion in oil until lightly browned; drain. Stir in wine or broth, thyme and marjoram. Bring to a boil. Reduce heat; simmer, uncovered, for 10 minutes.

Remove sausage; keep warm. Stir the sugar, mustard, 1-1/2 teaspoons parsley, 1-1/2 teaspoons chives, vinegar, salt and pepper into pan juices; heat through. Whisk a small amount of hot liquid into egg yolks; return all to the pan, stirring constantly. Cook and stir until thickened and bubbly. Stir in sausage and potatoes; heat through. Sprinkle with remaining parsley and chives. **Yield:** 3-4 servings.

Fruited Pork Picante

1 pound boneless pork loin, trimmed and cut into 1/2-inch cubes

1 tablespoon taco seasoning mix

1 cup julienned sweet red pepper

1-1/2 cups chunky salsa

1/3 cup peach preserves *or* peach spreadable fruit

1 package (6 ounces) frozen snow peas

Hot cooked rice, optional

Toss pork with taco seasoning mix. In a skillet sprayed with nonstick cooking spray, brown pork over medium heat. Add red pepper; cook for 1 minute. Add salsa and preserves; mix well. Bring to a boil. Reduce heat; cover and simmer for 15-20 minutes or until pork is tender. Add peas; cook and stir over medium heat until tender. Serve over rice if desired. **Yield:** 4 servings.

Cordon Bleu Pork Chops

4 bone-in pork rib chops (1 inch thick)

1/2 cup water

1/2 cup ketchup

1/4 cup white vinegar

2 tablespoons brown sugar

2 tablespoons dried minced onion

2 tablespoons Worcestershire sauce

1 tablespoon lemon juice

1 tablespoon soy sauce

1 teaspoon garlic powder

1 teaspoon ground mustard

4 thin slices part-skim mozzarella cheese

4 thin slices fully cooked ham

Cut a pocket in each chop by slicing almost to the bone. Combine the next 10 ingredients. Set aside 1/2 cup for basting and refrigerate. Pour remaining marinade into a large resealable plastic bag; add pork chops. Seal bag and turn to coat; refrigerate overnight, turning meat occasionally.

Place a slice of cheese on each slice of ham; roll up jelly-roll style. Drain pork and discard marinade. Insert a ham-cheese roll in each pocket; fasten with toothpicks.

Grill, covered, over medium heat, turning and basting occasionally with reserved marinade, for 25-35 minutes or until juices run clear. Remove toothpicks. **Yield:** 4 servings.

Pork-Stuffed Eggplant

1 large eggplant (1-1/2 pounds)
1 pound ground pork
1 egg
1/2 cup dry bread crumbs
1/2 cup grated Parmesan *or*
    Romano cheese

1/4 cup chopped fresh parsley
1-1/2 teaspoons dried oregano
1/2 teaspoon salt
1/2 teaspoon pepper
1 can (15 ounces) tomato sauce

Cut off stem of eggplant; cut eggplant in half lengthwise. Scoop out and reserve center, leaving a 1/2-in. shell. Steam shells for 3-5 minutes or just until tender; drain. Cube reserved eggplant. In a saucepan, cook eggplant cubes in boiling water for 6-8 minutes or until tender; drain and set aside.

In a skillet over medium heat, cook pork until no longer pink; drain. Add the eggplant cubes, egg, bread crumbs, cheese, parsley, oregano, salt and pepper; mix well.

Fill shells; place in a greased 9-in. square baking dish. Pour tomato sauce over eggplant. Cover and bake at 350° for 25-30 minutes or until heated through. **Yield:** 4 servings.

Pork Lo Mein

1 pound ground pork
1 cup thinly sliced carrots
1 cup chopped onion
1 garlic clove, minced
2 packages (3 ounce *each*)
    Oriental *or* Chicken-flavored
    Ramen noodles

1-1/2 cups water
1 cup frozen peas
6 cups shredded romaine

In a large skillet coated with nonstick cooking spray, cook pork, carrots, onion and garlic over medium heat until pork is no longer pink; drain.

Break noodles into skillet, stir in seasoning packets. Stir in water and peas. Bring to a boil; reduce heat and simmer for about 6-8 minutes or until noodles and vegetables are tender, stirring several times. Add romaine; heat and stir until wilted. **Yield:** 4 servings.

Inside-Out Pork Chops

4 pork chops (1 inch thick)
1 tablespoon butter
1/4 cup water
1 package (8-1/2 ounces) corn bread/muffin mix

1 egg
1/2 cup milk
1 to 2 teaspoons chili powder
2 to 3 tablespoons vegetable oil

In a skillet, brown pork chops on each side in butter over medium heat. Add water; bring to a boil. Reduce heat; cover and simmer for 20 minutes or until juices run clear and pork is tender. Drain pork chops on paper towels. Drain all drippings from pan.

In a bowl, combine muffin mix, egg, milk and chili powder; mix until blended. Immediately coat chops with batter. In the same skillet over medium heat, fry chops in oil until batter is golden brown and cooked through. **Yield:** 4 servings.

Ham Hot Dish

1/4 cup chopped onion
1/4 cup butter
3 tablespoons all-purpose flour
1/2 teaspoon salt
Dash ground nutmeg
Dash pepper
2-3/4 cups milk
1/4 cup chopped green pepper

1 can (4 ounces) mushrooms stems and pieces, drained
1 jar (4 ounces) diced pimientos, drained
1 package (7 ounces) macaroni, cooked and drained
1-1/2 cups cubed fully cooked ham
1/2 cup plus 2 tablespoons grated Parmesan cheese, *divided*

In a saucepan, saute onion in butter for 3 minutes or until tender. Stir in flour, salt, nutmeg and pepper. Gradually add milk, stirring constantly. Add the green pepper, mushrooms and pimientos. Bring to a boil; cook and stir for 2 minutes or until thickened. Remove from the heat; add macaroni and mix well.

Spoon half into a greased 13-in. x 9-in. x 2-in. baking pan. Sprinkle with ham and 1/2 cup Parmesan cheese. Top with the remaining macaroni mixture. Sprinkle with remaining cheese. Bake, uncovered, at 375° for 20-30 minutes or until heated through. **Yield:** 6-8 servings.

Rhubarb Pork Roast

1 boneless pork loin roast (about 3 pounds)

2 garlic cloves, minced

1 teaspoon dried rosemary, crushed

1/2 teaspoon poultry seasoning

2 cups diced fresh *or* frozen rhubarb, thawed and drained

1/3 cup honey

1/4 cup cider vinegar

6 whole cloves

3/4 teaspoon ground mustard

1/2 teaspoon salt

Rub the roast with garlic, rosemary and poultry seasoning. Place roast fat side up on a greased rack in a roasting pan. Bake, uncovered, at 350° for 1-1/4 hours.

Meanwhile, in a saucepan, combine the remaining ingredients; bring to a boil. Reduce heat; simmer, uncovered, for 10 minutes. Pour half over roast.

Bake 30-45 minutes longer or until a meat thermometer reads 160°, basting with remaining rhubarb sauce. Let stand for 10 minutes before slicing.

If desired, combine pan drippings and any remaining sauce; serve with the roast. **Yield:** 8 servings.

Stuffed Ham Bake

1/4 cup finely chopped onion

3 tablespoons butter

2 cups soft bread crumbs

1/4 cup whole kernel corn

3 tablespoons minced celery

1 tablespoon minced green pepper

1/8 teaspoon poultry seasoning

2 pounds fully cooked ham, cut into 1/2-inch slices

1 teaspoon honey

In a skillet, saute onion in butter until tender; remove from the heat. Stir in the bread crumbs, corn, celery, green pepper and poultry seasoning. Place half the ham slice in a greased 13-in. x 9-in. x 2-in. baking dish; spread stuffing over ham. Top with remaining ham.

Bake, uncovered, at 350° for 20 minutes. Brush top slices with honey. Bake 5-10 minutes longer or until heated through. **Yield:** 6-8 servings.

Sausage Stroganoff

1 pound bulk pork sausage	1/4 teaspoon pepper
1 medium onion, chopped	1/4 cup all-purpose flour
1/2 pound fresh mushrooms, sliced	1 cup (8 ounces) sour cream
1-1/4 cups chicken broth, *divided*	2 tablespoons minced fresh parsley, optional
1 tablespoon Worcestershire sauce	Hot cooked noodles

In a large skillet, cook sausage and onion over medium heat until meat is no longer pink; drain. Stir in mushrooms; cook for 1 minute. Add 1 cup broth, Worcestershire sauce and pepper; cover and simmer for 5 minutes or until heated through.

In a small bowl, combine the flour and remaining broth until smooth. Gradually stir into skillet. Bring to a boil; cook and stir for 2 minutes or until thickened. Reduce heat; add sour cream. Stir until heated through (do not boil). Add parsley if desired. Serve with noodles. **Yield:** 4 servings.

Pork Patties Oriental

1 pound ground pork	1 medium green pepper, cut into chunks
1 egg	3 green onions, sliced
1/2 cup bread crumbs	3 tablespoons brown sugar
2 tablespoons soy sauce	2 tablespoons cornstarch
3/4 teaspoon ground ginger	3 tablespoons water
3/4 teaspoon ground mustard	3 tablespoons cider vinegar
1 can (20 ounces) unsweetened pineapple chunks, undrained	Hot cooked rice

In a bowl, combine the first six ingredients. Shape into four patties.

In a large greased skillet, brown patties over medium heat on both sides; drain. Add the pineapple and juice, green pepper and onions; bring to a boil. Reduce heat; cover and simmer for 10 minutes.

In a small bowl, combine the brown sugar and cornstarch. Stir in water and vinegar until smooth. Stir into pineapple mixture. Bring to a boil; cook and stir for 2 minutes or until thickened. Serve over rice. **Yield:** 4 servings.

Pork Souvlaki

1/4 cup olive oil

2 tablespoons lemon juice

1 garlic clove, minced

1 teaspoon dried oregano

1/2 teaspoon chicken bouillon granules

1/4 teaspoon pepper

1/8 teaspoon cayenne pepper

1 pound boneless pork, cut into 1-1/4-inch cubes

In a large resealable plastic bag, combine the first seven ingredients; add pork. Seal bag and turn to coat; refrigerate overnight.

Drain and discard marinade. Thread meat on metal or soaked bamboo skewers, leaving a small space between pieces. Grill, covered, over medium heat for 15-20 minutes or until meat is no longer pink. **Yield:** 4 servings.

Stuffed Easter Ham

1/2 cup chopped onion

3 tablespoons chopped celery

3 tablespoons butter

2-3/4 cups cubed French bread (1/4-inch cubes)

1 cup chopped baking apple

3/4 cup chicken broth

3 tablespoons raisins

1 tablespoon chopped fresh parsley

1/8 teaspoon ground cinnamon

1 fully cooked ham (3 pounds), cut into 3/8-inch slices

1/2 cup pineapple preserves, melted

In a skillet, saute onion and celery in butter until tender; add the next six ingredients and mix well. Line an 11-in. x 7-in. x 2-in. baking pan with foil; place kitchen string on foil. Place one ham slice on top of string; spread with 1 cup of stuffing. Top with another ham slice. Repeat the process, using two ham slices between stuffing layers. Tie securely with string. Cover loosely with foil.

Bake at 350° for 1-1/4 hours. Uncover; baste ham with preserves. Bake, uncovered, for 45 minutes or until a meat thermometer inserted into the stuffing in the center of ham reads 140°, basting several times. Let stand for 10 minutes. Remove the string and separate the double ham slices; cut into desired portions. **Yield:** 8-10 servings.

Tangy Reuben Bake

- 3 medium potatoes, peeled, sliced and cooked
- 8 ounces smoked kielbasa *or* Polish sausage, thinly sliced
- 1 can (8 ounces) sauerkraut, rinsed and drained
- 1/2 cup Thousand Island salad dressing
- 2 tablespoons sugar
- 2 tablespoons minced fresh parsley
- 1 tablespoon dried minced onion
- 1/2 to 1 teaspoon caraway seeds
- 3/4 cup shredded cheddar cheese

In a bowl, combine the first eight ingredients. Transfer to a greased 8-in. square baking dish. Bake, uncovered, at 350° for 25 minutes. Sprinkle with cheese. Bake 5 minutes longer or until cheese is melted. **Yield:** 4 servings.

Sparerib Casserole

- 4 to 5 pounds pork spareribs, cut into individual ribs
- 2 teaspoons salt, *divided*
- 1/2 teaspoon pepper, *divided*
- 5 tablespoons vegetable oil, *divided*
- 6 cups cubed potatoes
- 1 medium onion, sliced
- 2 garlic cloves, minced
- 4 teaspoons all-purpose flour
- 2 tablespoons dried parsley flakes
- 1 can (12 ounces) evaporated milk
- 1/8 teaspoon paprika

Sprinkle ribs with 1 teaspoon salt and 1/4 teaspoon pepper. In a large skillet, brown ribs in 3 tablespoons oil in batches. Place ribs on a rack in shallow roasting pan. Bake, uncovered, at 350° for 20 minutes. Turn ribs; bake 20 minutes longer. Pat dry.

Place potatoes in a saucepan and cover with water; cover and bring to a boil over medium-high heat. Cook for 15-20 minutes or until tender.

Meanwhile, in a saucepan, saute onion and garlic in remaining oil until tender. Stir in the flour, parsley, and remaining salt and pepper until blended. Gradually stir in milk. Bring to a boil; cook and stir for 2 minutes or until thickened.

Drain potatoes; place in a greased 13-in. x 9-in. x 2-in. baking dish. Top with sauce and ribs. Cover and bake at 350° for 15 minutes. Uncover; sprinkle with paprika. Bake 5-10 minutes longer or until ribs are tender and potatoes are heated through. **Yield:** 6 servings.

Pork Fajita Pasta

1 package (7 ounces) angel hair pasta

4 boneless pork loin chops (1/2 inch thick and 4 ounces *each*), cut into thin strips

1 medium green pepper, julienned

1 medium onion, sliced and separated into rings

1 envelope (1.4 ounces) fajita seasoning

1/3 cup water

1 cup (4 ounces) shredded cheddar cheese

1 medium tomato, seeded and chopped

Cook pasta according to package directions. Meanwhile, in a large skillet, cook pork over medium heat until juices run clear. Add green pepper and onion; cook and stir for 1-2 minutes or until vegetables are crisp-tender.

Stir in fajita seasoning and water; cook 1 minute longer. Drain pasta. In a large bowl, layer the pasta, pork mixture, cheese and tomato. **Yield:** 4 servings.

Pork Chop and Rice Dinner

6 boneless pork chops (3/4 inch thick)

1 tablespoon butter

Salt and pepper to taste, optional

1 cup uncooked long grain rice

1 small onion, chopped

1 garlic clove, minced

1 can (10-3/4 ounces) condensed cream of broccoli soup, undiluted

1-1/2 cups water

1 cup (4 ounces) shredded sharp cheddar cheese

1/2 teaspoon pepper

1/4 teaspoon salt

In a skillet, brown pork chops in butter; season with salt and pepper if desired. Remove from the skillet and set aside. Reserve 2 tablespoons drippings; add rice, onion and garlic. Mix well. Stir in the soup, water, cheese, pepper and salt.

Transfer to a greased 13-in. x 9-in. x 2-in. baking dish; arrange chops over rice mixture. Cover and bake at 350° for 1 hour. Uncover; bake 15 minutes longer or until rice is tender and pork juices run clear. **Yield:** 6 servings.

Ham Loaf Pie

1-1/2 cups finely crushed cheese
    crackers
1/4 cup butter, melted
2 eggs
1 can (5 ounces) evaporated milk
1/2 cup finely chopped onion

1/4 cup chopped green pepper
1 tablespoon prepared mustard
1 tablespoon prepared
    horseradish
1 pound fully cooked ham,
    ground

Combine cracker crumbs and butter. Reserve 2 tablespoons for topping. Press remaining crumbs into the bottom and up the sides of a 9-in. pie plate. Bake at 350° for 8-10 minutes or until lightly browned.

Meanwhile, in a medium bowl, beat eggs. Blend in the milk, onion, green pepper, mustard and horseradish; stir in ham. Carefully spoon and spread into crust. Sprinkle with reserved crumbs.

Bake at 350° for 45-50 minutes or until set and a meat thermometer reads 160°. (A knife inserted halfway between the center and edge will be wet.) Let stand for 5 minutes before cutting. **Yield:** 6 servings.

Plum-Barbecued Spareribs

4 pounds spareribs *or* baby back
    pork ribs
1 tablespoon salt
1 can (16-1/2 ounces) purple
    plums in heavy syrup,
    undrained

1 tablespoon chopped onion
2 teaspoons soy sauce
1/4 teaspoon grated lemon peel
1/4 teaspoon ground cinnamon
Dash *each* ground cloves and nutmeg

Placed ribs on two foil-lined 15-in. x 10-in. x 1-in. baking pans. Cover and bake at 325° for 2 hours; drain.

Drain plums, reserving syrup. Remove and discard pits from plums. In a blender, combine the plums, syrup, onion, soy sauce, lemon peel, cinnamon, cloves and nutmeg; cover and process until smooth. Pour into a saucepan; bring to a boil. Cook for 3 minutes, stirring constantly. Remove from the heat.

Cut ribs into serving-size pieces. Place ribs meat side up in a 13-in. x 9-in. x 2-in. baking dish; spread 2/3 cup plum sauce over ribs. Bake, uncovered, at 325° for 30 minutes or until ribs are tender, basting three times with remaining sauce. **Yield:** 6 servings.

Apple Pork Pie

CRUST:
1 cup all-purpose flour
1/4 teaspoon salt
2/3 cup shredded cheddar cheese
1/3 cup shortening
3 tablespoons cold water

FILLING:
1-1/2 pounds boneless pork, cut into
1/2-inch cubes
1 cup water
1/4 cup finely chopped onion
3/4 teaspoon dried sage
3/4 teaspoon salt
1/4 cup all-purpose flour
3/4 cup milk
1-1/2 cups thinly sliced peeled
apples
1 tablespoon sugar

In a bowl, combine flour and salt. Add cheese; toss to coat. Cut in shortening until mixture resembles coarse crumbs. Gradually add water, tossing with a fork until dough forms a ball. Roll two-thirds of the ball into an 11-in. circle; transfer to a 9-in. pie plate. Roll remaining pastry into an 8-in. circle; cut into eight wedges. Chill pastry shell and wedges while preparing filling.

Brown pork in a skillet over medium-high heat. Add the water, onion, sage and salt. Reduce heat; cover and simmer for 30-40 minutes or until meat is tender. Combine flour and milk until smooth; gradually add to pork mixture. Bring to a boil; cook and stir for 2 minutes. Spoon half into prepared shell. Top with apples and sprinkle with sugar. Spoon remaining pork mixture over apples. Arrange pastry wedges on top.

Bake, uncovered, at 450° for 10 minutes. Reduce heat to 350°; bake 30-40 minutes longer or until pastry is lightly browned and crisp. **Yield:** 6 servings.

Western Ribs

3 pounds pork spareribs
1 cup barbecue sauce
1/2 cup tomato juice
2 tablespoons Italian salad
dressing
1 tablespoon dried parsley flakes
1 small onion, diced

Place the ribs in an ungreased 13-in. x 9-in. x 2-in. baking pan. Cover with foil. Bake at 325° for 1-1/2 hours or until just tender; drain. Combine remaining ingredients; spoon over ribs.

Bake, uncovered, 45 minutes longer, basting occasionally. Cut into serving-size pieces. **Yield:** 4 servings.

Spareribs Cantonese

4 pounds pork spareribs
1 cup orange marmalade
3/4 cup water
1/2 cup soy sauce
1/2 teaspoon garlic powder

1/2 teaspoon ground ginger or
2 teaspoons grated fresh
gingerroot
1/4 teaspoon salt, optional
Dash pepper
Lemon wedges, optional

Cut the ribs into serving-size pieces; place meat side down in a shallow roasting pan. Cover with foil; bake at 450° for 45 minutes. Drain; turn ribs.

Combine marmalade, water, soy sauce and seasonings; spoon over ribs. Bake, uncovered, 1 hour longer or until tender, basting occasionally with sauce. Garnish with lemon wedges if desired. **Yield:** 4-6 servings.

Italian Sausage and Sauerkraut

1-1/2 pounds bulk Italian sausage
1 small onion, chopped
2 cans (one 16 ounces, one 8 ounces) sauerkraut, undrained
1-1/2 teaspoons brown sugar
3/4 teaspoon poultry seasoning
7 to 8 medium potatoes

1/3 cup milk
Pinch pepper
1/2 teaspoon salt, optional
2 tablespoons butter
Paprika and chopped fresh parsley, optional

In a large skillet, cook sausage and onion over medium heat until sausage is no longer pink; drain. Add the sauerkraut, brown sugar and poultry seasoning; cover and simmer for 1 hour. Transfer to an ungreased 13-in. x 9-in. x 2-in. baking dish.

Meanwhile, cook potatoes until tender; drain and mash slightly. Add the milk, pepper and salt if desired; mash until smooth. Spread evenly over sausage mixture; dot with butter.

Bake at 350° for 20-25 minutes or until potatoes are lightly browned. Garnish with paprika and parsley if desired. **Yield:** 8 servings.

Pork Chop Suey

1-1/2 pounds pork chop suey meat
2 tablespoons vegetable oil
1 cup sliced onion
2-1/2 cups water
1-1/2 cups sliced celery
1 can (4 ounces) mushroom
  stems and pieces, drained

2 chicken bouillon cubes
1 teaspoon ground ginger
1/4 cup cornstarch
1/4 cup soy sauce
Hot cooked rice *or* mashed potatoes

In a skillet, brown pork in oil over medium heat. Add onion and saute for 10 minutes. Add the water, celery, mushrooms, bouillon and ginger; cover and cook for 30-40 minutes or until pork is tender.

Combine cornstarch and soy sauce until smooth; stir into skillet. Bring to a boil; cook and stir for 2 minutes or until thickened. Serve over rice or mashed potatoes. **Yield:** 6 servings.

Ham-Noodle Bake

1/4 cup butter
1/4 cup all-purpose flour
1/2 teaspoon salt
1/8 teaspoon pepper
2-1/2 cups milk
3 to 4 teaspoons prepared
  horseradish

1 tablespoon prepared mustard
6 cups cooked wide egg noodles
2 cups cubed fully cooked ham
1 cup cubed cheddar cheese
1/2 cup bread crumbs, toasted

In a saucepan, melt butter over medium heat. Stir in the flour, salt and pepper until smooth. Gradually add milk, stirring constantly. Bring to a boil; cook and stir for 2 minutes or until thickened. Add horseradish and mustard; mix well. Stir in the noodles, ham and cheese.

Pour into a greased 2-1/2-qt. baking dish. Cover and bake at 350° for 20 minutes. Uncover; sprinkle with bread crumbs. Bake 10-15 minutes longer or until bubbly and heated through. **Yield:** 4-6 servings.

Scalloped Potatoes 'n' Ham

1 small onion, chopped
1 small green pepper, thinly
  sliced
1 tablespoon butter
2 tablespoons all-purpose flour
1/2 teaspoon salt

1/8 teaspoon pepper
1 cup milk
1-1/2 cups (6 ounces) shredded
  cheddar cheese, *divided*
4 medium potatoes, peeled,
  cooked and sliced
1-1/2 cups diced fully cooked ham

In a skillet, saute onion and green pepper in butter until tender. Stir in the flour, salt and pepper until blended. Gradually add milk, stirring constantly. Bring to a boil; cook and stir for 2 minutes or until thickened. Remove from the heat; add half of the cheese, stirring until melted. Gently stir in potatoes and ham. Cover and cook over low heat for 10 minutes or until heated through, stirring occasionally. Sprinkle with remaining cheese; cover and let stand until cheese melts.

Microwave Directions: In a covered microwave-safe bowl, cook onion, green pepper in butter until tender. Stir in the flour, salt and pepper until blended. Gradually stir in milk. Cook on medium for 2-3 minutes or until thickened, stirring occasionally. Stir in half of the cheese; set aside.

In a 1-1/2-qt. microwave-safe baking dish, layer half the potatoes, ham and cheese sauce. Repeat layers. Cover and cook on high for 2-3 minutes or until heated through, stirring occasionally. Sprinkle with remaining cheese. Cover and let stand until cheese is melted. **Yield:** 4 servings.

Editor's Note: This recipe was tested in a 1,100-watt microwave.

Ham and Asparagus Roll-Ups

1 pound fresh asparagus
8 to 10 thin ham slices
1 can (10-3/4 ounces) condensed
  cream of celery soup, undiluted

1/4 cup milk
3 tablespoons sliced almonds

Steam asparagus until tender; pat dry. Roll a slice of ham around two to three asparagus stalks. Place ham rolls seam side down in a greased 11-in. x 7-in. x 2-in. baking dish. Combine the soup and milk; pour over the ham rolls. Top with almonds.

Bake, uncovered, at 350° for 30 minutes or microwave on high for 3-5 minutes or until heated through. **Yield:** 5 servings.

Old-Fashioned Kraut Dinner

1 pound fully cooked smoked
Polish sausage, cut into 1-inch
pieces
6 pork chops (3/4 inch thick)
1 tablespoon vegetable oil
1/2 cup chopped onion
1/4 cup chopped green pepper
1/2 teaspoon garlic powder

1/2 teaspoon pepper
1/2 teaspoon curry powder
1 can (15 ounces) tomato sauce
1/4 cup water
2 cans (14 ounces *each*)
sauerkraut, rinsed and well
drained
1 teaspoon sugar

In a large skillet, brown sausage and pork chops in oil; drain. Add the
next five ingredients; cook until vegetables are tender. Stir in tomato
sauce and water; cover and simmer for 40 minutes.

Remove pork chops to a serving platter; keep warm. Add sauerkraut
and sugar to skillet; mix well. Heat through. Serve with pork chops.
Yield: 6 servings.

Barbecued Pork with Beans

4 bone-in pork loin chops (3/4
inch thick)
1 tablespoon vegetable oil
2 cans (11 ounces *each*) pork and
beans

3 tablespoons Worcestershire
sauce, *divided*
1/4 cup ketchup
1/4 to 1/2 teaspoon chili powder

In a large skillet, brown pork chops in oil on both sides. Combine pork
and beans and 2 tablespoons Worcestershire sauce; place in a greased
11-in. x 7-in. x 2-in. baking dish. Top with chops.

Combine the ketchup, chili powder and remaining Worcestershire
sauce; spoon over chops. Bake, uncovered, at 350° for 50-55 minutes or
until meat is tender. **Yield:** 4 servings.

Herbed Pork Roast

6 garlic cloves, minced
1-1/2 teaspoons salt
3 tablespoons minced fresh parsley
1 tablespoon paprika
1/2 teaspoon dried oregano
1/4 cup olive oil
1 boneless pork loin roast (3 pounds)
14 to 16 unpeeled small red potatoes (about 2 pounds), halved

Combine garlic and salt in a small bowl until a paste forms. Add the parsley, paprika and oregano; mix well. Whisk in oil. Rub over roast. Cover and refrigerate overnight.

Place roast and any extra oil mixture in a roasting pan. Bake, uncovered, at 450° for 15 minutes. Add potatoes to pan. Reduce heat to 350°; bake for 1 to 1-1/4 hours or until a meat thermometer reads 160°. Spoon drippings over potatoes. Let roast stand for 10 minutes before slicing. **Yield:** 10 servings.

Cranberry-Stuffed Pork Chops

2 teaspoons dried rosemary, crushed
1/2 teaspoon rubbed sage
1/2 teaspoon dried tarragon
1/2 teaspoon salt
1/2 teaspoon pepper
1/4 cup butter, melted
5 slices day-old bread, cut into 1/2-inch cubes
3/4 cup whole-berry cranberry sauce
2 tablespoons water
6 bone-in pork rib chops (1 inch thick)
1 tablespoon vegetable oil

Combine the rosemary, sage, tarragon, salt and pepper; set half aside. In a large bowl, combine remaining seasonings and butter. Add the bread cubes, cranberry sauce and water; toss to coat. Cut a pocket in each chop by slicing almost to the bone. Spoon 1/4 cup stuffing into each pocket. Rub reserved seasonings over chops.

In a large skillet, brown chops in oil. Transfer to a 13-in. x 9-in. x 2-in. baking pan. Bake, uncovered, at 325° for 1 to 1-1/4 hours or until pork juices run clear and a meat thermometer reads 160°. **Yield:** 6 servings.

Pork Chops with Sauteed Plums

4 pork chops (1 inch thick)	1 pound fresh plums, pitted and sliced
1 teaspoon salt, *divided*	
1/4 teaspoon pepper	1/2 cup chopped onion
1 tablespoon vegetable oil	2 tablespoons water
	1/2 teaspoon dried thyme

Sprinkle pork chops with 1/2 teaspoon salt and pepper. In a skillet over medium heat, brown the pork chops in oil; set chops aside. Reserve 1 tablespoon drippings; saute plums and onion for 4-6 minutes or until plums begin to brown. Stir in the water, thyme and remaining salt. Return pork chops to pan. Reduce heat; cover and simmer for 13-16 minutes or until pork is tender. **Yield:** 4 servings.

Jalapeno Ribs

4 teaspoons light brown sugar	**JALAPENO BARBECUE SAUCE:**
2 teaspoons chili powder	2 cans (8 ounces *each*) tomato sauce
1 teaspoon paprika	
1 teaspoon salt	2/3 cup packed light brown sugar
1 teaspoon pepper	1/3 cup lemon juice
1/8 teaspoon garlic powder	1/4 cup Worcestershire sauce
3-1/2 to 4 pounds pork spareribs	1 small onion, finely chopped
	2 jalapeno peppers, seeded and finely chopped
	2 beef bouillon cubes

Combine the first six ingredients. Rub all of the mixture onto both sides of ribs. Place ribs meat side up on a rack in a foil-lined roasting pan. Bake at 325° for 1-1/2 to 1-3/4 hours or until tender.

Meanwhile, combine sauce ingredients in a saucepan; bring to a boil. Reduce heat; simmer, uncovered, for 30-40 minutes or until thickened.

Transfer ribs to grill. Grill, uncovered, over medium heat, basting with sauce and turning several times, for 10-15 minutes. Reheat remaining sauce and serve with ribs. **Yield:** 4 servings.

Orange Dijon Pork

4 boneless pork chops (1/2 inch thick)
1/4 teaspoon salt
1/4 teaspoon pepper

2 tablespoons butter
1/4 cup Dijon-mayonnaise blend
1/4 cup orange marmalade

Sprinkle chops with salt and pepper. In a skillet, brown chops in butter over medium heat for 3-5 minutes on each side. Remove from the heat; place chops in an 8-in. square baking dish. Add Dijon-mayonnaise blend and marmalade to drippings in the skillet; stir until smooth. Cook over low heat for 2 minutes or until heated through. Pour over chops.

Cover and bake at 350° for 20-25 minutes. Uncover; bake 5-10 minutes longer or until chops are tender and sauce is thickened. **Yield:** 4 servings.

Hawaiian Pizza Pasta

1/2 pound fresh mushrooms, sliced
1 medium onion, chopped
1 medium green pepper, chopped
2 garlic cloves, minced
3 tablespoons vegetable oil
1 can (15 ounces) tomato sauce
2 bay leaves
1 teaspoon dried oregano

1 teaspoon dried basil
1/2 teaspoon sugar
3-1/2 cups uncooked spiral pasta
6 cups (24 ounces) shredded part-skim mozzarella cheese, *divided*
1 can (20 ounces) pineapple chunks, drained
1 cup cubed fully cooked ham

In a large saucepan, saute the mushrooms, onion, green pepper and garlic in oil for 5 minutes or until tender. Add the tomato sauce, bay leaves, oregano, basil and sugar. Bring to a boil. Reduce heat; simmer, uncovered, for 20-30 minutes or until thickened, stirring frequently.

Meanwhile, cook pasta according to package directions; drain. Discard bay leaves from sauce. Add the pasta, 5 cups mozzarella cheese, pineapple and ham.

Transfer to a greased shallow 3-qt. baking dish. Sprinkle with remaining cheese. Bake, uncovered, at 350° for 30-35 minutes or until heated through. **Yield:** 12-14 servings.

Oven-Baked Ribs

4 pounds pork spareribs
2 medium oranges
1 bottle (28 ounces) barbecue sauce
1 cup coarsely chopped onion
2/3 to 1 cup packed brown sugar

1 tablespoon Worcestershire sauce
1-1/2 teaspoons chili powder
1 to 1-1/2 teaspoons hot pepper sauce
1/4 to 1/2 teaspoon cayenne pepper

Place ribs in two foil-lined 15-in. x 10-in. x 1-in. baking pans. Bake at 325° for 2 hours; drain. Cut into serving-size portions.

Place ribs in an ungreased 13-in. x 9-in. x 2-in. baking dish. Squeeze oranges, reserving 1/2 cup juice and the peel. Combine the juice, barbecue sauce, onion, brown sugar, Worcestershire sauce, chili powder, hot pepper sauce and cayenne. Cut orange peel into large chunks and add to sauce; pour sauce over ribs.

Bake, uncovered, at 325° for 30-45 minutes longer or until ribs are tender and sauce is thickened, turning ribs several times to coat with sauce. Remove orange peel. **Yield:** 4-6 servings.

Sausage-Stuffed Potatoes

2 baking potatoes
1 package (12 ounces) bulk pork sausage
1 tablespoon butter

2 tablespoons grated Parmesan cheese
Dash pepper
1/4 cup shredded cheddar cheese

Scrub and pierce potatoes; bake at 400° for 1 hour or until tender.

In a skillet, cook sausage over medium heat until no longer pink; drain. Cool potatoes slightly; cut in half lengthwise. Scoop out the pulp and place in a mixing bowl; add butter and mash. Stir in Parmesan cheese, pepper and sausage. Spoon into potato shells.

Place in an 11-in. x 7-in. x 2-in. baking dish. Bake, uncovered, at 350° for 20-25 minutes or until heated through. Sprinkle with cheddar cheese. Bake 5 minutes longer or until cheese is melted. **Yield:** 2 servings.

Hungarian Pork Loaf

2 cups crushed herb-seasoned
  stuffing mix
1 cup buttermilk
1 egg

1 tablespoon minced fresh
  parsley
1 teaspoon garlic salt
1 teaspoon paprika, *divided*
2 pounds ground pork

In a bowl, combine stuffing mix and buttermilk; let stand for 15 minutes. Add the egg, parsley, garlic salt and 1/2 teaspoon paprika. Crumble pork over mixture and mix well.

Press into a greased 9-in. x 5-in. x 3-in. loaf pan. Bake at 350° for 1-1/2 to 1-3/4 hours or until a meat thermometer reads 160°; drain. Sprinkle with remaining paprika. **Yield:** 8-10 servings.

Mustard Baked Ham with Gravy

2 tablespoons all-purpose flour
1 tablespoon brown sugar
1 tablespoon ground mustard
4 teaspoons water

1 teaspoon cider vinegar
4 fully cooked ham steaks
  (1/2 inch thick)
1-1/4 cups milk

In a small bowl, combine the flour, brown sugar and mustard. Stir in water and vinegar to form a paste; spread 1 teaspoon on each side of ham steaks.

Place in an ungreased 13-in. x 9-in. x 2-in. baking dish. Pour milk over ham. Bake, uncovered, at 325° for 35 minutes. Serve immediately.

If milk gravy is desired, transfer ham to a serving platter and keep warm. Pour pan juices into a blender; cool slightly. Cover and process until smooth. Transfer to a small saucepan; bring to a boil, stirring constantly. Serve immediately with ham. **Yield:** 4 servings.

Spanish Pork Steaks

6 pork shoulder *or* sirloin steaks (1/2 inch thick)
3/4 teaspoon salt, *divided*
1/8 teaspoon pepper
1/2 cup sliced fresh mushrooms
1/2 cup sliced pimiento-stuffed olives
1/4 cup chopped green pepper
1/4 cup finely chopped onion
1 garlic clove, minced
1 tablespoon all-purpose flour
1 tablespoon sugar
2 cups tomato juice

In a skillet over medium-high heat, brown steaks. Place in an ungreased 13-in. x 9-in. x 2-in. baking dish. Sprinkle with 1/4 teaspoon salt and pepper. Top with the mushrooms, olives, green pepper, onion and garlic.

Combine the flour, sugar and remaining salt; gradually stir in tomato juice until smooth. Pour over vegetables. Bake, uncovered, at 350° for 1 hour or until meat is tender. **Yield:** 6 servings.

Curried Pork Chops

4 pork chops (1/2 inch thick)
2 tablespoons butter, *divided*
1/2 cup chopped onion
1 cup water
1-1/2 cups diced unpeeled tart apples
1/2 cup raisins, optional
3 tablespoons orange marmalade
2 tablespoons lemon juice
1 to 2 tablespoons curry powder
4 teaspoons sugar
1/2 teaspoon pepper
2 tablespoons all-purpose flour
1/4 cup cold water
Hot cooked rice *or* macaroni

In a large skillet, brown pork chops on each side in 1 tablespoon of butter over medium heat; drain and set aside.

In the same skillet, saute onion in remaining butter until tender. Add the water, apples, raisins if desired, marmalade, lemon juice, curry, sugar and pepper; mix well. Bring to a boil.

Return pork chops to skillet. Reduce heat; cover and simmer for 10-15 minutes or until pork juices run clear and apples are crisp-tender. Remove pork chops; keep warm.

Combine flour and cold water until smooth; stir into skillet. Bring to a boil; cook and stir for 2 minutes or until thickened. Serve over rice or macaroni. **Yield:** 4 servings.

Shaker Pork Sandwiches

1 teaspoon rubbed sage	3/4 cup sugar
1/2 teaspoon salt	2 tablespoons cornstarch
1/4 teaspoon pepper	3/4 cup water
1 garlic clove, minced	1/2 cup cider vinegar
1 boneless pork loin roast (4 to 5 pounds)	1/4 cup soy sauce
	12 to 16 hamburger buns, split

Combine the sage, salt, pepper and garlic; rub over roast. Place on a rack in a shallow roasting pan. Cover and bake at 350° for 1-3/4 to 2-1/4 hours or a meat thermometer reads 160° and meat is tender. Remove meat and shred with a fork.

In a large saucepan, combine the sugar and cornstarch; add water, vinegar and soy sauce until smooth. Bring to a boil; cook and stir for 2 minutes or until thickened. Add shredded pork; stir until meat is coated and heated through. Serve on buns. **Yield:** 12-16 servings.

Zucchini Sausage Squares

5 small zucchini, cut into 1/4-inch slices (about 4 cups)	1/4 teaspoon garlic powder
1 large onion, chopped	1/4 teaspoon dried basil
1/2 cup butter	1/4 teaspoon dried oregano
1 pound bulk Italian sausage, cooked and drained	2 eggs
2 teaspoons minced fresh parsley	2 cups (8 ounces) shredded part-skim mozzarella cheese
1/2 teaspoon pepper	1 tube (8 ounces) refrigerated crescent rolls
	2 tablespoons prepared mustard

In a large skillet, saute the zucchini and onion in butter. Stir in the sausage, parsley and seasonings. In a large bowl, combine the eggs, cheese and sausage mixture.

Unroll crescent roll dough and place in a greased 13-in. x 9-in. x 2-in. baking dish. Press onto the bottom and up the sides to form a crust; seal seams and perforations. Brush with mustard. Spoon sausage mixture over crust. Bake, uncovered, at 375° for 18-20 minutes or until crust is golden brown. **Yield:** 6-8 servings.

Crunch Top Ham And Potato Casserole

2 pounds frozen Southern-style hash brown potatoes, thawed

2 cups sour cream

2 cups cubed fully cooked ham

1-1/2 cups (6 ounces) shredded cheddar cheese

1 can (10-3/4 ounces) condensed cream of chicken soup, undiluted

1/2 cup butter, melted

1/3 cup chopped green onions

1/2 teaspoon ground pepper

TOPPING:

2 cups crushed cornflakes

1/4 cup butter, melted

In a large bowl, combine the first eight ingredients. Transfer to a greased 13-in. x 9-in. x 2-in. baking dish. Combine topping ingredients; sprinkle over casserole. Bake at 350° for 1 hour or until heated through. **Yield:** 10 servings.

Italian Cabbage and Rice

1-1/2 pounds ground pork

1 cup chopped onion

2 garlic cloves, minced

4 cups shredded cabbage

1 can (8 ounces) tomato sauce

1 cup chicken broth

2 tablespoons red wine vinegar

1/2 teaspoon dried oregano

1/2 teaspoon dried basil

1/2 teaspoon fennel seed

1/4 teaspoon pepper

1/4 teaspoon sugar

3 cups cooked long grain rice

6 bacon strips, cooked and crumbled

1/4 teaspoon crushed red pepper flakes, optional

Grated Parmesan cheese, optional

In a large skillet, cook pork, onion and garlic over medium heat until pork is no longer pink; drain. Add the next nine ingredients; cover and simmer for 5 minutes.

Stir in rice, bacon and red pepper flakes if desired; cover and simmer 5 minutes longer or until cabbage is tender. Sprinkle with Parmesan cheese if desired. **Yield:** 6 servings.

Grilled Stuffed Pork Chops

1 cup medium picante sauce
2 tablespoons honey
1 teaspoon Worcestershire sauce
4 bone-in pork rib chops (1 inch thick)

1/2 pound bulk hot pork sausage
1/2 teaspoon garlic powder
1/4 teaspoon pepper
1/4 cup prepared zesty Italian salad dressing

Combine the picante sauce, honey and Worcestershire sauce; stir until honey is dissolved. Divide the sauce into two small bowls; set aside.

Cut a pocket in each chop by slicing almost to the bone. Stuff with sausage; secure with toothpicks. Sprinkle chops with garlic powder and pepper. Brush each side with Italian dressing.

Grill, covered, over medium heat for 5 minutes on each side. Grill 10-15 minutes longer or until meat juices run clear, basting twice with sauce from one bowl. Remove toothpicks. Serve with sauce from the second bowl. **Yield:** 4 servings.

Herb-Marinated Pork Loin

1/2 cup tomato juice
1/2 cup vegetable oil
1/2 cup finely chopped onion
1/4 cup lemon juice
1/4 cup chopped fresh parsley
1 garlic clove, minced

1 teaspoon salt
1 teaspoon dried marjoram
1 teaspoon dried thyme
1/2 teaspoon pepper
1 boneless pork loin roast (3 pounds)

In a large resealable plastic bag, combine the first 10 ingredients; add pork. Seal bag and turn to coat; refrigerate overnight, turning meat occasionally. Drain and discard marinade.

Grill, covered, over indirect heat, turning occasionally, for 1-1/4 to 1-3/4 hours or until a meat thermometer reads 160°. Let stand for 5 minutes before slicing. **Yield:** 10-12 servings.

Parmesan Pork Sandwiches

1 garlic clove, minced
4 tablespoons vegetable oil, *divided*
1 can (15 ounces) tomato puree
1 egg, lightly beaten
2 tablespoons water
1/4 cup seasoned bread crumbs
4 boneless pork loin chops (1/4 inch thick)
1/2 cup shredded part-skim mozzarella cheese
1/4 cup grated Parmesan cheese
4 sandwich rolls, split

In a saucepan, saute garlic in 2 tablespoons oil. Add the tomato puree. Bring to a boil. Reduce heat; simmer, uncovered, for 5 minutes.

Meanwhile, combine the egg and water in a shallow bowl. Place bread crumbs in another shallow bowl. Dip pork chops in egg mixture, then coat with crumbs. In a large skillet, brown chops on both sides in remaining oil over medium-high heat.

Spread half of the tomato mixture in a greased 11-in. x 7-in. x 2-in. baking dish. Top with pork chops; drizzle with remaining tomato mixture. Sprinkle with cheeses. Bake, uncovered, at 425° for 8-10 minutes or until meat juices run clear. Serve on rolls. **Yield:** 4 servings.

Ham Rolls Continental

6 thin slices fully cooked ham (about 5-inch square)
6 thin slices Swiss cheese (about 4-inch square)
6 thin slices cheddar cheese (about 4-inch square)
12 frozen broccoli spears, thawed
1 small onion, thinly sliced into rings
2 tablespoons butter
2 tablespoons all-purpose flour
1/2 teaspoon salt
Dash white pepper
1-1/4 cups milk

Top each ham slice with a slice of Swiss cheese, a slice of cheddar and two broccoli spears (floret ends out); roll up jelly-roll style. Place seam side down in an ungreased 11-in. x 7-in. x 2-in. baking dish. Arrange onion rings on top.

In a small saucepan, melt butter. Stir in the flour, salt and pepper until smooth. Gradually add milk, stirring constantly. Bring to a boil; cook and stir for 2 minutes or until thickened. Pour over center of ham rolls. Bake, uncovered, at 350° for 25-30 minutes or until the broccoli is tender. **Yield:** 6 servings.

Lemon Pork Ribs

1 can (12 ounces) frozen
   lemonade concentrate, thawed
2/3 cup soy sauce
1 teaspoon seasoned salt
1 teaspoon celery salt
2 garlic cloves, minced
6 pork steaks (1/2 inch thick)

In a bowl, combine the first five ingredients. Reserve 1/2 cup for basting and refrigerate. Pour remaining marinade into a large resealable plastic bag; add pork. Seal bag and turn to coat; refrigerate overnight, turning meat several times.

Drain and discard marinade. Grill, covered, over medium heat for 5 minutes. Turn; baste with reserved marinade. Cook 15-20 minutes longer, basting occasionally, or until juices run clear. **Yield:** 6 servings.

Pork and Cabbage Rolls

1 medium head cabbage (3
   pounds)
1 pound ground pork
1/2 pound sage-flavored pork
   sausage
1 cup chopped onion
2 cups cooked brown rice
1/4 teaspoon pepper
2 cups chicken broth *or* 2 cans
   (15 ounces *each*) seasoned
   tomato sauce

Remove core from the cabbage. Place cabbage in a large saucepan and cover with water. Bring to a boil; boil until outer leaves loosen from head. Remove cabbage; set softened leaves aside. Return cabbage to boiling water to soften more leaves. Repeat until all leaves are softened. Cut out the thick vein from the bottom of each reserved leaf, making a V-shaped cut. Set aside 12 large leaves for rolls. Coarsely chop enough of the remaining leaves to measure 8 cups. Place chopped cabbage in an ungreased 13-in. x 9-in. x 2-in. baking dish.

In a skillet over medium heat, cook the pork, sausage and onion over medium heat until meat is no longer pink; drain. Stir in rice. Place 1/2 cup meat mixture on each cabbage leaf. Fold in sides, beginning from the cut end. Roll up completely to enclose filling.

Place rolls seam side down in the baking dish. Sprinkle with pepper. Pour broth or tomato sauce over rolls. Cover and bake at 325° for 1 to 1-1/4 hours. **Yield:** 6 servings.

Pork with Peanuts

1 pound pork cutlets (1/4 inch thick)

4 green onions, cut into 1-inch pieces

1 garlic clove, minced

1 tablespoon vegetable oil

1 can (14 ounces) bean sprouts, drained

1/2 cup thinly sliced celery

1/2 cup thinly sliced carrots

1/2 cup thinly sliced green *or* sweet red pepper

1 tablespoon cornstarch

1 cup chicken broth

2 tablespoons soy sauce

1/4 to 1/2 teaspoon crushed red pepper flakes

1/2 cup dry roasted peanuts

Hot cooked rice *or* thin spaghetti

Cut pork into 1/2-in. strips. In a skillet, stir-fry pork, onions and garlic in oil over medium-high heat for 2-3 minutes or until pork is no longer pink. Add the bean sprouts, celery, carrots and green pepper; stir-fry for 2-3 minutes.

Combine cornstarch, broth and soy sauce until smooth; add to skillet. Stir in red pepper flakes. Bring to a boil; cook and stir for 2 minutes or until thickened. Stir in peanuts. Serve over rice or spaghetti. **Yield:** 4-6 servings.

Microwave Corn Bread Casserole

2 cups frozen mixed vegetables

1-1/2 cups cubed fully cooked ham

1 package (6 ounces) corn bread stuffing mix

3 eggs

2 cups milk

1/4 teaspoon salt

1/4 teaspoon pepper

1 cup (4 ounces) shredded cheddar cheese

In a greased 11-in. x 7-in. x 2-in. microwave-safe dish, combine the vegetables, ham and stuffing mix. In a bowl, combine the eggs, milk, salt and pepper. Pour over corn bread mixture. Cover and refrigerate for at least 5 hours or overnight.

Remove from the refrigerator 30 minutes before cooking. Cover and microwave on high for 14-18 minutes or until a knife inserted in the center comes out clean. Sprinkle with cheese. Cover and let stand for 5 minutes before serving. **Yield:** 4-6 servings.

Editor's Note: This recipe was tested in a 1,100-watt microwave.

Crunchy Baked Pork Tenderloin

1 pork tenderloin (1 pound), cut crosswise into 1-inch medallions

1/4 cup butter, melted

1/4 cup mayonnaise

4 to 5 teaspoons prepared mustard

1-1/4 cups crushed herb-seasoned stuffing mix

Flatten pork tenderloin pieces to 1/4-in. to 1/2-in. thickness. In a shallow bowl, combine the butter, mayonnaise and mustard; dip pork in butter mixture, then roll in stuffing crumbs.

Place in a greased 13-in. x 9-in. x 2-in. baking pan. Bake, uncovered, at 425° for 13-16 minutes or until juices run clear. Let stand for 5 minutes before slicing. **Yield:** 4 servings.

Pork Ribs and Chilies

2-1/2 to 3 pounds boneless country-style pork ribs

2 cans (14-1/2 ounces *each*) diced tomatoes, undrained

2 cans (14-1/2 ounces *each*) chicken broth

1 jar (16 ounces) salsa

1 can (4 ounces) chopped green chilies

2 to 3 garlic cloves, minced

2 teaspoons ground cumin

1 teaspoon crushed red pepper flakes

1/2 teaspoon ground coriander, optional

1/4 teaspoon salt

1/8 teaspoon pepper

2 tablespoons cornstarch

1/4 cup cold water

Hot cooked rice

Shredded cheddar *or* Monterey Jack cheese, optional

Sour cream and guacamole, optional

Place ribs in a deep roasting pan. Cover and bake at 450° for 30 minutes; drain. Reduce temperature to 350°. Bake, uncovered, 45 minutes longer; drain. Let stand until cool.

Cut meat into 1-in. cubes; return to pan. Combine the tomatoes, broth, salsa, chilies and seasonings; pour over ribs. Cover and bake for 2 hours.

Combine cornstarch in water until smooth; stir into rib mixture. Bake, uncovered, 15 minutes longer. Serve over rice. Top with cheese, sour cream and guacamole if desired. **Yield:** 8 servings.

Ribs with Caraway Kraut And Stuffing Balls

3 pounds boneless country-style pork ribs
1 can (14 ounces) sauerkraut, drained
1-1/2 cups tomato juice
1/2 cup chicken broth
1 medium apple, diced
1 tablespoon brown sugar
2 to 3 teaspoons caraway seeds
1/8 teaspoon salt
1/8 teaspoon pepper

STUFFING BALLS:
1 package (8 ounces) herb-seasoned stuffing mix
1-1/3 cups hot water
1/2 cup butter, melted
2 eggs

In a large skillet, brown ribs; drain. Combine the sauerkraut, tomato juice, broth, apple, brown sugar, caraway, salt and pepper; pour over ribs. Cover and simmer 1-1/2 hours or until meat is very tender.

For stuffing balls, combine the stuffing mix, water and butter; mix lightly and let stand for 5 minutes. Stir in eggs. Shape into 2-in. balls; place over ribs and sauerkraut. Cover and simmer for 20 minutes. **Yield:** 6 servings.

Glazed Pork Tenderloin

1/2 cup currant jelly
1 tablespoon prepared horseradish
2 pork tenderloins (3/4 pound *each*)
1/2 cup chicken broth
1/4 cup white grape juice
1/4 teaspoon salt
1/4 teaspoon pepper

In a microwave-safe bowl, combine the jelly and horseradish. Microwave on high for 1 minute or until jelly is melted; stir until smooth.

Place the tenderloins on a rack in a shallow roasting pan. Brush with half of the jelly mixture. Bake, uncovered, at 425° for 20 minutes. Turn the meat over; brush with the remaining jelly mixture. Bake 10 minutes longer or until a meat thermometer reads 160°. Remove the meat and keep warm.

Add broth and grape juice to roasting pan; stir to loosen browned bits. Transfer to a saucepan. Cook over medium-high heat until liquid is reduced to 1/2 cup, about 5 minutes. Strain sauce; add salt and pepper. Slice pork; serve with sauce. **Yield:** 6 servings.

Poultry

Turkey Rice Casserole

4 cups chicken broth
1/4 cup uncooked wild rice
1-3/4 cups uncooked long grain rice
2 cups sliced fresh mushrooms
1/2 cup fresh broccoli florets
1 small onion, chopped
1/4 cup grated carrot
1/4 cup sliced celery
2 tablespoons olive oil
5 cups cubed cooked turkey
1 jar (2 ounces) diced pimientos, drained

1 teaspoon salt
1/2 teaspoon dried marjoram
1/2 teaspoon dried oregano
5 tablespoons all-purpose flour
3 cups milk
1/4 cup white wine *or* chicken broth
2 cups (8 ounces) shredded Swiss cheese
2 cups (8 ounces) shredded cheddar cheese, *divided*

In a large saucepan, bring broth to a boil; add the wild rice. Cover and simmer for 25 minutes. Add the long grain rice; simmer 25 minutes longer or until tender.

In a large skillet, saute the mushrooms, broccoli, onion, carrot and celery in oil until tender. Add the turkey, pimientos, salt, marjoram and oregano. Stir in the rice.

In a large saucepan, combine the flour, milk and wine or broth until smooth. Bring to a boil; cook and stir for 2 minutes or until thickened. Reduce heat; add Swiss cheese and 1 cup cheddar cheese, stirring until melted. Add to turkey mixture.

Transfer to a greased 13-in. x 9-in. x 2-in. baking dish. Sprinkle with the remaining cheddar cheese. Bake, uncovered, at 350° for 25-30 minutes or until heated through. **Yield:** 12 servings.

Asparagus-Lover's Stir-Fry

4 tablespoons vegetable oil, *divided*

1 cup sliced celery

4 cups fresh asparagus pieces

1/2 cup sliced green onions

4 boneless skinless chicken breast halves, cut into 1-inch strips

2 teaspoons grated orange peel

1 garlic clove, minced

4 teaspoons cornstarch

1/2 cup water

1/4 cup orange juice

2 tablespoons orange juice concentrate

2 tablespoons soy sauce

1/2 cup sliced almonds

Hot cooked rice

In a large skillet or wok, heat 2 tablespoons oil. Stir-fry celery over medium-high heat for 1 minute. Add asparagus and onions; stir-fry for 3-5 minutes or until asparagus is crisp-tender. Transfer to a bowl; set aside. Add remaining oil to the skillet. Stir-fry chicken, orange peel and garlic for 3-4 minutes or until chicken juices run clear.

Combine cornstarch, water, orange juice, orange juice concentrate and soy sauce until smooth; stir into skillet along with reserved vegetables. Cook and stir for 3 minutes or until sauce is thickened and vegetables are heated through. Stir in almonds. Serve over rice. **Yield:** 6-8 servings.

Corny Bread Bake

2 cups cubed cooked chicken

1-1/2 cups (6 ounces) shredded Monterey Jack cheese

1 can (11 ounces) Mexican-style corn, drained

1 can (4 ounces) chopped green chilies, drained

1 cup biscuit/baking mix

3 eggs, *separated*

1 cup milk

1/2 teaspoon salt

In a bowl, combine the chicken, cheese, corn and chilies; place in a greased shallow 2-1/2-qt. baking dish.

In a mixing bowl, beat biscuit mix, egg yolks, milk and salt until smooth. In another mixing bowl, beat egg whites until stiff peaks form; fold into yolk mixture. Pour over chicken mixture.

Bake, uncovered, at 350° for 40-45 minutes or until browned and a knife inserted near the center comes out clean. **Yield:** 4-6 servings.

Texas Turkey Tacos

1 medium onion, chopped
2 garlic cloves, minced
1 tablespoon olive oil
1/2 pound ground turkey
1/3 cup frozen corn
3 tablespoons picante sauce
3 tablespoons chicken broth
1/2 teaspoon salt
1/4 teaspoon ground cumin
1/8 teaspoon cayenne pepper
4 flour tortillas (7 inches), warmed
Chopped tomato, shredded lettuce, shredded cheddar cheese *and/or* sour cream, optional

In a saucepan, saute onion and garlic in oil until tender. Add turkey; cook over medium until meat is no longer pink. Drain if necessary. Stir in the corn, picante sauce, broth, salt, cumin and cayenne. Cook and stir for 5 minutes or until corn is tender. Spoon over tortillas. Top with tomato, lettuce, cheese and sour cream if desired. Roll up. **Yield:** 2 servings.

Chicken Crescent Casserole

1 celery rib, sliced
3 tablespoons butter, *divided*
1 can (10-3/4 ounces) condensed cream of mushroom soup, undiluted
2/3 cup mayonnaise
1/2 cup sour cream
2 tablespoons dried minced onion
3 cups cubed cooked chicken
1 can (8 ounces) sliced water chestnuts, drained
1 jar (4-1/2 ounces) sliced mushrooms, drained
2/3 cup shredded Swiss cheese
1 tube (8 ounces) refrigerated crescent rolls
1/2 cup sliced almonds

In a large saucepan, saute celery in 1 tablespoon butter until tender. Stir in the soup, mayonnaise, sour cream, onion, chicken, water chestnuts and mushrooms. Cook and stir over medium heat just until mixture begins to boil. Transfer to an ungreased 13-in. x 9-in. x 2-in. baking dish. Sprinkle with cheese.

Unroll crescent roll dough into a rectangle; seal seams and perforations. Place over cheese. Melt the remaining butter; toss with nuts and sprinkle over top. Bake, uncovered, at 375° for 20-25 minutes or until golden brown. **Yield:** 8-10 servings.

Picante Chicken

4 boneless skinless chicken breast halves, cubed
1 tablespoon vegetable oil
1 cup chopped onion
1 cup chopped celery
1 cup chopped green *or* sweet red pepper

1 jar (12 ounces) picante sauce
1/2 teaspoon lemon-pepper seasoning
1/4 teaspoon salt, optional
Hot cooked rice, optional

In a large skillet or wok, saute chicken in oil for 10-12 minutes or until juices run clear. Add the onion, celery and pepper; saute until crisp-tender. Add picante sauce, lemon-pepper and salt if desired. Bring to a boil. Reduce heat; simmer, uncovered, for 30 minutes. Serve over rice if desired. **Yield:** 4 servings.

Hot Turkey Sandwiches

4 slices bread, toasted and buttered
4 slices cooked turkey
1/2 cup shredded cheddar *or* process cheese (Velveeta)

8 bacon strips, cooked and drained
4 slices tomato, optional
1/4 cup grated Parmesan cheese

Place toast in a shallow baking pan. Top with the turkey, cheddar cheese, two bacon strips and tomato if desired. Sprinkle with Parmesan cheese. Broil 5 in. from the heat for 3-4 minutes or until cheddar cheese is melted. **Yield:** 4 servings.

Cola Chicken

1 can (12 ounces) diet cola
1/2 cup ketchup
2 to 4 tablespoons minced onion

1/4 teaspoon dried oregano
1/4 teaspoon garlic powder
8 chicken pieces, skin removed

In a large skillet, combine the first five ingredients. Bring to a boil; boil for 1 minute. Add chicken; stir to coat. Reduce heat to medium; cover and simmer for 20 minutes. Uncover; simmer for 45 minutes or until chicken juices run clear. **Yield:** 4 servings.

Turkey Burritos

1 pound ground turkey
1/2 cup chopped onion
1 can (14-1/2 ounces) diced tomatoes, undrained
1 can (16 ounces) refried beans with green chilies
1 can (4 ounces) chopped green chilies
1 can (2-1/4 ounces) sliced ripe olives, drained
1 envelope taco seasoning mix
1/4 cup frozen corn
1/4 cup uncooked instant rice
10 to 12 flour tortillas (7 to 8 inches)
Shredded cheddar *or* Monterey Jack cheese, optional

In a large nonstick saucepan, cook turkey and onion over medium heat until no longer pink; drain. Add the tomatoes, beans, chilies, olives, taco seasoning and corn; bring to a boil. Reduce heat; cover and simmer for 15 minutes.

Return to a boil. Stir in rice; remove from the heat. Cover; let stand for 5 minutes. Place about 1/2 cup filling down the center of each tortilla; sprinkle with cheese if desired. Fold in sides of tortilla. **Yield:** 10-12 servings.

Dijon Chicken

1/3 cup Dijon mustard
1/3 cup sour cream
6 boneless skinless chicken breast halves
1-1/4 cups Italian-style bread crumbs
24 stuffed green *or* pitted ripe olives
1/4 cup butter, melted
1 tablespoon fresh lemon juice
1/8 teaspoon cayenne pepper
6 lemon slices

In a shallow bowl, combine mustard and sour cream. Dip chicken in mixture, coating both sides, then roll in bread crumbs. Place four olives in the center of each chicken breast; fold in half.

Place in an ungreased 11-in. x 7-in. x 2-in. baking dish. Combine the butter, lemon juice and cayenne; drizzle over chicken. Place a slice of lemon on each chicken breast.

Bake, uncovered, at 325° for 40-45 minutes or until juices run clear and a meat thermometer reads 170°. **Yield:** 6 servings.

Turkey Broccoli Bake

1 package (10 ounces) frozen chopped broccoli, thawed
2-1/2 cups (10 ounces) shredded cheddar cheese, *divided*
1-1/2 cups cubed cooked turkey
2/3 cup chopped onion
3/4 cup biscuit/baking mix
3/4 teaspoon salt
1/4 teaspoon pepper
3 eggs, beaten
1-1/3 cups milk

In a bowl, combine the broccoli, 2 cups cheese, turkey and onion. Spoon into a greased 9-in. deep-dish pie plate.

In a bowl, combine the biscuit mix, salt, pepper, eggs and milk. Pour over broccoli mixture; sprinkle with remaining cheese.

Bake at 400° for 30-35 minutes or until a knife inserted near the center comes out clean. Let stand for 5 minutes before cutting. **Yield:** 6-8 servings.

South Seas Skillet

4 boneless skinless chicken breast halves, cut into thin strips
1/4 cup butter
1/3 cup sliced green onions
3 garlic cloves, minced
1 cup water
1/3 cup raisins
3 tablespoons chopped fresh parsley, *divided*
2 teaspoons brown sugar
1 teaspoon chicken bouillon granules
1/8 teaspoon salt
1 orange, cut into 8 wedges
Hot cooked rice

In a large skillet, saute chicken in butter for 6-8 minutes or until juices run clear. Remove from skillet; set aside.

Saute onions and garlic in drippings until tender. Add the water, raisins, 2 tablespoons parsley, brown sugar, bouillon and salt. Simmer for 15 minutes or until liquid is reduced by half. Add chicken and heat through. Sprinkle with remaining parsley. Squeeze juice from orange wedges over chicken. Serve over rice. **Yield:** 4 servings.

Chicken Barbecued in Foil

3/4 cup chopped onion
1/2 cup ketchup
1/4 cup lemon juice
3 tablespoons butter
2 tablespoons Worcestershire sauce
1 tablespoon brown sugar

1 teaspoon ground mustard
1 teaspoon cider vinegar
1 broiler/fryer chicken (3-1/2 to 4 pounds), cut up and skin removed
Salt and pepper to taste
4 sheets heavy-duty aluminum foil (18 inches x 12 inches)

In a saucepan, combine the first eight ingredients; bring to a boil. Reduce heat; simmer, uncovered, for 15 minutes. Place 2 pieces of chicken in the center of each piece of foil; fold up edges to hold sauce. Sprinkle chicken with salt and pepper. Spoon sauce over chicken. Bring opposite long edges of foil together over the top and fold down several times. Fold the short ends toward the chicken and crimp tightly to prevent leaks.

Place packets on a baking sheet. Bake at 350° for 1 hour. Carefully open packets and turn down foil. Broil chicken for 5 minutes or until browned. **Yield:** 4 servings.

Creole Fried Chicken

1 cup all-purpose flour
2 teaspoons salt
1-1/2 teaspoons Creole seasoning
1/2 teaspoon pepper

1 broiler/fryer chicken (3-1/2 to 4 pounds), cut up
3 tablespoons vegetable oil
2 cups water

In a shallow bowl, combine the flour, salt, seasoning and pepper. Coat chicken with flour mixture. Heat oil in a large skillet, fry chicken, a few pieces at a time, until brown on all sides. Add water; bring to a boil. Reduce heat; cover and simmer for 45 minutes or until juices run clear. Thicken gravy if desired. **Yield:** 4 servings.

Editor's Note: The following spices may be substituted for 1 teaspoon Creole seasoning: 1/4 teaspoon *each* salt, garlic powder and paprika; and a pinch *each* of dried thyme, ground cumin and cayenne pepper.

Sweet-and-Sour Chicken

3 tablespoons all-purpose flour
1/2 teaspoon garlic powder
1/2 teaspoon salt
1/2 teaspoon pepper
1-1/2 pounds boneless skinless chicken breasts, cut into 1-inch cubes
3 tablespoons vegetable oil, *divided*

3 celery ribs, sliced
2 medium green peppers, diced
1 medium onion, diced
1/2 cup ketchup
1/2 cup lemon juice
1/2 cup crushed pineapple with syrup
1/3 cup packed brown sugar
Hot cooked rice

In a shallow dish, combine the flour, garlic powder, salt and pepper; coat chicken. In a skillet, saute chicken in 2 tablespoons oil over medium-high heat for 8-10 minutes or until tender. Remove and set aside.

Saute the celery, green peppers and onion in remaining oil for 5 minutes or until crisp-tender. Return chicken pan. Combine the ketchup, lemon juice, pineapple and brown sugar; add to skillet. Bring to a boil; cook and stir for 1-2 minutes or until heated through. Serve over rice. **Yield:** 6 servings.

Chicken with Cucumber Sauce

1/4 cup yellow cornmeal
1-1/2 teaspoons ground mustard
1/4 teaspoon ground nutmeg
1/8 to 1/4 teaspoon cayenne pepper
1/2 teaspoon seafood seasoning, optional
8 boneless skinless chicken breast halves

2 tablespoons vegetable oil

CUCUMBER SAUCE:
1 bottle (8 ounces) ranch salad dressing
1 cup diced peeled cucumber
1 tablespoon sliced green onion
1/2 teaspoon dill weed

In a shallow dish, combine the cornmeal, mustard, nutmeg, cayenne pepper and seafood seasoning if desired; coat chicken. In a skillet, cook chicken in oil over medium heat for 5-7 minutes on each side or until browned and juices run clear.

Meanwhile, combine sauce ingredients in a saucepan; cook over low heat until heated through. Serve over chicken. **Yield:** 8 servings.

Summer Squash Enchiladas

3/4 cup chopped onion

2 garlic cloves, minced

1 tablespoon vegetable oil

3 cups chopped yellow squash

2 cups cubed cooked chicken

1 can (4 ounces) chopped green chilies

2 tablespoons butter

2 tablespoons all-purpose flour

2 teaspoons chili powder

1/4 teaspoon salt

1/8 teaspoon pepper

1-1/4 cups milk

10 flour tortillas (6 to 8 inches)

1-1/2 cups (6 ounces) shredded Monterey Jack cheese, *divided*

1 cup chopped fresh tomatoes

Sour cream

In a skillet, saute onion and garlic in oil until tender. Add squash and saute until tender. Add chicken and chilies; heat through.

In a saucepan, melt butter. Stir in flour, chili powder, salt and pepper until smooth. Gradually add milk, stirring constantly. Bring to a boil; cook and stir for 2 minutes or until thickened. Add 1/3 cup sauce to chicken mixture; mix well. Place 1/3 to 1/2 cup chicken mixture down the center of each tortilla; top with 1 tablespoon cheese. Roll up and place seam side down in a greased 13-in. x 9-in. x 2-in. baking dish. Spread remaining sauce on top.

Cover and bake at 400° for 25 minutes. Uncover; sprinkle with tomatoes and remaining cheese. Bake 5 minutes longer or until cheese is melted. Serve with sour cream. **Yield:** 4-6 servings.

Zesty Turkey

2 tablespoons rubbed sage

1 tablespoon pepper

2 teaspoons curry powder

2 teaspoons garlic powder

2 teaspoons dried parsley flakes

2 teaspoons celery seed

1 teaspoon paprika

1/2 teaspoon ground mustard

1/4 teaspoon ground allspice

1 turkey breast (4 to 4-1/2 pounds)

2 cups reduced-sodium chicken broth

In a small bowl, combine spices and mix well. Place turkey on a rack in a roasting pan; rub with spice mixture. Add broth to pan. Bake at 350° for 2-3 hours or until thermometer reads 170°, basting every 30 minutes. **Yield:** 6 servings.

Chicken Tamale Pie

1 package (8-1/2 ounces) corn
  bread/muffin mix
1 egg, beaten
1/3 cup milk
1/2 cup shredded cheddar cheese
1 can (10-3/4 ounces) condensed
  cream of chicken soup,
  undiluted

2 cups cubed cooked chicken
1 cup frozen corn, thawed
1/2 cup chopped green onions
1 can (4 ounces) chopped green
  chilies
1 garlic clove, minced
1/2 to 3/4 teaspoon chili powder

In a mixing bowl, combine the muffin mix, egg and milk; add cheese.
Spread in the bottom and up the sides of a greased 9-in. pie plate.

In a saucepan, combine the soup, chicken, corn, onions, chilies, garlic
and chili powder; heat through. Immediately pour into crust.

Bake at 400° for 20-25 minutes or until crust is golden and filling is
hot. **Yield:** 6 servings.

Dilly Chicken and Potatoes

1 broiler/fryer chicken (3-1/2 to 4
  pounds), cut up
1 pound new potatoes, cut into
  chunks
2 tablespoons vegetable oil
1 cup half-and-half cream

1 to 1-1/2 teaspoons salt
1/2 teaspoon seasoned pepper
3/4 cup sliced green onions
1/4 cup snipped fresh dill or 1
  tablespoon dill weed
1/2 cup sour cream

In a large skillet, brown chicken and potatoes in oil over medium heat
for 10-15 minutes. Remove chicken and potatoes; set aside.

Drain skillet, reserving 1 tablespoon drippings. To drippings, add the
cream, salt and pepper; stir to mix. Return chicken and potatoes to
skillet. Sprinkle with onions and dill. Cover and simmer for 50-60
minutes or until chicken juices run clear and potatoes are tender.

With a slotted spoon, remove chicken and potatoes to a serving
platter; keep warm. Add sour cream to pan; stir to mix and heat through
(do not boil). Serve with chicken and potatoes. **Yield:** 4-6 servings.

Crescent Chicken Squares

1 package (3 ounces) cream
  cheese, softened
3 tablespoons butter, melted,
  divided
1/4 teaspoon salt
1/8 teaspoon pepper
2 cups cubed cooked chicken

2 tablespoons milk
1 tablespoon chopped onion
1 tablespoon diced pimientos
1 tube (8 ounces) refrigerated
  crescent rolls
1/4 cup seasoned bread crumbs

In a mixing bowl, beat cream cheese, 2 tablespoons butter, salt and pepper until smooth. Stir in chicken, milk, onion and pimientos. Unroll crescent roll dough and separate into four rectangles; place on an ungreased baking sheet and press perforations together.

Spoon 1/2 cup chicken mixture into the center of each rectangle. Bring edges up to the center and pinch to seal. Brush with remaining butter; sprinkle with crumbs.

Bake at 350° for 20-25 minutes or until golden. **Yield:** 2-4 servings.

Turkey Squash Casserole

1 pound ground turkey
1 tablespoon vegetable oil
2 cups sliced yellow summer
  squash
1 medium onion, chopped
2 eggs
1 cup evaporated milk

1 cup (4 ounces) shredded
  part-skim mozzarella cheese
6 tablespoons butter, melted
1/2 teaspoon salt
1/4 teaspoon pepper
1 cup crushed saltines (about 30
  crackers)

In a large skillet, cook turkey in oil over medium heat until meat is no longer pink. Add the squash and onion. Cook until vegetables are crisp-tender; drain.

In a bowl, combine the eggs, milk, cheese, butter, salt and pepper. Stir into the turkey mixture. Transfer to a greased 8-in. square baking dish. Sprinkle with the cracker crumbs.

Bake, uncovered, at 375° for 35-40 minutes or until heated through. **Yield:** 6 servings.

Stuffed Cornish Hens

2 tablespoons finely chopped onion
1/3 cup uncooked long grain rice
4 tablespoons butter, *divided*
3/4 cup water
1/2 cup condensed cream of celery soup
1 tablespoon lemon juice
1 teaspoon minced chives
1 teaspoon dried parsley flakes
1 teaspoon chicken bouillon granules
2 Cornish game hens (1 to 1-1/4 pounds *each*)
Salt and pepper to taste
1/2 teaspoon dried tarragon

In a small skillet, saute onion and rice in 2 tablespoons butter until rice is golden. Add the water, soup, lemon juice, chives, parsley and bouillon. Bring to a boil. Reduce heat; cover and simmer for 25 minutes or until rice is tender and liquid is absorbed. Remove from the heat and cool slightly.

Sprinkle hen cavities with salt and pepper; stuff with rice mixture. Place breast side up on a rack in an ungreased 13-in. x 9-in. x 2-in. baking pan. Melt remaining butter and add tarragon; brush some over the hens.

Cover loosely and bake at 375° for 30 minutes. Uncover; bake 30-45 minutes longer or until a meat thermometer reads 180° for hens and 165° for stuffing, basting frequently with tarragon butter. **Yield:** 2 servings.

Turkey Schnitzel

1/4 cup seasoned bread crumbs
1/4 cup grated Parmesan cheese
1/2 teaspoon garlic powder
1/4 teaspoon salt
1/4 teaspoon pepper
1 egg
1 tablespoon water
4 uncooked turkey breast slices (1/4 inch thick)
1/4 cup lemon juice
1/4 cup vegetable oil

In a shallow bowl, combine the first five ingredients. In another shallow bowl, beat egg and water. Dip turkey slices in lemon juice, then the egg mixture and coat with bread crumbs.

In a skillet, cook turkey in oil until browned on both sides and juices run clear. **Yield:** 4 servings.

Chicken Potpie

1 cup chopped celery
1/4 cup chopped onion
2 tablespoons butter
2-1/4 cups water, *divided*
1-1/2 cups diced cooked chicken
1 cup frozen mixed vegetables
3/4 cup uncooked thin egg noodles
1 tablespoon chicken bouillon granules
1/4 teaspoon pepper
2 tablespoons cornstarch
Pastry for single-crust pie (10 inches)

In a medium saucepan, saute celery and onion in butter until tender. Add 2 cups water, chicken, vegetables, noodles, bouillon and pepper. Cook, uncovered, over medium heat for 5 minutes or just until noodles are tender, stirring occasionally.

Combine cornstarch and remaining water until smooth; stir into saucepan. Bring to a boil; cook and stir for 2 minutes or until thickened. Pour into an ungreased 10-in. pie plate. Roll out pastry to fit plate; place over filling. Cut several 1-in. slits in the top.

Bake at 350° for 45-55 minutes or until lightly browned. Let stand for 5 minutes before serving. **Yield:** 6 servings.

Ginger Chicken Stir-Fry

4 boneless skinless chicken breast halves, cut into bite-size pieces
2 tablespoons vegetable oil
2 cups *each* broccoli florets, cauliflowerets and carrot pieces
1 cup chopped onion
3 tablespoons cornstarch
1/4 cup cold water
2 cups chicken broth
1/4 cup teriyaki sauce
1/4 cup soy sauce
1/2 teaspoon pepper
1/2 teaspoon ground ginger
1/8 to 1/4 teaspoon cayenne pepper
1 garlic clove, minced

In a large skillet or wok, stir-fry chicken in oil over medium-high heat for 10 minutes or until juices run clear. Remove chicken and set aside.

In the same skillet, stir-fry the broccoli, cauliflower, carrots and onion for 5-8 minutes or until tender. Combine the cornstarch and water until smooth. Add the remaining ingredients; stir into skillet. Bring to a boil; cook and stir for 2 minutes or until thickened. Return chicken to skillet and heat through. **Yield:** 8 servings.

German Chicken

1 broiler/fryer chicken (3-1/2 to 4 pounds), cut up
3/4 cup all-purpose flour
3 tablespoons butter
3 tablespoons vegetable oil
3/4 teaspoon garlic powder, *divided*
1/2 teaspoon pepper, *divided*

1 large head green cabbage (3 pounds), coarsely chopped
1 large onion, chopped
1 can (29 ounces) sauerkraut, rinsed and drained
1 can (15 ounces) tomato sauce
1/3 cup packed brown sugar
1/4 cup cider vinegar

Coat chicken pieces with flour. In a large skillet, heat butter and oil; brown chicken on all sides. Place in a large Dutch oven or roaster; sprinkle with 1/4 teaspoon garlic powder and 1/8 teaspoon pepper. Top with half of the cabbage and onion.

In a bowl, combine the sauerkraut, tomato sauce, brown sugar, vinegar and remaining garlic powder and pepper. Pour half over the cabbage and onion. Repeat layers.

Cover and bake at 350° for 1-1/2 hours or until a meat thermometer reads 170° for breast pieces and 180° for thighs and drumsticks and cabbage is tender. **Yield:** 4 servings.

Spicy Chicken Corn Skillet

1 pound boneless skinless chicken breasts, cut into thin strips
1 tablespoon vegetable oil
1 medium onion, chopped
1 medium green pepper, chopped
1 tablespoon butter
1 can (14-1/2 ounces) stewed tomatoes, cut up

1 cup frozen corn, thawed
1/2 teaspoon salt
1/2 teaspoon dried oregano
1/2 teaspoon paprika
1/4 teaspoon pepper
1/8 to 1/4 teaspoon cayenne pepper
1 cup cooked rice

In a large skillet, stir-fry chicken in oil until no longer pink; remove and set aside. In the same skillet, saute onion and green pepper in butter until tender. Stir in the tomatoes, corn and seasonings. Bring to a boil. Stir in chicken and rice. Reduce heat; cover and cook until heated through. **Yield:** 4 servings.

Sunshine Chicken

1 package (3 ounces) lemon
  gelatin
3 tablespoons butter, melted
3 tablespoons prepared mustard
2 teaspoons garlic salt

1/4 teaspoon pepper
4 large boneless skinless chicken
  breast halves
2 tablespoons thinly sliced
  almonds
Hot cooked rice, optional

In a small bowl, combine the gelatin, butter, mustard, garlic salt and
pepper. Brush over both sides of the chicken breasts and place in an
ungreased 11-in. x 7-in. x 2-in. baking dish. Spoon remaining mixture
around chicken.

Cover and bake at 350° for 20-25 minutes, basting once. Uncover;
baste and sprinkle with almonds. Bake 15 minutes longer or until a
meat thermometer reads 170°. Serve over rice if desired. **Yield:** 4
servings.

Ground Turkey Turnovers

1-1/2 pounds ground turkey
1 can (10-3/4 ounces) condensed
  cream of chicken soup,
  undiluted
1 egg, lightly beaten
2 tablespoons all-purpose flour
1/2 teaspoon salt
1/4 teaspoon pepper

1 can (8-1/4 ounces) mixed
  vegetables, drained
1 jar (2 ounces) diced pimientos,
  drained
1/2 cup shredded part-skim
  mozzarella cheese
2 tubes (17.3 ounces *each*)
  Southern-style biscuits

In a nonstick saucepan, cook turkey over medium heat until no longer
pink; drain. Combine the soup, egg, flour, salt and pepper; add to
turkey. Cook for 5 minutes, stirring occasionally. Add vegetables and
pimientos; cook for 2 minutes. Remove from the heat; stir in cheese.

On a floured surface, pat eight of the biscuits into circles; top each
with about 2/3 cup turkey mixture. Pat remaining biscuits into 5-in.
circles and place on top of turkey mixture. Seal edges with water. Press
edges together with a fork dipped in flour. Place on an ungreased baking
sheet.

Bake at 375° for 12-14 minutes or until golden brown. **Yield:** 8
servings.

Chicken with Tomato-Cream Sauce

8 boneless skinless chicken
  breast halves
1/4 cup butter
1 small onion, thinly sliced
2 garlic cloves, minced
1 can (14-1/2 ounces) diced
  tomatoes, undrained

1 teaspoon salt
2 tablespoons all-purpose flour
1 cup (8 ounces) sour cream
2/3 cup grated Parmesan cheese
Hot cooked noodles

In a large skillet, brown chicken in butter on each side. Remove and set aside. Add onion and garlic; saute until tender. Stir in tomatoes and salt. Bring to a boil. Reduce heat; return chicken to pan. Cover and simmer for 30 minutes or until chicken juices run clear.

Remove chicken and keep warm. Combine the flour and sour cream. Reduce heat to low; stir in sour cream mixture and Parmesan cheese. Heat through (do not boil). Serve chicken and sauce over noodles. **Yield:** 8 servings.

Sunday Fried Chicken

3 cups all-purpose flour
2 to 3 teaspoons poultry
  seasonings
2 teaspoons paprika
2 to 3 teaspoons onion powder
1 to 2 teaspoons garlic powder
1/2 teaspoon salt

Dash pepper
2 eggs
1 tablespoon milk
2 broiler/fryer chickens (3
  pounds *each*), cut up *or* 16 of
  your favorite poultry pieces
Oil for deep-fat frying

Combine dry ingredients in a plastic bag. In a bowl, lightly beat eggs and milk. Dip chicken pieces in egg mixture and shake off excess. Place chicken in bag, a few pieces at a time, and shake to coat.

In an electric skillet, heat 1/4 in. of oil to 350°; brown chicken on all sides. Cook, uncovered, for 15-25 minutes or until a meat thermometer reads 170° for breast pieces and 180° for thighs and drumsticks. **Yield:** 6-8 servings.

Overnight Chicken Casserole

8 slices day-old white bread

4 cups chopped cooked chicken

1 jar (4-1/2 ounces) sliced mushrooms, drained

1 can (8 ounces) sliced water chestnuts, drained

4 eggs

2 cups milk

1/2 cup mayonnaise

1/2 teaspoon salt

6 to 8 slices (6 ounces) process American cheese

1 can (10-3/4 ounces) condensed cream of celery soup, undiluted

1 can (10-3/4 ounces) condensed cream of mushroom soup, undiluted

1 jar (2 ounces) chopped pimientos, drained

2 tablespoons butter, melted

Remove the crusts from bread and set aside. Arrange bread slices in a greased 13-in. x 9-in. x 2-in. baking dish. Top with chicken; cover with the mushrooms and water chestnuts.

In a bowl, beat eggs; blend in milk, mayonnaise and salt. Pour over chicken. Arrange cheese on top. Combine soups and pimientos; pour over cheese. Cover and refrigerate overnight.

Remove from the refrigerator 30 minutes before baking. Crumble reserved crusts; toss with melted butter. Sprinkle over casserole. Bake, uncovered, at 325° for 1-1/4 hours or until set. Let stand for 10 minutes before cutting. **Yield:** 8-10 servings.

Editor's Note: Reduced-fat or fat-free mayonnaise is not recommended for this recipe.

Bacon and Blue Cheese Chicken

3 tablespoons dried minced onion

2 tablespoons dried parsley flakes

2 teaspoons dried basil

1 teaspoon poppy seeds

8 chicken thighs

1 cup chunky blue cheese salad dressing

6 bacon strips, cooked and crumbled

In a small bowl, combine the onion, parsley, basil and poppy seeds; rub over chicken. Place in an ungreased 11-in. x 7-in. x 2-in. baking dish. Pour dressing over chicken.

Bake, uncovered, at 350° for 40 minutes. Sprinkle with bacon. Bake 5-10 minutes longer or until a meat thermometer reads 180°. **Yield:** 6-8 servings.

Coconut Chicken with Pineapple Vinaigrette

1 cup crushed shredded wheat cereal

3/4 cup flaked coconut

1 broiler/fryer chicken (3-1/2 to 4 pounds), cut up

2 eggs, beaten

1 tablespoon cornstarch

1 tablespoon sugar

1/3 cup water

1/3 cup white vinegar

1 tablespoon butter

1/2 cup chopped green pepper

1 small onion, chopped

1 cup drained pineapple chunks

1 tablespoon chopped pimientos

In a shallow bowl, combine cereal and coconut. Remove skin from chicken if desired. Dip chicken pieces in eggs, then coat with coconut mixture.

Place in a greased 13-in. x 9-in. x 2-in. baking dish. Bake, uncovered, at 375° for 50-60 minutes or until juices run clear.

Meanwhile, in a small saucepan, combine cornstarch and sugar. Stir in water until smooth. Add vinegar and butter. Bring to a boil; cook and stir for 2 minutes or until thickened. Add green pepper and onion; cook until onion is softened. Stir in pineapple and pimientos; heat through. Serve with chicken. **Yield:** 4 servings.

Orange Barbecued Turkey

1/2 cup orange juice

1 teaspoon grated orange peel

1 tablespoon vegetable oil

2 teaspoons Worcestershire sauce

1 teaspoon ground mustard

1/2 teaspoon ground pepper

1/8 teaspoon garlic powder *or* 1 garlic clove, minced

4 turkey breast steaks (about 1-1/4 pounds)

In a large resealable plastic bag, combine the first seven ingredients; add turkey. Seal bag and turn to coat; refrigerate for 4 hours or overnight, turning occasionally.

Drain and discard marinade. Grill or broil steaks for 3-5 minutes on each side or until juices run clear. Do no overcook. **Yield:** about 4 servings.

Smothered Ginger Chicken

1/2 cup plus 3 tablespoons
all-purpose flour, *divided*
1-1/2 teaspoons salt, *divided*
1/4 teaspoon pepper
1 broiler/fryer chicken (3-1/2 to
4 pounds), cut up
3 tablespoons vegetable oil

1 cup chopped onion
1/4 cup *each* chopped green and
sweet red pepper
3 garlic cloves, minced
3 cups chicken broth
1/2 teaspoon ground ginger

In a shallow dish, combine 1/2 cup flour, 1 teaspoon salt and pepper;
coat chicken pieces. Heat oil in a large skillet, fry chicken, a few pieces
at a time, until well browned. Remove from skillet and set aside.

Add the onion, peppers and garlic to drippings; saute until tender.
Combine remaining flour and 1/2 cup chicken broth until smooth; set
aside. Stir ginger and remaining broth and salt into vegetable mixture.
Add chicken; cover tightly and simmer for 45 minutes or until a meat
thermometer reads 170° for breast pieces and 180° for thighs and
drumsticks. Stir flour mixture; stir into skillet. Bring to a boil; cook and
stir for 2 minutes or until thickened. **Yield:** 4 servings.

Grilled Chicken Kabobs

1/2 cup olive oil
1/4 cup lemon juice
4 garlic cloves, minced
2 teaspoons honey
1-1/2 teaspoons dried thyme

1 teaspoon salt, optional
1 teaspoon crushed red pepper
flakes
1 teaspoon pepper
4 boneless skinless chicken
breast halves (4 ounces *each*)

In a small bowl, combine the oil, lemon juice, garlic, honey, thyme, salt
if desired, red pepper flakes and pepper and salt if desired. Reserve half
of marinade for basting; cover.

Cut chicken into 1-in.-wide strips; weave onto metal or soaked
wooden skewers. Place in an 11-in. x 7-in. x 2-in. baking dish. Pour
remaining marinade over chicken. Cover and refrigerate for at least 4
hours.

Drain and discard marinade. Grill kabobs, uncovered, over medium
heat for 5-7 minutes on each side or until chicken juices run clear. Brush
frequently with reserved marinade. **Yield:** 4 servings.

Open-Faced Chicken Benedict

6 boneless skinless chicken
  breast halves
1/2 cup all-purpose flour
1 teaspoon paprika
1/2 teaspoon salt
1/4 teaspoon pepper
2 tablespoons vegetable oil
6 slices Canadian bacon

SAUCE:
1/2 cup sour cream
1/2 cup mayonnaise
1 tablespoon lemon juice
1 teaspoon yellow mustard
1/8 teaspoon pepper
3 English muffins, split and
  toasted

Pound chicken to 1/4-in. thickness. In a large resealable plastic bag, combine the flour, paprika, salt and pepper. Add chicken, one piece at a time, and shake to coat.

In a large skillet, cook chicken in oil until browned and juices run clear. Transfer to a platter and keep warm. Brown bacon in the same skillet, turning once; remove and keep warm.

For sauce, combine the sour cream, mayonnaise, lemon juice, mustard and pepper in a small saucepan. Cook, stirring constantly, until heated through; hold over low heat (do not boil).

Place English muffin halves on a baking sheet. Top each with a slice of bacon, one chicken breast half and 2 tablespoons sauce. Broil until bubbly. **Yield:** 6 servings.

Editor's Note: Reduced-fat or fat-free mayonnaise is not recommended for this recipe.

Peach-Glazed Chicken

1 broiler/fryer chicken (3-1/2 to 4
  pounds), cut up
1 jar (4 ounces) peach baby food
1/3 cup packed brown sugar
1/3 cup ketchup
1/3 cup white vinegar

1 tablespoon soy sauce
1/2 teaspoon ground ginger
1 teaspoon salt
1/4 teaspoon garlic powder
1/4 teaspoon pepper

Place chicken in a single layer in a greased or foil-lined 13-in. x 9-in. x 2-in. baking dish. Bake, uncovered, at 350° for 20 minutes.

Combine remaining ingredients; pour over chicken. Bake, uncovered, 45 minutes longer or until a meat thermometer reads 170° for breast pieces and 180° for thighs and drumsticks. **Yield:** 4 servings.

Apple Butter Barbecued Chicken

4 boneless skinless chicken breast halves (1 pound)
1/3 cup apple butter
2 tablespoons salsa
2 tablespoons ketchup
1 tablespoon vegetable oil
1/2 teaspoon salt, optional
1/4 teaspoon garlic powder
2 drops Worcestershire sauce
2 drops Liquid Smoke, optional

Place chicken in a greased 8-in. square baking dish. Combine remaining ingredients; pour over chicken. Bake, uncovered, at 375° for 25 minutes or until meat juices run clear. **Yield:** 4 servings.

Ranch Chicken 'n' Rice

2 cups uncooked instant rice
1-1/2 cups milk
1 cup water
1 envelope ranch salad dressing mix
1 pound boneless skinless chicken breasts, cut into 1/2-inch strips
1/4 cup butter, melted
Paprika

Place rice in a greased shallow 2-qt. baking dish. In a bowl, combine the milk, water and salad dressing mix; set aside 1/4 cup. Pour remaining mixture over rice. Top with chicken strips. Drizzle with butter and reserved milk mixture.

Cover and bake at 350° for 35-40 minutes or until rice is tender and chicken juices run clear. Sprinkle with paprika. **Yield:** 4 servings.

Marmalade Drumsticks

12 chicken drumsticks (about 2-1/2 pounds)
3/4 cup orange marmalade
2 cups herb-seasoned stuffing mix, crushed
1/2 cup butter

Spread the drumsticks with marmalade. Coat evenly with stuffing crumbs. Place in a single layer in a greased shallow baking pan. Drizzle with butter. Bake at 350° for 40 minutes or until a meat thermometer reads 180°. **Yield:** 6 servings.

Stir-Fried Chicken Fajitas

1/4 cup vegetable oil

3 tablespoon red wine vinegar

1-1/2 teaspoons sugar

1-1/2 teaspoons chili powder

1 teaspoon dried oregano

1/2 teaspoon garlic powder

1/2 teaspoon salt

1/4 teaspoon pepper

1-1/2 pounds boneless skinless chicken breasts, cut into thin strips

8 flour tortillas (10 inches), warmed

2 cups shredded lettuce

2 cups (8 ounces) shredded cheddar *or* Monterey Jack cheese

1 large tomato, diced

3/4 cup sour cream

Taco sauce

In a large resealable plastic bag, combine the first eight ingredients; add chicken. Seal bag and turn to coat; refrigerate for 4 hours.

Drain and discard marinade. Saute chicken in a large skillet over medium heat for 6-7 minutes or until juices run clear.

Spoon about 1/2 cup chicken down the center of each tortilla. Top with lettuce, cheese, tomato, sour cream and taco sauce. Fold in sides of tortilla and serve immediately. **Yield:** 8 servings.

Baked Crumbled Chicken

1-1/2 cups crushed cornflakes

2 tablespoons minced fresh parsley

2 teaspoons paprika

1-1/2 teaspoons salt

1-1/2 teaspoons dried basil

1/2 teaspoon pepper

2 eggs

1/2 cup milk

1 broiler/fryer chicken (3-1/2 to 4 pounds), cut up

1/4 cup butter, melted

In a shallow bowl or large resealable plastic bag, combine cornflakes, parsley, paprika, salt, basil and pepper.

In another bowl, beat eggs and milk. Dip chicken pieces in egg mixture, then coat generously with crumb mixture. Place in an ungreased 13-in. x 9-in. x 2-in. baking dish. Drizzle with butter.

Bake, uncovered, at 375° for 50-60 minutes or until golden brown and juices run clear. **Yield:** 4 servings.

South-of-the-Border Thighs

1 cup olive oil
4-1/2 teaspoons chili powder
1 tablespoon lime juice
2 teaspoons ground cumin
1 teaspoon ground coriander
1 teaspoon salt
1/2 teaspoon ground cloves
1/2 teaspoon cayenne pepper
1/2 teaspoon pepper
6 garlic cloves, minced
6 chicken thighs (4 ounces *each*)

In a small bowl, combine the first 10 ingredients. Reserve half the marinade for basting; cover and refrigerate. Pour remaining marinade in a large resealable plastic bag; add chicken. Seal bag and turn to coat; refrigerate for at least 4 hours.

Drain and discard marinade. Grill chicken, uncovered, over medium-low heat, for 20-40 minutes or until a meat thermometer reads 180°, turning and basting frequently with reserved marinade. **Yield:** 4-6 servings.

Extra-Crispy Italian Chicken

1-1/4 cups pancake mix
2 envelopes (.6 ounce *each*) zesty Italian salad dressing mix, *divided*
1 egg
1/3 cup club soda
1 broiler/fryer chicken (3-1/2 to 4 pounds), cut up
Oil for deep-fat frying

In a shallow bowl, combine pancake mix and one envelope salad dressing mix. In another shallow bowl, combine the egg, club soda and remaining envelope of salad dressing mix. Dip chicken pieces in egg mixture, then coat with the seasoned pancake mix. Place chicken pieces on a rack; let stand for 5 minutes.

In a deep-fat fryer, heat oil to 375°. Fry chicken, several pieces at a time, for 6 minutes or until golden brown. Place on an ungreased 15-in. x 10-in. x 1-in. baking pan.

Bake, uncovered, at 350° for 30 minutes or until a meat thermometer reads 170° for breast pieces and 180° for thighs and drumsticks. **Yield:** 4 servings.

Cheesy Turkey Burgers

3 ounces reduced-fat cream
  cheese
1/2 cup shredded reduced-fat
  Mexican cheese blend
1 small onion, grated
3 tablespoons old-fashioned oats
2 tablespoons minced chives

1 garlic clove, minced
1/2 to 1 teaspoon caraway seeds
1/2 teaspoon salt
1-1/2 pounds lean ground turkey
8 onion rolls, split
8 lettuce leaves
8 tomato slices

In a bowl, combine the first eight ingredients. Crumble turkey over mixture and mix well. Shape into eight 1/2-in.-thick patties.

If using the grill, coat grill rack with nonstick cooking spray before starting the grill. Grill burgers, uncovered, over medium heat or broil 4-6 in. from the heat for 8-10 minutes on each side or until a meat thermometer reads 165°. Serve on rolls with lettuce and tomato. **Yield:** 8 servings.

Chicken-Mushroom Deluxe

1-1/2 cups sliced fresh mushrooms
1/2 cup chopped onion
1/2 cup chopped green pepper
2 tablespoons butter
1 can (10-3/4 ounces) condensed
  cream of chicken soup,
  undiluted
1/2 cup milk
1/4 cup chopped pimientos

3/4 teaspoon dried basil
1 package (8 ounces) rotini
  pasta, cooked and drained
2 cups (16 ounces) 4% cottage
  cheese
1-1/2 cups (6 ounces) shredded
  cheddar cheese
1/2 cup grated Parmesan cheese,
  divided
3 cups cubed cooked chicken

In a skillet, saute the mushrooms, onion and green pepper in butter until tender. Add the soup, milk, pimientos and basil; mix well and heat through.

Place pasta in the bottom of a greased 13-in. x 9-in. x 2-in. baking dish. Combine the cottage cheese, cheddar and 1/4 cup Parmesan; spread over pasta. Top with chicken. Pour sauce over chicken. Sprinkle with remaining Parmesan.

Cover and bake at 350° for 50-55 minutes or until bubbly. **Yield:** 6-8 servings.

Mexican-Style Chicken Kiev

4 large boneless skinless chicken breast halves

1 can (4 ounces) chopped green chilies, drained

2 ounces Monterey Jack cheese, cut into 4 strips

1/4 cup fine dry bread crumbs

2 tablespoons grated Parmesan cheese

3-1/2 teaspoons chili powder

1/4 teaspoon salt

1/8 teaspoon ground cumin

4 tablespoons butter, melted

2 teaspoons cornstarch

1/2 teaspoon chicken bouillon granules

1/2 cup cold water

1 cup picante sauce

Flatten chicken to 1/4-in. thickness. Place about 2 tablespoons chilies and one strip of Monterey Jack cheese on long end of each chicken breast. Fold in sides and ends; secure with a toothpick.

In a shallow bowl, combine the crumbs, Parmesan cheese, chili powder, salt and cumin. Dip chicken in 3 tablespoons butter, then roll in crumb mixture. Place chicken rolls seam side down in an ungreased 11-in. x 7-in. x 2-in. baking dish. Drizzle with remaining butter. Cover and refrigerate at least 4 hours. Bake, uncovered, at 400° for 20-25 minutes or until chicken is tender.

Meanwhile, in a small saucepan, combine the cornstarch, bouillon and water until smooth; stir in picante sauce. Bring to a boil over medium heat; cook and stir for 1 minute or until slightly thickened. Remove toothpicks from chicken and serve with sauce. **Yield:** 4 servings.

Garlic-Brown Sugar Chicken

1 cup packed brown sugar

2/3 cup white vinegar

1/4 cup lemon-lime soda

2 to 3 tablespoons minced garlic cloves

2 tablespoons soy sauce

1 teaspoon pepper

1 broiler/fryer chicken (3-1/2 to 4 pounds), cut up

In a large resealable plastic bag, combine the first six ingredients; add chicken. Seal bag and turn to coat; refrigerate for 2-4 hours.

Transfer chicken and marinade to a large skillet; bring to a boil. Reduce heat; cover with lid ajar and simmer 45 minutes or until juices run clear and a meat thermometer reads 170° for breast pieces and 180° for thighs and drumsticks. **Yield:** 4 servings.

Turkey Bean Bake

1 pound ground turkey
1 large onion, chopped
2 garlic cloves, minced
1 can (16 ounces) baked beans
1 can (16 ounces) kidney beans, rinsed and drained
1 can (15 ounces) black beans, rinsed and drained

1/2 cup ketchup
2 tablespoons brown sugar
2 tablespoons molasses
1 tablespoon red wine vinegar
1 teaspoon prepared mustard
1/4 teaspoon pepper

In a large skillet, cook the turkey, onion and garlic over medium heat until meat is no longer pink; drain. Stir in the remaining ingredients.

Transfer to a greased 1-1/2-qt. baking dish. Bake, uncovered, at 350° for 25-30 minutes or until bubbly. **Yield:** 4-6 servings.

Hearty Chicken and Beans

3-1/2 to 4 pounds chicken thighs
1/2 cup soy sauce, *divided*
2 tablespoons brown sugar
1 garlic clove, minced
1/2 teaspoon ground cumin, optional
2 tablespoons vegetable oil
2 celery ribs, thinly sliced

1 can (15 ounces) spicy chili beans, undrained
1 can (8 ounces) sliced water chestnuts, drained
1 can (4 ounces) mushroom stems and pieces, drained
3 tablespoons cornstarch
1-1/4 cups water
Hot cooked rice

Bone and skin chicken; cut into bite-size pieces. In a large resealable plastic bag, combine 1/4 cup soy sauce, brown sugar, garlic and cumin if desired; add chicken. Seal bag and turn to coat; refrigerate for 4 hours or overnight.

Drain chicken, discarding marinade. In a large skillet, heat oil over medium-high. Cook chicken for 6-8 minutes or until juices run clear. Remove chicken with a slotted spoon; set aside. Saute celery in drippings for 2 minutes or until crisp-tender. Add the beans, water chestnuts and mushrooms; cook for 5 minutes or until heated through. Add chicken.

Combine cornstarch and water until smooth; stir remaining soy sauce. Stir into chicken mixture. Bring to a boil; cook and stir for 2 minutes or until thickened. Serve over rice. **Yield:** 6-8 servings.

Cornish Hens with Veggies

4 Cornish game hens (22 ounces *each*)

1/3 cup butter, melted

1-1/2 teaspoons minced fresh rosemary *or* 1/2 teaspoon dried rosemary, crushed

1 tablespoon minced fresh parsley

1 teaspoon salt

1/2 teaspoon pepper

2 pounds small red potatoes

1 pound carrots, cut into 2-inch slices, optional

Place the hens breast side up on a rack in a roasting pan; tie drumsticks together with kitchen string. Combine the butter, rosemary, parsley, salt and pepper; spoon over hens. Bake, uncovered, at 375° for 1 hour.

Meanwhile, peel a 1-in. strip around the center of each potato. Place potatoes and carrots if desired in a saucepan; cover with water. Bring to a boil. Reduce heat; cover and simmer for 15 minutes. Drain; add to roasting pan.

Baste hens and vegetables with pan drippings. Bake for 15-20 minutes or until a meat thermometer reads 180° for hens and vegetables are tender. Strain pan drippings and thicken for gravy if desired. **Yield:** 4 servings.

Orange-Coated Chicken

2 eggs

1/3 cup orange juice

1 cup seasoned bread crumbs

1 teaspoon paprika

1 teaspoon salt

1 teaspoon grated orange peel

1 broiler/fryer chicken (3-1/2 to 4 pounds), cut up

1/4 cup butter, melted

Orange slices

2 tablespoons minced fresh parsley

In a shallow bowl, beat eggs and orange juice. In another bowl, combine the bread crumbs, paprika, salt and orange peel. Dip chicken pieces in egg mixture, then coat with the crumb mixture. Place skin side down in a greased 13-in. x 9-in. x 2-in. baking dish; drizzle with butter.

Bake, uncovered, at 400° for 30 minutes. Turn chicken. Reduce heat to 350°; bake for 20 minutes. Top with orange slices and sprinkle with parsley. Bake 5-10 minutes longer or until a meat thermometer reads 170° for breast pieces and 180° for thighs and drumsticks. **Yield:** 4 servings.

Lemon Almond Chicken

1-1/4 cups all-purpose flour
2-3/4 teaspoons salt
3/4 teaspoon pepper
6 large boneless skinless chicken breast halves
2 eggs, beaten
2 tablespoons vegetable oil
2 tablespoons plus 1/4 cup butter, *divided*

1 tablespoon minced green onion
1 garlic clove, minced
1-1/2 cups chicken broth
1/2 cup dry white wine *or* ginger ale
3 tablespoons fresh lemon juice
1/2 cup slivered almonds, toasted
Minced fresh parsley
1 lemon, thinly sliced

In a shallow bowl or large resealable plastic bag, combine the flour, salt and pepper; set aside 1/4 cup for sauce. Dredge chicken in remaining flour mixture, then dip in eggs.

Heat oil and 2 tablespoons butter in a large skillet over medium-high heat. Add chicken; cook until golden brown on both sides. Drain on paper towels. Place in a greased 13-in. x 9-in. x 2-in. baking dish.

For sauce, melt remaining butter in a small saucepan. Add onion and garlic; cook for 1 minute. Stir in reserved flour mixture; cook and stir for 1 minute. Gradually add the broth, ginger ale and lemon juice. Bring to a boil; cook and stir for 2 minutes or until slightly thickened. Pour over chicken.

Bake, uncovered, at 375° for 20-30 minutes. Top with almonds, parsley and lemon. Serve immediately. **Yield:** 6 servings.

Chicken Crouton Hot Dish

1 can (14-1/2 ounces) chicken broth
1 can (10-3/4 ounces) condensed cream of chicken soup, undiluted

1 cup (8 ounces) sour cream
1/2 cup butter, melted
1 package (14 ounces) seasoned stuffing croutons
4 cups shredded cooked chicken

In a large bowl, combine the broth, soup, sour cream and butter. Stir in croutons and chicken.

Transfer to a greased 13-in. x 9-in. x 2-in. baking dish. Bake, uncovered, at 375° for 20-25 minutes or until heated through. **Yield:** 8 servings.

Chicken a la King

1/2 cup chopped onion
1/4 cup butter
1/4 cup all-purpose flour
3/4 teaspoon salt
1/2 teaspoon pepper
1/4 teaspoon dried sage
1-1/2 cups milk

1 cup chicken broth
2 cups sliced fresh mushrooms
1 cup sliced carrots, cooked
1 cup peas, cooked
1/2 cup green pepper, cooked
2 cups cubed cooked chicken
Warm biscuits

In saucepan, saute onion in butter until tender. Stir in the flour, salt, pepper and sage until smooth. Gradually add milk and broth, stirring constantly. Bring to a boil; cook and stir for 2 minutes or until thickened. Add vegetables and chicken; heat through. Serve over biscuits. **Yield:** 4-6 servings.

Turkey Patties Oriental

1 tablespoon sugar
1 tablespoon cornstarch
1/8 teaspoon ground ginger
1 cup chicken *or* turkey broth
3 tablespoons reduced-sodium soy sauce
2 teaspoons white vinegar
1 egg
1/3 cup dry bread crumbs

1/4 teaspoon salt
1/4 teaspoon garlic powder
1-1/4 pounds lean ground turkey
1 large green pepper, cut into 1-inch pieces
1 cup sliced celery
2 medium tomatoes, cut into wedges
Hot cooked rice

In a small bowl, combine sugar, cornstarch and ginger. Whisk in the broth, soy sauce and vinegar until smooth; set aside.

In another bowl, lightly beat egg. Add bread crumbs, salt and garlic powder; mix well. Crumble turkey over mixture and mix well. Shape into five patties.

In a nonstick skillet coated with cooking spray, cook patties over medium-high heat for 3-5 minutes on each side or until browned and juices run clear. Add the green pepper and celery. Stir reserved broth mixture; add to pan and bring to a boil. Reduce heat; cover and simmer for 5 minutes or until vegetables are crisp-tender. Add tomatoes; simmer 6 minutes longer. Serve over rice. **Yield:** 5 servings.

Swiss Chicken Bake

1 package (7 ounces) thin spaghetti, cooked and drained
1 package (10 ounces) frozen chopped spinach, thawed and well drained
1/2 cup half-and-half cream
1/3 cup Parmesan cheese, *divided*
1/2 teaspoon salt
1/4 teaspoon pepper
1/8 to 1/4 teaspoon ground nutmeg
2 cups diced cooked chicken
1 cup (4 ounces) shredded Swiss cheese
1/2 cup sliced fresh mushrooms
2 bacon strips, cooked and crumbled
4 eggs, lightly beaten
1 cup ricotta cheese
1/4 cup chopped onion
1 garlic clove, minced

In a large bowl, combine the spaghetti, spinach, cream, 4 tablespoons Parmesan cheese, salt, pepper and nutmeg. Place in the bottom of a greased 8-in. square baking dish. Top with chicken, Swiss cheese, mushrooms and bacon.

In a bowl, combine the eggs, ricotta, onion and garlic; spread over chicken. Sprinkle with remaining Parmesan. Bake, uncovered, at 350° for 30-35 minutes or until bubbly. **Yield:** 4-6 servings.

Grilled Turkey Sandwiches

1/2 cup chicken broth
1/4 cup olive oil
4-1/2 teaspoons finely chopped onion
1 tablespoon white wine vinegar
2 teaspoons dried parsley flakes
1/2 teaspoon salt
1/2 teaspoon rubbed sage
1/8 teaspoon pepper
6 turkey breast slices (1 pound)
6 whole wheat hamburger buns, split
6 lettuce leaves
6 tomato slices

In a large resealable plastic bag, combine the first eight ingredients; add turkey. Seal bag and turn to coat; refrigerate for 12 hours or overnight, turning occasionally.

If grilling the turkey, coat grill rack with nonstick cooking spray before starting the grill. Drain and discard marinade.

Grill turkey, covered, over indirect medium heat or broil 6 in. from the heat for 3-4 minutes on each side or until juices run clear. Serve on buns with lettuce and tomato. **Yield:** 6 servings.

Pecan Oven-Fried Fryer

1-1/2 cups biscuit/baking mix
3/4 cup finely chopped pecans
1 tablespoon paprika
1-1/2 teaspoons salt
3/4 teaspoon pepper

3/4 teaspoon poultry seasoning
1 can (5 ounces) evaporated milk
1 broiler/fryer chicken (3-1/2 to 4 pounds), cut up
1/2 cup butter, melted

In a shallow bowl, combine the biscuit mix, pecans, paprika, salt, pepper and poultry seasoning. Place milk in another shallow bowl. Dip chicken pieces in milk, then coat generously with pecan mixture.

Place in a greased 13-in. x 9-in. x 2-in. baking dish. Drizzle with butter. Bake, uncovered, at 350° for 1 hour or until a meat thermometer reads 170° for breast pieces and 180° for thighs and drumsticks. **Yield:** 4 servings.

Curried Chicken and Rice

1 cup chicken broth
1 teaspoon curry powder
1/2 teaspoon paprika
1 package (6 ounces) long grain and wild rice mix
3 cups sliced fresh mushrooms (8 ounces)
10 ounces fresh pearl onions, cooked according to package directions
1/2 medium green pepper, julienned

1 broiler/fryer chicken (3-1/2 to 4 pounds), cut up

CURRY SAUCE:
1 carton (8 ounces) plain yogurt
1/2 cup ricotta cheese
1/3 cup chutney
1 tablespoon all-purpose flour
2 teaspoons curry powder
2 tablespoons slivered almonds

In an ungreased 13-in. x 9-in. x 2-in. baking dish, combine the broth, curry powder, paprika and seasoning mix from the rice. Top with rice, mushrooms, onions and green pepper. Arrange chicken pieces on top. Cover and bake at 425° for 50 minutes.

Meanwhile, in a blender or food processor, combine the yogurt, ricotta cheese, chutney, flour and curry powder. Process until smooth; pour over chicken. Sprinkle with almonds. Increase oven temperature to 475°. Bake, uncovered, for 5-10 minutes. **Yield:** 4-6 servings.

Ranch-Style Thighs

1/2 cup dry bread crumbs
1/4 cup grated Parmesan cheese
2 tablespoons yellow cornmeal
1/2 teaspoon Italian seasoning
6 chicken thighs (skin removed if desired)
1/2 cup ranch salad dressing

In a shallow bowl, combine the crumbs, Parmesan cheese, cornmeal and Italian seasoning. Place salad dressing in another shallow bowl. Dip chicken in salad dressing, then coat with crumb mixture.

Place in a greased 13-in. x 9-in. x 2-in. baking dish. Bake, uncovered, at 375° for 45-50 minutes or until juices run clear. **Yield:** 3-4 servings.

Honey Baked Chicken

1 broiler/fryer chicken (3 pounds), cut up
1/3 cup butter, melted
1/3 cup honey
2 tablespoons prepared mustard
1 teaspoon salt
1 teaspoon curry powder
Cooked rice

Place chicken skin side up in a 13-in. x 9-in. x 2-in. baking pan. Combine the butter, honey, mustard, salt and curry powder; pour over chicken.

Bake, uncovered, at 350° for 1-1/4 hours, basting with the pan juices every 15 minutes. Serve with rice. **Yield:** 4-6 servings.

Tasty Texas Tenders

1 pound chicken tenders *or* boneless skinless chicken breasts
3 cups crisp rice cereal, crushed
1 teaspoon garlic salt
1 teaspoon dill weed
1/4 cup vegetable oil
Sour cream, optional

If using chicken breasts, cut into 4-in. strips; set aside. In a shallow dish, combine the cereal, garlic salt and dill. Place oil in another shallow dish. Dip chicken tenders or strips in oil, then roll in cereal mixture. Place on a foil-lined baking sheet.

Bake, uncovered, at 350° for 30 minutes or until juices run clear. Serve with sour cream for dipping if desired. **Yield:** 4-6 servings.

Turkey Potato Supper

2 cups water
1/4 cup butter
1 teaspoon salt
2-2/3 cups mashed potato flakes
2 eggs, lightly beaten
1 can (10-3/4 ounces) condensed cream of chicken soup, undiluted
1/4 cup mayonnaise
1 teaspoon lemon juice
1/2 teaspoon curry powder
2 cups cubed cooked turkey
1 package (10 ounces) frozen chopped broccoli, thawed
1/4 cup slivered almonds, toasted, optional

In a large saucepan, bring the water, butter and salt to a boil. Remove from the heat; stir in potato flakes. Let stand for 30 seconds. Whip with a fork. Stir in eggs. Spoon the potatoes onto the bottom and up the sides of a greased 8-in. square baking dish, forming a shell.

In a bowl, combine the soup, mayonnaise, lemon juice and curry. Stir in turkey and broccoli. Bake, uncovered, at 350° for 20 minutes. Sprinkle with almonds if desired.

Bake 15-20 minutes longer or until potato edges are golden brown and filling is heated through. Let stand for 10 minutes before serving. **Yield:** 4-6 servings.

Editor's Note: Reduced-fat or fat-free mayonnaise is not recommended for this recipe.

Southwestern Fried Rice

1 pound boneless skinless chicken breasts, cubed
1 package (10 ounces) frozen corn, thawed
1 small green pepper, chopped
1 small onion, chopped
2 teaspoons canola oil
1 cup chicken broth
1 cup salsa
1 teaspoon chili powder
1/4 teaspoon cayenne pepper
1-1/2 cups uncooked instant rice
1/2 cup shredded reduced-fat cheddar cheese

In a large nonstick skillet, saute the chicken, corn, green pepper and onion in oil until chicken juices run clear. Stir in the broth, salsa, chili powder and cayenne; bring to a boil. Add the rice. Cover and remove from the heat; let stand for 5 minutes. Fluff with a fork. Sprinkle with cheese; cover and let stand for 2-3 minutes or until cheese is melted. **Yield:** 6 servings.

Chicken Parmesan

2 boneless skinless chicken breast halves
1/4 cup plain yogurt
1/2 cup seasoned bread crumbs
3 tablespoons olive oil, *divided*
3 ounces uncooked spaghetti
1 medium onion, chopped

2 garlic cloves, minced
1/2 teaspoon *each* dried basil, oregano and parsley flakes
1 can (8 ounces) tomato sauce
1/2 cup water
1/4 cup shredded part-skim mozzarella cheese
1/4 cup shredded Parmesan cheese

Pound chicken to 1/4-in. thickness; coat with yogurt and bread crumbs. In a large skillet, brown chicken on both sides in 2 tablespoons oil until juices run clear. Remove and keep warm.

Cook spaghetti according to package directions. Meanwhile, in the skillet, saute the onion, garlic, basil, oregano and parsley in remaining oil until onion is tender. Add the tomato sauce and water; simmer for 1 minute.

Drain spaghetti; add to skillet and toss to coat. Top with chicken; sprinkle with cheeses. Cover and let stand for 5 minutes or until cheese is melted. **Yield:** 2 servings.

Cheesy Chicken Roll-Ups

8 large boneless skinless chicken breast halves
1 block (6 ounces) cheddar cheese

1 cup crushed cheddar cheese crackers (about 2 cups whole crackers)
4-1/2 teaspoons taco seasoning mix
1/4 cup butter, melted

Pound chicken breasts to 1/4-in. thickness. Cut cheese into eight 3-1/2-in. x 3/4-in. sticks. Place one cheese stick in the center of each chicken breast. Fold long sides over cheese; fold ends up and secure with a toothpick if necessary.

In a bowl, combine crackers and taco seasoning. Dip chicken in butter, then roll in crumb mixture. Place seam side down in a greased 13-in. x 9-in. x 2-in. baking dish.

Cover and bake at 400° for 20-25 minutes or until chicken is no longer pink. **Yield:** 8 servings.

Chicken and Tomato Scampi

2 to 3 garlic cloves, minced
1/4 cup chopped green onions
2 tablespoons butter
1 tablespoon olive oil
4 boneless skinless chicken breast halves, cut into 1-inch pieces
1 teaspoon salt, optional
1/2 teaspoon pepper
1 can (14-1/2 ounces) Italian stewed tomatoes
1/4 cup lemon juice
1/2 teaspoon sugar
2 teaspoons cornstarch
2 teaspoons cold water
1/4 cup chopped fresh parsley
Hot cooked rice, optional

In a skillet, saute garlic and onions in butter and oil until onions are tender. Add chicken, salt if desired and pepper. Cook for 6-8 minutes or until chicken juices run clear. Add the tomatoes, lemon juice and sugar; heat through.

Combine cornstarch and water until smooth; stir into chicken mixture. Bring to a boil; cook and stir for 1 minute or until thickened. Add parsley. Serve over rice if desired. **Yield:** 4 servings.

Corny Turkey Burgers

1/4 cup yellow cornmeal
1 egg, lightly beaten
1/2 to 1 jalapeno pepper, seeded and chopped
1 tablespoon lime juice
2 to 4 drops hot pepper sauce
1/2 to 1 teaspoon ground cumin
1/4 teaspoon salt
1/8 teaspoon pepper
1 pound ground turkey
2 tablespoons vegetable oil

SAUCE:
1 cup fresh corn, cooked
1 cup picante sauce
1 tablespoon lime juice
Hamburger buns, optional

In a medium bowl, combine the first eight ingredients. Crumble turkey over mixture and mix well. Shape into four patties. Heat oil in skillet; fry patties over medium heat for about 4 minutes on each side or until a meat thermometer reads 165°.

In a small saucepan, heat the corn, picante sauce and lime juice; serve over burgers. Serve on hamburger buns if desired. **Yield:** 4 servings.

Editor's Note: When cutting or seeding hot peppers, use rubber or plastic gloves to protect your hands. Avoid touching your face.

Easy Fried Rice

2 eggs, beaten
1/4 teaspoon salt
3 tablespoons vegetable oil,
    divided
4 cups cold cooked rice
1-1/2 cups frozen oriental blend
    vegetables
1/2 cup sliced green onions
1 garlic cloves, minced
1 cup diced cooked chicken
3 tablespoons soy sauce
1 tablespoon chicken broth
1/2 teaspoon pepper
1/4 teaspoon ground ginger
4 bacon strips, cooked and
    crumbled

In a bowl, whisk the eggs and salt. In a skillet, heat 1 teaspoon oil until hot. Add egg mixture; cook and stir over medium heat until eggs are completely set, breaking into small pieces. Remove from skillet and set aside.

Add remaining oil to skillet. Stir-fry rice over medium-high heat for 5 minutes. Add the vegetables, onions and garlic; stir-fry for 5 minutes. Add chicken; stir-fry for 3-5 minutes or until heated through. Combine the soy sauce, broth, pepper and ginger. Add to rice; stir to coat. Add bacon and eggs; heat through. **Yield:** 4 servings.

Mediterranean Chicken

1 broiler/fryer chicken (3-1/2 to 4
    pounds), cut up
3 tablespoons vegetable oil,
    divided
3 medium onions, thinly sliced
3 garlic cloves, minced
1/4 cup chopped fresh parsley
1 tablespoon chopped fresh
    tarragon *or* 1 teaspoon dried
    tarragon
1 teaspoon salt
1/2 teaspoon pepper
1 cup chopped stuffed olives
Hot cooked rice *or* noodles

In a large skillet, brown chicken on all sides in 2 tablespoons oil over medium heat. Remove chicken and set aside. Add remaining oil to skillet. Saute onions and garlic until tender. Add the parsley, tarragon, salt and pepper; mix well.

Return chicken to skillet; cover with onion mixture. Sprinkle with olives. Reduce heat; cover and simmer 40-45 minutes or until chicken is tender and juices run clear. Serve over rice or noodles. **Yield:** 4-6 servings.

Picnic Potato Chip Chicken

3 cups crushed ridged potato chips (any flavor)
3/4 to 1 teaspoon garlic powder

1/2 cup butter, melted
1 broiler/fryer chicken (3-1/2 to 4 pounds), cut up

In a shallow bowl, combine potato chips and garlic powder. Place butter in another shallow bowl. Dip chicken pieces in butter, then roll in potato chip mixture.

Place in a greased 15-in. x 10-in. x 1-in. baking pan. Sprinkle with any remaining butter and coating. Bake, uncovered, at 350° for 1 hour or until a meat thermometer reads 170° for breast pieces and 180° for thighs and drumsticks. **Yield:** 4 servings.

Comforting Chicken 'n' Noodles

6 ounces uncooked wide egg noodles
1/2 cup butter, *divided*
1/3 cup all-purpose flour
3 teaspoons salt, *divided*
1-1/2 cups milk
1 cup chicken broth
2 tablespoons white wine *or* additional chicken broth, optional

4 tablespoons grated Parmesan cheese, *divided*
1/2 pound fresh mushrooms, sliced
1 garlic clove, minced
1/8 teaspoon pepper
4 cups cubed cooked chicken
Paprika

Cook noodles according to package directions; drain. In a saucepan, melt 1/4 cup butter. Stir in flour and 1-1/2 teaspoons salt until smooth. Gradually add milk and broth. Bring to a boil; cook and stir for 2 minutes or until thickened. Remove from the heat; stir in wine or additional broth if desired.

In a bowl, combine the noodles, 1 cup white sauce, 2 tablespoons Parmesan cheese, 2 tablespoons butter and 1 teaspoon salt. Transfer to a greased 3-qt. baking dish; set aside.

In a skillet, saute mushrooms and garlic in remaining butter until tender. Stir in pepper and remaining salt. Spoon over noodle mixture. Top with chicken. Pour the remaining white sauce over chicken. Sprinkle with remaining Parmesan. Garnish with paprika.

Cover and bake at 350° for 30-35 minutes or until bubbly. **Yield:** 6 servings.

Turkey a la King

1 medium onion, chopped
3/4 cup sliced celery
1/4 cup diced green pepper
1/4 cup butter, cubed
1/4 cup all-purpose flour
1 teaspoon sugar
1-1/2 cups chicken broth
1/4 cup half-and-half cream
3 cups cubed cooked turkey *or* chicken
1 can (4 ounces) sliced mushrooms, drained
6 pastry shells *or* pieces of toast

In a large skillet, saute the onion, celery and green pepper in butter until tender. Stir in flour and sugar until blended. Gradually stir in broth. Bring to a boil; cook and stir for 1 minute or until thickened. Reduce heat. Add the cream, turkey and mushrooms; heat through. Serve either in pastry shells or over toast. **Yield:** 6 servings.

Chicken Livers Royale

1/2 cup seasoned croutons
1 pound chicken livers, cut into bite-size pieces
2 tablespoons olive oil, *divided*
1 cup sliced fresh mushrooms
1/2 cup chopped onion
1 garlic clove, minced
16 pitted ripe olives, halved, optional
4 bacon strips, cooked and crumbled
1/2 cup spaghetti sauce
4 eggs
1 cup (4 ounces) shredded part-skim mozzarella cheese
1/4 cup chopped fresh parsley

Coat four individual 10-oz. custard cups or ramekins with nonstick cooking spray. Divide croutons among dishes; set aside.

In a large skillet, saute chicken livers in 1 tablespoon oil for about 8 minutes or until outsides are lightly browned and centers are still slightly pink. Remove with a slotted spoon and place over croutons. Discard drippings from the skillet.

In same skillet, saute the mushrooms, onion, garlic and olives if desired in remaining oil until vegetables are tender. Remove with a slotted spoon and place over chicken livers. Sprinkle with bacon; top with spaghetti sauce. Break an egg into each dish, then sprinkle with cheese.

Bake, uncovered, at 325° for 25-30 minutes or until whites are completely set and the yolks begin to thicken. Sprinkle with parsley. Serve immediately. **Yield:** 4 servings.

Pesto Mushroom Chicken

4 boneless skinless chicken breast halves
Salt and pepper to taste
5 tablespoons olive oil
1 cup loosely packed fresh basil leaves
1/2 cup chopped walnuts
2 garlic cloves, minced
1/2 teaspoon salt
1/3 cup grated Parmesan cheese
4 slices part-skim mozzarella cheese
1 cup sliced fresh mushrooms

Flatten chicken to 1/4-in. thickness; sprinkle with salt and pepper. In a large skillet, cook chicken in 1 tablespoon oil for 5-10 minutes on each side or until juices run clear.

Meanwhile, for pesto, combine the basil, nuts, garlic, salt and Parmesan cheese in a blender or food processor; cover and process until well blended. While processing, gradually add remaining oil in a stream.

Spoon pesto over chicken. Top each with a slice of mozzarella. Sprinkle mushrooms around chicken. Cover and cook for 5 minutes or until cheese is melted and mushrooms are tender. **Yield:** 4 servings.

Turkey in the Strawganoff

1 cup chopped onion
1/2 cup butter
2 garlic cloves, minced
1/4 cup all-purpose flour
1 to 2 teaspoons salt
1/2 teaspoon pepper
2 cans (10-3/4 ounces *each*) condensed cream of chicken soup, undiluted
4 cups cubed cooked turkey
1 can (8 ounces) mushroom stems and pieces, drained
2 cups (16 ounces) sour cream
1/4 cup plus 2 tablespoons minced fresh parsley, *divided*
1 pound fine noodles, cooked
1 tablespoon diced pimientos, drained

In a large skillet, saute onion in butter. Add garlic; saute 2 minutes longer. Stir in the flour, salt and pepper until blended. Add the soup, turkey and mushrooms. Bring to a boil. Reduce heat; simmer, uncovered, for 10 minutes.

Stir in sour cream and 1/4 cup parsley; heat for 6 minutes, stirring frequently. Serve over noodles. Garnish with pimientos and remaining parsley. **Yield:** 6-8 servings.

Famous Fried Chicken

3/4 cup all-purpose flour
3/4 cup biscuit/baking mix
3-1/2 teaspoons seasoned salt
1-1/2 teaspoons chili powder
1/2 teaspoon salt
1/4 teaspoon garlic powder

1 egg
1/2 cup milk
1 broiler/fryer chicken (3-1/2 to 4 pounds), cut up
Oil for deep-fat frying

In a shallow bowl, combine the first six ingredients. In another shallow bowl, beat egg and milk. Dip chicken pieces in egg mixture, then coat with flour mixture.

In a deep-fat fryer, heat oil to 375°. Fry chicken, several pieces at a time, until browned on all sides, about 4 minutes.

Place in an ungreased 13-in. x 9-in. x 2-in. baking dish. Bake, uncovered, at 350° for 40 minutes or until juices run clear. **Yield:** 4 servings.

Chicken and Spinach Supper

4 packages (10 ounces *each*) frozen chopped spinach, thawed and well drained
1/4 teaspoon ground nutmeg
1 teaspoon salt, *divided*, optional
4 cups diced cooked chicken
1/4 cup butter
1/4 cup all-purpose flour
1/4 teaspoon pepper

1/8 teaspoon paprika
2 cups chicken broth
1 tablespoon lemon juice
1/2 teaspoon dried rosemary, crushed

TOPPING:
1 tablespoon butter, melted
1/2 cup bread crumbs
1/3 cup grated Parmesan cheese

In a bowl, combine the spinach, nutmeg and 1/2 teaspoon salt if desired. Pat in the bottom of a greased 13-in. x 9-in. x 2-in. baking dish. Top with chicken.

Melt butter in a saucepan. Stir in the flour, pepper, paprika and remaining salt if desired until smooth. Gradually add the broth, lemon juice and rosemary, stirring constantly. Bring to a boil; cook and stir for 2 minutes or until thickened. Pour over chicken. Combine the topping ingredients; sprinkle over casserole.

Bake, uncovered, at 350° for 40-45 minutes or until bubbly. **Yield:** 8 servings.

Barbecued Raspberry Chicken

1/4 cup raspberry vinegar

2 tablespoons vegetable oil

1 to 2 teaspoons dried tarragon *or* 1 tablespoon fresh tarragon

4 chicken breast halves, skinned and boned

Salt to taste

Fresh ground pepper

SAUCE:

1 cup undiluted frozen raspberry juice

1 tablespoon cornstarch

Fresh raspberries

Combine the vinegar, oil and tarragon; pour half into a large resealable plastic bag and set aside remaining marinade. Add chicken to bag. Seal bag and turn to coat; marinate for 30 minutes.

Grease grill lightly with oil. Drain and discard marinade from chicken. Season with salt and pepper. Grill chicken over medium heat for 5-8 minutes on each side or until a meat thermometer reads 170°, basting frequently with reserved marinade.

While chicken cooks, whisk together sauce ingredients in saucepan. Cook over medium-low heat for 5-7 minutes or until thickened and smooth, stirring constantly.

When chicken is done, place sauce in a pool on warm platter; place chicken on top of sauce. Garnish with a few fresh berries and a sprig of fresh tarragon. **Yield:** 4 servings.

Onion-Baked Chicken

1/2 cup spicy brown mustard

1/4 cup soy sauce

2 tablespoons dried minced onion

1 cup dry bread crumbs *or* crushed cornflakes

1/2 teaspoon chicken bouillon granules

4 boneless skinless chicken breast halves

In a shallow bowl, combine mustard and soy sauce; set aside. In a small skillet, toast onion over medium heat until lightly browned, about 3 minutes. Pour into a shallow bowl. Add crumbs and bouillon; mix well. Dip chicken in mustard mixture, then coat with crumb mixture.

Place on a rack over a greased 15-in. x 10-in. x 1-in. baking pan. Bake, uncovered, at 350° for 25 minutes or until a meat thermometer reads 170°. **Yield:** 4 servings.

Oven-Baked Sesame Chicken

4 boneless skinless chicken
  breast halves
1 cup buttermilk
1/3 cup butter, melted
1 tablespoon lemon juice
1 garlic clove, minced

1 cup dry bread crumbs
1/4 cup sesame seeds
1 tablespoon grated Parmesan
  cheese
1 teaspoon salt
1/4 teaspoon white pepper

Place chicken in a large resealable plastic bag; add buttermilk. Seal bag and turn to coat; refrigerate for at least 4 hours.

In a shallow bowl, combine the butter, lemon juice and garlic. In another shallow bowl, combine the bread crumbs, sesame seeds, Parmesan cheese, salt and pepper. Drain chicken, discarding buttermilk; pat dry with paper towels. Dip chicken in butter mixture, then coat with crumb mixture.

Place in an ungreased 11-in. x 7-in. x 2-in. baking dish. Drizzle with remaining butter mixture. Bake, uncovered, at 450° for 10 minutes. Reduce heat to 350°; bake 20 minutes longer or until a meat thermometer reads 170°. **Yield:** 4 servings.

Chicken Spaghetti

8 ounces spaghetti
1 medium onion, chopped
1/2 cup chopped green pepper
2 celery ribs, chopped
4 tablespoons butter, *divided*
2 cans (10-3/4 ounces *each*)
  condensed cream of mushroom
  soup, undiluted

1 can (4 ounces) mushroom
  stems and pieces, drained
2-1/2 cups cubed cooked chicken
2 cups (8 ounces) shredded
  cheddar cheese
1/2 cup dry bread crumbs
5 bacon strips, cooked and
  crumbled

Cook spaghetti according to package directions; drain. In a small skillet, saute the onion, green pepper and celery in 2 tablespoons butter until tender. Transfer to a large bowl. Add the soup, mushrooms, spaghetti, chicken and cheese; toss to coat.

Transfer to a greased 13-in. x 9-in. x 2-in. baking dish. Sprinkle with bread crumbs and bacon; dot with remaining butter. Bake, uncovered, at 350° for 30-35 minutes or until heated through. **Yield:** 8-10 servings.

Chick-a-Roni

2 cups cubed cooked chicken

2 cups cooked macaroni

1 can (10-3/4 ounces) condensed cream of chicken soup, undiluted

1 jar (4 ounces) diced pimientos, drained

4 ounces process cheese (Velveeta), cubed

1 cup (4 ounces) shredded cheddar cheese

1 package (3 ounces) cream cheese, cubed

In a large bowl, combine all the ingredients. Transfer to a greased 3-qt. baking dish. Cover and bake at 350° for 20 minutes. Uncover; bake 20 minutes longer or until heated through. **Yield:** 6-8 servings.

Chicken Lasagna Rolls

1 medium onion, chopped

1/2 cup chopped sweet red pepper

1/2 cup chopped almonds

1/3 cup butter

1/2 cup cornstarch

1-1/2 teaspoons salt

2 cans (10-1/2 ounces *each*) condensed chicken broth, undiluted

2 cups chopped cooked chicken

1 package (10 ounces) frozen chopped spinach, thawed and well drained

1/4 teaspoon pepper

1/4 teaspoon ground nutmeg

10 lasagna noodles, cooked and drained

2 cups milk

1 cup (4 ounces) shredded Swiss cheese, *divided*

1/4 cup dry white wine *or* water

In a large saucepan, saute the onion, red pepper and almonds in butter until onion is tender and almonds are toasted. Stir in the cornstarch and salt until blended. Stir in broth. Bring to a boil; cook and stir for 2 minutes or until thickened.

Transfer half of the sauce to a bowl; stir in the chicken, spinach, pepper and nutmeg. Spread about 3 tablespoons over each lasagna noodle. Roll up and place seam side down in a greased 11-in. x 7-in. x 2-in. baking dish.

Add the milk, 1/2 cup Swiss cheese and wine or water to remaining sauce. Cook and stir over medium heat until thickened and bubbly. Pour over roll-ups.

Bake, uncovered, at 350° for 20-25 minutes. Sprinkle with remaining cheese; bake 5 minutes longer or until cheese is melted. **Yield:** 5 servings.

Chicken Florentine

10 boneless skinless chicken breast halves
2 tablespoons honey
1 package (10 ounces) frozen chopped spinach, thawed and well drained
2 cups (8 ounces) shredded cheddar cheese
1/3 cup all-purpose flour
2 teaspoons garlic salt
1 teaspoon pepper
1 egg
1/3 cup milk
1 cup dry bread crumbs
Oil for deep-fat frying

Pound chicken breasts to 1/4-in. thickness; brush each with honey. Combine spinach and cheese; place about 2 tablespoons in the center of each chicken breast. Fold long sides over filling; fold ends up and secure with a toothpick. Place seam side down in a shallow pan. Cover and refrigerate for several hours.

In a shallow bowl, combine the flour, garlic salt and pepper. In another shallow bowl, beat egg and milk. Dredge chicken in flour mixture, dip in egg mixture and roll in bread crumbs.

Heat oil in a deep-fat fryer to 375°. Fry chicken, several rolls at a time, for 1-1/2 minutes or until golden brown. Place in an ungreased 13-in. x 9-in. x 2-in. baking dish.

Bake, uncovered, at 350° for 30 minutes or until juices run clear. Remove toothpicks before serving. **Yield:** 6-8 servings.

Pine Nut Chicken

3/4 cup all-purpose flour
1/4 teaspoon salt
1/8 teaspoon pepper
2 eggs
6 boneless skinless chicken breast halves (4 ounces *each*)
2 cups chopped pine nuts *or* almonds
1/3 cup butter

In a shallow bowl, combine the flour, salt and pepper. Beat eggs in another shallow bowl. Flatten chicken to 1/2-in. thickness. Coat with flour mixture; dip into eggs. Pat the nuts firmly onto both sides of chicken.

In a large skillet over medium heat, cook the chicken in butter for 4-5 minutes on each side or until browned and juices run clear. **Yield:** 4-6 servings.

Chicken Tetrazzini

1/2 cup butter
1 can (10-3/4 ounces) cream of mushroom soup, undiluted
1 can (10-3/4 ounces) cream of chicken soup, undiluted
1 jar (4-1/2 ounces) sliced mushrooms, drained
2 tablespoons chopped pimiento
2 cups cubed cooked chicken
4 ounces spaghetti, cooked and drained
1 cup (8 ounces) sour cream
Grated Parmesan cheese
Paprika

In a saucepan, melt butter over low heat. Add soups and mushrooms. Stir until well blended. Remove from the heat; add pimiento, chicken, spaghetti and sour cream.

Pour mixture into a greased 13-in. x 9-in. x 2-in. baking pan. Sprinkle with Parmesan cheese and paprika. Bake, uncovered, at 350° for 30-35 minutes. **Yield:** 4-6 servings.

Roast Goose with Apple-Raisin Stuffing

1 domestic goose (10 to 12 pounds)
Salt

STUFFING:
1 cup chopped celery
1 cup chopped onion
2 tablespoons butter
3 cups chopped peeled apples
2 cups raisins
8 cups cubed day-old white bread
2 to 3 tablespoons sugar
1 teaspoon salt
2 eggs
1/2 cup apple cider
1/2 cup water

Sprinkle the inside of the goose with salt. Prick skin well; set aside. In a skillet, saute the celery and onion in butter; transfer to a large bowl. Add the apples, raisins, bread, sugar and salt.

In a small bowl, beat eggs, cider and water. Pour over bread mixture and toss lightly. Stuff the goose. Place goose breast side up on a rack in a large shallow roasting pan.

Bake, uncovered, at 350° for 3 to 3-1/2 hours or until a meat thermometer reads 180°. Drain fat from pan as it accumulates. Tent with foil and let stand for 15 minutes before carving. Remove all dressing. **Yield:** 8-10 servings.

Chicken Amondine

1 cup sliced celery
1 cup chopped green pepper
1/2 cup chopped onion
1 tablespoon butter
3 cups cubed cooked chicken
2 cups cooked rice
1 cup chicken broth
1 package (10 ounces) frozen peas, thawed
1 jar (2 ounces) diced pimientos, drained
1/2 teaspoon salt
1/4 teaspoon pepper
2 cans (10-3/4 ounces *each*) condensed cream of chicken soup, undiluted
3/4 cup mayonnaise

TOPPING:
7 ounces sage and onion stuffing
2/3 cup sliced almonds
3/4 cup butter, melted

In a large skillet, saute the celery, green pepper and onion in butter until tender; remove from the heat. Add the chicken, rice, broth, peas, pimientos, salt and pepper; mix well. Spoon into a greased 13-in. x 9-in. x 2-in. baking dish.

Combine soup and mayonnaise; spread over chicken mixture. For topping, combine stuffing and almonds; sprinkle over top. Drizzle with butter.

Cover and bake at 350° for 30 minutes. Uncover; bake 15 minutes longer or until bubbly. **Yield:** 6-8 servings.

Editor's Note: Reduced-fat or fat-free mayonnaise is not recommended for this recipe.

Chicken Pilaf Saute

2 cups cubed cooked chicken
1 cup uncooked long grain rice
1/4 cup chopped onion
3 tablespoons butter
3 chicken bouillon cubes
2-1/2 cups boiling water
1/2 teaspoon salt
1/2 teaspoon dried thyme
1/4 teaspoon pepper
1 cup chopped fresh tomatoes
1/2 cup slivered almonds, toasted

In a skillet, cook the chicken, rice and onion in butter over medium heat for 10 minutes. Dissolve bouillon in water. Add the salt, thyme and pepper. Pour into skillet; bring to a boil. Reduce heat; cover and simmer for 15 minutes. Stir in tomatoes and almonds. Cover and cook for 15-20 minutes or until rice is tender. **Yield:** 2-4 servings.

Fish & Seafood

Seafood in Tomato Sauce

3 tablespoons vegetable oil, *divided*

1/4 pound fresh mushrooms, sliced

1 garlic clove, minced

1 can (16 ounces) whole tomatoes, diced

1 teaspoon dried thyme

1-1/2 teaspoons dried oregano

1 teaspoon sugar

Salt and pepper to taste

1/2 pound bay scallops

1/2 pound small shrimp, peeled and deveined

1 cup cooked rice

1/2 pound cooked real *or* imitation crabmeat chunks

3/4 cup grated *or* shredded Parmesan cheese

In a large saucepan, heat 1 tablespoon oil. Saute mushrooms and garlic for 3-4 minutes. Add the tomatoes, herbs, sugar, salt and pepper. Cover and bring to a boil. Reduce heat; simmer for 30 minutes. Uncover; simmer 10 minutes longer.

Meanwhile, heat remaining oil in a skillet over medium heat. Add scallops and shrimp; cook for 3-4 minutes or until scallops are opaque and shrimp turn pink.

Divide rice over the bottoms of four individual ovenproof baking dishes. Top with shrimp and scallops. Stir crab into tomato mixture and spoon into the casseroles. Sprinkle each with Parmesan cheese. Broil 4-6 in. from heat until the cheese is melted. Serve immediately. **Yield:** 4 servings.

Cream Cheese-Stuffed Catfish

4 bacon strips
1/2 cup soft bread crumbs
4-1/2 teaspoons cream cheese, softened
2 teaspoons lemon juice, *divided*
1-1/2 teaspoons finely chopped onion

1-1/2 teaspoons finely chopped celery
1-1/2 teaspoons dried parsley flakes
1/2 teaspoon dried thyme
1/4 teaspoon pepper, *divided*
1/8 teaspoon salt
2 catfish fillets (6 ounces *each*)

In a skillet, cook bacon over medium heat until cooked but not crisp. Remove to paper towels; keep warm. In a bowl, combine the bread crumbs, cream cheese, 1-1/2 teaspoons lemon juice, onion, celery, parsley, thyme, 1/8 teaspoon pepper and salt. Sprinkle catfish fillets with remaining lemon juice and pepper. Spread crumb mixture over each fillet; roll from one end. Wrap two strips of bacon around each fillet and secure with toothpicks.

Place in a greased 8-in. square baking dish. Bake, uncovered, at 350° for 25-30 minutes or until fish flakes easily with a fork. Remove toothpicks before serving. **Yield:** 2 servings.

Crunchy Tuna Surprise

1 can (12 ounces) tuna, drained and flaked
1-1/2 cups cooked rice
1 can (10-3/4 ounces) condensed cream of mushroom soup, undiluted

1/2 cup milk
1/4 cup minced fresh parsley
3/4 cup crushed cornflakes
2 tablespoons butter, melted

In a bowl, combine the first five ingredients. Transfer to a greased shallow 1-1/2-qt. baking dish. Combine the cornflake crumbs and butter; sprinkle over the top. Bake, uncovered, at 350° for 25-30 minutes or until bubbly. **Yield:** 4 servings.

Orange Roughy Parmesan

1 orange roughy, red snapper, cod *or* haddock fillet (about 6 ounces)

1 tablespoon butter, melted

1/8 teaspoon salt, optional

Dash garlic powder

1 tablespoon seasoned bread crumbs

1 tablespoon grated Parmesan cheese

Place fish in a greased 11-in. x 7-in. x 2-in. baking dish. Brush fillet with butter. Sprinkle with salt if desired and garlic powder.

In a shallow bowl, combine bread crumbs and Parmesan. Coat fish with bread crumb mixture and return to prepared pan. Bake, uncovered, at 425° for 12-15 minutes or until fish flakes easily with a fork. **Yield:** 1 serving.

Broiled Lime Shrimp

3/4 cup lime juice

4 green onions, thinly sliced

2 serrano peppers, seeded and minced, optional

4 teaspoons olive oil

2 teaspoons minced garlic

1/2 teaspoon salt

36 extra-large uncooked shrimp, peeled and deveined

Shredded lettuce *or* sliced cucumbers, optional

2 tablespoons minced sweet red pepper, optional

In a small bowl, combine the first six ingredients. Pour half of the marinade into a large resealable plastic bag; add the shrimp. Seal bag and turn to coat; refrigerate for 2-3 hours, turning occasionally. Cover and refrigerate remaining marinade for basting.

Drain and discard marinade from shrimp. Thread shrimp on metal or soaked wooden skewers. Grill, covered over medium heat or broil 3-4 in. from the heat for 2-3 minutes on each side or until shrimp turn pink, basting cooked sides of shrimp frequently with reserved marinade. Serve shrimp over lettuce or cucumbers and sprinkle with red pepper if desired. **Yield:** 6 servings.

Editor's Note: When cutting or seeding hot peppers, use rubber or plastic gloves to protect your hands. Avoid touching your face.

Grilled Salmon Sandwiches

1 can (8 ounces) red *or* pink
  salmon, well drained
1/3 cup finely chopped celery
2 tablespoons sweet pickle
  relish, well drained

1/8 teaspoon ground pepper
1/4 cup mayonnaise
  8 slices white *or* Italian bread
  1 egg, beaten
2/3 cup milk

In a small bowl, combine first five ingredients. Divide and spread over 4 slices of bread. Top with remaining bread slices and dip each sandwich into combined egg and milk mixture. Toast sandwiches on a well-greased griddle or skillet until bread is lightly browned on both sides. Serve immediately. **Yield:** 4 sandwiches.

Mediterranean Shrimp and Pasta

4 ounces uncooked linguine
3 green onions, thinly sliced
2 garlic cloves, minced
2 tablespoons olive oil
1/2 cup sliced fresh mushrooms
3 plum tomatoes, chopped
1 jar (6 ounces) marinated
  artichoke hearts, drained
1/4 cup white wine *or* chicken
  broth

1 teaspoon Italian seasoning
1/4 teaspoon salt
1/8 teaspoon dried rosemary,
  crushed
1/8 teaspoon pepper
1/2 pound medium shrimp, peeled
  and deveined
Grated Parmesan cheese, optional

Cook linguine according to package directions. Meanwhile, in a skillet, saute onions and garlic in oil until tender. Add mushrooms and tomatoes; cook and stir for 3 minutes. Stir in the artichoke hearts, wine or broth, Italian seasoning, salt, rosemary and pepper. Bring to a boil. Reduce heat; simmer, uncovered, for 5 minutes or until mixture reaches desired thickness.

Add shrimp; cook and stir for 3 minutes or until shrimp turn pink. Drain linguine; top with shrimp mixture and toss to coat. Sprinkle with Parmesan cheese if desired. **Yield:** 2 servings.

Broccoli Tuna Roll-Ups

1 can (10-3/4 ounces) condensed cream of mushroom soup, undiluted

1 cup milk

1 can (12-1/2 ounces) tuna, drained and flaked

2-1/2 cups broccoli florets, cooked

1 cup (4 ounces) shredded cheddar cheese, *divided*

1 can (2.8 ounces) french-fried onions, *divided*

6 small flour tortillas (6 to 7 inches)

1/2 cup chopped tomatoes, optional

In a small bowl, combine soup and milk; set aside. In a medium bowl, combine tuna, broccoli, 1/2 cup cheddar cheese, half of the onions and 3/4 cup soup mixture. Divide mixture among tortillas and roll up.

Place seam side down in a greased 13-in. x 9-in. x 2-in. baking dish. Pour remaining soup mixture over tortillas. Sprinkle with tomatoes if desired.

Cover and bake at 350° for 35 minutes. Uncover; sprinkle with remaining cheese and onions. Bake 5 minutes longer or until cheese is melted. **Yield:** 3-6 servings.

Simple Herbed Scallops

3 tablespoons butter, *divided*

3/4 teaspoon lemon juice

1/2 teaspoon minced chives

1/4 teaspoon dried parsley flakes

1/8 teaspoon garlic salt

1/8 teaspoon dried tarragon

Dash pepper

1/2 to 3/4 pound fresh *or* frozen sea scallops, thawed

2 tablespoons dry bread crumbs

In a small saucepan, melt 2 tablespoons butter. Add the lemon juice, chives, parsley, garlic salt, tarragon and pepper; stir well.

Place scallops in a greased 1-qt. baking dish. Pour butter mixture over scallops. Melt remaining butter and toss with bread crumbs; sprinkle over scallops. Bake, uncovered, at 350° for 20-25 minutes or until scallops are opaque and topping is lightly browned. **Yield:** 2 servings.

Pineapple Shrimp Rice Bake

2 cups chicken broth
1 cup uncooked long grain rice
1 garlic clove, minced
1 medium onion, chopped
1 medium green pepper, julienned
2 tablespoons vegetable oil
2 teaspoons soy sauce
1/4 teaspoon ground ginger
1-1/2 pounds cooked medium shrimp, peeled and deveined
1-1/2 cups cubed fully cooked ham
3/4 cup pineapple tidbits, drained

In a large saucepan, bring broth to a boil. Stir in rice. Reduce heat; cover and simmer for 25 minutes or until tender.

Meanwhile, in a large skillet, saute the garlic, onion and green pepper in oil until tender. Stir in soy sauce and ginger. Add shrimp, ham and pineapple. Stir in rice.

Transfer to a greased 2-qt. baking dish. Bake, uncovered, at 350° for 15-20 minutes or until heated through. Stir before serving. **Yield:** 8 servings.

Pepper and Salsa Cod

1 teaspoon olive oil
1/2 pound cod, haddock *or* orange roughy fillet
1/4 teaspoon salt
Dash pepper
1/3 cup orange juice
1/4 cup salsa
1/3 cup julienned green pepper
1/3 cup julienned sweet red pepper
Hot cooked rice

Coat a 1-qt. baking dish with nonstick cooking spray. Place fish in dish; sprinkle with salt and pepper. Pour orange juice over fish. Top with salsa and peppers.

Cover and bake at 350° for 18-22 minutes or until peppers are tender and fish flakes easily with a fork. Serve with rice. **Yield:** 2 servings.

Sesame Shrimp

2 tablespoons soy sauce

2 tablespoons sesame oil, *divided*

2 teaspoons lemon juice

1/4 teaspoon garlic powder

Dash lemon-pepper seasoning

1/2 pound medium shrimp, peeled and deveined

Hot cooked rice, optional

1 tablespoon sesame seeds, toasted

In a resealable plastic bag, combine the soy sauce, 1 tablespoon sesame oil, lemon juice, garlic powder and lemon-pepper; add shrimp. Seal bag and turn to coat; refrigerate for 30 minutes.

Drain and discard marinade. In a skillet, saute shrimp in remaining sesame oil for 3 minutes or until shrimp turn pink. Serve with rice if desired. Sprinkle with sesame seeds. **Yield:** 2 servings.

Cheesy Tuna Lasagna

1 medium onion, chopped

2 tablespoons butter

1 can (12 ounces) tuna, drained and flaked

1 can (10-3/4 ounces) condensed cream of mushroom soup, undiluted

1/2 cup milk

1/2 teaspoon garlic salt

1/2 teaspoon dried oregano

1/4 teaspoon pepper

9 lasagna noodles, cooked and drained

1-1/2 cups small-curd cottage cheese

8 ounces sliced part-skim mozzarella cheese

1/4 cup grated Parmesan cheese

In a large saucepan, saute onion in butter until tender. Stir in the tuna, soup, milk, garlic salt, oregano and pepper until combined. Spread 3/4 cupful into a greased 11-in. x 7-in. x 2-in. baking dish.

Layer with three noodles (trimming if necessary), 3/4 cup tuna mixture, half of the cottage cheese and a third of the mozzarella cheese. Repeat layers. Top with remaining noodles, tuna mixture and mozzarella. Sprinkle with Parmesan cheese.

Bake, uncovered, at 350° for 25-30 minutes or until bubbly. Let stand for 10-15 minutes before serving. **Yield:** 6-8 servings.

Salmon with Herb-Mustard Sauce

2 cups mayonnaise
1 tablespoon Dijon mustard
1 tablespoon snipped fresh dill
  or 1 teaspoon dill weed
1 tablespoon minced fresh
  marjoram or 1 teaspoon dried
  marjoram
1 teaspoon minced fresh thyme
  or 1/2 teaspoon dried thyme

1 whole salmon (5 to 7 pounds),
  head and tail removed
2 teaspoon coarsely ground
  pepper
1/2 teaspoon salt
1 tablespoon balsamic vinegar
2 medium lemons, sliced
1/2 cup butter, melted

In a small bowl, combine the mayonnaise, mustard, dill, marjoram and thyme; cover and refrigerate until serving.

Place fish in the center of a large greased sheet of aluminum foil. Sprinkle inside of salmon with pepper and salt and drizzle with vinegar. Place overlapping lemon slices inside salmon to completely cover. Use wooden toothpicks to secure cavity along opening. Drizzle butter over the top.

Fold foil over fish and seal. Place on a large baking sheet. Bake at 325° for 80-95 minutes or until fish flakes easily with a fork. Serve with the herb-mustard sauce. **Yield:** 10 servings.

Spectacular Shrimp Salad

1 medium cucumber
1/2 pound frozen medium cooked
  shrimp, thawed
1 can (15 ounces) garbanzo
  beans, rinsed and drained
1/4 cup minced fresh parsley
1/3 cup olive oil

2 tablespoons cider vinegar
1 garlic clove, minced
1/8 teaspoon salt
1/8 teaspoon lemon-pepper
  seasoning
Leaf lettuce, optional

Slice cucumber in quarters lengthwise; cut into thin pieces and place in a bowl. Add the shrimp, beans and parsley.

In a small bowl, combine the oil, vinegar, garlic, salt and lemon-pepper; pour over salad and toss to coat. Chill for at least 1 hour. Serve over lettuce if desired. **Yield:** 4 servings.

Linguine with Garlic Clam Sauce

1 package (8 ounces) linguine
2 to 3 garlic cloves, minced
5 tablespoons butter
1/4 cup olive oil
1 tablespoon all-purpose flour

2 cans (6-1/2 ounces *each*) minced clams
1 cup (4 ounces) shredded Monterey Jack cheese
1/4 cup minced fresh parsley

Cook linguine according to package directions. Meanwhile, in a skillet, saute garlic in butter and oil until golden. Stir in flour until blended. Drain clams, reserving juice; set clams aside. Gradually add juice to the skillet. Bring to a boil; cook and stir for 2 minutes or until thickened. Reduce heat; stir in clams, cheese and parsley. Cook and stir until cheese is melted and sauce has thickened. Drain linguine; top with clam sauce. **Yield:** 4 servings.

Poached Teriyaki Salmon

2 cups orange juice
1/3 cup teriyaki sauce
6 salmon fillets (6 ounces *each*), skin removed

6 thin orange slices
2 teaspoons cornstarch
4 teaspoons cold water

In a large nonstick skillet, bring orange juice and teriyaki sauce to a boil. Place salmon fillets in skillet; top each with an orange slice. Return to a boil. Reduce heat; cover and simmer for 15-20 minutes or until fish flakes easily with a fork. Remove fillets and keep warm.

Strain cooking liquid; return 3/4 cup to the skillet. Combine cornstarch and water until smooth; stir into skillet. Bring to a boil; cook and stir for 1-2 minutes or until thickened. Serve over salmon. **Yield:** 6 servings.

Sole Amondine

5 tablespoons butter, *divided*
1 tablespoon olive oil
1 pound sole *or* whitefish fillets
All-purpose flour
1 egg, beaten

1/4 cup slivered almonds, toasted
2 tablespoons lemon juice
1/4 cup dry white wine, optional
Lemon wedges

In a skillet, heat 4 tablespoons butter and oil over medium heat. Dip fillets in flour, then in egg. Place in skillet; cook for 2-3 minutes on each side or until lightly browned and the fish flakes easily with a fork. Transfer to a platter and keep warm.

In the same skillet, melt remaining butter. Add almonds, lemon juice, and wine if desired; heat through. Pour over fillets and garnish with lemon wedges. Serve immediately. **Yield:** 2-4 servings.

Shrimp and Asparagus Casserole

2 packages (10 ounces *each*) frozen asparagus cuts
1/4 cup butter
1/4 cup all-purpose flour
1 cup milk
3/4 cup half-and-half cream
1/4 cup dry white wine *or* 1/4 cup additional cream *or* 1/4 cup chicken broth

1/2 teaspoon salt
1/8 teaspoon pepper
1 egg yolk, slightly beaten
1/2 cup grated Parmesan cheese
1 pound cooked small shrimp
1/2 cup buttered soft bread crumbs

Cook asparagus for 3 minutes. Drain well; set aside. In a small saucepan, melt butter. Stir in the flour; until smooth. Gradually add milk and cream. Bring to a boil; cook and stir for 2 minutes or until thickened. Stir in wine, additional cream or broth. Season with salt and pepper. Stir in egg yolk, cheese and shrimp.

In a greased 2-1/2-qt. baking dish, arrange half the asparagus; top with half the sauce. Repeat layers. Top with buttered crumbs. Bake, uncovered, at 350° for 30 minutes or until heated through. **Yield:** 6 servings.

Parmesan Salmon Fillets

TOMATO LOVAGE COMPOTE:
- 2 large tomatoes, seeded and chopped
- 1/2 cup finely chopped red onion
- 1/3 cup minced lovage *or* celery leaves
- 1/4 cup lemon juice
- 1/4 cup olive oil
- 1 tablespoon grated lemon peel
- 1/2 teaspoon salt
- 1/2 teaspoon hot pepper sauce

SALMON:
- 1 egg
- 2 tablespoons milk
- 1 cup dry bread crumbs
- 1/2 cup grated Parmesan cheese
- 4 salmon fillets (6 ounces *each*)
- 3 tablespoons vegetable oil

In a large bowl, gently toss the compote ingredients. Cover and let stand at room temperature for 1 hour.

In a shallow bowl, whisk the egg and milk. In another shallow bowl, combine bread crumbs and Parmesan cheese. Pat salmon dry with paper towels. Dip in milk mixture, then coat with crumb mixture. In a large nonstick skillet, cook the salmon in oil over medium-high heat until fish flakes easily with a fork, turning once. Serve with compote. **Yield:** 4 servings.

Crab Quiche

- 1/2 cup mayonnaise
- 2 tablespoons all-purpose flour
- 2 eggs, beaten
- 1/2 cup milk
- 2 cans (6 ounces *each*) flaked crabmeat, drained
- 1/3 cup chopped green onions
- 1 tablespoon finely chopped parsley
- 2 cups (8 ounces) shredded Swiss cheese
- 1 unbaked pastry shell (9 inches)

In a bowl, combine the mayonnaise, flour, eggs and milk. Stir in the crab, onion, parsley and cheese. Spoon into the pastry shell. Bake at 350° for 1 hour. **Yield:** 6-8 servings.

Editor's Note: Reduced-fat or fat-free mayonnaise is not recommended for this recipe.

Salmon Biscuit Bake

1 can (14-3/4 ounces) salmon, drained, bones and skin removed
1 cup frozen peas, thawed
1/4 cup milk
1/4 cup mayonnaise
2 tablespoons finely chopped green pepper

1/4 teaspoon lemon-pepper seasoning
1 cup (4 ounces) shredded cheddar cheese

TOPPING:
1 cup biscuit/baking mix
1/3 cup milk
2 tablespoons mayonnaise

In a bowl, combine the salmon, peas, milk, mayonnaise, green pepper and lemon-pepper. Transfer to a greased 9-in. pie plate. Sprinkle with cheese.

Combine the biscuit mix, milk and mayonnaise just until moistened. Drop eight mounds onto salmon mixture. Bake, uncovered, at 425° for 10-15 minutes or until bubbly and biscuits are golden brown. **Yield:** 4-6 servings.

Editor's Note: Reduced-fat or fat-free mayonnaise is not recommended for this recipe.

Potato Salmon Casserole

2-1/2 cups cubed cooked potatoes
2 cups frozen peas, thawed
1 cup mayonnaise
1 can (14-3/4 ounces) salmon, drained, bones and skin removed

5 ounces process cheese (Velveeta), cubed
1 cup finely crushed cornflakes
1 tablespoon butter, melted

Place potatoes in a greased 2-qt. baking dish. Sprinkle with peas; spread with mayonnaise. Top with salmon and cheese.

Bake, uncovered, at 350° for 30 minutes. Combine cornflake crumbs and butter; sprinkle over top. Bake 5-10 minutes longer or until golden brown. **Yield:** 4-6 servings.

Editor's Note: Reduced-fat or fat-free mayonnaise is not recommended for this recipe.

Baked Whole Salmon

3/4 cup white wine *or* chicken broth

3/4 cup chopped celery leaves

1 small onion, minced

2 lemon slices

8 fresh basil leaves

2 teaspoons dried tarragon

1 teaspoon dried rosemary, crushed

1/4 teaspoon dried thyme

1 whole salmon (about 10 pounds)

1-1/2 teaspoons salt

WINE SAUCE:

2 green onions, chopped

1/2 cup butter

6 tablespoons all-purpose flour

2-1/3 cups water

2-1/3 cups white wine *or* chicken broth

2 egg yolks, lightly beaten

1/2 cup heavy whipping cream

Salt and pepper to taste

In a saucepan, combine the first eight ingredients. Bring to a boil over medium heat. Reduce heat; simmer, uncovered, for 30 minutes.

Remove head and tail from salmon if desired. Place a double thickness of heavy-duty foil on a baking sheet (longer than the length of the fish). Grease foil. Place salmon on foil; sprinkle the cavity with salt. Pour herb sauce over fish. Fold foil over fish and seal tightly. Bake at 375° for 60-75 minutes or until fish flakes easily with a fork.

Place salmon on a serving platter and keep warm. Strain cooking juices, reserving 1/3 cup. In a large saucepan, saute green onions in butter until tender. Stir in flour until blended. Gradually stir in the water, wine or broth and reserved cooking juices. Bring to a boil over medium-high heat; cook and stir for 2 minutes or until thickened.

Reduce heat. Stir a small amount of hot liquid into the egg yolks; return all to the pan, stirring constantly. Add the cream, salt and pepper. Cook and stir until mixture reaches 160°. Serve with the salmon. **Yield:** 12-14 servings.

Fillets with Ginger Sauce

1 tablespoon olive oil
1 tablespoon butter
1 flounder *or* sole fillet (about 8 ounces)
2 garlic cloves, minced
1/4 teaspoon ground ginger *or* 1-1/2 teaspoons minced fresh gingerroot

4 teaspoons sugar
1 tablespoon cider vinegar
1 tablespoon soy sauce
1 tablespoon cornstarch
2/3 cup water
2 tablespoons thinly sliced chives
Thinly sliced green onion, optional

In a skillet, heat olive oil and butter until butter is melted. Fry fish over medium heat for 4 minutes on each side or until fish flakes easily with a fork. Remove to a plate and keep warm.

Add garlic and ginger to skillet; cook and stir for 1-2 minutes. Stir in the sugar, vinegar and soy sauce. Combine cornstarch and water until smooth. Stir into skillet. Bring to a boil; cook and stir for 1-2 minutes or until thickened. Pour over fish. Sprinkle with chives and onion if desired. **Yield:** 2 servings.

Pecan Fish

2 tablespoons plus 2 teaspoons seasoned bread crumbs
2 tablespoons finely chopped pecans, toasted
1-1/2 teaspoons toasted wheat germ
1/4 teaspoon dried thyme
1/8 teaspoon garlic powder

1/8 teaspoon onion powder
1/8 teaspoon salt
1/8 teaspoon pepper
2 tablespoons butter, melted, *divided*
1/2 pound cod, haddock *or* orange roughy fillets

In a shallow bowl, combine the bread crumbs, pecans, wheat germ, thyme, garlic powder, onion powder, salt and pepper. Place half of the butter in another shallow dish. Dip fillet in butter, then coat with bread crumb mixture.

Place in a greased 8-in. square baking dish. Bake, uncovered, at 425° for 13-15 minutes or until fish flakes easily with a fork. Drizzle with remaining butter. **Yield:** 2 servings.

Skillet Fish Dinner

1 celery rib, chopped
1/2 cup chopped green pepper
1/2 cup chopped onion
1 teaspoon olive oil
2 to 3 plum tomatoes, chopped
1/4 teaspoon salt

Dash pepper
1/2 pound cod, haddock *or* orange
   roughy fillets
1/4 to 1/2 teaspoon seafood
   seasoning
Hot cooked rice
Hot pepper sauce, optional

In a skillet, saute the celery, green pepper and onion in oil until almost tender. Add tomatoes; cook and stir for 1-2 minutes. Sprinkle with salt and pepper.

Top with fish fillets and sprinkle with seafood seasoning. Reduce heat; cover and simmer for 6 minutes. Break fish into chunks. Cook about 3 minutes longer or until fish flakes easily with a fork. Serve over rice. Serve with hot pepper sauce if desired. **Yield:** 2 servings.

Crab Thermidor

3 tablespoons butter
3 tablespoons all-purpose flour
1/4 teaspoon salt
1/8 teaspoon paprika
1/8 teaspoon ground nutmeg
1-1/2 cups half-and-half cream

2 ounces process cheese
   (Velveeta), cubed
1 tablespoon lemon juice
1/2 cup shredded cheddar cheese
2 packages (8 ounces *each*)
   imitation crabmeat, flaked
Additional paprika, optional

In a large saucepan, melt butter. Stir in the flour, salt, paprika and nutmeg until smooth. Gradually add cream. Bring to a boil; cook and stir for 2 minutes or until thickened. Reduce heat; add process cheese and lemon juice, stirring until cheese is melted. Remove from the heat; add cheddar cheese, stirring until melted. Stir in crab.

Transfer to a greased 1-qt. baking dish. Sprinkle with additional paprika if desired. Bake, uncovered, at 350° for 20-25 minutes or until bubbly. **Yield:** 4 servings.

Shrimp Crepes

1-1/2 cups milk
4 eggs
1-1/2 teaspoons sugar
1/8 teaspoon salt
1 cup all-purpose flour
Butter

FILLING:
3 tablespoons butter
4-1/2 cups chopped fresh broccoli
6 green onions, chopped

2 teaspoons minced garlic, *divided*
1/4 teaspoon Worcestershire sauce, *divided*
1/2 teaspoon salt
1/4 teaspoon pepper
1 pound uncooked shrimp, peeled and deveined
1/4 cup white wine *or* chicken broth
1 envelope bearnaise sauce

In a mixing bowl, combine the milk, eggs, sugar and salt. Add flour; beat until smooth.

Melt 1 teaspoon butter in an 8-in. nonstick skillet. Pour 2 tablespoons batter into center of skillet; lift and turn pan to cover the bottom. Cook until top appears dry; turn and cook 15-20 seconds longer. Remove to a wire rack. Repeat with remaining batter, adding butter to skillet as needed. When cool, stack crepes with waxed paper or paper towels in between.

For filling, in a large skillet, melt butter over medium heat. Add broccoli, onions, 1 teaspoon garlic, 1/8 teaspoon Worcestershire sauce, salt and pepper. Cook and stir for 7-9 minutes or until broccoli is crisp-tender. Remove mixture from the pan and set aside. Add the shrimp, wine or broth, and remaining garlic and Worcestershire sauce to the pan. Saute until shrimp for 4 minutes or until shrimp turn pink. Return broccoli mixture to skillet.

Spoon filling down center of crepes; roll. Place in an ungreased 15-in. x 10-in. x 1-in. baking pan. Bake, uncovered, at 350° for 15-20 minutes or until heated through. Meanwhile, prepare bearnaise sauce according to package directions. Serve over crepes. **Yield:** 8 servings (16 crepes).

Sweet Sensations

Candy

Soft Rum Caramels

1 teaspoon plus 1/4 cup butter,
softened, *divided*

1 cup heavy whipping cream

1 cup packed brown sugar

1 cup light corn syrup

1/4 cup sugar

1/4 teaspoon salt

1 to 2 teaspoons rum extract

Line an 8-in. square pan with foil and grease the foil with 1 teaspoon
butter; set aside. In a mixing bowl, cream remaining butter. Beat in
cream until smooth; set aside.

In a heavy saucepan, combine the brown sugar, corn syrup, sugar and
salt. Bring to a boil over medium heat, stirring constantly. Reduce heat
to medium-low; cook until a candy thermometer reads 244° (firm-ball
stage). Gradually add cream mixture. Continue cooking until a candy
thermometer reads 242°. Remove from the heat; stir in extract.

Pour into prepared pan (do not scrape sides of saucepan). Cool
completely. Invert pan onto cutting board; remove foil. Cut candy into
squares. Wrap individually in waxed paper or foil; twist ends. **Yield:**
1-1/2 pounds.

Editor's Note: We recommend that you test your candy thermometer
before each use by bringing water to a boil; the thermometer should read
212°. Adjust your recipe temperature up or down based on your test.

Candied Pecans

2-3/4 cups pecan halves
  2 tablespoons butter, softened, *divided*
  1 cup sugar

1/2 cup water
1/2 teaspoon salt
1/2 teaspoon ground cinnamon
  1 teaspoon vanilla extract

Place pecans in a shallow baking pan in a 250° oven for 10 minutes or until warmed. Grease a 15-in. x 10-in. x 1-in. baking pan with 1 table-spoon butter; set aside.

Grease the sides of a large heavy saucepan with remaining butter; add the sugar, water, salt and cinnamon. Cook and stir over low heat until sugar is dissolved. Continue to cook and stir over medium heat until mixture comes to a boil. Cover and cook for 2 minutes to dissolve sugar crystals around sides of pan.

Cook, without stirring, until a candy thermometer reads 236° (soft-ball stage). Remove from the heat; add vanilla. Stir in warm pecans until evenly coated. Spread onto prepared baking pan. Bake at 250° for 30 minutes, stirring every 10 minutes. Spread on a waxed paper-lined baking sheet to cool. **Yield:** about 1 pound.

Editor's Note: We recommend that you test your candy thermometer before each use by bringing water to a boil; the thermometer should read 212°. Adjust your recipe temperature up or down based on your test.

Peppermint Patties

1 can (14 ounces) sweetened condensed milk
1/2 cup butter, melted
  1 tablespoon peppermint extract

3 pounds confectioners' sugar
3 pounds chocolate candy coating

In a large mixing bowl, combine the milk, butter, extract and sugar. Form into 1/2-in. balls and flatten into patties. Place on a waxed paper-lined baking sheet. Freeze for 30 minutes.

In a microwave or heavy saucepan, melt half of the chocolate coating at a time; stir until smooth. Dip patties into chocolate to coat. Let stand on waxed paper-lined baking sheets until set. **Yield:** 12-13 dozen.

White Chocolate Truffles

18 ounces white candy coating, cut into pieces

9 tablespoons butter

2 tablespoons heavy whipping cream

1/4 cup confectioners' sugar

Additional confectioners' sugar

In a microwave or heavy saucepan, melt candy coating with butter and cream; stir until smooth. Stir in sugar. (If mixture separates, beat with a mixer for 30 seconds.) Pour into an 8-in. square pan. Refrigerate for 20 minutes or until slightly hardened.

Using a melon baller or spoon, scoop out and shape into 1-in. balls. Roll in additional sugar. Store in an airtight container in the refrigerator. **Yield:** about 5 dozen.

Bavarian Mint Fudge

1-1/2 teaspoons plus 1 tablespoon butter, *divided*

2 cups (12 ounces) semisweet chocolate chips

1 package (11-1/2 ounces) milk chocolate chips

1 can (14 ounces) sweetened condensed milk

1 teaspoon peppermint extract

1 teaspoon vanilla extract

Line an 11-in. x 7-in. x 2-in. pan with foil and grease the foil with 1-1/2 teaspoons butter; set aside.

In a heavy saucepan, melt the chocolate chips and remaining butter over low heat; stir until smooth. Remove from the heat; stir in the milk and extracts until well blended. Spread into prepared pan. Refrigerate until set.

Using the foil, lift fudge out of the pan. Discard the foil; cut fudge into 1-in. squares. Store in the refrigerator. **Yield:** About 2-1/2 pounds.

Almond Toffee

1-1/2 teaspoons plus 2 cups butter, softened, *divided*

2 cups sugar

1/3 cup water

2 tablespoons light corn syrup

1 package (11-1/2 ounces) milk chocolate chips

1 cup finely chopped almonds, toasted

Line the bottom and sides of a 15-in. x 10 in. x 1-in. baking pan with foil. Grease the foil with 1-1/2 teaspoons butter; set aside.

In a large heavy saucepan, melt remaining butter. Add the sugar, water and corn syrup. Cook and stir over medium heat until a candy thermometer reads 290° (soft-crack stage).

Pour into prepared pan. Cool for 4 minutes. Sprinkle with chocolate chips; let stand for 3 minutes. Spread melted chocolate evenly over candy. Sprinkle with almonds; press down lightly. Cool until chocolate is firm. Break into bite-size pieces. Store in airtight containers. **Yield:** about 1 pound.

Editor's Note: We recommend that you test your candy thermometer before each use by bringing water to a boil; the thermometer should read 212°. Adjust your recipe temperature up or down based on your test.

Chocolate Billionaires

1 tablespoon butter

1 package (14 ounces) caramels

3 tablespoons water

1-1/2 cups chopped pecans

1 cup crisp rice cereal

3 cups milk chocolate chips

1-1/2 teaspoons shortening

Line two baking sheets with waxed paper; grease the paper with the 1 tablespoon butter and set aside. In a large heavy saucepan, combine the caramels and water; cook and stir over low heat until smooth. Stir in pecans and cereal until coated. Drop by teaspoonfuls onto prepared pans. Refrigerate for 10 minutes or until firm.

Meanwhile, in a small heavy saucepan, melt chocolate chips and shortening over low heat; stir until smooth. Dip candy into chocolate, coating all sides; place on prepared pans. Refrigerate until set. Store in an airtight container. **Yield:** about 2 pounds.

Raisin Peanut Clusters

2 cups (12 ounces) semisweet
    chocolate chips
2 tablespoons shortening

2 cups raisins
2 cups dry roasted peanuts

In a heavy 3-qt. saucepan, melt chocolate and shortening; stir until smooth. Remove from the heat; add raisins and peanuts. Drop by heaping tablespoonfuls onto a lightly greased baking sheet. Refrigerate until firm, about 2 hours. Store in airtight containers in refrigerator. **Yield:** 3 dozen.

Orange Apricot Balls

1 pound dried apricots (3 cups)
1/2 medium unpeeled navel
    orange

1 cup sugar, *divided*

In a food processor or grinder, coarsely chop apricots and orange. Add 2/3 cup sugar; mix well. Shape into 3/4-in. balls; roll in remaining sugar. Store in refrigerator. **Yield:** 1-1/2 pounds (5 dozen).

Haystacks

1 package (6 ounces) butterscotch
    chips
1/2 cup peanut butter

1 can (3 ounces) chow mein
    noodles
1 cup miniature marshmallows

In a saucepan, melt butterscotch chips and peanut butter over low heat. Fold in the chow mein noodles, then marshmallows. Drop by teaspoonfuls onto greased waxed paper. Let stand until set. **Yield:** 2 dozen.

Peanut Butter Fingers

2 cups peanut butter
2 cups ground pitted dates
2 cups confectioners' sugar

2 cups chopped walnuts
5 tablespoons butter, melted
2 cups (12 ounces) semisweet chocolate chips

In a large bowl, combine the peanut butter, dates, sugar, walnuts and butter. Shape into "fingers" and place on baking sheets; freeze until firm.

Meanwhile, melt chocolate chips in a microwave or heavy saucepan. Insert a toothpick into each end of a frozen finger and dip into the chocolate. Place on waxed paper until set. Store in the refrigerator. **Yield:** 4-5 dozen.

Easy Mint Chocolate Truffles

1 tablespoon plus 3/4 cup butter, *divided*
3 cups sugar
1 can (5 ounces) evaporated milk
2 cups (12 ounces) semisweet chocolate chips

1/2 teaspoon peppermint extract
1 jar (7 ounces) marshmallow creme
1 teaspoon vanilla extract
Baking cocoa, finely chopped nuts *or* chocolate sprinkles

Line a 15-in. x 10-in. x 1-in. baking pan with foil. Grease the foil with 1 tablespoon butter; set aside.

In a heavy saucepan, combine the sugar, milk and remaining butter. Bring to a boil over medium heat. Cook, stirring constantly, until a candy thermometer reads 234° (soft-ball stage). Remove from the heat; stir in chips and peppermint extract until chocolate is melted. Stir in marshmallow creme and vanilla until smooth. Spread into prepared pan.

Refrigerate, uncovered, for 3 hours or until firm. Lift out of pan; cut into 1-1/2-in. squares. Roll into 1-in. balls. Roll in the cocoa, nuts or sprinkles. Refrigerate in an airtight container. **Yield:** 70 truffles.

Editor's Note: We recommend that you test your candy thermometer before each use by bringing water to a boil; the thermometer should read 212°. Adjust your recipe temperature up or down based on your test.

Mocha Nut Fudge

1 cup packed brown sugar
1/3 cup evaporated milk
2 tablespoons light corn syrup
1 cup (6 ounces) semisweet
   chocolate chips

2 teaspoons vanilla extract
1 teaspoon instant coffee
   granules
1 cup chopped walnuts

In a heavy saucepan, combine the brown sugar, milk and corn syrup. Cook and stir over medium heat until sugar is dissolved and mixture comes to a boil; boil for 2 minutes.

Remove from the heat; stir in chocolate chips, vanilla and coffee granules with a wooden spoon. Continue stirring until mixture is smooth and thick, about 5 minutes. Stir in walnuts.

Shape into two 9-in. logs; wrap each in plastic wrap. Refrigerate for 2 hours or overnight. Unwrap and cut into slices. **Yield:** 1 pound.

Creamy Pastel Mints

1 package (8 ounces) cream
   cheese, softened
1 teaspoon mint extract

6-2/3 cups confectioners' sugar
Red, green and yellow food coloring
Sugar

In a small mixing bowl, beat cream cheese and mint extract until smooth. Gradually beat in as much confectioners' sugar as possible; knead in remaining confectioners' sugar.

Divide mixture into four portions. Tint one pink, one green and one yellow, leaving one portion white. For each color, shape into 1/2-in. balls. Dip one side of each ball into sugar. Press sugared side into small candy molds; unmold and place on waxed paper. Let stand for 1 hour or until dry before storing in airtight containers; refrigerate. May be stored for up to 1 week before serving. **Yield:** about 12-1/2 dozen.

Crunchy Chocolate Cups

1 package (12 ounces) semisweet chocolate chips

1 package (11 ounces) butterscotch chips

1 package (10 ounces) peanut butter chips

1 cup coarsely crushed cornflakes

1/2 cup chopped peanuts, optional

In a large heavy saucepan, melt the chocolate chips, butterscotch chips and peanut butter chips over low heat. Remove from the heat; stir in the cornflakes. Add the peanuts if desired. Let stand for 10-15 minutes or until slightly cooled.

Drop by teaspoonfuls into miniature foil cups placed on a 15-in. x 10-in. x 1-in. baking sheet. Refrigerate until firm. **Yield:** about 5 dozen.

Coconut Almond Bars

1 package (3 ounces) cream cheese, softened

3-1/2 cups sifted confectioners' sugar

1 teaspoon vanilla extract

1-1/2 cups flaked coconut

50 whole almonds

2 cups (12 ounces) semisweet chocolate chips

2 tablespoons shortening

In a large mixing bowl, beat cream cheese; add sugar and vanilla. Stir in coconut. Turn out onto a 12-in. x 9-in. piece of buttered foil; pat into at 10-in. x 5-in. rectangle. Cut into 25 rectangles, each 2 in. x 1 in. Press two almonds into the top of each rectangle. Chill.

Meanwhile, in a microwave or heavy saucepan, melt chocolate chips and shortening; stir until smooth. Carefully dip rectangles in melted chocolate one at a time; set on waxed paper to dry. Store in an airtight container in the refrigerator or freeze. **Yield:** 25 candies.

Date Pecan Fudge

3/4 cup butter
3 cups sugar
2/3 cup evaporated milk
1/2 cup chopped dates

12 ounces white candy coating,
 coarsely chopped
4 cups miniature marshmallows
1 cup chopped pecans
1 teaspoon vanilla extract

In a large heavy saucepan, combine the butter, sugar and milk. Cook and stir over low heat until sugar is dissolved. Bring to a boil; boil and stir for 4 minutes. Add dates; boil and stir for 1 minute.

Remove from the heat; stir in candy coating and marshmallows until melted. Beat until smooth. Add pecans and vanilla; beat with a wooden spoon until glossy.

Pour into a buttered 13-in. x 9-in. x 2-in. pan. Let stand at room temperature overnight. Cut into squares. **Yield:** 3 pounds.

Chocolate Chews

1/4 cup butter
1/2 cup dark corn syrup
6 tablespoons baking cocoa

1/2 teaspoon vanilla extract
3-1/4 cups confectioners' sugar,
 divided
3/4 cup nonfat dry milk powder

In a saucepan, melt butter over medium heat. Stir in corn syrup and cocoa; bring to a boil. Remove from the heat; stir in the vanilla, 2 cups confectioners' sugar and milk powder. (Mixture will be stiff.)

Turn out onto a surface lightly dusted with confectioners' sugar. Knead in remaining confectioners' sugar; knead 3-4 minutes longer or until stiff. Divide into four pieces and roll each into an 18-in. rope. Cut into 3/4-in. pieces. Wrap each candy in cellophane or waxed paper. Store in refrigerator. **Yield:** 8 dozen.

Pink Ice

10 ounces white candy coating
7 peppermint candies, crushed (about 2 tablespoons)

1/4 teaspoon peppermint extract
2 drops red food coloring

In a microwave, melt candy coating; stir until smooth. Stir in the candies, peppermint extract and food coloring. Spread onto waxed paper to cool completely. Break into small pieces; store in an airtight container. **Yield:** 10 ounces.

Crunchy Peanut Candy

1 package (18 ounces) white candy coating
1 cup chunky peanut butter

2 cups dry roasted peanuts
2 cups miniature marshmallows
3 cups crisp rice cereal

In a large roasting pan or Dutch oven, heat candy coating in a 200° oven for 15 minutes or until melted. Stir in peanut butter. Fold in remaining ingredients. Drop by tablespoonfuls onto waxed paper-lined baking sheets. Refrigerate until set. **Yield:** 7 dozen.

Coconut Drops

1 package (14 ounces) flaked coconut
6 drops red food coloring

6 drops green food coloring
1 pound white candy coating

Divide coconut between two bowls. Add red food coloring to one bowl and green to the other; toss to coat.

In a heavy saucepan over low heat, melt candy coating. Drop by tablespoonfuls onto waxed paper. While coating is still warm, sprinkle half of each drop with pink coconut and the other half with green; press down gently. Refrigerate until firm. **Yield:** 1-1/4 pounds.

Chocolate Covered Cherries

2-1/2 cups confectioners' sugar
1/4 cup butter, softened
1 tablespoon milk
1/2 teaspoon almond extract

2 jars (8 ounces *each*) maraschino cherries with stems, well drained
2 cups (12 ounces) semisweet chocolate chips
2 tablespoons shortening

In a mixing bowl, combine the sugar, butter, milk and extract. Knead into a large ball. Roll into 1-in. balls and flatten each into a 2-in. circle. Wrap around cherries and lightly roll in hands. Place with stems up on waxed paper-lined baking sheet. Cover loosely and refrigerate 4 hours or overnight.

In a microwave or heavy saucepan, melt chocolate chips and shortening; stir until smooth. Holding on to stem, dip cherries into chocolate; set on waxed paper to harden. Store in a covered container. Refrigerate 1-2 weeks before serving. **Yield:** 3 dozen.

White Chocolate Fudge

1 tablespoon plus 1/2 cup butter, *divided*
3 cups sugar
1 cup evaporated milk

1 jar (7 ounces) marshmallow creme
1-2/3 cups white chocolate chips
1 cup chopped pecans *or* almonds, toasted

Grease a 13-in. x 9-in. x 2-in. baking dish with 1 tablespoon butter; set aside. In a heavy saucepan, bring the sugar, milk and remaining butter to a boil over low heat, stirring constantly. Cook until mixture reaches 234° (soft-ball stage) on a candy thermometer.

Remove from the heat; add the marshmallow creme, chocolate chips and nuts, stirring until marshmallow and chocolate are melted. Spread in prepared dish. Cool before cutting. **Yield:** 8-9 dozen.

Editor's Note: We recommend that you test your candy thermometer before each use by bringing water to a boil; the thermometer should read 212°. Adjust your recipe temperature up or down based on your test.

Speedy Oven Fudge

1 tablespoon plus 1 cup butter, *divided*
1/2 cup milk
2/3 cup baking cocoa

2 pounds confectioners' sugar
2 teaspoons vanilla extract
1 cup chopped nuts

Grease an 11-in. x 7-in. x 2-in. baking dish with 1 tablespoon butter; set aside. In a 3-qt. baking dish, place the milk then remaining butter. Top with the cocoa, then the sugar (do not stir). Place in a 350° oven for 15 minutes or until butter is melted.

Carefully transfer to a mixing bowl. Add vanilla; beat on high for 2 minutes. Stir in nuts. Pour into prepared dish. Cool before cutting. **Yield:** 3 pounds.

Apricot Bonbons

1/2 cup butter, cubed
1 cup sugar
1 egg, beaten
1 package (7 ounces) dried apricots, finely chopped

1 teaspoon vanilla extract
Pinch salt
2 cups crisp rice cereal
1 cup finely chopped pecans
Confectioners' sugar

In a heavy saucepan, combine the butter, sugar, egg, apricots, vanilla and salt. Bring to a boil over medium heat, stirring constantly. Cook and stir for 8 minutes or until thickened. Remove from the heat; stir in cereal and pecans. Let stand until cool enough to handle.

Shape into 1-in. balls; roll in confectioners' sugar. Place on baking sheets; let stand until completely cool. Reroll in sugar if desired. Refrigerate in an airtight containers. **Yield:** about 3-1/2 dozen.

Chocolate Caramel Clusters

1 package (14 ounces) caramels
4-1/2 teaspoons milk
1 package (6 ounces) pecan
   halves

1 cup (6 ounces) semisweet
   chocolate chips
1 tablespoon shortening

In a microwave or heavy saucepan, melt caramels and milk; stir until smooth. Place pecan halves in groups of three on a greased baking sheet. Spoon melted caramel over pecans (about 1 tablespoon over each cluster).

Refrigerate. Melt chocolate chips and shortening; spread over clusters. Store in the refrigerator. **Yield:** 3 dozen.

Pecan Fondant

1/3 cup butter, softened
1/3 cup light corn syrup
1/8 teaspoon salt
3-1/2 cups confectioners' sugar,
   divided

Additional confectioners' sugar
About 180 pecan halves, toasted
   (about 3/4 pound)

In a bowl, stir the butter, corn syrup and salt with a wooden spoon until smooth. Add 1 cup sugar; stir until completely blended. Gradually add remaining sugar, stirring until completely blended.

Dust work surface with additional sugar. Knead dough until smooth, about 5 minutes. Shape into 1/2-in. balls. Place each ball between two pecan halves; gently press together. Place on waxed paper-lined baking sheets. Cover and refrigerate for 3 hours or until set. Keep refrigerated until serving (candies will be soft). **Yield:** about 7-1/2 dozen.

Coconut Snacks

1 cup creamy peanut butter
1 cup confectioners' sugar
1/2 cup nonfat dry milk powder

4 tablespoons water
1 cup (6 ounces) semisweet
chocolate chips
1-1/2 cups flaked coconut

In a mixing bowl, beat peanut butter, sugar, milk and water until smooth. Fold in chocolate chips. Form into 1-in. balls; roll in coconut. Refrigerate until firm. **Yield:** 4 dozen.

Chocolate-Dipped Treats

1 cup (6 ounces) semisweet
chocolate chips
1 tablespoon shortening

1/4 teaspoon ground cinnamon
Large marshmallows, miniature
pretzel twists *and/or* whole fresh
strawberries

In a microwave or heavy saucepan, melt chocolate chips and shortening. Stir in cinnamon. Dip three-quarters of each marshmallow, pretzel and/or strawberry in chocolate. Place on a waxed paper-lined baking sheet. Refrigerate until set, about 30 minutes. **Yield:** about 4 dozen.

Peanut Butter Mallow Candy

2 packages (10 ounces *each*)
peanut butter *or* butterscotch
chips
3/4 cup butter
1/2 cup peanut butter

1 package (10-1/2 ounces)
miniature marshmallows
3/4 cup chopped peanuts
3/4 cup flaked coconut

In a microwave or heavy saucepan, melt chips, butter and peanut butter; stir until smooth. Add remaining ingredients and mix well. Spread into a lightly greased 15-in. x 10-in. x 1-in. baking pan. Refrigerate until firm. Cut into squares. **Yield:** about 5 dozen.

Cookies, Bars & Brownies

Lemon Coconut Bars

1/2 cup butter, softened
1 cup sugar
1 egg
1/4 cup molasses
2-1/4 cups all-purpose flour
1 teaspoon ground cinnamon
1/2 teaspoon baking soda
1/4 teaspoon salt

FILLING:
1/2 cup sugar
1/4 cup lemon juice
1 tablespoon grated lemon peel
1 tablespoon butter
2 eggs
1/8 teaspoon salt
1 cup flaked coconut

In a mixing bowl, cream butter and sugar. Beat in egg and molasses. Combine the flour, cinnamon, baking soda and salt; gradually add to creamed mixture and mix well. Cover and refrigerate for 2 hours or overnight.

For filling, in a saucepan, combine the sugar, lemon juice, peel, butter, eggs and salt. Cook and stir over low heat until thickened, about 10 minutes. Remove from the heat; stir in coconut. Cool slightly; chill.

Divide dough into fourths. Roll each portion into a 15-in. x 3-1/2-in. rectangle. Spread 1/4 cup filling off-center down each rectangle. Bring long edges together over filling; seal edges. Cut into 1-1/2-in. bars; place on ungreased baking sheets.

Bake at 350° for 12-15 minutes or until edges are lightly browned. Cool for 2 minutes; remove to a wire rack to cool completely. **Yield:** about 3-1/2 dozen.

Saucepan Fudgies

4 squares (1 ounce *each*)
unsweetened chocolate
1/4 cup butter
2 cups sugar
2 eggs
1 teaspoon vanilla extract

2 cups all-purpose flour
2 teaspoons baking powder
1/4 teaspoon salt
1/4 cup chopped pecans
Confectioners' *or* granulated sugar

In a large heavy saucepan, melt chocolate and butter over low heat, stirring constantly. Remove from the heat and cool slightly. Stir in sugar. Add eggs, one at a time, beating well after each addition. Beat in vanilla.

Combine the flour, baking powder and salt; gradually add to chocolate mixture. Stir in pecans. Refrigerate for 30 minutes or until easy to handle. Roll into 1-in. balls, then roll in sugar. Place 2 in. apart on ungreased baking sheets.

Bake at 300° for 18-20 minutes or until edges are set and tops crack. Remove to wire racks to cool. **Yield:** about 6 dozen.

Apple Crumb Bars

3 cups all-purpose flour
1-1/2 cups old-fashioned oats
1-1/2 cups packed brown sugar
3/4 teaspoon baking soda
1-1/4 cups butter, *divided*

5 to 6 cups thinly sliced pared
apples
1 cup sugar
3 tablespoons cornstarch
1 cup boiling water
1 teaspoon vanilla extract

In a bowl, combine the flour, oats, brown sugar and baking soda. Cut in 1 cup plus 2 tablespoons butter. Reserve 2 cups for topping; lightly pat remaining crumbs into a greased 13-in. x 9-in. x 2-in. baking pan. Arrange apples on top of crumbs; set aside.

In a saucepan, combine sugar and cornstarch. Stir in water and remaining butter. Bring to a boil; cook and stir for 2 mintues or until thickened. Remove from the heat; stir in vanilla. Spread on apples. Sprinkle reserved crumbs on top.

Bake at 350° for 35-45 minutes or until top is lightly browned. Cool on a wire rack. **Yield:** 3-4 dozen.

Baki's Old-World Cookies

1 cup butter, softened
1 cup sugar
2 eggs
2 teaspoons vanilla extract
1 cup ground walnuts

1-1/2 cups all-purpose flour
1 teaspoon ground cloves
1-1/2 teaspoons ground cinnamon
Shortening
Confectioners' sugar

In a mixing bowl, cream butter and sugar. Add eggs, one at a time, beating well after each addition. Beat in vanilla. Add nuts. Sift together the flour and spices; gradually add to the creamed mixture. Cover and refrigerate for 1 hour.

Using shortening, liberally grease muffin cups or individual 3-in. tins or tart shells. Fill 1/3 to 1/2 full and press dough around sides, leaving depression in center. (If dough is too soft as you press into tins, add more flour.)

Bake at 350° for about 18 minutes or until light brown. Cool 2 minutes; tap several times to remove cookies. Dust with confectioners' sugar. **Yield:** 2-3 dozen.

Soft Chocolate Cookies

1 cup butter, softened
1 1/2 cups sugar
2 eggs
2 teaspoons vanilla extract
2 cups all-purpose flour

2/3 cup baking cocoa
3/4 teaspoon baking soda
1/2 teaspoon salt
Confectioners' sugar

In a mixing bowl, cream butter and sugar. Add eggs, one at a time, beating well after each addition. Beat in vanilla. Combine the flour, cocoa, baking soda and salt; gradually add to creamed mixture. Cover and refrigerate for 1 hour or until easy to handle.

Roll into 1-in. balls. Place 2 in. apart on ungreased baking sheets. Flatten with a fork if desired. Bake at 350° for 8-10 minutes or until the edges are firm. Remove to wire racks. Dust warm cookies with confectioners' sugar. **Yield:** 5-1/2 dozen.

Sugar Cookie Slices

1-1/2 cups butter, softened
1-1/2 cups sugar
1/2 teaspoon vanilla extract

3 cups all-purpose flour
1 teaspoon baking soda
1/2 teaspoon salt

In a mixing bowl, cream butter and sugar. Beat in vanilla. Combine the flour, baking soda and salt; gradually add to the creamed mixture. Shape into two 8-in. rolls; wrap each in plastic wrap. Refrigerate for 4 hours or until firm.

Unwrap and cut into 1/4-in. slices. Place 2 in. apart on ungreased baking sheets. Bake at 350° for 12-14 minutes or until set (do not brown). Remove to wire racks to cool. **Yield:** 5 dozen.

Dipped Sandwich Cookies

1/2 cup peanut butter
1 sleeve (4 ounces) round butter-flavored crackers

1 cup (6 ounces) white *or* milk chocolate chips
1 tablespoon shortening

Spread peanut butter on half of the crackers; top with other half to make sandwiches. Refrigerate. Melt chocolate chips and shortening in a microwave or heavy saucepan; stir until smooth. Dip sandwiches and place on waxed paper until chocolate sets. **Yield:** 1-1/2 dozen.

Gold Rush Brownies

2 cups graham cracker crumbs (about 32 squares)
1 cup (6 ounces) semisweet chocolate chips

1/2 cup chopped pecans
1 can (14 ounces) sweetened condensed milk

In a bowl, combine the crumbs, chocolate chips and pecans. Stir in milk until blended (batter will be stiff). Spread into a greased 8-in. square baking dish.

Bake at 350° for 25-30 minutes or until a toothpick inserted near the center comes out clean. Cool on a wire rack. Cut into bars. **Yield:** 1 dozen.

Tom Thumb Treats

1 cup all-purpose flour	1 teaspoon vanilla extract
1/2 cup packed brown sugar	2 tablespoons all-purpose flour
1/2 teaspoon salt	1/2 teaspoon baking powder
1/2 cup shortening	1/4 teaspoon salt
	1-1/2 cups flaked coconut
TOPPING:	1 cup chopped walnuts
2 eggs	
1 cup packed brown sugar	

In a bowl, combine the flour, brown sugar and salt. Cut in shortening until the mixture resembles coarse crumbs. Press into a greased 13-in. x 9-in. x 2-in. baking pan. Bake at 325° for 12-15 minutes or until golden brown.

In a mixing bowl, beat eggs, brown sugar and vanilla until foamy. Combine the flour, baking powder and salt; gradually add to the egg mixture. Stir in coconut and nuts. Spread over crust. Bake for 20 minutes or until golden brown. Cool on a wire rack. Cut into bars. **Yield:** 3-1/2 dozen.

No-Bake Cornflake Cookies

4 cups cornflakes	1/2 cup light corn syrup
1-1/2 cups flaked coconut	1/2 cup evaporated milk
3/4 cup chopped pecans	1/4 cup butter
1-1/2 cups sugar	Dash salt

In a large heatproof bowl, combine the cornflakes, coconut and pecans; set aside. Place remaining ingredients in a 1-qt. saucepan. Bring mixture to 240° (soft-ball stage), stirring constantly. Add syrup mixture to dry ingredients; stir well. Drop by tablespoonfuls onto waxed paper. Let stand until set. **Yield:** 3-4 dozen.

Editor's Note: We recommend that you test your candy thermometer before each use by bringing water to a boil; the thermometer should read 212°. Adjust your recipe temperature up or down based on your test.

Raisin Sheet Cookies

1 cup raisins	1-1/2 teaspoons baking soda
1-1/4 cups water	1/4 teaspoon ground nutmeg
1 cup shortening	1/4 teaspoon ground cinnamon
1-1/2 cups sugar	1/2 teaspoon salt
2 eggs	1 cup chopped nuts
3 cups all-purpose flour	Confectioners' sugar icing, optional

In a small saucepan, combine raisins and water; bring to a boil. Drain; reserve 1 cup liquid and set raisins aside.

In a mixing bowl, cream shortening and sugar; add eggs. Sift together the flour, baking soda, nutmeg, cinnamon and salt; add alternately with raisin liquid to creamed mixture. Stir in raisins and nuts. Spread in a lightly greased 15-in. x 10-in. x 1-in. baking pan.

Bake at 350° for 25-30 minutes. If desired, glaze with confectioners' sugar icing while warm. Cut while warm. **Yield:** 5-6 dozen.

Banana Cocoa Brownies

1 cup quick-cooking oats	2 tablespoons vegetable oil
1 cup boiling water	1 teaspoon vanilla extract
4 egg whites	1 cup all-purpose flour
1-1/2 cups mashed ripe bananas (about 3 medium)	1/4 cup baking cocoa
3/4 cup packed brown sugar	1 teaspoon baking soda
1/2 cup sugar	1/2 teaspoon salt

In a small bowl, combine oats and boiling water; let stand for 5 minutes. In a large mixing bowl, beat the egg whites, bananas, sugars, oil and vanilla until blended. Combine the dry ingredients; gradually add to creamed mixture. Stir in the oat mixture.

Spread into a 13-in. x 9-in. x 2-in. baking pan coated with nonstick cooking spray. Bake at 350° for 20-25 minutes or until a toothpick inserted near the center comes out clean (do not overbake). Cool on a wire rack. Cut into bars. **Yield:** 4 dozen.

Austrian Chocolate Balls

2 squares (1 ounce *each*)
   unsweetened chocolate
1/3 cup butter
1 cup sugar
1 egg
1 egg yolk
1/2 teaspoon almond extract
1-1/3 cups all-purpose flour
1/2 cup finely chopped almonds

GLAZE:

1 square (1 ounce) unsweetened
   chocolate
1 tablespoon butter, softened
1/4 teaspoon almond extract
1-1/4 cups confectioners' sugar
3 to 4 tablespoons milk

In a medium saucepan, melt chocolate and butter over low heat. Remove from the heat; transfer to a large mixing bowl. Add the sugar, egg, yolk and extract. Add flour and nuts; blend thoroughly.

Shape into 3/4-in. balls and place 1 in. apart on ungreased baking sheets. Bake at 350° for 10-12 minutes or until set. Cool.

For glaze, melt chocolate and butter in a small saucepan. Add the extract, sugar and milk; blend well. Dip tops of cookies into glaze. Allow to dry completely before storing in airtight containers. **Yield:** 2-3 dozen.

Spicy Molasses Cookies

1 cup shortening
1-1/2 cups packed brown sugar
1/4 cup light *or* dark molasses
3 eggs
3-1/2 cups all-purpose flour
3 teaspoons ground cinnamon
1 teaspoon baking soda

1/2 teaspoon salt
1/2 teaspoon ground nutmeg
1/4 teaspoon ground cloves
1/4 teaspoon ground allspice
1 cup chopped walnuts, optional
1 cup raisins, optional

In a large mixing bowl, cream shortening and sugar. Add molasses. Add eggs, one at a time, beating well after each addition. Combine the dry ingredients and spices; add to batter and mix lightly. Stir in nuts and raisins if desired; mix well.

Drop by teaspoonfuls 2 in. apart onto greased baking sheets. Bake at 350° for 10-12 minutes. Remove to wire racks to cool. **Yield:** about 12 dozen.

No-Guilt Brownies

3 egg whites
3/4 cup low-fat cottage cheese
1 teaspoon vanilla extract
1 cup sugar
3/4 cup all-purpose flour

1/2 teaspoon baking powder
1/4 teaspoon salt
3 squares (1 ounce *each*)
  unsweetened chocolate,
  melted and cooled
2 teaspoons confectioners' sugar

Place the egg whites, cottage cheese and vanilla in a blender or food processor; cover and process until smooth. Combine the sugar, flour, baking powder and salt; add to cottage cheese mixture. Cover and process for 30 seconds. Add chocolate; cover and process just until blended, about 15 seconds.

Spread into an 8-in. square baking dish coated with nonstick cooking spray. Bake at 350° for 20-25 minutes or until a toothpick inserted near the center comes out clean (do not overbake). Cool on a wire rack. Dust with confectioners' sugar. Cut into bars. **Yield:** 16 brownies.

Cheesecake Dreams

1 cup all-purpose flour
1/3 cup packed brown sugar
1/2 cup chopped pecans
1/3 cup butter, melted

FILLING:
1 package (8 ounces) cream
  cheese, softened

1/4 cup sugar
1 egg
2 tablespoons milk
1 tablespoon lemon juice
1 teaspoon vanilla extract

In a bowl, combine the flour, brown sugar and pecans. Stir in butter; mix well. Set aside 1/3 cup for topping. Press remaining mixture into a greased 8-in. square baking dish. Bake at 350° for 12-15 minutes or until lightly browned.

Meanwhile, in a mixing bowl, beat cream cheese and sugar. Beat in the egg, milk, lemon juice and vanilla. Pour over crust; sprinkle with reserved pecan mixture.

Bake for 20-25 minutes or until firm. Cool on a wire rack. Cut into 16 squares, then cut each in half diagonally. Store in the refrigerator. **Yield:** 32 bars.

Potato Chip Crunchies

2 cups butter, softened
1-1/2 cups sugar
1 egg
1 teaspoon vanilla extract

4 cups all-purpose flour
1 cup crushed potato chips
1 cup chopped pecans

In a mixing bowl, cream butter and sugar. Beat in egg and vanilla. Gradually add flour. Fold in the potato chips and pecans.

Drop by tablespoonfuls 1-1/2 in. apart onto ungreased baking sheets. Flatten with a fork. Bake at 350° for 12-14 minutes or until golden brown. Remove to wire racks to cool. **Yield:** 8 dozen.

Flourless Peanut Butter Cookies

4 egg whites
2 cups peanut butter

1-2/3 cups sugar

In a mixing bowl, beat egg whites until stiff peaks form. In another bowl, combine peanut butter and sugar; fold in egg whites.

Drop by heaping teaspoonfuls 2 in. apart onto lightly greased baking sheets. Flatten slightly with a fork. Bake at 325° for 15-20 minutes or until set. Remove to wire racks to cool. **Yield:** about 6-1/2 dozen.

Brown Butter Refrigerator Cookies

1 cup butter
2 cups brown sugar
2 eggs
3 cups all-purpose flour

1 teaspoon baking soda
1 teaspoon cream of tartar
1/4 teaspoon salt
1 cup chopped pecans

In a small saucepan, cook butter over low heat until lightly browned. Remove from the heat; stir in sugar. Mix well. Add remaining ingredients. Dough will be thick and crumbly. Shape into rolls; wrap each in plastic wrap. Refrigerate for 4 hours or until firm.

Unwrap and cut into 1/4-in. slices. Place 2 in. apart on ungreased baking sheets. Bake at 375° for 10-12 minutes. Remove to wire racks to cool. **Yield:** 3 dozen.

Popcorn Cookies

1/2 cup butter, softened
1 cup sugar
1 egg
1 teaspoon vanilla extract
1-1/4 cups all-purpose flour
1/2 teaspoon baking soda

Pinch salt
2 cups popped popcorn, slightly crushed
1 cup (6 ounces) semisweet chocolate chips
1/2 cup chopped pecans

In a large mixing bowl, cream butter and sugar. Beat in egg and vanilla. Combine the flour, baking soda and salt; gradually add to the creamed mixture. Stir in the popcorn, chocolate chips and pecans.

Drop by tablespoonfuls 2 in. apart onto greased baking sheets. Bake at 350° for 13-14 minutes or until golden brown. Remove to wire racks to cool. **Yield:** 2-1/2 dozen.

Chocolate Mint Cookies

3/4 cup butter
1-1/2 cups packed dark brown sugar
2 tablespoons water
2 cups (12 ounces) semisweet chocolate chips
2 eggs

2-1/2 cups all-purpose flour
1-1/4 teaspoons baking soda
1/2 teaspoon salt
2 packages (4.67 ounces *each*) mint Andes candies, halved

In a heavy saucepan, combine the butter, brown sugar and water; cook over low heat until butter is melted. Remove from the heat; stir in chips until melted.

Transfer to a mixing bowl; cool for 10 minutes. Add eggs, one at a time, beating well after each addition. Combine the flour, baking soda and salt; gradually add to the chocolate mixture. Cover and refrigerate for 1 hour or until easy to handle.

Roll into 1-in. balls. Place 2 in. apart on ungreased baking sheets. Bake at 350° for 10-12 minutes or until surface cracks. Remove to wire racks. Immediately place half of a mint candy on each cookie. Let stand until candy begins to melt; spread with a knife. **Yield:** about 9 dozen.

Orange-Date Bars

1 cup chopped dates
1/3 cup sugar
1/3 cup vegetable oil
1/2 cup orange juice
1 egg, beaten

1 cup all-purpose flour
1-1/2 teaspoons baking powder
1 tablespoon grated orange rind
1/2 cup chopped pecans

In a saucepan, combine the dates, sugar, oil and juice. Cook for 5 minutes to soften dates. Cool. Add egg; mix well. Combine all remaining ingredients and stir into date mixture.

Spread into a greased 8-in. square baking dish. Bake at 350° for 25-30 minutes. Cool on a wire rack. Cut into bars. **Yield:** 2 dozen.

Raspberry Delights

1 cup butter, softened
1 cup sugar
2 egg yolks

2 cups all-purpose flour
1 cup coarsely ground pecans
1 cup raspberry jam

In a mixing bowl, cream butter and sugar. Add egg yolks; mix well. Gradually add flour. Stir in the pecans.

Spread half into a lightly greased 13-in. x 9-in. x 2-in. baking pan. Top with jam. Drop remaining dough by teaspoonfuls over jam. Bake at 350° for 25-30 minutes or until top is golden brown. Cool on a wire rack. Cut into bars. **Yield:** 3 dozen.

Scotch Shortbread Bars

1 cup butter, softened
1/2 cup confectioners' sugar
2 cups all-purpose flour

1/4 teaspoon baking powder
1/4 teaspoon salt
Additional confectioners' sugar

In a mixing bowl, cream butter and sugar. Combine flour, baking powder and salt; gradually add to the creamed mixture. Spread into an ungreased 11-in. x 7-in. x 2-in. baking pan. Prick several times with a fork.

Bake at 350° for 20-22 minutes or until edges begin to brown. Dust with confectioners' sugar. Cool on a wire rack. Cut into bars. **Yield:** 2 dozen.

Rhubarb Squares

1-1/2 cups all-purpose flour
3 tablespoons sugar
3/4 cup cold butter

FILLING:
3 tablespoons all-purpose flour

3/4 cup heavy whipping cream
2 cups sugar, *divided*
4 eggs, *separated*
2 teaspoons vanilla extract
5 cups diced rhubarb

Combine flour and sugar; cut in butter until crumbly. Press into the bottom of a 13-in. x 9-in. x 2-in. baking pan. Bake at 350° for 10 minutes. Cool slightly.

For filling, blend flour and cream in a mixing bowl until smooth. Add 1-1/4 cups sugar and egg yolks; mix well. Fold in vanilla and rhubarb. Pour into crust. Bake at 325° for 55-60 minutes or until a sharp knife inserted near center comes out clean.

Meanwhile, beat egg whites on medium speed until soft peaks form. Gradually beat in remaining sugar, 1 tablespoon at a time, on high until stiff peaks form. Remove from oven; immediately top with meringue and broil lightly. Cool on a wire rack. Cut into squares. **Yield:** about 2 dozen.

Swiss Treat Bars

1 cup butter, softened
1-1/4 cups sugar
1 egg
1 teaspoon vanilla extract
2-1/2 cups all-purpose flour
1-1/2 teaspoons baking powder

1/2 teaspoon salt
1 cup (6 ounces) semisweet chocolate chips
1/2 cup finely chopped nuts
1/2 cup maraschino cherries, drained and chopped
1/2 cup flaked coconut

In a large mixing bowl, cream butter and sugar. Beat in egg and vanilla. Combine the flour, baking powder and salt; gradually add to creamed mixture. Fold in the chocolate chips, nuts, cherries and coconut (mixture will be thick).

Press into a greased 15-in. x 10-in. x 1-in. baking pan. Bake at 375° for 18-22 minutes or until lightly browned. Cool on a wire rack before cutting. **Yield:** 5 dozen.

Frosted Cherry Nut Bars

1/2 cup butter, softened
1/2 cup sugar
1/2 cup packed brown sugar
2 eggs
1 teaspoon vanilla extract
2 cups all-purpose flour
1-1/2 teaspoons baking powder
1/2 teaspoon salt
3/4 cup milk
1 cup mixed nuts, coarsely chopped

1 cup halved maraschino cherries
1 cup (6 ounces) semisweet chocolate chips

FROSTING:
1/4 cup butter
2 tablespoons milk
1/2 teaspoon vanilla extract
2 cups confectioners' sugar

In a mixing bowl, cream butter and sugars. Add eggs, one at a time, beating well after each addition. Beat in vanilla. Combine the flour, baking powder and salt; add to creamed mixture alternately with milk. Stir in the nuts, cherries and chocolate chips.

Spread into a greased 15-in. x 10-in. x 1-in. baking pan. Bake at 325° for 25-30 minutes or until golden brown.

Meanwhile, in a saucepan over medium heat, melt butter until golden brown, about 7 minutes. Add milk and vanilla. Remove from the heat; beat in confectioners' sugar until smooth. Frost warm bars. Cool on a wire rack. Cut into bars. **Yield:** about 6 dozen.

Tea Cakes

1 cup butter, softened
1-1/2 cups sugar
3 eggs
1 tablespoon vanilla extract

3 cups all-purpose flour
1 tablespoon baking powder
1/4 teaspoon salt

In a mixing bowl, cream butter and sugar. Add eggs, one at a time, beating well after each addition. Beat in vanilla. Combine the flour, baking powder and salt; gradually add to the creamed mixture (the dough will be soft).

Drop by teaspoonfuls 2 in. apart onto greased baking sheets. Bake at 375° for 7-8 minutes or until the edges are golden brown. Remove to wire racks to cool. **Yield:** 9 dozen.

Crunch Bars

1/2 cup butter, softened
3/4 cup sugar
2 eggs
1 teaspoon vanilla extract
3/4 cup all-purpose flour
1/4 teaspoon baking powder

1/4 teaspoon salt
2-1/2 cups miniature marshmallows

TOPPING:
1 cup (6 ounces) chocolate chips
1 cup chunky peanut butter
1-1/2 cups crisp rice cereal

In a large mixing bowl, cream butter and sugar. Add eggs and vanilla. Combine dry ingredients; add to creamed mixture. Spread in a greased 13-in. x 9-in. x 2-in. baking pan. Bake at 350° for 15-20 minutes. Arrange marshmallows evenly over bars; bake 2 minutes longer. Cool on a wire rack for 30 minutes.

For topping, melt chocolate chips and peanut butter in a microwave or heavy saucepan; stir until smooth. Stir in cereal. Spread over marshmallow layer. Cover and refrigerate until firm. **Yield:** 2 dozen.

Whoopee Pies

6 tablespoons shortening
3/4 cup sugar
1 cup milk
1 teaspoon vanilla extract
2 cups all-purpose flour
2 tablespoons baking cocoa
1-1/2 teaspoons baking soda
1 teaspoon salt

FILLING:
1/2 cup shortening
3/4 cup confectioners' sugar
6 tablespoons marshmallow creme
1 teaspoon vanilla extract
Milk

For cookies, cream the shortening and sugar. Beat in milk and vanilla. Combine the flour, cocoa, baking soda and salt. Gradually add to creamed mixture.

Drop cookies 2 in. apart on ungreased baking sheets. Bake at 425° for 10-12 minutes or until set. (If cookies rise too much, press down with spatula.) Remove to wire racks to cool.

Meanwhile, combine the first four filling ingredients. Stir in enough milk to achieve spreading consistency. Spread filling on the bottoms of half of the cooled cookies; top with remaining cookies. **Yield:** about 2 dozen.

Toffee Nut Squares

1/2 cup butter, softened
1/2 cup packed brown sugar
1 cup all-purpose flour
1/4 cup heavy whipping cream

FILLING:
1 cup packed brown sugar
2 eggs

1 teaspoon vanilla extract
2 tablespoons all-purpose flour
1 teaspoon baking powder
1/4 teaspoon salt
1 cup flaked coconut
1 cup chopped nuts

In a large mixing bowl, cream the butter and brown sugar until light and fluffy. Gradually add flour. Add cream, 1 tablespoon at a time, until a soft dough forms. Press into an ungreased 9-in. square baking pan. Bake at 350° for 15 minutes.

Meanwhile, in a small mixing bowl, beat the brown sugar, eggs and vanilla until blended. Combine flour, baking powder and salt; gradually add to mixture. Stir in coconut and nuts.

Spread over crust. Bake for 25-20 minutes or until a toothpick inserted near the center comes out clean. Cool on a wire rack before cutting. **Yield:** about 1-1/2 dozen.

Pecan Sandies

1/3 cup butter, softened
1/3 cup shortening
1/2 cup sugar
1/2 cup packed brown sugar

1 egg
1 teaspoon vanilla extract
1-1/2 cups self-rising flour
1/2 cup chopped pecans

In a mixing bowl, cream the butter, shortening and sugars. Beat in egg and vanilla. Gradually add flour. Stir in pecans. Drop by rounded teaspoonfuls 2 in. apart onto ungreased baking sheets.

Bake at 375° for 9-11 minutes or until edges are lightly browned. Cool for 1-2 minutes before removing to wire racks. **Yield:** about 3-1/2 dozen.

Editor's Note: As a substitute for the self-rising flour, place 2-1/4 teaspoons baking powder and 3/4 teaspoon salt in a measuring cup. Add all-purpose flour to measure 1 cup. Add an additional 1/2 cup all-purpose flour.

Sweet-as-Sugar Cookies

1 cup butter, softened
1 cup sugar
1 cup confectioners' sugar
1 cup vegetable oil
2 eggs
4-1/4 cups all-purpose flour

1 teaspoon salt
1 teaspoon cream of tartar
1 teaspoon baking soda
1 teaspoon vanilla extract
Additional sugar
Nutmeg

In a mixing bowl, cream butter, sugars and oil. Add eggs, one at a time, beating well after each addition. Add dry ingredients and vanilla; mix well. Refrigerate dough overnight.

Form into walnut-size balls and place on greased baking sheets. Combine sugar and nutmeg; dip glass in mixture and flatten cookies with it. Bake at 375° for 8 minutes. Remove to wire racks to cool. **Yield:** about 5 dozen.

Grandma Brubaker's Orange Cookies

1 cup shortening
2 cups sugar
2 eggs, *separated*
1 cup buttermilk
5 cups all-purpose flour
2 teaspoons baking powder
2 teaspoons baking soda

Pinch salt
Juice and peel of 2 medium oranges

ICING:
2 cups confectioners' sugar
1/4 cup orange juice
1 tablespoon butter
1 tablespoon grated orange peel

In a mixing bowl, cream shortening and sugar. Beat in egg yolks and buttermilk. Sift together the flour, baking powder, soda and salt; add alternately with orange juice and peel to creamed mixture. Add egg whites and beat until smooth.

Drop by rounded teaspoonfuls onto greased baking sheets. Bake at 325° for 10 minutes.

For icing, combine all ingredients and beat until smooth. Frost cookies when cool. **Yield:** about 6 dozen.

Chocolate Buttermilk Brownies

1 cup butter
1/4 cup baking cocoa
1 cup water
2 cups sugar
2 cups all-purpose flour
1 teaspoon baking soda
1/2 teaspoon salt
1/2 cup buttermilk
2 eggs, beaten
1 teaspoon vanilla extract
3 to 4 drops red food coloring, optional

FROSTING:
1/2 cup butter
1/4 cup baking cocoa
1/4 cup buttermilk
1 pound confectioners' sugar
1 teaspoon vanilla extract
Dash salt
3/4 cup chopped almonds, optional

In a saucepan, bring the butter, cocoa and water to a boil. Cool. Meanwhile, in a large mixing bowl, combine the sugar, flour, baking soda and salt. Pour cocoa mixture over dry ingredients; mix well.

Add the buttermilk, eggs, vanilla, and food coloring if desired. Mix until well combined. Pour into a greased and floured 15-in. x 10-in. x 1-in. baking pan. Bake at 350° for 20 minutes.

For frosting, melt butter with cocoa and buttermilk in a saucepan. Stir in the sugar, vanilla and salt. Spread over warm brownies. Sprinkle with nuts if desired. **Yield:** 35 brownies.

Fruitcake Squares

6 tablespoons butter, melted
4 cups crushed vanilla wafers
1 cup pecan halves
3/4 cup chopped dates
3/4 cup chopped mixed candied fruit

1/2 cup chopped candied pineapple
1 can (14 ounces) sweetened condensed milk
1 teaspoon vanilla extract

Pour butter into a 15-in. x 10-in. x 1-in. baking pan. Sprinkle with wafer crumbs. Arrange pecans and fruit over crumbs; press down gently. Combine milk and vanilla; pour evenly over fruit. Bake at 350° for 20-25 minutes or until lightly browned. Cool on a wire rack. Cut into squares. **Yield:** about 3 dozen.

Amish Raisin Cookies

1 cup raisins	1 teaspoon vanilla extract
1 cup water	3 cups all-purpose flour
3/4 cup butter, softened	1 teaspoon baking powder
2 cups packed brown sugar	1 teaspoon baking soda
1 egg	1/8 teaspoon salt

In a small saucepan, combine raisins and water. Bring to a boil; cook until liquid is reduced to 1/2 cup. Set aside to cool.

In a large mixing bowl, cream butter and brown sugar until light and fluffy. Beat in egg and vanilla. Combine the flour, baking powder, baking soda and salt; gradually add to creamed mixture. Stir in raisins with liquid.

Drop by tablespoonfuls 2 in. apart onto ungreased baking sheets. Bake at 375° for 10-12 minutes or until the surface cracks. Remove to wire racks to cool. **Yield:** 6 dozen.

Crisp Chocolate Chip Cookies

1 cup butter, softened	1 tablespoon baking soda
1 cup sugar	1/2 teaspoon salt
1 cup packed brown sugar	2 cups (12 ounces) chocolate chips
1 cup vegetable oil	
1 egg	1 cup quick-cooking or old-fashioned oats
1 teaspoon vanilla extract	
3-1/2 cups all-purpose flour	1 cup cornflakes or crisp rice cereal

In a large mixing bowl, cream butter and sugars. Add the oil, egg and vanilla. Combine the flour, baking soda and salt; add to creamed mixture. Stir in the chocolate chips, oats, and cornflakes or cereal.

Drop by spoonfuls 2 in. apart onto greased baking sheets. Bake at 350° for 12-14 minutes. Remove to wire racks to cool. **Yield:** about 3 dozen.

Hearty Whole Wheat Cookies

1 cup butter, softened
2 cups packed brown sugar
3 eggs
3 tablespoons half-and-half cream
2 teaspoons vanilla extract
2 cups quick-cooking oats

2 cups whole wheat flour
1 teaspoon baking soda
1 teaspoon baking powder
1/2 teaspoon salt
1 package (12 ounces) miniature semisweet chocolate chips
2 cups coarsely chopped peanuts

In a mixing bowl, cream butter and brown sugar. Add eggs, one at a time, beating well after each addition. Beat in the cream and vanilla.

In a blender or food processor, process oats until finely ground. Combine the oats, flour, baking soda, baking powder and salt; gradually add to the creamed mixture. Stir in chocolate chips and peanuts.

Drop by tablespoonfuls 1-1/2 in. apart onto ungreased baking sheets. Bake at 350° for 10-12 minutes or until golden brown. Remove to wire racks to cool. **Yield:** 6 dozen.

Pineapple Delights

1 cup butter, softened
1 cup sugar
1 cup packed brown sugar
2 eggs
1 teaspoon vanilla extract
4 cups all-purpose flour
2 teaspoons baking powder

1/2 teaspoon baking soda
1/2 teaspoon salt
1 can (8 ounces) crushed pineapple, drained
1 cup chopped walnuts
1/4 cup chopped maraschino cherries

In a mixing bowl, cream butter and sugars. Add the eggs, one at a time, beating well after each addition. Beat in vanilla. Combine the flour, baking powder, baking soda and salt; gradually add to the creamed mixture. Stir in the pineapple, walnuts and cherries.

Drop by rounded tablespoonfuls 2 in. apart onto ungreased baking sheets. Bake at 425° for 7-9 minutes or until lightly browned. Remove to wire racks to cool. **Yield:** 7 dozen.

Pecan Icebox Cookies

1 cup butter, softened
1 cup sugar
1 cup packed brown sugar
3 eggs
4 cups all-purpose flour

2 teaspoons baking powder
1 teaspoon baking soda
1 teaspoon ground cinnamon
1/2 teaspoon salt
1 cup chopped pecans

In a mixing bowl, cream butter and sugars. Add the eggs, one at time, beating well after each addition. Combine flour, baking powder, baking soda, cinnamon and salt; gradually add to the creamed mixture. Stir in pecans. Shape into four 6-1/2-in. rolls; wrap each in plastic wrap. Refrigerate overnight.

Unwrap and cut into 1/8-in. slices. Place 1 in. apart on ungreased baking sheets. Bake at 375° for 7-10 minutes or until lightly browned. Remove to wire racks to cool. **Yield:** about 9 dozen.

Coffee Almond Crisps

1 cup shortening
2 cups packed brown sugar
2 eggs
1/2 cup brewed coffee, room
  temperature
3-1/2 cups all-purpose flour

1 teaspoon baking soda
1 teaspoon salt
1-1/2 teaspoons ground cinnamon,
  divided
1 cup chopped almonds, toasted
3 tablespoons sugar

In a mixing bowl, cream shortening and brown sugar. Add eggs, one at a time, beating well after each addition. Beat in coffee. Combine the flour, baking soda, salt and 1 teaspoon cinnamon; gradually add to the creamed mixture. Stir in almonds.

Drop by rounded teaspoonfuls 2 in. apart onto ungreased baking sheets. Combine sugar and remaining cinnamon; sprinkle over cookies. Flatten slightly. Bake at 375° for 10-12 minutes or until firm. Remove to wire racks to cool. **Yield:** 6 dozen.

Pumpkin Cheesecake Bars

1 cup all-purpose flour

1/3 cup packed brown sugar

5 tablespoons cold butter

1 cup finely chopped pecans

1 package (8 ounces) cream cheese, softened

3/4 cup sugar

1/2 cup canned pumpkin

2 eggs

1 teaspoon vanilla extract

1-1/2 teaspoons ground cinnamon

1 teaspoon ground allspice

In a bowl, combine flour and brown sugar. Cut in butter until crumbly. Stir in pecans; set aside 3/4 cup for topping. Press remaining crumb mixture into a greased 8-in. square baking dish. Bake at 350° for 15 minutes or until edges are lightly browned. Cool on a wire rack.

In a mixing bowl, beat cream cheese and sugar. Beat in the pumpkin, eggs, vanilla, cinnamon and allspice. Pour over crust. Sprinkle with reserved crumb mixture.

Bake for 30-35 minutes or until golden brown. Cool on a wire rack. Cut into bars. Store in the refrigerator. **Yield:** 16 bars.

Fudgy Brownies

2 cups sugar

3/4 cup baking cocoa

2/3 cup vegetable oil, *divided*

1/2 cup boiling water

1-1/3 cups all-purpose flour

1/2 teaspoon baking soda

1/4 teaspoon salt

2 eggs

1 teaspoon vanilla extract

1 cup chopped walnuts

In a mixing bowl, combine the sugar and cocoa. Add 1/3 cup oil and water; beat until smooth. Combine the flour, baking soda and salt. Add to cocoa mixture along with the eggs, vanilla and remaining oil. Stir in walnuts.

Spread into a greased 13-in. x 9-in. x 2-in. baking pan. Bake at 350° for 35-40 minutes or until a toothpick inserted near the center comes out clean. Cool on a wire rack. Cut into bars. **Yield:** 6 dozen.

Favorite Cake Brownies

1/4 cup butter
2/3 cup sugar
1/4 cup baking cocoa
1 egg white
1/3 cup fat-free milk
1/2 teaspoon vanilla extract
3/4 cup all-purpose flour
1/4 teaspoon baking powder

1/4 teaspoon baking soda
1/3 cup chopped nuts
1 teaspoon confectioners' sugar

TOPPING:
1/2 cup confectioners' sugar
1 tablespoon baking cocoa
1 tablespoon fat-free milk
1/4 teaspoon vanilla extract

In a large saucepan, melt butter; remove from the heat. Stir in sugar and cocoa until smooth. Add the egg white, milk and vanilla; stir just until blended. Combine the flour, baking powder and baking soda; stir into chocolate mixture just until blended. Stir in nuts.

Pour into a 9-in. square baking pan coated with nonstick cooking spray. Bake at 350° for 16-18 minutes or until a toothpick inserted near the center comes out clean. Cool on a wire rack. Dust with confectioners' sugar.

In a small bowl, combine topping ingredients until smooth. Drizzle over brownies. **Yield:** 16 brownies.

Lemon Drop Cookies

1/2 cup butter, softened
3/4 cup sugar
1 egg
1 tablespoon half-and-half cream
1 teaspoon grated lemon peel

1-1/2 cups all-purpose flour
1/2 cup finely crushed lemon drops
1 teaspoon baking powder
1/4 teaspoon salt

In a large mixing bowl, cream butter and sugar. Beat in the egg, cream and lemon peel. Combine the flour, lemon drops, baking powder and salt; gradually add to the creamed mixture.

Drop by rounded teaspoonfuls 3 in. apart onto greased baking sheets. Bake at 350° for 8-10 minutes or until edges are lightly browned. Cool for 2 minutes before removing to wire racks. **Yield:** about 3-1/2 dozen.

Old-Fashioned Chocolate Chip Cookies

2 cups shortening
2 cups sugar
2 cups packed brown sugar
4 eggs

5 cups all-purpose flour
2 teaspoons baking powder
1 teaspoon salt
2 cups (12 ounces) semisweet chocolate chips

In a large mixing bowl, cream shortening and sugars until fluffy. Add eggs, one at a time, beating well after each addition. Combine the dry ingredients; add to creamed mixture and mix well. Stir in chocolate chips.

Drop by spoonfuls 3 in. apart onto greased baking sheets. Bake at 350° for 8-10 minutes. Remove to wire racks to cool. **Yield:** 7-8 dozen.

Applesauce Brownies

1/4 cup butter, softened
3/4 cup sugar
1 egg
1 cup all-purpose flour
1 tablespoon baking cocoa
1/2 teaspoon baking soda
1/2 teaspoon ground cinnamon
1 cup applesauce

TOPPING:
1/2 cup chocolate chips
1/2 cup chopped walnuts *or* pecans
1 tablespoon sugar

In a large mixing bowl, cream butter and sugar. Beat in egg. Combine the flour, cocoa, baking soda and cinnamon; add to creamed mixture along with applesauce. Mix well. Pour into a greased 8-in. square baking dish.

Combine topping ingredients; sprinkle over batter. Bake at 350° for 25 minutes or until toothpick comes out clean. Cool on a wire rack. Cut into squares. **Yield:** 16 brownies.

Chocolate Chip Marshmallow Bars

1 cup shortening
3/4 cup sugar
3/4 cup packed brown sugar
2 eggs
1 teaspoon vanilla extract
2-1/4 cups all-purpose flour

1 teaspoon baking soda
1 teaspoon salt
2 cups miniature marshmallows
1-1/2 cups semisweet chocolate chips
3/4 cup chopped walnuts

In a mixing bowl, cream shortening and sugars. Add eggs, one at a time, beating well after each addition. Beat in vanilla. Combine the flour, baking soda and salt; gradually add to creamed mixture. Stir in the marshmallows, chips and walnuts.

Spread into a greased 13-in. x 9-in. x 2-in. baking pan. Bake at 350° for 25-30 minutes or until golden brown. Cool on a wire rack. Cut into bars. **Yield:** 3 dozen.

Peanut Butter Brownies

1 package (18-1/4 ounces) chocolate cake mix
1/3 cup vegetable oil
1 egg
1 can (14 ounces) sweetened condensed milk

2 cups (12 ounces) semisweet chocolate chips, melted
1/2 cup peanut butter
1 teaspoon vanilla extract

In a bowl, combine the cake mix, oil and egg until crumbly. Set aside 1 cup for topping. Firmly press remaining mixture into a greased 13-in. x 9-in. x 2-in. baking pan; set aside.

In a bowl, combine the milk, chocolate chips, peanut butter and vanilla until smooth. Spread over crust. Sprinkle with reserved crumb mixture.

Bake at 350° for 25-30 minutes or until brownies pull away from the pan. Cool on a wire rack. Cut into bars. **Yield:** 4-1/2 dozen.

Pies & Tarts

All-American Strawberry Pie

3/4 cup sugar

1/2 cup all-purpose flour

1/4 teaspoon salt

3 cups milk

3 egg yolks, lightly beaten

2 tablespoons butter

1-1/2 teaspoons vanilla extract

1 cup heavy whipping cream

4-1/2 teaspoons confectioners' sugar

1 pastry shell (9 inches), baked

1 pint fresh strawberries, halved

1 cup fresh *or* frozen blueberries

In a large saucepan, combine the sugar, flour and salt. Stir in milk until smooth. Cook and stir over medium-high heat until thickened and bubbly. Reduce heat; cook and stir 2 minutes longer. Remove from the heat. Stir a small amount of hot filling into egg yolks; return all to pan, stirring constantly. Bring to a gentle boil; cook and stir 2 minutes longer. Remove from the heat; stir in butter and vanilla. Cool for 20 minutes without stirring.

Pour into pie shell; chill several hours until firm. In a small mixing bowl, beat cream until it begins to thicken. Add sugar; beat until stiff peaks form. Spread half over pie filling. Arrange berries on cream. Dollop or pipe remaining cream around edge of pie. **Yield:** 8 servings.

Ozark Blueberry Pie

FILLING:
- 1 can (16 ounces) whole-berry cranberry sauce
- 1/3 cup packed brown sugar
- 1/4 cup sugar
- 2 tablespoons all-purpose flour
- 2 tablespoons cornstarch
- 2 tablespoons orange juice
- 1/2 teaspoon grated orange peel
- 1/8 teaspoon salt
- 2 cups fresh *or* frozen blueberries

CRUST:
- 2-2/3 cups all-purpose flour
- 1 teaspoon salt
- 1/2 teaspoon ground mace
- 1 cup shortening
- 6 tablespoons ice water
- 2 tablespoons butter
- 1 egg
- 1 tablespoon water

In a large bowl, combine first eight ingredients. Stir in blueberries; set aside.

For crust, in another large bowl, combine the flour, salt and mace; cut in shortening until mixture is crumbly. Gradually add ice water, 1 tablespoon at a time, and toss lightly with a fork until dough forms a ball. Divide dough in half.

On a floured surface and using a floured rolling pin, roll one half to a 10-in. circle. Place into 9-in. pie pan. Trim pastry even with edge. Spoon filling into crust; dot with butter. Roll out remaining pastry to fit top of pie. Place over filling. Trim, seal and flute edges. Cut slits in pastry. Beat egg with water; brush over crust.

Bake at 425° for 40 minutes or until golden brown. Cool on a wire rack. **Yield:** 8 servings.

Tree-Mendous No-Bake Cherry Pie

- 2 tablespoons cornstarch
- 3/4 cup sugar
- 1-1/2 cups water
- 1 package (6 ounces) cherry gelatin
- 1 quart (4 cups) fresh *or* frozen pitted, chopped red tart cherries
- 2 cups whipped topping
- 2 pastry shells (8 inches *each*), baked

In a saucepan, bring the cornstarch, sugar and water to a boil over low heat; cook and stir for 2 minutes or until thick and clear. Stir in gelatin until dissolved. Add cherries. Chill until mixture starts to set, then fold in whipped topping. Pour into pastry shells. Cover and chill. **Yield:** 2 pies (6-8 servings each).

Peanut Butter-Chocolate Chip Pie

1-1/2 cups chocolate wafer crumbs
1/4 cup butter, melted
1/2 cup chunky peanut butter
1 package (8 ounces) cream cheese, softened
1 cup confectioners' sugar
1 teaspoon vanilla extract
1 carton (8 ounces) frozen whipped topping, thawed
3/4 cup semisweet chocolate chips, *divided*

Combine wafer crumbs and butter; press into the bottom and up the sides of a 9-in. pie plate. Bake at 350° for 10 minutes. Cool.

Meanwhile, in a large mixing bowl, cream the peanut butter, cream cheese and sugar. Add vanilla. By hand, fold in whipped topping and 1/2 cup chocolate chips. Pile into cooled crust; chill for several hours. Sprinkle remaining chocolate chips on top. Store in the refrigerator. **Yield:** 8 servings.

Lemon Meringue Pie

1-1/2 cups sugar
6 tablespoons cornstarch
Dash salt
1-1/2 cups water
3 egg yolks, lightly beaten
2 tablespoons butter
1/3 cup fresh lemon juice (about 3 lemons)
2 teaspoons grated lemon peel
1 pastry shell (9 inches), baked

MERINGUE:
3 egg whites
1/2 teaspoon vanilla extract
1/4 teaspoon cream of tartar
6 tablespoons sugar

In a saucepan, combine the sugar, cornstarch and salt. Stir in water. Cook and stir over medium-high heat until thickened. Reduce heat; cook and stir 2 minutes longer. Gradually stir in 1 cup of hot filling to egg yolks; return all to the saucepan, stirring constantly. Bring to a gentle boil; cook and stir 2 minutes longer. Remove from the heat. Gently stir in the butter, lemon juice and peel. Pour hot filling into pastry shell.

For meringue, in a large mixing bowl, beat the egg whites, vanilla and cream of tartar at medium speed until soft peaks form. Add sugar gradually, 1 tablespoon at a time, beating on high until stiff and glossy. Immediately spread over pie, sealing edges to pastry.

Bake at 350° for 12-15 minutes or until meringue is golden. Cool. Store in refrigerator. **Yield:** 8 servings.

Lemonade Pie

1 can (14 ounces) sweetened
  condensed milk

1 can (12 ounces) frozen pink
  lemonade, thawed and
  undiluted

1 carton (6 ounces) frozen
  whipped topping, thawed

1 graham cracker crust
  (9 inches)

Graham cracker crumbs

In a bowl, combine the milk, lemonade and whipped topping. Pour into the crust. Refrigerate for at least 12 hours. Garnish with graham cracker crumbs. **Yield:** 8 servings.

Maple Walnut Pie

1 cup maple syrup

4 eggs, beaten

1/2 cup sugar

1/3 cup butter, melted

Dash salt

1-1/3 cups walnuts, broken

Pastry for single-crust pie (9 inches)

In a bowl, combine the syrup, eggs, sugar, butter and salt until smooth. Fold in walnuts. Pour into pie crust; cover edge of pastry with foil. Bake at 350° for 15 minutes. Remove foil and bake 25 minutes more or until the filling is set. Cool on a wire rack. **Yield:** 8 servings.

French Coconut Pie

3 eggs, beaten

1-1/2 cups sugar

1 cup milk

1/2 cup butter, melted

1 tablespoon all-purpose flour

1 teaspoon vanilla extract

1 teaspoon white vinegar

1 cup flaked coconut

1 unbaked pastry shell (9 inches)

In a mixing bowl, combine the first eight ingredients; pour into the pie shell. Bake at 400° for 10 minutes. Reduce heat to 325° and bake 40 minutes longer or until top is golden and the center is almost set. Cool on a wire rack. Store in the refrigerator. **Yield:** 8 servings.

Harvest Watermelon Pie

3 cups chopped watermelon rind (peel and fruit removed)

1-1/3 cups (6 ounces) dried cranberries

3/4 cup chopped walnuts

1/3 cup cider vinegar

1/2 cup sugar

2 teaspoons pumpkin pie spice

1 teaspoon all-purpose flour

1/4 teaspoon salt

Pastry for double-crust pie (9 inches)

ORANGE GLAZE:

1/2 cup confectioners' sugar

2 teaspoons grated orange peel

1 tablespoon orange juice

Place watermelon rind in a saucepan and cover with water; bring to a boil. Reduce heat; simmer, uncovered, for 10 minutes or until the rind is tender and translucent. Remove from the heat; drain. Place in a large bowl; add the cranberries, walnuts and vinegar.

Combine the sugar, pie spice, flour and salt; add to rind mixture and stir well. Line a 9-in. pie plate with bottom pastry; trim the pastry even with edge. Add filling.

Roll out remaining pastry; make a lattice crust. Seal and flute edges. Cover edges loosely with foil. Bake at 425° for 20 minutes. Remove foil; bake 20-25 minutes longer or until crust is golden brown.

Combine glaze ingredients; spoon over hot pie. Cool on a wire rack. **Yield:** 6-8 servings.

Frozen Coconut Caramel Pie

2 tablespoons butter

1 cup flaked coconut

1/4 cup chopped pecans

1 package (8 ounces) cream cheese, softened

1 can (14 ounces) sweetened condensed milk

1 carton (16 ounces) frozen whipped topping, thawed

2 graham cracker crusts (9 inches *each*)

1 jar (12 ounces) caramel ice cream topping

In a skillet, melt butter; add coconut and pecans. Cook and stir over medium heat for 10 minutes or until golden brown and toasted; set aside.

In a mixing bowl, beat cream cheese and milk until smooth. Fold in whipped topping. Pour into crusts. Drizzle with caramel topping; sprinkle with coconut mixture.

Cover and freeze for 8 hours or overnight or until firm. Remove from the freezer 5 minutes before slicing. **Yield:** 2 pies (6-8 servings each).

Frozen Cranberry Velvet Pie

1 package (8 ounces) cream
  cheese, softened
1 cup heavy whipping cream
1/4 cup sugar

1/2 teaspoon vanilla extract
1 can (16 ounces) whole
  cranberry sauce
1 pastry shell (9 inches), baked

In a mixing bowl, beat cream cheese until fluffy. In another bowl, whip whipping cream, sugar and vanilla until thick but not stiff. Add to cream cheese, beating until smooth and creamy. Fold in cranberry sauce.

Spoon into pie crust; freeze until firm, at least 4 hours. Remove from freezer 10 minutes before serving. **Yield:** 8-10 servings.

Lemon Pear Pie

2 eggs, lightly beaten
1 cup sugar
1/4 cup lemon juice
1 tablespoon butter

1 teaspoon grated lemon peel
3 cans (15 ounces *each*) pear
  halves, drained and cubed
1 unbaked pastry shell (9 inches)

In a saucepan, combine the first five ingredients. Cook and stir over low heat for 10 minutes or until thickened and bubbly. Remove from the heat; fold in pears. Pour into pastry shell.

Bake at 350° for 50-55 minutes or until crust is golden brown and filling is bubbly. Cool on a wire rack for 1 hour. Store in the refrigerator. **Yield:** 6-8 servings.

Coconut Walnut Tart

Pastry for a single-crust pie (9 inches)
2 eggs
1-1/2 cups packed brown sugar
1/2 cup butter, melted

3 tablespoons milk
1-1/2 teaspoons vanilla extract
1-1/2 cups flaked coconut
1/3 cup chopped walnuts

Place pastry in a 9-in. fluted tart pan with a removable bottom; set aside. In a mixing bowl, beat eggs for 1 minute. Add the brown sugar, butter, milk and vanilla; mix well. Stir in coconut and walnuts. Pour into crust.

Bake at 450° for 8 minutes. Reduce heat to 350°; bake 20-25 minutes longer or until puffed and golden brown. **Yield:** 12-14 servings.

Pecan Pie

4 eggs
1 cup sugar
1/8 teaspoon salt
1-1/2 cups dark corn syrup

2 tablespoons plus 1 teaspoon
  butter, melted and cooled
1 teaspoon vanilla extract
1 cup pecan halves
1 unbaked pastry shell (9 inches)

In a mixing bowl, beat eggs just until blended but not frothy. Add sugar, salt and corn syrup. Add butter and vanilla, mixing just enough to blend. Spread pecans in the bottom of pastry shell. Pour in filling.

Place in a 350° oven and immediately reduce heat to 325°. Bake for 50-60 minutes. **Yield:** 8-10 servings.

Lime Pie

1 can (14 ounces) sweetened
  condensed milk
1/2 cup lime juice
1 carton (8 ounces) frozen
  whipped topping, thawed

Few drops green food coloring,
  optional
1 graham cracker crust
  (9 inches)
Additional whipped topping and fresh
  mint, optional

In a medium bowl, combine milk and juice; let stand for a few minutes. Stir in whipped topping. Add food coloring if desired. Spoon into crust. Chill until firm. Garnish with whipped topping and mint if desired. **Yield:** 6 servings.

Oatmeal Pie

3/4 cup old-fashioned oats
1/2 cup sugar
1/2 cup flaked coconut
1/2 cup corn syrup
1/2 cup butter, melted

2 eggs, well beaten
1 teaspoon vanilla extract
1 unbaked pastry shell (9 inches)
1 package (3 ounces) pecan
  halves

In a large bowl, combine the oats, sugar, coconut, corn syrup, butter, eggs and vanilla. Pour into crust. Bake at 350° for 15-20 minutes. Arrange pecans on top of pie; bake 30 minutes longer or until well browned. **Yield:** 8 servings.

Sweet Cherry Pie

1-1/4 cups all-purpose flour
1/2 teaspoon salt
1/3 cup shortening
4 to 5 tablespoons cold water
1/4 cup sugar

2 tablespoons cornstarch
1 can (15 ounces) pitted dark
  sweet cherries
1-1/2 teaspoons lemon juice
Dash almond extract
1 tablespoon butter

In a bowl, combine flour and salt; cut in shortening until crumbly. Gradually add water, tossing with a fork until a ball forms. Divide dough in half so that one ball is slightly larger than the other. Roll out larger ball to fit a 7-in. pie plate. Transfer pastry to pie plate. Trim pastry even with edge.

For filling, combine sugar with cornstarch in a microwave-safe bowl. Drain cherries and reserve 2 tablespoons juice. Stir in cherries; reserved juice and lemon juice. Microwave on high for 2-3 minutes until mixture comes to a boil and is thickened, stirring occasionally. Stir in almond extract. Pour into crust. Dot with butter.

Roll out remaining pastry to fit top of pie. Place over filling. Flute edges. Cut slits in pastry.

Bake at 400° for 15 minutes. Reduce heat to 350° and bake 25-30 minutes longer or until golden brown. Cool on a wire rack. **Yield:** 4 servings.

Crustless Pear Pie

4 cups sliced peeled pears
1/2 cup sugar
1 tablespoon cornstarch
1/4 teaspoon ground cinnamon
1/4 teaspoon ground ginger
1/4 teaspoon ground nutmeg

2 tablespoons chopped almonds
3/4 cup all-purpose flour
1/3 cup packed brown sugar
1/2 teaspoon baking powder
1/8 teaspoon salt
1/4 cup cold butter

In a bowl, combine the pears, sugar, cornstarch, cinnamon, ginger and nutmeg; toss to coat. Transfer to a 9-in. pie plate coated with nonstick cooking spray. Sprinkle with almonds.

In a bowl, combine the flour, brown sugar, baking powder and salt; cut in butter until crumbly. Sprinkle over the top.

Bake at 350° for 40-45 minutes or until golden. Cool on a wire rack. Store in the refrigerator. **Yield:** 8 servings.

Coconut Pineapple Pie

2-1/4 cups flaked coconut, *divided*
2 tablespoons butter, melted
1 can (20 ounces) crushed pineapple, undrained
32 large marshmallows

2 teaspoons rum *or* vanilla extract
1/4 teaspoon salt
1 cup heavy whipping cream, whipped

In a bowl, combine 2 cups coconut and butter. Press into the bottom and up the sides of a greased 9-in. pie plate. Bake at 325° for 8-10 minutes or until golden brown. Cool on a wire rack. Toast the remaining coconut; set aside.

Drain pineapple, reserving 1/2 cup juice (discard remaining juice or refrigerate for another use); set pineapple aside. In a saucepan, combine marshmallows and reserved juice. Cook and stir over medium heat until marshmallows are melted. Remove from the heat. Add the pineapple, extract and salt; mix well. Refrigerate for 2 hours or until cool.

Fold in the whipped cream; spoon into prepared crust. Sprinkle with toasted coconut. Cover and refrigerate for 2 hours or until set. Refrigerate leftovers. **Yield:** 8 servings.

Fresh Blueberry Tarts

1 package (8 ounces) cream cheese, softened
1/4 cup packed light brown sugar
1 package (6 count) individual graham cracker tart shells

2 cups fresh blueberries, *divided*
3 tablespoons sugar
1 teaspoon fresh lemon juice
1 teaspoon grated lemon peel

In bowl, beat cream cheese and brown sugar until smooth. Spread in tart shells. In a bowl, mash 3 tablespoons blueberries with sugar, lemon juice and peel. Add remaining berries and toss. Spoon into tarts. Chill for 1 hour. **Yield:** 6 servings.

Apple Graham Pie

2 cups graham cracker crumbs
3/4 cup sugar, *divided*
1/2 cup butter, melted

4 cups sliced peeled tart apples (about 4 medium)
1 teaspoon ground cinnamon

In a bowl, combine the cracker crumbs, 1/4 cup sugar and butter until crumbly; press two-thirds onto the bottom and up the sides of an ungreased 9-in. microwave-safe pie plate. Set remaining crumb mixture aside.

In a bowl, toss apples with cinnamon and remaining sugar. Arrange in crust; sprinkle with reserved crumbs. Microwave, uncovered, on high for 6 minutes; rotate. Cook 5-6 minutes longer or until apples are tender. Cool on a wire rack. Store in the refrigerator. **Yield:** 6-8 servings.

Editor's Note: This recipe was tested in a 1,100-watt microwave.

Peanut Butter Pie

3/4 cup confectioners' sugar
1/2 cup creamy peanut butter
1 pastry shell (9 inches), baked and cooled
2/3 cup plus 3 tablespoons sugar, *divided*
1/3 cup plus 1 tablespoon cornstarch, *divided*

2-1/2 cups milk
3 eggs, *separated*
2 tablespoons butter
1 teaspoon vanilla extract
1/2 cup water

Place confectioners' sugar in a bowl. Cut in the peanut butter with a pastry blender until crumbly. Set aside 2 tablespoons for garnish. Sprinkle remaining crumbs into the pie shell.

In a saucepan, combine 2/3 cup sugar and 1/3 cup cornstarch. Stir in milk until smooth. Cook and stir over medium-high heat until thickened and bubbly. Reduce heat; cook and stir 2 minutes longer. Remove from the heat. Stir a small amount of hot filling into egg yolks; return all to pan, stirring constantly. Bring to a gentle boil; cook and stir 2 minutes longer. Remove from the heat. Gently stir in butter and vanilla. Pour into pie shell.

In a small saucepan, combine remaining sugar and cornstarch with water; cook over low heat until thickened. Cool slightly. Beat egg whites until stiff; fold in cornstarch mixture. Spread meringue over the hot filling, sealing to edges. Sprinkle reserved peanut butter mixture over top. Bake at 350° for 12-15 minutes or until golden brown. **Yield:** 8 servings.

Bumbleberry Pie

1-1/2 cups all-purpose flour
1 teaspoon salt
1 teaspoon sugar
1 cup cold butter
1/4 cup cold water

FILLING:
1 medium tart apple, peeled and diced
1 cup diced fresh *or* frozen rhubarb, thawed
1 cup fresh *or* frozen raspberries, thawed and drained
1 cup fresh *or* frozen blueberries, thawed and drained
1 cup sliced fresh *or* frozen strawberries, thawed and drained
1 cup sugar
1/2 cup all-purpose flour
1 tablespoon lemon juice
Heavy whipping cream, optional
Coarse sugar, optional

In a bowl, combine the flour, salt and sugar. Cut in butter until mixture resembles coarse crumbs. Gradually add water, tossing with a fork until a ball forms. Cover and refrigerate for 1 hour.

On a lightly floured surface, roll out half of the dough to fit a 9-in. pie plate. Transfer pastry to pie plate. Trim pastry to within 1 in. beyond edge of plate.

In a large bowl, combine the filling ingredients; pour into crust. Roll out the remaining pastry; make a lattice crust. Seal and flute edges. If desired, brush with cream and sprinkle with coarse sugar. Cover edges loosely with foil.

Bake at 400° for 20 minutes. Reduce heat to 350°; remove foil. Bake 40-45 minutes longer or until crust is golden brown and filling is bubbly. Cool on a wire rack. **Yield:** 6-8 servings.

Sour Cream Rhubarb Pie

4 cups cubed rhubarb
1 unbaked pastry shell (10 inches)
2 eggs
1-1/2 cups sugar
1 cup (8 ounces) sour cream
3 tablespoons quick-cooking tapioca
Ground cinnamon

Place rhubarb in pie shell. In a bowl, beat eggs. Add the sugar, sour cream and tapioca. Pour over rhubarb; let stand for 15 minutes. Sprinkle with cinnamon.

Bake at 400° for 15 minutes. Reduce heat to 350° and bake 30 minutes longer. Cool on a wire rack. Store in the refrigerator. **Yield:** 8-10 servings.

Cinnamon Chocolate Angel Pie

2 egg whites
1/2 teaspoon white vinegar
1/2 cup sugar
1/8 to 1/4 teaspoon ground
cinnamon
1 pastry shell (9 inches), baked

FILLING:
2 egg yolks
1/4 cup water
1 cup (6 ounces) semisweet
chocolate chips
1 cup heavy whipping cream
1/4 cup sugar
1/4 teaspoon ground cinnamon

In a mixing bowl, beat egg whites and vinegar on medium speed until foamy. Combine sugar and cinnamon; gradually beat into egg whites, 1 tablespoon at a time, on high until stiff peaks form. Spread into the pastry shell. Bake at 325° for 20-25 minutes or until meringue is lightly browned. Cool.

For filling, whisk egg yolks and water in a saucepan. Add chocolate chips; cook and stir over low heat until a thermometer reads 160° and mixture is thickened (do not boil). Cool. Spread 3 tablespoons over meringue; set remainder aside.

In a mixing bowl, beat the cream until it begins to thicken. Add sugar and cinnamon; beat until stiff peaks form. Spread half over the chocolate layer. Fold reserved chocolate mixture into remaining whipped cream; spread over top. Cover and chill for 6 hours or overnight. Refrigerate any leftovers. **Yield:** 8-10 servings.

Banana Cream Pie

1 cup cold milk
1 cup (8 ounces) sour cream
1 package (3.4 ounces) instant
vanilla pudding mix

1 pastry shell (9 inches), baked
3 medium firm bananas, cut into
1/2-inch slices
1 carton (8 ounces) frozen
whipped topping, thawed

In a large mixing bowl, beat the milk, sour cream and pudding mix until smooth. Place a third of the banana slices into pastry shell. Top with half of the pudding mixture. Repeat layers.

Arrange the remaining bananas on top; cover with whipped topping. Cover and chill for at least 2 hours. **Yield:** 6-8 servings.

Rhubarb Apple Pie

2 cups sliced fresh *or* frozen rhubarb, thawed

1 can (21 ounces) apple pie filling

1/4 cup sugar

1/4 teaspoon ground cinnamon

1/4 teaspoon ground nutmeg

Pastry for double-crust pie (9 inches)

1/4 cup butter

TOPPING:

1 tablespoon sugar

1/4 teaspoon ground cinnamon

Water

In a bowl, combine the first five ingredients. Line a 9-in. pie plate with bottom pastry; trim to 1 in. beyond edge of plate. Add filling; dot with butter. Roll out remaining pastry dough. Place over filling. Trim, seal and flute edges. Cut slits in top.

Combine sugar and cinnamon. Brush crust with water; sprinkle with cinnamon-sugar. Cover edges loosely with foil.

Bake at 400° for 20 minutes. Remove foil. Reduce heat to 350° and bake 15 minutes longer or until crust is golden brown. Cool on a wire rack. Store in the refrigerator. **Yield:** 6-8 servings.

Blueberry Cream Pie

1/2 cup sugar

1/2 cup packed brown sugar

3 tablespoons plus 1-1/2 teaspoons all-purpose flour

1/4 teaspoon salt

1/4 teaspoon ground nutmeg

4 cups fresh *or* frozen blueberries, thawed, *divided*

1 tablespoon butter

1 tablespoon lemon juice

1 pastry shell (9 inches), baked

TOPPING:

2 cups whipped topping

1 tablespoon sugar

1/2 teaspoon vanilla extract

In a saucepan, combine the sugars, flour, salt and nutmeg. Add 2 cups blueberries. Bring to a boil over medium-low heat, stirring constantly. Cook and stir for 2 minutes or until thickened. Remove from the heat; gently stir in butter and lemon juice. Refrigerate for 15 minutes. Stir in remaining berries.

Pour into pastry shell. Refrigerate for 3 hours or until set. Combine topping ingredients; serve with pie. Refrigerate leftovers. **Yield:** 6-8 servings.

Old-Time Buttermilk Pie

CRUST:
1-1/2 cups all-purpose flour
1 teaspoon salt
1/2 cup shortening
1/4 cup cold milk
1 egg, beaten

FILLING:
1/2 cup butter, softened
2 cups sugar
3 tablespoons all-purpose flour
3 eggs
1 cup buttermilk
1 teaspoon vanilla extract
1 teaspoon ground cinnamon
1/4 cup lemon juice

In a bowl, combine flour and salt; cut in shortening until crumbly. Gradually add milk and egg, tossing with a fork until dough forms a ball blend well. On a floured surface, roll dough out very thin. Place in a 10-in. pie pan; set aside.

For filling, in a mixing bowl, cream butter and sugar. Add flour. Add eggs, one at a time, beating well after each addition. Stir in remaining ingredients and mix well. Pour into crust.

Bake at 350° for 45 minutes. Cool pie completely before serving. Store in the refrigerator. **Yield:** 8-10 servings.

Peach Praline Pie

4 cups sliced peeled ripe peaches (about 3 pounds)
1/2 cup sugar
2 tablespoons quick-cooking tapioca
1 teaspoon lemon juice

1/2 cup all-purpose flour
1/4 cup packed brown sugar
1/2 cup chopped pecans
1/4 cup butter
1 unbaked deep-dish pie shell (9 inches)

In a large bowl, combine the peaches, sugar, tapioca and lemon juice; let stand for 15 minutes.

Meanwhile, combine the flour, brown sugar and pecans in a small bowl; cut in butter until crumbly. Sprinkle 1/3 of crumbs over bottom of pie shell; cover with peach mixture. Sprinkle remaining crumbs on top, allowing peaches to show if desired.

Bake at 450° for 10 minutes. Reduce heat to 350° and bake 20 minutes longer or until peaches are tender and topping is golden brown. **Yield:** 8-10 servings.

German Chocolate Pie

1 package (4 ounces) German sweet chocolate

1/4 cup butter

1 can (12 ounces) evaporated milk

1-1/2 cups sugar

3 tablespoons cornstarch

1/8 teaspoon salt

2 eggs

1 teaspoon vanilla extract

1 unbaked deep-dish pastry shell (9 inches)

1-1/2 cups coconut

1 cup pecans, chopped

In a saucepan, melt chocolate and butter over low heat; stir until smooth. Remove from the heat and blend in milk; set aside.

In a mixing bowl, combine the sugar, cornstarch and salt. Beat in eggs and vanilla. Blend in melted chocolate; pour into pie shell. Combine coconut and pecans; sprinkle on top of pie.

Bake at 375° for 45 minutes. Cool on a wire rack. Store in the refrigerator. **Yield:** 8-10 servings.

Pink Velvet Company Pie

1 can (12 ounces) evaporated milk

2-1/2 cups graham cracker crumbs (about 32 squares)

1/4 cup butter, melted

1 package (3 ounces) strawberry gelatin

1/2 cup boiling water

1/4 cup lemon juice

1/4 cup sugar

1 teaspoon grated lemon peel

Pour milk into a large mixing bowl; place mixer beaters in the bowl. Cover and refrigerate for at least 2 hours.

In a small bowl, combine cracker crumbs and butter. Set aside 1/4 cup for topping. Press remaining crumb mixture onto the bottom and 1 in. up the sides of a greased 9-in. springform pan. Set aside.

In a bowl, dissolve gelatin in boiling water; stir in lemon juice and sugar. Cool to room temperature. Remove mixing bowl from refrigerator; beat milk until soft peaks form. Gradually add gelatin mixture, beating until stiff peaks form. Fold in lemon peel. Spoon into crust; sprinkle with reserved crumbs. Chill for at least 4 hours or until set.

Carefully run a knife around edge of pan to loosen. Remove sides of pan. Refrigerate leftovers. **Yield:** 10-12 servings.

Prize-Winning Apple Pie

CRUST:
- 2 cups all-purpose flour
- 1 teaspoon salt
- 1/2 teaspoon baking powder
- 2/3 cup butter-flavored shortening
- 1 tablespoon vegetable oil
- 4 to 5 tablespoons milk

FILLING:
- 1 cup sugar
- 4 tablespoons cornstarch
- 3/8 teaspoon ground nutmeg
- 3/8 teaspoon ground cinnamon
- Dash salt
- 4-1/2 cups thinly sliced, pared tart apples (Jonathans work well)
- 1 tablespoon water
- 2 tablespoons butter

In a large bowl, combine the flour, salt and baking powder; cut in shortening until mixture is crumbly. Sprinkle in oil, then milk, 1 tablespoon at a time, tossing with a fork until dough forms a ball. Divide dough in half so that one ball is slightly larger than the other. Roll out larger ball to fit a 9-in. pie plate. Transfer pastry to pie plate. Trim pastry even with edge.

In a bowl, combine the sugar, cornstarch, nutmeg, cinnamon and salt; mix with apples and water. Spoon filling into crust; dot with butter. Roll out remaining pastry to fit top of pie. Place over filling. Trim, seal and flute edges. Cut slits in pastry. Cover edge with aluminum foil to prevent over-browning.

Bake at 425° for 25 minutes. Remove foil; bake 15 minutes longer. Cool on a wire rack. **Yield:** 8 servings.

Mock Pecan Pie

- 2 cups packed brown sugar
- 1/2 cup butter, melted
- 4 eggs, beaten
- 1 tablespoon vanilla extract
- 1 cup cooked pinto beans, mashed
- 1 unbaked pastry shell (10 inches)
- Whipped cream *or* vanilla ice cream

In a mixing bowl, beat together the sugar, butter, eggs and vanilla. Stir in beans. Pour into pastry shell.

Bake at 350° for 45-50 minutes or until a knife inserted in the center comes out clean. Serve warm or chilled with whipped cream or ice cream. **Yield:** 8-10 servings.

Banana Fudge Pie

1/2 cup miniature semisweet
  chocolate chips, melted
3 cups frozen whipped topping,
  thawed, *divided*
2 eggs

1/4 cup sugar
1 unbaked pastry shell (9 inches)
2 bananas, sliced
Additional miniature chocolate chips
  for garnish, optional

In a large mixing bowl, combine the melted chocolate, 1 cup whipped topping, eggs and sugar. Pour into pastry shell. Bake at 350° for 30 minutes. Cool for 10 minutes, then refrigerate for 1 hour.

Layer sliced bananas over pie and top with remaining whipped topping. Sprinkle miniature chocolate chips on top if desired. Chill until serving. **Yield:** 8 servings.

Orange Meringue Pie

1-1/2 cups sugar
1/4 cup plus 2 tablespoons
  cornstarch
1/4 teaspoon salt
3 cups orange juice
4 egg yolks, well beaten
1/4 cup plus 2 tablespoons lemon
  juice

3 tablespoons butter
1-1/2 teaspoons grated orange peel
1 pastry shell (9 inches), baked

MERINGUE:
4 egg whites
1/4 teaspoon cream of tartar
1/2 cup sugar

In a large saucepan, combine the sugar, cornstarch and salt. Stir in orange juice until smooth. Cook and stir over medium-high heat until thickened and bubbly. Reduce heat; cook and stir 2 minutes longer. Remove from the heat. Stir a small amount of hot filling into egg yolks; return all to pan, stirring constantly. Bring to a gentle boil; cook and stir 2 minutes longer. Remove from the heat. Gently stir in lemon juice, butter and orange peel. Pour hot filling into pie shell.

Meanwhile, for meringue, in a small mixing bowl, beat egg whites and cream of tartar on medium speed until soft peaks form. Gradually beat in sugar, 1 tablespoon at a time, on high until stiff peaks form. Spread over hot filling, sealing edges to crust. Swirl meringue into center of pie.

Bake at 350° for 12-15 minutes or until golden brown. Cool on a wire rack for 1 hour; refrigerate for 1-2 hours before serving. Refrigerate leftovers. **Yield:** 8 servings.

Chocolate Shoofly Pie

1-1/3 cups boiling water
1 can (16 ounces) chocolate syrup
1 teaspoon baking soda, *divided*
1-1/2 cups all-purpose flour
1/2 cup sugar
1/3 cup butter, softened
1 unbaked deep-dish pie crust (9 inches)

In a small bowl, stir together water, chocolate syrup and 1/4 teaspoon baking soda; set aside. In a large mixing bowl, blend the flour, sugar, butter and remaining baking soda; reserve 1 cup for topping.

Place pie crust on a baking sheet. Pour 1 cup of chocolate syrup mixture into shell; gently combine rest of chocolate syrup mixture with remaining crumb mixture and add to pie crust. Sprinkle reserved crumbs on top.

Bake at 375° for 50-60 minutes or until a toothpick comes out clean. **Yield:** 8 servings.

Cranberry-Apple Mincemeat Pies

4 cups fresh *or* frozen cranberries, thawed
4 cups chopped peeled tart apples
1-1/2 cups chopped dried apricots
1-1/2 cups golden raisins
1 medium unpeeled navel orange, finely chopped
1/4 cup *each* red and green candied cherries
2-3/4 cups sugar
1 cup apple juice
1/4 cup orange marmalade
1 teaspoon ground ginger
3/4 teaspoon *each* ground allspice, cinnamon and nutmeg
1/4 cup butter
Pastry for double-crust pie (9 inches)

In a Dutch oven or large kettle, combine the fruit, sugar, apple juice, marmalade and spices. Bring to a boil over medium heat. Reduce heat; simmer, uncovered, for 50-60 minutes, stirring occasionally. Remove from the heat; gently stir in butter. Cool completely or refrigerate for up to 1 week.

Line two 9-in. pie plates with pastry; trim and flute edges. Divide filling between crusts. Cover edges loosely with foil. Bake at 400° for 20 minutes. Remove foil.

Bake 20-25 minutes longer or until crust is golden brown and filling is bubbly. Cool on wire racks. **Yield:** 2 pies (6-8 servings each).

Bride's Peach Pie

Pastry for a double-crust pie
  (9 inches)
    5 cups sliced peeled peaches
    1 tablespoon lemon juice
    1/2 cup sugar
    1/4 cup packed brown sugar

    3 tablespoons all-purpose flour
    1/4 teaspoon ground nutmeg
    1/8 teaspoon salt
    1/2 teaspoon almond extract
    2 tablespoons butter, cubed

Line a 9-in. pie plate with bottom crust; trim pastry even with edge and set aside. In a bowl, toss peaches with lemon juice. Combine the sugars, flour, nutmeg and salt; add to peaches and toss. Sprinkle with almond extract; toss gently.

Transfer to prepared crust; dot with butter. Roll out remaining pastry to fit top of pie; place over filling. Cut slits in pastry. Trim, seal and flute edges. Cover edges loosely with foil.

Bake at 425° for 15 minutes. Reduce heat to 350°; remove foil and bake for 45-50 minutes longer or until crust is golden brown and filling is bubbly. Cool on a wire rack. **Yield:** 6-8 servings.

Walnut-Crunch Pumpkin Pie

    2 eggs
    1 can (15 ounces) solid-pack
      pumpkin
    1 can (12 ounces) evaporated
      milk
    3/4 cup packed brown sugar
    2 teaspoons vanilla extract
1-1/2 teaspoons ground cinnamon

    1/2 teaspoon salt
    1/2 teaspoon ground ginger
    1/2 teaspoon ground nutmeg
    1 unbaked pastry shell (9 inches)

TOPPING:
    1 cup chopped walnuts
    3/4 cup packed brown sugar
    1/4 cup butter, melted

In a mixing bowl, beat eggs. Add the pumpkin, milk, brown sugar, vanilla, cinnamon, salt, ginger and nutmeg; mix well. Pour into pastry shell.

Cover edges loosely with foil. Bake at 425° for 15 minutes. Reduce heat to 350°. Remove foil; bake 35-40 minutes longer or until set and a knife inserted near the center comes out clean. Cool on a wire rack for 2 hours.

Combine the topping ingredients; sprinkle over pie. Cover edges loosely with foil. Broil 3-4 in. from the heat for about 2 minutes or until golden brown. Remove foil. Store in the refrigerator. **Yield:** 6-8 servings.

Fudge Pecan Brownie Tart

PASTRY:
- 1 cup all-purpose flour
- 1/4 cup packed light brown sugar
- 1/4 cup finely chopped pecans
- 1/2 cup cold butter
- 2 tablespoons milk
- 1 teaspoon vanilla extract

BROWNIE FILLING:
- 3 squares (1 ounce *each*) unsweetened chocolate
- 1/2 cup chocolate chips
- 1/2 cup butter, cut into pieces
- 1-1/2 cups sugar
- 3 eggs
- 2 teaspoons vanilla extract
- 3/4 cup all-purpose flour
- 1 cup chopped pecans

FUDGE FROSTING:
- 1-1/2 squares (1-1/2 ounces) unsweetened chocolate
- 2/3 cup sweetened condensed milk
- 1/4 cup butter
- 1/2 teaspoon vanilla extract
- Whipped cream and whole pecans for garnish, optional

In a large bowl, combine flour, brown sugar and nuts; cut in butter until mixture resembles coarse crumbs. Mix in milk and vanilla with a fork just until blended. Pat onto bottom and up the sides of an 11-in. tart pan; set aside.

For filling, in a microwave or heavy saucepan, melt chocolate squares and chips; stir until smooth. Stir in butter. Transfer to a large bowl and stir in with sugar. Add eggs and vanilla; blend well. Gradually add flour, stirring well after each addition. Add nuts. Pour over pastry.

Bake at 350° for 30-35 minutes, or until center is just set and toothpick comes out clean. Cool on wire rack.

Meanwhile, for frosting, in a small heavy saucepan, melt chocolate over low heat. Add the milk and butter. Heat for 5 minutes or until smooth and thick, stirring constantly. Remove from the heat; stir in vanilla. Spread over tart. Garnish with whipped cream and pecans if desired. **Yield:** 10-12 servings.

Cakes

Fresh Apple Cake With Caramel Sauce

1/2 cup butter, softened
3/4 cup sugar
1 egg
1 cup all-purpose flour
1/2 teaspoon baking soda
1/2 teaspoon ground nutmeg
1/2 teaspoon ground cinnamon
2 cups chopped peeled baking apples
1/2 cup chopped walnuts

CARAMEL SAUCE:
1/2 cup packed brown sugar
2 tablespoons cornstarch
1/2 cup light corn syrup
1/4 cup half-and-half cream *or* evaporated milk
1/4 cup butter
1/4 teaspoon salt
1 egg, beaten

In a mixing bowl, cream butter and sugar. Beat in the egg. Combine the flour, baking soda, nutmeg and cinnamon; add to creamed mixture and mix well. Stir in apples and walnuts. Transfer to a greased 8-in. square baking dish.

Bake at 350° for 30-35 minutes or until a toothpick inserted near the center comes out clean. Cool on a wire rack.

Meanwhile, for caramel sauce, blend brown sugar and cornstarch in a saucepan. Add remaining ingredients; cook and stir until thickened, about 3 minutes. Serve cake warm or cold with warm caramel sauce.
Yield: 9 servings.

Strawberry Chiffon Cake

1 cup all-purpose flour
3/4 cup sugar
1-1/2 teaspoons baking powder
1/2 teaspoon salt
1/4 cup vegetable oil
3 eggs, *separated*

1/3 cup orange juice
1/4 teaspoon cream of tartar
1-1/2 to 2 quarts fresh strawberries, sliced
Vanilla ice cream
Whipped cream

Sift together the flour, sugar, baking powder and salt. Place in a large bowl and make a well in the center. Add oil, egg yolks and orange juice; beat with a spoon until smooth.

In a mixing bowl, beat egg whites and cream of tartar until stiff peaks form. Gradually add to batter, folding gently until blended. Pour into an ungreased 9-in. x 5-in. x 3-in. loaf pan.

Bake at 325° for 50-55 minutes or until top springs back when lightly touched. Invert immediately on a wire rack, but keep in pan. When cool, remove cake from pan and slice into 12 pieces. Top each slice with berries, ice cream and whipped cream. **Yield:** 12 servings.

Snowball Cake

2 tablespoons unflavored gelatin
1/4 cup cold water
1 cup boiling water
1 cup sugar
1 tablespoon lemon juice
1 can (20 ounces) crushed pineapple, drained

1 carton (16 ounces) frozen whipped topping, thawed, *divided*
1 prepared angel food cake (8 inches), cut into cubes
1-1/2 cups flaked coconut

In a bowl, sprinkle gelatin over cold water; let stand for 1 minute. Add boiling water; stir until gelatin is dissolved. Stir in sugar and lemon juice until sugar is dissolved. Add pineapple. Refrigerate until partially thickened, about 20 minutes. Fold in 4 cups whipped topping.

Line a 3-qt. round bowl with plastic wrap. Spoon about 2 cups pineapple mixture into bowl. Layer with half of the cake cubes and half of the remaining pineapple mixture. Repeat layers. Refrigerate for at least 4 hours.

Unmold onto a serving plate. Spread remaining whipped topping over dessert. Sprinkle with coconut. **Yield:** 16 servings.

Quick Graham Cracker Cake

1-1/4 cups graham cracker crumbs,
 divided
 1 package (18-1/4 ounces) white
  cake mix
 2 tablespoons sugar
1-1/2 cups water

2 egg whites
4 tablespoons vegetable oil
1 pint whipping cream, whipped
 or 1 carton (12 ounces) frozen
 whipped topping, thawed

Set aside 2 tablespoons graham cracker crumbs. In a large mixing bowl, combine the remaining crumbs, cake mix, sugar, water, egg whites and oil; beat for 2 minutes. Pour into two greased and floured 9-in. round baking pans.

 Bake at 350° for 25-30 minutes or until a toothpick inserted near the center comes out clean. Cool for 10 minutes before removing from pans to wire racks to cool completely.

 Split each cake in half horizontally. Spread whipped cream between layers and frost entire cake. Sprinkle reserved graham cracker crumbs on top. Refrigerate until serving time. **Yield:** 16-20 servings.

Surprise-Inside Cupcakes

 2 cups sugar
 3 cups all-purpose flour
1/2 cup baking cocoa
 2 teaspoons baking soda
 2 cups water
2/3 cup vegetable oil
 2 tablespoons white vinegar
 2 teaspoons vanilla extract

FILLING:
 1 package (8 ounces) cream
  cheese, softened
1/3 cup sugar
 1 egg
Dash salt

In a large mixing bowl, combine all the cake ingredients and blend well. Fill paper-lined muffin cups two-thirds full.

 For filling, cream all ingredients in a small mixing bowl. Drop a teaspoonful of filling into each cupcake.

 Bake at 350° for 20 minutes or until a toothpick inserted in the cupcake, not filling, comes out clean. Cool for 10 minutes before removing from the pans to wire racks to cool completely. Store in the refrigerator. **Yield:** 2 dozen.

Fresh Coconut Pound Cake

1 cup butter, softened
3 cups sugar
6 eggs
1 teaspoon vanilla extract
1 teaspoon coconut extract
3 cups all-purpose flour
1/4 teaspoon baking soda
1/4 teaspoon salt
1 carton (8 ounces) sour cream

1 cup fresh *or* frozen, thawed coconut

ICING:
1/2 cup vegetable shortening
4 cups confectioners' sugar
1/4 cup water
1 teaspoon vanilla extract (preferably clear)
1/8 teaspoon salt

In a large mixing bowl, cream butter, gradually adding sugar; beat until mixture is light and fluffy. Add eggs, one at a time, beating well after each addition. Beat in extracts.

Combine the flour, baking soda and salt; add to creamed mixture alternately with sour cream, beginning and ending with flour mixture. Stir in the coconut. Pour batter into greased and floured 10-in. tube pan.

Bake at 350° for 1 hour and 20 minutes, or until a toothpick inserted in center comes out clean. Cool for 10-15 minutes before removing from pan to a wire rack to cool completely.

To make icing, combine all ingredients in large mixing bowl. Beat until fluffy. Frost top and sides. **Yield:** 16 servings.

Banana Upside-Down Cake

1/4 cup butter
1/2 cup packed brown sugar
3 medium firm bananas, cut into 1/2-inch slices

1 package (9 ounces) yellow cake mix
Whipped cream

Place butter in a 9-in. square baking pan. Heat at 350° for 4-5 minutes or until melted; sprinkle with brown sugar. Arrange bananas in pan; set aside. Prepare cake mix according to package directions; pour over bananas.

Bake at 350° for 30-35 minutes or until a toothpick inserted near the center comes out clean. Immediately invert cake onto a serving platter. Let stand for 5 minutes before removing pan. Serve warm with whipped cream. **Yield:** 9 servings.

Root Beer Float Cake

1 package (18-1/4 ounces) white cake mix

1-1/4 cups root beer

2 eggs

1/4 cup vegetable oil

FROSTING:

1 envelope whipped topping mix

1/2 cup chilled root beer

In a mixing bowl, combine the first four ingredients. Beat on low speed for 30 seconds; beat on high for 2 minutes. Pour into a greased 13-in. x 9-in. x 2-in. baking pan.

Bake at 350° for 35-40 minutes or until a toothpick inserted near the center comes out clean. Cool completely on a wire rack.

In another mixing bowl, beat frosting ingredients until stiff peaks form. Frost cake. Store in the refrigerator. **Yield:** 12-15 servings.

Sauerkraut Brownie Cake

1/2 cup butter

3 squares (1 ounce *each*) unsweetened chocolate

1-1/4 cups sugar

1 teaspoon vanilla extract

3 eggs

1 cup all-purpose flour

1 teaspoon baking powder

1/2 teaspoon salt

2/3 cup sauerkraut, rinsed, drained and finely chopped

1/2 cup chopped walnuts

CHOCOLATE GLAZE:

1/2 cup packed brown sugar

1/4 cup butter

2 to 3 tablespoons milk

1 square (1 ounce) unsweetened chocolate

1/2 cup chopped walnuts

1/2 cup confectioners' sugar

1/2 teaspoon vanilla extract

In a small saucepan, melt butter and chocolate over low heat, stirring until smooth. Remove from the heat; place chocolate mixture in a large mixing bowl along with sugar, vanilla and eggs. Beat well. Combine dry ingredients; stir in to batter until well blended. Stir in sauerkraut and nuts. Spread into a greased 9-in. square baking pan.

Bake at 350° for 30 minutes or until a toothpick inserted near the center comes out clean. Cool completely on a wire rack.

For glaze, bring first four ingredients to boil in a heavy saucepan. Boil for 3 minutes; do not stir. Remove from the heat; immediately stir in the nuts, sugar and vanilla. Pour hot glaze onto center of cooled cake and spread to edges. Cool before cutting. **Yield:** 9 servings.

Cherry Pineapple Cake

2 cans (16 ounces *each*) pitted
tart red cherries, drained
1 can (20 ounces) crushed
pineapple in syrup, undrained
1/3 cup finely chopped walnuts

1 package (18-1/4 ounces) white
cake mix
1/2 cup butter, melted
Whipped cream, optional

Spread cherries and pineapple with juice over bottom of an ungreased
13-in. x 9-in. x 2-in. baking dish. Top with nuts. Sprinkle dry cake mix
over all. Pour butter evenly over cake mix.

Bake at 350° for 1 hour. Cool. Invert onto a serving plate. Cut into
squares. Top with whipped cream if desired. **Yield:** 12-15 servings.

Apple Kuchen

6 large tart apples, peeled, cored
and sliced
2 teaspoons ground cinnamon
1 cup sugar, *divided*
1 tablespoon butter, softened
1/2 cup milk
1 cup all-purpose flour
1 teaspoon baking powder

VANILLA SAUCE:
1 cup sugar
2 tablespoons cornstarch
1/2 teaspoon salt
2 cups cold water
2 tablespoons butter
1 teaspoon vanilla extract

Arrange apples in a 13-in. x 9-in. x 2-in. baking pan. Combine cinnamon
and 1/2 cup sugar. Reserve 1 tablespoon; sprinkle remaining mixture
over apples.

In a mixing bowl, combine the butter, milk, flour, baking powder and
remaining sugar. Drop by tablespoonfuls over apples; sprinkle reserved
cinnamon-sugar over top. Bake at 350° for 35-40 minute or until golden
brown.

Meanwhile, for sauce, combine the sugar, cornstarch, salt and water
in a saucepan until smooth. Bring to a boil over medium heat; cook and
stir for 2 minutes or until thickened. Remove from the heat; stir in
butter and vanilla. Serve sauce and kuchen warm. **Yield:** 10-12 servings.

Danish Christmas Cake

1 package (18-1/4 ounces) yellow
   cake mix
2 cups cold milk
1 package (3 ounces) instant
   vanilla pudding mix

1 package (11-1/2 ounces)
   macaroons, crushed
1 jar (10 ounces) currant jelly
1 cup heavy whipping cream
2 tablespoons sugar
1/2 teaspoon vanilla extract

Bake cake according to package directions, using two greased 9-in.
round baking pans. Cool for 10 minutes before removing from pans to
wire racks to cool completely.

In a bowl, whisk milk and pudding mix for 2 minutes. Let stand for 2
minutes or until soft-set. Stir in macaroons. Cut each cake horizontally
in half. Place one bottom layer on a serving plate; spread with half of
pudding mixture. Top with another cake layer; spread with jelly. Top
with another cake layer; spread with remaining pudding mixture. Top
with remaining cake layer.

In a small mixing bowl, beat cream until it begins to thicken. Add
sugar and vanilla; beat until stiff peaks form. Frost top and sides of
cake. Store in the refrigerator. **Yield:** 16-20 servings.

Eggless-Milkless-Butterless Cake

1 cup packed brown sugar
1 cup raisins
1 cup water
1/3 cup shortening
1 teaspoon ground cinnamon
1/2 teaspoon ground cloves

1/4 teaspoon ground nutmeg
2 cups all-purpose flour
1 teaspoon baking powder
1 teaspoon baking soda
1/2 teaspoon salt

In a heavy saucepan, combine first seven ingredients. Bring to a boil and
boil for 5 minutes. Cool. Place in a mixing bowl. Combine the flour,
baking powder, baking soda and salt; add to batter. Pour into a greased
9-in. x 5-in. x 3-in. loaf pan.

Bake at 350° for about 45 minutes or until a toothpick inserted near
the center comes out clean. Cool for 10 minutes before removing from
pan to a wire rack. **Yield:** 8-10 servings.

Zucchini Cake

3 cups all-purpose flour
3 cups sugar
2-1/2 teaspoons ground cinnamon
1-1/2 teaspoons baking soda
1 teaspoon salt
1-1/2 cups vegetable oil
4 eggs, lightly beaten
1 teaspoon vanilla extract

3 cups shredded zucchini
1 cup chopped walnuts

FROSTING:
1 package (8 ounces) cream cheese, softened
1/2 cup butter, softened
4 cups confectioners' sugar
1 teaspoon vanilla extract

In a mixing bowl, combine the flour, sugar, cinnamon, baking soda and salt. In a separate bowl, beat the oil, eggs and vanilla; add to flour mixture and beat well. Stir in zucchini and nuts. Pour into three well-greased 9-in. round baking pans.

Bake at 325° for 30-40 minutes or until toothpick inserted near the center comes out clean. Cool for 10 minutes before removing from pans to wire racks to cool completely.

For frosting, beat cream cheese and butter; blend in sugar and vanilla. Beat until smooth. Frost between layers and top and sides of cake. **Yield:** 10-12 servings.

Brown Sugar Pudding Cake

1 cup packed brown sugar
1 tablespoon all-purpose flour
2 tablespoons butter, melted
1/4 teaspoon salt
2 cups boiling water

PUDDING:
2 tablespoons butter, melted
1/2 cup packed brown sugar
1 cup all-purpose flour
1 teaspoon baking powder
1/2 teaspoon salt
1/2 cup milk
1/2 cup chopped nuts

In a bowl, combine the first five ingredients. Pour into a 1-1/2-qt. baking dish; set aside.

For pudding, in a mixing bowl, beat butter and sugar until blended. Combine the flour, baking powder and salt. Add to the sugar mixture alternately with milk. Stir in nuts. Spoon into baking dish. Bake at 350° for 40-45 minutes. Serve warm. **Yield:** 6-8 servings.

Raspberry-Filled Cake

1/4 cup butter, softened
1/2 cup sugar
1 egg
1/2 teaspoon vanilla extract
1 cup cake flour
1-1/2 teaspoons baking powder
1/4 teaspoon salt
1/3 cup milk

FILLING:
2 cups fresh raspberries, *divided*
1 tablespoon sugar
2-1/2 teaspoons cornstarch
1 teaspoon lemon juice
1/8 teaspoon vanilla extract
1/4 cup sour cream
1 cup whipped topping
Additional raspberries, optional

In a mixing bowl, cream butter and sugar. Beat in egg and vanilla. Combine the flour, baking powder and salt; add to creamed mixture alternately with milk. Pour into a greased and floured 9-in. round baking pan.

Bake at 350° for 20-25 minutes or until a toothpick inserted near the center comes out clean. Cool for 5 minutes before removing from the pan to a wire rack to cool completely.

Meanwhile, for filling, heat 1 cup raspberries in microwave for 30 seconds, then mash and measure 1/4 cup juice. Discard seeds.

In a small saucepan, combine sugar and cornstarch; gradually add raspberry juice until smooth. Bring to a boil; cook and stir for 1 minute or until thickened. Remove from the heat. Stir in lemon juice and vanilla; cool.

In a bowl, combine sour cream and whipped topping. Fold in cooled raspberry mixture and remaining berries. Cut cake horizontally in half. Place one layer on a serving plate. Spread with half of the filling. Top with remaining layer and filling. Garnish with additional berries if desired. Store in the refrigerator. **Yield:** 6 servings.

Picnic Cake

1/2 cup butter, softened
1-1/2 cups sugar
2 eggs
1 teaspoon vanilla extract
2-1/2 cups all-purpose flour
3 teaspoons baking powder
1/2 teaspoon salt
1 cup milk
10 large marshmallows, cut in half diagonally
1/2 cup packed brown sugar
1/2 cup chopped pecans

In a mixing bowl, cream butter and sugar. Add eggs, one at a time, beating well after each addition. Add vanilla; mix well. Combine the flour, baking powder and salt; add to creamed mixture alternately with milk.

Pour into a greased 13-in. x 9-in. x 2-in. baking pan. Place the marshmallows cut side up on batter; lightly press into batter. Sprinkle with brown sugar and nuts.

Bake at 350° for 38-40 minutes or until a toothpick inserted near the center comes out clean. Cool on a wire rack. **Yield:** 12-16 servings.

Angel Food Cake

1 cup cake flour
1-1/2 cups sugar, *divided*
1-1/4 cups egg whites (about 10 eggs)
1-1/4 teaspoons cream of tartar
1 teaspoon vanilla extract
1/4 teaspoon almond extract
1/4 teaspoon salt

In a bowl, combine cake flour and 1/2 cup sugar; set aside. In a mixing bowl, beat egg whites, cream of tartar, extracts and salt on medium speed until soft peaks form. Gradually beat in the remaining sugar, 1 tablespoon at a time, on high until stiff glossy peaks form and sugar is dissolved. Gently fold in reserved flour mixture, about 1/3 cup at a time.

Gently spoon into an ungreased 10-in. tube pan. Cut through the batter with a knife to remove air pockets. Bake on the lowest oven rack at 350° for 35-40 minutes or until lightly browned and entire top appears dry. Immediately invert pan; cool completely, about 1 hour.

Run a knife around side and center tube of pan. Remove cake to a serving plate. **Yield:** 12-16 servings.

Hot Fudge Pudding Cake

1 cup all-purpose flour
2/3 cup sugar
1/2 cup baking cocoa, *divided*
2 teaspoons baking powder
1/4 teaspoon salt
1/2 cup milk
1/4 cup vegetable oil
1 teaspoon vanilla extract
1/2 cup chopped pecans
3/4 cup packed brown sugar
1-1/4 cups hot water
Ice cream *or* whipped cream

In a large mixing bowl, combine the flour, sugar, 1/4 cup cocoa, baking powder and salt. Blend in the milk, oil and vanilla. Stir in nuts. Pour into a greased 9-in. square baking pan. Combine brown sugar and remaining cocoa; sprinkle evenly over batter. Pour hot water over top. Do not stir.

Bake at 350° for 45 minutes or until cake tests done. Cool for 10 minutes on a wire rack. Cut into squares and invert onto plates. Serve with ice cream or whipped cream. If cake is not served immediately, pieces can also be warmed in the microwave. **Yield:** 9 servings.

Chocolate Mayonnaise Cake

2 cups all-purpose flour
1 cup sugar
3 tablespoons baking cocoa
2 teaspoons baking soda
1 cup water
1 cup mayonnaise
1 teaspoon vanilla extract

BROWN SUGAR FROSTING:
1/4 cup butter
1/2 cup packed brown sugar
2 tablespoons milk
1-3/4 cups sifted confectioners' sugar

In a large mixing bowl, combine the flour, sugar, cocoa and baking soda. Add water, mayonnaise and vanilla; beat at medium speed until thoroughly combined.

Pour into a greased 9-in. square or an 11-in. x 7-in. x 2-in. baking pan. Bake at 350° for 30-35 minutes or until a toothpick inserted near the center comes out clean. Cool completely on a wire rack.

For frosting, melt butter in a saucepan. Stir in brown sugar; cook and stir until bubbly. Remove from the heat and stir in milk. Gradually add confectioners' sugar; beat by hand until frosting achieves spreading consistency. Immediately frost cake. **Yield:** 9-12 servings.

Pear Cake with Sour Cream Topping

1/2 cup butter, softened
1/2 cup sugar
3 eggs, lightly beaten
1 teaspoon grated lemon peel
1-3/4 cups all-purpose flour
2 teaspoons baking powder
1 teaspoon salt

1/2 cup milk
1 can (29 ounces) pear halves, drained

TOPPING:
1 cup (8 ounces) sour cream
2 tablespoons brown sugar
1 tablespoon grated lemon peel

In a mixing bowl, cream butter and sugar. Add eggs and lemon peel; mix well. Combine the flour, baking powder and salt; add to creamed mixture alternately with milk. Beat well.

Spread batter into a greased 13-in. x 9-in. x 2-in. baking pan. Slice pear halves and arrange in rows on top of batter. Combine the topping ingredients until smooth; spread over the pears. Bake at 350° for 30-35 minutes or until toothpick inserted near the center comes out clean. Cool on a wire rack. **Yield:** 12-16 servings.

Rice Pudding Cake

1/2 cup raisins
Boiling water
1 cup uncooked long grain rice
Water
1 quart milk
3/4 cup butter, softened

1 cup sugar
5 eggs, *separated*
2 tablespoons grated orange peel
2 tablespoons graham cracker crumbs
Confectioners' sugar

In a small bowl, cover raisins with boiling water. Let stand for 5 minutes; drain and set aside.

In a large saucepan, cover rice with water; bring to a boil. Drain the liquid; add milk to rice. Bring to a boil. Reduce heat; cover and simmer for 15-20 minutes or until rice is tender.

In a mixing bowl, cream butter and sugar. Add egg yolks; beat well. Add rice mixture, raisins and orange peel. Beat egg whites until stiff; fold into the batter. Spoon into a greased 10-in. tube pan. Sprinkle with crumbs.

Bake at 350° for 55-60 minutes or until set. Cool in pan for 20 minutes. Loosen sides and center with a knife. Carefully invert onto a serving plate. Dust with confectioners' sugar. **Yield:** 12-16 servings.

Apple Gingerbread

4 to 5 cups sliced peeled tart
   apples
1-1/2 cups sugar, *divided*
1 cup dark molasses
1/2 cup butter, softened
2 eggs, lightly beaten
2-1/2 cups all-purpose flour

1 teaspoon baking soda
1 teaspoon ground ginger
1 teaspoon ground cinnamon
1 teaspoon ground cloves
1/2 teaspoon salt
1/2 cup boiling water

Arrange apples in greased 17-in. x 11-in. x 1-in. baking pan. Sprinkle with 1/2 cup sugar. Bake at 350° for 5 minutes. Remove from the oven.

In a small mixing bowl, combine molasses, butter and remaining sugar until smooth. Beat in eggs.

In a large bowl, combine the flour, baking soda, ginger, cinnamon, cloves and salt. Add molasses mixture and beat until smooth. Add boiling water; mix well. Pour batter over apples and spread evenly in pan.

Bake for 30 minutes or until a toothpick inserted near the center comes out clean. Cool on a wire rack. **Yield:** 20-24 servings.

Carrot Cake

1-1/3 cups vegetable oil
4 eggs
1-1/2 cups sugar
2 cups all-purpose flour
2 teaspoons baking powder
2 teaspoons baking soda
2 teaspoons ground cinnamon
2-1/2 cups finely shredded carrots
1/2 cup chopped walnuts

CREAM CHEESE ICING:
1 package (3 ounces) cream
   cheese, softened
3 cups confectioners' sugar
1 teaspoon vanilla extract
Dash salt
2 to 3 tablespoons milk

In a large mixing bowl, combine the oil, eggs and sugar. Combine the flour, baking powder, soda and cinnamon; add to mixing bowl. Beat well. Stir in carrots and nuts. Pour into a greased 13-in. x 9-in. x 2-in. baking pan. Bake at 350° for about 50 minutes or until a toothpick inserted near the center comes out clean. Cool on a wire rack.

For frosting, beat cream cheese, sugar, vanilla and salt in a mixing bowl. Beat in enough milk to achieve spreading consistency. Spread over cooled cake. **Yield:** 12 servings.

Grandma's Spring & Summer Torte

2 cups all-purpose flour
3 tablespoons sugar
1/4 teaspoon salt
1 cup butter, softened
2 egg yolks
1 teaspoon vanilla extract

FILLING:
1-1/2 cups sugar
1/4 cup all-purpose flour

4 cups sliced fresh *or* frozen rhubarb
1 cup half-and-half cream *or* evaporated milk
4 egg yolks, lightly beaten
2 tablespoons butter, softened

MERINGUE:
4 egg whites
1/4 teaspoon cream of tartar
1/2 cup sugar

For crust, combine the flour, sugar and salt in a medium bowl. Cut in butter, egg yolks and vanilla until crumbly. Press mixture into the bottom of 13-in. x 9-in. x 2-in. baking pan. Combine all filling ingredients and pour over crust. Bake at 375° for 45-50 minutes or until filling is set.

Meanwhile, in a mixing bowl, beat egg whites and cream of tartar until soft peaks form. Gradually add sugar, beating until stiff and glossy. Spread over filling. Bake 10-12 minutes longer or until meringue is lightly browned. **Yield:** 15 servings.

One-Bowl Chocolate Cake

1 cup sugar
1 egg
1/2 cup milk
1/2 cup butter, softened
1/4 teaspoon salt
1 teaspoon baking soda

1 teaspoon vanilla extract
1-1/2 cups all-purpose flour
1/2 cup baking cocoa
1/2 cup boiling water
Frosting *or* confectioners' sugar

Place the first 10 ingredients in order listed in a large mixing bowl; beat well. Pour into a greased and floured 8-in. square baking dish.

Bake at 375° for 35 minutes or until a toothpick inserted near the center comes out clean. Cool on a wire rack. Frost as desired or dust with confectioners' sugar. **Yield:** 9 servings.

Orange Date Cake

4 cups all-purpose flour
2 teaspoons baking soda
1 teaspoon salt
1-1/2 cups chopped dates
1 cup chopped walnuts
1 cup butter-flavored shortening
2 cups sugar

4 eggs
Grated peel of 1 orange
2 cups buttermilk

ORANGE SYRUP:
Juice of 1 orange
1/2 to 3/4 cup sugar

Sift together the flour, baking soda and salt; combine 1 cup with dates and walnuts. Set both mixtures aside.

In a large mixing bowl, cream shortening and sugar. Add eggs, one at a time, beating well after each addition. Add orange peel. Add flour mixtures. Stir in buttermilk just until blended. Spoon into a greased and floured 10-in. tube pan. Bake at 300° for 1-1/2 to 1-3/4 hours or until cake tests done. Cool for 10 minutes before removing from pan to wire rack.

For syrup, heat orange juice and sugar in saucepan until sugar dissolves. Let stand for 30 minutes. Cool 10 minutes longer before pouring over cake. **Yield:** 16-20 servings.

Chocolate Oat Cake

1 cup quick-cooking *or* old-fashioned oats
1/2 cup butter
1-1/2 cups boiling water
1/4 cup baking cocoa
1 cup sugar
1 cup packed brown sugar
2 eggs

1 teaspoon vanilla extract
1-1/2 cups all-purpose flour
1 teaspoon salt
1 teaspoon baking soda
1 cup (6 ounces) chocolate chips
1 cup chopped walnuts *or* pecans

Place oats and butter in a large mixing bowl; pour water over and let cool for 20 minutes. Add cocoa and beat well. Beat in sugars, eggs and vanilla. Combine the flour, salt and baking soda; add to batter.

Pour into a greased 13-in. x 9-in. x 2-in. baking pan. Sprinkle with chocolate chips and nuts. Bake at 350° for 45 minutes or until a toothpick inserted near the center comes out clean. Cool on a wire rack. **Yield:** 12-15 servings.

Devil's Food Cake

3/4 cup baking cocoa
2 cups sugar, *divided*
3 eggs
1-1/2 cups milk, *divided*
3/4 cup shortening

2 cups cake flour
1 teaspoon baking soda
1/8 teaspoon salt
1 teaspoon vanilla extract

In a heavy saucepan over low heat or the top of a double boiler, combine cocoa and 1 cup sugar. Beat 1 egg; add to cocoa mixture. Stir in 1 cup milk; cook until thick and smooth. Set aside to cool.

Meanwhile, cream shortening and remaining sugar in a large mixing bowl. Add remaining eggs, one at a time, beating well after each addition.

Sift together the flour, baking soda and salt; add to creamed mixture alternately with remaining milk. Add vanilla and cooled cocoa mixture; beat thoroughly. Pour into two greased 9-in. round baking pans.

Bake at 375° for 20-25 minutes or until toothpick inserted near the center comes out clean. Cool for 10 minutes before removing from pans to wire racks. Frost as desired. **Yield:** 12 servings.

Pineapple Bundt Cake

1 can (20 ounces) crushed pineapple
1/3 cup packed brown sugar
3 tablespoons butter, melted
8 maraschino cherries
8 pecan halves

1 package (16 ounces) pound cake mix
1 teaspoon grated lemon peel
1 teaspoon vanilla extract

Drain pineapple, reserving juice. Combine 1/2 cup pineapple, brown sugar, butter and 3 tablespoons of pineapple juice. Spoon into a greased 10-in. fluted tube pan. Alternate cherries and pecans over the sugar mixture.

Prepare cake batter according to package directions, substituting reserved pineapple juice for water. Stir in lemon peel, vanilla and remaining pineapple. Spoon over cherries and pecans.

Bake at 325° for 60-70 minutes or until a toothpick inserted near the center comes out clean. Cool for 10 minutes before removing from pan to a wire rack to cool completely. **Yield:** 12-16 servings.

Caramel Butter Cake

1 cup butter, softened
2 cups sugar
4 eggs
2 teaspoons vanilla extract
4 cups all-purpose flour
4 teaspoons baking powder
1-1/3 cups milk

CARAMEL SAUCE:
1/2 cup packed brown sugar
2 cups sugar
3/4 cup evaporated milk
2 egg yolks
2 tablespoons butter, softened
1 teaspoon vanilla extract
Confectioners' sugar, optional

In a mixing bowl, cream butter and sugar. Add eggs, one at a time, beating well after each addition. Add vanilla; mix well. Combine flour and baking powder; add to creamed mixture alternately with milk. Pour into three greased and floured 9-in. round baking pans.

Bake at 350° for 25-30 minutes or until a toothpick inserted near the center comes out clean. Cool for 10 minutes before removing from the pans to wire racks. When completely cooled, split each cake into two layers.

For caramel sauce, melt the brown sugar in a heavy skillet over low heat for about 25 minutes. Remove from the heat; set aside.

In a heavy saucepan, combine the sugar, milk and egg yolks. Bring to a boil over medium heat, stirring constantly. Add melted brown sugar. Cook and stir until a thermometer reads 238° (soft-ball stage). Remove from the heat; stir in the butter and vanilla until the mixture is smooth and spreadable.

To assemble, quickly spread 1/3 cup caramel sauce over five cake layers; stack on a serving plate. Top with the plain layer. Dust cake with confectioners' sugar if desired. **Yield:** 12 servings.

Editor's Note: We recommend that you test your candy thermometer before each use by bringing water to a boil; the thermometer should read 212°. Adjust your recipe temperature up or down based on your test.

Chocolate Nougat Cake

1/3 cup butter, softened
1-1/4 cups plus 2 tablespoons sugar, *divided*
2 eggs, *separated*
2 squares (1 ounce *each*) unsweetened chocolate, melted
1-1/3 cups all-purpose flour
1-1/4 teaspoons baking powder
1/2 teaspoon salt
3/4 cup plus 2 tablespoons milk
1/2 cup finely chopped nuts

SEVEN-MINUTE FROSTING:
1-1/2 cups sugar
2 egg whites
1/3 cup cold water
1/4 teaspoon cream of tartar
1 teaspoon vanilla extract

In a large mixing bowl, cream butter and 3/4 cup plus 2 tablespoons sugar until fluffy. Blend in egg yolks and chocolate. Sift together the flour, baking powder and salt; add to creamed mixture alternately with milk. Stir in nuts. In a mixing bowl, beat egg whites with remaining sugar until stiff peaks form; fold gently into batter.

Pour into two greased and floured 8-in. round baking pans. Bake at 350° for 30-35 minutes or until a toothpick inserted near the center comes out clean. Cool for 10 minutes before removing from pans to wire racks to cool completely.

For frosting, combine the sugar, egg whites, water and cream of tartar in a heavy saucepan over low heat. With a portable mixer, beat on low speed for 1 minute. Continue beating on low over low heat until frosting reaches 160°, about 8-10 minutes. Pour into a large mixing bowl; add vanilla. Beat on high until frosting forms stiff peaks, about 7 minutes. Spread frosting between layers and over top and sides of cake. Store in the refrigerator. **Yield:** 12 servings.

Editor's Note: A stand mixer is recommended for beating the frosting after it reaches 160°.

Poppy Seed Bundt Cake

6 tablespoons poppy seeds
1 cup buttermilk
1 cup butter, softened
1-1/2 cups sugar
4 eggs, *separated*
2-1/2 cups all-purpose flour
2 teaspoons baking powder

1 teaspoon baking soda
1/2 teaspoon salt

FILLING:
1/3 cup sugar
2 teaspoons baking cocoa
1 teaspoon ground cinnamon

Place poppy seeds and buttermilk in a bowl; soak for 2 hours. In a large mixing bowl, cream butter until fluffy. Add sugar and egg yolks; beat well. Combine the remaining dry ingredients; add alternately with poppy seeds-buttermilk to creamed mixture.

In another bowl, beat egg whites until stiff. Fold into batter; set aside. Combine filling ingredients; sprinkle a third into bottom of a greased and floured 10-in. fluted tube pan. Pour in half of batter; "swirl" in half of remaining filling. Add remaining batter and filling, again swirling together.

Bake at 350° for 1 hour or until cake tests done. Turn out immediately onto a wire rack to cool. **Yield:** 16-20 servings.

Chocolate Angel Food Cake

2 cups egg whites (12 to 16 large eggs)
1 cup cake flour
1/2 cup baking cocoa

2 teaspoons cream of tartar
1 teaspoon vanilla extract
2 cups sugar

Place egg whites in a large mixing bowl; let stand at room temperature for 30 minutes. Sift flour and cocoa together three times; set aside.

Add cream of tartar and vanilla to egg whites; beat on medium speed until soft peaks form. Gradually add sugar, about 2 tablespoons at a time, beating on high until glossy peaks form and sugar is dissolved. Gradually fold in flour mixture, about 1/2 cup at a time.

Gently spoon into an ungreased 10-in. tube pan. Cut through the batter with a knife to remove air pockets. Bake on the lowest oven rack at 325°; for 60 minutes. Turn off the oven and let cake sit in the oven for 5 minutes. Remove from the oven and immediately invert pan; cool completely, about 1 hour.

Run a knife around side and center tube of pan. Remove cake to a serving plate. **Yield:** 12 servings.

Lemon Blueberry Tea Cake

1 cup fresh *or* frozen blueberries
1 tablespoon plus 1-2/3 cups
  all-purpose flour, *divided*
1/2 cup butter, softened
1 cup sugar
2 eggs
1-1/2 teaspoons baking powder
1/4 teaspoon salt
1/2 cup milk
1 tablespoon grated lemon peel

GLAZE:
1/2 cup sugar
1/4 cup lemon juice

Toss blueberries with 1 tablespoon flour; set aside. In a large mixing bowl, cream butter and sugar. Add eggs, one at a time, beating well after each. Combine the baking powder, salt and remaining flour; add to creamed mixture alternately with milk. Fold in lemon peel and berries.

Pour into a greased and floured 9-in. x 5-in. x 3-in. loaf pan. Bake at 350° for 60-65 minutes or until a toothpick inserted near center comes out clean. Cool for 10 minutes before removing from pan to a wire rack.

Meanwhile, combine glaze ingredients in a small saucepan. Heat to boiling, stirring until sugar dissolves. Brush glaze on top and sides of cake. Cool. To serve, cut into 1/2-in. slices. **Yield:** 18 servings.

Editor's Note: If using frozen blueberries, do not thaw.

Banana Cupcakes

1/3 cup shortening
2/3 cup sugar
1 egg
1 teaspoon vanilla extract
3/4 cup mashed ripe bananas
  (about 2 small bananas)
1-1/3 cups cake flour
1 teaspoon baking powder
1/2 teaspoon salt
1/2 teaspoon baking soda
1/2 teaspoon ground cinnamon
1/2 teaspoon ground cloves
1/4 teaspoon ground nutmeg
1 tablespoon confectioners'
  sugar

In a mixing bowl, cream the shortening and sugar. Add the egg, vanilla and bananas; mix well. Combine flour, baking powder, salt, baking soda, cinnamon, cloves and nutmeg; add to creamed mixture just until combined.

Fill paper-lined muffin cups two-thirds full. Bake at 375° for 18-20 minutes or until a toothpick comes out clean. Cool for 10 minutes before removing from the pan to a wire rack to cool completely. Dust with confectioners' sugar. **Yield:** 1 dozen.

Special Birthday Cake

1/3 cup vanilla *or* white chips
1/2 cup hot water
1 cup butter, softened
1-1/2 cups sugar
4 eggs, *separated*
1 cup buttermilk
1 teaspoon vanilla extract
2-1/2 cups all-purpose flour
1 teaspoon baking soda

WHITE CHOCOLATE FROSTING:
1 cup sugar
1/2 cup plus 1 tablespoon evaporated milk
6 tablespoons butter
3 cups vanilla *or* white chips
2-1/4 teaspoons vanilla extract

In a small bowl, combine the chips and water; stir until chips are melted. In a large mixing bowl, cream the butter and sugar. Add egg yolks, one at a time, beating well after each addition. Add melted chip mixture, buttermilk and vanilla; beat well. Combine flour and baking soda; gradually add to the creamed mixture.

In a small mixing bowl, beat egg whites until stiff peaks form. Gently fold into the creamed mixture. Pour into three greased and floured 9-in. round baking pans.

Bake at 350° for 25-30 minutes or until a toothpick inserted near the center comes out clean. Cool for 10 minutes before removing from pans to wire racks to cool completely.

For frosting, combine the sugar, milk and butter in a saucepan; bring to a boil, stirring constantly. Boil for 1 minute; remove from the heat. Stir in chips and vanilla until smooth; cool. Spread frosting between layers and over top and sides of cake. **Yield:** 12-14 servings.

Red Velvet Cake

1/2 cup shortening

1-1/2 cups sugar

2 eggs

1/4 cup (2 ounces) red food
coloring

3 tablespoons baking cocoa

2-1/4 cups all-purpose flour

1 teaspoon baking soda

1/2 teaspoon salt

1 cup buttermilk

1 tablespoon vanilla extract

1 tablespoon white vinegar

FLUFFY WHITE FROSTING:

1 cup milk

5 tablespoons all-purpose flour

3/4 cup butter

4 tablespoons shortening

1-1/2 cups sugar

2 teaspoons vanilla extract

Grease two 9-in. round baking pans and line with waxed paper; set aside. In a large mixing bowl, cream shortening and sugar until fluffy. Add eggs, one at a time, beating well after each addition. Combine food coloring and cocoa; add to creamed mixture. Combine the flour, baking soda and salt; add to cream mixture alternately with buttermilk. Stir in vanilla and vinegar. Pour into prepared pans.

Bake at 350° for 35 minutes or until toothpick inserted near center comes out clean. Cool for 10 minutes before removing from pans to wire racks to cool completely.

For frosting, whisk together milk and flour in a saucepan. Cook over medium heat for 5 minutes or until thick (like paste), stirring constantly. Cool. Place in a mixing bowl with remaining frosting ingredients. Beat at high speed until consistency of whipped cream. Spread frosting between layers and over the top and sides of cake. **Yield:** 12 servings.

Desserts

Edna's Cream Sticks

STICKS:

    2 packages (1/4 ounce *each*) dry yeast
    1 cup warm water (110° to 115°)
    1 cup warm milk (110° to 115°)
2/3 cup sugar
1/2 cup butter
1/2 teaspoon salt
    2 eggs, beaten
    6 to 7 cups all-purpose flour

FILLING:

    3 tablespoons all-purpose flour
    1 cup milk
    1 cup butter, softened
    1 cup sugar
    1 teaspoon vanilla extract
Confectioners' sugar
Oil for deep-fat frying

In a large mixing bowl, dissolve yeast in warm water. Add the milk, sugar, butter, salt, eggs and 2 cups flour. Beat until smooth. Stir in enough remaining flour to form a firm dough. Do not knead.

Place in a greased bowl, turning once to grease the top. Cover and let rise in a warm place until doubled, about 45 minutes hour.

Meanwhile, for filling, in a saucepan, combine flour and milk smooth. Bring to a boil over medium heat cook and stir for 2 minutes or until thickened. Refrigerate for 1 hour.

Punch dough down. Turn onto a floured surface; roll out and cut into oblong pieces. Cover and let rise until doubled, about 45 minutes.

In a mixing bowl, cream butter and sugar; beat in vanilla. Add to cooled flour mixture and beat until sugar is dissolved and filling is fluffy. Gradually beat in enough confectioners' sugar to achieve spreading consistency.

In an electric skillet or deep-fat fryer heat oil to 375°. Fry sticks, a few at a time, until golden brown on each side. Drain on paper towels. While sticks are still warm, make a cut in the top of each; fill with filling. Frost with your favorite icing. **Yield:** 40 servings.

Chocolate Velvet Cream

2 squares (1 ounce *each*) semisweet chocolate, coarsely chopped
2 cups milk, *divided*

2 envelopes unflavored gelatin
2/3 cup sugar
2 teaspoons vanilla extract
2 cups heavy whipping cream

In a heavy saucepan, heat chocolate and 1-1/2 cups milk until chocolate is melted, stirring until smooth. Meanwhile, in a small saucepan, sprinkle gelatin over remaining cold milk; let stand for 1 minute. Heat over low heat, stirring until gelatin is completely dissolved; add to melted chocolate. Remove from the heat; add sugar and vanilla. Mix well. Let stand just until mixture starts to gel.

Meanwhile, in a mixing bowl, whip the cream until stiff peaks form. Fold into chocolate mixture. Cover and chill until firm. **Yield:** 10 servings (5 cups).

Fruit Kuchen

1 cup heavy whipping cream
3/4 cup sugar
2/3 cup soft bread crumbs
1 loaf (1 pound) frozen bread dough, thawed

3 tablespoons cherry *or* raspberry pie filling

TOPPING:
3 tablespoons all-purpose flour
2 tablespoons butter, melted
1 tablespoon sugar

In a saucepan, combine the cream, sugar and bread crumbs. Cook over medium heat until mixture begins to thicken. Remove from the heat; cook for 15 minutes.

Meanwhile, divide the dough in half; press into the bottom and up the sides of two 9-in. pie plates to form a crust.

Pour half of cream mixture into each crust. Drop spoonfuls of pie filling over cream layer. Combine topping ingredients; sprinkle over filling.

Bake at 350° for 25-30 minutes or until edges are golden brown and center is set. **Yield:** 2 kuchens (8-10 servings each).

Skillet Chocolate Dumplings

CHOCOLATE SAUCE:
- 3/4 cup packed brown sugar
- 1/4 cup baking cocoa
- 1 tablespoon cornstarch
- Dash salt
- 2 cups water
- 2 tablespoons butter

DUMPLINGS:
- 1 cup sifted all-purpose flour
- 1/2 cup sugar
- 2 tablespoons baking cocoa
- 2 teaspoons baking powder
- 1/2 teaspoon salt
- 3 tablespoons cold butter
- 1 egg, lightly beaten
- 1/3 cup milk
- 1 teaspoon vanilla extract
- Whipped cream *or* ice cream

For sauce, in a heavy skillet, combine the brown sugar, cocoa, cornstarch and salt. Stir in water; cook until mixture begins to boil and thicken slightly, stirring constantly. Add butter; mix well. Remove sauce from the heat while make dumplings.

For dumplings, sift together the flour, sugar, cocoa, baking powder and salt. Cut in butter until mixture resembles fine crumbs. Combine the egg, milk and vanilla; blend gradually into flour mixture.

Return skillet to heat, bring the chocolate sauce to a boil. Reduce heat to low. Drop by tablespoonfuls onto simmering chocolate sauce. Cover and simmer for 20 minutes or until a toothpick inserted in a dumpling comes out clean (do not lift the cover while simmering). Serve warm with whipped cream or ice cream. **Yield:** 6-8 servings.

Dirty Ice Cream

- 2 quarts vanilla ice cream, softened
- 1 package (16 ounces) cream-filled chocolate sandwich cookies, crushed
- 1 carton (8 ounces) frozen whipped topping, thawed
- Additional cookies, halved *and/or* crushed, optional
- Fresh mint, optional

In a large bowl, combine ice cream and cookies. Fold in whipped topping. Pour into an ungreased 13-in. x 9-in. x 2-in. pan. Cover and freeze overnight.

Remove from freezer 10 minutes before serving. Garnish with additional cookies and mint if desired. **Yield:** 16-20 servings.

Grandma's Apple Dumplings

SAUCE:
1-1/2 cups sugar
1-1/2 cups water
1/4 cup red cinnamon candies
1/4 teaspoon ground cinnamon
1/4 teaspoon ground nutmeg

DUMPLINGS:
2 cups all-purpose flour
2 teaspoons baking powder

1 teaspoon salt
2/3 cup shortening
2/3 cup cold milk
6 small baking apples, peeled and cored
3 tablespoons butter
1 egg white, beaten
1 tablespoon sugar
Half-and-half cream, optional

In a large saucepan, combine all sauce ingredients. Bring to a full rolling boil, stirring occasionally. Set aside.

For dumplings, in a large mixing bowl, combine the flour, baking powder and salt. Using a fork or pastry blender, cut in shortening until mixture resembles coarse crumbs. Gradually add milk, mixing lightly with a fork until a soft dough forms. Shape into a ball.

On a lightly floured surface, roll dough to an 18-in. x 12-in. rectangle. Cut into six squares. Place an apple in the center of each square; dot with butter. Bring corners of pastry up to top of apple; press edges to seal.

Place in an ungreased 13-in. x 9-in. x 2-in. baking dish. Pour sauce into pan around dumplings. Brush dumplings with egg white and sprinkle with sugar.

Bake at 375° for 50 minutes or until light golden brown and apples are tender. Serve warm with cream if desired. **Yield:** 6 servings.

Frozen Dream Dessert

1 cup sugar
1 envelope unsweetened soft drink mix, any flavor

2 cups milk
1 cup heavy whipping cream

In a bowl, combine the sugar, drink mix and milk; stir until the sugar and drink mix are dissolved. Pour into a freezer container. Freeze for 1 hour or until slushy.

In a mixing bowl, beat cream until stiff. Add drink mix mixture and mix just until combined. Return to the freezer container. Freeze until solid, about 2 hours. **Yield:** 1 quart.

Cherry Grunt

1 can (16 ounces) pitted tart red
cherries, undrained
1-1/2 cups water
3/4 cup sugar, *divided*
1/4 cup cold butter, *divided*

1 cup all-purpose flour
1-1/2 teaspoons baking powder
Pinch salt
1/3 cup milk
1/2 teaspoon vanilla extract

In a large saucepan, combine the cherries with juice, water, 1/2 cup
sugar and 2 tablespoons butter. Bring to a boil. Reduce heat; simmer,
uncovered, for 5 minutes.

Meanwhile, sift together the flour, baking powder, salt and remaining
sugar. Cut in remaining butter with a pastry blender. Add milk and
vanilla.

Drop by teaspoonfuls over simmering cherry mixture. Cover and
simmer for 20 minutes or until a toothpick inserted in a dumpling comes
out clean (do not lift the cover while simmering). **Yield:** 8-10 servings.

German Cheesecake

1/2 cup graham cracker crumbs
2 cups (16 ounces) 4% cottage
cheese
2 packages (8 ounces *each*)
cream cheese, softened
1 cup sugar

4 eggs, lightly beaten
1 tablespoon lemon juice
1 teaspoon vanilla extract
1/4 cup all-purpose flour
2 cups (16 ounces) sour cream

Sprinkle the crumbs over the bottom and up the sides of a greased 10-
in. springform pan. In a blender or food processor, puree cottage cheese;
set aside.

In a mixing bowl, beat cream cheese and sugar. Add eggs; beat on low
speed just until combined. Stir in the lemon juice, vanilla, flour, sour
cream and pureed cottage cheese.

Pour into pan. Place on a baking sheet. Bake at 325° for 60-70
minutes. Cool on a wire rack for 10 minutes. Carefully run a knife
around edge of pan; cool 1 hour longer. Refrigerate overnight. Slice with
a wet knife. Refrigerate leftovers. **Yield:** 16 servings.

Mom's Fried Apples

1/2 cup butter
6 medium unpeeled tart red apples, sliced

3/4 cup sugar, *divided*
3/4 teaspoon ground cinnamon

Melt butter in a large skillet. Add apples and 1/2 cup sugar; stir to mix well. Cover and cook over low heat for 20 minutes or until apples are tender, stirring frequently. Add cinnamon and remaining sugar. Cook and stir over medium-high heat for 10 minutes. **Yield:** 6-8 servings.

Rhubarb Cloud

3 cups sliced fresh *or* frozen rhubarb, thawed
1/2 cup sugar

1 tablespoon lemon juice
1 teaspoon grated orange peel
1 cup whipping cream

In a large saucepan, bring rhubarb, sugar, lemon juice and orange peel to a boil. Reduce heat; cook, uncovered, over medium heat until mixture is reduced to about 1 cup, about 15 minutes. Cool completely. In a mixing bowl, beat cream until soft peaks form. Fold in rhubarb mixture. Serve immediately. **Yield:** 4 servings.

Editor's Note: If using frozen rhubarb, measure rhubarb while still frozen, then thaw completely. Drain in a colander, but do not press liquid out.

Baked Custard

4 eggs
2/3 cup sugar
1/2 teaspoon salt
1/4 teaspoon ground nutmeg

1/4 teaspoon ground cinnamon
3 teaspoons vanilla extract
2-2/3 cups milk

In a mixing bowl, combine the eggs, sugar, spices and vanilla. Blend in milk. Pour into a 1-1/2-qt. baking dish. Place baking dish in a large baking pan; add 1 in. of hot water to larger pan. Bake at 325° for 1 hour or until a knife inserted near middle comes out clean. Store leftovers in the refrigerator. **Yield:** 6 servings.

Icebox Cookie Cheesecake

1-1/4 cups chocolate wafer crumbs
4 tablespoons butter, melted
2 cups heavy whipping cream, *divided*
3 packages (8 ounces *each*) cream cheese, softened
1 cup sugar

1-1/4 pounds cream-filled chocolate cookies (54 cookies), *divided*
4 squares (1 ounce *each*) semisweet chocolate
1/2 teaspoon vanilla extract
Whipped cream

Combine crumbs and butter; press into bottom of a 9-in. or 10-in. springform pan. Freeze. In a mixing bowl, beat 1-1/2 cups whipping cream until stiff peaks form; refrigerate.

In a large mixing bowl, beat cream cheese until smooth. Gradually add sugar; blend thoroughly. Break 38 of the cookies each into three pieces; fold into filling along with chilled whipped cream. Spread filling evenly into crust, smoothing top and spreading to edges. Cover and refrigerate 4 hours or overnight.

Meanwhile, melt chocolate in a saucepan over low heat, stirring constantly. Remove from the heat; cool slightly. Whisk in vanilla and remaining whipping cream. Loosen cheesecake from pan by running knife around edge; remove sides of pan.

Glaze top and sides of cake with chocolate mixture. Refrigerate until glaze hardens, about 20 minutes. To serve, cut into 16 pieces; top each piece with a dollop of whipped cream and stand a whole cookie upright in cream. **Yield:** 16 servings.

Easy Apple Betty

10 cups sliced peeled tart apples (about 3 pounds)
1/4 cup unsweetened apple juice

1-3/4 cups crushed oatmeal cookies (about 18)
1/4 cup butter, melted
1/2 teaspoon ground cinnamon

In a bowl, toss apples with apple juice; arrange half in a 13-in. x 9-in. x 2-in. baking dish coated with nonstick cooking spray. Combine the cookie crumbs, butter and cinnamon; sprinkle half over apples. Repeat layers.

Bake, uncovered, at 375° for 40-45 minutes or until apples are tender and topping is golden brown. Serve warm. **Yield:** 12 servings.

Pumpkin Pudding

1 cup canned pumpkin
1 tablespoon molasses
1/2 teaspoon ground cinnamon
1/8 teaspoon ground cloves
1/4 teaspoon salt
1-1/2 cups cold milk

1 package (3.4 ounces) instant vanilla pudding mix
1/2 cup heavy whipping cream, whipped
Additional whipped cream, optional
Additional ground cinnamon, optional

In a mixing bowl, combine the pumpkin, molasses and spices. Gradually add milk. Add pudding mix; beat slowly with an electric mixer until thick, about 1 minute. Fold in whipped cream.

Pour into a serving bowl or individual serving dishes. Cover and chill for 1 hour. If desired, top each serving with a dollop of whipped cream and a sprinkle of cinnamon. **Yield:** 9-12 servings.

Cranberry Baklava

40 sheets phyllo dough (14 inch x 9 inch)
1 cup butter, melted
1-1/2 cups fresh or frozen cranberries, finely chopped

1 cup finely chopped walnuts
1 cup sugar
1 teaspoon ground cinnamon
1-1/2 cups honey

Grease two 13-in. x 9-in. x 2-in. baking dishes. Layer six sheets of phyllo dough in one dish, brushing each sheet with butter. (Keep remaining phyllo dough covered with plastic wrap and a damp towel to prevent it from drying out.)

In a bowl, combine the cranberries, walnuts, sugar and cinnamon. Sprinkle about 2/3 cup over top layer of phyllo. Layer and brush six sheets of dough with butter. Top with about 2/3 cup cranberry mixture. Layer and brush six more sheets of dough with butter; top with 1/3 cup cranberry mixture. Top with two more sheets of dough, brushing each sheet with butter.

In the remaining dish, repeat layering with remaining dough and filling. Using a sharp knife, cut halfway through each stack to make 12 pieces. Bake at 325° for 60-70 minutes or until golden brown.

In a small saucepan, heat the honey over low heat just until warm and thin. Pour over warm baklava. Cool on wire racks for 1 hour. **Yield:** 24 servings.

Tuxedo Strawberries

18 medium fresh strawberries
1 cup vanilla *or* white chips
3-1/2 teaspoons shortening, *divided*
1-1/3 cups semisweet chocolate chips

Pastry bag *or* small heavy-duty
resealable plastic bag
#2 pastry tip, optional

Line a tray or baking sheet with waxed paper; set aside. Wash berries and pat completely dry. In microwave, melt vanilla chips and 1-1/2 teaspoons shortening; stir until smooth. Dip each berry until two-thirds is coated, allowing excess to drip off. Place on waxed paper-lined baking sheet; chill 30 minutes or until set.

Melt chocolate chips and remaining shortening; stir until smooth. Dip each side of berry into chocolate from the tip of the strawberry to the top of vanilla coating. Set aside remaining chocolate. Chill berries for 30 minutes or until set.

Melt reserved chocolate if necessary. Cut a small hole in the corner of a pastry or plastic bag; insert tip or pipe directly from bag. Fill with melted chocolate. Pipe a "bow tie" at the top of the white "v" and two or three buttons down the front of the "shirt." Chill for 30 minutes or until set. Cover and store in the refrigerator for 1 day. **Yield:** 1-1/2 dozen.

Pineapple Bread Pudding

10 slices white bread
3/4 cup butter, melted
5 eggs
1 can (20 ounces) crushed
pineapple, drained

1/4 cup dried currants *or* raisins
1 cup sugar
1-1/2 teaspoons vanilla extract
3/4 teaspoon ground cinnamon
Whipped cream, optional

Place bread on a baking sheet. Bake at 375° for 4 minutes; turn bread over and bake 4 minutes longer or until very light brown. Cut toasted bread into 1-in. cubes. Toss with melted butter; set aside.

In a bowl, beat eggs until thick and lemon-colored. Add the pineapple, currants, sugar and vanilla; mix well. Fold in bread cubes.

Pour into a greased 2-1/2-qt. baking dish. Sprinkle with cinnamon. Cover and bake at 350° for 30-35 minutes or until bubbly and golden brown. Serve warm with whipped cream if desired. **Yield:** 8-10 servings.

Raspberry Supreme Cheesecake

2 cups graham cracker crumbs
1 cup chopped toasted almonds
1/2 cup sugar
2/3 cup butter, melted
1 package (8 ounces) cream cheese, softened
1 can (14 ounces) sweetened condensed milk
1/3 cup lemon juice

1 teaspoon vanilla extract
1 package (6 ounces) raspberry gelatin
2 cups hot water
2 packages (10 ounces *each*) frozen raspberries, partially thawed
2 cups whipped cream
1/4 cup toasted slivered almonds

In a bowl, combine the first four ingredients. Press into the bottom of a 13-in. x 9-in. x 2-in. baking pan; chill for 30 minutes.

Meanwhile, in a large mixing bowl, beat the cream cheese, milk, lemon juice and vanilla until smooth. Pour over crust; chill. Dissolve gelatin in water. Add raspberries and stir until completely thawed; chill until very thick. Pour over filling. Chill until set.

Before serving, top with whipped cream and almonds. Store in the refrigerator. **Yield:** 16-20 servings.

Zucchini Apple Crisp

8 cups sliced zucchini (cut like apple slices)
3/4 cup lemon juice
1/2 cup sugar
2 teaspoons ground cinnamon
1 teaspoon ground nutmeg

TOPPING:
1-1/3 cups packed brown sugar
1 cup all-purpose flour
1 cup old-fashioned oats
2/3 cup butter, softened
Whipped cream *or* ice cream, optional

Place zucchini and lemon juice in a large saucepan. Cover and cook over medium heat for about 15 minutes or until zucchini is tender, stirring occasionally. Add the sugar, cinnamon and nutmeg; stir until sugar is dissolved. Remove from the heat. Pour into a greased 13-in. x 9-in. x 2-in. baking pan.

For topping, combine the brown sugar, flour, oats and butter until crumbly. Sprinkle over zucchini. Bake at 375° for 50 minutes or until topping is golden brown. Serve warm with whipped cream or ice cream if desired. **Yield:** 12-16 servings.

Apricot Burritos

1 cup chopped dried apricots
1 cup water
1/4 cup sugar
1/4 cup packed brown sugar
1/4 teaspoon ground cinnamon

1/4 teaspoon ground nutmeg
8 flour tortillas (6 inches)
Oil for frying
Cinnamon-sugar

In a saucepan, combine the first six ingredients. Bring to a boil; reduce heat. Simmer, uncovered, for 10 minutes or until thickened. Place 1 tablespoon on each tortilla. Fold sides and ends over filling; roll up.

In an electric skillet, heat 1 in. of oil to 375°. Fry burritos, in batches, for 1 minute on each side or until golden brown. Drain on paper towels. Sprinkle with cinnamon-sugar. **Yield:** 8 burritos.

Blueberry Orange Cups

1/3 cup orange marmalade
1 pint orange sherbet

1 cup fresh *or* frozen blueberries

In a saucepan, heat marmalade over low until melted; add blueberries. Spoon sherbet into individual dessert dishes. Top with marmalade mixture. **Yield:** 4 servings.

Butterscotch Pudding

1 cup packed dark brown sugar
1/4 cup all-purpose flour
1/8 teaspoon salt

2 cups milk
2 eggs
1 teaspoon vanilla extract

In a large saucepan, combine the sugar, flour and salt. Stir in milk until smooth. Cook and stir over medium-high heat until thickened and bubbly. Reduce heat; cook and stir 2 minutes longer. Remove from the heat. Stir a small amount of hot filling into eggs; return all to pan, stirring constantly. Bring to a gentle boil; cook and stir 2 minutes longer. Remove from the heat. Gently stir vanilla. Pour into dessert cups and chill. **Yield:** 4 servings.

Layered Icebox Dessert

CRUST:
- 1 package (18-1/4 ounces) German chocolate cake mix
- 1 egg
- 1/2 cup butter, melted
- 1/2 cup chopped pecans

FILLING/TOPPING:
- 1 package (8 ounces) cream cheese, softened
- 1 cup sugar
- 1 carton (12 ounces) frozen whipped topping, thawed, *divided*
- 3 cups cold milk
- 2 packages (3.4 ounces *each*) instant French vanilla pudding mix
- 1/4 teaspoon ground nutmeg
- 1/4 teaspoon rum extract
- 2 tablespoons chopped pecans, toasted

In a mixing bowl, combine the dry cake mix, egg, butter and pecans. Press into a greased 13-in. x 9-in. x 2-in. baking dish. Bake at 350° for 15-20 minutes or until toothpick inserted near the center comes out clean. Cool completely. (As crust cools, it will fall in the center to form a shell.)

In a mixing bowl, beat cream cheese and sugar for 2 minutes. Fold in 1 cup whipped topping. Spread over crust. Refrigerate for 10 minutes.

In a bowl, whisk milk and pudding mix for 2 minutes. Whisk in nutmeg and extract. Let stand for 2 minutes or until soft-set. Spread over cream cheese layer. Top with remaining whipped topping. Sprinkle with pecans. Refrigerate for at least 2 hours. **Yield:** 16-20 servings.

Fruit and Cream Parfaits

- 1 cup heavy whipping cream
- 3 tablespoon sugar
- 1 teaspoon vanilla extract
- Dash salt
- 1 cup (8 ounces) sour cream
- 1 can (21 ounces) cherry, strawberry, raspberry *or* blueberry pie filling, *divided*

In a mixing bowl, beat cream until soft peaks form. Gradually add sugar, vanilla and salt; beat until stiff peaks form. Fold in sour cream. Set aside six cherries from pie filling.

Spoon half of the remaining pie filling into parfait glasses; top with half of the cream mixture. Repeat layers. Top with reserved cherries. **Yield:** 6 servings.

Peppermint Stick Dessert

8 ounces peppermint candy, crushed
1/2 cup half-and-half cream
1-1/4 teaspoons unflavored gelatin
1 tablespoon cold water
1-1/2 cups heavy whipping cream, whipped
27 chocolate wafers

In a small saucepan, combine crushed candy and half-and-half cream. Cook over low heat until candy is melted, stirring occasionally.

In a small bowl, sprinkle gelatin over water; let stand for 1 minute. Stir into hot peppermint mixture until dissolved. Refrigerate for 20 minutes or until mixture begins to set. Fold in whipped cream.

Crush three chocolate wafers; set aside for garnish. Line a 1-1/2-qt. serving bowl with 12 wafers. Top with half of the peppermint mixture. Repeat layers. Sprinkle with chocolate crumbs. Refrigerate for at least 8 hours. **Yield:** 9-12 servings.

Moon Cake

CRUST:
1 cup water
1/2 cup butter
1 cup all-purpose flour
4 eggs

FILLING:
3 cups cold milk
2 packages (3.4 ounces *each*) instant vanilla pudding mix
1 package (8 ounces) cream cheese, softened

TOPPING:
1 carton (8 ounces) frozen whipped topping, thawed
Chocolate sauce
Chopped nuts

In a saucepan, bring water and butter to a boil. Add flour all at once and stir until mixture forms a ball. Remove from the heat and cool slightly. Add eggs, one at a time, beating well after each addition. Spread on a greased 15-in. x 10-in. x 1-in. baking pan.

Bake at 400° for 30 minutes. Cool but do not prick, leaving surface with its "moon-like" appearance.

Meanwhile, for filling, whisk together milk and pudding mix for 2 minutes. Let stand for 2 minutes or until soft-set. Add cream cheese; blend well. Spread on crust; cover and refrigerate for 20 minutes. Top with whipped topping. Drizzle chocolate sauce over top and sprinkle with nuts. **Yield:** about 15 servings.

Orange-Glazed Bananas

3/4 cup orange juice concentrate
3 tablespoons butter
3 tablespoons brown sugar
2 tablespoons grated orange
  peel

3/4 teaspoon ground ginger
4 medium firm bananas, sliced
Vanilla ice cream

In a saucepan over medium heat, combine the first five ingredients. Cook and stir until the sugar is dissolved. Add bananas and heat through. Serve over ice cream. **Yield:** about 3 cups.

Honey Fruit Dessert

2 medium ripe nectarines *or* peaches *or* 4 apricots, halved and pitted
4 medium ripe plums, halved and pitted

2 tablespoons honey
Vanilla ice cream
1/4 cup chopped cashews *or* peanuts, optional

Line a 13-in. x 9-in. x 2-in. baking pan with foil; coat foil with nonstick cooking spray. Place fruit cut side up in pan. Bake, uncovered, at 425° for 18-20 minutes or until tender. Drizzle with honey; bake 2-3 minutes longer or until golden brown. Serve warm with ice cream and nuts if desired. **Yield:** 4-6 servings.

Blueberry Raspberry Crunch

1 can (21 ounces) blueberry pie filling
1 can (21 ounces) raspberry pie filling

1 package (18-1/4 ounces) white cake mix
1/2 cup chopped walnuts
1/2 cup butter, melted

Combine pie fillings in a greased 13-in. x 9-in. x 2-in. baking dish. In a bowl, combine the cake mix, walnuts and butter until crumbly; sprinkle over filling.

Bake, uncovered, at 375° for 25-30 minutes or until filling is bubbly and topping is golden brown. Serve warm. **Yield:** 12 servings.

Heavenly Cheesecake

1-1/2 cups chocolate wafer crumbs
5 tablespoons butter, melted
1 envelope unflavored gelatin
1 cup milk
5 Milky Way candy bars (2.05 ounces *each*), *divided*

2 packages (8 ounces *each*) cream cheese, softened
2 tablespoons sugar
1 teaspoon vanilla extract
1 cup heavy whipping cream

In a bowl, combine wafer crumbs and butter. Press onto the bottom and 1 in. up the sides of a greased 9-in. springform pan. Refrigerate.

In a saucepan, sprinkle gelatin over milk; let stand for 1 minute. Cook and stir over low heat until gelatin is dissolved. Cut four candy bars into quarters; add to gelatin mixture. Cook until candy bars are melted and mixture is smooth. Remove from the heat; set aside.

In a mixing bowl, beat cream cheese and sugar; add gelatin mixture and vanilla. Add cream; beat on high speed for 4 minutes. Pour into crust. Refrigerate for at least 4 hours or until firm. Slice or chop remaining candy bar for garnish. **Yield:** 12 servings.

Strawberry Rhubarb Dumplings

4 cups sliced fresh *or* frozen rhubarb, thawed
1-1/2 cups water
1 cup sugar
1/8 teaspoon salt

1-1/2 cups mashed strawberries
1 cup biscuit/baking mix
1/3 cup milk
Whipped cream

In a large saucepan, bring the rhubarb, water, sugar and salt to a boil. Reduce heat; simmer, uncovered, for 6-8 minutes or until rhubarb is tender. Stir in strawberries; return to a boil.

Meanwhile, in a large bowl, combine biscuit mix and milk just until moistened. Drop batter in four mounds onto rhubarb mixture. Cook, uncovered, for 10 minutes. Cover and cook 5-8 minutes longer or until a toothpick inserted in a dumpling comes out clean. Serve warm with whipped cream. **Yield:** 4 servings.

Editor's Note: If using frozen rhubarb, measure rhubarb while still frozen, then thaw completely. Drain in a colander, but do not press liquid out.

Lemon Snowball

2 envelopes unflavored gelatin
1/4 cup cold water
1 cup boiling water
1 cup sugar
1 can (12 ounces) frozen orange juice concentrate, thawed
2 tablespoons grated lemon peel
2 tablespoons lemon juice
Dash salt
3 cups heavy whipping cream, *divided*
1 angel food cake, cubed
1/4 cup confectioners' sugar
1/2 cup flaked coconut

In a large bowl, sprinkle gelatin over cold water. Let stand for 5 minutes. Add boiling water; stir until gelatin is dissolved. Add the sugar, orange juice, lemon peel, lemon juice and salt; mix well. Refrigerate until mixture begins to thicken, about 1 hour, stirring occasionally.

In a large mixing bowl, beat 2 cups cream until stiff; fold into lemon mixture. Line 12-cup bowl with plastic wrap. Spoon 1 cup lemon filling into lined bowl. Sprinkle with a layer of cake. Alternate filling cake, ending with filling. Cover and refrigerate 6 hours or overnight.

To serve, invert bowl onto a large serving platter. Remove plastic wrap. Beat confectioners' sugar and remaining cream until stiff. Frost entire cake; sprinkle with coconut. **Yield:** 16-20 servings.

Strawberry Trifle

1 cup cold milk
1 cup (8 ounces) sour cream
1 package (3.4 ounces) instant vanilla pudding mix
1 teaspoon grated orange peel
2 cups heavy whipping cream, whipped
8 cups cubed angel food cake
4 cups sliced fresh strawberries

In a bowl, whisk the milk, sour cream, pudding mix and orange peel for 2 minutes. Let stand for 2 minutes or until soft-set. Fold in whipped cream.

Place half of the cake cubes in a 3-qt. glass bowl. Arrange a third of the strawberries around sides of bowl and over cake; top with half of the pudding mixture. Repeat layers once. Top with remaining berries. Refrigerate for 2 hours before serving. **Yield:** 8-10 servings.

Cranberry-Chocolate Ice Cream

2 cups fresh *or* frozen
  cranberries
1/2 cup orange juice
1/2 teaspoon almond extract
1 quart vanilla ice cream,
  softened

4 squares (1 ounce *each*)
  semisweet chocolate, coarsely
  chopped *or* 3/4 cup miniature
  semisweet chocolate chips

In a small saucepan, combine cranberries and orange juice. Cook over medium heat until the berries pop, about 8 minutes. Cool slightly. Place in food processor or blender; add extract and pulse for about 5 minutes or until coarsely chopped. Freeze for 10 minutes.

Place ice cream in a large bowl; fold in the cranberry mixture and chocolate. Serve immediately or cover and freeze. **Yield:** 6-8 servings.

Cocoa Rice Pudding

2-1/2 cups milk
1/2 cup uncooked long grain rice
1 egg, beaten
1/4 cup sugar
1/4 cup packed brown sugar

3 tablespoons baking cocoa
1/4 teaspoon salt
1 teaspoon butter
1/2 teaspoon vanilla extract
Whipped cream *or* additional milk

In a large saucepan, bring milk and rice to a boil. Reduce heat; cover and simmer for 30 minutes. Remove from the heat and let stand for 10 minutes. Stir together the egg, sugars, cocoa and salt in a bowl; add a small amount of rice mixture to bowl and mix well.

Return all to saucepan along with butter. Cook over low heat for 5 minutes or until thermometer reads 160°, stirring constantly. Remove from the heat; gently stir in vanilla. Cover and let cool in a saucepan for 1 hour. Serve with whipped cream or milk. Refrigerate leftovers. **Yield:** 6 servings.

Crispy Rhubarb Cobbler

1 cup sugar
1/3 cup pancake mix
4 cups diced fresh *or* frozen
   rhubarb, thawed and drained

TOPPING:
  1 egg, beaten
1/4 cup vegetable oil
2/3 cup sugar
1/2 cup pancake mix

In a bowl, combine sugar and pancake mix. Add the rhubarb and toss to coat. Transfer to a greased 8-in. square baking dish. Combine topping ingredients; spread over rhubarb mixture.

Bake, uncovered, at 350° for 45 minutes or until filling is bubbly and top is golden brown. **Yield:** 6 servings.

Strawberry Dessert

1 loaf (10-1/2 ounces) angel food
   cake, cubed
1 cup cold fat-free milk
1 package (1 ounce) sugar-free
   instant vanilla pudding mix
2 cups sugar-free low-fat vanilla
   ice cream, softened

1 package (.3 ounce) sugar-free
   strawberry gelatin
1 cup boiling water
1 cup cold water
1 package (20 ounces) frozen
   unsweetened strawberries,
   partially thawed and sliced

Place cake in the bottom of a 13-in. x 9-in. x 2-in. baking dish. In a bowl, whisk milk and pudding mix and milk for 2 minutes. Let stand for 2 minutes or until soft-set. Add ice cream; beat on low 1 minute. Pour over cake; chill.

Dissolve gelatin in boiling water. Add cold water and strawberries; mix until partially set. Spoon over pudding layer. Cover and chill overnight. **Yield:** 24 servings.

Frozen Mocha Cheesecake

CRUST:
  1-1/2 cups chocolate wafer crumbs
    2 tablespoons sugar
    1/3 cup butter, melted

FILLING:
    2 packages (8 ounces *each*)
      cream cheese, softened

  1 can (14 ounces) sweetened
    condensed milk
2/3 cup chocolate syrup
  1 tablespoon instant coffee
    granules
  1 teaspoon hot water
  1 cup whipped cream

In a bowl, combine the crust ingredients. Press into the bottom of a 9-in. springform pan; set aside.

For filling, in a large mixing bowl, beat cream cheese until smooth. Gradually add milk and syrup. Dissolve coffee in water; add to cream cheese mixture. Fold in whipped cream. Pour into crust; freeze at least 6 hours. Remove from the freezer 10 minutes before serving. **Yield:** 12-16 servings.

Broiled Banana Crisp

    2 small firm bananas
    1 tablespoon lemon juice
    2 tablespoons quick-cooking oats
    2 tablespoons brown sugar
4-1/2 teaspoons all-purpose flour

  1/4 teaspoon ground cinnamon
  1/8 teaspoon ground nutmeg
    2 tablespoons cold butter
Vanilla ice cream, optional

Peel bananas; cut in half lengthwise, then widthwise. Place bananas in a greased 9-in. square baking pan. Sprinkle with lemon juice. Combine the oats, brown sugar, flour, cinnamon and nutmeg. Cut in butter until mixture resembles coarse crumbs. Sprinkle over bananas. Broil 4-6 in. from the heat for 3-4 minutes or until bubbly. Serve with ice cream if desired. **Yield:** 2 servings.

Aunt Rose's Peach Cobbler

2 cans (29 ounces *each*) sliced peaches, drained
7 slices white bread, crusts removed
1-1/2 cups sugar
2 tablespoons all-purpose flour

1/2 cup butter, melted
1 egg

TOPPING:
1 tablespoon sugar
1/4 teaspoon ground cinnamon
Vanilla ice cream

Place the peaches in a greased 11-in. x 7-in. x 2-in. baking dish. Cut each slice of bread into four strips; place over peaches.

In a bowl, combine the sugar, flour, butter and egg. Spread over bread. Combine sugar and cinnamon; sprinkle over the top.

Bake, uncovered, at 350° for 40-45 minutes or until golden brown. Serve warm with ice cream. **Yield:** 6-8 servings.

Butter Brickle Dessert

1 cup butter, melted
2 cups all-purpose flour
1/2 cup packed brown sugar
1/2 cup quick-cooking oats

1 cup chopped pecans
1 jar (12-1/2 ounces) caramel topping *or* sauce
1/2 gallon (rectangular) vanilla ice cream

In a bowl, combine the butter, flour, sugar, oats and pecans; spread into a greased 15-in. x 10-in. x 1-in. baking pan. Bake at 350° for 15 minutes. Cool for 5 minutes; break into pieces while still warm.

Pat half of the crumbs into a 13-in. x 9-in. x 2-in. baking pan. Drizzle with half of the caramel topping. Cut ice cream into 1-in. slices; place in a single layer in pan. Sprinkle with remaining crumbs. Drizzle with remaining topping. Freeze until firm, about 2-3 hours. Remove from freezer 10 minutes before cutting. **Yield:** 16-20 servings.

Coconut Trifle

1 prepared angel food cake (8 inches), cut into 1-inch cubes

2 cups cold milk

2 packages (3.4 ounces *each*) instant coconut cream pudding mix

1 quart vanilla ice cream, softened

1 carton (8 ounces) frozen whipped topping, thawed

1/4 cup flaked coconut, toasted

Place cake cubes in a large bowl. In a bowl, whisk milk and pudding mixes for 2 minutes. Let stand for 2 minutes or until soft-set. Stir in ice cream until well mixed. Pour over cake cubes; stir just until combined.

Transfer to a 5-qt. trifle bowl. Spread with whipped topping and sprinkle with coconut. Cover and refrigerate for at least 30 minutes before serving. **Yield:** 20 servings.

Apple Honey Tapioca Pudding

4 cups sliced peeled tart apples (cut in eighths)

3/4 cup honey

3 tablespoons butter

1/2 teaspoon salt

1 tablespoon lemon juice

1/2 teaspoon ground cinnamon

1/3 cup quick-cooking tapioca

2-1/2 cups water

Cream, ice cream *or* whipped cream

In a large saucepan, combine the first six ingredients. Bring to a boil. Reduce heat; cover and simmer just until apples are tender. Meanwhile, combine the tapioca and water; let stand for 5 minutes.

Using a slotted spoon, move apples into a bowl. Add tapioca and water to saucepan. Cook and stir until thickened and clear. Pour over apples. Serve warm with cream or ice cream, or cold with whipped cream. **Yield:** 6 servings.

Homemade Cocoa Pudding

3/4 cup plus 2 tablespoons sugar
2/3 cup baking cocoa
1/2 cup plus 2 tablespoons
  all-purpose flour

1/2 teaspoon salt
2-1/2 cups milk
2 cups heavy whipping cream
2 teaspoons vanilla extract

In a 2-1/2-qt. microwave-safe bowl, combine the sugar, cocoa, flour and salt. Gradually whisk in milk and cream until smooth. Cover with waxed paper. Microwave on high for 8-9 minutes or until thickened, whisking every 4 minutes. Whisk in the vanilla.

Pour into dessert dishes. Serve warm, or press a piece of waxed paper or plastic wrap on top of pudding and refrigerate. **Yield:** 6 servings.

Editor's Note: This recipe was tested in a 1,100-watt microwave.

Maple Raisin Pudding

2 tablespoons butter, softened
1/4 cup sugar
2 eggs
1-1/2 cups all-purpose flour
1 tablespoon baking powder

1/2 teaspoon salt
1/2 cup raisins
1 cup milk
1-1/2 cups pure maple syrup
Whipping cream *or* ice cream,
  optional

In a mixing bowl, cream butter and sugar. Add the eggs, one at a time, beating well after each addition. Combine the flour, baking powder, salt and raisins; add alternately with milk to creamed mixture.

In a small saucepan, bring syrup to a boil; pour into a greased 1-1/2-qt. baking dish. Pour batter over hot syrup; do not stir.

Bake, uncovered, at 375° for 30-35 minutes. Serve hot with cream or ice cream if desired. **Yield:** 6-8 servings.

Russian Cream

3/4 cup sugar
1 envelope unflavored gelatin
1/2 cup cold water
1 cup heavy whipping cream

1-1/2 cups (12 ounces) sour cream
1 teaspoon vanilla extract
4 to 5 cups cut up fresh fruit
   (bite-size pieces)

In a saucepan, combine sugar and gelatin. Stir in water; let stand for 1 minute. Bring to a boil, stirring constantly. Remove from the heat; stir in whipping cream.

In a bowl, combine sour cream and vanilla. Add gradually to hot mixture; mix until smooth. Pour into a 4-cup bowl or mold coated with nonstick cooking spray. Cover and chill for 4 hours or overnight. Serve over fruit. **Yield:** 8 servings.

Chocolate Snappers

3/4 cup shortening
1 cup sugar
1 egg
1-3/4 cups all-purpose flour
1/3 cup baking cocoa
1/4 cup light corn syrup

2 tablespoons vegetable oil
2 teaspoons baking soda
1 teaspoon ground cinnamon
1/4 teaspoon salt
Additional sugar

In a mixing bowl, cream shortening and sugar. Add egg; beat well. Add the flour, cocoa, corn syrup, oil, baking soda, cinnamon and salt; mix well. Shape by rounded teaspoonfuls into balls; roll in additional sugar.

Place 2 in. apart on greased baking sheets. Bake at 350° for 12-15 minutes. Cool on wire racks. **Yield:** 5 dozen.

Caramel Cashew Cheesecake

1/4 cup cold butter
1/2 cup all-purpose flour
3/4 cup chopped unsalted cashews
2 tablespoons confectioners' sugar
Pinch salt

FILLING:
4 packages (8 ounces *each*) cream cheese, softened
1-1/4 cups sugar

1 tablespoon vanilla extract
5 eggs, lightly beaten
2 tablespoons heavy whipping cream

TOPPING:
1 cup sugar
3 tablespoons water
3/4 cup heavy whipping cream
1 cup coarsely chopped unsalted cashews

In a bowl, cut butter into flour until mixture resembles coarse crumbs. Stir in the cashews, confectioners' sugar and salt. Press onto the bottom and 1/2 in. up the sides of a greased 9-in. springform pan. Place on a baking sheet. Bake at 350° for 15 minutes. Cool on a wire rack. Reduce heat to 325°.

In a mixing bowl, beat cream cheese, sugar and vanilla until smooth. Add eggs and cream; beat on low speed just until combined. Pour over crust. Place on a baking sheet. Bake at 325° for 55-60 minutes or until center is almost set. Cool on a wire rack for 10 minutes. Carefully run a knife around edge of pan to loosen. Cool 1 hour longer.

In a saucepan, combine sugar and water. Cook over medium-low heat until sugar is dissolved. Bring to a boil over medium-high heat; cover and boil for 2 minutes. Uncover; boil until mixture is golden brown and a candy thermometer reads 300° (hard-cracked stage), about 8 minutes.

Remove from the heat. Stir in cream until smooth, about 5 minutes (mixture will appear lumpy at first). Add cashews; cool to lukewarm. Carefully spoon over cheesecake. Refrigerate overnight. Remove sides of pan. Refrigerate leftovers. **Yield:** 12 servings.

Editor's Note: We recommend that you test your candy thermometer before each use by bringing water to a boil; the thermometer should read 212°. Adjust your recipe temperature up or down based on your test.

General Recipe Index

APPLES
Apple Butter Barbecued Chicken, 331
Apple Cider Salad, 113
Apple-Cinnamon Coleslaw, 168
Apple Cottage Cheese Salad, 118
Apple Crumb Bars, 388
Apple Gingerbread, 443
Apple Graham Pie, 420
Apple Honey Tapioca Pudding, 473
Apple Kuchen, 436
Apple Pie a la Mode Shake, 25
Apple Pork Pie, 292
Apple-Raisin Meat Loaf, 230
Apple-Strawberry Peanut Salad, 161
Apples, Berries and Yams, 165
Applesauce Brownies, 409
Applesauce-Sauerkraut Spareribs, 281
Baked Pork Chops and Apples, 279
Bumbleberry Pie, 421
Chicken-Apple Croissants, 69
Chunky Applesauce, 182
Cranberry-Apple Mincemeat Pies, 428
Cranberry Apple Punch, 27
Easy Apple Betty, 459
Ethan's Apple-Nut Pancakes, 57
Fresh Apple Cake with Caramel Sauce, 431
Grandma's Apple Dumplings, 456
Grandma's Apple Salad, 132
Mom's Fried Apples, 458
Morning Glory Muffins, 196
Orange-Pecan Baked Apples, 52
Prize-Winning Apple Pie, 426
Rhubarb Apple Pie, 423
Roast Goose with Apple-Raisin Stuffing, 355
Rose's Apple Turnover Coffee Cake, 207
Sausage Apple Roll, 270
Sticky Apple Biscuits, 184
Sugar-Topped Applesauce Muffins, 186
Toasted Apple-Cheese Sandwiches, 67
Westerfield Wassail, 20
Zucchini Apple Crisp, 462

APRICOTS
Almond Apricot Bread, 206
Apricot Bonbons, 384
Apricot Burritos, 463
Hot Jam Breakfast Sandwiches, 58
Orange Apricot Balls, 377

ARTICHOKES
Artichoke 'n' Olive Salad, 118
Cheesy Artichoke Garlic Loaf, 5
Stuffed Artichokes, 231

ASPARAGUS
Almond Asparagus, 134
Asparagus-Chicken Pie, 59
Asparagus-Lover's Stir-Fry, 312
Asparagus with Blue Cheese Sauce, 164
Breaded Asparagus Sticks, 30
Cream of Asparagus Soup, 87
Creamed Asparagus and Tomato, 157
Ham and Asparagus Roll-Ups, 295

Shrimp and Asparagus Casserole, 366
Warm Asparagus Salad, 119

AVOCADOS
Garbanzo Avocado Salad, 150
Roasted Corn and Avocado Dip, 34

BACON & CANADIAN BACON
Bacon and Blue Cheese Chicken, 327
Bacon Onion Breadsticks, 201
Bacon-Potato Burritos, 56
Bacon Veggie Roll-Ups, 102
Bacon-Wrapped Water Chestnuts, 15
Canadian Bacon Breakfast, 51
Cheesy Egg Casserole, 62
Down-on-the-Farm Breakfast, 45
Hawaiian Roll-Ups, 29
Hot Bacon Cheese Spread, 33
Hot Bacon Dressing, 171
Individual Egg Bakes, 49
Open-Faced Chicken Benedict, 330
Pepper Lover's BLT, 86
Sausage Bacon Tidbits, 36
Spanish-Style Breakfast Bake, 43
Swiss 'n' Bacon Pizza, 35
Tomato-Bacon Rarebit, 83
Turkey BLT, 81
Wake-Up Bacon Omelet, 50

BANANAS
Banana Cocoa Brownies, 392
Banana Cream Pie, 422
Banana Cupcakes, 450
Banana Fritters, 46
Banana Fudge Pie, 427
Banana Nut Bread, 185
Banana Smoothie, 26
Banana Upside-Down Cake, 434
Broiled Banana Crisp, 471
Chocolate Banana Smoothie, 28
Orange-Glazed Bananas, 466
Wholesome Quick Bread, 211

BARLEY
Mixed Grain and Wild Rice Cereal, 57
Tomato Barley Salad, 148
Turkey Barley Soup, 104

BEANS
Baked Chili, 75
Barbecued Pork with Beans, 296
Basil Beans, 111
Black Bean Potato Chili, 68
Black Bean Salsa, 21
Blue Cheese Green Beans, 112
Chili Rice Pie, 246
Church Supper Chili, 91
Classic Red Beans 'n' Rice, 159
Cranberry Baked Beans, 165
Favorite Chili, 65
Fiesta Black Bean Salad, 127
Four-Bean Salad, 142
Garbanzo Avocado Salad, 150
Green Bean Bundles, 169

Green Beans with Mushrooms, 135
Hearty Chicken and Beans, 336
Lima Bean Casserole, 167
Mini Green Bean Casserole, 160
Old-Fashioned Baked Beans, 163
Pumpkin Chili, 107
Quick Bean Soup, 86
Sweet Succotash Chili, 84
Tex-Mex Bean Dip, 28
Three Bean Casserole, 155
Turkey Bean Bake, 336
Two-Bean Tuna Salad, 120
Vegetable Bean Soup, 94
Vegetarian Chili, 76
White Christmas Chili, 97

BEEF (also see Corned Beef; Ground Beef)
Appetizer
Dried Beef Spread, 19
Main Dishes
Barbecued Short Ribs, 229
Beef 'n' Pepper Stir-Fry, 251
Beef Burgundy, 236
Beef Pinwheels, 235
Beef Rouladen, 241
Brisket with Gingersnap Gravy, 222
Cheesy Beef Stroganoff, 246
Chicken-Fried Cube Steaks, 249
Frank's Sauerbraten, 221
Hungarian Goulash, 241
Italian-Style Round Steak, 256
Lemon Rib Eyes, 262
Parsley-Stuffed Flank Steak, 249
Pepper Steak, 259
Perfect Prime Rib Roast, 219
Red-Eye Beef Roast, 257
Rhubarb Beef, 260
Roast Beef with Mushroom Sauce, 229
Sesame Flank Steak, 258
Short Ribs with Plums, 240
Sirloin with Bernaise Sauce, 219
Smoky Beef Brisket, 235
Spiced Pot Roast, 217
Stuffed Round Steak, 234
Stuffed Sirloin Roast, 220
Sweet and Spicy Steak, 222
Tenderloin Diane, 216
Vegetable Beef Kabobs, 245
Soup & Sandwiches
Favorite Chili, 65
Italian Beef Sandwiches, 250
Sirloin Steak Sandwiches, 248

BEETS
Glazed Beets, 149
Harvard Beets, 141

BISCUITS & SCONES
Baking Powder Drop Biscuits, 188
Cheddar Biscuits, 201
Cinnamon Chip Raisin Scones, 200
Corn Scones, 205
Cranberry Scones, 193

Frosted Cinnamon-Raisin Biscuits, 204
Lemon Blueberry Drop Scones, 202
Mom's Buttermilk Biscuits, 187
Sage Cornmeal Biscuits, 191
Savory Biscuits, 187
Sticky Apple Biscuits, 184
Sunshine Biscuits, 203
Sweet Potato Biscuits, 208

BLUEBERRIES
Best-Ever Blueberry Muffins, 195
Blueberry Brunch Loaf, 48
Blueberry Cream Pie, 423
Blueberry Milk Shake, 21
Blueberry Orange Cups, 463
Blueberry Raspberry Crunch, 466
Blueberry Streusel Coffee Cake, 197
Bumbleberry Pie, 421
Fresh Blueberry Tarts, 419
Lemon Blueberry Drop Scones, 202
Lemon Blueberry Tea Cake, 450
Ozark Blueberry Pie, 412

BREADS (see Biscuits & Scones; Coffee
Cakes; Muffins; Quick Breads; Rolls &
Buns; Yeast Breads)

BROCCOLI
Broccoli, Hamburger and Cheese Soup, 79
Broccoli Supreme, 156
Broccoli Tomato Cups, 150
Broccoli Tuna Roll-Ups, 361
Cheesy Broccoli Rice, 122
Golden Broccoli Bake, 218
Hamburger-Broccoli Dip, 19
Herbed Broccoli Spears, 160
Italian Broccoli Salad, 123
Turkey Broccoli Bake, 316

CABBAGE (also see Sauerkraut)
Acorn Cabbage Bake, 166
Apple-Cinnamon Coleslaw, 168
Cabbage-Potato Saute, 110
Cabbage Rolls, 215
Chinese Noodle Slaw, 117
Cranberry Cabbage Salad, 147
German Chicken, 324
Hungarian Cabbage with Noodles, 116
Italian Cabbage and Rice, 304
Kielbasa Cabbage Soup, 90
New England Boiled Dinner, 238
Nutty Coleslaw, 147
Pork and Cabbage Rolls, 307
Tangy Cabbage Salad, 114
Turkey Cabbage Soup, 83

CARROTS
Carrot Cake, 443
Carrot Casserole, 141
Carrot Soup, 87
Crown Jewel Patties, 111
Curry Carrot Dip, 38
Nutty Carrot Salad, 122
Tangerine Carrots, 161
Zesty Carrots, 131

CASSEROLES
Beef
Baked Spaghetti, 218
Cashew Noodle Casserole, 227
Cheeseburger Macaroni, 244
Cheesy Casserole, 261
Cheesy Tortilla Bake, 242
Company Casserole, 223
Corn 'n' Beef Pasta Bake, 247
Corn Bread Beef Bake, 243
Creamy Corned Beef Casserole, 256
Farmhouse Dinner, 224
Golden Broccoli Bake, 218
Lazy Lasagna, 253
Manicotti, 216
Mexi-Corn Lasagna Dish, 233
Mock Ravioli, 252
Pizza Casserole, 254
Tater-Topped Casserole, 221
Zucchini Lasagna, 214
Fish & Seafood
Cheesy Tuna Lasagna, 363
Crab Thermidor, 371
Crunchy Tuna Surprise, 358
Pineapple Shrimp Rice Bake, 362
Potato Salmon Casserole, 368
Salmon Biscuit Bake, 368
Seafood in Tomato Sauce, 357
Shrimp and Asparagus Casserole, 366
Pork
Cheesy Zucchini Medley, 274
Crunch Top Ham and Potato Casserole, 304
Depression Casserole, 277
Ham Hot Dish, 285
Ham-Noodle Bake, 294
Hawaiian Pizza Pasta, 299
Italian Sausage and Sauerkraut, 293
Jambalaya, 280
Potato Ham au Gratin, 271
Sparerib Casserole, 289
Tangy Reuben Bake, 289
Poultry
Chick-a-Roni, 353
Chicken Amondine, 356
Chicken and Spinach Supper, 350
Chicken Crescent Casserole, 313
Chicken Crouton Hot Dish, 338
Chicken-Mushroom Deluxe, 334
Chicken Spaghetti, 352
Chicken Tetrazzini, 355
Comforting Chicken 'n' Noodles, 347
Corny Bread Bake, 312
Jambalaya, 280
Overnight Chicken Casserole, 327
Ranch Chicken 'n' Rice, 331
Swiss Chicken Bake, 340
Turkey Bean Bake, 336
Turkey Broccoli Bake, 316
Turkey Rice Casserole, 311
Turkey Squash Casserole, 321

CAULIFLOWER
Cauliflower Lettuce Salad, 140
Cheddar Cauliflower, 132
Colorful Cauliflower Salad, 125
Cottage-Cauliflower Spread, 28
Creamy Cauliflower Salad, 115
Tangy Cauliflower, 137

CHEESE
Appetizers
Beef 'n' Cheddar Biscuits, 12
Cheese Olive Appetizers, 26
Cheese Straws, 18
Cheesy Artichoke Garlic Loaf, 5
Cheesy Mushroom Appetizers, 30
Chili Cheese Dip, 7
Cottage-Cauliflower Spread, 28
Creamy Red Pepper Dip, 18
Creamy Shrimp Dip, 22
Crunchy Swiss-n-Ham Snacks, 23
Ham 'n' Cheese Puffs, 25
Ham and Cheese Spread, 11
Hot Bacon Cheese Spread, 33
Swiss 'n' Bacon Pizza, 35
Tomato-Cheese Snack Bread, 13
Breads
Cheddar Biscuits, 201
Golden Cheese Yeast Bread, 197
Spinach Cheese Muffins, 205
Breakfast & Brunch
Cheesy Egg Casserole, 62
Ham and Cheese Waffles, 49
Condiments
Blue Cheese Dressing, 178
Cheddar Cheese Sauce, 176
Evelyn's Original Roquefort Dressing, 177
Main Dishes
Bacon and Blue Cheese Chicken, 327
Beef 'n' Veggie Cheddar Pie, 252
Cheeseburger Macaroni, 244
Cheesy Beef Stroganoff, 246
Cheesy Casserole, 261
Cheesy Chicken Roll-Ups, 344
Cheesy Tortilla Bake, 242
Cheesy Tuna Lasagna, 363
Cheesy Zucchini Medley, 274
Chicken Lasagna Rolls, 353
Chicken Parmesan, 344
Cordon Bleu Pork Chops, 283
Cream Cheese-Stuffed Catfish, 358
Lazy Lasagna, 253
Mozzarella Meat Whirl, 232
Orange Roughy Parmesan, 359
Parmesan Ham Pasta, 275
Parmesan Salmon Fillets, 367
Pork Chops Parmesan, 277
Potato Ham au Gratin, 271
Scalloped Potatoes 'n' Ham, 295
Swiss Chicken Bake, 340
Zucchini Lasagna, 214
Sides & Salads
Apple Cottage Cheese Salad, 118
Asparagus with Blue Cheese Sauce, 164
Baked Hominy and Cheese, 136
Blue Cheese Green Beans, 112
Cheddar Cauliflower, 132
Cheesy Broccoli Rice, 122

Mother's Manicotti, 162
My Mother's Mac and Cheese, 165
Parmesan Potato Sticks, 115
Spinach Cheese Bake, 134
Stove-Top Macaroni and Cheese, 133
Swiss Bake, 137
Tomato Mozzarella Bake, 127
Turkey-Blue Cheese Pasta Salad, 148
Soups & Sandwiches
Broccoli, Hamburger and Cheese Soup, 79
Cheesy Chicken Corn Soup, 78
Cheesy Turkey Burgers, 334
Dilly Cheese Soup, 106
Grilled Blue Cheese Sandwiches, 91
Lasagna in a Bun, 67
Parmesan Pork Sandwiches, 306
Special Ham 'n' Cheese Sandwiches, 92
Three-Cheese Tomato Melt, 99
Toasted Apple-Cheese Sandwiches, 67

CHERRIES
Bishop's Bread, 202
Cheery Cherry Bread, 187
Cherry Grunt, 457
Cherry Honey Relish, 182
Cherry Pineapple Cake, 436
Chocolate Covered Cherries, 383
Frosted Cherry Nut Bars, 399
Molded Cherry-Pineapple Salad, 138
Sweet Cherry Pie, 418
Swiss Treat Bars, 398
Tree-Mendous No-Bake Cherry Pie, 412

CHICKEN
Appetizers
Aunt Shirley's Liver Pate, 29
Buttery Chicken Spread, 23
Curried Chicken Balls, 22
Hot Wings, 32
Mandarin Chicken Bites, 6
Sweet and Sour Chicken Nuggets, 16
Breakfast & Brunch
Asparagus-Chicken Pie, 59
Main Dishes
Apple Butter Barbecued Chicken, 331
Asparagus-Lover's Stir-Fry, 312
Bacon and Blue Cheese Chicken, 327
Baked Crumbled Chicken, 332
Barbecued Raspberry Chicken, 351
Cheesy Chicken Roll-Ups, 344
Chick-a-Roni, 353
Chicken a la King, 339
Chicken Amondine, 356
Chicken and Spinach Supper, 350
Chicken and Tomato Scampi, 345
Chicken Barbecued in Foil, 317
Chicken Crescent Casserole, 313
Chicken Crouton Hot Dish, 338
Chicken Florentine, 354
Chicken Lasagna Rolls, 353
Chicken Livers Royale, 348
Chicken-Mushroom Deluxe, 334
Chicken Parmesan, 344
Chicken Pilaf Saute, 356

Chicken Potpie, 323
Chicken Spaghetti, 352
Chicken Tamale Pie, 320
Chicken Tetrazzini, 355
Chicken with Cucumber Sauce, 318
Chicken with Tomato-Cream Sauce, 326
Coconut Chicken with Pineapple Vinaigrette, 328
Cola Chicken, 314
Comforting Chicken 'n' Noodles, 347
Corny Bread Bake, 312
Creole Fried Chicken, 317
Crescent Chicken Squares, 321
Curried Chicken and Rice, 341
Dijon Chicken, 315
Dilly Chicken and Potatoes, 320
Easy Fried Rice, 346
Extra-Crispy Italian Chicken, 333
Famous Fried Chicken, 350
Garlic-Brown Sugar Chicken, 335
German Chicken, 324
Ginger Chicken Stir-Fry, 323
Grilled Chicken Kabobs, 329
Hearty Chicken and Beans, 336
Honey Baked Chicken, 342
Jambalaya, 280
Lemon Almond Chicken, 338
Marmalade Drumsticks, 331
Mediterranean Chicken, 346
Mexican-Style Chicken Kiev, 335
Onion-Baked Chicken, 351
Open-Faced Chicken Benedict, 330
Orange-Coated Chicken, 337
Oven-Baked Sesame Chicken, 352
Overnight Chicken Casserole, 327
Peach-Glazed Chicken, 330
Pecan Oven-Fried Fryer, 341
Pesto Mushroom Chicken, 349
Picante Chicken, 314
Picnic Potato Chip Chicken, 347
Pine Nut Chicken, 354
Ranch Chicken 'n' Rice, 331
Ranch-Style Thighs, 342
Smothered Ginger Chicken, 329
South-of-the-Border Thighs, 333
South Seas Skillet, 316
Southwestern Fried Rice, 343
Spicy Chicken Corn Skillet, 324
Stir-Fried Chicken Fajitas, 332
Summer Squash Enchiladas, 319
Sunday Fried Chicken, 326
Sunshine Chicken, 325
Sweet-and-Sour Chicken, 318
Swiss Chicken Bake, 340
Tasty Texas Tenders, 342
Salad
Chicken Tortellini Salad, 168
Soups & Sandwiches
California Clubs, 82
Cheesy Chicken Corn Soup, 78
Chicken-Apple Croissants, 69
Chicken Salad on Buns, 81
Chicken Stew, 106

Chicken Tortellini Soup, 105
Chickenwiches, 84
Curried Chicken Pita Pockets, 92
Dilled Chicken Soup, 102
Farmhouse Chicken Soup, 63
Fried Chicken Pitas, 74
Grandmother's Chicken 'n' Dumplings, 96
Hot Chicken Heroes, 88
Make-Ahead Saucy Sandwiches, 78
Mom's Chicken Soup, 77
Southwestern Chicken Soup, 88
Tarragon Chicken Salad, 99

CHILI
Baked Chili, 75
Black Bean Potato Chili, 68
Favorite Chili, 65
Pumpkin Chili, 107
Sweet Succotash Chili, 84
Vegetarian Chili, 76
White Christmas Chili, 97

CHOCOLATE
Applesauce Brownies, 409
Austrian Chocolate Balls, 393
Banana Cocoa Brownies, 392
Banana Fudge Pie, 427
Bavarian Mint Fudge, 375
Chocolate Angel Food Cake, 449
Chocolate Banana Smoothie, 28
Chocolate Billionaires, 376
Chocolate Buttermilk Brownies, 403
Chocolate Caramel Clusters, 385
Chocolate Chews, 381
Chocolate Chip Marshmallow Bars, 410
Chocolate Chip Pumpkin Bread, 206
Chocolate Cinnamon Rolls, 198
Chocolate Covered Cherries, 383
Chocolate Dipped Treats, 386
Chocolate Mayonnaise Cake, 441
Chocolate Mint Cookies, 396
Chocolate Nougat Cake, 448
Chocolate Oat Cake, 445
Chocolate Peanut Butter, 172
Chocolate Shoofly Pie, 428
Chocolate Snappers, 475
Chocolate Velvet Cream, 454
Cinnamon Chocolate Angel Pie, 422
Cocoa Rice Pudding, 469
Cranberry-Chocolate Ice Cream, 469
Crisp Chocolate Chip Cookies, 404
Crunchy Chocolate Cups, 380
Devil's Food Cake, 446
Easy Mint Chocolate Truffles, 378
Easy Mint Hot Chocolate, 17
Favorite Cake Brownies, 408
Frappe Mocha, 6
Fudge Pecan Brownie Tart, 430
Fudgy Brownies, 407
German Chocolate Pie, 425
Gold Rush Brownies, 390
Homemade Cocoa Pudding, 474
Hot Chocolate Mix, 31
Hot Fudge Pudding Cake, 441

Mocha Nut Fudge, 379
No-Guilt Brownies, 394
Old-Fashioned Chocolate Chip Cookies, 409
One-Bowl Chocolate Cake, 444
Peanut Butter Brownies, 410
Peanut Butter-Chocolate Chip Pie, 413
Saucepan Fudgies, 388
Sauerkraut Brownie Cake, 435
Skillet Chocolate Dumplings, 455
Soft Chocolate Cookies, 389
Speedy Oven Fudge, 384
White Chocolate Fudge, 383
White Chocolate Truffles, 375
Whoopee Pies, 400

COCONUT
Coconut Almond Bars, 380
Coconut Chicken with Pineapple
    Vinaigrette, 328
Coconut Drops, 382
Coconut Pineapple Pie, 419
Coconut Snacks, 386
Coconut Trifle, 473
Coconut Walnut Tart, 416
French Coconut Pie, 414
Fresh Coconut Pound Cake, 434
Frozen Coconut Caramel Pie, 415
German Chocolate Pie, 425
Lemon Coconut Bars, 387
Lemon Snowball, 468
Snowball Cake, 432
Tom Thumb Treats, 391

COFFEE CAKES
Blueberry Streusel Coffee Cake, 197
Buttermilk Coffee Cake, 54
Cinnamon-Raisin Coffee Cake, 196
Danish Coffee Cake, 212
Graham-Streusel Coffee Cake, 53
Rose's Apple Turnover Coffee Cake, 207

CONDIMENTS (also see Salads &
    Dressings)
All Seasons Marinade, 178
Cheddar Cheese Sauce, 176
Cherry Honey Relish, 182
Chivey Potato Topper, 180
Chocolate Peanut Butter, 172
Chunky Applesauce, 182
Elegant Holiday Ham Glaze, 172
Fresh Salsa, 180
Horseradish Sauce, 181
Lemon Butter Topping, 177
Lemon Curd, 176
Light Pesto, 175
Microwave Hollandaise Sauce, 174
Mushroom Pasta Sauce, 175
Orange Barbecue Sauce, 181
Raspberry Vinegar, 177
Roasted Garlic Spread, 173
Salad Croutons, 179
Salt Substitute, 174
Sweet Dill Refrigerator Pickles, 176
Tarragon Butter, 178
White Sauce for Pasta, 173

CORN
Baked Corn Casserole, 144
Cajun Corn Soup with Shrimp, 64
Cheesy Corn Chip Soup, 78
Corn 'n' Beef Pasta Bake, 247
Corn Medley, 161
Corn Scones, 205
Corn Wheels with Lime Butter, 153
Corny Bread Bake, 312
Corny Turkey Burgers, 345
Golden Corn Puff, 151
Mexi-Corn Lasagna Dish, 233
Patio Salad, 138
Peppery Corn Salad, 157
Roasted Corn and Avocado Dip, 34
Scalloped Corn, 129
Spicy Chicken Corn Skillet, 324
Sweet Succotash Chili, 84

CORNED BEEF
Corned Beef Hash and Eggs, 41
Creamy Corned Beef Casserole, 256
New England Boiled Dinner, 238
Wake-Up Sandwiches, 58

CORNISH HENS
Cornish Hens with Veggies, 337
Stuffed Cornish Hens, 322

CRANBERRIES
Apples, Berries and Yams, 165
Cranberry-Apple Mincemeat Pies, 428
Cranberry Apple Punch, 27
Cranberry Baked Beans, 165
Cranberry Baklava, 460
Cranberry Cabbage Salad, 147
Cranberry-Chocolate Ice Cream, 469
Cranberry Gelatin Salad, 118
Cranberry-Glazed Spareribs, 273
Cranberry Nut Stuffing, 130
Cranberry Scones, 193
Cranberry-Stuffed Pork Chops, 297
Elegant Holiday Ham Glaze, 172
Frozen Cranberry Velvet Pie, 416
Thanksgiving Sandwiches, 104
Westerfield Wassail, 20

CUCUMBERS
Chicken with Cucumber Sauce, 318
Cool Cucumber Sandwich, 108
Sour Cream Cucumber Salad, 152
Stuffed Cucumbers, 162
Sweet Dill Refrigerator Pickles, 176

DATES
Bishop's Bread, 202
Date Nut Bread, 198
Date Pecan Fudge, 381
Orange-Date Bars, 397
Orange Date Cake, 445
Peanut Butter Fingers, 378
Spiced Date Oatmeal, 44

EGGS
Appetizers
Chutney Stuffed Eggs, 25

Crab-Stuffed Deviled Eggs, 21
Deviled Ham and Egg Appetizer, 6
Pickled Eggs, 18
Breakfast & Brunch
Asparagus-Chicken Pie, 59
Bacon-Potato Burritos, 56
Cheesy Egg Casserole, 62
Corned Beef Hash and Eggs, 41
Crab Quiche, 367
Creamed Ham and Eggs, 42
Curried Scrambled Egg, 42
Down-on-the-Farm Breakfast, 45
Garden Fresh Breakfast, 55
Home-Style Hominy Casserole, 61
Individual Egg Bakes, 49
Rice-Crust Quiche, 62
Salmon Scramble, 60
Sausage Potato Wraps, 276
Spanish-Style Breakfast Bake, 43
Wake-Up Bacon Omelet, 50
Wake-Up Sandwiches, 58
Zucchini Oven Omelet, 41
Sandwiches
Creamy Egg Salad Sandwiches, 97
Egg Salad Tuna Wraps, 93
Humpty-Dumpty Sandwich Loaf, 72
Sausage Potato Wraps, 276
Triple Tasty Sandwich Spread, 89

FISH
Appetizer
Salmon Pate, 15
Breakfast & Brunch
Salmon Scramble, 60
Main Dishes
Baked Whole Salmon, 369
Broccoli Tuna Roll-Ups, 361
Cheesy Tuna Lasagna, 363
Cream Cheese-Stuffed Catfish, 350
Crunchy Tuna Surprise, 358
Fillets with Ginger Sauce, 370
Orange Roughy Parmesan, 359
Parmesan Salmon Fillets, 367
Pecan Fish, 370
Pepper and Salsa Cod, 362
Poached Teriyaki Salmon, 365
Potato Salmon Casserole, 368
Salmon Biscuit Bake, 368
Salmon with Herb-Mustard Sauce, 364
Skillet Fish Dinner, 371
Sole Amondine, 366
Salads
Salmon Salad, 153
Two-Bean Tuna Salad, 120
Sandwiches
Egg Salad Tuna Wraps, 93
Grilled Salmon Sandwiches, 360
Vegetable Tuna Sandwiches, 100

FRUIT (also see specific kinds)
Fluffy Fruit Salad, 113
Fruit and Cream Parfaits, 464
Fruit Kuchen, 454
Fruit Slush, 12

FRUIT *(continued)*
Fruitcake Squares, 403
Fruited Pork Picante, 283
Fruity Pasta Salad, 158
Fruity Thirst Quencher, 16
Fruity-Toot-Toot, 140
Honey Fruit Dessert, 466
Hot Curried Fruit, 158
Scrumptious Breakfast Fruit Soup, 47
Yogurt Honey Fruit Bowl, 47

GROUND BEEF
Appetizers
Barbecued Mini-Balls, 13
Beef 'n' Cheddar Biscuits, 12
Chili Cheese Dip, 7
Easy Egg Rolls, 38
Hamburger-Broccoli Dip, 19
Hawaiian Roll-Ups, 29
Nutty Beef Turnovers, 34
Super Nachos, 8
Sweet-and-Sour Meatballs Appetizer, 33
Tiny Taco Meatballs, 20
Main Dishes
Apple-Raisin Meat Loaf, 230
Baked Nachos, 225
Baked Spaghetti, 218
Baked Ziti with Fresh Tomatoes, 245
Beef 'n' Veggie Cheddar Pie, 252
Beef Florentine, 243
Beef Fried Rice, 238
Beef-Stuffed Onions, 240
Beefy Enchiladas, 226
Cabbage Rolls, 215
Cashew Noodle Casserole, 227
Cheeseburger Macaroni, 244
Cheesy Casserole, 261
Cheesy Tortilla Bake, 242
Chili Rice Pie, 246
Chop Suey, 231
Classic Meat Loaf, 220
Company Casserole, 223
Corn 'n' Beef Pasta Bake, 247
Corn Bread Beef Bake, 243
Cornmeal Empanadas, 237
Crazy Crust Pizza, 250
Creamy Beef Stroganoff, 232
Curried Meat Loaf, 215
Farmhouse Dinner, 224
German Skillet Meal, 234
Golden Broccoli Bake, 218
Hobo Knapsacks, 244
Hot Tamale Pie, 254
Kid-Pleasing Spaghetti, 258
Lazy Lasagna, 253
Mandarin Beef Skillet, 247
Manicotti, 216
Meatballs with Spaetzle, 255
Mexi-Corn Lasagna Dish, 233
Mexican Meat Loaf Roll, 239
Mock Pot Roast, 259
Mock Ravioli, 252
Mozzarella Meat Whirl, 232
Oven Porcupines, 236

Pizza Casserole, 254
Poached Meatballs in Lemon Sauce, 260
Southwestern Deep-Dish Pizza, 223
Spaghetti-Style Rice, 242
Stuffed Acorn Squash, 224
Stuffed Artichokes, 231
Stuffed Green Peppers, 233
Stuffed Meat Loaf, 262
Stuffed Pizza, 213
Swedish Meatballs, 228
Taco Rice, 222
Tater-Topped Casserole, 221
Topsy-Turvy Pie, 257
Willie Hoss' Meat Loaf, 253
Zesty Corn Cakes, 251
Zucchini Lasagna, 214
Sides
Cheesy Broccoli Rice, 122
Classic Red Beans 'n' Rice, 159
Three Bean Casserole, 155
Soups & Sandwiches
ABC Soup, 69
Autumn Soup, 85
Baked Chili, 75
Beef Crescent Loaf, 225
Black Bean Potato Chili, 68
Broccoli, Hamburger and Cheese Soup, 79
Church Supper Chili, 91
Deviled English Muffins, 88
Hearty Steak Soup, 66
Herbed Pasties, 93
Homemade Pinwheel Noodles, 248
Lasagna in a Bun, 67
Lemon-Herb Gyros, 239
Meatball Noodle Soup, 101
Meaty Pita Pockets, 226
Open-Faced Pizza Burgers, 261
Oriental Patties, 237
Pepper Soup, 74
Pizza Buns, 76
Pumpkin Chili, 107
Pumpkin Sloppy Joes, 228
Saucy Herb Hamburgers, 227
Sausage-Stuffed French Loaf, 217
Sweet Potato Stew, 92
Sweet Succotash Chili, 84
Taco Crescents, 214
Zesty Meatball Sandwiches, 230

HAM
Appetizers
Crunchy Swiss-n-Ham Snacks, 23
Deviled Ham and Egg Appetizer, 6
Ham 'n' Cheese Puffs, 25
Ham and Cheese Spread, 11
Ham Pickle Pinwheels, 17
Hawaiian Roll-Ups, 29
Breakfast & Brunch
Creamed Ham and Eggs, 42
Early-Riser Muffins, 48
Ham and Cheese Waffles, 49
Rice-Crust Quiche, 62
Southwest Skillet Dish, 61

Main Dishes
Cordon Bleu Pork Chops, 283
Crunch Top Ham and Potato Casserole, 304
Ham and Asparagus Roll-Ups, 295
Ham Balls with Mustard Dill Sauce, 281
Ham Fried Rice, 282
Ham Hot Dish, 285
Ham Loaf Pie, 291
Ham-Noodle Bake, 294
Ham Rolls Continental, 306
Hasty Heartland Dinner, 269
Hawaiian Pizza Pasta, 299
Jambalaya, 280
Microwave Corn Bread Casserole, 308
Mustard Baked Ham with Gravy, 301
Parmesan Ham Pasta, 275
Potato Ham au Gratin, 271
Saucy Ham and Rice, 268
Scalloped Potatoes 'n' Ham, 295
Stuffed Easter Ham, 288
Stuffed Ham Bake, 286
Side & Salads
Classic Red Beans 'n' Rice, 159
Ham, Turkey and Wild Rice Salad, 143
Pesto Pasta Salad, 170
Soups & Sandwiches
Barbecued Ham Sandwiches, 278
Ham and Spinach Loaf, 68
Ham-Stuffed Bread, 103
Humpty-Dumpty Sandwich Loaf, 72
Mock Monte Cristos, 73
Quick Calzones, 77
Rosemary's Ham Reubens, 69
Special Ham 'n' Cheese Sandwiches, 92
Stuffed Ham Slices, 95
Sweet 'n' Sour Pockets, 71
Triple Tasty Sandwich Spread, 89
Wild Rice Soup, 108

HONEY
Apple Honey Tapioca Pudding, 473
Cherry Honey Relish, 182
Honey Baked Chicken, 342
Honey-Baked French Toast, 54
Honey Cereal Bites, 9
Honey Fruit Dessert, 466
Honey Mustard Dressing, 174
Honey White Loaves, 208
Yogurt Honey Fruit Bowl, 47

LAMB
Lamb and Potato Stew, 80

MARSHMALLOWS &
MARSHMALLOW CREME
Chocolate Chip Marshmallow Bars, 410
Crunchy Peanut Candy, 382
Date Pecan Fudge, 381
Peanut Butter Mallow Candy, 386
Picnic Cake, 440
White Chocolate Fudge, 383
Whoopee Pies, 400

MEAT LOAVES
Apple-Raisin Meat Loaf, 230

Classic Meat Loaf, 220
Curried Meat Loaf, 215
Hungarian Pork Loaf, 301
Mexican Meat Loaf Roll, 239
Mock Pot Roast, 259
Mozzarella Meat Whirl, 232
Sausage Apple Roll, 270
Stuffed Meat Loaf, 262
Willie Hoss' Meat Loaf, 253

MEATBALLS
Barbecued Meatballs, 275
Barbecued Mini-Balls, 13
Ham Balls with Mustard Dill Sauce, 281
Meatballs with Spaetzle, 255
Oven Porcupines, 236
Poached Meatballs in Lemon Sauce, 260
Swedish Meatballs, 228
Sweet-and-Sour Meatballs Appetizer, 33
Tangy Turkey Meatballs, 7
Zesty Meatball Sandwiches, 230

MUFFINS
Best-Ever Blueberry Muffins, 195
Easy Oat Bran Muffins, 189
Ginger Yeast Muffins, 209
Lemon-Raspberry Muffins, 211
Montana Mountain Muffins, 199
Morning Glory Muffins, 196
Roasted Red Pepper Muffins, 192
Spinach Cheese Muffins, 205
Sugar-Topped Applesauce Muffins, 186

MUSHROOMS
Cheesy Beef Stroganoff, 246
Cheesy Mushroom Appetizers, 30
Chicken-Mushroom Deluxe, 334
Chicken Tetrazzini, 355
Green Beans with Mushrooms, 135
Mixed Greens with Mushrooms, 130
Mushroom 'n' Tomato Salad, 119
Mushroom Pasta Sauce, 175
Pesto Mushroom Chicken, 349
Roast Beef with Mushroom Sauce, 229
Sausage Stroganoff, 287
Stuffed Mushrooms, 10

NUTS
Almond Apricot Bread, 206
Almond Asparagus, 134
Almond Toffee, 376
Apple-Strawberry Peanut Salad, 161
Banana Nut Bread, 185
Bishop's Bread, 202
Candied Pecans, 374
Caramel Cashew Cheesecake, 476
Cashew Noodle Casserole, 227
Chicken Amondine, 356
Chocolate Billionaires, 376
Chocolate Caramel Clusters, 385
Cinnamon Walnut Crescents, 189
Coconut Almond Bars, 380
Coconut Walnut Tart, 416
Coffee Almond Crisps, 406
Cranberry Nut Stuffing, 130

Crunchy Peanut Candy, 382
Danish Coffee Cake, 212
Date Nut Bread, 198
Date Pecan Fudge, 381
Ethan's Apple-Nut Pancakes, 57
Frosted Cherry Nut Bars, 399
Frosted Hazelnuts, 17
Fudge Pecan Brownie Tart, 430
Lemon Almond Chicken, 338
Maple Walnut Pie, 414
Mocha Nut Fudge, 379
Nutty Beef Turnovers, 34
Nutty Caramel Popcorn, 14
Nutty Carrot Salad, 122
Nutty Coleslaw, 147
Nutty Mandarin Salad, 135
Nutty Shrimp Salad Sandwiches, 74
Orange-Pecan Baked Apples, 52
Peach Praline Pie, 424
Pecan Fish, 370
Pecan Fondant, 385
Pecan Icebox Cookies, 406
Pecan Oven-Fried Fryer, 341
Pecan Pie, 417
Pecan Sandies, 401
Pine Nut Chicken, 354
Pork with Peanuts, 308
Raisin Peanut Clusters, 377
Sole Amondine, 366
Toffee Nut Squares, 401
Walnut-Crunch Pumpkin Pie, 429

OATS
Apple Crumb Bars, 388
Chocolate Oat Cake, 445
Crispy Breakfast Slices, 59
Four-Grain Bread, 190
Garlic Oatmeal Soup, 72
Mixed Grain and Wild Rice Cereal, 57
Oatmeal Pie, 417
Pear-Oatmeal Breakfast Pudding, 56
Spiced Date Oatmeal, 44
Vanilla Granola, 53

ONIONS
Bacon Onion Breadsticks, 201
Beef-Stuffed Onions, 240
Dad's Onion Rings, 110
French Onion Soup, 95
Marinated Onion Salad, 143
Onion-Baked Chicken, 351
Onion Pie, 148
Onions and Cream Appetizer, 27

ORANGES & TANGERINES
Blueberry Orange Cups, 463
Citrus Pork Skillet, 271
Creamy Citrus Salad, 159
Grandma Brubaker's Orange Cookies, 402
Mandarin Beef Skillet, 247
Mandarin Chicken Bites, 6
Marmalade Drumsticks, 331
Nutty Mandarin Salad, 135
One-Pan Pork a la Orange, 272
Orange Apricot Balls, 377

Orange Barbecue Sauce, 181
Orange Barbecued Turkey, 328
Orange-Coated Chicken, 337
Orange Colada, 20
Orange-Date Bars, 397
Orange Date Cake, 445
Orange Dijon Pork, 299
Orange-Glazed Bananas, 466
Orange Meringue Pie, 427
Orange-Pecan Baked Apples, 52
Tangerine Carrots, 161
Teriyaki Tangerine Ribs, 264

PASTA
ABC Soup, 69
Baked Spaghetti, 218
Baked Ziti with Fresh Tomatoes, 245
Beef Ravioli Soup, 75
Cashew Noodle Casserole, 227
Cheeseburger Macaroni, 244
Cheesy Beef Stroganoff, 246
Cheesy Tuna Lasagna, 363
Chick-a-Roni, 353
Chicken Lasagna Rolls, 353
Chicken Spaghetti, 352
Chicken Tetrazzini, 355
Chicken Tortellini Salad, 168
Chicken Tortellini Soup, 105
Comforting Chicken 'n' Noodles, 347
Corn 'n' Beef Pasta Bake, 247
Creamy Beef Stroganoff, 232
Creamy Veggie Vermicelli, 155
Elbow Macaroni Salad, 125
Fruity Pasta Salad, 158
Garlic-Buttered Pasta, 164
Ham-Noodle Bake, 294
Hawaiian Pizza Pasta, 299
Herbed Egg Noodles, 111
Homemade Noodles, 167
Homemade Pinwheel Noodles, 248
Hungarian Cabbage with Noodles, 116
Kid-Pleasing Spaghetti, 258
Lazy Lasagna, 253
Linguine with Garlic Clam Sauce, 365
Manicotti, 216
Meatball Noodle Soup, 101
Mediterranean Shrimp and Pasta, 360
Mock Ravioli, 252
Mother's Manicotti, 162
My Mother's Mac and Cheese, 165
Noodle Nibblers, 145
Parmesan Ham Pasta, 275
Pesto Pasta Salad, 170
Pork Fajita Pasta, 290
Quick Pantry Salad, 154
Sausage Stroganoff, 287
Spicy Spaghetti Salad, 157
Stove-Top Macaroni and Cheese, 133
Tortellini Bake, 120
Turkey-Blue Cheese Pasta Salad, 148
Turkey in the Strawganoff, 349
Zucchini-Garlic Pasta, 126

PEACHES
Aunt Rose's Peach Cobbler, 472

Bride's Peach Pie, 429
Peach-Glazed Chicken, 330
Peach Praline Pie, 424
Peachy Yogurt Shake, 11

PEANUT BUTTER
Chocolate Peanut Butter, 172
Easy Peanut Butter Pretzels, 12
Flourless Peanut Butter Cookies, 395
Haystacks, 377
Peanut Butter 'n' Jelly Shake, 16
Peanut Butter Brownies, 410
Peanut Butter-Chocolate Chip Pie, 413
Peanut Butter Fingers, 378
Peanut Butter Mallow Candy, 386
Peanut Butter Pie, 420

PEARS
Crustless Pear Pie, 418
Lemon Pear Pie, 416
Lime Pear Salad, 164
Pear Cake with Sour Cream Topping, 442
Pear-Oatmeal Breakfast Pudding, 56
Pork Chops with Pear Stuffing, 273

PEAS
Creamed Sweet Peas, 169
Hopping John, 117
Italian-Style Peas, 132
Pea Soup for a Crowd, 100
Picnic Peas, 123
Zesty Buttered Peas, 129

PEPPERS
Beef 'n' Pepper Stir-Fry, 251
Chicken Tamale Pie, 320
Chili Cheese Dip, 7
Chili Rellenos Sandwiches, 94
Creamy Red Pepper Dip, 18
Green Chili 'n' Rice Casserole, 160
Italian-Sausage Pepper Sandwiches, 90
Jalapeno Ribs, 298
Mexican Pork Stew, 101
Pepper and Salsa Cod, 362
Pepper Lover's BLT, 86
Pepper Soup, 74
Pepper Steak, 259
Peppery Corn Salad, 157
Pork Fajita Pasta, 290
Pork Fajitas, 276
Pork Ribs and Chilies, 309
Roasted Red Pepper Muffins, 192
Southwest Skillet Dish, 61
Southwestern Chicken Soup, 88
Stuffed Banana Peppers, 264
Stuffed Green Peppers, 233
Tasty Tortilla Roll-Ups, 35

PINEAPPLE
Cherry Pineapple Cake, 436
Coconut Chicken with Pineapple
  Vinaigrette, 328
Coconut Pineapple Pie, 419
Creamy Citrus Salad, 159
Hawaiian Pizza Pasta, 299
Hawaiian Roll-Ups, 29

Molded Cherry-Pineapple Salad, 138
Pineapple Bread Pudding, 461
Pineapple Bundt Cake, 446
Pineapple Delights, 405
Pineapple Shrimp Rice Bake, 362
Sweet 'n' Sour Pockets, 71
Tropical Pork Kabobs, 272

PIZZAS
Crazy Crust Pizza, 250
Mexican Pizza, 11
Southwestern Deep-Dish Pizza, 223
Stuffed Pizza, 213
Swiss 'n' Bacon Pizza, 35

PLUMS
Plum-Barbecued Spareribs, 291
Pork Chops with Sauteed Plums, 298
Short Ribs with Plums, 240

PORK (also see Bacon & Canadian Bacon;
  Ham; Ribs; Sausage)
Appetizer
Tasty Pork Nuggets, 37
Main Dishes
Apple Pork Pie, 292
Baked Pork Chops and Apples, 279
Barbecued Meatballs, 275
Barbecued Pork with Beans, 296
Braised Pork Chops, 274
Cajun Pork Roast, 270
Citrus Pork Skillet, 271
Cordon Bleu Pork Chops, 283
Cranberry-Stuffed Pork Chops, 297
Creamy Pork Tenderloin, 280
Creole-Style Pork Roast, 278
Crunchy Baked Pork Tenderloin, 309
Curried Pork and Green Tomatoes, 279
Curried Pork Chops, 302
Fruited Pork Picante, 283
Glazed Pork Tenderloin, 310
Grilled Stuffed Pork Chops, 305
Herb-Marinated Pork Loin, 305
Herbed Pork Roast, 297
Hungarian Pork Loaf, 301
Inside-Out Pork Chops, 285
Italian Cabbage and Rice, 304
Marinated Pork Loin Roast, 267
Mom's Chinese Dish, 269
Mozzarella Meat Whirl, 232
Old-Fashioned Kraut Dinner, 296
Old-Fashioned Pork Roast, 265
One-Pan Pork a la Orange, 272
Orange Dijon Pork, 299
Pork and Cabbage Rolls, 307
Pork Chop and Rice Dinner, 290
Pork Chop Suey, 294
Pork Chops Parmesan, 277
Pork Chops with Pear Stuffing, 273
Pork Chops with Sauteed Plums, 298
Pork Fajita Pasta, 290
Pork Fajitas, 276
Pork Lo Mein, 284
Pork Patties Oriental, 287
Pork Souvlaki, 288

PORK
Main Dishes (continued)
Pork-Stuffed Eggplant, 284
Pork Tenderloin Florentine, 263
Pork Wellington, 268
Pork with Peanuts, 308
Rhubarb Pork Roast, 286
Sesame Pork Kabobs, 266
Shredded Pork Tacos, 267
Spanish Pork Steaks, 302
Stuffed Crown Roast of Pork, 266
Swedish Meatballs, 228
Tropical Pork Kabobs, 272
Soups & Sandwiches
Mexican Pork Stew, 101
Parmesan Pork Sandwiches, 306
Pea Soup for a Crowd, 100
Shaker Pork Sandwiches, 303

POTATOES (also see Sweet Potatoes
& Yams)
Bacon-Potato Burritos, 56
Black Bean Potato Chili, 68
Bratwurst Potato Skillet, 282
Cabbage-Potato Saute, 110
Corned Beef Hash and Eggs, 41
Crunch Top Ham and Potato Casserole, 304
Dilly Chicken and Potatoes, 320
Down-on-the-Farm Breakfast, 45
Instant Party Potatoes, 110
Lamb and Potato Stew, 80
Mom's Monday Lunch Potato Soup, 99
New Potatoes with Dill, 114
Old-Fashioned Potatoes Anna, 168
Parmesan Potato Sticks, 115
Pennsylvania Dutch Potato Doughnuts, 44
Potato Casserole, 153
Potato Chip Crunchies, 395
Potato Ham au Gratin, 271
Potato Salmon Casserole, 368
Potato Volcano, 146
Potatoes Forradas, 114
Sausage Potato Wraps, 276
Sausage-Stuffed Potatoes, 300
Scalloped Potatoes 'n' Ham, 295
Sheepherder's Potatoes, 142
Skinny Fries, 145
Sour Cream Potato Salad, 121
Southern Potato Salad, 145
Southwest Skillet Dish, 61
Surprise Potatoes, 156
Swiss Bake, 137
Tater-Topped Casserole, 221
Turkey Potato Supper, 343

PUMPKIN
Chocolate Chip Pumpkin Bread, 206
Pumpkin Cheesecake Bars, 407
Pumpkin Chili, 107
Pumpkin Pudding, 460
Pumpkin Sloppy Joes, 228
Walnut-Crunch Pumpkin Pie, 429

QUICK BREADS
Almond Apricot Bread, 206
Banana Nut Bread, 185
Bishop's Bread, 202
Cheery Cherry Bread, 187
Chocolate Chip Pumpkin Bread, 206
Date Nut Bread, 198
Irish Soda Bread, 193
Monkey Bread, 184
Pimiento-Stuffed Olive Bread, 192
Wholesome Quick Bread, 211
Zucchini Snack Bread, 209

RAISINS
Amish Raisin Cookies, 404
Apple-Raisin Meat Loaf, 230
Cinnamon Chip Raisin Scones, 200
Cinnamon-Raisin Coffee Cake, 196
Frosted Cinnamon-Raisin Biscuits, 204
Hot Cross Buns, 183
Irish Soda Bread, 193
Maple Raisin Pudding, 474
Raisin Peanut Clusters, 377
Raisin Sheet Cookies, 392
Rice Pudding Cake, 442
Roast Goose with Apple-Raisin Stuffing, 355

RASPBERRIES
Barbecued Raspberry Chicken, 351
Blueberry Raspberry Crunch, 466
Bumbleberry Pie, 421
Lemon-Raspberry Muffins, 211
Raspberry Delights, 397
Raspberry-Filled Cake, 439
Raspberry Supreme Cheesecake, 462
Raspberry Vinegar, 177
Rosy Raspberry Salad, 133

RHUBARB
Baked Rhubarb, 156
Bumbleberry Pie, 421
Crispy Rhubarb Cobbler, 470
Grandma's Spring & Summer Torte, 444
Rhubarb Apple Pie, 423
Rhubarb Beef, 260
Rhubarb Cloud, 458
Rhubarb Pork Roast, 286
Rhubarb Punch, 31
Rhubarb Squares, 398
Sour Cream Rhubarb Pie, 421
Spiced Rhubarb Soup, 107
Strawberry Rhubarb Dumplings, 467

RIBS
Applesauce-Sauerkraut Spareribs, 281
Country-Style Pork Ribs, 270
Cranberry-Glazed Spareribs, 273
Jalapeno Ribs, 298
Lemon Pork Ribs, 307
Oven-Baked Ribs, 300
Plum-Barbecued Spareribs, 291
Pork Ribs and Chilies, 309
Ribs with Caraway Kraut and
Stuffing Balls, 310
Sparerib Casserole, 289
Spareribs Cantonese, 293

Teriyaki Tangerine Ribs, 264
Western Ribs, 292

RICE
Authentic Spanish Rice, 140
Beef Fried Rice, 238
Cheesy Broccoli Rice, 122
Chicken Pilaf Saute, 356
Chili Rice Pie, 246
Classic Red Beans 'n' Rice, 159
Cocoa Rice Pudding, 469
Curried Chicken and Rice, 341
Curried Turkey and Rice Salad, 112
Easy Fried Rice, 346
Greek Rice Salad, 149
Green Chili 'n' Rice Casserole, 160
Ham Fried Rice, 282
Ham, Turkey and Wild Rice Salad, 143
Hopping John, 117
Hot Dogs 'n' Rice, 277
Italian Cabbage and Rice, 304
Jambalaya, 280
Lemon Rice Pilaf, 141
Mixed Grain and Wild Rice Cereal, 57
Oven Porcupines, 236
Pineapple Shrimp Rice Bake, 362
Pork Chop and Rice Dinner, 290
Ranch Chicken 'n' Rice, 331
Rice-Crust Quiche, 62
Rice Pudding Cake, 442
Saucy Ham and Rice, 268
Skillet Seasoned Rice, 115
Southwestern Fried Rice, 343
Spaghetti-Style Rice, 242
Spanish-Style Breakfast Bake, 43
Taco Rice, 222
Turkey Rice Casserole, 311
Wild Rice Soup, 108

ROLLS & BUNS
Bacon Onion Breadsticks, 201
Caraway Puffs, 200
Chocolate Cinnamon Rolls, 198
Cinnamon Walnut Crescents, 189
Cornmeal Cinnamon Rolls, 210
Easy Crescent Rolls, 204
Golden Dinner Rolls, 199
Hot Cross Buns, 183
Iones's Parker House Rolls, 195
Rye Breadsticks, 194
Skillet Rolls, 191

SALADS & DRESSINGS
Bean Salads
Fiesta Black Bean Salad, 127
Four-Bean Salad, 142
Garbanzo Avocado Salad, 150
Cabbage Salads & Coleslaw
Apple-Cinnamon Coleslaw, 168
Chinese Noodle Slaw, 117
Cranberry Cabbage Salad, 147
Nutty Coleslaw, 147
Tangy Cabbage Salad, 114
Dressings
Blue Cheese Dressing, 178

Evelyn's Original Roquefort Dressing, 177
French Salad Dressing, 179
Honey Mustard Dressing, 174
Hot Bacon Dressing, 171
Maple-Dijon Salad Dressing, 173
Milly's Salad Dressing, 172
Paprika Salad Dressing, 180
Sweet-and-Sour Dressing, 181
Tangy Poppy Seed Dressing, 175
Zesty Buttermilk Salad Dressing, 179
Fruit Salads
Apple-Strawberry Peanut Salad, 161
Fluffy Fruit Salad, 113
Fruity Pasta Salad, 158
Fruity-Toot-Toot, 140
Grandma's Apple Salad, 132
Gelatin Salads
Apple Cider Salad, 113
Cranberry Gelatin Salad, 118
Creamy Citrus Salad, 159
Lime Pear Salad, 164
Mini Molded Salads, 116
Molded Cherry-Pineapple Salad, 138
Rosy Raspberry Salad, 133
Spinach Salad Ring, 131
Green Salads
Cauliflower Lettuce Salad, 140
Mary's Caesar Salad, 152
Mixed Greens with Mushrooms, 130
Nutty Mandarin Salad, 135
Main-Dish Salads
Chicken Tortellini Salad, 168
Curried Turkey and Rice Salad, 112
Ham, Turkey and Wild Rice Salad, 143
Salmon Salad, 153
Spectacular Shrimp Salad, 364
Turkey-Blue Cheese Pasta Salad, 148
Turkey Shrimp Salad, 166
Two-Bean Tuna Salad, 120
Pasta Salads
Chicken Tortellini Salad, 168
Elbow Macaroni Salad, 125
Fruity Pasta Salad, 158
Pesto Pasta Salad, 170
Quick Pantry Salad, 154
Spicy Spaghetti Salad, 157
Turkey-Blue Cheese Pasta Salad, 148
Potato Salads
Sour Cream Potato Salad, 121
Southern Potato Salad, 145
Rice & Barley Salads
Greek Rice Salad, 149
Ham, Turkey and Wild Rice Salad, 143
Tomato Barley Salad, 148
Vegetable Salads
Artichoke 'n' Olive Salad, 118
Chopped Salad, 152
Colorful Antipasto, 154
Colorful Cauliflower Salad, 125
Creamy Cauliflower Salad, 115
Italian Broccoli Salad, 123
Marinated Onion Salad, 143
Mushroom 'n' Tomato Salad, 119

Nutty Carrot Salad, 122
Patio Salad, 138
Peppery Corn Salad, 157
Sour Cream Cucumber Salad, 152
Stuffed Cucumbers, 162
Warm Asparagus Salad, 119

SANDWICHES
Cold Sandwiches
Arkansas Travelers, 104
California Clubs, 82
Chicken-Apple Croissants, 69
Chickenwiches, 84
Cool Cucumber Sandwich, 108
Creamy Egg Salad Sandwiches, 97
Curried Chicken Pita Pockets, 92
Egg Salad Tuna Wraps, 93
Fried Chicken Pitas, 74
Ham and Spinach Loaf, 68
Hearty Krautwiches, 65
Hearty Muffuletta Loaf, 80
Humpty-Dumpty Sandwich Loaf, 72
Liverwurst Deluxe, 82
Meat Loaf Sandwiches, 85
Nutty Shrimp Salad Sandwiches, 74
Special Ham 'n' Cheese Sandwiches, 92
Stuffed Ham Slices, 95
Sweet 'n' Sour Pockets, 71
Tarragon Chicken Salad, 99
Thanksgiving Sandwiches, 104
Triple Tasty Sandwich Spread, 89
Turkey Tomato Club, 64
Vegetable Tuna Sandwiches, 100
Hot Sandwiches
Bacon Veggie Roll-Ups, 102
Barbecued Ham Sandwiches, 278
Beef Crescent Loaf, 225
Cheesy Turkey Burgers, 334
Chicken Salad on Buns, 81
Chili Rellenos Sandwiches, 94
Corny Turkey Burgers, 345
Creamy Turkey Melt, 79
Deviled English Muffins, 88
Easy Stromboli, 70
Grilled Blue Cheese Sandwiches, 91
Grilled Salmon Sandwiches, 360
Grilled Turkey Sandwiches, 340
Ground Turkey Turnovers, 325
Ham-Stuffed Bread, 103
Herbed Pashes, 93
Hot Chicken Heroes, 88
Hot Jam Breakfast Sandwiches, 58
Hot Turkey Salad Pitas, 66
Hot Turkey Sandwiches, 314
Humpty-Dumpty Sandwich Loaf, 72
Italian Beef Sandwiches, 250
Italian-Sausage Pepper Sandwiches, 90
Lasagna in a Bun, 67
Lemon-Herb Gyros, 239
Make-Ahead Saucy Sandwiches, 78
Meaty Pita Pockets, 226
Mock Monte Cristos, 73
Open-Faced Pizza Burgers, 261
Oriental Patties, 237

Parmesan Pork Sandwiches, 306
Pepper Lover's BLT, 86
Pizza Buns, 76
Pumpkin Sloppy Joes, 228
Quick Calzones, 77
Rosemary's Ham Reubens, 69
Saucy Herb Hamburgers, 227
Sausage 'n' Spinach Pockets, 105
Sausage Potato Wraps, 276
Sausage Sloppy Joes, 265
Sausage-Stuffed French Loaf, 217
Shaker Pork Sandwiches, 303
Sirloin Steak Sandwiches, 248
Taco Crescents, 214
Three-Cheese Tomato Melt, 99
Toasted Apple-Cheese Sandwiches, 67
Tomato-Bacon Rarebit, 83
Turkey BLT, 81
Veggie Delights, 71
Wake-Up Sandwiches, 58
Zesty Meatball Sandwiches, 230

SAUERKRAUT
Applesauce-Sauerkraut Spareribs, 281
German Chicken, 324
German Skillet Meal, 234
Hearty Krautwiches, 65
Italian Sausage and Sauerkraut, 293
Old-Fashioned Kraut Dinner, 296
Ribs with Caraway Kraut and
    Stuffing Balls, 310
Rosemary's Ham Reubens, 69
Sauerkraut Brownie Cake, 435
Sauerkraut Side Dish, 139
Tangy Reuben Bake, 289

SAUSAGE
Appetizers
Pepperoni Bread, 27
Sausage Bacon Tidbits, 36
Speedy Pizza Rings, 37
Stuffed Mushrooms, 10
Sweet-and-Sour Meatballs Appetizer, 33
Breakfast & Brunch
Breakfast Pizza, 40
Country Sausage Gravy, 55
Hearty Sausage Loaf, 45
Home-Style Hominy Casserole, 61
Pigs in a Blanket, 46
Pork Sausage Ring, 52
Sausage Potato Wraps, 276
Simple Sausage Ring, 265
Main Dishes
Bratwurst Potato Skillet, 282
Cheesy Zucchini Medley, 274
Grilled Stuffed Pork Chops, 305
Italian Sausage and Sauerkraut, 293
Jambalaya, 280
Old-Fashioned Kraut Dinner, 296
Sausage Apple Roll, 270
Sausage Stroganoff, 287
Sausage-Stuffed Potatoes, 300
Stuffed Banana Peppers, 264
Stuffed Meat Loaf, 262
Tangy Reuben Bake, 289

Zucchini Sausage Squares, 303
Salad
Colorful Antipasto, 154
Soups & Sandwiches
Easy Stromboli, 70
Hearty Krautwiches, 65
Hearty Muffuletta Loaf, 80
Italian-Sausage Pepper Sandwiches, 90
Kielbasa Cabbage Soup, 90
Meat Loaf Sandwiches, 85
Quick Bean Soup, 86
Sausage 'n' Spinach Pockets, 105
Sausage Potato Wraps, 276
Sausage Sloppy Joes, 265
Sausage-Stuffed French Loaf, 217
Triple Tasty Sandwich Spread, 89

SEAFOOD (also see Fish)
Appetizers
Crab Roll-Ups, 24
Crab-Stuffed Celery, 19
Crab-Stuffed Deviled Eggs, 21
Creamy Shrimp Dip, 22
Hot Crab Dip, 36
Perfect Scalloped Oysters, 8
Main Dishes
Broiled Lime Shrimp, 359
Crab Quiche, 367
Crab Thermidor, 371
Linguine with Garlic Clam Sauce, 365
Mediterranean Shrimp and Pasta, 360
Pineapple Shrimp Rice Bake, 362
Seafood in Tomato Sauce, 357
Sesame Shrimp, 363
Shrimp and Asparagus Casserole, 366
Shrimp Crepes, 372
Simple Herbed Scallops, 361
Salads
Mini Molded Salads, 116
Spectacular Shrimp Salad, 364
Turkey Shrimp Salad, 166
Soups & Sandwiches
Cajun Corn Soup with Shrimp, 64
Crab Bisque, 89
Nutty Shrimp Salad Sandwiches, 74

SIDES
Asparagus
Almond Asparagus, 134
Asparagus with Blue Cheese Sauce, 164
Creamed Asparagus and Tomato, 157
Beans
Basil Beans, 111
Blue Cheese Green Beans, 112
Classic Red Beans 'n' Rice, 159
Cranberry Baked Beans, 165
Green Bean Bundles, 169
Green Beans with Mushrooms, 135
Lima Bean Casserole, 167
Mini Green Bean Casserole, 160
Old-Fashioned Baked Beans, 163
Three Bean Casserole, 155
Beets
Glazed Beets, 149
Harvard Beets, 141

Broccoli & Cauliflower
Broccoli Supreme, 156
Broccoli Tomato Cups, 150
Cheddar Cauliflower, 132
Herbed Broccoli Spears, 160
Tangy Cauliflower, 137
Cabbage & Sauerkraut
Acorn Cabbage Bake, 166
Cabbage-Potato Saute, 110
Hungarian Cabbage with Noodles, 116
Sauerkraut Side Dish, 139
Carrots
Carrot Casserole, 141
Crown Jewel Patties, 111
Tangerine Carrots, 161
Zesty Carrots, 131
Corn & Hominy
Baked Corn Casserole, 144
Baked Hominy and Cheese, 136
Corn Medley, 161
Corn Wheels with Lime Butter, 153
Golden Corn Puff, 151
Scalloped Corn, 129
Fruit
Baked Rhubarb, 156
Hot Curried Fruit, 158
Onions
Dad's Onion Rings, 110
Onion Pie, 148
Pasta
Creamy Veggie Vermicelli, 155
Garlic-Buttered Pasta, 164
Herbed Egg Noodles, 111
Homemade Noodles, 167
Mother's Manicotti, 162
My Mother's Mac and Cheese, 165
Noodle Nibblers, 145
Stove-Top Macaroni and Cheese, 133
Tortellini Bake, 120
Zucchini-Garlic Pasta, 126
Peas
Creamed Sweet Peas, 169
Italian-Style Peas, 132
Picnic Peas, 123
Zesty Buttered Peas, 129
Potatoes
Cabbage-Potato Saute, 110
Instant Party Potatoes, 110
New Potatoes with Dill, 114
Old-Fashioned Potatoes Anna, 168
Parmesan Potato Sticks, 115
Potato Casserole, 153
Potato Volcano, 146
Potatoes Forradas, 114
Sheepherder's Potatoes, 142
Skinny Fries, 145
Surprise Potatoes, 156
Swiss Bake, 137
Rice
Authentic Spanish Rice, 140
Cheesy Broccoli Rice, 122
Classic Red Beans 'n' Rice, 159
Green Chili 'n' Rice Casserole, 160

SIDES

Rice *(continued)*
Hopping John, 117
Lemon Rice-Pilaf, 141
Skillet Seasoned Rice, 115
Spinach
Acorn Squash with Spinach Stuffing, 121
Creamed Spinach, 119
Spinach Cheese Bake, 134
Squash & Zucchini
Acorn Cabbage Bake, 166
Acorn Squash with Spinach Stuffing, 121
Autumn Squash Bake, 137
Broiled Zucchini with Rosemary Butter, 124
Candied Acorn Squash Rings, 128
Ratatouille, 133
Sesame Zucchini, 123
Spectacular Spaghetti Squash, 139
Zucchini-Garlic Pasta, 126
Zucchini Patties, 149
Stuffing
Cranberry Nut Stuffing, 130
Skillet Stuffing, 151
Stuffing Balls, 169
Sweet Potatoes & Yams
Apples, Berries and Yams, 165
Sweet Potato Balls, 129
Twice-Baked Sweet Potatoes, 146
Tomatoes
Baked Stuffed Tomatoes, 126
Broccoli Tomato Cups, 150
Creamed Asparagus and Tomato, 157
Fried Green Tomatoes, 128
Ratatouille, 133
Tomato Crouton Casserole, 170
Tomato Mozzarella Bake, 127
Vegetables
Fresh Vegetable Kabobs, 144
Layered Vegetable Loaf, 109
Mixed Vegetable Side Dish, 163
Pocket Veggies, 124
Roasted Root Veggies, 122
Skillet Vegetables, 128
Vegetable Pancakes, 136

SOUPS *(also see Chili; Stews)*
ABC Soup, 69
Autumn Soup, 85
Beef Ravioli Soup, 75
Broccoli, Hamburger and Cheese Soup, 79
Cajun Corn Soup with Shrimp, 64
Carrot Soup, 87
Cheesy Chicken Corn Soup, 78
Chicken Tortellini Soup, 105
Church Supper Chili, 91
Crab Bisque, 89
Cream of Asparagus Soup, 87
Cream of Zucchini Soup, 98
Curried Acorn Squash Soup, 98
Dilled Chicken Soup, 102
Dilly Cheese Soup, 106
Farmhouse Chicken Soup, 63
French Onion Soup, 95
Garlic Oatmeal Soup, 72

Gazpacho, 81
Grandmother's Chicken 'n' Dumplings, 96
Hearty Steak Soup, 66
Homemade Pinwheel Noodles, 248
Kielbasa Cabbage Soup, 90
Meatball Noodle Soup, 101
Mom's Chicken Soup, 77
Mom's Monday Lunch Potato Soup, 99
Pea Soup for a Crowd, 100
Pepper Soup, 74
Quick Bean Soup, 86
Scrumptious Breakfast Fruit Soup, 47
Southwestern Chicken Soup, 88
Spiced Rhubarb Soup, 107
Spinach Bisque, 70
Summer Garden Soup, 73
Tomato Soup with a Twist, 82
Turkey Barley Soup, 104
Turkey Cabbage Soup, 83
Vegetable Bean Soup, 94
Wild Rice Soup, 108

SPINACH
Acorn Squash with Spinach Stuffing, 121
Beef Florentine, 243
Chicken and Spinach Supper, 350
Chicken Florentine, 354
Creamed Spinach, 119
Ham and Spinach Loaf, 68
Pork Tenderloin Florentine, 263
Sausage 'n' Spinach Pockets, 105
Spinach Bisque, 70
Spinach Cheese Bake, 134
Spinach Cheese Muffins, 205
Spinach Salad Ring, 131

SQUASH
Acorn Cabbage Bake, 166
Acorn Squash with Spinach Stuffing, 121
Autumn Squash Bake, 137
Candied Acorn Squash Rings, 128
Curried Acorn Squash Soup, 98
Ratatouille, 133
Spectacular Spaghetti Squash, 139
Stuffed Acorn Squash, 224
Summer Squash Enchiladas, 319
Turkey Squash Casserole, 321

STEWS
Chicken Stew, 106
Lamb and Potato Stew, 80
Mexican Pork Stew, 101
Sweet Potato Stew, 92

STRAWBERRIES
All-American Strawberry Pie, 411
Apple-Strawberry Peanut Salad, 161
Bumbleberry Pie, 421
Strawberry Chiffon Cake, 432
Strawberry Dessert, 470
Strawberry Punch, 9
Strawberry Rhubarb Dumplings, 467
Strawberry Trifle, 468
Tuxedo Strawberries, 461

SWEET POTATOES & YAMS
Apples, Berries and Yams, 165
Sweet Potato Balls, 129
Sweet Potato Biscuits, 208
Sweet Potato Stew, 92
Twice-Baked Sweet Potatoes, 146

TOMATOES
Baked Stuffed Tomatoes, 126
Baked Ziti with Fresh Tomatoes, 245
Broccoli Tomato Cups, 150
Chicken and Tomato Scampi, 345
Chicken with Tomato-Cream Sauce, 326
Creamed Asparagus and Tomato, 157
Curried Pork and Green Tomatoes, 279
Fresh Salsa, 180
Fried Green Tomatoes, 128
Mushroom 'n' Tomato Salad, 119
Pepper Lover's BLT, 86
Ratatouille, 133
Seafood in Tomato Sauce, 357
Three-Cheese Tomato Melt, 99
Tomato-Bacon Rarebit, 83
Tomato Barley Salad, 148
Tomato Bread, 203
Tomato-Cheese Snack Bread, 13
Tomato Crouton Casserole, 170
Tomato Fondue, 14
Tomato Mozzarella Bake, 127
Tomato Soup with a Twist, 82
Turkey BLT, 81
Turkey Tomato Club, 64

TURKEY
Appetizer
Tangy Turkey Meatballs, 7
Main Dishes
Orange Barbecued Turkey, 328
Texas Turkey Tacos, 313
Turkey a la King, 348
Turkey Bean Bake, 336
Turkey Broccoli Bake, 316
Turkey Burritos, 315
Turkey in the Strawganoff, 349
Turkey Patties Oriental, 339
Turkey Potato Supper, 343
Turkey Rice Casserole, 311
Turkey Schnitzel, 322
Turkey Squash Casserole, 321
Zesty Turkey, 319
Salads
Curried Turkey and Rice Salad, 112
Greek Rice Salad, 149
Ham, Turkey and Wild Rice Salad, 143
Quick Pantry Salad, 154
Turkey-Blue Cheese Pasta Salad, 148
Turkey Shrimp Salad, 166
Soups & Sandwiches
Arkansas Travelers, 104
Cheesy Turkey Burgers, 334
Corny Turkey Burgers, 345
Creamy Turkey Melt, 79
Grilled Turkey Sandwiches, 340

Ground Turkey Turnovers, 325
Hot Turkey Salad Pitas, 66
Hot Turkey Sandwiches, 314
Liverwurst Deluxe, 82
Mock Monte Cristos, 73
Pepper Lover's BLT, 86
Thanksgiving Sandwiches, 104
Turkey Barley Soup, 104
Turkey BLT, 81
Turkey Cabbage Soup, 83
Turkey Tomato Club, 64
White Christmas Chili, 97

VEGETABLES *(also see specific kinds)*
Autumn Soup, 85
Bacon Veggie Roll-Ups, 102
Beef 'n' Veggie Cheddar Pie, 252
Chop Suey, 231
Cornish Hens with Veggies, 337
Creamy Veggie Vermicelli, 155
Fresh Vegetable Kabobs, 144
Garden Fresh Breakfast, 55
Gazpacho, 81
Layered Vegetable Loaf, 109
Mixed Vegetable Side Dish, 163
Pocket Veggies, 124
Roasted Root Veggies, 122
Skillet Vegetables, 128
Summer Garden Soup, 73
Vegetable Bean Soup, 94
Vegetable Beef Kabobs, 245
Vegetable Pancakes, 136
Vegetable Tuna Sandwiches, 100
Vegetarian Chili, 76
Veggie Delights, 71
Veggie Loaves, 185

YEAST BREADS
Cinnamon Swirl Bread, 194
English Muffin Loaf, 190
Four-Grain Bread, 190
Golden Cheese Yeast Bread, 197
Honey White Loaves, 208
Quick Homemade Bread, 186
Sour Cream Herb Bread, 188
Tomato Bread, 203
Veggie Loaves, 185

ZUCCHINI
Broiled Zucchini with Rosemary Butter, 124
Cheesy Zucchini Medley, 274
Cream of Zucchini Soup, 98
Sesame Zucchini, 123
Speedy Pizza Rings, 37
Zucchini Apple Crisp, 462
Zucchini Cake, 438
Zucchini-Garlic Pasta, 126
Zucchini Lasagna, 214
Zucchini Oven Omelet, 41
Zucchini Patties, 149
Zucchini Sausage Squares, 303
Zucchini Snack Bread, 209
Zucchini Spread, 10

Alphabetical Recipe Index

ABC Soup, 69
Acorn Cabbage Bake, 166
Acorn Squash with Spinach Stuffing, 121
All-American Strawberry Pie, 411
All Seasons Marinade, 178
Almond Apricot Bread, 206
Almond Asparagus, 134
Almond Tea, 31
Almond Toffee, 376
Amish Raisin Cookies, 404
Angel Food Cake, 440
Apple Butter Barbecued Chicken, 331
Apple Cider Salad, 113
Apple-Cinnamon Coleslaw, 168
Apple Cottage Cheese Salad, 118
Apple Crumb Bars, 388
Apple Gingerbread, 443
Apple Graham Pie, 420
Apple Honey Tapioca Pudding, 473
Apple Kuchen, 436
Apple Pie a la Mode Shake, 25
Apple Pork Pie, 292
Apple-Raisin Meat Loaf, 230
Apple-Strawberry Peanut Salad, 161
Apples, Berries and Yams, 165
Applesauce Brownies, 409
Applesauce-Sauerkraut Spareribs, 281
Apricot Bonbons, 384
Apricot Burritos, 463
Arkansas Travelers, 104
Artichoke 'n' Olive Salad, 118
Asparagus-Chicken Pie, 59
Asparagus-Lover's Stir-Fry, 312
Asparagus with Blue Cheese Sauce, 164
Aunt Rose's Peach Cobbler, 472
Aunt Shirley's Liver Pate, 29
Austrian Chocolate Balls, 393
Authentic Spanish Rice, 140
Autumn Soup, 85
Autumn Squash Bake, 137

Bacon and Blue Cheese Chicken, 327
Bacon Onion Breadsticks, 201
Bacon-Potato Burritos, 56
Bacon Veggie Roll-Ups, 102
Bacon-Wrapped Water Chestnuts, 15
Baked Chili, 75
Baked Corn Casserole, 144
Baked Crumbled Chicken, 332
Baked Custard, 458
Baked Hominy and Cheese, 136
Baked Nachos, 225
Baked Pork Chops and Apples, 279
Baked Rhubarb, 156
Baked Spaghetti, 218
Baked Stuffed Tomatoes, 126
Baked Whole Salmon, 369
Baked Ziti with Fresh Tomatoes, 245
Baki's Old-World Cookies, 389
Baking Powder Drop Biscuits, 188
Banana Cocoa Brownies, 392

Banana Cream Pie, 422
Banana Cupcakes, 450
Banana Fritters, 46
Banana Fudge Pie, 427
Banana Nut Bread, 185
Banana Smoothie, 26
Banana Upside-Down Cake, 434
Barbecued Ham Sandwiches, 278
Barbecued Meatballs, 275
Barbecued Mini-Balls, 13
Barbecued Pork with Beans, 296
Barbecued Raspberry Chicken, 351
Barbecued Short Ribs, 229
Basil Beans, 111
Bavarian Mint Fudge, 375
Beef 'n' Cheddar Biscuits, 12
Beef 'n' Pepper Stir-Fry, 251
Beef 'n' Veggie Cheddar Pie, 252
Beef Burgundy, 236
Beef Crescent Loaf, 225
Beef Florentine, 243
Beef Fried Rice, 238
Beef Pinwheels, 235
Beef Ravioli Soup, 75
Beef Rouladen, 241
Beef-Stuffed Onions, 240
Beefy Enchiladas, 226
Best-Ever Blueberry Muffins, 195
Bishop's Bread, 202
Black Bean Potato Chili, 68
Black Bean Salsa, 21
Blue Cheese Dressing, 178
Blue Cheese Green Beans, 112
Blueberry Brunch Loaf, 48
Blueberry Cream Pie, 423
Blueberry Milk Shake, 21
Blueberry Orange Cups, 463
Blueberry Raspberry Crunch, 466
Blueberry Streusel Coffee Cake, 197
Braised Pork Chops, 274
Bratwurst Potato Skillet, 282
Breaded Asparagus Sticks, 30
Breakfast Pizza, 40
Bride's Peach Pie, 429
Brisket with Gingersnap Gravy, 222
Broccoli, Hamburger and Cheese Soup, 79
Broccoli Supreme, 156
Broccoli Tomato Cups, 150
Broccoli Tuna Roll-Ups, 361
Broiled Banana Crisp, 471
Broiled Lime Shrimp, 359
Broiled Zucchini with Rosemary Butter, 124
Brown Butter Refrigerator Cookies, 395
Brown Sugar Pudding Cake, 438
Brunch Tidbits Bread, 42
Bumbleberry Pie, 421
Butter Brickle Dessert, 472
Buttermilk Coffee Cake, 54
Butterscotch Pudding, 463
Buttery Chicken Spread, 23

Cabbage-Potato Saute, 110
Cabbage Rolls, 215
Cajun Corn Soup with Shrimp, 64
Cajun Pork Roast, 270
California Clubs, 82
Canadian Bacon Breakfast, 51
Candied Acorn Squash Rings, 128
Candied Pecans, 374
Caramel Butter Cake, 447
Caramel Cashew Cheesecake, 476
Caraway Puffs, 200
Carrot Cake, 443
Carrot Casserole, 141
Carrot Soup, 87
Cashew Noodle Casserole, 227
Cauliflower Lettuce Salad, 140
Cheddar Biscuits, 201
Cheddar Cauliflower, 132
Cheddar Cheese Sauce, 176
Cheery Cherry Bread, 187
Cheese Olive Appetizers, 26
Cheese Straws, 18
Cheeseburger Macaroni, 244
Cheesecake Dreams, 394
Cheesy Artichoke Garlic Loaf, 5
Cheesy Beef Stroganoff, 246
Cheesy Broccoli Rice, 122
Cheesy Casserole, 261
Cheesy Chicken Corn Soup, 78
Cheesy Chicken Roll-Ups, 344
Cheesy Egg Casserole, 62
Cheesy Mushroom Appetizers, 30
Cheesy Tortilla Bake, 242
Cheesy Tuna Lasagna, 363
Cheesy Turkey Burgers, 334
Cheesy Zucchini Medley, 274
Cherry Grunt, 457
Cherry Honey Relish, 182
Cherry Pineapple Cake, 436
Chick-a-Roni, 353
Chicken a la King, 339
Chicken Amondine, 356
Chicken and Spinach Supper, 350
Chicken and Tomato Scampi, 345
Chicken-Apple Croissants, 69
Chicken Barbecued in Foil, 317
Chicken Crescent Casserole, 313
Chicken Crouton Hot Dish, 338
Chicken Florentine, 354
Chicken-Fried Cube Steaks, 249
Chicken Lasagna Rolls, 353
Chicken Livers Royale, 348
Chicken-Mushroom Deluxe, 334
Chicken Parmesan, 344
Chicken Pilaf Saute, 356
Chicken Potpie, 323
Chicken Salad on Buns, 81
Chicken Spaghetti, 352
Chicken Stew, 106
Chicken Tamale Pie, 320
Chicken Tetrazzini, 355

Chicken Tortellini Salad, 168
Chicken Tortellini Soup, 105
Chicken with Cucumber Sauce, 318
Chicken with Tomato-Cream Sauce, 326
Chickenwiches, 84
Chili Cheese Dip, 7
Chili Rellenos Sandwiches, 94
Chili Rice Pie, 246
Chinese Noodle Slaw, 117
Chivey Potato Topper, 180
Chocolate Angel Food Cake, 449
Chocolate Banana Smoothie, 28
Chocolate Billionaires, 376
Chocolate Buttermilk Brownies, 403
Chocolate Caramel Clusters, 385
Chocolate Chews, 381
Chocolate Chip Marshmallow Bars, 410
Chocolate Chip Pumpkin Bread, 206
Chocolate Cinnamon Rolls, 198
Chocolate Covered Cherries, 383
Chocolate-Dipped Treats, 386
Chocolate Mayonnaise Cake, 441
Chocolate Mint Cookies, 396
Chocolate Nougat Cake, 448
Chocolate Oat Cake, 445
Chocolate Peanut Butter, 172
Chocolate Shoofly Pie, 428
Chocolate Snappers, 475
Chocolate Velvet Cream, 454
Chop Suey, 231
Chopped Salad, 152
Chunky Applesauce, 182
Church Supper Chili, 91
Chutney Stuffed Eggs, 25
Cinnamon Chip Raisin Scones, 200
Cinnamon Chocolate Angel Pie, 422
Cinnamon-Raisin Coffee Cake, 196
Cinnamon Swirl Bread, 194
Cinnamon Walnut Crescents, 189
Citrus Pork Skillet, 271
Classic Meat Loaf, 220
Classic Red Beans 'n' Rice, 159
Cocoa Rice Pudding, 469
Coconut Almond Bars, 380
Coconut Chicken with Pineapple
   Vinaigrette, 328
Coconut Drops, 382
Coconut Pineapple Pie, 419
Coconut Snacks, 386
Coconut Trifle, 473
Coconut Walnut Tart, 416
Coffee Almond Crisps, 406
Cola Chicken, 314
Colorful Antipasto, 154
Colorful Cauliflower Salad, 125
Comforting Chicken 'n' Noodles, 347
Company Casserole, 223
Cool Cucumber Sandwich, 108
Cordon Bleu Pork Chops, 283
Corn 'n' Beef Pasta Bake, 247
Corn Bread Beef Bake, 243

Corn Medley, 161
Corn Scones, 205
Corn Wheels with Lime Butter, 153
Corned Beef Hash and Eggs, 41
Cornish Hens with Veggies, 337
Cornmeal Cinnamon Rolls, 210
Cornmeal Empanadas, 237
Corny Bread Bake, 312
Corny Turkey Burgers, 345
Cottage-Cauliflower Spread, 28
Country Sausage Gravy, 55
Country-Style Pork Ribs, 270
Crab Bisque, 89
Crab Quiche, 367
Crab Roll-Ups, 24
Crab-Stuffed Celery, 19
Crab-Stuffed Deviled Eggs, 21
Crab Thermidor, 371
Cranberry-Apple Mincemeat Pies, 428
Cranberry Apple Punch, 27
Cranberry Baked Beans, 165
Cranberry Baklava, 460
Cranberry Cabbage Salad, 147
Cranberry-Chocolate Ice Cream, 469
Cranberry Gelatin Salad, 118
Cranberry-Glazed Spareribs, 273
Cranberry Nut Stuffing, 130
Cranberry Scones, 193
Cranberry-Stuffed Pork Chops, 297
Crazy Crust Pizza, 250
Cream Cheese-Stuffed Catfish, 358
Cream of Asparagus Soup, 87
Cream of Zucchini Soup, 98
Creamed Asparagus and Tomato, 157
Creamed Ham and Eggs, 42
Creamed Spinach, 119
Creamed Sweet Peas, 169
Creamy Beef Stroganoff, 232
Creamy Cauliflower Salad, 115
Creamy Citrus Salad, 159
Creamy Corned Beef Casserole, 256
Creamy Egg Salad Sandwiches, 97
Creamy Pastel Mints, 379
Creamy Pork Tenderloin, 280
Creamy Red Pepper Dip, 18
Creamy Shrimp Dip, 22
Creamy Turkey Melt, 79
Creamy Veggie Vermicelli, 155
Creole Fried Chicken, 317
Creole-Style Pork Roast, 278
Crescent Chicken Squares, 321
Crisp Chocolate Chip Cookies, 404
Crispy Breakfast Slices, 59
Crispy Rhubarb Cobbler, 470
Crown Jewel Patties, 111
Crunch Bars, 400
Crunch Top Ham and Potato Casserole, 304
Crunchy Baked Pork Tenderloin, 309
Crunchy Chocolate Cups, 380
Crunchy Peanut Candy, 382
Crunchy Swiss-n-Ham Snacks, 23
Crunchy Tuna Surprise, 358
Crustless Pear Pie, 418
Curried Acorn Squash Soup, 98
Curried Chicken and Rice, 341

Curried Chicken Balls, 22
Curried Chicken Pita Pockets, 92
Curried Meat Loaf, 215
Curried Pork and Green Tomatoes, 279
Curried Pork Chops, 302
Curried Scrambled Egg, 42
Curried Turkey and Rice Salad, 112
Curry Carrot Dip, 38

Dad's Onion Rings, 110
Dairy Hollow House Herbal Cooler, 22
Danish Christmas Cake, 437
Danish Coffee Cake, 212
Date Nut Bread, 198
Date Pecan Fudge, 381
Depression Casserole, 277
Deviled English Muffins, 88
Deviled Ham and Egg Appetizer, 6
Devil's Food Cake, 446
Dijon Chicken, 315
Dilled Chicken Soup, 102
Dilly Cheese Soup, 106
Dilly Chicken and Potatoes, 320
Dipped Sandwich Cookies, 390
Dirty Ice Cream, 455
Down-on-the-Farm Breakfast, 45
Dried Beef Spread, 19

Early-Riser Muffins, 48
Easy Apple Betty, 459
Easy Crescent Rolls, 204
Easy Egg Rolls, 38
Easy Fried Rice, 346
Easy Mint Chocolate Truffles, 378
Easy Mint Hot Chocolate, 17
Easy Oat Bran Muffins, 189
Easy Peanut Butter Pretzels, 12
Easy Stromboli, 70
Edna's Cream Sticks, 453
Egg Salad Tuna Wraps, 93
Eggless-Milkless-Butterless Cake, 437
Eggnog Dip, 24
Elbow Macaroni Salad, 125
Elegant Holiday Ham Glaze, 172
English Muffin Loaf, 190
Ethan's Apple-Nut Pancakes, 57
Evelyn's Original Roquefort Dressing, 177
Extra-Crispy Italian Chicken, 333

Famous Fried Chicken, 350
Farmhouse Chicken Soup, 63
Farmhouse Dinner, 224
Favorite Cake Brownies, 408
Favorite Chili, 65
Feather-Light Breakfast Puffs, 50
Fiesta Black Bean Salad, 127
Fillets with Ginger Sauce, 370
Flourless Peanut Butter Cookies, 395
Fluffy Fruit Salad, 113
Four-Bean Salad, 142
Four-Grain Bread, 190
Frank's Sauerbraten, 221
Frappe Mocha, 6
Freezer French Toast, 51
French Coconut Pie, 414
French Onion Soup, 95

French Salad Dressing, 179
Fresh Apple Cake with Caramel Sauce, 431
Fresh Blueberry Tarts, 419
Fresh Coconut Pound Cake, 434
Fresh Salsa, 180
Fresh Vegetable Kabobs, 144
Fried Chicken Pitas, 74
Fried Cornmeal Mush, 60
Fried Green Tomatoes, 128
Fried Shredded Wheat, 52
Frosted Cherry Nut Bars, 399
Frosted Cinnamon-Raisin Biscuits, 204
Frosted Hazelnuts, 17
Frozen Coconut Caramel Pie, 415
Frozen Cranberry Velvet Pie, 416
Frozen Dream Dessert, 456
Frozen Mocha Cheesecake, 471
Fruit and Cream Parfaits, 464
Fruit Kuchen, 454
Fruit Slush, 12
Fruitcake Squares, 403
Fruited Pork Picante, 283
Fruity Pasta Salad, 158
Fruity Popcorn Balls, 9
Fruity Thirst Quencher, 16
Fruity-Toot-Toot, 140
Fudge Pecan Brownie Tart, 430
Fudgy Brownies, 407

Garbanzo Avocado Salad, 150
Garden Fresh Breakfast, 55
Garlic-Brown Sugar Chicken, 335
Garlic-Buttered Pasta, 164
Garlic Oatmeal Soup, 72
Gazpacho, 81
German Cheesecake, 457
German Chicken, 324
German Chocolate Pie, 425
German Skillet Meal, 234
Ginger Chicken Stir-Fry, 323
Ginger Yeast Muffins, 209
Glazed Beets, 149
Glazed Pork Tenderloin, 310
Gold Rush Brownies, 390
Golden Broccoli Bake, 218
Golden Cheese Yeast Bread, 197
Golden Corn Puff, 151
Golden Dinner Rolls, 199
Graham-Streusel Coffee Cake, 53
Grandma Brubaker's Orange Cookies, 402
Grandma's Apple Dumplings, 456
Grandma's Apple Salad, 132
Grandma's Spring & Summer Torte, 444
Grandmother's Chicken 'n' Dumplings, 96
Grape Juice Crush, 10
Greek Rice Salad, 149
Green Bean Bundles, 169
Green Beans with Mushrooms, 135
Green Chili 'n' Rice Casserole, 160
Grilled Blue Cheese Sandwiches, 91
Grilled Chicken Kabobs, 329
Grilled Salmon Sandwiches, 360
Grilled Stuffed Pork Chops, 305
Grilled Turkey Sandwiches, 340
Ground Turkey Turnovers, 325

Ham and Asparagus Roll-Ups, 295
Ham 'n' Cheese Puffs, 25
Ham and Cheese Spread, 11
Ham and Cheese Waffles, 49
Ham and Spinach Loaf, 68
Ham Balls with Mustard Dill Sauce, 281
Ham Fried Rice, 282
Ham Hot Dish, 285
Ham Loaf Pie, 291
Ham-Noodle Bake, 294
Ham Pickle Pinwheels, 17
Ham Rolls Continental, 306
Ham-Stuffed Bread, 103
Ham, Turkey and Wild Rice Salad, 143
Hamburger-Broccoli Dip, 19
Harvard Beets, 141
Harvest Watermelon Pie, 415
Hasty Heartland Dinner, 269
Hawaiian Pizza Pasta, 299
Hawaiian Roll-Ups, 29
Haystacks, 377
Hearty Chicken and Beans, 336
Hearty Krautwiches, 65
Hearty Muffuletta Loaf, 80
Hearty Sausage Loaf, 45
Hearty Steak Soup, 66
Hearty Whole Wheat Cookies, 405
Heavenly Cheesecake, 467
Herb-Marinated Pork Loin, 305
Herbed Broccoli Spears, 160
Herbed Egg Noodles, 111
Herbed Pasties, 93
Herbed Pork Roast, 297
Hobo Knapsacks, 244
Home-Style Hominy Casserole, 61
Homemade Cocoa Pudding, 474
Homemade Noodles, 167
Homemade Pinwheel Noodles, 248
Honey Baked Chicken, 342
Honey-Baked French Toast, 54
Honey Cereal Bites, 9
Honey Fruit Dessert, 466
Honey Mustard Dressing, 174
Honey White Loaves, 208
Hopping John, 117
Horseradish Sauce, 181
Hot Bacon Cheese Spread, 33
Hot Bacon Dressing, 171
Hot Chicken Heroes, 88
Hot Chocolate Mix, 31
Hot Crab Dip, 36
Hot Cross Buns, 183
Hot Curried Fruit, 158
Hot Dogs 'n' Rice, 277
Hot Fudge Pudding Cake, 441
Hot Jam Breakfast Sandwiches, 58
Hot Tamale Pie, 254
Hot Turkey Salad Pitas, 66
Hot Turkey Sandwiches, 314
Hot Wings, 32
Humpty-Dumpty Sandwich Loaf, 72
Hungarian Cabbage with Noodles, 116
Hungarian Goulash, 241
Hungarian Pork Loaf, 301

Icebox Cookie Cheesecake, 459
Individual Egg Bakes, 49
Inside-Out Pork Chops, 285
Instant Party Potatoes, 110
Iones's Parker House Rolls, 195
Irish Soda Bread, 193
Italian Beef Sandwiches, 250
Italian Broccoli Salad, 123
Italian Cabbage and Rice, 304
Italian Sausage and Sauerkraut, 293
Italian-Sausage Pepper Sandwiches, 90
Italian-Style Peas, 132
Italian-Style Round Steak, 256

Jalapeno Ribs, 298
Jambalaya, 280

Kid-Pleasing Spaghetti, 258
Kielbasa Cabbage Soup, 90

Lamb and Potato Stew, 80
Lasagna in a Bun, 67
Layered Icebox Dessert, 464
Layered Vegetable Loaf, 109
Lazy Lasagna, 253
Lemon Almond Chicken, 338
Lemon Blueberry Drop Scones, 202
Lemon Blueberry Tea Cake, 450
Lemon Butter Topping, 177
Lemon Coconut Bars, 387
Lemon Curd, 176
Lemon Drop Cookies, 408
Lemon-Herb Gyros, 239
Lemon Meringue Pie, 413
Lemon Pear Pie, 416
Lemon Pork Ribs, 307
Lemon-Raspberry Muffins, 211
Lemon Rib Eyes, 262
Lemon Rice Pilaf, 141
Lemon Snowball, 468
Lemonade Pie, 414
Light Pesto, 175
Lima Bean Casserole, 167
Lime Pear Salad, 164
Lime Pie, 417
Linguine with Garlic Clam Sauce, 365
Liverwurst Deluxe, 82

Make-Ahead Saucy Sandwiches, 78
Mandarin Beef Skillet, 247
Mandarin Chicken Bites, 6
Manicotti, 216
Maple-Dijon Salad Dressing, 173
Maple Raisin Pudding, 474
Maple Walnut Pie, 414
Marinated Onion Salad, 143
Marinated Pork Loin Roast, 267
Marmalade Drumsticks, 331
Mary's Caesar Salad, 152
Meat Loaf Sandwiches, 85
Meatball Noodle Soup, 101
Meatballs with Spaetzle, 255
Meaty Pita Pockets, 226
Mediterranean Chicken, 346
Mediterranean Shrimp and Pasta, 360

Mexi-Corn Lasagna Dish, 233
Mexican Meat Loaf Roll, 239
Mexican Pizza, 11
Mexican Pork Stew, 101
Mexican-Style Chicken Kiev, 335
Microwave Corn Bread Casserole, 308
Microwave Hollandaise Sauce, 174
Milly's Salad Dressing, 172
Mini Garlic Bread, 23
Mini Green Bean Casserole, 160
Mini Molded Salads, 116
Mixed Grain and Wild Rice Cereal, 57
Mixed Greens with Mushrooms, 130
Mixed Vegetable Side Dish, 163
Mocha Nut Fudge, 379
Mock Monte Cristos, 73
Mock Pecan Pie, 426
Mock Pot Roast, 259
Mock Ravioli, 252
Molded Cherry-Pineapple Salad, 138
Mom's Buttermilk Biscuits, 187
Mom's Chicken Soup, 77
Mom's Chinese Dish, 269
Mom's Fried Apples, 458
Mom's Monday Lunch Potato Soup, 99
Monkey Bread, 184
Montana Mountain Muffins, 199
Moon Cake, 465
Morning Glory Muffins, 196
Mother's Manicotti, 162
Mozzarella Meat Whirl, 232
Mushroom 'n' Tomato Salad, 119
Mushroom Pasta Sauce, 175
Mustard Baked Ham with Gravy, 301
Mustard Dip, 26
My Mother's Mac and Cheese, 165

New England Boiled Dinner, 238
New Potatoes with Dill, 114
No-Bake Cornflake Cookies, 391
No-Guilt Brownies, 394
Noodle Nibblers, 145
Nutty Beef Turnovers, 34
Nutty Caramel Popcorn, 14
Nutty Carrot Salad, 122
Nutty Coleslaw, 147
Nutty Mandarin Salad, 135
Nutty Shrimp Salad Sandwiches, 74

Oatmeal Pie, 417
Old-Fashioned Baked Beans, 163
Old-Fashioned Chocolate Chip Cookies, 409
Old-Fashioned Kraut Dinner, 296
Old-Fashioned Popcorn Balls, 32
Old-Fashioned Pork Roast, 265
Old-Fashioned Potatoes Anna, 168
Old-Time Buttermilk Pie, 424
One-Bowl Chocolate Cake, 444
One-Pan Pork a la Orange, 272
Onion-Baked Chicken, 351
Onion Pie, 148
Onions and Cream Appetizer, 27
Open-Faced Chicken Benedict, 330
Open-Faced Pizza Burgers, 261
Orange Apricot Balls, 377
Orange Barbecue Sauce, 181

Orange Barbecued Turkey, 328
Orange-Coated Chicken, 337
Orange Colada, 20
Orange-Date Bars, 397
Orange Date Cake, 445
Orange Dijon Pork, 299
Orange-Glazed Bananas, 466
Orange Meringue Pie, 427
Orange-Pecan Baked Apples, 52
Orange Roughy Parmesan, 359
Oriental Patties, 237
Oven-Baked Ribs, 300
Oven-Baked Sesame Chicken, 352
Oven Porcupines, 236
Overnight Caramel French Toast, 43
Overnight Chicken Casserole, 327
Ozark Blueberry Pie, 412

Paprika Salad Dressing, 180
Parmesan Ham Pasta, 275
Parmesan Pork Sandwiches, 306
Parmesan Potato Sticks, 115
Parmesan Salmon Fillets, 367
Parsley-Stuffed Flank Steak, 249
Party Barbecued Franks, 7
Patio Salad, 138
Pea Soup for a Crowd, 100
Peach-Glazed Chicken, 330
Peach Praline Pie, 424
Peachy Yogurt Shake, 11
Peanut Butter 'n' Jelly Shake, 16
Peanut Butter Brownies, 410
Peanut Butter-Chocolate Chip Pie, 413
Peanut Butter Fingers, 378
Peanut Butter Mallow Candy, 386
Peanut Butter Pie, 420
Pear Cake with Sour Cream Topping, 442
Pear-Oatmeal Breakfast Pudding, 56
Pecan Fish, 370
Pecan Fondant, 385
Pecan Icebox Cookies, 406
Pecan Oven-Fried Fryer, 341
Pecan Pie, 417
Pecan Sandies, 401
Pennsylvania Dutch Potato Doughnuts, 44
Pepper and Salsa Cod, 362
Pepper Lover's BLT, 86
Pepper Soup, 74
Pepper Steak, 259
Peppermint Patties, 374
Peppermint Stick Dessert, 465
Pepperoni Bread, 27
Peppery Corn Salad, 157
Perfect Prime Rib Roast, 219
Perfect Scalloped Oysters, 8
Pesto Mushroom Chicken, 349
Pesto Pasta Salad, 170
Picante Chicken, 314
Pickled Eggs, 18
Picnic Cake, 440
Picnic Peas, 123
Picnic Potato Chip Chicken, 347
Pigs in a Blanket, 46
Pimiento-Stuffed Olive Bread, 192
Pine Nut Chicken, 354

Pineapple Bread Pudding, 461
Pineapple Bundt Cake, 446
Pineapple Delights, 405
Pineapple Shrimp Rice Bake, 362
Pink Ice, 382
Pink Velvet Company Pie, 425
Pizza Buns, 76
Pizza Casserole, 254
Plum-Barbecued Spareribs, 291
Poached Meatballs in Lemon Sauce, 260
Poached Teriyaki Salmon, 365
Pocket Veggies, 124
Popcorn Cookies, 396
Poppy Seed Bundt Cake, 449
Pork and Cabbage Rolls, 307
Pork Chop and Rice Dinner, 290
Pork Chop Suey, 294
Pork Chops Parmesan, 277
Pork Chops with Pear Stuffing, 273
Pork Chops with Sauteed Plums, 298
Pork Fajita Pasta, 290
Pork Fajitas, 276
Pork Lo Mein, 284
Pork Patties Oriental, 287
Pork Ribs and Chilies, 309
Pork Sausage Ring, 52
Pork Souvlaki, 288
Pork-Stuffed Eggplant, 284
Pork Tenderloin Florentine, 263
Pork Wellington, 268
Pork with Peanuts, 308
Potato Casserole, 153
Potato Chip Crunchies, 395
Potato Ham au Gratin, 271
Potato Salmon Casserole, 368
Potato Volcano, 146
Potatoes Forradas, 114
Prize-Winning Apple Pie, 426
Puffed Eggnog Pancake, 58
Pull-Apart Morning Rolls, 40
Pumpkin Cheesecake Bars, 407
Pumpkin Chili, 107
Pumpkin Pudding, 460
Pumpkin Sloppy Joes, 228

Quick and Easy Waffles, 60
Quick Bean Soup, 86
Quick Calzones, 77
Quick Graham Cracker Cake, 433
Quick Homemade Bread, 186
Quick Pantry Salad, 154

Raisin Peanut Clusters, 377
Raisin Sheet Cookies, 392
Ranch Chicken 'n' Rice, 331
Ranch-Style Thighs, 342
Raspberry Delights, 397
Raspberry-Filled Cake, 439
Raspberry Supreme Cheesecake, 462
Raspberry Vinegar, 177
Ratatouille, 133
Red-Eye Beef Roast, 257
Red Velvet Cake, 452
Rhubarb Apple Pie, 423
Rhubarb Beef, 260

Rhubarb Cloud, 458
Rhubarb Pork Roast, 286
Rhubarb Punch, 31
Rhubarb Squares, 398
Ribs with Caraway Kraut and Stuffing Balls, 310
Rice-Crust Quiche, 62
Rice Pudding Cake, 442
Roast Beef with Mushroom Sauce, 229
Roast Goose with Apple-Raisin Stuffing, 355
Roasted Corn and Avocado Dip, 34
Roasted Garlic Spread, 173
Roasted Red Pepper Muffins, 192
Roasted Root Veggies, 122
Root Beer Float Cake, 435
Rose's Apple Turnover Coffee Cake, 207
Rosemary's Ham Reubens, 69
Rosy Raspberry Salad, 133
Russian Cream, 475
Rye Breadsticks, 194

Sage Cornmeal Biscuits, 191
Salad Croutons, 179
Salmon Biscuit Bake, 368
Salmon Pate, 15
Salmon Salad, 153
Salmon Scramble, 60
Salmon with Herb-Mustard Sauce, 364
Salt Substitute, 174
Saucepan Fudgies, 388
Saucy Ham and Rice, 268
Saucy Herb Hamburgers, 227
Sauerkraut Brownie Cake, 435
Sauerkraut Side Dish, 139
Sausage 'n' Spinach Pockets, 105
Sausage Apple Roll, 270
Sausage Bacon Tidbits, 36
Sausage Potato Wraps, 276
Sausage Sloppy Joes, 265
Sausage Stroganoff, 287
Sausage-Stuffed French Loaf, 217
Sausage-Stuffed Potatoes, 300
Savory Biscuits, 187
Scalloped Corn, 129
Scalloped Potatoes 'n' Ham, 295
Scotch Shortbread Bars, 397
Scrumptious Breakfast Fruit Soup, 47
Seafood in Tomato Sauce, 357
Sesame Flank Steak, 258
Sesame Pork Kabobs, 266
Sesame Shrimp, 363
Sesame Zucchini, 123
Shaker Pork Sandwiches, 303
Sheepherder's Potatoes, 142
Short Ribs with Plums, 240
Shredded Pork Tacos, 267
Shrimp and Asparagus Casserole, 366
Shrimp Crepes, 372
Simple Herbed Scallops, 361
Simple Sausage Ring, 265
Sirloin Steak Sandwiches, 248
Sirloin with Bernaise Sauce, 219
Skillet Chocolate Dumplings, 455
Skillet Fish Dinner, 371
Skillet Rolls, 191

Skillet Seasoned Rice, 115
Skillet Stuffing, 151
Skillet Vegetables, 128
Skinny Fries, 145
Smoky Beef Brisket, 235
Smothered Ginger Chicken, 329
Snowball Cake, 432
Soft Chocolate Cookies, 389
Soft Run Caramels, 373
Sole Amondine, 366
Sour Cream Cucumber Salad, 152
Sour Cream Herb Bread, 188
Sour Cream Potato Salad, 121
Sour Cream Rhubarb Pie, 421
South-of-the-Border Thighs, 333
South Seas Skillet, 316
Southern Potato Salad, 145
Southwest Skillet Dish, 61
Southwestern Chicken Soup, 88
Southwestern Deep-Dish Pizza, 223
Southwestern Fried Rice, 343
Spaghetti-Style Rice, 242
Spanish Pork Steaks, 302
Spanish-Style Breakfast Bake, 43
Sparerib Casserole, 289
Spareribs Cantonese, 293
Special Birthday Cake, 451
Special Ham 'n' Cheese Sandwiches, 92
Spectacular Shrimp Salad, 364
Spectacular Spaghetti Squash, 139
Speedy Oven Fudge, 384
Speedy Pizza Rings, 37
Spiced Date Oatmeal, 44
Spiced Pot Roast, 217
Spiced Rhubarb Soup, 107
Spicy Chicken Corn Skillet, 324
Spicy Molasses Cookies, 393
Spicy Spaghetti Salad, 157
Spinach Bisque, 70
Spinach Cheese Bake, 134
Spinach Cheese Muffins, 205
Spinach Salad Ring, 131
Sticky Apple Biscuits, 184
Stir-Fried Chicken Fajitas, 332
Stove-Top Macaroni and Cheese, 133
Strawberry Chiffon Cake, 432
Strawberry Dessert, 470
Strawberry Punch, 9
Strawberry Rhubarb Dumplings, 467
Strawberry Trifle, 468
Stuffed Acorn Squash, 224
Stuffed Artichokes, 231
Stuffed Banana Peppers, 264
Stuffed Cornish Hens, 322
Stuffed Crown Roast of Pork, 266
Stuffed Cucumbers, 162
Stuffed Easter Ham, 288
Stuffed Green Peppers, 233
Stuffed Ham Bake, 286
Stuffed Ham Slices, 95
Stuffed Meat Loaf, 262
Stuffed Mushrooms, 10
Stuffed Pizza, 213
Stuffed Round Steak, 234
Stuffed Sirloin Roast, 220

Stuffing Balls, 169
Sugar Cookie Slices, 390
Sugar-Topped Applesauce Muffins, 186
Summer Garden Soup, 73
Summer Squash Enchiladas, 319
Sunday Fried Chicken, 326
Sunshine Biscuits, 203
Sunshine Chicken, 325
Super Nachos, 8
Surprise-Inside Cupcakes, 433
Surprise Potatoes, 156
Swedish Meatballs, 228
Sweet-and-Sour Chicken, 318
Sweet and Sour Chicken Nuggets, 16
Sweet-and-Sour Dressing, 181
Sweet-and-Sour Meatballs Appetizer, 33
Sweet 'n' Sour Pockets, 71
Sweet and Spicy Steak, 222
Sweet-as-Sugar Cookies, 402
Sweet Cherry Pie, 418
Sweet Dill Refrigerator Pickles, 176
Sweet Potato Balls, 129
Sweet Potato Biscuits, 208
Sweet Potato Stew, 92
Sweet Succotash Chili, 84
Swiss 'n' Bacon Pizza, 35
Swiss Bake, 137
Swiss Chicken Bake, 340
Swiss Treat Bars, 398

Taco Crescents, 214
Taco Rice, 222
Tangerine Carrots, 161
Tangy Cabbage Salad, 114
Tangy Cauliflower, 137
Tangy Poppy Seed Dressing, 175
Tangy Reuben Bake, 289
Tangy Turkey Meatballs, 7
Tarragon Butter, 178
Tarragon Chicken Salad, 99
Tasty Pork Nuggets, 37
Tasty Texas Tenders, 342
Tasty Tortilla Roll-Ups, 35
Tater-Topped Casserole, 221
Tea Cakes, 399
Tenderloin Diane, 216
Teriyaki Tangerine Ribs, 264
Tex-Mex Bean Dip, 28
Texas Turkey Tacos, 313
Thanksgiving Sandwiches, 104
Three Bean Casserole, 155
Three-Cheese Tomato Melt, 99
Tiny Taco Meatballs, 20
Toasted Apple-Cheese Sandwiches, 67
Toffee Nut Squares, 401
Tom Thumb Treats, 391
Tomato-Bacon Rarebit, 83
Tomato Barley Salad, 148
Tomato Bread, 203
Tomato-Cheese Snack Bread, 13
Tomato Crouton Casserole, 170
Tomato Fondue, 14
Tomato Mozzarella Bake, 127
Tomato Soup with a Twist, 82
Topsy-Turvy Pie, 257

Tortellini Bake, 120
Tree-Mendous No-Bake Cherry Pie, 412
Triple Tasty Sandwich Spread, 89
Tropical Pork Kabobs, 272
Turkey a la King, 348
Turkey Barley Soup, 104
Turkey Bean Bake, 336
Turkey BLT, 81
Turkey-Blue Cheese Pasta Salad, 148
Turkey Broccoli Bake, 316
Turkey Burritos, 315
Turkey Cabbage Soup, 83
Turkey in the Strawganoff, 349
Turkey Patties Oriental, 339
Turkey Potato Supper, 343
Turkey Rice Casserole, 311
Turkey Schnitzel, 322
Turkey Shrimp Salad, 166
Turkey Squash Casserole, 321
Turkey Tomato Club, 64
Tuxedo Strawberries, 461
Twice-Baked Sweet Potatoes, 146
Two-Bean Tuna Salad, 120

Vanilla Granola, 53
Vegetable Bean Soup, 94
Vegetable Beef Kabobs, 245
Vegetable Pancakes, 136
Vegetable Tuna Sandwiches, 100
Vegetarian Chili, 76
Veggie Delights, 71
Veggie Loaves, 185
Viennese Pancakes, 39

Wake-Up Bacon Omelet, 50
Wake-Up Sandwiches, 58
Walnut-Crunch Pumpkin Pie, 429
Warm Asparagus Salad, 119
Westerfield Wassail, 20
Western Ribs, 292
White Chocolate Fudge, 383
White Chocolate Truffles, 375
White Christmas Chili, 97
White Sauce for Pasta, 173
Wholesome Quick Bread, 211
Whoopee Pies, 400
Wild Rice Soup, 108
Willie Hoss' Meat Loaf, 253

Yogurt Honey Fruit Bowl, 47

Zesty Buttered Peas, 129
Zesty Buttermilk Salad Dressing, 179
Zesty Carrots, 131
Zesty Corn Cakes, 251
Zesty Meatball Sandwiches, 230
Zesty Turkey, 319
Zucchini Apple Crisp, 462
Zucchini Cake, 438
Zucchini-Garlic Pasta, 126
Zucchini Lasagna, 214
Zucchini Oven Omelet, 41
Zucchini Patties, 149
Zucchini Sausage Squares, 303
Zucchini Snack Bread, 209
Zucchini Spread, 10